Allen K. Philbrick

Department of Geography, Michigan State University

THIS

HUMAN WORLD

John Wiley & Sons, Inc.   *New York • London*

To my father, ALLEN E. PHILBRICK, who taught me that
"there is no such word as can't."

Preface

The subject matter of geography is the earth as the estate of man. The objective of geographic study is to portray and interpret the patterns of man's occupancy of the earth. At an elementary level this means concern with the "where" of countries, cities, rivers, and mountains—all of the individual elements of the traditionally descriptive inventory of things in their places. At a more advanced level geography is concerned with understanding how and why the human race has organized the earth's surface as it has. Fantastic technological advances make the world seem smaller. While advances in both production of necessities and amenities have brought about great changes, the world has also witnessed a sixfold increase in its human population within the past five centuries.

The context of this book is the world today. It is a world seemingly poised on the brink of destruction by the very people who represent its most enlightened and complex form of life; yet it is a world, also, which stands at the threshold of attainments which could make the past accomplishments of the human race dwindle to insignificance by comparison.

Because of the increasing scope of human knowledge, there is a tendency toward greater and greater specialization. With extreme specialization it is difficult for the individual to maintain his perspective in relation to society as a whole. Geography provides an approach to knowledge of the world which can help each of us develop more meaningful relationships within it.

The occupancy of the world is ever changing. New combinations of phenomena are ever in the process of becoming, as man evolves his occupancy of the earth on the basis of accumulated and transmitted knowledge and through creative innovations. The result is a continuous series of painfully striven for solutions to an endless progression of problems represented by innumerable specific decisions in the process of daily living by nearly three billion human beings. The evolution of the pattern and organization of area characteristic of man's occupancy of the earth is the product of two elements, human culture and material resources, which are united in life by the force of human volition. Regional analysis will demonstrate ways in which the cutting edge of human creative imagination provides leadership, while the natural and cultural environments supply challenge and opportunity. The perspective used throughout the book is that perceptive innovation is the force by which man has evolved his own pattern of occupancy using the materials of his earthly estate. The transmission and acceptance of creative innovation in the activities of an increasing number of people result in a spatial distribution of human culture which is the subject of cultural geography.

The plan of *This Human World* is the interweaving of several threads, which are commented on below. The traditional division of geography into systematic and regional treatments may be observed in the organization of the material of the first five chapters and the remaining fifteen. The first five chapters describe the world systematically in three main subdivisions—physical, cultural, and organizational. The remaining fifteen regional chapters are also divided into three parts. Six chapters (Chapters 6–11) are arranged around the analysis of Europe. Chapters 12–14 deal with the Americas and their focus on the United States and Canada. Then the division of the old-world Eurasian land mass into the Communist Bloc and the regions of the Eurasian perimeter is treated in Chapters 15–19. Chapter 20 summarizes world regional organization.

The major theme of this book is the origin and spread of a wider-than-local division of labor, defined as exchange-type area organization. In developing this idea it is demonstrated that only the processes of cultural evolution can account for the specific innovations which brought about this revolution in the geographical distribution of human activities and their complex interconnections.

The regional treatment begins with England and Europe because the evolution of a wider-than-local division of labor involves the geography of the English and European industrial revolution and its dissemination by Europeans throughout the world. The impact of the distribution of European culture is traced geographically in England, Europe, Africa south of the Sahara, and in selected Commonwealth countries.

The scene then shifts to the Americas, where the great migration of European and African peoples from the time of the Age of Discovery is examined in its geographic context of material resources and divergent cultural evolution. A return to the Old World portrays the very different cultural evolution as the double continent of Eurasia is analyzed in terms of the Communist Bloc and the complex cultures of the Eurasian perimeter regions—North Africa and Southwest, South, Southeast, and East Asia.

In the concluding chapter the schism in the world between Communist, free world, and neutral regions is brought into sharp focus. The relation to the theme of the book of the present stalemate in the struggle for power and influence within the human race is made clear. The struggle is being waged primarily by the peoples of three regions represented by the Americas, Europe, and the Communist Bloc. The importance of Eurasia lies in the large proportion of the human race living there, and the relatively undeveloped state of its patterns of occupancy compared to available resources. Successive waves of European culture have swept across the face of the earth and have broken around and over the unyielding masses of Asians. The impact of the Industrial Revolution is only now for the first time substantially affecting the reorganization of area there. The processes of cultural evolution and the understanding and use of the earth's resources for the development of a truly stable pattern of world organization are approaching a crisis of leadership. The perspective of geography is essential to an understanding of the future of *this human world.*

Acknowledgments

In the ten years it has taken to write this book I have had the advice and sympathy of many friends. I was privileged to participate almost annually during the mid-1950's in field discussions, organized for the purpose of evolving geographic-research concepts, with Dr. Robert S. Platt of the University of Chicago, Dr. Lawrence M. Sommers of Michigan State University, Dr. Elaine M. Bjorklund of Vassar College, Dr. Robert H. Brown of St. Cloud State College, and Dr. Ann Larimore Kolars of Rutgers University.

Dr. Platt's counsel has provided many intellectual bases from which I have started and derived stimulus. Professor Sommers, chairman of the Geography Department at Michigan State University, where I have done most of the writing of this book since 1956, has contributed more than he is aware by affording me every opportunity to complete it. In the evolution of my ideas Dr. Bjorklund has given much constructive criticism, particularly with reference to cultural geography.

I have had the technical assistance of many of my young colleagues among the graduate-student fraternity. They have borne with patience their roles as "guinea pigs" as I have tried out various aspects of the book in conversations and teaching situations. Many of these students have also worked for me in the drafting of maps. Chief among the latter have been Judith Sweetser Allen, Patricia Asiala, Robert G. Janke, Yasuo Masai, and Martha Palmer. Jane Phillips read and typed much of the manuscript and made many valuable editorial suggestions. Notwithstanding these acknowledgments, I accept full responsibility for the form and content of this book.

Allen K. Philbrick

EAST LANSING, MICHIGAN
APRIL 1963

Contents

Contents *(Continued)*

Maps, photographs, and tables are identified under appropriate subject entries in the Index.

PART I SYSTEMATIC GEOGRAPHY

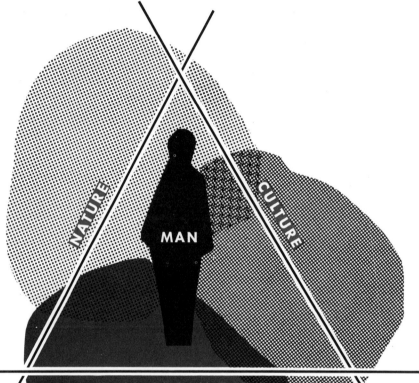

1 *A Geographic Point of View*

Geography portrays man occupying and using the earth, an image that gives significance to the title— *This Human World*. This first chapter explains the *what, where,* and *how* involved in the portrayal. The "what" concerns the classification of the subject matter of geography, the "where" deals with the parts of the planet earth with which the subject deals, and the "how" concerns the manner in which the study of geography is conducted.

The development of this theme requires definition, analysis, and interpretation of the *physical, cultural,* and *organizational* features of the world. Visualized upon the map these unevenly distributed features become a world portrait, as one might create the portrait of a person.

Each of the many features concerned is complex and has been the subject of detailed inquiry by scholars from many disciplines. The selection of ideas and facts with which to represent the world is the science and art of geographic generalization. The basic question "how does one significantly generalize about the world?" requires answers in terms of the features to be studied and presented.

Systematic Basis of Regional Geography

The two basic types of geographic study are systematic and regional. Systematic geography analyzes the world feature by feature; it is the geographic study of particular types of features. Regional world geography is a region-by-region synthesis in which each region is characterized by a distinctly different combination of many features. It combines the systematic features of the differing parts of the whole into one world made up of many regions. No geographic study, therefore, can avoid using both systematic and regional approaches in some combination. In this book the emphasis is regional, although the first five chapters are systematic.

Without some consistent restrictive basis for the selection of data, regional world geography is encyclopedic description, a smattering of knowledge about virtually everything which yields a profound understanding of nothing. To avoid this situation it is necessary to have a selective basis for the subject matter to be included in regional analysis. Such a basis is provided by a classification of the systematic subject matter to be treated.

The diagram on the facing page illustrates a classification of the subject matter of geography into three categories. The three subdivisions— *physical, cultural,* and the *human organization of area*—are the basis for understanding humanity in its regional units. Each category may be treated as covering a particular set of phenomena; but at the same time each of the three categories overlaps the other two. While each one is a distinctive body of knowledge representing a systematic viewpoint, it can also be treated as a subdivision of either of the other two categories. All three together represent the whole of geography.

The basic facts within these three sets of subject matter provide the ingredients of regions in this human world. By means of the *physical* aspect of geography we can understand the nature and distribution of material resources. The dispersion of human knowledge which has been transmitted from past generations and is evolving through the processes of innovation is the concern of *cultural* geography. We cannot even attempt an explanation of the progress mankind has made in occupying and using the earth unless we study the innovation and dispersion of human knowledge. In the final analysis the geography of man is the study of his *organization of area,* which embodies the evolution of human culture through occupancy and use of the earth and its resources.

Mankind cannot be understood out of context. Without material resources, without experience transmitted from the past, and without innovations evolving into the future, man would have remained indistinguishable from any other species of animal.

Instead he has used his capacity of mind and coordinated muscle to combine material resources and transmitted "know how" in a continuously evolving pattern of organized area on the face of the earth.

The overlapping character of the three aspects of systematic geography can be readily appreciated. One underlying purpose of studying the physical earth is ultimate use of nature by man. Such knowledge has made possible the evolution of culture and the organization of area. Looking at the same three aspects from the viewpoint of human culture, the categories in any classification of nature reflect man's interpretation of nature in relation to himself. The very organization of area by man can be interpreted as the vital expression of his culture. From the standpoint of area organization, both nature and culture are the ingredients which are combined in the evolving pattern of society's occupancy of the earth. Each aspect will be discussed in some detail in Chapters 2 through 5. They will only be introduced in this chapter.

The Physical Aspect of Geography. The significance of physical geography to human life lies in understanding the distribution of material resources and natural conditions. It analyzes the physical world from which man must take the material basis of his existence. A useful classification of resources related to human life is divided into three parts:

1. The resources from which foods are produced and which, therefore, indirectly sustain life.

2. The materials from which men build or manufacture useful articles.

3. The resources of nonanimal energy with which men supplement the force of their own muscles in the performance of work.

In the discussions of world regions throughout this book there will be many opportunities to realize the importance of the physical aspect of geography in terms of the resources and natural conditions which are characteristic of particular regions. It is almost impossible to evaluate the significance of a given resource at any one time in absolute terms since relative ignorance about a given natural phenomenon may either minimize or exaggerate the importance of a particular material. For example, appreciation of the importance of uranium depended upon discovery of radium and the development of nuclear physics. The significance to man of specific resources is constantly changing with the state of our knowledge. As discoveries are made materials which were previously unimportant become vital. As geographical discoveries of new locations yielding vital resources are made, they become more available to society. Accordingly, at a given moment society's state of awareness of resources provides a framework within which the significance of the physical aspect of geography must be acknowledged.

The Cultural Aspect of Geography. Like material things, cultural phenomena may also be subdivided into three groups.

1. Ideas and values.

2. Ways of doing things, including customs and technologies.

3. The works of man.

Among these works are the innumerable relatively permanent capital goods which constitute the productive plant by which society operates from day to day, including the systems of transportation and communication which interconnect the parts. How these items are also part of the human organization of area will be seen in more detail later.

Concepts and basic beliefs represent the implicit assumptions or values upon which a people base their outlook on life. Values represent motivation on which people base decisions and action.

Ways of doing things are so numerous as almost to defy classification. They extend from purely personal habits to traditional customs, and from inconsequental whims to intensely practical means of solving important technological problems.

Innovation, adaptation, and adoption of concepts and ways of doing things provide a continuing source of new motives and procedures by which society and its distribution pattern evolves. For example, the invention of many farm implements and machines in the United States has had a profound impact on the organization of area in agriculture. The invention of the steel plow by John Deere led to the opening of the prairies to farm settlement in the Middle West. The world-famous McCormick reaper revolutionized the harvesting of grain. Use of such innovations during the past century has had an ever-widening effect upon the production of food. Geographical analysis of cultural evolution is accomplished by locating the places of origin and tracing the spread of innovations as they have developed impact upon the way people live. In the transmission of information or "know-how" each person is a link in the chain of development. The spread of culture is therefore both an individual and a social process. By tracing the geography of this process we may study the evolution of human occupancy within world regions.

The Area Organizational Aspect of Geography. By living in the world people create an organized pattern through their activities, which represent the actions necessary to carry out the established way of life of a society. The organization of area can be mapped and studied just as can the patterns of natural phenomena and of culture. Three categories of activity result in related but distinctive patterns of area organization: (1) economic, (2) political, and (3) social.

Analysis of units of regional organization necessitates understanding how people who have particular cultural backgrounds and insight into the uses of natural resources have created their own distinctive patterns of occupancy. The main concern in this book is with the results of such processes, not with natural or social evolution in themselves. Great and small, the units or organized area which cover and characterize the earth make it this human world. The geographer makes use of subject matter from all three systematic aspects of the discipline in analyzing the world region by region.

The Earth's Surface Zone

It has been said that man lives at the bottom of a "sea of air." All life appears to occupy a narrow zone between the atmosphere and the litho-hydrosphere. The home of man is the outside surface of the earth sphere, which at the same time is the inside surface of the covering shell of atmosphere. This outside-inside situation emphasizes existence of *three* concentric shells—the *atmosphere,* the *litho-hydrosphere,* and the *biosphere.*

The Litho-Hydrosphere. The lithosphere is the mass of the planet. It begins at the surface and extends inward, including the water bodies (hydrosphere resting upon the more solid portions of the earth's crust. The lithosphere contains the earth's mineral resources, out of which man has fashioned so many of his important works. It also contains subsurface structural features which are the earth's crustal foundation for land and water-surface features.

The Atmosphere. The gaseous envelope of the atmosphere rests upon the outer surface of the litho-hydrosphere. No fixed distance marks the end of the atmosphere outward from the surface of the earth. The air is densest at the inside surface of the concentric ball-like shell of atmosphere and becomes progressively thinner or rarer with altitude above the earth. The average outer limit of the atmosphere may be taken to be the burn-out zone where speeding meteors and returning satellites are heated by friction to the point of ignition, approximately one hundred miles outward from the surface.

The Biosphere. Geographic interest focuses upon the biosphere, the sphere of living organisms which penetrate the litho-hydrosphere and the atmosphere. Within this thin, spherical shell life extends only a few miles outward into the atmosphere and inward into the litho-hydrosphere. The average thickness of the shell is approximately fifteen miles.

The biosphere is the spatial context of the human race. In addition it contains the distributional patterns of vegetation, all animal life, and soil. The soil contains minerals from the earth, nitrogen and other elements from the atmosphere, and organic materials from both vegetable and animal life; it is a living product of the unity of solar, earth, and life forces, which partakes of all three of the concentric earthly spheres.

Forces, Agents, Processes, and Distributions

How are the elements in physical, cultural, and organizational geography brought into relationship with each other? Elemental forces, which have produced mankind and set in motion the drama of man's occupancy and use of the earth, intertwine their energies within this spherical shell around the globe. Different combinations of forces, agents, and processes are responsible for the distribution of natural and cultural phenomena within the world. If we are to understand how man has attempted to control and organize his domain, the steps in these chains of relationship must be identified.

What forces are at work upon the surface of the world? External forces of the universe, principal among which is *solar* energy, penetrate the atmosphere; internal forces of the earth reach outward to affect all things on its surface. Major sources of energy from within the earth sphere are *earth heat, radioactivity,* and *gravity.* In addition to these there is also the force of *living matter* which is operative within the biosphere.

It is beyond the scope of this book to account for these forces or to attempt to explain them. It is fundamental, however, to point out examples of their power and to portray the distributional pat-

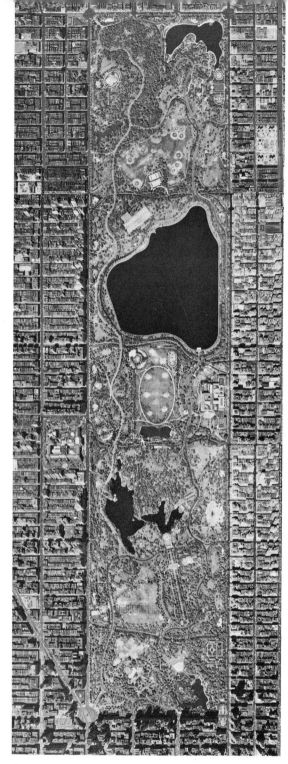

Figure 1. Central Park, New York City, contrasts sharply with its surroundings. The tall skyscrapers on the west and south sides of the park can be seen clearly by their shadows. The two distinctive homogeneous associations of elements inside and outside the park can be recognized readily. (*Courtesy of U. S. Coast and Geodetic Survey, Washington, D.C.*)

terns of their results. These forces alter matter and energy through diverse *processes* of particular kinds applied by specific *agents*. The forces, processes, and agents of nature and of human nature are partly expressed in the distribution of characteristic phenomena of the three aspects of geography.

Explicit recognition of *human creative imagination* as a force is of particular importance in understanding the impact of man upon the world. Creative imagination has produced the many evolving patterns of human society throughout the world. However unpredictable and little understood this force may be, unless it is *explicitly* recognized, the spark of innovation and of leadership in human affairs goes unnoticed. Unless creative imagination is taken into account interpretation of man becomes mechanistic and deterministic, which is to view man as if he were a machine rather than a living force.

The diagram facing page 1 of the book shows the relationship intended. Man is at the center with respect to each of the three facets of geography. This means that it is human creative imagination which unites all three facets in the processes of human existence and evolution.

It has been shown that the world may be studied from an intellectual position emphasizing any one, any two, or all three sides of the subject equally or in various ratios. Any combination is permissible under appropriate circumstances; but a full geographic treatment of a region or of the world must achieve a balance between all three aspects of the subject.

Geographic analysis of society starts with people in specific places. These people use the materials of nature within the active framework of a culture. Individual lives focused in human enterprises of a bewildering variety are combined within areas of human organization. Such areas express both nature and human culture. Individuals in the course of solving the problems of living, in the aggregate, account for the social evolution of the patterns of society. Answers to questions like "how has the world become what we find it to be?" are found by studying forces, processes, and agents which are responsible for the distributions of physical, cultural, and human organizational patterns.

Concepts of Area

Certain concepts of area must be defined and understood before they can be used in geographic study. An area or region is a particular extent or tract of the earth's surface. Such units of surface will be discussed under three headings: (1) arbitrary, (2) homogeneous, and (3) focal. These ideas about area represent distinctly different uses of the general idea of area or region; they are not necessarily mutually exclusive.

Arbitrary Area. An arbitrary area is one the boundaries of which are selected at random for convenience in establishing an area for some particular purpose. This concept should be compared with other ideas such as the homogeneous and focal area.

Homogeneous Area. A homogeneous area is one with a specified degree of similarity with respect to the criteria by which it is defined. The picture in Figure 1, showing Central Park in New York City, is an example. The park is defined by its criteria of curved roadways, paths, grass, trees, outcrops of bedrock, and surface ponds. The limits of the park are marked by the different characteristics of adjacent areas—straight streets, traffic congestion, and tall buildings, which dominate the surrounding land.

The central business district of Lansing, Michigan, and its surrounding wooded residential blocks shown in Figure 2 also illustrates homogeneity of two contrasting kinds. In this instance the boundary between the two associations of cultural elements is not quite so sharply defined as was the New York City example. Both of these examples are based on cultural facts. Natural features afford equally distinctive associations of elements within areas defined as homogeneous. Marked differences, for example, between sloping and level land define the boundaries of a plain. Delimitation of areas on the basis of homogeneity is one of the foundations of geographic generalization.

Focal Area. An area may also be defined in terms of dissimilar elements which are united in having a common focus of human organization. A focal area is divided into two parts—core and periphery. Because a focal area of human organization is the expression of human enterprises it may be characterized in terms of people and their activities. The core portion contains people and activities upon which surrounding population and activities come to a focus; the periphery contains population and activities which focus upon that core. The area of human organization as a whole is defined by the focal relationship between these two parts.

Figure 2. The buildings of the central business district of Lansing, Michigan, are virtually surrounded by wooded residential blocks, prompting the title of Lansing as "city in a forest." The capitol dome is visible just west of the main intersection of the city, marked by the tallest structures. The Grand River cuts across both the foreground and the left background. (*Courtesy of Abrams Aerial Survey Co., Lansing, Mich.*)

Figure 3 shows the two parts of a town. The concept of homogeneity is employed in the periphery on the basis of the repeated occurrence of residences in the community; and in the core on the basis of numerous business establishments in the downtown area. People who live in the residential neighborhoods, however, depend upon the tradesmen of the business district for their daily needs. The focal-area concept defines the whole town and its surrounding service hinterland. It is an area of human organization on the grounds of the focal interrelationship between internally homogeneous but mutually dissimilar subareas.

An area of human organization or focal area might be considered a special case of the homogeneous concept of area in the sense that the dissimilar elements in the area are similar in possessing a common focus. Separate concepts of homogeneity and focality, however, are more useful for the sake of clarity than is the emphasis upon their overlapping quality. The core and periphery as

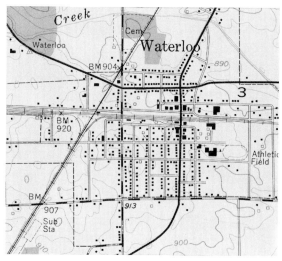

Figure 3. The aerial photograph and map of Waterloo, Indiana, afford a useful comparison of what can be read from these two kinds of representation. Three contrasting types of homogeneity which are roughly concentric—city center, residential blocks, and surrounding farmlands—are depicted. Interest centers on the focal relationships among the elements of each ring of homogeneity. The two outer associations contain elements which through the daily lives of people are focused on the center of Waterloo. (*Courtesy of Abrams Aerial Survey Co., Lansing, Mich., and Army Map Service, Washington, D.C.*)

defined above are each internally similar; but with respect to each other they are *dis*similar. The people of the core and periphery are interdependent as is expressed in the focality of the periphery upon the core. Such focality in function combines the two subregions into one area of human organization.

The map in Figure 4 is a second example of the focal area. It shows two international units of regional organization—the Commonwealth of Nations,[1] and the Communist Bloc.

The Communist Bloc is virtually a single continental unit of territory extending across Eurasia from the Baltic to the China Seas, and from the North Pole to the seventeenth parallel in North Vietnam. By contrast the Commonwealth, which is nearly equal in area to the Communist Bloc, is a widely scattered intercontinental grouping of independent states and dependent territories. These are interconnected across great distances by shipping routes and communications systems.

The concept of the focal area, or region of human organization, provides a key to understand-

ing the two international combinations of countries and territories. They differ markedly from one another in their political, economic, and social organization. The cultural backgrounds of their peoples are different in many important respects; yet each possesses a common focus upon a core or upon more than one core region. Within the Commonwealth there is a common focus upon England which is the core region of the United Kingdom, and within England upon the city of London. Within the Communist Bloc there are two core regions—the western Soviet Union, and Northeast China. Their respective focal centers are Moscow and Peiping. These two regions will be discussed in greater detail in Chapters 11 and 17.

The Role of the Map

The examples of types of area concepts were illustrated visually by maps. A map is a generalized representation on a plane surface of any portion or the whole of the earth's surface zone at a greatly reduced scale, and it is the principal means by which geographers visually study the distribution patterns characteristic of the three systematic aspects of geography and the world's various regions. The map is the most convenient form of recording geographical information, providing

[1] A number of predominantly non-European countries, India, Pakistan, and Ceylon, have become members and the title "British" has been dropped from the official title which is now "Commonwealth of Nations."

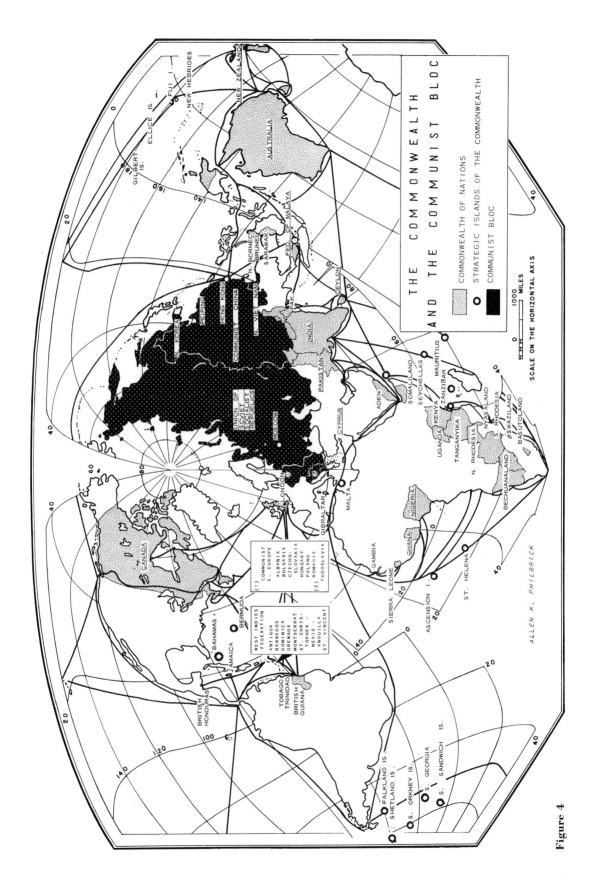

THE COMMONWEALTH
AND THE COMMUNIST BLOC

COMMONWEALTH OF NATIONS

STRATEGIC ISLANDS OF THE COMMONWEALTH

COMMUNIST BLOC

0   1000
|||||
MILES

SCALE ON THE HORIZONTAL AXIS

(1) COMMUNIST
E. EUROPE

ALBANIA
BULGARIA
CZECHO-
SLOVAKIA
HUNGARY
POLAND
ROMANIA

(2) YUGOSLAVIA

WEST INDIES
FEDERATION

ANTIGUA
BARBADOS
DOMINICA
GRENADA
MONTSERRAT
ST.-CHRIS-
TOPHER-
NEVIS-A
ANGUILLA
ST. VINCENT

ALLEN K. PHILBRICK

Figure 4

7

thereby the most effective means of visual comparison between phenomena in a given area, and between regions. Such comparisons are one of the means of geographical analysis, after which comes presentation of the results in which maps also play a prominent role.

Generalization. Mapping geographic phenomena involves two phases of generalization: the first phase involves ideas; the second, graphical presentation. The idea phase of generalization involves the classification of data: selected data must be classified into categories before they can be presented graphically.

A map to show annual precipitation, for example, might be made on the basis of a classification using ten inches of precipitation as the interval between lines of equal precipitation (isohyets). The degree of detail expressed on the map and the degree of verbal detail which might be based upon it in discussion depends directly upon the scale of classification and of the graphical presentation made on the map itself.

Scale. Scale is the ratio between the dimensions of the subject on the earth and the dimensions of the portrayal of that subject on the map. For example, a map on which one inch of paper equals one mile of the earth's surface has a scale in the ratio of one inch to the mile. All generalization is proportional to scale. The detail of representation on any map varies with scale just as does the degree of detail in the classification of data. Study of the world makes use of a wide range of scales, extending from those appropriate to visualizing the world as a whole to those scales pertinent for regions and localities.

Visualizing the Globe

The ability to visualize the distribution of phenomena and the shapes of regions defined by their contents is essential to geographic study. Such a "sense of place," including direction, is the equivalent of a "sense of history" in historical study. The ability to visualize mentally as well as actually on paper has to be cultivated. Neither ability is automatic. People without a developed sense of place can have no real conception of the grand design into which the locations of the world's regions fit.

The only true reproduction of the earth to scale is a model of the world in the form of a globe. Unfortunately we can see only one-half of the globe at a time. Since it is important to be able to see both hemispheres simultaneously, maps which transform the spherical surfaces of the earth onto a plane have to be used to visualize the global surface as a whole.

The distortions introduced in making a flat representation of a spherical surface do not make much difference in maps of local, regional, and even continental-sized portions of the earth. However, they may completely invalidate ideas of the world as a whole. The ideas inherent in a map depend in great part upon what kind of projection is used for the map of the world. Maps in Figures 5 and 6 illustrate this point. Figure 5 projects the relative sizes of the continents correctly. This type projection is called equal area. The interrupted form of the projection in Figure 5 shows each of the seven continents as a separate land mass at the sacrifice of their mutual relation to each other. Map A of Figure 6 is designed to demonstrate the nearly continuous alignment of the continents as one great land realm. The map, which is called the "clam-shell" projection, in this case is an equal-area hemisphere, modified by the addition of two arbitrary "wings" (which are not equal-area) representing the other half of the globe.

The problem of visualizing the pattern of the world's surface is made difficult by irregular distribution of the land and water regions of the earth. Only 28 per cent of the surface is land. The land tends to be concentrated in one hemisphere, the water in the other. However, the dispersion of the continents is such that the land realm occupies something *more* than a hemisphere, so that no hemispheric projection can adequately portray all of the land. Map A in Figure 6 is an attempt to show the global relationships of the continents to each other. On this map it is possible to see correctly how the world's lands are a ring of continents virtually enclosing the Atlantic-Arctic-Indian Oceans on one side of the earth. Except for Europe and Africa, five of the continents, as shown on map B—North and South America, Asia, Australia, and Antarctica—form a similar ring around the Pacific Ocean on the opposite side of the world. These maps will be referred to again in Chapter 3 when it is important to demonstrate the continuity of subsurface structural zonation of the earth's crust. The visual image of the globe in two parts, as a land-water realm on one side and a water realm on the other side of the earth, is a generalization of geographical pattern made possible through the use of maps.

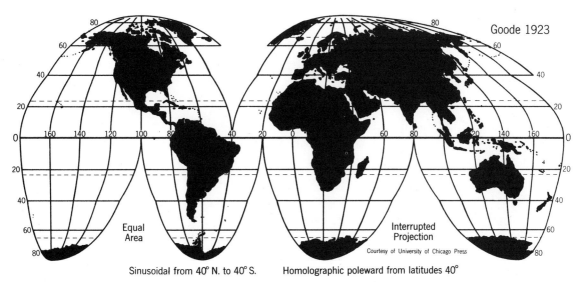

Figure 5. Homolosine projection.

Continuity of the Continents. A not otherwise obvious global continuity of the continents is illustrated in maps A and B of Figure 6. From Antarctica at the bottom of map A, the Palmer Peninsula points northward (to the left of the map) toward the southern tip of South America. South America is connected by Central America to North America. Alaska at the northwestern extremity of North America is only sixty miles across the Bering Strait from Eurasia. The clockwise circuit follows the Asian mainland to its southernmost tip near the equator in southern Malaya, on the doorstep of Singapore. A series of short hops from island to island over the Republic of Indonesia links Asia with Australia. Somewhat greater distances over water complete the circuit from Australia to New Zealand and back to Antarctica.

If the view of the globe is now reversed, as shown by map B, it may be seen that the journey just made was also a trip around the rim of the Pacific Basin. This second view makes the direction of the same trip counterclockwise. The Palmer Peninsula extends to the *right* from Antarctica toward South America, northward to North America and across the Bering Strait to Asia. This time the circuit continues through the Ryukyu Islands to the Philippines, New Guinea, the New Hebrides, and past Australia by way of New Zealand and back again to Antarctica.

If a cylinder of paper tangent to the surface of the globe over the rim of the Pacific were to receive an imaginary imprint of the Pacific Ocean's coastline and that cylinder were unfurled, the resulting line would follow a long strip map as in Figure 6C. On such a map it is clear that the Pacific coastline and the outer edges of the world's land-water realm would be the same. In detail this line is anything but straight; but the general alignment for 25,000 miles around the circumference of the earth seldom varies from a great circle by more than 10 per cent of the earth's circumference.

Global Patterns. It will help fix the global image in the mind to summarize the pattern of the world's lands in words. The globe has three pairs of continents and one single continent. Two pairs of continents and the single one are aligned in an approximate great circle, which is any circuit of the globe dividing it into two equal parts. These five continents, as has been shown on maps A and B of Figure 6, contain the common border between the land-water and water realms of the earth. The third pair of continents is Europe and Africa, located within the center of the world's land realm. It is around Africa on the globe that the "U"-shaped alignment of Arctic-Atlantic-Indian Oceans bends.

The three pairs of continents may be thought of as joining at opposite ends of the earth, at Antarctica in the Southern Hemisphere and in the Arctic Ocean of the Northern Hemisphere. The continents in each pair are arranged radially from a common "hinge" region at the Arctic end. They are like

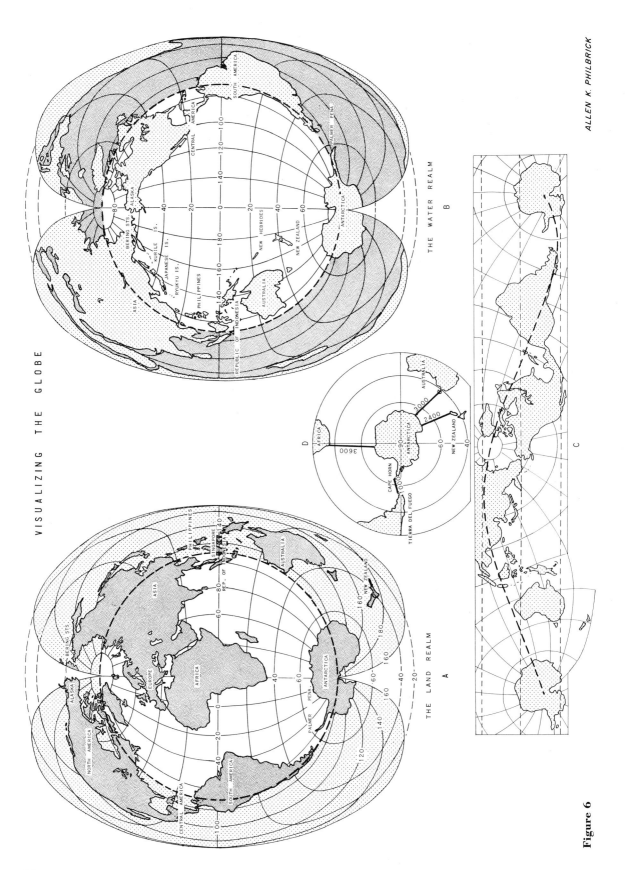

VISUALIZING THE GLOBE

ALLEN K. PHILBRICK

THE WATER REALM

B

THE LAND REALM

A

D

C

Figure 6

three links of two sausages each with the three links tied together at one end; the seventh continent is at the other end. Each of the pairs approaches Antarctica from a different global direction, but does not reach that continent. In each case the "different" direction can only be described as south, since the South Pole lies within Antarctica. This three-pointed pattern of Southern Hemisphere continents in relation to Antarctica is shown on map D in Figure 6. The gaps are long. New Zealand is 2,400 miles from the nearest point on the coast of Antarctica. Australia is nearly 3,000 miles away, while Africa (at 3,600 miles) is the most distant from Antarctica. South America is the closest, since only 1,000 miles separate Tierra del Fuego at the famous Cape Horn from the northernmost tip of the Palmer Peninsula.

Map A in Figure 6 shows how this radial pattern of pairs of continents encloses the three oceans, the Arctic, the Atlantic, and the Indian, as if they were giant-sized "inland seas." The three pairs of continents and Antarctica, along with the three enclosed oceans comprise the world's "land-water realm," as contrasted with the "water realm" on the Pacific side of the globe. Such are the patterns creating a spherical image of the biosphere. They have to be shown flat, but they should be remembered spherically as a global pattern.

This chapter has explained the "what, where, and how" involved in the study of geography. It has revealed how the discipline may be divided sys-tematically into three facets dealing with the physical and cultural world combined by mankind in the pattern of human organization of area. This subject matter has been visualized within the three concentric shells of the litho-hydrosphere, atmosphere, and biosphere. Relationships between phenomena may be traced within the biosphere by studying the forces, processes, and agents responsible for the distributions of pertinent physical, cultural, and organizational patterns of the world. Maps are to be the principal tool by means of which these patterns will be visualized. The data of geography will be analyzed on maps using two types of area concept—homogeneous and focal.

The next four chapters are an overview of the basic regional distributions of phenomena presented systematically for each of the three aspects of geography; they summarize the systematic basis of regional geography. Each chapter presents primarily the results of forces, processes, and agents operative within one of the facets of the discipline's subject matter; these chapters cannot present a full explanation of these phenomena. Only sufficient analysis is described to demonstrate that connections exist between the forces, agents, and processes producing the distributional patterns which are the main objects of presentation. These patterns of subject matter are the "vocabulary" of geography, with which we must have familiarity in order to "read the language" of the world's regions and understand the portrait of "this human world."

2 Principles and Regions of Human Organization

This chapter presents principles and regions of human organization and explains more fully the idea that activities of people can be generalized as units of organized area. The principles defined govern the geographical arrangement of world society, and the world regions of human organization outlined constitute the framework for later regional chapters.

Everyone has a routine of daily activity which takes place in one or more establishments. A family, for instance, living in a house or apartment in a city has a pattern of activity. In the morning the husband drives or rides some distance to his job in a factory, an office, or some other type of establishment. The children go to school. The housewife does the shopping in the various stores of the community business district. During the course of the day they make many contacts with people in various places. The husband, for example, comes into contact with a number of localities through communication with them: traveling in person, telephoning, writing letters, or by using materials from other places. When the day's work is done he returns home where he and his family may participate in the social life of the community to which they belong. Each day is a repetition of the preceding one, with some variations. Although the specific details vary considerably from person to person, each has some basic pattern of daily living.

Such a pattern can be described by diagramming it on a map. The diagram records activity in terms of the location of establishments and the routes or other interconnections between them. Even though the details vary for each individual as the course of his life unfolds, it is surprising how fixed the daily pattern of his life tends to be both in timing and in location. Most important, however, is the idea that the patterns of activity have a spatial dimension. The movements of people and things take place some*where*—in specific places. Locating and mapping these particular places of human activity and organization of area provide a geographic basis for analysis of human society.

Principles of the Human Organization of Area

The principles on the basis of which it is possible to analyze the area organization of human life are so simple that they might easily escape notice. Yet they are so basic that the distribution and functioning of world society cannot be understood without them.

The Focality of Human Activity. Human activity has focus. Although present in all animals, this focal quality seems to be immeasurably more significant for man because he is able to bring the powers of human intellect to bear on whatever he does. Focality of human activity is the result of purposeful application of energy in a basic geographic unit: the establishment or facility, such as a farm or a field, a residence or a room, a factory or a machine, a mine or a rock face within a mine. Much of human culture is expressed in such focal human enterprises. The pattern, however, is not static. New focal enterprises are constantly being developed as the pattern of life is "written" on the surface of the earth.

Localization of Human Focality. Focality is specifically located. Every discipline is troubled by the uniqueness of particulars and the validity of generalizations based on combinations of things which, though taken to be so, are not absolutely the same. History never repeats itself exactly. No two pine trees, fruit flies, mineral samples, or human establishments are completely identical. Geography begins with the unique location of a multitude of specific objects. On the one hand they are classifiable in terms of relative similarity. In this way focal establishments in which people are doing the same kinds of things are classified as the same kind of activity. But they are also classifiable in terms of relative location. The relative locations of many

Figure 7. The wide swath through the woods in the bottom of the aerial photograph indicates the location of a power line. The curved street and many branching driveways on the right margin form a nonplatted informal subdivision. The large square, a 160-acre quarter section composed of fields bordered on the bottom by the power line and on the right by the residences, comes to a focus in the farm yard in the upper left corner of the unit. The system of internal roadways and paths which coordinates the operation of the fields in their focusing on the farm yard is readily discernible. (*Courtesy of Abrams Aerial Survey Co., Lansing, Mich.*)

similar or dissimilar people, places, and objects are organized focally within any given area or region of human organization.

Techniques of defining and recording relative locations have evolved over a long period, but formalized systems have come into being only relatively recently.[1] Such systems are of three main kinds: (1) the network of latitude and longitude grid lines on the globe; (2) arbitrary grid coordinates, like those of the military grids and of various land survey systems for purposes of defining the location of properties; and (3) descriptive systems such as the verbal description of property or the number and street address.

The Interconnecting of Focal Establishments. *Establishments become interconnected during the normal course of the activities of people in the fulfillment of their needs. These interconnected establishments become larger units of area organization.* This principle is the basis on which occurs the development of a large number of such units of different complexity. They range from the neighborhood, community, settlement, town, village, city, or national state to the larger region and even world society.

Interconnection may be due to the fact that people like to be with other people, but it usually represents a more complex need for the pooling of effort and activity toward common objectives. In any event, such functional interconnections produce larger regions of organization from combinations of smaller ones.

Innumerable lines of movement develop within and between all kinds of establishments. Such interconnections are expressed not only in the many existing facilities of transportation and com-

---

[1] A detailed account of the origins, history, and applications of these overlapping systems is not appropriate here. They are ably dealt with in the *Story of Maps* by Lloyd A. Brown, Boston: Little, Brown, and Company, 1949.

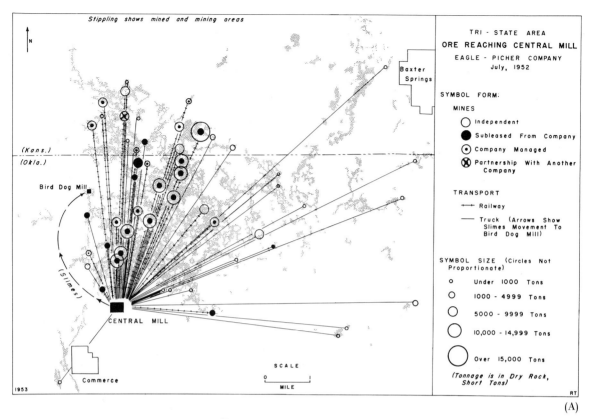

Figure 8. The area organization of a mine. (*Courtesy of Richard S. Thoman.*)

munication but also in less tangible ways. Such relationships as contracts, ownership, adherence to ideas, loyalties, and faith bind people and their establishments together just as surely as do material forms of interconnection.

The Force of Creative Imagination. As previously indicated, the determining force behind the evolution of a pattern of world occupancy is the human mind, which creates and transmits culture. Man has the ability to think, the power to exercise conscious will—to choose between alternatives. He has the capacity to innovate. The complex application of this creative imagination is primarily responsible for the distinctive character and distribution of man's organization of the areas he occupies. *The evolution of regions is the outgrowth of creative imagination in a setting of accumulated cultural experience and the use of resources in space and in time.*

A number of examples will be given to illustrate the range of focal establishments and the ways in which they are interconnected.

Focal Establishments as Basic Units of Area Organization

Activity in any establishment focuses in some one part of it more than in other parts, although there may be more than one focus in a single establishment. The following examples illustrate the focal character of individual establishments as the elementary areal unit of organization with which geography deals.

A Farm. The whole farm pictured in Figure 7 constitutes one establishment. The farmer undoubtedly focuses attention and activity on every part of the farm in the course of time, but all of the farming operations regularly come to a focus in the farmyard area, where house, barns, and other farm buildings mark the headquarters of farm life. Functionally each building may be the focus of a different type of activity. When differences within the farmyard are noted, structure by structure, distinctions lead finally to the farm house as the main headquarters of the farm as a functional unit. It is

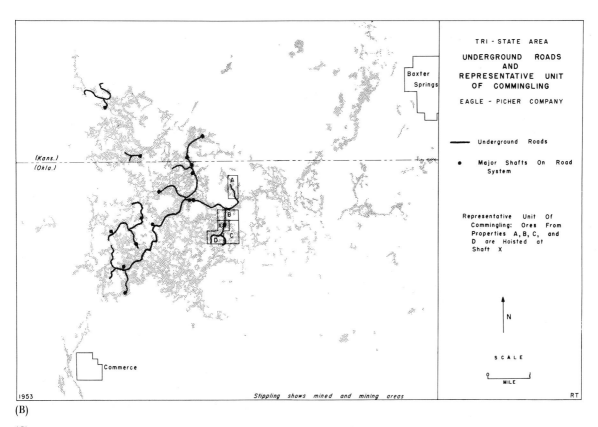

TRI - STATE AREA

UNDERGROUND ROADS
AND
REPRESENTATIVE UNIT
OF COMMINGLING

EAGLE - PICHER COMPANY

—————— Underground Roads

• Major Shafts On Road
System

Representative Unit Of
Commingling: Ores From
Properties A, B, C, and
D are Hoisted at
Shaft X

N

SCALE

0 |———————| 1
MILE

Stippling shows mined and mining areas

1953   RT

(B)

(C)

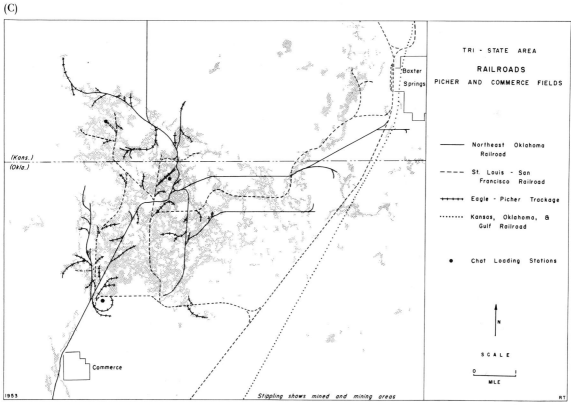

TRI - STATE AREA

RAILROADS
PICHER AND COMMERCE FIELDS

—————— Northeast Oklahoma
Railroad

– – – – St. Louis – San
Francisco Railroad

+++++ Eagle - Picher Trackage

········· Kansas, Oklahoma, &
Gulf Railroad

• Chat Loading Stations

N

SCALE

0 |———————| 1
MILE

Stippling shows mined and mining areas

1953   RT

15

therefore correct to say that the farm house is the headquarters of both the farmyard and the fields, and that the farmyard is the core area of the farm as a whole.

A Mining Field. The central mill of the Tri-State mining area in Missouri, Kansas, and Oklahoma is shown in Figure 8.[1] This mill has ceased operation, but until recently it was the principal focus of the lead and zinc mining of the Eagle-Picher Mining Company in the mining field of the same name. Here ore was concentrated before shipment to smelters elsewhere. The honeycomb pattern in the figure is the underground system of shaft and tunnel workings. A pattern of underground roads and a representative unit of the assembling of ores from several properties before hoisting (known as commingling) is shown in Figure 8B. The pattern of surface railroads is shown in Figure 8C.

Together, the complex of mining activities within this large areal unit belonged to an even larger corporate establishment, composed of a primary focus—the central mill—and a large number of peripheral mining locations, serviced by shafts, hoists, underground roads, and surface railways. Mining activity and its supporting functions focused upon every part of the mining field in the course of time, but all of the mining operations came to a focus regularly in the central mill, supplemented by some additional mills located within the field.

A Lumber Mill. The Brooks-Scanlon Lumber Company of Bend, Oregon, is shown in Figure 9.[2] The component parts of this establishment in relation to its timberlands are shown in Figure 9A, B, and C. Here the lumber mill is the focus of the establishment as a whole, as was the farmyard to the farm and the central mill to the mining field. Trains bring saw logs from the logging camps where they are dumped into the Deschutes River, which is dammed to form a mill pond. From this pond they are "fed" to each of two sawmills. Other specialized functions take place as indicated in the different buildings and facilities of the mill area. The activity of logging focuses on every part of the company's properties in the course of time, but all the lumbering operations come to a focus regularly in the lumber mill at Bend.

A Ranch. The Chiaraviglio ranch north of Buenos Aires, Argentina, is depicted in the map in Figure 10. The largest fenced areas are grazing units, each of which is stocked with a complete set of component cattle, sheep, and horses, as if it were a separate ranch. At opposite ends of the assemblage of ranch units are the land and quarters for two ranch-hand families. Each of the two families gardens for its own subsistence and rides circuit in its own half of the ranch units, locating and treating sick animals, repairing fences, and gathering information for the ranch manager.

The owner and his family, the ranch foreman-manager and his family, and the cowhands who live in dormitory bachelor's quarters occupy separate buildings and facilities in the core area of the ranch where all of the activities of the whole ranch come to a focus. Here the animals are processed, sheep are sheared, and all the animals are classified and then moved back to the individual breeding grounds or assembled for shipment to market.

A Residence. A single-family residence is diagrammed in Figure 11. Although the parcel of land occupied by this house is the smallest of the examples discussed, it too can be divided into its various parts. The house is the focus but the lot is further devoted to parkway, front lawn, sidewalks, driveway, garden, trash collection, and garage, which represent peripheral areas in relation to the house.

Illustrations could be continued indefinitely, each describing a different areal unit of organization in terms of focality within establishments, and each having a core and one or more subordinate peripheral parts.

Interconnections among Units of Area Organization

The following examples illustrate the ways in which interconnections are the means by which units of area organization are held together and may combine small units of area organization into larger ones. Interconnections are of two kinds, *internal* and *external*. Within an establishment internal connections bind it together and enable it to function as a unit. No establishment is without internal means of access to its parts, or external access to the rest of the community or the world at large. External connections link any establishment

[1] Richard S. Thoman, "The Changing Occupance Pattern of the Tri-state Area, Missouri, Kansas, and Oklahoma," Research Paper No. 31, University of Chicago, Dept. of Geography, 1953.

[2] Sheldon D. Ericksen, "Occupance in the Upper Deschutes Basin, Oregon," Research Paper No. 32, University of Chicago, Dept. of Geography, 1953.

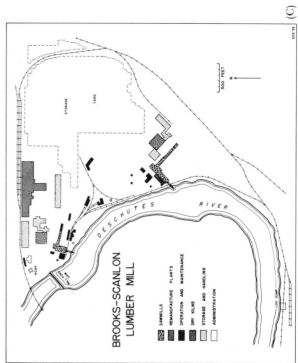

(B)

(C)

BROOKS-SCANLON
LUMBER MILL

SAWMILLS
REMANUFACTURE PLANTS
OPERATION AND MAINTENANCE
DRY KILNS
STORAGE AND HANDLING
ADMINISTRATION

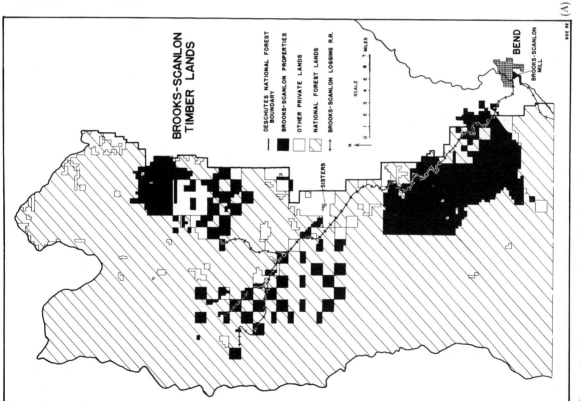

(A)

BROOKS-SCANLON
TIMBER LANDS

DESCHUTES NATIONAL FOREST
BOUNDARY
BROOKS-SCANLON PROPERTIES
OTHER PRIVATE LANDS
NATIONAL FOREST LANDS
BROOKS-SCANLON LOGGING R.R.

SCALE
0 1 2 3 4 5 6 7 MILES

SISTERS

BEND

BROOKS-SCANLON
MILL.

Figure 9. The area organization of a lumber mill. (*Courtesy of Sheldon D. Ericksen.*)

17

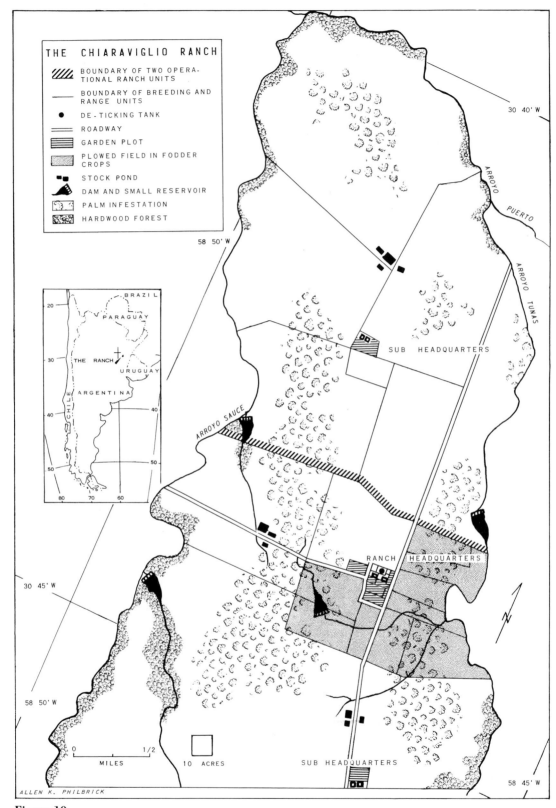

THE CHIARAVIGLIO RANCH

BOUNDARY OF TWO OPERA-
TIONAL RANCH UNITS

BOUNDARY OF BREEDING AND
RANGE UNITS

DE-TICKING TANK

ROADWAY

GARDEN PLOT

PLOWED FIELD IN FODDER
CROPS

STOCK POND

DAM AND SMALL RESERVOIR

PALM INFESTATION

HARDWOOD FOREST

30 40' W

58 50' W

ARROYO PUERTO

ARROYO TUNAS

BRAZIL

PARAGUAY

THE RANCH

URUGUAY

ARGENTINA

CHILE

20

30

40

50

80 70 60

40

50

ARROYO SAUCE

SUB HEADQUARTERS

RANCH HEADQUARTERS

30 45' W

58 50' W

N

0 1/2

MILES

10 ACRES

SUB HEADQUARTERS

58 45' W

ALLEN K. PHILBRICK

Figure 10

18

with others within a particular area of organization, and unite establishments among any number of separate areas of organization.

Internal Connections. Lines of movement are created within establishments resulting from the activities taking place in them. Traces, for example, are visible in agricultural fields along rows of crops. These are made by farm machinery in modern mechanized farming, or by the feet of farmers and domestic animals in nonmechanized agriculture. Paths and roadways follow the edges of fields and interconnect fields with the focal points of individual farmsteads.

In the Eagle-Pitcher mining field the underground roads and surface railways were the lines of movement of ore to the central mill. The logging railroads, the Deschutes River (converted into a mill pond with slips by which logs are guided to the saws), and the rail lines leaving the lumber mill are evidence of the movements of logs into and lumber out of the Brooks-Scanlon lumber mill.

External Interconnections. The road from a farm to the village interconnects the farm and the market within a larger community area. The railroad leading away from the mine and the lumber mill interconnect them with other places serving them and requiring their products. Many of these kinds of external connection exist as patterns of relatively fixed and permanent routes. The pictures and maps in Figures 12–17 show a number of the more important types of facilities and means of external interconnection which unite the regions of the world.

Mark Jefferson called the pattern which evolved from use of the steam locomotive "the civilizing rails."[1] The railroad building era during one hundred years from 1830 to 1930 saw the linking of vast areas of the world's lands when more than a million and a quarter miles of railroad track were constructed. Jefferson's maps in Figure 12 show the land surface within ten miles of operating railroads in 1920. The pattern is substantially the same today.

The first half of the twentieth century ushered in the air transportation age, exemplified by the view of the New York International Airport, Idlewild, one of the world's busiest (Figure 13). The map in Figure 14 shows the major flight lines connecting the world's lands through the services of commercial airlines.[2]

During the same period, the internal combustion engine, powered by gasoline, led not only to the

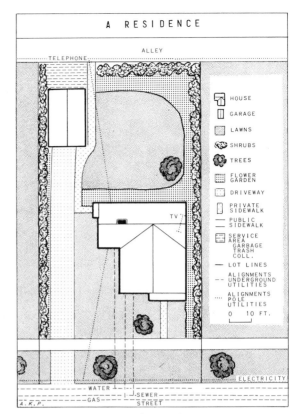

Figure 11

development of air transportation, but through the automobile made individual mobility a reality on land. There are today more than sixty million self-propelled vehicles on the highways of the United States, including cars, trucks, and busses. Traffic congestion produced by the automobile in the United States has made necessary such engineering feats as the "stack" in Los Angeles, shown in Figure 15. This is a four-decker expressway interchange to handle the interweaving of the huge streams of traffic.

The nationwide pattern of roads and highways which has evolved in the United States is similar in extent to that of the railroads. In the future, as shown by the map in Figure 16, a new interstate highway system consisting of four-lane, limited-access divided highways will link every major metropolitan center of the nation.

[1] Mark Jefferson, "The Civilizing Rails," *Economic Geography*, 4:217–231, 1928.
[2] Ernst Kremling, "Luftverkehr" (map) *Welt wirtschafts Atlas fur Politik und Zeitgesihicte*, Munich, Germany: JRO-Verlag, 1961, Karte Nr 139.

Until these developments in land and air transportation began leadership in interregional traffic, movement belonged to water transportation. Water is still the most economical means of moving bulk freight long distances, and is keeping pace with land and air forms as technological innovations in navigational aids and ship construction multiply. For example, atomic submarines are now in operation, and a subpolar route to the old world has been projected. It will only be a matter of time before this new source of energy is applied effectively to commercial water movement of freight.

The map in Figure 17 shows the major ocean shipping lanes of the world. The widths of the lines on the map are proportional to the net register tonnage of vessels moving along them. The routes represented interconnect the major ports of the world, of which the port of New York is the world's largest, illustrated by the harbor facilities shown in Figure 18.

Communication is an equally basic type of interconnection. Networks of telephone, telegraph, teletype, radio, and television communication today blanket heavily populated areas and interconnect all of the world's regions. This means that news and information can be almost instantaneously disseminated to all parts of the globe.

Other less tangible ties both unite and separate units of regional organization. The mine field used in an earlier example is a unit based on ownership, leases, contracts, and working agreements between a considerable number of independent subunits. While these contractual relationships bind the mining field together, they also serve to make it separate and distinct from other units of organized area. The inherent nature of private and public property rights is to recognize distinctions within which people acknowledge degrees of exclusiveness separating units of organized area from each other along sharp and legally defined lines. The existence of national states and blocs of nations having international agreements among them proves how fundamentally divisive as well as unifying the ideas and values in which people believe can be.

Regions of Human Organization

On the basis of these principles the human race has occupied and organized various parts of the earth's surface in a very unevenly distributed pattern of different kinds of activities. It is the task of the regional chapters of this book to visualize these

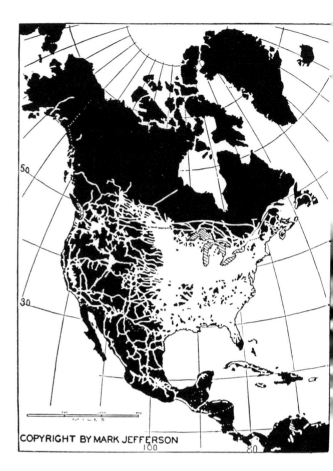

patterns and to illustrate the processes by which they have been created. It is the purpose of the remaining portion of the present chapter to outline the major division of the world into regions which can serve as a framework for that analysis and discussion.

Types of Area Organization. The occupied surface of the earth may be divided among three types of area organization. These are given the names (1) subsistence, (2) transitional, and (3) exchange organization of area. The titles of the categories imply a development from one to the other by stages. This is properly the subject of Chapter 5 dealing with cultural evolution, which is climaxed in present world patterns by the exchange organization of area. Each type will be defined in the present discussion and the patterns of their world distribution shown.

Subsistence area organization. The subsistence organization of area is defined by *local* self-sufficiency. Local isolation has been characteristic of the entire world throughout most of recorded

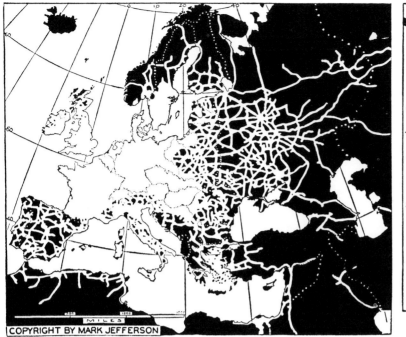

Figure 12. The areas in white on the continents represent the territories within ten miles of a railroad.

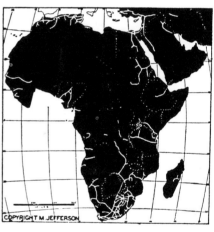

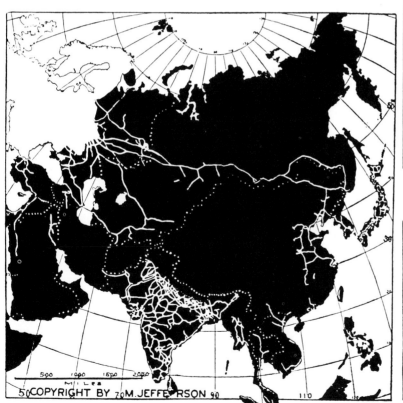

Figure 13. This aerial view of New York International Airport (Idlewild) was taken from 15,000 feet looking west across Brooklyn toward Manhattan and the Hudson River in the background. The air terminal itself has been created by filling in the swampy margins of Jamaica Bay on the southwestern corner of Long Island. (*Courtesy of The Port of New York Authority.*)

history. Only in the past several centuries has regional and worldwide interdependence developed. Subsistence represents individual, family, tribe, or other group effort to wrest a living directly from the earth's resources. In this form of local organization whatever is collected, trapped, killed, or grown to be eaten is consumed locally. Production, distribution, and consumption are oriented toward individual or group self-sufficiency. Many different groups of people fall into this category. Tribal areas occupied by primitive hunters and gatherers, rudimentary migratory subsistence farmers, and extensive subsistence pastoral peoples are represented. Emerging from this stage are the regions of intensive subsistence agricultural villages in China, India, Japan, and Java.

To describe the characteristics of subsistence the following selection is quoted from *A Chinese Village*[1], and is representative of the traditional agricultural village. The culture is Chinese, and the resources are those of Shantung Province in northeastern China. The mode of area organization is that of the subsistence agricultural village. With allowances for individual cultural differences, for variations in the degree of intensity of resource use, and for contrasts in material environment, examples of this same system of area organization could have been found throughout every part of the world as

[1] Martin C. Yang, *A Chinese Village, Taitou, Shantung Province,* London: Routledge and Kegan Paul Ltd., 1948, pp. 1, 4, 14, 16, 18, 19, 25, and 27.

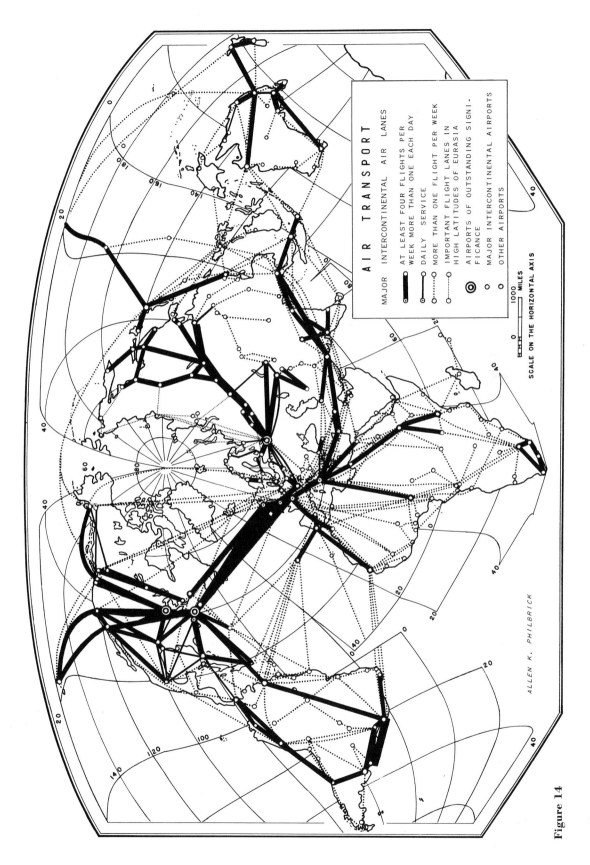

AIR TRANSPORT

MAJOR INTERCONTINENTAL AIR LANES

- AT LEAST FOUR FLIGHTS PER WEEK MORE THAN ONE EACH DAY
- DAILY SERVICE
- MORE THAN ONE FLIGHT PER WEEK
- IMPORTANT FLIGHT LANES IN HIGH LATITUDES OF EURASIA

- AIRPORTS OF OUTSTANDING SIGNIFICANCE
- MAJOR INTERCONTINENTAL AIRPORTS
- OTHER AIRPORTS

1000   0   1000
MILES

SCALE ON THE HORIZONTAL AXIS

ALLEN K. PHILBRICK

Figure 14

23

Figure 15. Four layers of concrete ribbons interweave part of Los Angeles traffic. Automobiles and trucks like zooming bugs symbolize the speed and intricacy of movement necessary for the functioning of modern cities. (*Courtesy of Los Angeles Chamber of Commerce.*)

little as two hundred years ago. In the not too distant future this mode of area organization may well become extinct.

The village of Taitou is located on a stretch of level land ringed with mountains on the southwestern shore of Kiaochow Bay. . . . This region is one of the oldest agricultural areas in China. Its people are almost all farmers who cultivate their own land and live in compact villages. . . .

The crop fields lie beyond and around the village. While the boundaries of neighboring villages frequently overlap, usually the boundary line is recognizable. . . . The village site can be divided roughly into two parts: the residential area and the immediate outskirts.

In this area, as in all other parts of the country, the cultivated land has for long been elaborately partitioned into very small fragments.[1] A farmer, or a

---

[1]Fields range in size from fragments of an acre to slightly more than one acre. Family holdings composed of many fragments will vary from one-quarter acre to a high of ten acres.

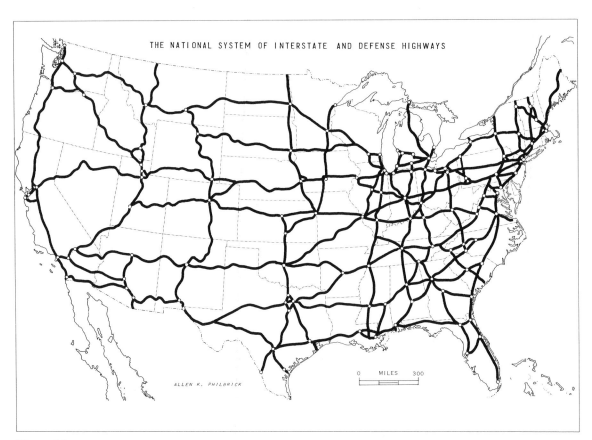

THE NATIONAL SYSTEM OF INTERSTATE AND DEFENSE HIGHWAYS

ALLEN K. PHILBRICK

0 MILES 300

Figure 16

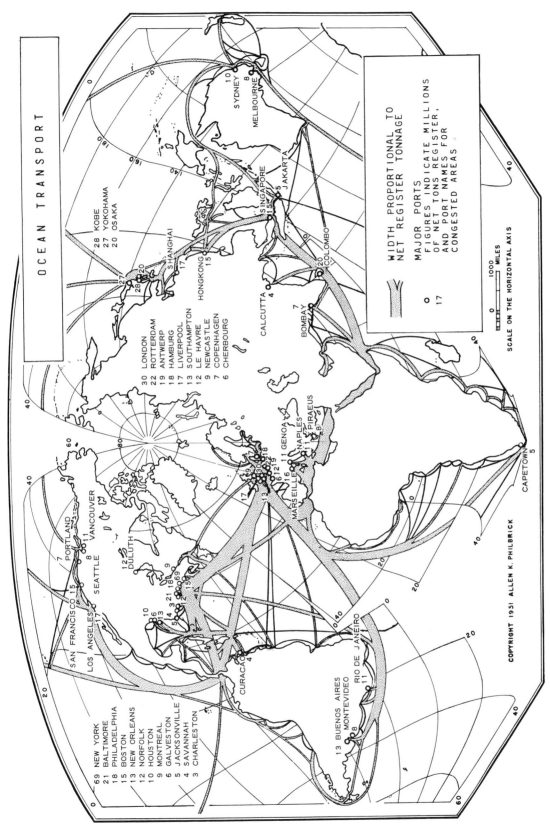

WIDTH PROPORTIONAL TO
NET REGISTER TONNAGE

MAJOR PORTS
FIGURES INDICATE MILLIONS
OF NET TONS REGISTER,
AND PORT NAMES FOR
CONGESTED AREAS

o
17

SCALE ON THE HORIZONTAL AXIS

0   1000
MILES

28 KOBE
27 YOKOHAMA
20 OSAKA

30 LONDON
22 ROTTERDAM
19 ANTWERP
18 HAMBURG
17 LIVERPOOL
13 SOUTHAMPTON
12 LE HAVRE
9 NEWCASTLE
7 COPENHAGEN
6 CHERBOURG

69 NEW YORK
21 BALTIMORE
18 PHILADELPHIA
15 BOSTON
13 NEW ORLEANS
12 NORFOLK
10 HOUSTON
9 MONTREAL
6 GALVESTON
5 JACKSONVILLE
4 SAVANNAH
3 CHARLESTON

COPYRIGHT 1951 ALLEN K. PHILBRICK

Figure 17. (*Courtesy of Prentice-Hall, Inc., from Lucille Carlson, Geography and World Politics, Englewood Cliffs, N.J., 1958, p. 69.*)

Figure 18. This aerial view of part of New York's more than 400 miles of shoreline available for harbor shows the Brooklyn shoreline with Manhattan in the background. The view from 6,500 feet is looking north up the Hudson River. (*Courtesy of The Port of New York Authority.*)

family, does not own one but a number of plots, and these are generally scattered in a number of localities. Homes are not on the cultivated land but in the village. . . . Each field belongs to a different owner and each owner must have some way of reaching his field, so there are numerous roads or paths crossing the land. In summer, or during the growing season, the land resembles many small strips of different colors lying side by side.

The main crops are wheat, millet, barley, soybean, corn, sweet potatoes, and peanuts. A variety of vegetables are grown in the gardens. . . .

The crop is threshed and the grain is dried and stored. . . . Millet is harvested as wheat is. Women . . . cut the seed-heads from the stalks with pieces of sharpened iron when the crop is gathered on the threshing ground.

Although agriculture is the main means of livelihood, many subsidiary occupations supplement income in the slack periods of the farm work calendar. . . .

None of the artisans in this village makes his living entirely from his trade, with the exception of the Christian church and the teacher of the Christian school. All the masons, carpenters, weavers, workers in the small foundry, the village schoolteacher, the crop watcher, and the several village officers work on their land with their families during the sowing and harvesting seasons. . . .

A number of important points may be summarized from the quotation: (1) the division of labor was extremely localized within the family or within the village; (2) whatever was produced was consumed largely at home; (3) principles of area organization define the core and periphery of the village as a subsistent unit; and (4) the facts of the account underscore the vegetarian diet and hand-labor basis of production. This contrasts with the greater emphasis upon meat in the diet and with mechanization of production in the exchange organization example to be examined next.

Exchange area organization. Exchange beyond the local area means trade and commerce, which assumes a division of labor beyond the family, tribe, small village, or group. It further involves the development of media of exchange. Some barter and money exchange is found in subsistence economies, but there it was primarily concerned with luxury goods rather than necessities. Today, without a continued high volume of trade in the necessities of life, whole countries and hundreds of cities would perish in a short time.

The modern exchange world and its component, the industrial world, evolved out of subsistence predecessors. For at least the last century, all mankind has been controlled and dominated by that portion of its members belonging to the large exchange economies. This most fundamental economic evolution in organization has been in progress for the past five centuries. It is largely the expression of European culture and is the product of the scientific and industrial revolution. Geographically it has meant the development of wider and wider geographic division of labor, larger and more discontinuous areas and regions of human organization, and also the further spread of European culture to many additional parts of the world.

The inherent geographical difference between *subsistence* and *exchange* organization of area is the more-than-local geographic division of labor characteristic of the latter. This fact is, of course, implicit in the world *exchange*. Gradual growth of exchange on a more-than-local basis was accompanied by exploration and the development of interregional division of labor or functions. Today many of these divisions have long since become intercontinental and worldwide in scope.

The significance of the degree of geographical division of labor in the exchange world can perhaps best be appreciated through an example. Consider the production of meat through its various stages in the United States. Each stage of production involves people and their establishments. Cattle from a ranch are rounded up and shipped to a Middle Western corn-belt farm for fattening. The farmer has cultivated corn on a large part of his land expressly for this purpose (Figure 19A). After some weeks of corn feeding, (Figure 19B) the fattened cattle are trucked either to a railhead or directly to a regional market such as the Chicago Stock Yards (Figure 19C and D). There the animals are sold, butchered, and processed. The processed meat is sold or kept in warehouses until it can be sold. The finished beef is purchased by a wholesaler or perhaps by a large chain grocery. The meat, which started out from a western ranch is then trucked to the freight yard, loaded into refrigerator cars, and shipped to a distant city. There the shipment is divided among several retail stores. Clerks wrap portions cut by the local butchers into attractive cellophane packages and arrange them in self-service meat counters (Figure 19E). The customers pick out their favorite cuts, and in due course the meat is consumed.

Many individuals in a long chain of establishments have participated in the geographically di-

Figure 19. Stages of meat production from field to store counter.

(A) Corn is mechanically harvested.

(B) Corn is placed in a feeding trough. (*Courtesy of U. S. Dept. of Agriculture.*)

vided production, distribution, processing, transportation, marketing, and consumption of meat. The entire organization of the activities in their respective places and in a particular sequence has depended upon the coordinated effort of a large number of persons distributed at specific places over a region thousands of miles in extent.

In a commercial economy each step takes place in not only different but often very widely separated establishments. Between all steps in the chain, trade or exchange must take place to keep the products flowing and the system operating. It is a system wherein *exchange* is the necessary ingredient in the cycle of production, distribution, and consumption in contrast to the subsistence economy, where each step characteristically takes place within the same establishment, or, if in a different one, within the same locality.

Geographically, therefore, the essential difference between the two main categories of world occupance is in the degree of development of a geographical division of functions, that is, the degree of individual and local community self-sufficiency. In the subsistence category, agriculture including animal husbandry supports most of the population locally and directly through the efforts of individuals on behalf of themselves, their families, or, at most, of their village or tribal groups. Division of labor occurs essentially at the local level, and contact between establishments located beyond this is rare.

In the exchange category, on the other hand, direct consumption of food or other articles by the producers themselves has been replaced by an elaborate division of labor. Producer and consumer are usually unknown to one another. They are brought together only indirectly and through the agency of commercial exchange. Geographical division of labor exists between establishments

(D) The Chicago Stockyards. (*Courtesy of American Meat Institute.*)

(C) The animals are taken by truck to livestock centers such as shown in (D). (*Courtesy of U. S. Dept. of Agriculture.*)

(E) The finished product appears under cellophane in stores. (*Courtesy of American Meat Institute.*)

located at any economically feasible distance from one another, local to worldwide. In most cases the consumer may not even know where an article he has used was produced, let alone be acquainted with any of the persons involved in its production.

Transition: subsistence to exchange. In practice it is increasingly difficult to tell whether many areas previously organized on a subsistence basis may still be so classified. China and India, for example, are rapidly developing the specialized functions of an exchange economy. A third category—*transitional*—can be used for regions which cannot be placed in either subsistence or exchange categories. There are few if any large areas of the world which can still be said to be 100 per cent subsistence oriented. In classifying world regions, the following definitions will be used. If more than 60 per cent of the population within a region gains more than half its livelihood by participation in exchange-type occu-

pance, the region is one of exchange-type area organization. If more than 60 per cent of the population lives by subsistence agriculture, such regions are classified as subsistence-type occupance regions. If the population falls within the range of more than 40 but less than 60 per cent of either of the two categories of organization, it is classified as a *transitional* or combined type.

Unoccupied regions. There are still uninhabited parts of the world. These are the areas of ice-covered water and coastal lands in the Arctic, and the ice-capped continental land and coastal water areas of Antarctica, each covering about five million square miles. Although the Antarctic is currently the site of temporary habitation set up for scientific observation and potential development under international agreement, it is classified as unoccupied. The world's oceans are also classifiable in this category.

World Pattern of Regions of Human Organization. The regions into which the world is divided for the purposes of analysis in this book are shown on the map in Figure 20. They are classified under the three headings previously enumerated and the unoccupied world in Table I: the exchange world, the subsistence world, and the transitional or combined type.

The exchange world. The exchange world is divided into seven major regions, the boundaries of which do not necessarily correspond to those of existing political units. The regions are given general descriptive titles for identification rather than for boundary definition purposes.

If the world were united, three of these regions, United States-Canada, Western Europe, and the Soviet Union, would form a single world core

TABLE I WORLD REGIONS

I. *The Exchange World* (7 regions)
  A. World Core
     United States-Canada
     Western Europe
     Soviet Union
  B. Southern Hemisphere Periphery
     Southern South America
     South Africa
     Australia-New Zealand
  C. Japan

II. *Transitional or Combined* (1 region)
  A. Intensive-Extensive
     Mexi-Caribbean America

III. *The Subsistence World* (9 regions)
  A. Intensive
     East Asia
     South Asia
  B. Intensive and Extensive
     Southeast Asia
     Southwest Asia and North Africa
  C. Extensive
     Amazon-Andean South America
     Africa South of the Sahara
     Central Asian Highlands and Basins
     Arctic Rimland
     Pacific Islands

IV. *The Unoccupied World* (5 regions)
  A. Frozen-Water Surfaces
     Arctic Ice-Covered Water and Land
     Antarctic Ice-Covered Land and Water
  B. Ocean Basins
     Pacific
     Atlantic
     Indian

realm of nodal or focal[1] organization. The two giants of the mid-twentieth century, the United States and the Soviet Union, are both Western European in cultural origin. They represent conflicting western and eastern expansions of European culture within the central middle latitudes of the Northern Hemisphere. Like two huge satellites flung into orbit from a nucleus of common origin, their separate and antagonistic development and aspirations trouble the world. Yet, both of them, with their European source region, represent the most advanced of industrially developed countries, based upon industrial-scientific technology.

The area organization of all three regions is marked by transportation and communications interconnections based upon a highly developed regional division of labor. As will be seen in much greater detail in regional chapters, these three industrially developed Northern Hemisphere regions are the core of a three-fold or tripartite organization of the present day world. The rest of the world's peoples are dominated in one way or another—politically, economically, militarily, and psychologically—by people of one or another of these core units. From these three regional centers stream the greatest number of land, water, and air transportation and communications lines interconnecting them with all parts of the world.

Only two of the seven exchange-world regions—Western Europe and the Soviet Union—share a common land boundary. The "iron curtain" is the European boundary between Communism to the East and free enterprise systems to the West. The United States-Canada region and Western Europe are both separated and united by the North Atlantic Ocean.

Three of the remaining four regions of importance in the exchange world are in the Southern Hemisphere. If the world's land masses are considered as a single unit, a view discussed in Chapter 1, these three regions occupy peripheral positions with respect to the tripartite world core region. They are, respectively, southern South America, southern Africa, and Australasia. The fourth exchange region is Japan. All seven of the exchange world regions are urban focused, with economies based upon the most advanced technological developments in the production of the necessities and the amenities of life.

---

[1]Nodal and focal are used synonymously here, although nodal is usually applied to large regions and focal to smaller areas.

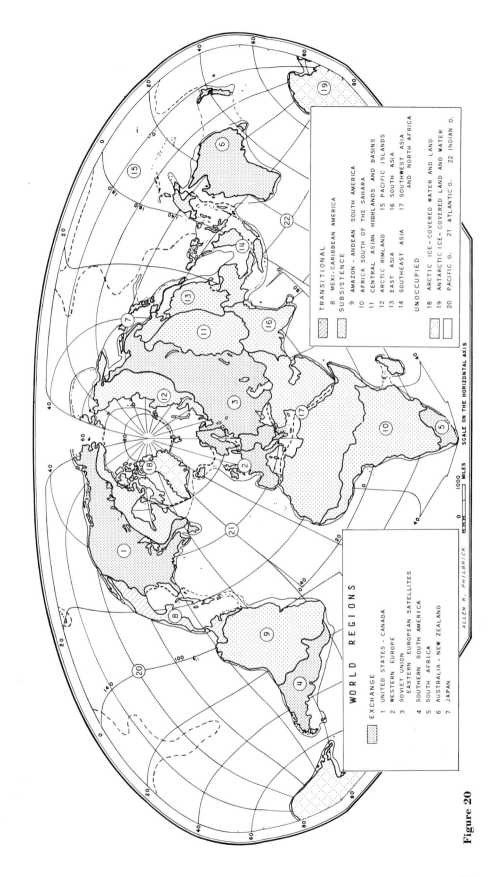

WORLD REGIONS

EXCHANGE
1 UNITED STATES - CANADA
2 WESTERN EUROPE
3 SOVIET UNION
  EASTERN EUROPEAN SATELLITES
4 SOUTHERN SOUTH AMERICA
5 SOUTH AFRICA
6 AUSTRALIA - NEW ZEALAND
7 JAPAN

TRANSITIONAL
8 MEXI-CARIBBEAN AMERICA

SUBSISTENCE
9 AMAZON - ANDEAN SOUTH AMERICA
10 AFRICA SOUTH OF THE SAHARA
11 CENTRAL ASIAN HIGHLANDS AND BASINS
12 ARCTIC RIMLAND   15 PACIFIC ISLANDS
13 EAST ASIA   16 SOUTH ASIA
14 SOUTHEAST ASIA   17 SOUTHWEST ASIA
                             AND NORTH AFRICA

UNOCCUPIED
18 ARCTIC ICE - COVERED WATER AND LAND
19 ANTARCTIC ICE - COVERED LAND AND WATER
20 PACIFIC O.   21 ATLANTIC O.   22 INDIAN O.

ALLEN K. PHILBRICK

SCALE ON THE HORIZONTAL AXIS

0   1000
MILES

Figure 20

31

The subsistence world. The rapidly changing subsistence world is divided into two major types of regions. One type is marked by scattered extensive and the other by concentrated intensive patterns of small local areal units of organization. The degree of concentration of settlement is measured in the average density of population and reflects the life-supporting capacity of natural resources as understood by the inhabitants of the areas in question.

The characteristics of *extensive subsistence regions* are: relatively few, small, scattered settlements; a sparse to very sparse population; and a low intensity of agricultural use of land. Characteristics of *intensive subsistence regions* are: relatively many, larger, and more frequently distributed settlements; a moderate to very dense population; and high intensity of agricultural use of the land. Varying degrees and mixtures of these two types of subsistence patterns occur within nine regions, constituting the subsistence category.

Dense and very dense concentrations of population (many closely packed small areal units of organization intensively cultivating the land for subsistence) are characteristic of the East Asia and South Asia regions. Two regions are mixtures of intensive and extensive subsistence occupance: Southeast Asia and the Middle East, including the Sahara of northern Africa. The remaining five regions, largely typical of extensive subsistence livelihood, are on the average very sparsely populated. Settlement within them is intermittent, separated by large unoccupied areas not specifically differentiated on the map. They are the Amazon-Andean region of South America, the region of Africa south of the Sahara, the central Asian highlands and basins, the Arctic rimland, and the ocean-dominated Pacific islands.

A transitional region in which both exchange and subsistence organization exist in somewhat equal quantities is represented by Mexi-Caribbean America. The proportion of urban to rural population is a useful indicator of the ratio of exchange organization to subsistence organization in a country such as Mexico. Large urban populations, not directly supported by individuals working the land, are indications of a commitment to more than local geographical division of labor. But large agricultural populations do not necessarily live primarily on a subsistence basis. In Mexico as a whole at least one-third of the population is urban.

The words core and periphery have been used in describing units of area organization of various scales. On the map of world regional organization in Figure 21, this concept is illustrated on a world scale. The core is the tripartite industrialized region composed of the United States, Western Europe, and the Soviet Union. The periphery is the rest of the world, interconnected radially with one or more of the centers in the core regions.

The same idea of regional organization with a core and periphery is repeated on a lesser scale within each of the seven regions of the exchange world. Generalized homogeneous regions of cropland, forest land, ranch land, and mineral-producing areas are united functionally by the centralized activities of manufacturing and trade. The activities within these peripheral regions come to a focus on the industrialized urban-core regions within the United States-Canada, Europe, and the Soviet Union. In a somewhat less fully developed way the same relationship exists in each of the countries of southern South America—Chile, Brazil, Uruguay, and Argentina; within the Republic of South Africa, Australia, and New Zealand; and within Japan.

The same idea of core and periphery is repeated on a still smaller scale within each of the subregions of the seven exchange world regions, and yet further down the scale within any community. Life is focused within cities and settlements wherever people live. Individual establishments, the basic geographical units of focality, it will be remembered, are composed of the same two parts—core and peripheral areas of activity which focus upon the core.

The progression of area units from individual establishments to world regions and the world as a whole are formed into a hierarchy of regions of human organization. The larger regions are functionally formed by the successive interconnections between the smaller ones.

Starting at the top, worldwide organization is composed of subparts (the seven exchange world regions), each of which is itself functionally organized internally. The pattern of human organization of area is such that the interconnections of different kinds of activity in a series of peripheral areas focus upon a hierarchically arranged series of cores, which extends right down to each individual establishment everywhere, and within each establishment to each person in human society.

Within regions of a subsistence organization of

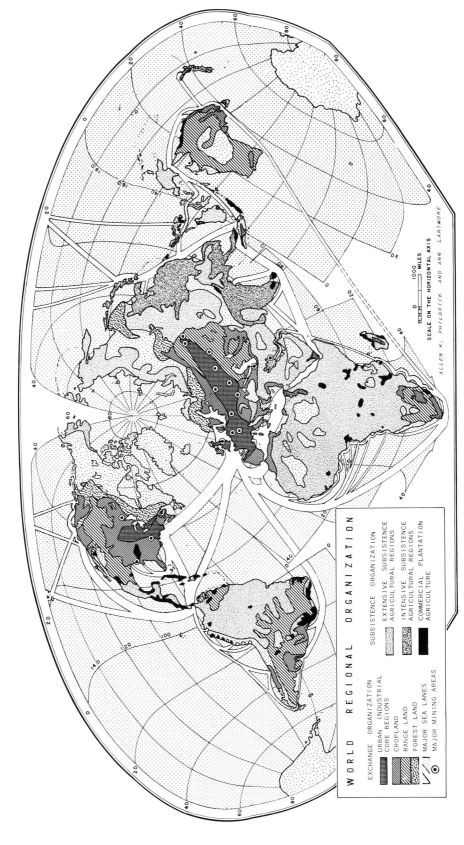

Figure 21. (*Courtesy of Economic Geography, taken from Allen K. Philbrick, "Principles of Areal Functional Organization in Regional Human Geography."*)

area the evolution of larger regional focality is weak or nonexistent. In these regions the presence of thousands of local units of area organization at the village and tribal levels attests to the vigorous existence of the human organization of area, but at a lower order of complexity. All parts of the world, however, are rapidly developing larger units of exchange-type regional organization. In this sense it would be fair to say that pure subsistence organization of area remains scarcely anywhere in the world. But the involvement of the population as a whole in exchange-type organization has not everywhere reached the same proportions. It is for this reason that the world regions of human organization shown on the map in Figure 20 distinguish between exchange, subsistence, transitional, and unoccupied categories.

The Pattern of World Population

The regions of human organization in Figure 21 classify world society into various categories. The pattern of world population shows more definitely within each region where the population fitting these categories is located. Visualizing how unevenly the population of the world is distributed will be used to set the stage for discussion of the other two aspects of geography. For it is the resources of nature and the processes of cultural evolution which supply the additional ingredients for an understanding of the distribution of world society.

The pattern of people shown on the map in Figure 22 is the result of long-continued application of human creative ability to the general problems of survival on this planet. The estimated 2.9 billion persons in the world are very unevenly distributed. One country, China, contains nearly one-fourth of this total. Four countries, China, India, the Union of Soviet Socialist Republics, and the United States of America account for one-half. Only sixteen countries have populations which contribute 1 per cent or more to the world total (29 million out of 2.9 billion). These first sixteen countries are listed by size of population in Table II. The total population of these countries is nearly three-fourths of the world's total. Out of more than 150 indepen-

TABLE II   THE FIRST SIXTEEN COUNTRIES BY POPULATION IN THE WORLD, 1959–1961[a]

Country	Rank	Population, millions	Per cent of world	Area,[b] sq. mi.	Per cent of world area	Average[b] population/sq. mi.
World		2,907.0	100.0	52,185.3	100.0	55.7
China	1	669.0	23.0	3,691.5	7.1	181.2
India	2	438.0	15.1	1,260.0	2.4	347.6
U.S.S.R.	3	210.5	7.2	8,649.4	16.6	24.3
U.S.A.	4	180.0	6.2	3,615.2	6.9	49.7
Pakistan	5	93.8	3.3	364.4	0.7	257.4
Japan	6	93.4	3.2	142.7	0.3	654.5
Indonesia	7	90.3	3.1	575.9	1.1	156.8
Brazil	8	64.2	2.2	3,287.9	6.3	19.5
West Germany	9	52.8	1.8	95.7	0.2	551.7
United Kingdom	10	52.2	1.8	94.2	0.2	554.1
Italy	11	49.0	1.7	116.3	0.2	421.3
France	12	45.1	1.5	212.8	0.4	211.9
Mexico	13	34.6	1.2	760.4	1.5	45.5
Nigeria	14	33.7	1.2	339.2	0.6	99.3
Spain	15	29.9	1.0	194.4	0.4	153.8
Poland	16	29.3	1.0	120.4	0.2	243.3
Total		2,165.8	74.5	23,520.4	45.1	92.1

[a] United Nations, *Demographic Yearbook 1960*, New York: 1961, pp. 99–118.
[b] Excluding uninhabited polar lands and uninhabited islands.

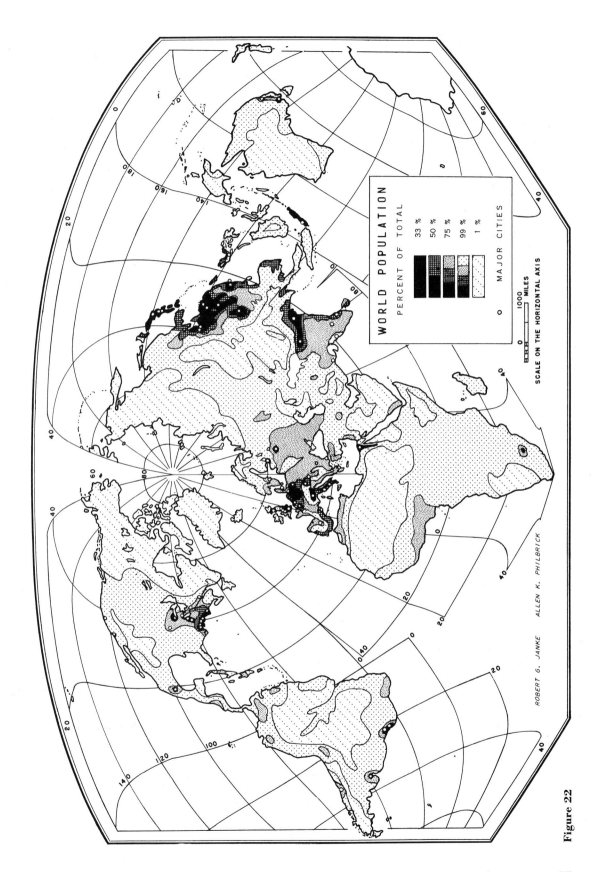

WORLD POPULATION

PERCENT OF TOTAL

33 %
50 %
75 %
99 %
1 %

○ MAJOR CITIES

SCALE ON THE HORIZONTAL AXIS

0   1000
MILES

ROBERT G. JANKE   ALLEN K. PHILBRICK

Figure 22

dent countries and dependent states existing in the world, these sixteen range from Poland's 29 million persons to China's nearly 670 million.

The extreme degree of concentration of population can be appreciated by the fact that one-third of humanity is included within twenty-four blacked-in areas on the map in Figure 22. These most heavily populated areas lie primarily within four distinct regions—Eastern Asia, Southern and Southeast Asia, Western Europe, and in Eastern North America. They occupy a total of less than 3 per cent of the world's land area. Each blacked-in area represents at least one-tenth of 1 per cent (2.9 million persons) at an average density per square mile of 640 persons. Around these major concentrations of people the map further shows the most densely populated one-half, two-thirds, and three-fourths of the human race. Such a map, based at it must be upon estimates, serves only to demonstrate the concentration of population. From it, however, in comparison with the map of regions of human organization, the concentrations of subsistence agricultural village populations in China and India can be distinguished from the heavily industrialized urban concentrations in Europe, Russia, and North America, as well as the secondary core regions of exchange-type regional organization in the Southern Hemisphere.

The significance of a density of 640 persons per square mile (one person per acre) is illustrated by comparison to average American Middle West rural population density. In the Middle West a typical square mile of farm land contains a density of sixteen–twenty persons. If each farm housed four persons, there would be four or five farms in one square mile. On this basis a density of 640 persons per square mile would require subdivision of a square mile into 160 four-acre farms. Such a density of agricultural population is inconceivable to those used to present circumstances and standards of living in the United States. Yet, the density of agricultural population in parts of China, India, Japan, and Java, for example, is actually two or three times that figure of 640 per square mile.

The world's largest concentration in area and population in North China, whose inhabitants total 9 per cent of the world's people (250 million) within an estimated area of only 290,000 square miles. The newest large concentration is the urban strip from Boston to Washington along the coastal fringe of the northeastern United States. Twenty-eight million Americans—approximately 1 per cent of the total world population—live in this 19,000-square-mile territory. North China is primarily agricultural. The northeastern United States coastal fringe is almost completely urban and suburban. It is difficult to imagine two heavily populated regions of the world more different from each other than the Eastern United States and Northern China. These differences are basically contrasts in types of area organization classifying parts of the pattern of world population.

Summary

This chapter has expanded the idea that the activities of people can be generalized as geographical units of organized area. Principles of *focality, localization* and *interconnection,* of *creative imagination,* and of the *hierarchical arrangement* of human society have been formulated. For purposes of summary these principles are repeated here.

1. Human activity has focus.

2. Focal activity is localized in specific places.

3. Establishments become interconnected during the normal course of the activities of people in the fulfillment of their needs. The interconnections of focal establishments form larger units of area organization.

4. The evolution of regions of human organization is ultimately the outgrowth of creative imagination in a setting of accumulated cultural experience and natural resources both in space and in time.

5. The progression of area units from individual establishments to world regions and the world as a whole are formed into a hierarchy of regions of human organization.

As the result of the operation of these principles it is possible to recognize the existence of three types of world regions. These are shown under the headings of subsistence, transitional, and exchange-type organization. The twenty-two regions of the map in Figure 20 subdivide the pattern of population distribution in Figure 22, thus providing the regional framework of this human world.

In the next two chapters the distribution of material resources, the primary basis of life, will be discussed. It is necessary to have a clear idea of the basic resources available for human use in order to understand how human beings, during the course of using them, have subdivided the world into regions. The next chapter deals with the distribution of the elements—sunlight, warmth, and water.

3 *Warmth and Water*

The atmosphere consists primarily of oxygen, nitrogen, and lesser amounts of carbon dioxide and water vapor as well as traces of rarer gases. Oxygen is necessary for survival of animal life, while carbon dioxide and nitrogen are essential ingredients of plant life. Both forms of life are dependent upon water, light, and warmth. Atmospheric constituents (oxygen, carbon dioxide, and nitrogen) remain fairly constant throughout the atmospheric shell around the world, but sunlight, heat energy stored in the atmosphere, and amounts of fresh water available to life on land differ greatly in their distribution. It will be the task of this chapter to present significant patterns of light, warmth, and fresh water over the surface of the earth.

Warmth

Some background information is necessary to understand the variable patterns of light energy and its transformation into warmth.

Earth-Sun Relations. Light energy, which comes to the earth from the sun, is distributed according to an orderly progression upon different parts of the earth in different amounts. These differences are a complex product of a number of factors.

1. The sun's rays fall upon a spherical or curved surface.

2. The rotation of the earth occurs once every 24 hours.

3. The revolution of the earth around the sun occurs once in every $365\frac{1}{4}$ days.

4. The earth's axis of rotation is consistently inclined at an angle of $23\frac{1}{2}$ degrees from the vertical in relation to the plane of the earth's orbit around the sun.

The curvature of the earth's surface causes variation from 90 to 180 degrees in the angle at which the sun's light strikes the outer shell of the earth including the atmosphere. Such variation produces a large difference in the concentration of energy received per unit of area.

The rotation of the earth makes daylight and darkness alternately within every 24-hour period. The yearly revolution of the earth around the sun produces the alternation of the seasons from spring to summer, to fall, and to winter.

These factors taken together produce a particular pattern and progression of energy receipt or *insolation.* For the whole year any given point on the earth has a characteristic progression in the amount of light energy received. At any given instant there is variation from place to place in the amount of energy being received over the whole earth.

Transformation of Light Energy into Heat. Light energy from the sun does not heat the atmosphere directly, since the air is capable of directly absorbing only about 14 per cent of the energy of sunlight. Instead, the surface materials of the earth absorb the relatively short wavelengths of light energy and transform them into the longer wavelengths of heat energy. The earth, in turn, is primarily responsible for warming the atmosphere. Thus, the average amount of light energy received at any point on the earth's surface will determine the amount of energy available to be transformed into heat.

A second major control of the transformation of light energy into heat is the heating and cooling characteristics of the different kinds of surface on which sunlight falls. Land and water heat and cool at different rates. Land heats faster and to a higher temperature and cools faster and to a lower temperature than does a corresponding body of water receiving an identical amount of solar energy. Hence, at any given latitude which receives identical average amounts of solar energy there is a greater average annual range of temperature over land than over water.

The most useful basis for the regional delineation of warmth regions is provided by two major criteria: (1) *average annual range* of temperature and (2) *seasonal cycles* of temperature.

Average Annual Range of Temperature.

Average annual temperature range is the difference between the average temperature of the warmest month and the average temperature of the coldest month of the year. Monthly averages are in turn averages of daily temperatures. Thus, the annual range generalizes the variation in temperatures characteristic of a place during the annual cycle of the season.

Figure 23 shows the position of lines passing through points of equal average annual range of temperature. The map reflects operation of the two principal controls of temperature—solar energy and difference between land and water as agents of heat transfer. In the first instance, differences in annual range from zero to more than 100 degrees generally accord with latitude. Little range is observed in equatorial latitudes. The range increases with latitude poleward. At the same time, lines of equal average annual range of temperature show remarkable agreement with the shapes of land masses, reflecting the difference between capacities of land and water to absorb light energy and transform it into heat.

From the map in Figure 23 the following five categories of average annual temperature range are defined in quantitative terms:

Small	0–10 degrees Fahrenheit
Moderate	10–30 degrees Fahrenheit
Great	30–50 degrees Fahrenheit
Severe	50–90 degrees Fahrenheit
Extreme	More than 90 degrees Fahrenheit

Solar control is most dominant in equatorial latitudes of small average annual temperature range, while average annual ranges poleward from the equator remain the smallest over water. Conversely, average annual ranges are greater much closer to the equator over land than they are over water, demonstrating the importance of difference between land and water as agents of heat transfer to the air. This difference obviously matters least in equatorial latitudes. Its effect becomes progressively greater poleward, particularly over land, but the influence of the land is also felt far out into the oceans *east* of the continents in middle latitudes. This latter effect is the result of consistent west-to-east movement of surface winds in the middle latitudes known as the Prevailing Westerlies. By the same token the influence of the sea is felt along the *west* coasts of continents in middle latitudes. It is not surprising, therefore, that names of temperature regions should allude to continental versus marine location and to general latitudinal position.

Marine, equatorial, and continental equatorial range regions have small average annual temperature ranges, while continental range regions, except in equatorial latitudes, have large average annual ranges. An estimate based on the map in Figure 23 shows that more than 80 per cent of the total square miles of the earth's surface which experiences a small annual range in temperature is water surface. More than 90 per cent of the additional area from 10–20 degree range (the lower half of the category called "moderate" average annual range) is ocean. Conversely, more than two-thirds of the remaining square miles of the earth having an excess of 20 degrees range in average annual temperature is land surface. It will be noted from the map that the largest ocean areas having temperature ranges greater than 20 degrees are adjacent to the eastern margins of North America and Asia. For Antarctica, location of the 20-degree range line can only be estimated. The ring of moderate average annual temperature range (10–30 degrees) is transitional between marine and continental regions, being partly subtropical continental in character and partly middle-latitude marine. Middle-latitude continental atmospheric regions which have average annual temperature ranges greater than 30 degrees lie over land. The correlation of *moderate, great, severe,* and *extreme continental* temperature ranges with land masses in middle latitudes is the primary and dramatic fact shown by the map in Figure 23.

Average annual temperature range, however, tells only part of the story. A difference of 15 degrees, for example, between an average *33 degrees* in January and a 48-degree average in July is the same amount in degrees as the range from a January average of 80 degrees to a July average of 95 degrees; yet the actual temperature regimes referred to are very different. One regime is cool all year round; the other is hot. Obviously, therefore, the actual temperatures characteristic of a place must be taken into account in addition to the average annual range of temperatures in defining warmth regions.

Table III shows the average temperature for the warmest and coldest months of a series of stations located within the "small" range ring. As may be seen, each has a range of less than 30 degrees and more than 10 degrees, yet the actual average temperatures for these stations vary from a 27-degree

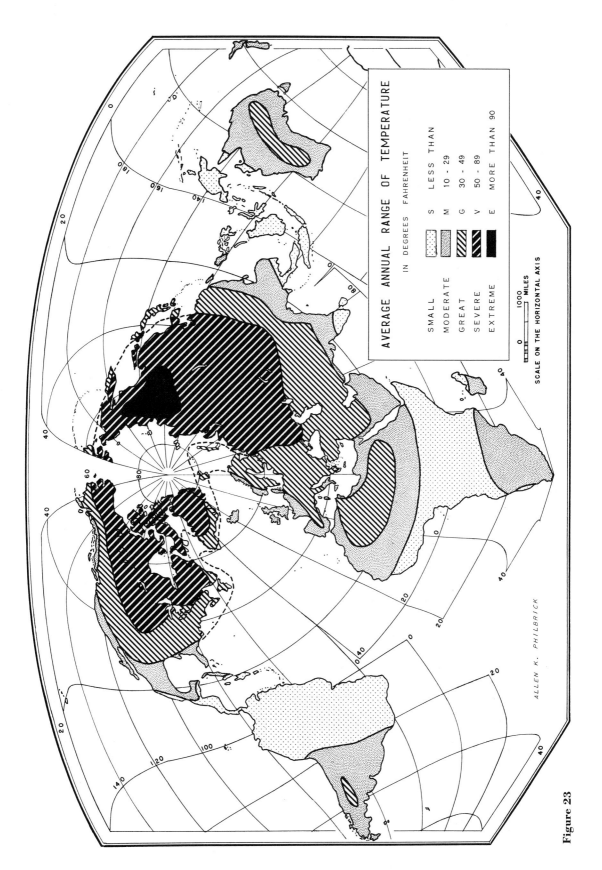

AVERAGE ANNUAL RANGE OF TEMPERATURE

IN DEGREES FAHRENHEIT

S LESS THAN
M 10 - 29
G 30 - 49
V 50 - 89
E MORE THAN 90

SMALL
MODERATE
GREAT
SEVERE
EXTREME

SCALE ON THE HORIZONTAL AXIS

0   1000
         MILES

ALLEN K. PHILBRICK

Figure 23

39

TABLE III SELECTED STATIONS WITH AVERAGE ANNUAL TEMPERATURE RANGES FROM 10–30 DEGREES

Station	*Av. temp., coldest month*[a]	*Av. temp., warmest month*	*Av. annual range*	*Station*	*Av. temp., coldest month*	*Av. temp., warmest month*	*Av. annual range*
Timbuktu	71	95	24	Gibraltar	55	75	20
Aden	76	89	13	Azores	58	73	15
Karachi	65	87	22	San Diego	54	68	14
Calcutta	65	86 (May)	20	Marseilles	44	72	28
Cairo	53	81	28	Salem	41	66	25
Bermuda	62 (Feb.-Mar.)	80 (Aug.)	26	London	39	63	24
Taihoku	57 (Feb.)	82	25	Atka	34	51	17
Hong Kong	58 (Feb.)	85 (July-Aug.)	27	Stykkisholm	29 (Feb.)	51 (Aug.)	22
				Tromsö	27	52	27

[a] Temperatures are in degrees Fahrenheit. Unless otherwise indicated warmest month is July and coldest is January.

January average at Tromsö, Norway, to 76 degrees for January at Aden. At the opposite end of the yearly range cycle, Tromsö has a July average of 52 degrees against a July average for Aden of 89 degrees or 95 degrees for Timbuktu.

Seasonal Cycles of Temperature. The seasonal character of temperatures may be defined in terms of varying degrees of warmth and their significance to people. As indicated earlier, for example, the freezing point of water at 32 degrees Fahrenheit is a critical point in its significance to man. According to Hartshorne[1] there are four kinds of seasons.

Cold Season: Mean daily temperatures below 32 degrees; snow and ice prominent.
Cool Season: Mean temperatures above 32 degrees but below 50; frosts occur, but do not dominate.
Warm Season: Mean temperatures above 50 degrees but below 68 degrees; free from frost, but without extreme heat.
Hot Season: Mean temperatures above 68 degrees.

The cycles of cold, cool, warm, and hot may be used to define the general conditions characteristic of the yearly regime of temperatures for any place. The map in Figure 24 shows these four cycles derived from temperature data for stations throughout the world, forming regions of seasonal cycles of temperature which fall into ten types of seasonal temperature regions.

1. Hot
2. Warm
3. Cool
4. Cold
5. Warm-Hot
6. Cool-Warm
7. Cold-Cool
8. Cool-Warm-Hot-Warm
9. Cold-Cool-Warm-Cool
10. Cold-Cool-Warm-Hot-Warm-Cool

[1]Richard Hartshorne, "Six Standard Seasons of the Year," *Ann. Assn. Am. Geographers*, 28:165–178 (1938).

Other "Controls" of Temperature. Many other agents and processes modify distribution of air temperatures in addition to those just defined in terms of latitudinal position and marine versus continental location. Important among these are elevation and the effect of ocean currents upon the distribution of heat energy. Cloudiness, humidity, and precipitation also affect warmth. Only elevation and ocean currents will be discussed, however.

Elevation. For every thousand feet of elevation above sea level the average temperature of the air drops 3 degrees Fahrenheit. Stations at the same latitude but at markedly different elevations demonstrate this temperature effect, as shown in the graphs in Figure 25. Pertinent locational facts for three such stations in South America are shown in Table IV.

The table and graphs show that while the three stations have nearly identical average annual ranges of temperature, actual temperatures vary directly with elevation. While the seasonal cycle of Cuyaba, Brazil, is hot all year round, La Paz, Bolivia, is cool-warm; and El Misti, on the Bolivian-Peruvian border, is cold.

When making world maps of temperature, data are reduced to sea level in order to eliminate the variation due to elevation. As shown in Figure 25

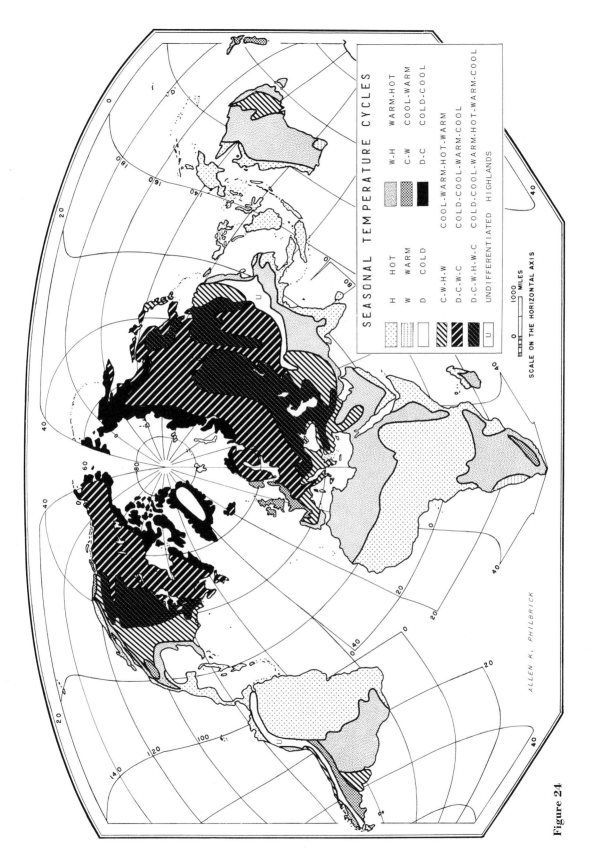

SEASONAL TEMPERATURE CYCLES

H HOT	W-H	WARM-HOT
W WARM	C-W	COOL-WARM
D COLD	D-C	COLD-COOL

C-W-H-W	COOL-WARM-HOT-WARM
D-C-W-C	COLD-COOL-WARM-COOL
D-C-W-H-W-C	COLD-COOL-WARM-HOT-WARM-COOL
	UNDIFFERENTIATED HIGHLANDS

SCALE ON THE HORIZONTAL AXIS

0   1000
MILES

ALLEN K. PHILBRICK

Figure 24

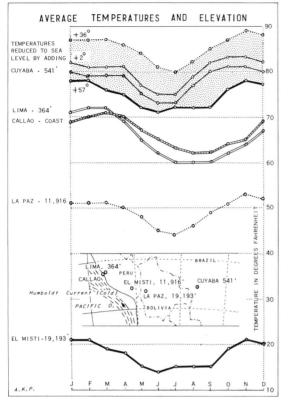

Figure 25

and Table IV, such manipulations show that except for elevation all three stations would have average readings within 10 degrees of one another every month of the year. All three would have only a "hot" seasonal cycle if they were all at sea level.

Ocean currents. Compare, now, the three inland station graphs (reduced to sea level) with the two additional lines on the graph in Figure 25 representing coastal temperatures at Lima and Callao. These two places are west coastal points, at 345 feet of elevation and at sea level, respectively. Why are the average monthly temperatures so consistently 10 to 20 degrees cooler than those of interior stations reduced to sea level? It cannot be due primarily to marine versus continental conditions, because at 15 degrees south latitude the prevailing winds in the Southern Hemisphere are the Southeast Trades, which blow offshore, not onshore, which would make the air warmer instead of cooler. The cooling effect is the result, rather, of a northward-flowing current of cool water from colder, more southerly locations in the Pacific. The cool current is made still colder by the upwelling of water from sea depths immediately adjacent to the coast, due to replacement of surface waters pushed offshore by offshore winds. In the Atlantic there is a similarly notable cold current off the coast of southwest Africa, known as the Benguela Current.

Perhaps the most famous current of all is the warm Gulf Stream in the Atlantic, a mighty "ocean river," which carries tropical waters, warming air temperatures poleward from equatorial latitudes past Miami, the Bahamas, and Bermuda. Farther north, this great stream within the ocean swings eastward and becomes the North Atlantic Drift. To it, in the main, may be attributed the relatively milder average annual ranges of temperature along the North Atlantic coast of Europe all the way past northern Scandinavia. It brings ice-free conditions, for example, to the port of Murmansk on the Kola Peninsula of the Soviet Union, well north of the Arctic Circle.

A similar current, known as the Kuroshio or Japanese Current, which flows northward off the east coast of Asia, helps to account for the smaller range of temperatures along the marine west coast of northern North America. It, too, swings eastward, as does the Gulf Stream North Atlantic Drift in the Atlantic, becoming the North Pacific Current. It brings both warmer water and warmer air masses to

TABLE IV   EFFECT OF ELEVATION ON AIR TEMPERATURE[a]

Stations	Latitude	Longitude	Elevation, feet	Av. annual temp.	Av. annual temp. reduced to sea level	Av. annual range
Cuiaba	15.30 S	56.10 W	541	78	80	8
La Paz	16.29 S	68.30 W	11,916	49	85	9
El Misti	16.15 S	70.58 W	19,193	18	75	7

[a] W. G. Kendrew, *The Climates of the Continents*, Oxford, England: Clarendon Press, 1953, pp. 522–523.

the west coast of the Pacific Northwest of the United States and western Canada.

The principal systems of ocean currents in the major ocean basins of the world are shown on the map in Figure 26. Cool currents are those moving equatorward from more poleward locations, and warm currents are those moving poleward from more equatorial regions.

Growing Season. In terms of its significance to human activities, perhaps the most important effect of the amount and seasonality of heat energy in the atmosphere is the length of time between the last frost in the spring and the first frost in the fall. This span of time is the normal period in which vegetation will grow during the year if it receives an adequate supply of moisture, sunlight, and carbon dioxide, plus other necessary mineral and organic nutrients from the soil. Every place has an average annual growing season, varying from a duration of no days in some places to the entire year in others, as shown in Figure 27. Minimum growing season for a great many crops is close to 120 days. If there are 240 consecutive days without frost, there is, accordingly, time for double cropping that is, two 120-day crops from the same land in the same growing season). If there are 360 days (nearly frost free), three crops are possible. Last, there are those tropical areas which never have a frost. These lands have no winter, though they may have a nongrowing season induced by drought. Thus, from the standpoint of the duration of warmth, regions vary from none to one, then two, then multiple growing seasons. In combinations with other conditions and circumstances of agriculture, the length of the growing season has great significance for the areal distribution of different kinds of agriculture.

Warmth Regions. When the two criteria of warmth—*average annual temperature range* and *seasonal cycles*—are combined as in the map in Figure 28, the resulting areas are designated as *warmth regions.* The criterion of average annual range bounds a series of ringlike zones, according to varying degrees of marine versus continentality of temperature extremes. Seasonal cycles of actual average temperatures subdivide the range belts or rings into individual sectors. Each combination of temperature zone and seasonal sector constitutes a *warmth region.* It can readily be appreciated that each seasonal cycle sector crosses several temperature range rings, and that each temperature belt crosses several seasonal cycle sectors.

With few exceptions the entire land surface of the world can be described adequately by less than two dozen warmth regional types. Specific individual warmth regions are shown by the map in Figure 28. The combinations of temperature and seasonal cycle for each type on the map are shown in the appendix at the end of this book. Individual temperature graphs for each average annual range ring are shown in Figure 29. The temperature lines in each graph are so designed that we may identify and read the average monthly temperatures for representative stations. The portion of the year during which any one of the seasonal categories occurs receives the name of that warmth category. In this manner, any period with average temperatures over 68 degrees is hot; from 50–68 degrees is warm; from 32–50 degrees is cool; below 32 degrees is cold.

The horizontal lines drawn on the temperature graphs in Figure 29 represent the same seasonal temperature limits. Accordingly, those stations in each range region belonging to specific seasonal-cycle categories are shown in separate groups on the graphs. Spans of temperature (in addition to *selected* individual line graphs) which summarize each warmth region type are shown in Figure 29.

The map in Figure 28 illustrates a number of relationships. Temperature ranges between extremes of warmth and of cold are greater over land than they are over water in corresponding latitudes. Water's moderating influence upon air temperatures is everywhere evident, because it warms more slowly, and, once heated, cools more slowly than land. The Arctic Ocean ice pack acts like a land bridge between North America and Asia. In response to such continuity of solid surface the *great* and *severe* temperature range rings extend from America across the Arctic into Asia. Great indentations in contours of average annual temperature range occur poleward over the North Atlantic. These indicate smaller ranges of temperature resulting from warm ocean currents. By contrast, the *severe, great,* and *moderate* range rings are U-shaped with the bases of the U's pointing equatorward over land areas. In the Southern Hemisphere the poleward ends of three of the Southern Hemisphere continents, South America, Africa, and Australia, which are isolated from one another by the South Atlantic and Indian Oceans, lie within moderate-temperature range zones of the Southern Hemisphere.

Warmth regions have been discussed in terms of

OCEAN CURRENTS

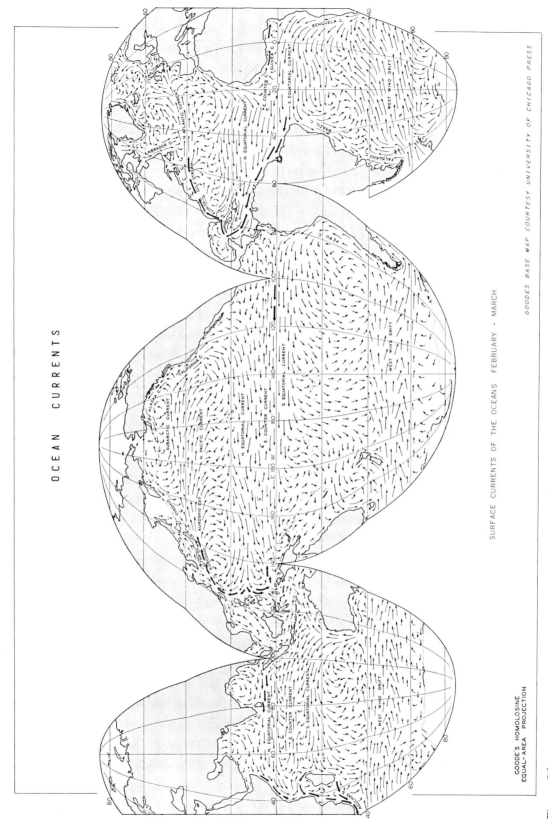

SURFACE CURRENTS OF THE OCEANS   FEBRUARY - MARCH

GOODES BASE MAP COURTESY UNIVERSITY OF CHICAGO PRESS

GOODE'S HOMOLOSINE
EQUAL-AREA PROJECTION

Figure 26

44

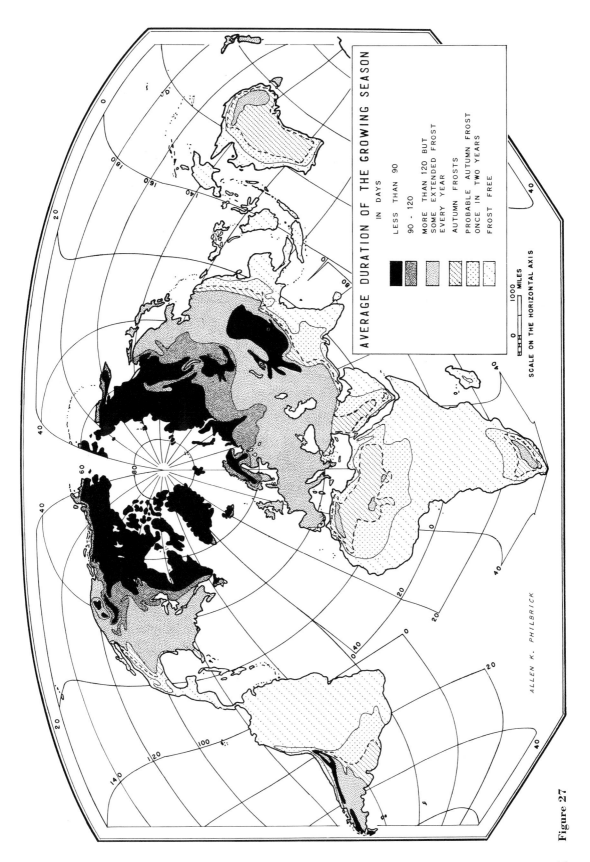

AVERAGE DURATION OF THE GROWING SEASON

IN DAYS

LESS THAN 90

90 - 120

MORE THAN 120 BUT
SOME EXTENDED FROST
EVERY YEAR

AUTUMN FROSTS

PROBABLE AUTUMN FROST
ONCE IN TWO YEARS

FROST FREE

0   1000
MILES

SCALE ON THE HORIZONTAL AXIS

ALLEN K. PHILBRICK

Figure 27

45

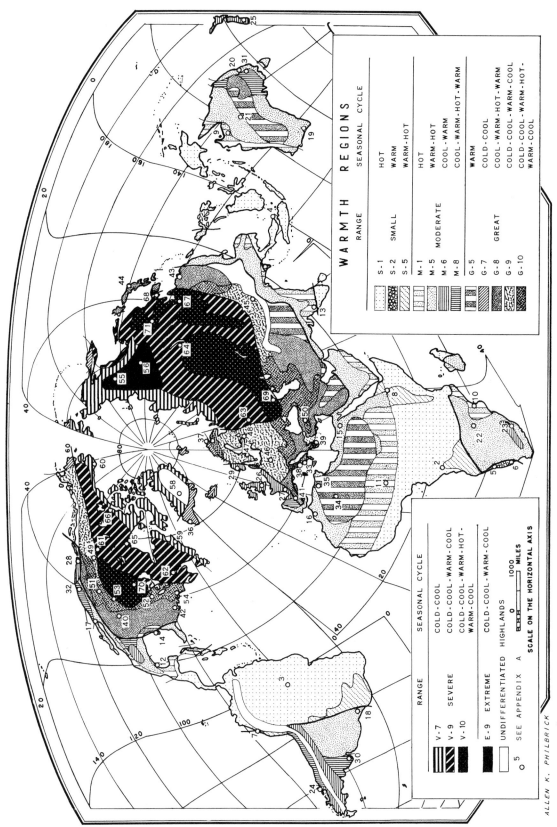

WARMTH REGIONS

	RANGE		SEASONAL CYCLE
S-1	SMALL		HOT
S-2			WARM
S-5			WARM-HOT
M-1	MODERATE		HOT
M-5			WARM-HOT
M-6			COOL-WARM
M-8			COOL-WARM-HOT-WARM
G-5	GREAT		WARM
G-7			COLD-COOL
G-8			COLD-COOL-WARM-WARM
G-9			COLD-COOL-WARM-COOL
G-10			COLD-COOL-WARM-HOT-WARM-COOL

	RANGE	SEASONAL CYCLE
V-7	SEVERE	COLD-COOL
V-9		COLD-COOL-WARM-COOL
V-10		COLD-COOL-WARM-HOT-WARM-COOL
E-9	EXTREME	COLD-COOL-WARM-COOL

UNDIFFERENTIATED HIGHLANDS

o 5   SEE APPENDIX A

SCALE ON THE HORIZONTAL AXIS

0   1000
MILES

ALLEN K. PHILBRICK

Figure 28

46

both yearly temperature range and actual warmth of varying seasonal cycles, as the result of forces, agents, and processes within the atmosphere recorded at the surface. Warmth measured in terms of the length of the growing season will be referred to again in more detail in later chapters dealing with specific world regions.

Water

Water is the most significant mineral resource to life, which would be impossible without it. Living tissues, both animal and vegetable, are composed primarily of water. Throughout the complicated and immensely varied evolution of living forms, biologists trace every branch of life back to oceanic origins. Understanding of the facts concerning the distribution of water resources is equally important, therefore, to that of the distribution of heat energy.

The Hydrologic Cycle. There is a mutual and direct relationship between the temperature of the air and the amount of water vapor it can hold. This relationship becomes apparent every time it rains: precipitation is caused by cooling moist air below the point at which a given mass of the air can hold all of its vapor content. Table V shows the relationship between warmth of the air and its ability to absorb and hold water vapor.

Evaporation and condensation constitute a cycle of change of water from liquid to gaseous and back to a liquid state in a hydrologic cycle, which, on a world scale, is essential to understanding the geographic distribution of water. Solar energy is responsible for the evaporation of water from the oceans which supply most of the atmosphere's water vapor. Circulation of the atmosphere carries moist air over the land, and condensation and run-

off are responsible for returning quantities of precipitation back to the oceans. In the processes of this geographic hydrologic cycle, maritime air becomes continental air, and the cycle is repeated endlessly. Both vegetation and soil intercept and store precipitation. Moisture transpires from vegetation and evaporates from both vegetation and soil. These relationships are illustrated in the diagram in Figure 30.[1]

The quantities of water involved in the hydrologic cycle are enormous. According to Wüst,[2] over the whole world the total evaporation and precipitation involved in the hydrologic cycle averages 96,000 cubic miles of water during the year. This is the equivalent of covering the states of New York and Pennsylvania with water one mile deep each year, with several thousand cubic miles of water left over. Spread over the entire area of the earth, this amount would cover the globe to a depth of 31 inches each year. Of the total water budget, 81,000 cubic miles return to the oceans. About 24,000 cubic miles of water—one-fourth of the total—is precipitated over land. Of this land share some 15,000 cubic miles re-evaporates from moist earth and is returned by the movement of air masses to be reprecipitated over the oceans. Nine thousand cubic miles of water flow back to the oceans as runoff from the world's land surface. Visualizing the variations in the amount of moisture available in different parts of the world is basic to understanding the distribution of human activities. In addition to amount, the timing, variability or dependability, and effectiveness of the moisture afforded any given place are also fundamental. In the following discussion, appropriate measures and patterns of distribution for each of the above characteristics of water are shown.

Three ranges of precipitation are distinguished on the map in Figure 31. Regions with less than 20 inches per year are relatively dry; those with 20 to 60 inches are humid; and areas having more than 60 inches are wet. The major dry region extends in a crescent shape more than three-fourths of the way around the world, from the African Sahara across the Middle East, into Soviet Asia and across Siberia into the Arctic, across the Arctic ice into northern Canada, and thence equatorward to south-

TABLE V   MAXIMUM WATER VAPOR CAPACITY IN GRAINS PER CUBIC FOOT OF AIR AT VARYING TEMPERATURES[a]

Temp., degrees F.	Water vapor grains	Difference between successive intervals, grains per 10° temp. change
−40	0.05	. . .
0	0.5	0.01
32	2.1	0.5
50	4.1	1.1
68	7.6	1.9
86	13.3	3.2
104	22.4	5.1

[a] After D. J. Kiefer, *Monthly Weather Review*, Vol. 69, Washington: Government Printing Office, 1941.

[1]"The Hydrologic Cycle," *Water*, The Yearbook of Agriculture, 1955 U.S.D.A., Washington, D.C., United States G.P.O., 1955, p. 42.

[2]G. Wüst, "Verdunstung und Niederschlag auf der Erde," *Gesellschaft Erdkunde*, Berlin: 1922, pp. 35–43.

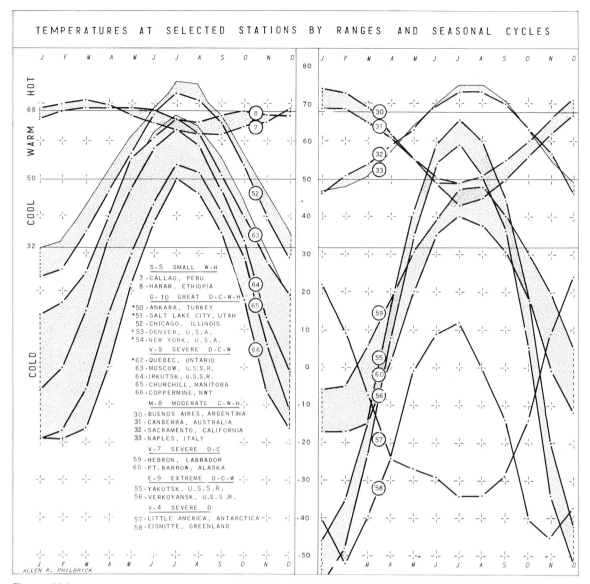

S-5 SMALL W-H
7 - CALLAO, PERU
8 - HARAR, ETHIOPIA
G-10 GREAT D-C-W-H
*50 - ANKARA, TURKEY
*51 - SALT LAKE CITY, UTAH
52 - CHICAGO, ILLINOIS
*53 - DENVER, U.S.A.
*54 - NEW YORK, U.S.A.
V-9 SEVERE D-C-W
*62 - QUEBEC, ONTARIO
63 - MOSCOW, U.S.S.R.
64 - IRKUTSK, U.S.S.R.
65 - CHURCHILL, MANITOBA
66 - COPPERMINE, NWT
M-8 MODERATE C-W-H
30 - BUENOS AIRES, ARGENTINA
31 - CANBERRA, AUSTRALIA
32 - SACRAMENTO, CALIFORNIA
33 - NAPLES, ITALY
V-7 SEVERE D-C
59 - HEBRON, LABRADOR
60 - PT. BARROW, ALASKA
E-9 EXTREME D-C-W
55 - YAKUTSK, U.S.S.R.
56 - VERKOYANSK, U.S.S.R.
V-4 SEVERE D
57 - LITTLE AMERICA, ANTARCTICA
58 - EISMITTE, GREENLAND

ALLEN K. PHILBRICK

Figure 29A

western North America. It is estimated to be 25,000 square miles in area, or nearly half the world's lands, and gives its name—the Arid Crescent—to the map as a whole.

Two major humid land regions—eastern North America and western Eurasia or Europe—face each other across the North Atlantic. They are nearly surrounded by the Arid Crescent, and the two concentric regions, one humid and one dry, are in turn surrounded by a ring of intermittently mixed wet and humid lands, interrupted in the American Southwest and along the Arctic rim by the Arid Crescent. A ring of wet territories within generally humid regions extends from the rainy west coast of northern North America southward, skips across the arid Southwest, to humid subtropical Caribbean lands, and thence to the tropical wet and humid lands extending from South America to Singapore. Wet lands of subtropical Asia extend along that continent's east coast and island chains as far as the tip of Kamchatka. In the Aleutian Islands, after bypassing the subhumid Siberian coast, humid marine conditions connect the ring, full circle, with the marine west coast wet lands of North America. Across the Equator in the Southern Hemisphere, continental dry spots are surrounded in turn by

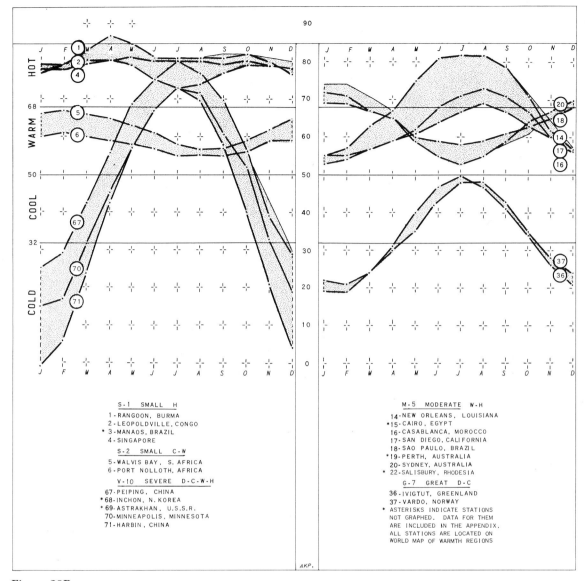

Figure 29B

humid marine conditions, in at least four separate continental locations—southern South America and Africa, and in Australia and Antarctica.

The Timing of Precipitation. Seasonal timing of precipitation in any given locality is just as important for plant growth as the total amount of moisture available. Ideally, the incidence of precipitation should correspond with moisture needs at the various stages of plant growth during the growing season. Much of the work of agriculture is devoted to the control and management of existing quantities of water in relation to the requirements of various kinds of crops at different stages of growth. Problems in draining excessive quantities of water or in storing water for use at a later time in the growing season necessitate employment of a wide range of conservation practices involving combined drainage and storage devices which make possible more effective application of moisture for the successful cultivation of specific crops. Thus, water resource management involves both amount and timing of precipitation.

The map in Figure 32 shows the generalized pattern of precipitation seasonality over the world. Once again, three major distinctions are made between regions in regard to precipitation distribu-

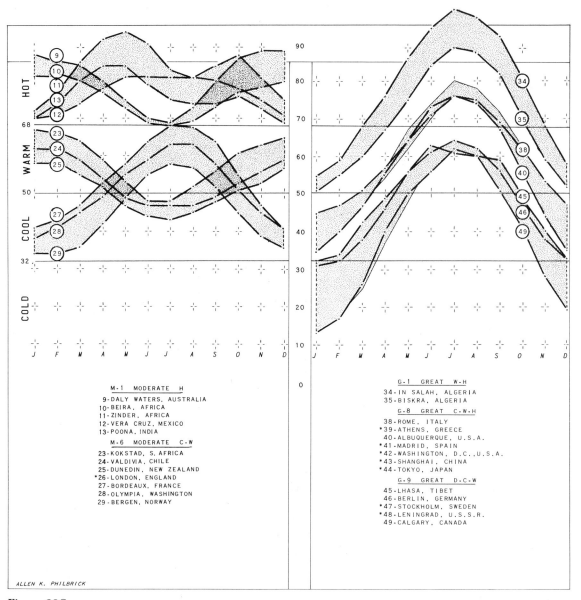

Figure 29C

tion (1) throughout the year, (2) primarily in the summer season, and (3) primarily in the winter season. Regions such as the Mediterranean, which has given its name to a type of climate characterized by winter rains and summer drought, are out of season with respect to the "normal" growing season. Regions of summer drought in such subtropical warmth regions, however, often have a long growing season, which modifies somewhat the impact of seasonal eccentricity of precipitation in such areas. Year round precipitation occurs in the rainy tropics and in certain temperate regions of the middle latitudes. In the middle latitudes, winter precipita-

tion often takes the form of snow cover which is a naturally occurring storage medium of moisture and serves as a ground cover to reduce effects of freezing. This effect is of considerable importance in areas where crops such as winter grains are sown in the fall to germinate during the winter.

Dependability and Variability of Precipitation. Variability of average annual precipitation is measured in terms of the departure from the normal or average amount of precipitation expected based on observations over a period of years. This measurement of variability, in terms of a percentage of the average amount of precipitation, serves as

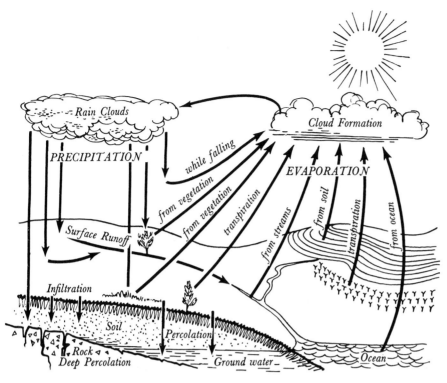

Figure 30. The hydrologic cycle. (*Courtesy of U. S. Dept. of Agriculture.*)

an index of precipitation dependability or average variability. The geographical pattern of average variability of precipitation is depicted on the map in Figure 33. A comparison of the maps in Figures 31 and 33 points to a relationship between amount and variability. When the amount is scanty, occurrence is unreliable. When the amount is moderate or ample, occurrence is more dependable. This is partially explained in the fact that smaller variations are proportionately larger when the total precipitation is small than when the total is large. By the same token, however, to crops dependent on scanty supplies of precipitation, even small variations in amount are more critical than if the supply were more plentiful.

Evaporation and Transpiration. Rapidity of evaporation from the surface and transpiration from vegetation, which affects the actual amount of moisture available in a place, is an additional consideration. The climatologist, Thornthwaite,[1] considers evaporation and transpiration basic elements in the measurement of precipitation effec-

tiveness. To him comparison of the amount of precipitation with potential evaporation is fundamental to a true measure of the availability of moisture at any given point. This comparison tells an observer whether amounts of precipitation occurring are greater than could be evaporated under existing average temperature conditions, are equal to that figure, or are less than could be evaporated were greater precipitation available. Such a measure, could it be generally applied, would tell accurately the timing of moisture surplus and deficiency at any point in relation to the timing of actual precipitation as it occurs.

Unfortunately, there is no simple means of measuring this timing relationship because it is not only a matter of evaporation, but of transpiration of moisture by vegetation. Thornthwaite calls the combination of evaporation and transpiration *evapotranspiration*. Potential evapotranspiration, in the absence of data from direct observation, can be calculated only indirectly from temperature, precipitation, and humidity observations. The map in Figure 34 shows potential evapotranspiration for the United States, but no map of potential evapotranspiration has yet been constructed for the world

[1]C. W. Thornthwaite, "An Approach toward a Rational Classification of Climate," *Geographical Review,* Vol. 33, January, 1948, p. 64.

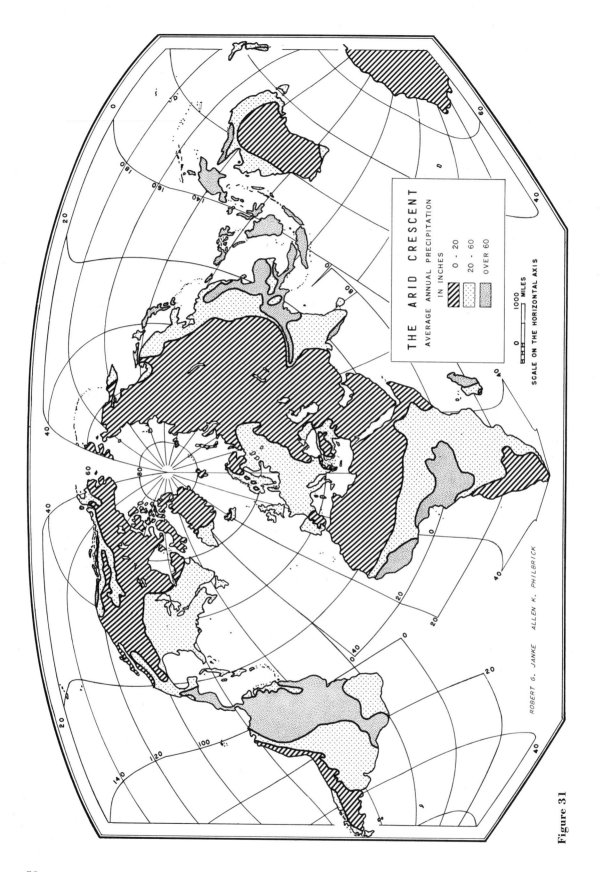

THE ARID CRESCENT

AVERAGE ANNUAL PRECIPITATION
IN INCHES

0 - 20
20 - 60
OVER 60

0   1000
└─────────┘ MILES
SCALE ON THE HORIZONTAL AXIS

ROBERT G. JANKE   ALLEN K. PHILBRICK

Figure 31

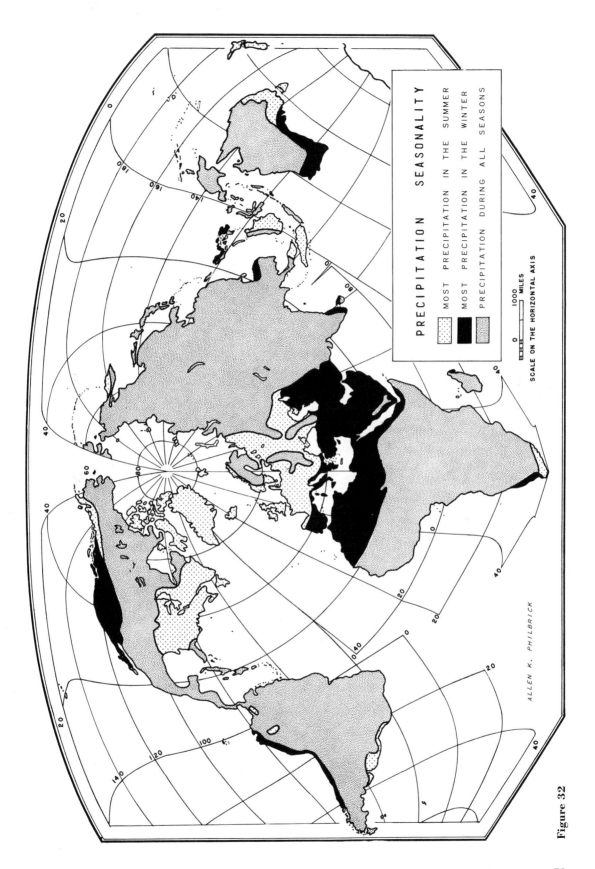

Figure 32

53

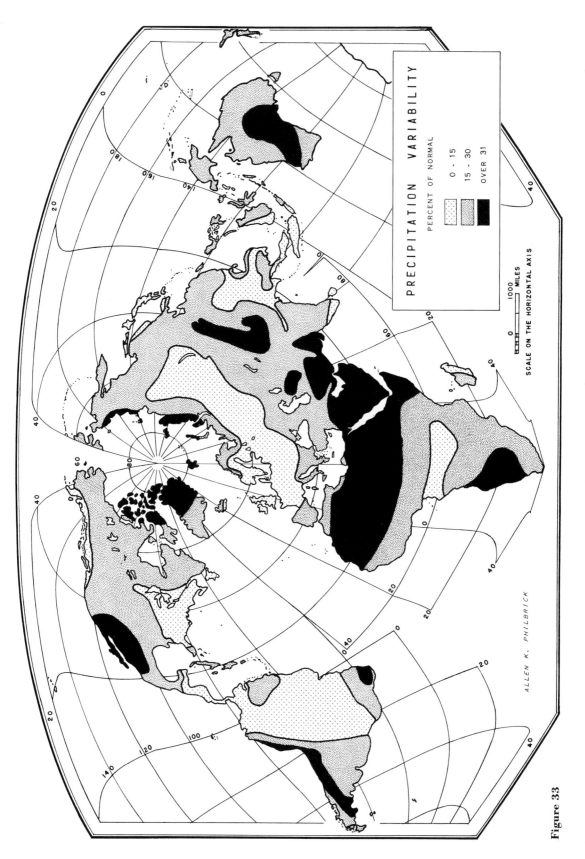

Figure 33

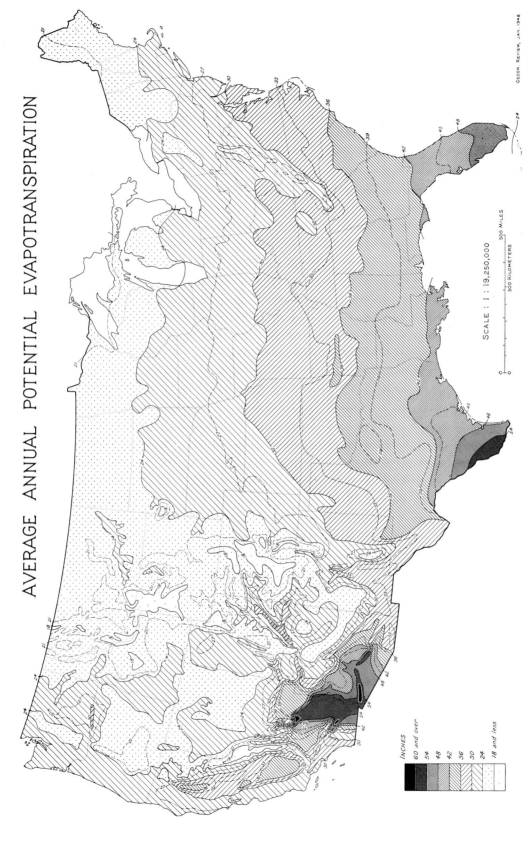

AVERAGE ANNUAL POTENTIAL EVAPOTRANSPIRATION

SCALE : 1 : 19,250,000

500 MILES

500 KILOMETERS

INCHES

60 and over
54
48
42
36
30
24
18 and less

GEOGR. REVIEW, JAN. 1948

Figure 34. (*Courtesy of Geographical Review, taken from C. W. Thornthwaite, "An Approach toward a Rational Classification of Climate."*)

as a whole. A great deal of research remains to be done before adequate and detailed measurement of evapotranspiration will make possible an evaluation, for the world as a whole, of precipitation effectiveness as a combination of amount, timing, dependability, and rates of evapotranspiration.

Relation of Precipitation Distribution to Different Agents and Processes.

Different agents and processes and their combinations are of primary importance in producing different portions of the pattern of precipitation shown in Figure 31. The three most important specific processes of precipitation are convectional, frontal, and orographic means of lifting moist air so that it will become cooled. Precipitation cannot occur without this cooling of moist air. Thus, there must be not only water vapor in the air, but such air must then be cooled so that the water vapor will be condensed into liquid form. The only natural means of condensation that can produce significant amounts of precipitation is cooling by the rising of moist air.

Warm air in contact with water absorbs moisture. When such warm air rises, the updraft is described as *convectional*. Convectional rising of air and the convectional precipitation which results when the air is cooled occurs in the tropics all year round and in continental areas of the middle latitudes in summer. The equatorial belt of humid and wet regions are essentially of convectional origin.

A *frontal* interaction, a warm air mass overriding a cold air mass, is associated with the *cyclonic* storms of the middle latitudes. Thus, precipitation produced by the uplifting of warm moist air over colder air is called cyclonic precipitation. Precipitation in the middle latitudes poleward of 30 degrees latitude is primarily of this type.

Another type of precipitation, called *orographic*, is of great importance over land areas where horizontally moving air masses rise upon contact with sharp elevations or other topographic features. On the world map in Figure 31 many areas of precipitation are primarily orographic. One example is the Atlantic coastal uplands of Central America and South America, where the Northeast Trade Winds bring moisture-laden air masses against highland areas. Others are the west coasts of continents in middle and high latitudes where the Prevailing Westerlies bring moisture-laden air against the Andes in southern Chile, or the coastal ranges of northwestern North America, and the west coast of South Island, New Zealand.

The Monsoon Effect.

Another instance in which moist air moves inland over major continental regions is described as the "monsoon effect." Reference has already been made to the important differences in heating capacities of water and of land. The maps of average annual range of temperature and warmth regions show the great contrasts in warmth over land and over water, particularly during summer when land areas warm more rapidly to a much higher temperature than do comparably located water bodies of the same latitude, and in winter when land areas cool off more quickly to a much lower temperature than do comparably located water bodies. The effect of such differences in temperature upon the relative densities of air masses of continental or marine nature is marked during the two opposing seasons. Warm air and low pressure areas tend to be associated with land in winter and oceans in summer. (In these cases, warm and cool are used in a purely relative sense.) The result is a tendency for air to move into regions of the land masses during periods of high sun, in summer, when air pressures over land are low. In the opposite season, in periods of low sun in winter, air tends to flow from high pressure areas over land outward to low pressure areas over the oceans. This influx and outflow of air between land and water bodies constitutes the monsoon effect.

In regions where such influx of air into continental areas brings moisture-laden air from the oceans over land, there is a marked increase in the quantity of water vapor available for all types of precipitation. Monsoon types of precipitation are best recognized and have the profoundest importance to great numbers of people in Asia—as in India and the mainland areas of southeastern Asia. Orographic precipitation produces the wet region confined to the coastal mountains of western peninsular India as the result of the impact between monsoon winds and the Western Ghats, from Bombay to Mysore. Fuller description of this phenomenon will be reserved for discussion of that world region.

When supplies of moist air arrive over warmed lands, convectional precipitation also occurs in large quantities. In other world regions, also, monsoon-type invasions of warm moist air participate in frontal collision with polar air masses moving equatorward across middle latitudes. When such frontal movements occur, moisture of monsoon origin is available for cyclonically produced as well as convectional and orographic precipitation.

Precipitation Regions. At the end of the discussion of warmth and the atmosphere, warmth regions were used to express the geographic summation of the significance of the heating of the atmosphere. In the same manner, water availability as the result of precipitation may be summarized by the precipitation regions shown on the map in Figure 35.

Precipitation regional types express combinations of three of the characteristics of water availability —*amount, variability,* and *seasonality.* Classification of measures of each of the three variables is shown in Table VI.

The variations shown in Table VI appear in the legends of the maps in Figures 31, 32, and 33. Combined, they become the legend of the map in Figure 35. Major regional types characterized by specific combinations of these elements have been generalized for clarity into three major groups, once again on the basis of significance to human life. In order to make this kind of generalization, certain assumptions have been made. It is assumed that for most people over the long range, humid precipitation conditions have advantages over those which are either wet or dry. This means it is better to have 20–60 inches of precipitation per year than more than 60 inches or less than 20 inches. Second, it is assumed that the less variable precipitation is from year to year the better it is. Third, it is assumed that year-round seasonal distribution is somewhat more advantageous than precipitation only in the summer, and that only winter precipitation is the least desirable.

Certainly the extremes in such value judgments are clear enough; that is, it is better to have water than not; it is better to be able to depend upon having the same amount of water every year than not; precipitation which occurs year round, or at least in the growing season, is better than water only in the winter time. On the basis of such assumptions, regions characterized by a combination of 20–60 inches of precipitation, with little variation from year to year, and well distributed throughout the year or occurring in summer, have distinct human advantages over regions with less than 20 inches of precipitation a year, experiencing wide variations in amount, with precipitation occurring primarily in the winter.

In between these wide contrasts are all the other possible combinations of the three sets of three variables under discussion. For purposes of general-

TABLE VI   VARIATIONS IN THREE CHARACTERISTICS OF PRECIPITATION

Amount		Variability		Seasonality	
1	Humid, 20–60 in.	1	Dependable, less than 15%	1	Year round
2	Wet, more than 60 in.	2	Moderate, 15–30%	2	Summer
3	Dry, less than 20 in.	3	Variable, more than 30%	3	Winter

izing this complex subject, some of the more favorable combinations based upon the above assumptions, which occur between the extremes, are classified with the *most* advantageous conditions, while some of the less advantageous combinations are classified with the *least* advantageous combinations. The three groups of circumstances are summarized in the legend of the map in Figure 35.

The map shows that the primary regions which experience moisture conditions within the range described as *humid, dependable, occurring year round or in the summer* are Eastern North America; Western Europe, including a portion of European Russia; and southeastern interior China centered on the Szechuan Basin. In addition, eastern Korea, Hokkaido and the coastal strip of Russia's Far Eastern provinces also belong to this category. These three are the largest middle-latitude regions having the above precipitation characteristics. Southern Hemisphere middle-latitude regions with these characteristics are much smaller; they include New Zealand, southeastern Australia, the eastern and southern tip of South Africa, and southernmost South America in Chile, Argentina, Uruguay, and Brazil.

One major difference between middle-latitude precipitation regions on the one hand, and tropical and subtropical ones on the other, is in the effectiveness of precipitation. The effectiveness of precipitation in the humid tropics and subtropics is greatly reduced by the increased evaporation accompanying higher temperatures of the air characteristic of warmth regions in those latitudes (map of the length of growing season, Figure 27). A second basic difference between them and their middle-latitude counterparts is the absence of frost in the humid tropical and subtropical precipitation regions. This condition means that there is a continuous high rate of biological and chemical activity.

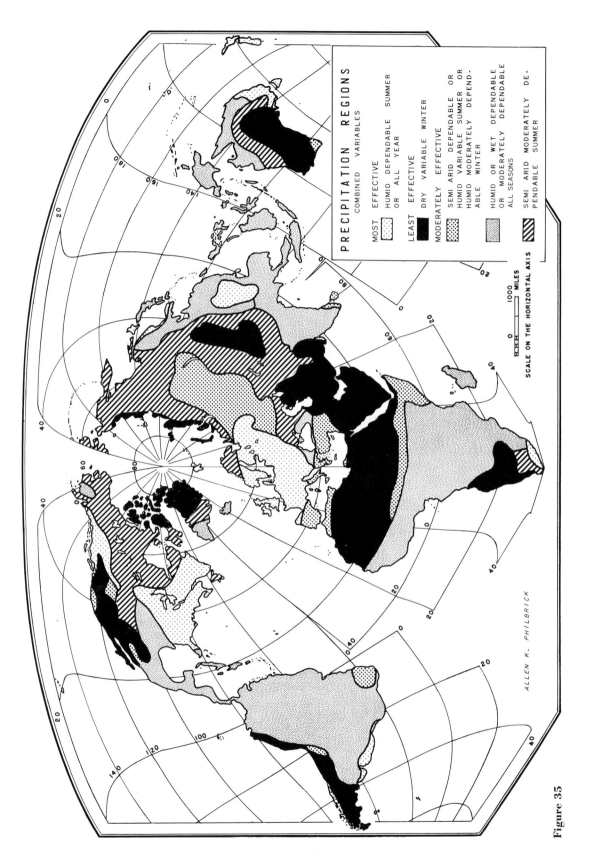

PRECIPITATION REGIONS
COMBINED VARIABLES

MOST EFFECTIVE
☐ HUMID DEPENDABLE SUMMER OR ALL YEAR

LEAST EFFECTIVE
■ DRY VARIABLE WINTER

MODERATELY EFFECTIVE
▨ SEMI ARID DEPENDABLE OR HUMID VARIABLE SUMMER OR HUMID MODERATELY DEPENDABLE WINTER
▨ HUMID OR WET DEPENDABLE OR MODERATELY DEPENDABLE ALL SEASONS
▨ SEMI ARID MODERATELY DEPENDABLE SUMMER

0 ___ 1000
MILES

SCALE ON THE HORIZONTAL AXIS

ALLEN K. PHILBRICK

Figure 35

58

The Arid Crescent shown on the map in Figure 31 can also be read from the map of precipitation regions in Figure 35, illustrating the many significant variations within the Arid Crescent. A wide range of water resource opportunities and problems are posed by the gamut of precipitation characteristics covered, from complete aridity in the hot or tropical deserts, to the frozen deserts of the Arctic ice cap. Between these extremes lie fertile subhumid grasslands and marginal agricultural regions experiencing less than 20 inches of precipitation but also experiencing low rates of evaporation which increase the efficiency of the available amounts of precipitation during the growing season. This combination of circumstances is particularly important in western Siberia within central Russia and in the western great plains of Canada and northern United States.

It will become evident in later chapters, just as in the case of warmth regions, how the differing combinations of resources, including water, which characterize specific regions of the world, present both opportunities and challenges to human perception and ingenuity in their development and use.

4 Land and Life

The processes which shape the land and water features of the earth and have brought into being living plants and animals upon the earth are the results of solar, earth, and life forces. The purpose of this second chapter dealing with the physical aspect of geography is to describe the patterns of the land and its mineral content and living matter. Along with the warmth and water regions discussed in the preceding chapter, patterns of *land and life* make it possible to understand variations in the resources of *food* production necessary to sustain human life. The patterns of subsurface and surface features of the earth's outer shell make it possible to understand the locations of various kinds of *minerals* upon which society has come to depend, including the principal *metallic* ores from which metals are extracted and mineral *fuels* which supply energy. Both of these types of minerals are the base upon which modern industrial society is constructed.

Subsurface Structural Zones

The earth's subsurface structure is subdivided into three zonal types on the map in Figure 36. To the first type belong several stable structural areas of ancient metamorphic-igneous rocks, which are often referred to as "crystalline shields" or as "the cornerstones of the continents." It is clear from the map that each of the continents has one or more of these stable blocks of land surface and subsurface. These territories have been permanent parts of the continents so long that their rocks predate the evolution of life forms which could leave fossil remains. The second type zone, nearly opposite in character, consists of unstable areas of crustal weakness. Instead of being widely separated and relatively isolated areas as are the stable crystalline shields, the unstable zone is virtually one continuous alignment of territory around the world. In contrast to the shield regions which are ancient, geologically speaking, the world's zone of crustal instability shown on the map is occupied by the most recently uplifted mountain ranges and deep depressions. The third structural type consists of sedimentary rock strata deposited in basins which were formerly shallow seas. These have been uplifted through time and are today the world's sedimentary lowlands. Some of the largest such regions are located between the separate shield regions and the continuous zone of crustal weakness, and appear on each of the seven continents.

Constructive and Destructive Forces. The earth's structural zones are the product of unending conflict between external and internal forces. In the long run, earth forces make the earth's surface rougher. Solar forces, indirectly through the agents of water, ice, and wind, and with the assistance of gravity, wear this rough surface down or level it. This "struggle" which has been in progress for at least three billion years finds each set of forces and circumstances counteracting the other.

What are the chief agents and processes by which earth forces tend to make the surface rougher? Internal earth forces break or bend the earth's crust, producing either vertical or horizontal movement of materials near the surface. The processes are called *vulcanism* when molten or viscous materials of the earth's interior intrude within the subsurface crust or are spewed forth onto the surface. Results of bending, thrusting, overthrusting, warping, squeezing, twisting, cracking or faulting of the earth's crust are called *diastrophism*. These combinations of movement may upend portions of the earth's crust, downthrust them, or displace them laterally. Results are regional differences in geologic patterns. The greatest movements are characteristic of the territories identified on the map in Figure 36 as the zones of crustal weakness. This zone appears as a world alignment of high mountains on land and deep trenches in the oceans, as well as festoons of islands representing the tops of submerged mountain chains. The entire linear arrangement may be thought of as the result of geologic processes within the last 100 million years out of a total of more than three billion years.

Equally great mountain ranges were built in the far-distant past, half a billion years ago or more in regions now known for their long-standing stability as "cornerstones of the continents." Such ancient "battlegrounds" between constructive and destructive processes have largely been leveled off by the agents and processes of erosion.

Weathering, Erosion, and Sorting Processes. The surfaces of the crystalline shield areas referred to are the worn-down and truncated stubs of ancient mountains which remain after long-continued weathering and erosion. When the surface is pitted, broken, and cracked as the result of alternate heat and cold, the processes are referred to as *physical* or *mechanical* weathering. Water and heat accelerate chemical changes, and occur concomitantly with the physical changes. Over long periods of time minerals are mechanically dissolved. In solution chemical combinations occur and new mineral products are precipitated out of solution to become concentrated in particular locations. Minerals in solution are carried away in moving water. When they come into contact with the right combinations of other minerals, the chemical processes of "exchange" may occur, producing new mineral solutions. Altogether these are the processes of *chemical weathering*. Physical and chemical weathering prepare materials from the earth's crust for movement by other agencies, soften and break bedrock into pieces which are movable by running water, moving ice, and wind.

The sizes of particles which can be moved vary with the steepness of slope, the amount of force available, and the mass and speed of the moving agent. In steep, mountainous terrain, for example, very large chunks of rock choke the beds of rapidly flowing mountain freshets. In the lower reaches of extensive plains near sea level, on the other hand, the gradient of streams is more gradual and the rate of flow of rivers is slowed down. Accordingly, only small particles of silt can be carried in suspension by such sluggish streams.

Gravity is the principal direct force of erosion, whether it produces an initial rockfall or the runoff from precipitation. During the carrying process gravity assists in further fragmenting previously weathered particles, as when rocks and pebbles are knocked, chipped, and ground against one another

in streams of running water. Wind—itself a direct product of gravitational force—blows fine particles against larger ones. Also, particles of many sizes are ground together under immense masses of moving ice beneath continental and mountain glaciers. Earth gravity produces all such movements and has a part in the reduction of the sizes of rock particles as they are transported gradually and intermittently from higher to lower elevations.

The movement of material in the processes of erosion also sorts and arranges the pieces by size. Great bodies of materials are created which are relatively homogeneous as to particle sizes. Beds of sand and gravel, silt and clay, or the talus slopes at the bases of young rough mountains are examples. In general, within any reasonably long period of time, the smaller pieces move the greater distances. Glacial ice, however, is capable of moving even large masses of rock great distances along with large quantities of smaller particles. As a consequence the relatively unsorted components of glacial debris vary in sizes from tiny bits to huge boulders.

Temporary Building Processes of Erosion. In the course of weathering and erosion of the surface rock of the lithosphere, many temporary halts occur in the journeys of individual rock bits from their original sites. Along the way many land-surface forms are constructed through deposition by water, wind, or ice. Landforms of aggradation may remain for varying periods of time under a great variety of circumstances; yet all depositional landforms are only stages in the great journey of surface materials from higher to lower elevations. Uneven as the pattern of landforms may be when viewed in detail, regularity and order is infinitely greater than would at first seem apparent.

World Landform Regions

The pattern of world lands results from the interaction of the constructional and destructional processes as sketched in the preceding section. The structural processes of vulcanism and diastrophism combine with the grading and aggrading processes of weathering and erosion to produce the continents and ocean basins as well as the entire range of landforms characterizing the configuration of the surface.

Base Level. The level of the oceans (mean sea level) is the base level of the erosion process of precipitation runoff from the land in the hydrologic cycle. The continued operation of the erosion process measured in millions of years has the

TABLE **VII**   MAJOR WATER-LAND RELATIONSHIPS OF THE EARTH

Ocean or continent		Area, sq. mi.	Per cent of world	
Earth as a whole		196,950,305	100	
Hydrosphere		139,405,122	70.7	
Lithosphere		57,545,183	29.3	
Hydrosphere				
Pacific Basin		69,374,182	35.2	50.1
Atlantic Basin		35,665,239	18.1	25.3
Arctic Basin		5,440,197	2.7	3.8
Indian Basin		28,925,504	14.7	20.8
	Total	139,405,122	70.7	100.0
Lithosphere			Per cent of lithosphere	
Asia		17,035,000	8.7	29.7
Africa		11,635,000	5.9	20.2
N. America		8,325,000	4.2	14.4
S. America		6,800,000	3.5	11.8
Antarctica		6,000,000	3.0	10.4
Australasia		4,000,000	2.0	7.0
Europe		3,750,000	1.9	6.5
	Total	57,545,000	29.3	100.0
Drainage area of lithosphere by ocean basins			Per cent of lithosphere	
Atlantic-Arctic		27,672,564	48.2	
Indian		10,358,496	18.0	
Pacific		7,162,123	12.4	
Internal		12,352,000	21.4	
	Total	57,545,183	100.0	
Drainage slope of lithosphere by "land and water realms"			Per cent of lithosphere	
"Land realm" drainage to Atlantic-Arctic-Indian Basins		38,031,060	66.2	
Estimated ⅔ of internal drainage region sloping toward Atlantic-Arctic-Indian Basin		8,234,666	14.3	
	Total	46,265,726	80.5	
"Land realm" drainage to Pacific "water realm"		7,162,132	12.4	
Estimated ⅓ of internal drainage sloping Pacific-ward		4,117,334	7.1	
	Total	11,279,457	19.5	
	Final total	57,545,183	100.0	

capability of reducing any landform including the continents themselves to the level of the sea. So far as is known, however, no continent has ever been eroded away completely because the processes of continental building go on simultaneously with the processes of wearing away.

Major Land-Water Relationships of the Earth. The present world pattern of continental lands and water drainage regions is a stage of development between opposing forces and processes of continental building and base leveling. The world's lands are characterized in terms of three major drainage units on the map in Figure 37. The largest drainage basin in the world covers the great bulk of the land-water realm referred to in Chapter 1 and outlined by the world-girdling alignment of continental divides on North and South America, Asia, Australia, and Antarctica. A relatively narrow ring of lands on these same continents drains into the Pacific Ocean basin. The remaining category consists of several regions of internal or no drainage. In these latter regions evaporation either exceeds precipitation so that there is no drainage, or water which starts its journey toward the sea is trapped within land basins for which there is no outlet, whence it evaporates.

Table VII enumerates the water and land area relationships of the earth. The lands draining into the nearly land-enclosed Arctic-Atlantic-Indian Ocean basins are two-thirds of the earth's land area (66.2 per cent). The drainage into the Pacific Basin is from only about one-eighth (12.4 per cent) of the world's total land area. The remainder, slightly more than one-fifth (21.4 per cent) of the world's lands, has no drainage or possesses drainage patterns which never reach the seas. It is estimated that the latter regions of internal or no drainage, if they were to receive sufficient precipitation to have surface runoff reaching the oceans, would be divided into surfaces sloping toward the oceans enclosed within the land realm and surfaces sloping toward the Pacific Basin in a ratio of 2 to 1 (14.2 to 7.1 per cent, respectively). This means, accordingly, that slightly more than four-fifths of the world's lands belong to the combined drainage region in which surface runoff flows generally to the combined Arctic-Atlantic-Indian Ocean basins (80.4 per cent); and that less than a fifth (19.6 per cent) of the land surfaces drains toward the Pacific Basin. Such facts emphasize the continuity of the world's lands as a single unit of land.

Table VII shows further that the Pacific Ocean, with 69,374,182 square miles, exceeds in size the world's total land area of some 57.5 million square miles. The Pacific approximates the areas of the

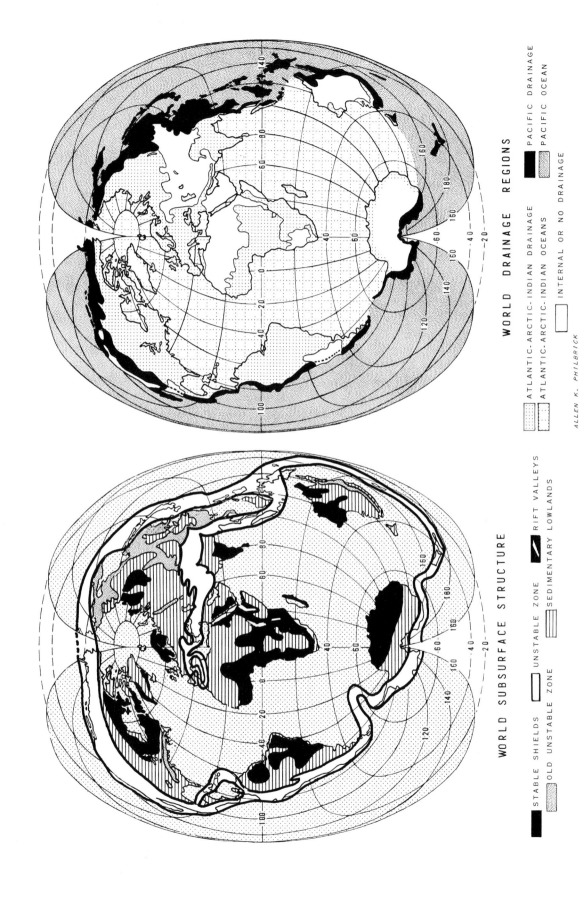

WORLD SUBSURFACE STRUCTURE

STABLE SHIELDS   UNSTABLE ZONE   RIFT VALLEYS

OLD UNSTABLE ZONE   SEDIMENTARY LOWLANDS

Figure 36

WORLD DRAINAGE REGIONS

ATLANTIC-ARCTIC-INDIAN DRAINAGE   PACIFIC DRAINAGE

ATLANTIC-ARCTIC-INDIAN OCEANS   PACIFIC OCEAN

INTERNAL OR NO DRAINAGE

ALLEN K. PHILBRICK

Figure 37

63

combined Atlantic-Arctic-Indian Oceans, which total 70,030,940 square miles. The total water area of the earth is 70.7 per cent of the surface of the globe, 139,405,000 out of a global surface of 196,000,000 square miles. The 80 per cent of the land realm draining into or sloping toward the land-enclosed Atlantic-Arctic-Indian Oceans added to the areas of those three bodies of water comprises just over 60 per cent of the world's total surface (60.1 per cent). Conversely, the areas of the Pacific Ocean and that portion of the land realm draining into or sloping toward the Pacific comprise the rest of the earth (39.9 per cent).

Landform Types. Within the context of the geological cycle of continental building and base leveling, it is possible to define and locate on the world map four major types of landforms—plains, mountains, plateaus, and hill lands.

Plains are primarily level or nearly level land, but may have differences in elevation locally (local relief) of as much as 500 feet. Plains can occur at any elevation above sea level, but are usually found below 5,000 feet. Along some border of their extent plains will have distinctly higher land. Plateaus are also primarily level land, but at considerably higher elevations than plains. They are bordered by a marked difference in height of land usually an escarpment or abrupt change in elevation. Since they are high land they are often deeply incised by rivers; and in humid regions may be so dissected by erosion as to become hill country. In both plains and plateau areas, however, flat or gently sloping land exceeds in total area the rougher or steeply sloping configurations.

Mountains are characterized by sloping land with local relief generally in excess of 2,000 feet. Hill country also slopes with local relief between 500 and 2,000 feet. It is difficult to be precise in defining the boundaries between hilly and mountainous terrain. In both mountains and hill country rough and steeply sloping land occupies a greater proportion of total area than does level or gently sloping land.

Patterns of Landform Regions. The world pattern of the landform types defined in the preceding paragraphs follows closely the pattern of subsurface structural zones already shown on the map in Figure 36. The global pattern of the unstable zone of crustal weakness is in the form of a huge Greek letter theta (θ). The bar of the theta is the Mediterranean-Alps-Caucasus-Himalayan mountain zone

from Gibraltar to Singapore. The bar separates the pattern of structural weakness characterizing the margins of the land-water realm into two parts. The circle of the theta girdles the earth and marks the divide between the land-water realm and the water realm in the Pacific Basin.

"Isolated" block-like metamorphic shield regions face one another across "enclosed oceans" in each of the two parts of the theta north and south of the central bar. The Canadian, Scandinavian, and Russian Angara shields face one another across the Arctic in the north. In the south portion Venezuelan-Brazilian shields, the crystalline plateaus of southern Africa, the Deccan Shield in India, and the Western Australian and Antarctic shield regions face one another across the South Atlantic-Indian Oceans. If these groupings of ancient rock regions are regarded as combined centers, each is surrounded by major plains regions or sedimentary lowlands, which are in turn surrounded by the mountain systems, deep sea trenches, and festoons of island arcs marking the world zone of crustal instability. These concentric relationships are shown graphically on the map in Figure 36.

Mountains. The major mountain systems of the world are shown in Figure 38. The larger cordilleran regions are youthful, geologically speaking. They have risen within the zone of crustal weakness. In a clockwise direction around the land realm, they are the Andes system of South America, the Sierra Madres and island arc systems of Central America, Mexico, and the Carribbean, the Rocky Mountain system of North America, and the island arc systems of eastern and southern Asia and Oceania east of Australia. Across the land-water realm from east to west are the Himalayan-Caucasus-Alpine systems.

Other older mountain systems are also important. They occur in relation to older zones of earlier instability in the earth's crust and in rejuvenated (reuplifted) portions of ancient crystalline shields. The Appalachians of eastern North America, the Urals—traditional boundary between Europe and Asia—the Great Dividing Range of the eastern highlands in Australia, are mountains of this type.

Plains. Between mountains and the ancient shield regions of each continent lie sedimentary lowlands. These are identified on the map in Figure 38. There are five extensive lowland regions in the southern half of the land realm and two in the northern half. The Antarctic lowland is buried

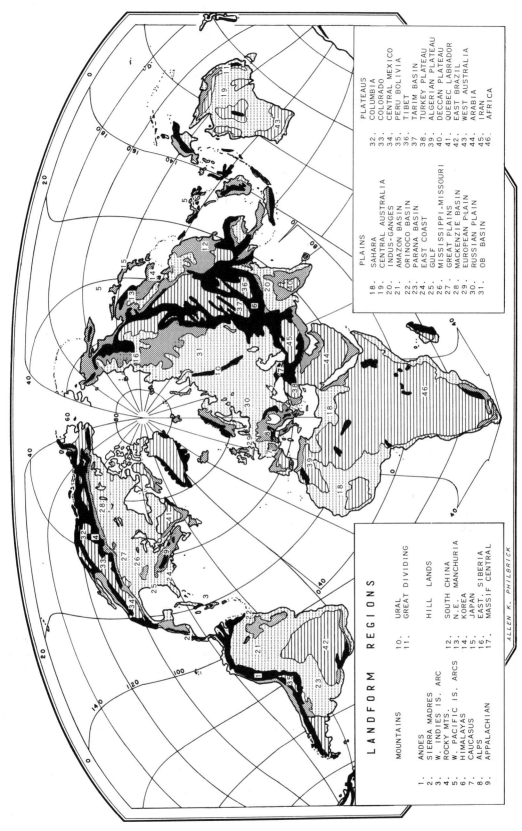

Figure 38

LANDFORM REGIONS

MOUNTAINS
1. ANDES
2. SIERRA MADRES
3. W. INDIES IS. ARC
4. ROCKY MTS.
5. W. PACIFIC IS. ARCS
6. HIMALAYAS
7. CAUCASUS
8. ALPS
9. APPALACHIAN
10. URAL
11. GREAT DIVIDING

HILL LANDS
12. SOUTH CHINA
13. N.E. MANCHURIA
14. KOREA
15. JAPAN
16. EAST. SIBERIA
17. MASSIF CENTRAL

PLAINS
18. SAHARA
19. CENTRAL AUSTRALIA
20. INDUS-GANGES
21. AMAZON BASIN
22. ORINOCO BASIN
23. PARANA BASIN
24. EAST COAST
25. GULF
26. MISSISSIPPI-MISSOURI
27. GREAT PLAINS
28. MACKENZIE BASIN
29. EUROPEAN PLAIN
30. RUSSIAN PLAIN
31. OB BASIN

PLATEAUS
32. COLUMBIA
33. COLORADO
34. CENTRAL MEXICO
35. PERU BOLIVIA
36. TIBET
37. TARIM BASIN
38. TURKEY PLATEAU
39. ALGERIAN PLATEAU
40. DECCAN PLATEAU
41. QUEBEC LABRADOR
42. EAST BRAZIL
43. WEST AUSTRALIA
44. ARABIA
45. IRAN
46. AFRICA

ALLEN K. PHILBRICK

under the only continental glacier existing today. A second plain, north of the Equator in Africa, is the Sahara, which is the world's largest desert. The third is the central desert basin of Australia. The other two large plains are on the subcontinent of India-Pakistan and in South America. Each of the latter is associated with great river systems. In the Indian subcontinent, the Indus and the Ganges Rivers have created great alluvial plains upon sedimentary rocks between the Himalayas on the north and the Deccan Shield of peninsular India on the south. In South America a great central continental lowland between the Andes on the west and the Venezuelan and Brazilian shield regions on the east is drained by the Parana, the Amazon, and the Orinoco River systems.

In the northern half of the land realm two great sedimentary plains lie between the crystalline shields and the highlands of the zone of weakness. These are the plains of North America and Eurasia. Between the Canadian Shield and the western Rocky Mountain cordillera is the huge North American central lowlands. It is roughly triangular in shape and may be subdivided into three parts—the gulf and coastal plain from Texas to Maine, the bulk of the Mississippi-Missouri drainage basin of the continental interior, and the high plains of Canada and the Mackenzie River basin of western and northern Canada between the Canadian Rockies and the Arctic. The Canadian Shield region could technically be classified as a plain except that its worn-down surface is the remnant of ancient mountains rather than the predominantly level surface of a sedimentary lowland. Its surface is also rough, ice-scoured, and pitted. Dotted with thousands of glacial lakes, the Canadian Shield presents a rough and stony surface which is not included with the North American plains regions.

In Eurasia the great northern Eurasian Plain is also triangular in shape. Narrow on the west between the Scandinavian Shield and the Alps, it widens rapidly eastward in Russia into the greatest extent of level land in the world. Although interrupted by the Ural Mountains, the plain may be said to continue in the form of the West Siberian or the Ob River Basin.

As distinct from these plains of major extent, there are numerous alluvial plains and delta regions of intermediate size. Medium-sized plains of annually deposited eroded materials from the world's uplands represent some of the earth's most inten-sively farmed territories. They include such world-famous river valleys and deltas as the Nile, the Tigris and Euphrates, the Po and the Rhine river plains and deltas in Europe, the Central Valley of California, and the Imperial Valley Delta of the Colorado River. There are also the deltas in Southeast Asia of the Irrawaddy, Mekong, and Menam Rivers; and the Canton Delta of South China. To these could be added a very large number of smaller alluvial plains and deltas throughout the world.

Plateaus. Other flat lands of extensive size are the major plateaus of the earth. Many of these are partly enclosed within major mountain systems. Examples are the Columbia and Colorado plateaus of the United States and the central plateau of Mexico. Mention should be made also of the high plateaus of Peru and Bolivia within the Andes of South America. In the same way, the Tibetan Plateau, the Tarim Basin, and the interior highland deserts and subhumid grasslands of Mongolia are enclosed within the mountain systems of central Asia. Within the Alpine system of Europe are the Spanish and French central massifs and the plateaus of Turkey and Algeria.

Other principal plateau regions are not so associated with mountain systems, but instead are the remnants of ancient metamorphic blocks. The great continental tableland of southern Africa is of this type. The Deccan Plateau of the Indian Peninsula and the plateaus of eastern Brazil, western Australia, Arabia, Iran, and eastern Quebec-Labrador in North America are examples.

Hill lands. The fourth category of landform—hill lands—is transitional in character. Rough land, with more sloping than level terrain, yet without local relief of truly mountainous country often occupies the territories between plains and mountains. Such are the foot hills or the piedmont sections which are transitional between the other two landform types. The dissected edges of plateaus and eroded highland plains also fall into this category. There are, accordingly, a great many small regions of hill land, too numerous to show upon a world map of the scale used in Figure 38.

Important hill regions are located in south China, in northeastern Manchuria, and in Korea. The great bulk of Japan and southeastern and coastal Siberia is of this type of landform. Most of the hilly regions of the world are narrow transitional territories between other landforms.

Land is important not only for its surface configuration which provides the platform of man's activities, but also for its contents. The contents are significant in at least two important ways—in supplying mineral ingredients for the soil from which human food is partly derived, and in supplying a wide range of minerals out of which goods are manufactured as from metallic ores or energy is derived, as from the mineral fuels. The patterns of landforms which in turn reflect patterns of subsurface structure can be used as indicators of the kinds of other resources contained within the land. This idea will be developed further in accounting for the distribution of important minerals.

Minerals

There are three kinds of rock with which the mineral contents of the lands are associated: *igneous, sedimentary,* and *metamorphic.* Igneous rocks are solidified from a molten state and originate within the subsurface. Sedimentary rocks are formed from eroded particles derived from other rocks. Deposited by water, wind, or ice, beds of eroded materials which have been buried under great thicknesses of such materials become indurated as rock by pressure over long periods of time. Metamorphic rocks are those changed by heat and pressure from their original form into rock of a different kind. Slate and marble are examples of metamorphic rocks— slate changed by pressure from shale and marble from limestone. Granite is an igneous rock, while sandstone and limestone are sedimentary rocks.

Relationship of Rock Type to Subsurface Structural Zone.

The sedimentary lowlands are regions where materials derived from older igneous and metamorphic formations have accumulated and covered up other older surfaces. Subsequently many of the horizontally bedded sedimentary strata have been warped, folded, faulted, or in some way altered by crustal movement. In these processes igneous intrusions or extrusions may also have occurred.

The most recent mountain-building in the unstable zone is characterized by all three of these types of rock. Metamorphic rocks and igneous rocks of any age have been upthrust. If there were covering strata they either have been eroded away or they occur now as flanking upturned or folded remnants; and, in some instances, they remain as cap rock many thousands of feet above their former position. Igneous and metamorphic rocks are the principal types in the zone of structural weakness. The shield regions are ancient igneous and very old metamorphosed rocks with a very few ancient sediments.

The Relationship of Mineral Types to Rock Types and Structural Zones.

A mineral is a chemical compound occurring naturally that has a particular molecular structure. It is nonliving material which in many mechanical mixtures, when solidified, familiarly appears as rock. Granite, for example, is a rock composed of three minerals— quartz, feldspar, and biotite. Present concern is with two principal classes of minerals—*metallic* minerals and the mineral *fuels.* The broad geographical patterns of mineral distributions are associated with the distinctions between various structural zones and between rock types. The mineral fuels are found almost exclusively in *sedimentary* rocks, and the metallic ores are only slightly less consistently associated with the *contact zone between* sedimentary and metamorphic or igneous rocks. It must be remembered, of course, that while all mineral fuels are sedimentary in origin, not all sedimentary rocks are mineral fuel-bearing. By the same token, just because many metallic minerals are found in or near igneous or metamorphic rock sources does not mean that all igneous or metamorphic rocks represent metal or metallic mineral-bearing ore bodies. The geographical pattern of concentrations of metallic content in minerals is perhaps best expressed by the idea that such ores have most frequently been found and mined within the "contact zone" where the sedimentary and the metamorphic-igneous rock regions meet. This has been true for a variety of reasons. First, the contact zone is one of increased physical and chemical reactions which concentrate particular minerals of a high metal content per unit of rock. Second, such areas tend to produce ore bodies which are at or near to the surface. This increases their chances of easy discovery, and, once found, increases their accessibility for mining. Third, locations of such ore bodies in the vicinity of sedimentary rocks are more likely to be close to workable bodies of coal of a sufficiently good quality for smelting purposes.

Mineral Concentrations.

In Table VIII, selected metals are listed in order of their average concentration in the earth's crust. It is quite clear that the metal content of most igneous rocks is quite small, which demonstrates why ore bodies in which metal content *is* high are at a premium. In only a relatively few places are there concentrations of ore in large enough amounts and with metallic

Metal	Per cent	Metal	Per cent
Aluminum	8.13	Cobalt	0.0023
Iron	5.00	Uranium	0.004
Magnesium	2.09	Lead	0.00016
Titanium	0.44	Tungsten	0.00015
Manganese	0.10	Antimony	0.0001
Chromium	0.02	Mercury	0.0005
Vanadium	0.015	Silver	0.0001
Zinc	0.0132	Gold	0.0000005
Nickel	0.008	Platinum	0.0000005
Copper	0.007	Radium	0.0000000013
Tin	0.004		

TABLE VIII AVERAGE PROPORTION OF SELECTED METALS IN THE EARTH'S CRUST[a]

[a] Gilluly, Waters, and Woodford, *Principles of Geology*, San Francisco: Freeman, 1951, p. 564.

content high enough per unit of rock to justify mining. The amount and richness of a given ore necessary before economic exploitation is feasible varies with the rarity of the material and the demand for its use. For example, high quality iron ores have more than 70 per cent metal content. Gold, on the other hand, is so valuable that ores having less than one-third of an ounce per ton of rock are mined.

Natural processes of mineral concentration are both mechanical and chemical. A simplified classification includes three primary processes which are called *segregation, replacement,* and *sedimentation. Segregation* is the concentration of minerals which occurs when molten material (magma) from inside the earth cools. The settling of denser minerals and crystallization at different temperatures tends to segregate minerals of different sorts homogeneously within magma during the cooling process. *Replacement,* as the name implies, means that one mineral is chemically exchanged for another, either through direct contact, or indirectly through chemical replacement in water solution. Last, the sorting and grading processes of erosion are themselves responsible for the concentration and deposition of many minerals. This is called *sedimentation.* Such concentration occurs either by deposition or removal. When heavier particles of ores with metallic content collect by falling to the bottom of the stream, concentration takes place by deposition. On the other hand, concentration may also be the result of purification through removal of lighter, valueless materials by washing away or through solution.

World Distribution of Major Iron Formations. As the result of many combinations of the above processes, metallic minerals originally associated with igneous and other metamorphic rocks have become concentrated in many localities. Iron ores are often concentrated as Precambrian sediments located adjacent to extensive surface outcroppings of ancient metamorphic rocks. The map in Figure 39 shows those iron ore deposits on each continent which we estimated to have reserves of ore exceeding one billion metric tons each. The position of each formation in the contact zone between metamorphic-igneous rock regions and with sediments is striking indication of the fact that iron occurs in association with igneous rocks, although most igneous rocks are not rich enough in iron content to justify recovery of iron from them.

In North America five separate districts have a potential tonnage of one billion metric tons of iron ore: Mesabi, Steep Rock, Schefferville, and Wabana associated with the Canadian Shield, and the Birmingham, Alabama formation associated with the Old Appalachians. In South America there are three such districts: the Cerro Bolivar of the Venezuelan Shield. Tofo of Chile in the Chilean coast ranges, and the Itabira formation in the Brazilian Shield. In Europe there are four districts: the Cleveland iron district in England, the Lorraine of France, Kiruna of Sweden, and Krivoi Rog in the Ukraine of the Soviet Union. Africa is represented by the Rustenberg region in South Africa, and Asia by Singhbhum in the Deccan Shield of peninsular India. Of the inhabited continents only Australia seems not to have an iron ore deposit containing more than a billion tons of good quality ore in a single locality. On every continent, however, there are many important additional iron ore formations of lesser size. The most important iron formation in Australia occurs in South Australia.

Other Metallic Minerals. Other metallic minerals may be grouped for discussion under several headings. First, there are a number of heavy metals which are important as alloys in the iron and steel industry. These are called the *ferroalloy metals* and include nickel, cobalt, tungsten, vanadium, molybdenum, chromium, and manganese. Second, there are the other *non-ferrous heavy metals*—copper, lead, zinc, tin, and antimony. A third class of heavy metals is the category of *precious metals*—gold, silver, and platinum. In a final category by themselves are the *light metals*—aluminum, magnesium, and titanium.

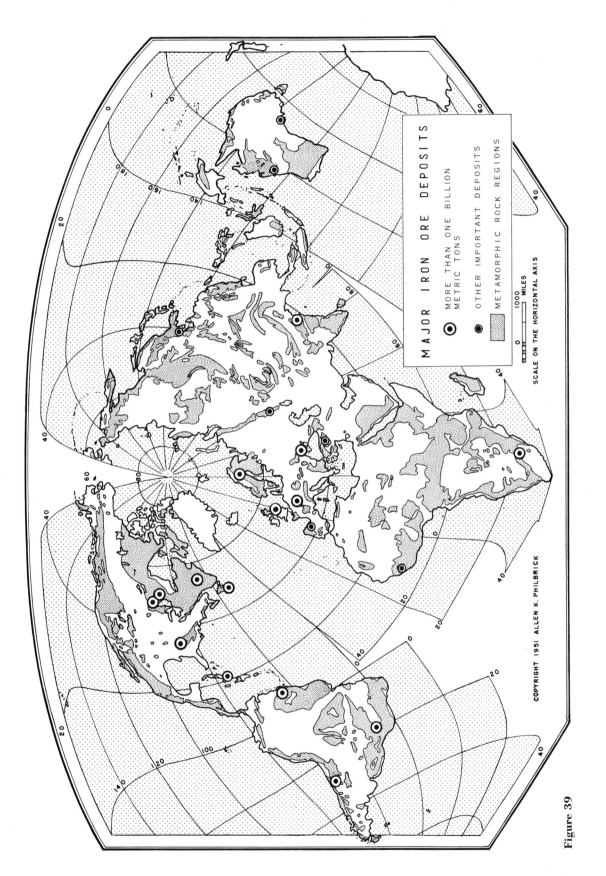

MAJOR IRON ORE DEPOSITS

⊙ MORE THAN ONE BILLION
   METRIC TONS

⦿ OTHER IMPORTANT DEPOSITS

▨ METAMORPHIC ROCK REGIONS

0   1000
|▭▭▭▭|
     MILES

SCALE ON THE HORIZONTAL AXIS

COPYRIGHT 1951 ALLEN K. PHILBRICK

Figure 39

69

In order to demonstrate the association of metallic minerals with the contact zone between igneous-metamorphic rocks and the sedimentaries, Figure 40 shows the principal locations of all of the above metallic ores against a background of the generalized pattern of igneous-metamorphic rocks. The principal ore deposits of each metal are shown by dots. Since the object of the map is to demonstrate the single idea of spatial association of metallic ores with the contact zone between igneous-metamorphic and sedimentary rocks, the types of individual ore bodies are not identified. There is an 85 per cent correlation between the patterns of metallic mineral deposits and adjacency to igneous or metamorphic rocks. Of the 15 per cent remainder on the map in Figure 40, which are clearly dissociated from the patterns of igneous-metamorphic rock regions, the majority are residual minerals concentrated by the processes of sedimentation—bauxite, lead, zinc, and iron oxides.

The Mineral Fuels. Among the more important resources related to the development of technology have been the *energy* resources. The mineral fuels, in particular, have played a special role in multiplying by hundreds the average power to perform work. Of the four basic minerals needed in the largest quantities by modern industrial societies, two are the mineral fuels, *coal* and *petroleum.* The other two are the nonfuels, *iron ore* and *water.*

The distribution of mineral fuels occurs primarily within the pattern of great sedimentary lowlands. Both coal and petroleum are of organic origins and have been deposited in sedimentary rocks. (See the map in Figure 41.) The necessary conditions for the entrapment of organic materials so that they might be preserved and transformed into coal and petroleum did not occur everywhere. Also, once formed, such deposits have not always survived subsequent natural processes such as surface erosion, in the case of coal measures.

According to Van Royen,[1]

Three essentials for the development of oil in a pool are (1) source beds, probably shales or limestones in which organic remains were deposited on ancient sea bottoms; (2) reservoir rock, probably sandstone or limestone in which the petroleum accumulated; and (3) a "structure" or "trap" (stratigraphic or structural) shaped to permit the oil and gas to enter but not to escape and disperse upward.

[1] William Van Royen, *Mineral Resources of the World,* New York: Prentice-Hall, Inc., 1952, p. 25.

Within the sedimentary rock regions where oil or natural gas is possible, the proven oil or gas fields of greatest importance are identified by a contour of dashed lines on the map in Figure 41. The sedimentary rock regions of the world are shown in white on the map. The metamorphic-igneous rock regions are stippled in grey. All important mineral-fuel districts of any type—coal, natural gas, or petroleum—are shown in black. The map clearly demonstrates the association of mineral fuels with sedimentary rocks.

The two maps—one of metallic minerals in Figure 40 and the other of mineral fuels in Figure 41—show striking contrasts in the location of the mineral content of the land. The distributional relationship of each pattern to specific rock types and structural zones attests to the significance of different processes by which each of the many different kinds of mineral resource has become concentrated.

In addition to natural processes which increase our understanding of the patterns of mineral occurrence, the maps also reflect certain human characteristics since they show districts where minerals have been found. Each was first observed and developed in some locality where it occurred at or near the surface. Relative quality, accessibility, ease of recovery, and inherent usefulness to human beings, however, have all been factors in the decisions which have governed prospecting, development, and use of mineral resources. These human circumstances, therefore, indirectly affect the state of human knowledge concerning the distribution of minerals.

In addition to the mineral content which is useful to man through his extracting it from the earth, still another important mineral ingredient of the land is the soil. Soil is only in part a product of the mineral content of the land; and it is vegetation which extracts the mineral content of the soil for man. The significance of soil in the direct and indirect support of life renders it an integral part of the geography of life within the biosphere, in which section it will be discussed.

The Biosphere

The biosphere has already been defined as the contact zone of atmosphere with the combined surfaces of lithosphere and hydrosphere. The actual surface of that contact has been described as the configuration of the land. Outward and inward from that contact surface lies the narrow band within which life exists. The biosphere is delimited vertically by the distribution of life. Life is a force which carries with it innumerable agents for its application in the form of an almost infinite variety of plants and animals.

Man is unable to answer the fundamental question—What is life? Yet no considerable extent of the earth is devoid of living substance in some form or other. Even the most extreme deserts and the frozen wastes of the Arctic and Antarctic are not so barren as to be completely devoid of life, although superficially they may seem so. Desert flowers, after a rare rain storm, attest to the latent life awaiting only the opportunity to blossom forth. In the icy fastness of Antarctica, in the recently discovered lakes district, where thawing takes place in the summer season, the edges of the rocky lakes are green with algae; and lichens cling stubbornly to life upon bare rock surfaces. Such facts are proof of the fundamental idea that living matter possesses extreme adaptability. Through processes of mutation and natural selection over long periods of time, life has evolved and continued to develop highly specialized forms suited to particular conditions. Life forms utilize the great variety of natural circumstances and materials distributed over the earth's surface. The major outlines of the more important of these circumstances and materials have been sketched in previous sections dealing with the atmosphere and lithosphere.

There are three great associations of living things which unite all the resources discussed systematically in the two chapters on the physical aspect of geography. *Vegetation, animals,* and the *soil* in one form or another embody within the biosphere *moisture, carbon dioxide, minerals,* and the *remains of previous life* within the physical context of different degrees of *warmth* and *humidity* of the atmosphere, and the various *surface configurations* of the land. The forces which combine these diverse elements appear to be *solar energy* and *life* itself. As the result of complex biological processes which are beyond the scope of this book, an almost bewildering variety of living forms are classifiable, and are distributed over the face of the earth. Each of the three great associations will be briefly characterized.

Vegetation. Vegetation is a result, an agent, and a living force. As an agent organic matter contributes to the formation of the soil and to the sustenance of other vegetation. Plant life serves as a cover for and provides sustenance for animal life.

As a force vegetative life combines solar energy and earth materials in the processes of its own growth and the evolution of species. In relation to other life forms vegetation occupies a key position to our understanding of all life within the biosphere because of its role in the formation of soil and in support of the animal kingdom.

Animals. Animals, too, are a result, an agent, and a living force. The natural distribution of fauna is determined primarily by the location of food sources. Both directly (in terms of herbivorous animals) and indirectly (in terms of carnivorous animals) major animal associations follow closely the patterns of established vegetation associations. The one outstanding exception to this rule is man—homo sapiens. Through the application of creative imagination and volition, man directly determines his own geographical distribution more than any other living creature. This fact is the key reason for acknowledging human force as a distinctive form of creative energy with the capacity of shaping the human pattern of the world.

Soil. Soil is a fitting climax to the discussion of the physical aspect of geography. Soil is the living and life-yielding embodiment of all the forces, agents, and processes of nature within the biosphere. In it are the mineral constituents of the subsurface rocks which constitute the parent materials. These minerals are the weathered and transported products of the agents of erosion. They have been mobilized by the same forces of the solar system responsible for the distribution of heat energy and moisture of the atmosphere. As features of the surface they have been alternately blown away, moistened, flooded, warmed, frozen, baked, and moved about in becoming the fragmented mantle of earth materials intermittently covering the lithosphere. Within this physical structure of soil materials, the countless forms of organic life have stirred and grown, died, decayed, and intermingled. This soil mantle which incompletely blankets the land surfaces of the earth is literally the fragile, often "tissue-thin," living contact between the subsurface crust of the earth and its enveloping atmosphere of oxygen, carbon dioxide, heat energy, and moisture.

Despite dramatic technological achievements of modern science, mankind is still dependent on the soil for life. It is a truism that man is a product of the soil. Its plant life feeds man directly, and by providing plant life to his livestock feeds him indirectly as well. Accordingly, *soil* is a primary resource

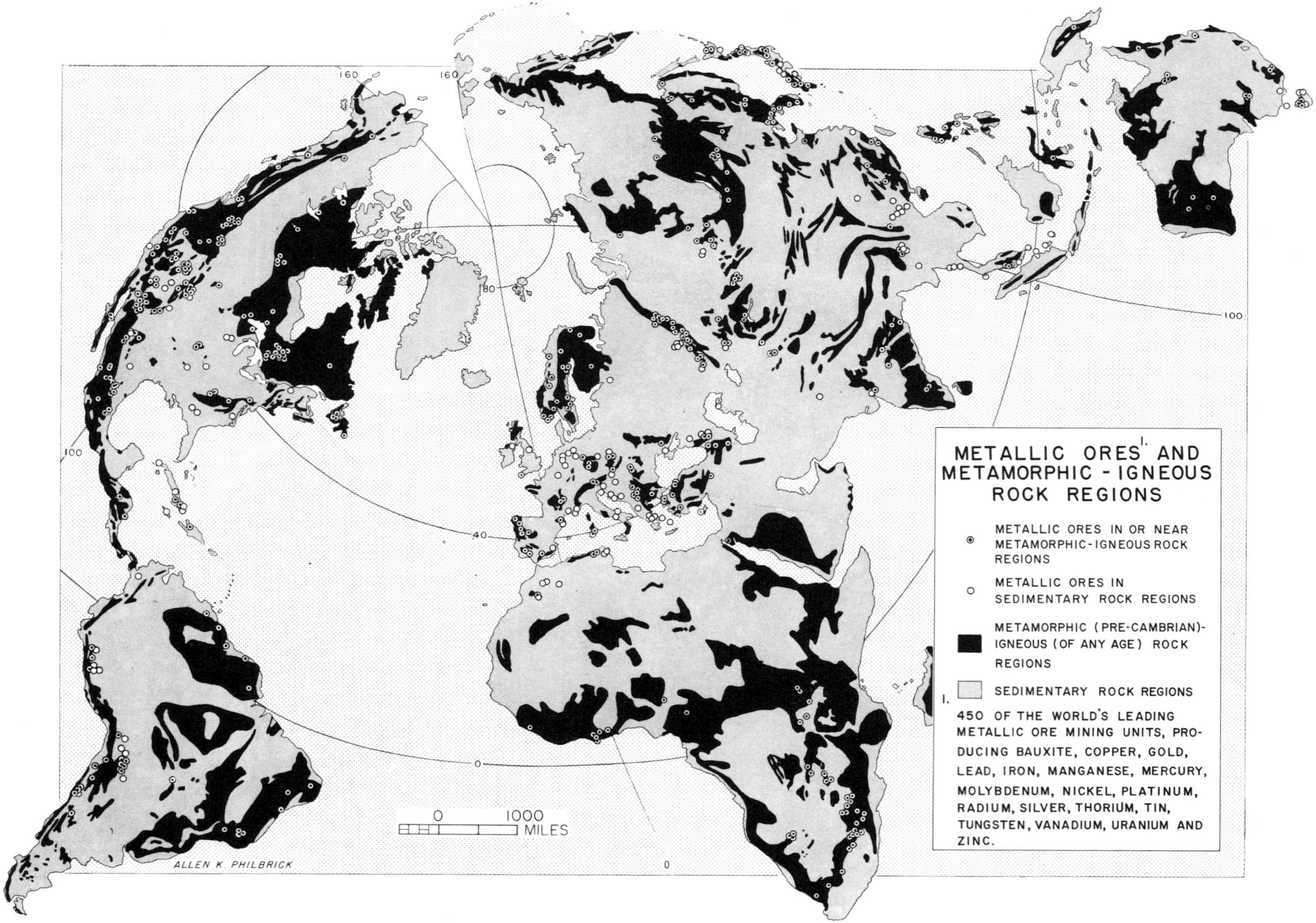

METALLIC ORES¹ AND
METAMORPHIC - IGNEOUS
ROCK REGIONS

⊙   METALLIC ORES IN OR NEAR
METAMORPHIC-IGNEOUS ROCK
REGIONS

○   METALLIC ORES IN
SEDIMENTARY ROCK REGIONS

■   METAMORPHIC (PRE-CAMBRIAN)-
IGNEOUS (OF ANY AGE) ROCK
REGIONS

☐   SEDIMENTARY ROCK REGIONS

1.   450 OF THE WORLD'S LEADING
METALLIC ORE MINING UNITS, PRO-
DUCING BAUXITE, COPPER, GOLD,
LEAD, IRON, MANGANESE, MERCURY,
MOLYBDENUM, NICKEL, PLATINUM,
RADIUM, SILVER, THORIUM, TIN,
TUNGSTEN, VANADIUM, URANIUM AND
ZINC.

ALLEN K PHILBRICK

0   1000   MILES

Figure 40

72

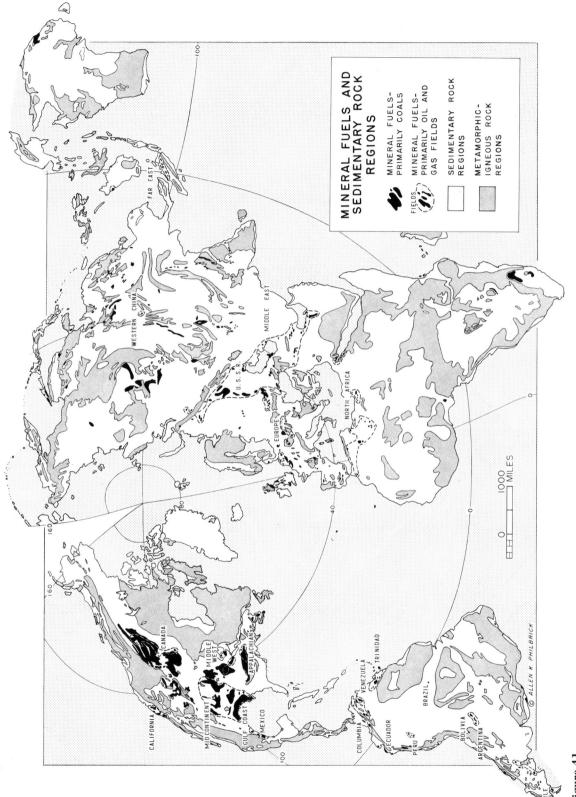

MINERAL FUELS AND
SEDIMENTARY ROCK
REGIONS

MINERAL FUELS-
PRIMARILY COALS

MINERAL FUELS-
PRIMARILY OIL AND
GAS FIELDS

FIELDS

SEDIMENTARY ROCK
REGIONS

METAMORPHIC-
IGNEOUS ROCK
REGIONS

FAR EAST

WESTERN CHINA

U.S.S.R.

MIDDLE EAST

EUROPE

NORTH AFRICA

CANADA

MIDDLE
WEST

APPALACHIAN

CALIFORNIA

MID CONTINENT

GULF COAST

MEXICO

COLUMBIA

ECUADOR

PERU

VENEZUELA

TRINIDAD

BRAZIL

BOLIVIA

ARGENTINA

CHILE

0   1000
        MILES

© ALLEN K PHILBRICK

Figure 41

73

of agriculture. Others in the association are *growing season,* a measure of warmth; *precipitation,* a measure of available water; and *surface configuration,* an expression of ease of cultivation, management, drainage, and susceptibility to erosion. Few resources of the earth are more basic to human sustenance than is the soil. Its use and conservation are, therefore, of paramount importance.

Role of Vegetation in the Distribution of Life

Of the three expressions of life—vegetation, animals, and soil—vegetation is the key to understanding the distribution of the other two. This is true because of the dual role of vegetation as both shelter and food for animals and as an agent in the formation of soils.

Adjustments of Vegetation to Water and Temperature Conditions. Vegetation reflects in its diversity the great variety of moisture and precipitation conditions prevailing over the earth. The principal distinction in vegetation is between *trees* and *grasses,* or, more generally, between *woody* and *herbaceous* plants. The principal determinants as to whether grass or trees dominate the living landscape are moisture, and, indirectly, temperature, through its effect on evaporation. Forest vegetation is a measure of precipitation effectiveness, reflecting both amount and evaporation of precipitation, as well as ground water storage. The regions where precipitation is more effective, from humid through wet conditions, are occupied by trees and other woody plants. Regions with less effective and less dependable precipitation are characterized by grasses and herbaceous plants. No single amount of precipitation sufficient for all forest vegetation can be cited. Toward the poleward limit of trees an annual precipitation of as little as 15 inches will support conifers. In middle latitudes at least 30 inches are required, while in the tropics as much as 90 to 150 inches of precipitation are optimal for some species of trees.

Not only is there variation in the amount of precipitation necessary with variations of temperature, but also the moisture requirements differ with the type of tree. Forests are either broad or needle-leafed, or evergreen or deciduous. Broad-leafed evergreen trees in the rainy tropics require the most water—more than 90 inches a year. Broad-leafed deciduous trees of the tropics are next, requiring 45–90 inches of precipitation a year. Broad-leafed deciduous trees of the middle latitudes are less demanding, while the needle-leafed evergreens or conifers of middle-latitude and subarctic regions require the least water.

The lower limit of annual precipitation necessary to grow trees characteristic of a given locality represents generally the beginning of predominance by grassy plants. Seasonal distribution of precipitation is also very important, since most trees are unable to withstand prolonged periods of drought unless stored water is available. The effectiveness as well as the amount of available moisture within regions of predominantly grassy vegetation determines the height and thickness of grassland cover.

The role of water is two-fold. It is a necessary constituent of plant tissue and a vital agent in the processes of plant nutrition. It unites the resources of the earth with those of the atmosphere in the bodies of plants. On the one hand, the mineral and organic food materials derived from the earth are made available by being dissolved in water. When they are dissolved in water, these nutrients are drawn into the roots and stems which lead to the leaves. On the other hand, the carbon content of vegetation is derived from the carbon dioxide of the atmosphere. Carbon is dissolved in the water supplied to certain cells within the leafy structure of plants. The all-important process of photosynthesis takes place in living vegetable matter when light energy and living cells through the agency of water combine the carbon dioxide of the air and the food nutrients of the earth into chlorophyl—the green matter of vegetation.

The amount of water available over the long range provides a control, along with a variety of other conditions, for the success of vegetative life. The range in water requirements of different plants is quite wide. It may be measured by the ratio of units of water required to make it possible for one unit of equivalent dry matter to be absorbed. This ratio varies from as little as 40–50 units of water for coniferous trees to as much as 2 to 3 thousand units of water per unit of dry matter absorbed by some domesticated vegetables. The principal variables which differentiate the amount and kinds of vegetation over the earth are (1) the amount of moisture effectively available, (2) the concentration of plant food (both mineral and organic) in the soil, and (3) other conditions. Other conditions include such items of indirect importance as type and texture of the soil, slope of the surface, relative humidity, temperature of the air, and exposure to air movements. Man takes many steps in his agri-

(A) A tropical jungle forest with mahogany trees in the Cameroons. On the edges of a tropical forest such as this, the profusion of undergrowth gives a two-storied effect to the forest profile. (*Courtesy of United Nations.*)

(B) The fine stand of mixed hardwoods in southeastern Pennsylvania includes tulip-poplar, various oaks, birches, sycamore, and maple. (*Courtesy of American Forest Products Industries.*)

Figure 42

(C) A well-managed spruce timberland lining both sides of a New Hampshire road. These trees are part of a second-growth forest belonging to a paper company. (*Courtesy of American Forest Products Industries.*)

cultural and horticultural practices to increase this efficiency. In many other ways, however, purposeful or not, man also has destroyed or altered natural vegetation—so much so that there is probably little truly natural vegetation over most of the earth.

Distinctive Vegetation Associations. There are four principal combinations of woody and herbaceous and grassy vegetation types: *forest, grassland, grassland and forest mixtures,* and *desert.*

Forest associations are of three principal kinds: the *tropical rainforest,* the *deciduous hardwood and mixed forests* of middle latitudes, and the *coniferous forests* of middle and relatively high latitudes as shown in Figure 42A, B, and C, respectively.

Grassland associations may also be subdivided into three major kinds. These are the tall grasses of the prairies, the shorter grasses of the steppe lands, and the semigrasslands of the tundra (Figure 43A, B, and C, respectively). The latter is an association of short grasses with herbs and many varieties of lichens and mosses. Again, the major controls are the adjustments through natural selection of the vegetation forms to precipitation and temperature conditions.

Transitional between the vegetation associations in which either trees or grasses are predominant are mixtures of trees with grasses. Such forest-grassland transitions predominate in the margins of tropical regions. These extensive regions, called *savannas,* are characterized by 25–50 inches of precipitation which occurs in markedly contrasting wet and dry seasons. Such precipitation seasonality, coupled with relatively high temperatures, produces sparsely distributed trees interspersed with tall stands of coarse grasses. The trees tend to be thorny and stunted, of the deciduous variety which lose their leaves during the dry season. Because they are subjected to drought their root systems probe the soil deeply in search of underground water. Within savanna regions tree cover is denser along permanent watercourses than on the higher land between streams. Savannas range in relative proportion of trees and grasses from almost complete forest to nearly total grassland cover. Variations in the amount of precipitation and length of the dry season bring about corresponding variations in the amount of tree cover and in the fullness of vegetative development. High grasses provide excellent cover for animal life. Toughness of stalks and depth of root systems make savanna grasses difficult to plow and discouraging to those attempting cultivation. Savanna grasses also harbor many insect pests. The

tsetse fly, the carrier of sleeping sickness among men and nagana, a similar disease among cattle, finds the tropical savanna of Africa an excellent habitat.

Typical savanna associations are shown in Figure 44A, B, and C. These include tall-grass, short-tree savannas, widely dispersed tall-tree, short-grass savannas, and short-grass, park-woodland savannas.

Extremes of drought and undependability of moisture represent desert conditions. Adjustment to such extreme conditions produces especially woody and stunted desert vegetation.

World Vegetation Regions. The map in Figure 45 shows the geographical distribution of principal vegetation types. It should be compared with maps of warmth regions, amount, seasonality, and variability of precipitation, and with the map of precipitation regions.

Patterns of vegetation show striking variations within the region with less than 20 inches of annual precipitation designated as the Arid Crescent. These differences are an expression of the effectiveness of precipitation, as well as the adjustment of plant forms to average moisture and temperature conditions. As we move poleward in the Arid Crescent from Saharan Africa through central Asia to Soviet Siberia, we pass from desert to steppe, to deciduous and coniferous forests, to tundra, and polar desert.

The great ring of coniferous forests in middle-latitude lands is the greatest stretch of continuous forest in the world. Between 55 and 60 degrees north latitude this belt girdles the earth for a distance of over 12,000 miles and ranges from 1,000 to 1,500 miles in width from north to south. South of these vast Northern Hemisphere coniferous forests there once were three particularly important middle-latitude deciduous forest regions which corresponded with the humid precipitation regions of the North Atlantic in Europe, eastern North America, and eastern China in Asia. Human settlement has virtually wiped out virgin forests in these regions. Deforestation is nearly complete in eastern China, but large amounts of second and third growth still characterize western Europe and eastern North America.

In the Southern Hemisphere, as may be observed from the map, correspondence is much closer between vegetation and moisture regions. Tropical rainforests coincide with wet lands where at least 2.5 inches of precipitation occur each month of the year. Savanna combinations poleward of the

Figure 43. Grassland associations.

(A) A man-altered prairie. Tall grasses with flowering weeds on the edges of the field represent the thick mat of grass typical of the natural prairie. In pioneer days, the billowing of prairie grasses waist high to a person walking through them made a scene never to be forgotten. The trees around the farmstead are a planted shelter belt. (*Courtesy of American Forest Products Industries.*)

(B) Short grass steppe vegetation in Wyoming. This view shows cattle grazing on the range land of the subhumid intermontane basin. (*Courtesy of Lew Merrim.*)

(C) The Canadian Northwest Territory tundra north of the tree line. The shrub vegetation in the foreground is willow; the other vegetation consists of mosses and lichens. The broken and altered bedrock is the metamorphic rough surface of the Canadian shield on the shores of Courageous Lake, Mackenzie District. (*Courtesy of William Hughes.*)

(A) Tall coarse grass with low trees.

Figure 44. Savanna associations. (*Photographs courtesy of American Geographical Society.*)

rainforests represent adjustments to the alternating wet and dry seasons of the warm tropics. Tropical steppes and deserts occupy the drier regions which have a high rate of evaporation. Only small middle-latitude portions of Southern Hemisphere continents possess humid conditions which can produce broad-leafed deciduous forests. These are in south central Chile, east coastal South Africa, and east coastal Australia south of the Tropic of Capricorn.

Forces, Agents, and Processes of Soil Formation

The interplay of processes involved in soil formation illustrates the way in which soil is a coordinated expression of all the physical elements of the contact between the litho-hydrosphere and the atmosphere within the spatial limits of the biosphere.

The mechanical and chemical processes of weathering break up and prepare solid rock materials of the lithosphere into the parent materials of future soils. This is the mantle of fragmented rocks beneath the surface soils, which in most places covers the solid crust of the earth. Weathering continues at every stage of the cycle of erosion from bedrock to base level. Unquestionably the geologic cycle is so long that the pattern of soils over the world at any one time may be regarded as quite stable; yet every soil particle is at some particular stage in the unending processes of wearing away of the continents or of their upbuilding.

Soil Formation. The basic processes of soil formation are those of weathering, of plant and animal life, and of erosion. Physical and chemical weathering produce the rocky materials of soil from

(B) Short grass with widely spaced trees.

(C) Park-type short grass tropical savanna in South Africa Kouger National Park.

the earth's crust and continually fragments such material still further into the individual soil particles of gravel, sand, silt, and clay. Processes of plant and animal growth and development produce organic materials. Through chemical processes of decay, aided by the life processes of bacteria and microorganisms, organic materials are altered so that their organic mineral content (humus) can be re-used in new plant growth. Chemical processes of ionization, replacement, and chemical precipitation render the mineral constituents of the earth's rocky materials available for mechanical solution in water which carries them into the vegetation. The processes of erosion explain the transference of soil from one place to another.

Elements are removed from the soil through the processes of *leaching*. The chemical constituents of the soil, either organic or inorganic, are dissolved and then washed out and away from soil particles by the percolation of water down through the structure of the soil. Elements are added to the soil by *accumulation*. Solid materials are deposited around the particles within the structure of the soil out of solution through the processes of evaporation or chemical precipitation. The differential rates at which leaching and accumulation occur may be classified under three special headings: *laterization, podzolization,* and *calcification.*

Laterization. This process of soil formation is characteristic of humid and wet tropical and subtropical forested regions. Both organic and mineral constituents are leached out of the surface layers of the soil to an excessive degree, leaving behind a residual concentration of insoluble hydroxides of

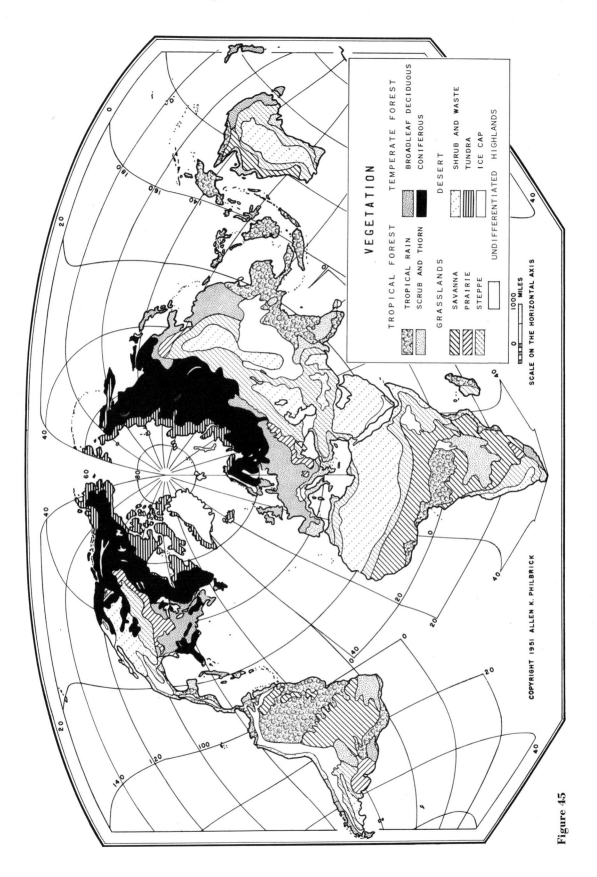

Figure 45

80

iron and aluminum. Completion of the process may produce concentrations of iron and aluminum (laterites) salts of sufficient metallic content to qualify as economically exploitable ores. Few soils become completely laterized to this extent, but most tropical and subtropical lands have lateritic soils. The rich humus of luxuriant tropical and subtropical vegetation is washed away (leached) before it can be assimilated. The remaining insoluble red and yellow hydroxides of iron and aluminum percolate downward and become concentrated at the base of the soil just above the subsoil or unaltered parent material. A wide variety of lateritic soils are produced by the different combinations in amounts of mineral content lost or accumulated through these processes. The name *pedalfers* has been coined for these soils as a group—*ped* for earth, *al* for aluminum, and *fer* for iron.

Podzolization. The opposite of laterization is podzolization, a process of weathering and soil formation characteristic of the subhumid to humid northern middle-latitude and subarctic coniferous forested regions. Under certain circumstances podzolization may extend throughout the middle latitudes and into the tropics. Under podzolization chemical activity is retarded by cold so that the entire regime of soil formation takes place at a slower pace. Small amounts of organic and mineral constituents are dissolved because of both lack of moisture and the slower rate of chemical action, which induces or permits the accumulation and deposition of a layer of incompletely decomposed organic matter. The thick brown mantle of pine needles on the floor of a coniferous forest is symptomatic of this condition. The incompletely decomposed layer of organic material is high in acid content. The organic acid near the top layer of the soil combines with hydroxides and oxides of iron and aluminum and renders them soluble. Their leaching produces a grayish-white zone of relative color absence which is characteristic of the gray-brown podzols. Middle-latitude forest soils generally have a blended brownish coloring midway between the gray of the highly podzolized soils of the subarctic and the red or yellow typical of laterized soils of tropics and subtropics. Highly laterized or podzolized soils at either extreme of the pedalfers are the least fertile of the forest soils. Podzols of deciduous hardwoods and mixed forests of the middle latitudes are the most fertile of the forest soils.

Calcification. Soils formed under a cover of grassland, particularly temperate humid grasslands, represent a balance between the processes of leaching and accumulation of extreme laterization and podzolization. They tend to conserve greater proportions of humus accumulation than any other soils on earth. Since they occur toward the drier margins of humid regions, they are less subject to leaching. Since they are less subject to shade, also, processes of decay of organic materials tend to occur faster than in temperate forests. The process of calcification is the accumulation of lime which is characteristic of grassland soils in their lower portions. The depth of the zone of lime accumulation varies directly with the amount of precipitation. Water working downward from the surface returns toward the surface by capillary action and brings lime up with it in solution. Under these circumstances grassland soils tend to maintain a good balance between acid and alkaline soil conditions. The grassland soils are probably the world's greatest store of natural fertility in existence. The fertility of grassland soils decreases as the average annual precipitation decreases because the amount of humus in the soil declines with the amount of moisture. Also, as grassland soils are formed under drier conditions, lime accumulations are nearer the surface which tends to make them more alkaline. Lack of water hinders the ability of the processes of weathering to complete their work so that extremely dry regions tend to be rough and stony with sharp angular edges on bedrock outcrops.

Regional Classification and Soils Regions.

It may be observed on the world map in Figure 46 that soil fertility decreases for different reasons in different directions from regions of highest fertility. The decreases in general fertility take place in the directions of greater calcification, more podzolization, and increased laterization. Calcification is associated with increasing aridity; podzolization occurs in regions of moderate precipitation under conditions of reduced evaporation rates at cool temperatures; and laterization is characteristic of warm to hot and humid conditions. Such generalizations as these concerning soils apply to residual soils formed in place under the associated conditions described. Two kinds of soil fertility are exceptions—the relatively high fertility of many transported soils, renewed periodically by the importation of fresh ingredients (flooding, for example), and the high fertility of soils formed from certain mineral-rich volcanic parent materials.

So complex are the possible combinations of

soil-forming processes that it is little wonder soils are classifiable in many different ways according to the purposes of the classification. Soils are sometimes classified according to the *type of rock* which supplied the parent material; or they may be classified descriptively by *attributes* such as color, size of particles, texture, and slope. Another approach to classification is according to circumstances of formation. In this way *physiographic* classification makes the distinction between residual and transported soils. Residual soils are formed in place, while transported soils might be alluvial (water-deposited), morainic (ice-deposited), and dune or loessial (wind-deposited) soils. Still another view is the classification of soils by their *stages of development,* as youthful or mature, in recognition of a cycle through which it is believed all soils will pass if circumstances do not disrupt or interrupt the processes of soil formation.

Each of the above is a useful and significant classification in the study of soils per se. For geographical purposes, however, the classification of soils into ten great soil groups on the basis of inherent characteristics and one category of undifferentiated mountainous areas is considered to be the most useful. It allows an overall summarization of great groups into four categories reflecting both the major soil-formation processes and also distinctions as to agricultural fertility. These categories are *lateritic, podzolized,* and *calcified* soils and one additional category which is *the most fertile* of the great soil groups. The soil groups of the first three categories are located marginally with respect to the soils of the last category as shown by the map in Figure 46.

The lateritic soils are represented by two great soil groups—the most highly lateritic soils of the *rainy tropics,* and the partially laterized red and yellow soils of the *wet and dry savanna* vegetation regions. By and large such soils are subject to excessive leaching and when cultivated are quickly exhausted of their small amounts of mineral and organic constituents. They require long periods of fallowing during which they return quickly to brush and bush. They are, accordingly, only intermittently cultivated.

Podzolized soils are located in the high middle latitudes and subarctic. They consist primarily of the soils beneath the great *coniferous forested belts* of the Northern Hemisphere, and the water-logged or permanently frozen soils of the *tundra.* These two

great soil groups tend to be infertile also. Whereas the laterites are infertile because of excessive chemical activity and leaching, the podzols are infertile because of the lack of sufficient warmth and moisture fully to decompose available organic material.

The third category is comprised of the calcified soils in arid lands. The three great soil groups within this category are the gray *desert* soils, brown *semi-desert* soils, and *semi-arid* chestnut soils. Within these soils fertility is directly related to the amount of moisture available. Long-range water availability has determined to a considerable extent both the amount of humus content and the depth of lime accumulation as already indicated. Soils of this category are relatively infertile because of drought.

The fourth category represents the most extensive regions of relatively high soil fertility on the earth. The geographical position of the three great soil groups of this category is central in relation to the other less fertile soil groups. The three soil groups of this central category are the *black or chernozem* soil groups formed under true grassland conditions, the *prairie grassland* soil group, humid enough for forest in many places but characterized by grass instead, and the *gray-brown forest podzols.* The last group is the most fertile of the soils formed under forest cover. All three of these more fertile soils regions occupy transitional zones between dry and wet, cold and warm. The pattern of great soil groups in North America demonstrates ideally this geographic relationship. The deciduous and mixed forests of the gray-brown forest soils region generally east of the Mississippi, north of the Ohio, and extending into the center of the Great Lakes Region occupy a transitional position between the conifers of the north and the conifers of the subtropical southland. On the north less fertility is associated with podzolization. To the south less fertility is associated with greater laterization. To the west humid conditions give way to drought and tree cover changes to grass. The western edges of the gray-brown forest zone merge with the humid prairies. West of the prairies and extending in a long narrow north-south, northwest-southeast belt are the chernozems of the Great Plains. Still further west decreased fertility is associated with less moisture.

A similar transitional zone of fertile soils is found in South America. In this instance greater laterization cuts down natural soil fertile to the north and east, while aridity is the limiting circumstance to the

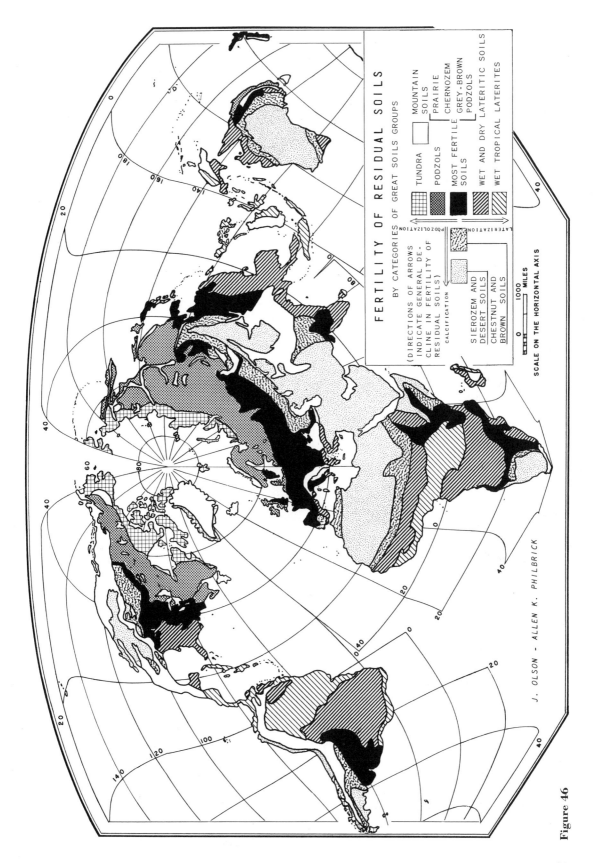

Figure 46

83

south and west. The narrowing of the continent in the middle latitudes restricts the area of the podzols to a small region in southern Chile. The more fertile gray-brown forest soils are limited to a small region of middle-latitude Chile.

In Eurasia fertile gray-brown forest soils give way on the east and north to less fertile podzols. In the center of the continent fertile grassland soils change toward the south into less fertile steppe-land and desert soils. In China the former residual soils of this once-forested region after a bordering zone of fertile grassland soils on the northwest match decreasing fertility with increasing drought. In South China, except for alluvial soils, fertility declines as laterization increases.

In Africa central laterites of the rainforest regions are almost surrounded by red and yellow soils of the wet and dry savanna. Between the savanna and the subtropical deserts of the Sahara in the north and the Kalahari in the southwest are more fertile grassland soils. These African grasslands are less fertile, however, than middle-latitude grasslands of North America and Eurasia. Only in the high plateaus of South Africa, in the Pampas of Argentina, and in the eastern interior plains of Australia can Southern Hemisphere grassland soils approach the fertility of the black earth soils of Russia and the American Middle West. The fifth category shown on the map is undifferentiated highlands. Comparison of the soils map with a world map of cultivated land in Figure 47 discloses the high degree of awareness of soil fertility by the world's farmers.

Comparison of the soils groups and categories shown on the map in Figure 46 with the other world maps in the chapters dealing with the physical aspect of geography demonstrates the way in which soils summarize the forces, agents, and processes of nature within the biosphere. Such comparison demonstrates the association of soils with *warmth regions*, with relative *amounts, reliability*, and *seasonality of precipitation*. Also clearly visible are the impact of differences in *landforms* and *drainage* upon the redistribution of soils by the agents of *erosion*. The role played by life itself through the impact of *vegetation* on the humus content of soil is apparent. From the coincidences of soil with vegetation regions we may infer that it is *life* which integrates warmth, moisture, surface, subsurface condition, drainage, vegetation, and soil into one complexly interwoven set of associations. This great pattern of the living soil unites many different natural processes. The study of the distribution of results from

these processes is properly the specialized subject matter of physical geography.

The Animal Kingdom

Animal life may be thought of in two groups. The first group is the human race and all domesticated animals; the second is all living animal forms except man and the animals he has domesticated. The study of animal forms as such is zoology. The phyla into which zoologists classify their subject matter taxonomically do not have clear-cut geographical distribution. The reason for this is the far greater mobility of animals than plants, even though animals, like vegetation forms, are dependent on their environment.

Pattern of Animal Regions. Animals tend to group themselves within each of several regional types in accordance with the kind of vegetation to which their food supply is related. This will be a direct relationship if the animals eat vegetation as food, or an indirect relationship if the animals eat other vegetation-eating animals. Generally valid animal associations may be segregrated on the basis of forest, savanna, grassland, and desert habitats.

The degree of geographical differentiation of animals forms is the result of processes of natural selection. These processes are partly a function of physical circumstances permitting or inhibiting migration. Thus, the relatively isolated positions of southern South America, Africa, and Australia have been instruments in the evolution of dissimilar types of animals because intermigration of species between similar environments is prevented by isolation. The contrary tends to be true of the continents in the Northern Hemisphere.

The map in Figure 48 shows five distinctive faunal regions of continental size.[1] Divisions are based upon relative barriers of two types—zonal climates which have caused most animal species to become regionally differentiated and limited; and barriers either of salt water or topography which have isolated and limited some fauna regionally. It is beyond the scope of the present discussion to enumerate the complex animal forms which fill these average geographical limits. It is important to realize that animal life is mobile, that it is on the threshold of the capacity to be thoughtful and decision-making life. Even though the thought processes of most animals are not "knowing" or

[1]Phillip J. Darlington, *Zoogeography*, New York: John Wiley and Sons, 1957, pp. 426–427.

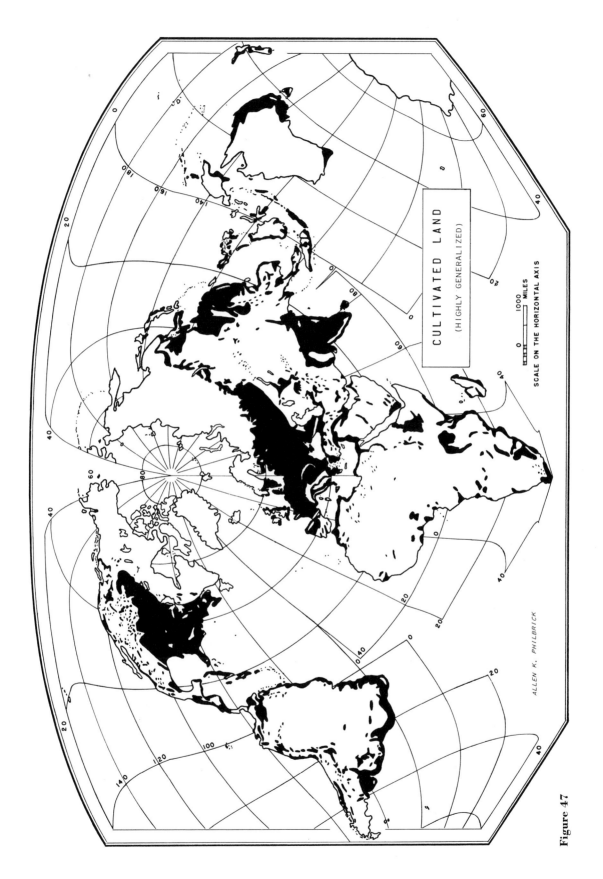

CULTIVATED LAND
(HIGHLY GENERALIZED)

0   1000
MILES
SCALE ON THE HORIZONTAL AXIS

ALLEN K. PHILBRICK

Figure 47

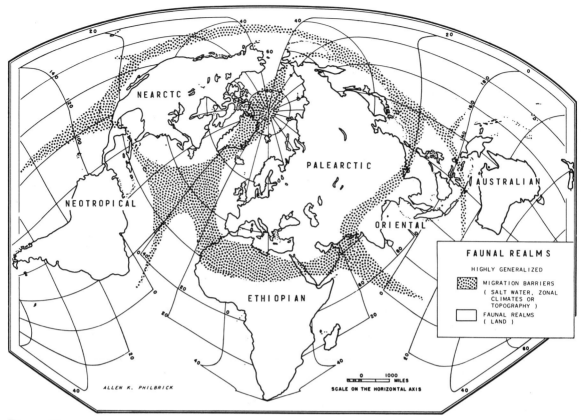

Figure 48

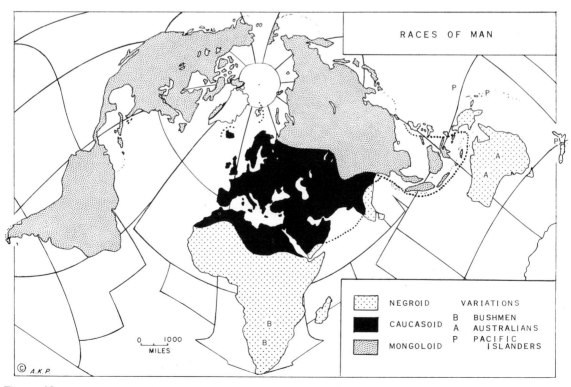

Figure 49

"reasoned" as can be the case with human beings, the elementary possibilities of reasoning along with physical mobility of animals is responsible for a much wider dispersal of individual animals forms in relation to environmental circumstances than is possible for vegetation.

Distribution of Primitive Man as an Animal. The map in Figure 49 illustrates the distribution of the races of primitive man.[1] It shows three major races and three peripheral variations: Negroid, Caucasoid, and Mongoloid as primary categories; and Bushmen, Australian, and Pacific island peoples as secondary variations.

From the standpoint of pattern it is significant that the part of the world which comes closest to having common borders with all six faunal regions on Figure 48 is also the most likely region of origin for the dispersal of the human race throughout the world. This is the region extending across North Africa and the Middle East to South Asia. Dispersal and racial evolution from the beginning of human history sets man apart as nature's most versatile animal form—the only vertebrate to dominate in all of the faunal regions.

Role of Creative Human Force in the Sociogeographic Evolution of Modern Society. The

[1]Carleton S. Coon, *The Story of Man*, New York: Alfred A. Knopf., Inc., 1954, p. 191.

critical transition from prehuman to homo sapiens is impossible to document. It is generally believed, however, that the transition occurred when prehumans became manlike by making tools. From the start the assumption made in the analysis of human evolution is that *cultural innovation* marks the difference between human and nonhuman animal existence. There may be a relationship between the purely physical evolution of man and the cultural evolution which is an expression of it. The transition from throwing stones at random to aiming and perfecting the skill of hitting objects with stones involves a *mental* difference. The development of such mental concepts on a simple plane must have led to the capacity to think of and use more complex concepts. Accordingly, the critical evolution in man was the brain. The use of the mind, in turn, could be related by processes of natural selection to other physiological changes in the evolution of man's biological structure. If this assumption is valid, it explains the fact that man, of all animal forms, early became dominant in all of the faunal regions of the world. It further explains the fact that man has developed the greatest range and flexibility in living on and making use of the resources of the earth. It is this distinction of man as a knowing, *cultural* being which makes it imperative to appraise the impact of human creative imagination in understanding the geographical distribution of man, his activities, and his works in "this human world."

5 *The Cultural Aspect of Geography*

Culture is studied as an end in itself by many disciplines within the social sciences—anthropology, archeology, sociology, as well as history and geography. In geography the analysis of culture is a means to an end as well as an end in itself.

When a geographer wishes to do more than describe a landform, he must account for its existence. He does this in terms of genetic interpretation. When he wishes to do more than describe the patterns of human activity or of human area organization he must account for the existence of them also. He, therefore, studies the processes of cultural evolution to account for the development of human activity patterns. Processes of innovation, adaptation, and imitation explain the origination of specific ways of living and their transmittal and dispersion from place to place. In addition, therefore, to understanding human cultures in themselves, the purpose of cultural geography is to demonstrate man's creative role in originating and applying innovation to the process of constructing the patterns of human occupancy of the earth.

Forces, Agents, and Processes of Culture

In order to accomplish this purpose it is necessary to have clearly in mind the forces, agents, and processes of cultural evolution, transmission, and dispersal.

Forces and Agents. The basic force of culture is human creative imagination. The hands of men have joined in building what the mind was also creating. In this sense the body is the agent of the mind. This applies both to individuals and to groups. Establishments and institutions of all sorts have been created which represent coordinated activity of mind and body. All the ramifications and extensions of the individual by means of human organization, however, have their root in man himself, who is both force and agent of culture processes.

Innovation, Transmission, and Dispersion. Fundamentally the processes of cultural evolution which account for the geographical pattern of human society are those of innovation, transmission, and dispersion.

Innovation includes not only original invention, but also adaptation and imitation as well. All three are acts of imagination, although they represent varying degrees of originality in their human creativity. Intuitive insight occurs in the mind when new solutions to old problems are generated, or when perception of possibilities latent in the relationship between things develops. No one can say that he knows how such ideas occur; but the human brain is the recognized source of this human quality called creativity. The increment of newness is usually a small "leap" or change which has been prepared for by the efforts of many people groping toward a solution of some problem. In this way most innovations or inventions are the result of many individuals' efforts, both separately and together. The process of innovation is a social one at the same time that it involves individual acts of creativity. This explains why many inventions are centers of controversy as to whom should be given the credit for them. Adaptation and imitation similarly involve perceptivity but in a lesser degree. From the standpoint of understanding the pattern of society, however, they are of fundamental importance in explaining the diversification and spread of culture.

Transmission of culture means the communication of culture from person to person. Without transmittal the threads of the continuity of culture through time would be broken. As it is, however, the accumulated experience of society is handed down from generation to generation, so that the individual has the possibility of benefiting from the innovations of millions of others who have preceded him. Culture transmission is accomplished by both formal and informal means. So important is the contribution of the past that it has recognized and organized expression in the recorded works of man. The specific task of formal education is both the cultivation of the means of understanding and the specific acts of teaching and transmitting the experiences of others. Also, in numberless informal ways the experience of people is communicated and absorbed from person to person, and through the contact of people of different ages a continuity of informal cultural exchange is maintained.

Dispersion of culture is the movement of culture from place to place. The acts of culture innovation are focused in particular places by the locations of the individuals involved. Through transmission and the movement of people, innovations move outward from a point of origin in one or more directions. In the course of time activities and interconnections of people bring about the dissemination of culture. The process is given the general name of culture dispersion.

Leading and Following. In order to understand the application of the above processes to the evolution of the patterns of human occupance it is necessary to relate the individuals engaged in the daily activities of society to those processes. This can be done by understanding that every individual in his daily life participates in the processes in some way—participates either through leading or following. This classification suggests a means of linking specific activities with the processes of innovation, transmission, and dispersion of culture.[1]

For example, if a farmer originates a farm practice, his innovation is an act of leadership. If he tries to get others to adopt his idea, such leadership may be said to be *active.* If he employs this new idea only on his own farm and either does not perceive its implications for others or does nothing about getting others to follow his example, which does not begin until someone actually imitates his innovation, his leadership may be said to be *passive.* There are both active and passive followers also. Those who go through the accepted motions of daily living with unthinking obedience, who simply follow the cultural practices of others, may be called *passive followers.* On the other hand, those individuals who are alert to improved ways of doing things, who seek means of bettering themselves and of rendering their services to others, may be classified as *active followers.*

The above elementary classification of peoples' reactions to life around them may be useful in accounting for the positive roles of innovators,

adapters, and imitators. Account also needs to be taken of negative reactions. Rejection and failure to appreciate what is new and different is probably more frequent than positive reactions. Human society is basically conservative in its resistance to change. Nor is all adoption or resistance to change voluntary. "Man's inhumanity to man" still compels acquiescence by the weak to the will of the strong. Oppression and dominance by force or threat of force, whether military, economic, or social, still affects the activities of millions.

There are varying degrees of overlap between the types in the above suggested classification, but all persons fit into the processes in one way or another. This means that the impact of cultural evolution through the agencies of countless individuals upon the patterns of occupance is continuous. The viewpoint supplies a means by which the new elements in culture as they become adapted and imitated may be understood as a "cutting edge" in the construction of the patterns of society.

Analysis of cultural evolution geographically reveals that there are regions from which innovations have come in great numbers and that there have been particular routes over which people and their cultures have moved in such numbers as to identify them as streams of culture dispersion. Before turning to an appraisal of the geographical patterns of culture it will be useful to present a classification of the results of the culture innovation process.

Cultures as Ways of Life

A culture is a way of life characteristic of a group of people within a definable area during a particular period of time. Culture can be further defined by classifying the elements of the way of living which it represents. It will include first of all the basic *assumptions, ideas, concepts* or *values* by which people guide or direct their lives. These principles will have a great many ramifications relating to all of the specific *ways of doing things,* which represent a second category in the classification of a way of life. In turn, the activities according to the ways of doing things which are characteristic of a given culture will result in specific *works* of man within the society.

Values, Ideas, or Concepts. Interwoven with the conduct of every day activities are certain basic human values, ideas, or concepts. These evolve over a period of time and are transmitted from generation to generation—from parents to children, from elder to younger, or from leaders to followers.

---

[1] The ideas of "leading and following," particularly, and much of the other contents of this chapter, in general, were worked out jointly by the author and Dr. E. M. Bjorklund, Department of Geography, Vassar College.

They often reflect principles of conduct, problems which a people have faced in their historical tradition, or fundamental attitudes with respect to nature and the material resources of a given region.

For example, one of the basic assumptions of the people in the early Middle East found expression in the Old Testament and is an underlying idea among Christians, Jews, and Moslems: the concept of man having dominion over all of the earth and its resources. With the spread particularly of Christianity by Europeans, this implicit attitude of people has had great influence on the way resources have been developed and used in many parts of the world.

The basic ideas of human rights which found expression in the English Magna Carta and the American Bill of Rights represent more specific and recorded values which are rooted in Anglo-American culture.

Ways of Doing. "Ways of doing" is the broadest possible expression of a great range of activities, customs, and procedures which answer the basic questions, "How is life conducted?" "How do people feed, clothe, and shelter themselves, and enjoy, in varying degrees, the amenities of life?" "What are the ways of doing things which are characteristic of a given society's technology and which, in turn, reflect its human values?"

Beyond those classified as economic other ways of doing apply to political or purely social phases of life. Uniformity in peoples' ways of doing things is one of the principal means of creating a distinctive culture and delimiting a homogeneous culture region.

Works of Man. The physical plant of structures and facilities in which men live represents in the aggregate a major part of the works of man. But not all of the works are visible. Not the least important is the particular organization of areas which results from the functioning of society. Less tangible works are also the works of man represented by deeds, which though without visible result, may nevertheless alter the course of the future.

In the historical sense, the world is truly cluttered with man's works, both useful and abandoned. Tangible remains range from hallowed art treasures such as the pyramids of Egypt and the Parthenon, to present-day networks of railways, the skyscrapers of modern cities, and the spoil dumps beside the gold fields of the Witwatersrand in South Africa, to mention only a few.

Innumerable elements in the values, ways, and works of man express the culture of any given people in a particular area at any certain time. The *intangibles* become visible indirectly. Along with the more obvious forms or traits of a people, they are embodied in the *tangible* results of a culture. When mapped and analyzed from the standpoint of their geographical distribution, all human phenomena may be the subject matter of cultural geography.

World Culture Systems

When viewed on a world scale the results of thousands of years of cultural evolution are difficult to generalize; yet distinctive patterns of general significance can be pointed out when particular elements of evolved culture, first taken separately, are then combined in their composite geographical distribution.

Combinations of Elements. Four specific attributes of human culture are separately classified and shown on the maps in Figures 50 to 53. Their composite patterns are used as the basis for the map of world culture systems which is recorded on the map in Figure 54. The four specific attributes are *religion, language, technology,* and *literacy.* Religions represent basic assumptions, ideas, and human values. Languages are the basic means of social communication between individuals and groups; and technologies illustrate the distinctive ways of conducting the business of living. Each of these attributes is mapped separately showing three major distinctions for each one. Simplicity in this classification is essential in selecting only the most basic distinguishing features so that the composite map does not become encumbered with innumerable combinations. In this way the more complex composite patterns of cultural combinations can be made to reveal major world culture systems on the broadest scale.

Religions. The map in Figure 50 shows the distribution of grouping of specific religions which are classified into three categories. These are the faiths which may be termed *individualistic* in that they provide a set of beliefs by which the individual person may relate himself to a supreme being while maintaining his own individual identity. These are the Christian, Jewish, and Mohammedan religions. They are broadly distinguished from other more *mystical faiths,* which have in common the idea of the submergence of the self in a nonworldly state of infinite being. This category includes Hinduism and Buddhism. Both of these first two categories are, in turn, contrasted with *animist* religions based on complex sets of superstitions attached to natural phenomena endowed with animate forms. Such nature worship characterizes the widely separated tribal religious groups throughout the world.

Languages. The map in Figure 51 shows the distribution of groups of languages classified under three main headings. These are the *alphabetized written* languages, the *ideographic written* languages based upon a picture-form principle, and *nonwritten* languages which had only a spoken form in their original cultural setting. The alphabetized tongues have a restricted number of abstract symbols for sounds. The ideographic languages have a much larger number of symbols than the alphabetized.

The alphabetized languages of the world are all derived from a common Sumerian alphabet which originated in the Middle East in ancient Sumeria, east of the Mediterranean Sea. The spread of the concept of the alphabet and its adaptation to the many different languages which possess alphabetized written form is in itself one of the most striking examples of the origin and dispersion of culture. Similarly the Chinese ideographic written language originated in northwestern China, and spread to Japan where it was adapted to and evolved further into the present-day Japanese language.

Technologies. The map in Figure 52 shows the distribution of technologies in terms of three broad stages of their historical evolution. Later stages of development have replaced or masked the previous existence of earlier ones. Since present-day technological development is changing rapidly in many parts of the world, a cutoff time at the beginning of the present century is used. This same time limitation may generally be applied to all the maps discussed in this section. Three categories of technology represent the initial *hunting and collecting* technology of early man, the *intensive subsistence husbandry* of the first agricultural revolution, and *industrialized urban-focused science* based on the industrial-urban revolution of recent times. The initial hunting and collecting stage is broadened to include the rudimentary beginnings of subsistence agriculture. The intensive subsistence husbandry of the first agricultural revolution refers particularly to the great agrarian societies of ancient times, whereas industrialized technology of the age of science is the offshoot of the renaissance of culture beginning in the fourteenth century in Europe.

Literacy. The map in Figure 53 shows a measure of the effectiveness of language communication in terms of literacy. It is striking how the effective application of alphabetized language by highly literate peoples corresponds closely with science-based industrial and urban-commercial technology.

Composite Culture Systems. The composite map in Figure 54 shows the distribution of five great culture systems on the basis of sets of combinations of these three elements (disregarding recent economic changes).

1. The association of tribal animist peoples with unwritten languages and hunting and gathering technology.

2. The Chinese-Japanese cultures combining Buddhist religious backgrounds, an ideographic written language, and a centuries-old tradition of intensive subsistence agricultural economy.

3. The Hindu-dominated culture of India, combining Hindu-Buddhist religious beliefs, diverse alphabetized languages, and intensive subsistence agricultural technology.

4. The individualistic Mohammedan faith of the Middle East, associated with alphabetized languages and intensive subsistence agricultural economy.

5. The individualistic Christian and Jewish peoples of European culture in six continental regions of the world, using alphabetized languages and operating within a science-based industrialized urban-commercial technology.

With the possible exception of Communist culture there is no other cultural group in the world which is not either buried within one of these five groups as a minority, or classifiable as a part of one or another of these categories. A logical case could be made in the Communist cultures for their inclusion within the appropriate categories over which Communist dictatorship has siezed power. If this is done the two principal powers of the Communist Bloc, the Union of Soviet Socialist Republics and Communist China, belong to the cultures of categories 5 and 2, respectively. Against these backgrounds the Communists are striving to replace previous cultures with the culture of Communism. In view of this situation the map in Figure 54 shows the outline of the Communist Bloc countries as a possible sixth category of *collectivist atheistic values* practiced by peoples using *alphabetized written language* operating within a *science-based industrialized urban-socialized technology.*

World Regions of Culture Innovation

Within the cultural framework of the five systems enumerated above and a possible sixth system representing Communist culture, there are at least a

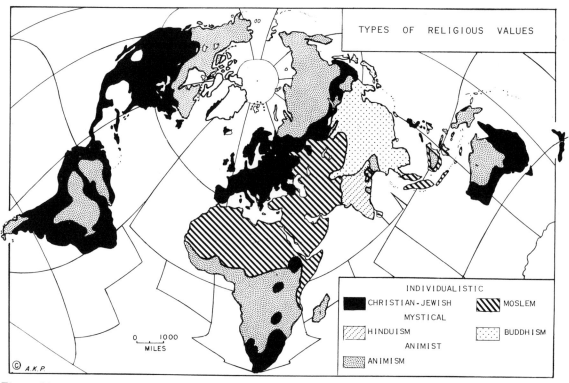

Figure 50

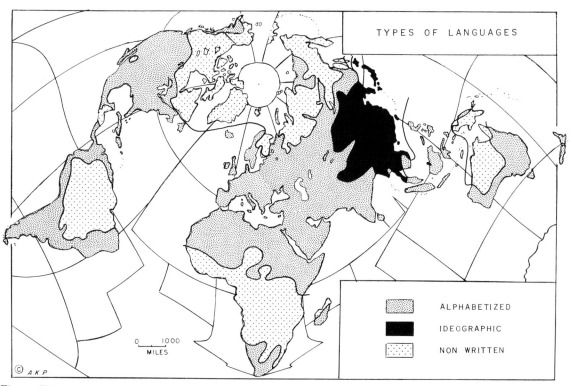

Figure 51

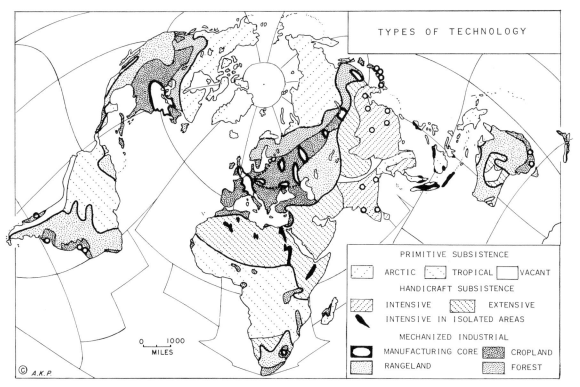

Figure 52

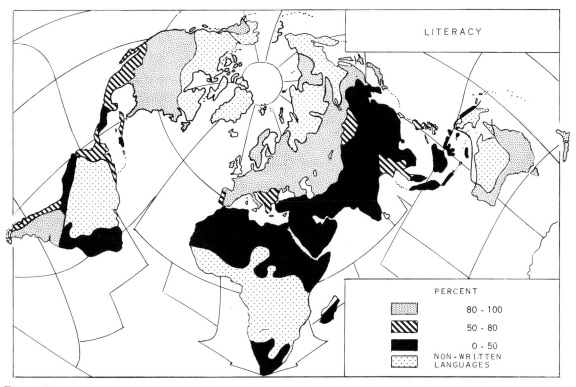

Figure 53

dozen culture source regions of importance on a world scale. Each of these regions has had a central area or main culture hearth. General location of each culture hearth is shown on the map in Figure 55. Around each central area the region of initial dispersion of significant innovations is also indicated. Each source region is important for a different combination of reasons. They will be discussed chronologically.

Significant Stages of Development. As mentioned earlier, it seems probable that mankind had its beginnings within the tropics somewhere between sub-Saharan Africa north of the equator and Southeast Asia. No culture hearths can be identified for man's ultimate beginnings. The first identifiable stage of development involves the transition from prehistoric to historic times. The major innovations in human history have involved revolutionary changes in technology. The agricultural revolution marks the first great stage of development and nine out of the twelve culture hearths represent centers of innovation at this stage of cultural evolution. The transition into modern times has been marked by a second agricultural revolution which accompanied the industrial revolution. The remaining three culture hearths and regions are represented by innovations from this more recent and continuing stage of cultural evolution today. From each of these principal culture hearths cultural innovations have spread and migrated as people have carried forth the ways of doing things which they represented.

The first agricultural revolution. The first agricultural revolution grew out of the hunting and gathering stages of societies which preceded it, and which still prevail in some parts of the world. The invention of agriculture had immense human geographic implication because it created the prerequisites for a sedentary rather than a nomadic way of life. These were the production of dependable surpluses of food so that men could remain in one settled place instead of moving about in the eternal search for sustenance.

Contrary to popular belief the first agricultural innovations were probably not seed planting and the domestication of herd animals. They were the horticultural practices of root planting and the taming of animals for ceremonial or ritual purposes. According to Sauer this occurred first in Southeast Asia.[1] The innovations of seed planting and herd animal domestication took place later. Seed agriculture, as indicated by Vavilov[2] (millets, wheat,

barley, and sorghums), probably originated in hill lands at widely separated points in the Middle East. Sauer shows three culture hearths as the most probable in this region. These were in southern Turkey, eastern Ethiopia, and in central west Pakistan. The dispersal of such knowledge to adjacent alluvial valleys and the development of relatively densely populated agricultural empires based upon seed agriculture was a subsequent development. The same sequence of events apparently occurred also in the uplands adjacent to the Wei Valley, a tributary of the Yellow River in North China. Prior to the discovery of the Americas by Europeans, cultures in the Americas seem to have evolved in isolation from other peoples. The invention of agriculture in the Americas is also divided into two phases by the same kind of agricultural innovations which took place in the Old World—root planting and seed planting. The culture hearths recording the location of the agricultural revolution in the Americas, again, are described by Sauer.[3] The places of origin are in the wet and dry tropics. The culture hearth of tropical root planters is shown to be in northwest South America on the map in Figure 55. Another area is that of the planters of the potato and other tubers which was located in the equivalent of more middle-latitude conditions in the Andean highlands. The map in Figure 55 also shows a Central American hearth of seed planting west of a line approximating the southern border of modern Mexico.

The complex of crops was different in the seed-planting hearth of North America from those in the corresponding culture hearths of the Old World. Instead of small grains, the dominant plants were corn, beans, and squash (pumpkin). They may have originated as attractive weeds within cultivated plots of root plantings.

The livestock associations of the New and Old Worlds were equally striking in their differences. While the pig, the dog, the cow, and the horse were domesticated in the culture hearths of Eurasia, the lone contribution of American seed planters to the domestication of animals was the turkey. In root-planting regions the domesticated animals in the Americas were the llama, alpaca, and the guinea

---

[1]Carl O. Sauer, *Agricultural Origins and Dispersals*, New York: The American Geographical Society, 1952.

[2] N. I. Vavilov, "The Origins, Variation, Immunity, and Breeding of Cultivated Plants," translated from the Russian by K. Starr Chester, *Chronica Botanica*, **13**: Nos. 1–6 (1949–1950).

[3] Sauer, *loc. cit.*

pig. It would seem from these differences that cultural developments of the Americas in pre-Columbian times could have had little if any contact with Eurasia. The subsequent contribution of the American Indian to the Euro-American culture after the occupation of the Americas by Europeans is represented more by the survival of certain traits including crops and animals than by the carrying over of ways of living as a whole.

Special importance of the Middle East. The three major alluvial agrarian societies of the Middle East which evolved as the result of the gradual dispersal of root-planting and seed-agricultural practices into the Indus, the Nile, and the Tigris-Euphrates valleys were of basic importance. Their granaries supported the first urban populations in such ancient military-cultural-administrative centers as Harappa and Mohenjo-Daro on the Indus, as Aphroditopolis and Thebes on the Nile, and Ur, Babylon, and Nineveh in the Tigris-Euphrates river valleys.

If Sauer's views of root-planting origins in Southeast Asia are valid the first agricultural revolution began to spread from that region as much as 10,000 years ago. This was followed by the evolution of seed agriculture in the Middle Eastern highlands from 7,000 to 8,000 years ago, which led ultimately to the first joint agricultural-urban societies of some 4,000 to 5,000 year's antiquity in both the Middle East and China.

The Middle East generally occupies a strategic position as crossroads for streams of culture dispersal between Asia, Europe, and Africa. The territory from the eastern end of the Mediterranean Sea to the Persian Gulf is known as the Fertile Crescent from what is now Syria through Iraq. Ancient caravans maintained contact through this region between Asia and the Middle East. Later the same routes were used by traders between Europe and the Orient. Many threads of cultural continuity of worldwide importance today may be traced back to the Middle East for their beginnings. Four of the world's leading religions originated in Middle Eastern culture hearths—Christianity and Judaism from the Holy Land, Mohammedanism from Arabia, and Hinduism from the Indus region of West Pakistan. Buddhism in China can also be traced back to beginnings in India as a "reformation" or reaction to Hinduism. The origin of the alphabet in the Middle East has already been mentioned. The cultures of the eastern shores of the Mediterranean Sea were the predecessors of the cultures of ancient Greece and, in turn, of Rome. Both Greek

and Roman societies lived by a colonial supply of food from many parts of the Mediterranean's shores, including the lands of the Middle East. Rome became the world's first really metropolitan center. The Roman Empire was Europe's first interregional unit of organization; and Rome was the bridge by which Middle Eastern Christianity became European.

The industrial revolution and the importance of Europe. The second great revolutionary epoch had its roots in Europe and the evolution of culture in that region after the fall of the Roman Empire. The spread of Middle Eastern Christianity, and its split into a western and eastern church accompanied the geographic division of the Roman world into two parts. The economic regional organization of the western or Latin portion of Christendom was focused on Rome, and that of the eastern or Byzantine part on Constantinople. The Roman system came to an end, as shown by Henri Pirenne,[1] with the loss of control of the Mediterranean to the Moslems in the seventh century A.D. The long period of the so-called Dark Ages in Europe saw a return of local subsistence agricultural livelihood with the collapse of larger regional organization of the Roman era. The gradual emergence of modern Europe dates from the slow revival of trade and commerce which led Europeans to the age of exploration and the industrial revolution of the eighteenth century.

The struggle between Latin Christendom and Mohammedanism for the control of the Mediterranean and of Europe itself isolated Europeans from the culture of the Middle East and from Asia for a time. These events encouraged merchants to seek new routes to the East by going around Africa and westward across the Atlantic in efforts to circumnavigate the globe. These were the explorations which led directly to the discovery of the Americas, Australia, New Zealand, and Antarctica, which discoveries, in turn, motivated the expansion of European culture to every continent in the world. There can be little doubt that the most significant events pertaining to the dispersion of culture during the past five hundred years have been the complex evolution and spread of Western European ideas, ways of doing things, and works, to the far corners of the earth. This historic process has seen the virtual *Europeanization* of the Americas, Russia, and Aus-

---

[1] Henri Pirenne, *Medieval Cities,* translated by Frank D. Halsey, Garden City, N.Y.: Doubleday and Co., Inc., 1956, p. 16.

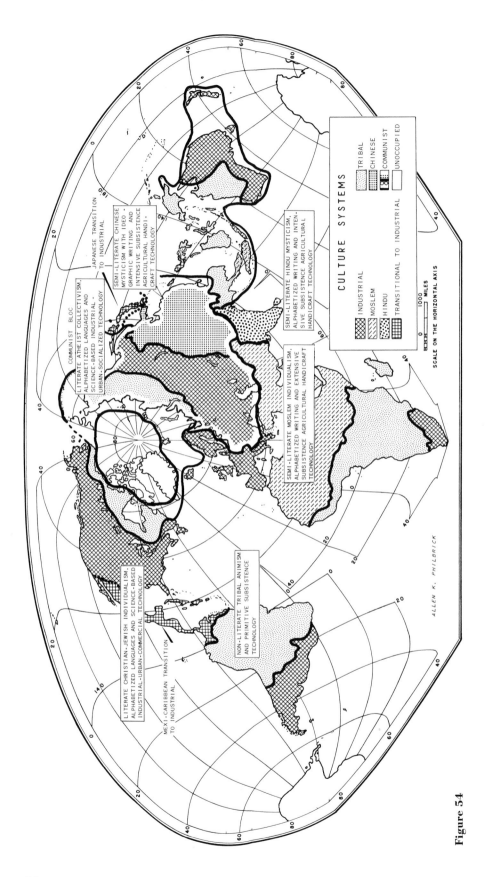

CULTURE SYSTEMS

INDUSTRIAL
MOSLEM
HINDU
TRANSITIONAL TO INDUSTRIAL

TRIBAL
CHINESE
COMMUNIST
UNOCCUPIED

0   1000
MILES
SCALE ON THE HORIZONTAL AXIS

COMMUNIST BLOC

JAPANESE TRANSITION TO INDUSTRIAL

SEMI-LITERATE CHINESE MYSTICISM WITH IDEO-GRAPHIC WRITING AND INTENSIVE SUBSISTENCE AGRICULTURAL HANDI-CRAFT TECHNOLOGY

SEMI-LITERATE HINDU MYSTICISM. ALPHABETIZED WRITING AND INTEN-SIVE SUBSISTENCE AGRICULTURAL HANDICRAFT TECHNOLOGY

LITERATE ATHEIST COLLECTIVISM. ALPHABETIZED LANGUAGES AND SCIENCE-BASED INDUSTRIAL-URBAN-SOCIALIZED TECHNOLOGY

SEMI-LITERATE MOSLEM INDIVIDUALISM, ALPHABETIZED WRITING AND EXTENSIVE SUBSISTENCE AGRICULTURAL HANDICRAFT TECHNOLOGY

LITERATE CHRISTIAN-JEWISH INDIVIDUALISM. ALPHABETIZED LANGUAGES AND SCIENCE-BASED INDUSTRIAL-URBAN-COMMERCIAL TECHNOLOGY

MEXI-CARIBBEAN TRANSITION TO INDUSTRIAL

NON-LITERATE TRIBAL ANIMISM AND PRIMITIVE SUBSISTENCE TECHNOLOGY

ALLEN K. PHILBRICK

Figure 54

96

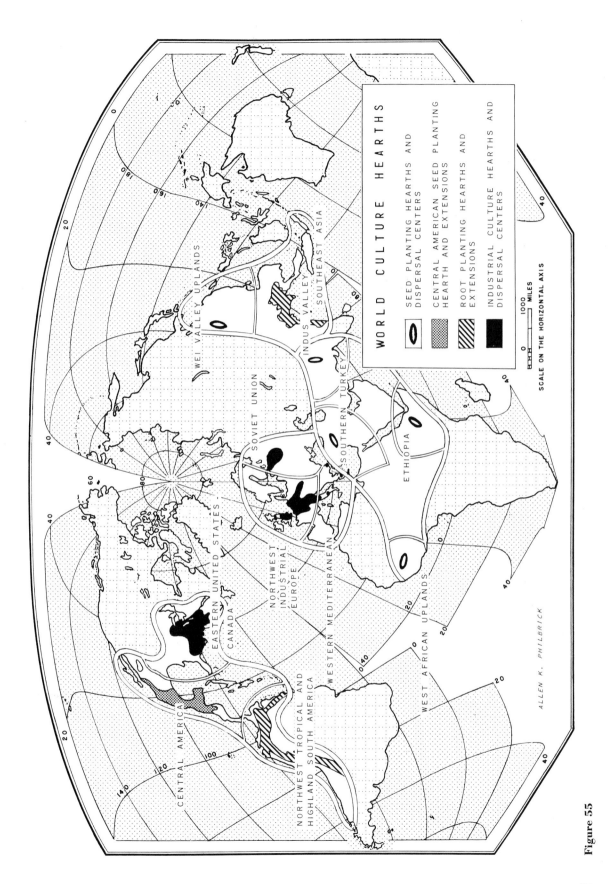

WORLD CULTURE HEARTHS

SEED PLANTING HEARTHS AND DISPERSAL CENTERS

CENTRAL AMERICAN SEED PLANTING HEARTH AND EXTENSIONS

ROOT PLANTING HEARTHS AND EXTENSIONS

INDUSTRIAL CULTURE HEARTHS AND DISPERSAL CENTERS

SCALE ON THE HORIZONTAL AXIS

0   1000
MILES

SOUTHEAST ASIA

WEI VALLEY UPLANDS

INDUS VALLEY

SOVIET UNION

SOUTHERN TURKEY

ETHIOPIA

NORTHWEST INDUSTRIAL EUROPE

CANADA

EASTERN UNITED STATES

WESTERN MEDITERRANEAN

WEST AFRICAN UPLANDS

CENTRAL AMERICA

NORTHWEST TROPICAL AND HIGHLAND SOUTH AMERICA

ALLEN K. PHILBRICK

Figure 55

tralasia, and the colonial exploitation of Africa. Emphasis here upon European culture is not intended to lessen the intrinsic importance of indigenous cultures within other distinctive regions of the world; yet it can scarcely be denied that the world pattern of occupancy everywhere is more and more under the influence and impact of European culture. This impact often combines or coexists with distinctive non-European cultures in many parts of the world.

Western Europeans created genuinely worldwide organization of area for the first time. This was an expression of the shift from local subsistence organization of area to regional and interregional exchange organization of area. World commerce developed from regional and local commerce. Local commerce motivated increased production of goods, such as wool textiles in northern Europe. This expanded production, in turn, provided the setting for the industrial revolution. The city-states of Italy, the ports of the Hanseatic League along the shores of the North and Baltic Seas, and the early guild-controlled manufacturers in the cities of the Low Countries were the medieval forerunners of the development of capitalism in Europe. The revolutionary innovations which transformed manufacturing, transportation, and communication technologies were the contributions of the English industrial revolution. While the first urban revolution rested on agricultural foundations, the second urban revolution rested on the cultural innovations of the industrial revolution. The geographic and social reorganization of society built around the factory system of production following the invention of the steam engine became focused in cities. Concentrations of these cities in industrialized regions became the core regions of modern national states.

The concentration of productive activity in cities created huge markets for agricultural products. This transformed agriculture from a subsistence basis into an exchange or commercial one. Technological improvements in agriculture brought about by the industrial revolution have constituted a second agricultural revolution.

The cities marking the concentration of west European industrial culture are located in a belt which extends from Glasgow to Rome. Generalized on the map in Figure 55 these cities fix the primary shape of the culture hearth designated *industrial European.*

Dispersion of ideas, "know how," and works have accompanied the explorations and colonizing activities of West Europeans wherever they have gone. Significant regional developments have taken shape on no less than five separate continents which are European in culture, outside of Europe herself. The Europeanized portions of these continents, along with Europe, dominate the world today. Two of these regional developments—the United States-Canada, and the Soviet Union—have become conflicting regional foci of industrial "know how," military power, and ideological convictions. Concentrations of their industrial cities have been generalized on the map in Figure 55, along with Europe's, as the three most influential industrial-scientific culture hearths in the world.

An important distinction may be made between European culture and all other cultures. In the context of what may be termed recent geographical events, against the background of possibly a million years of total human evolution, European culture during the past four and one-half centuries has brought about more changes over the surface of the earth than all human cultures before that time. During the past half-millenium European culture has been aggressive; non-European cultures have been relatively passive. No previous culture has ever exerted so widespread a geographical impact either upon so many people or over so vast a territory. European cultures have been carriers which have penetrated the territory of others. In understanding the pattern of world society one of the primary themes of world regional geography must be the recognition and analysis of the creative and leading role of Europeans.

Culture Systems and World Regions of Human Organization. The maps of culture systems and regions of cultural origin should now be compared with the map of world regions of human organization in Figure 20 of Chapter 2. Such comparison reveals that the two are closely related to each other. The exchange-world regions are all European in cultural origin except Japan. Those exchange-world regions which comprise the world core have as their internal-core regions the three industrial culture hearths in Europe, North America, and the Soviet Union. The exchange-world regions of the Southern Hemisphere are the peripheral recipients of European culture. Their core regions may be understood, also, as secondary industrial culture hearths.

The extensive subsistence world corresponds in general to the surviving areas of tribal cultures, where pockets of the hunting and collecting stage of technology may still be found, where languages are still spoken which have no indigenous written form, where animist religious ideas still persist behind a veneer of more sophisticated values superimposed from outside. In these regions transitional relations exist between subsistence technologies and the wage economies of the exchange units of area organization. However, traditional ways of life are still dominant in places where so-called backward peoples live under conditions which are euphemistically referred to as "underdeveloped."

An example of an intensive subsistence economy in varying stages of transition is China, whose ancient culture system is today being communized; or India, where efforts are underway to transform a national economy of subsistence agricultural villages into an industrial nation. In all such regions the efforts to bring about changes mean conflict with traditional beliefs and ways of living.

The specific organization of every region is a product of living cultures evolving in the present from a transmitted past tradition and moving into the future. The culture processes in every locality within these diverse world regions have many types of ingredients in common. In each, for instance, human creativity is at work molding the future from past experience. In this process people use the resources of the physical earth according to their understanding of the utility of the resources (cultural perception) in the performances of productive tasks. The activities take place within establishments and facilities (themselves products of the culture) which possess an organized functional pattern in area. When all of the ingredients are put together in the different kinds of regions within the world they comprise the portrait of this human world.

PART II WORLD REGIONAL GEOGRAPHY

The regional chapters in this book have one main theme. The world is organized into regions representing different stages to which people have brought their organization of area by making use of diverse physical resources and transmitted or innovated cultures. The most advanced regions are based upon exchange-type area organization. This type is still being expanded and evolved. In the shift from a local to a wider division of labor among people, subsistence organization continues to give way to exchange. This shift which began centuries ago is still in the process of development and is of fundamental importance in understanding the ways in which people continue to develop the patterns of society.

Part of this main theme is also the idea that only the processes of cultural evolution can account for the specific innovations and developments which continue to bring about changes in the organization of area. Location of places of culture origin and tracing the dispersion of ideas and ways of doing things from those places can explain the basis upon which the pattern of occupancy has developed.

Central to this main theme and its principal corollary is the importance of Europe and of England as the culture hearths of particular innovations during the industrial revolution which brought about the transition from a subsistence organization of area to one of regional and worldwide exchange. The spread of exchange area organization by people of English and then more broadly by people of European descent and its continued evolution by other peoples is the primary reason for many of the similarities among regions. The differences in stage of area organization represent, in turn, many of the differences among regions.

The regional portions of this book are arranged in three sections. Each section focuses on one of the three principal core regions of the world. Other regions of the world are examined in relationship to the core region with which their peoples have the most contact. Accordingly, the first section deals with Europe and with outlying Southern Hemisphere regions primarily connected with Europe. The second section is devoted to the Americas, and focuses principally upon the United States-Canada. The third section examines Eurasia in terms of its division into a central Communist Bloc which focuses upon the Soviet Union, and the Eurasian perimeter comprising a ring of five distinct additional cultures. A concluding chapter assesses world regional organization as a whole.

The three aspects of resources, culture, and area organization which were discussed systematically in the first five chapters of the book are the basic ingredients for regional synthesis. No attempt is made to treat each region in the same degree of detail, nor even with the same emphasis upon each aspect of geography. Instead, the degree of detail and emphasis among the ingredients varies from region to region in the interest of developing the main theme. The whole world is portrayed even though some of its regional features are subordinated in relation to the whole picture.

This explains why an entire chapter is devoted to the origins of the English industrial revolution—because of the importance of this culture hearth to the worldwide dissemination of European industrial culture. More emphasis is also given to the geographic progression of settlement in North America than is given to that subject for any other region. This was done because America affords the best example in the world of the geographical dispersion of cultures of European origin into a previously sparsely settled but resource-rich region. North America is also the continental milieu of the principal audience to whom this book is addressed so that greater emphasis, particularly on the United States, seems warranted.

6 *The United Kingdom*

In the light of the expressed theme of the regional sections in this book, there are a number of excellent reasons for beginning with the United Kingdom. First, English innovations started the industrial revolution. These provided a basis on which Europeans generally continued to exert worldwide influence. The United Kingdom is the oldest and most maturely developed example in the world of the exchange-type organization of area initiated by the industrial revolution. The English, in their original empire, and in the continuing commonwealth form of international organization, created the first worldwide interregional organization of territory. The Commonwealth affords a virtual cross-section of the entire world within one unit of organization which focuses traditionally upon the city of London and upon the United Kingdom as the mother country. The United Kingdom is of special significance to Americans because its people contributed dominant elements such as the English language and English law to the culture of the United States and Canada.

An Overview of the Patterns of Occupancy in England, Scotland, Wales and Northern Ireland

The United Kingdom has been called a nation of shopkeepers. This is the result of her traditional role in world commerce, a position of dominance now challenged by other world powers. Of her more than 50 million citizens (52,157,000 in 1959) well over 90 per cent are packed into urban settlements. Distribution of settlement is shown by the map in Figure 56. No other country in the world is so completely urbanized. This is the result of long concentration upon manufacturing products for sale to the world from her own and from imported raw materials.

Land Use. Yet, here is a country over half of which is covered with grassland, a fourth in arable land, and one-tenth divided among woodland-forest, moorland, heath, and bog. The pattern of concentrated settlements containing most of the residential, manufacturing, and commercial establishments consumes only one-eighth of the total land area. Remaining fractions belong to other categories of land use such as orchards, mining properties, and recreational land.

The maps in Figures 56 to 59 show the land use in Britain (excluding Northern Ireland).[1] They indicate the distribution of the major categories of economic activity—livestock raising on grassland, farming on arable land, manufacturing and commerce in built-up settlement areas, and range land in heath and moorland.

The degree of concentration of activity and population in cities indicates a highly developed geographical division of labor in the United Kingdom. According to census data, less than 6 per cent of the economically active population is involved in agriculture (which includes livestock raising). With the exception of mining (3.7 per cent of the economically active) which is also resource-oriented in distribution, more than 90 per cent of the working population is engaged in manufacturing, services, commerce, transportation, construction, or utilities. These people are located in the cities and other settlements. The fact that so small a proportion of the population is engaged in the production of food reflects the dependence of the United Kingdom on areas outside her borders and the long-continued existence of an organized interregional division of functions between the central country, her overseas possessions, and independent Commonwealth and other countries of the world market.

Resource Associations Used to Build the United Kingdom. The United Kingdom, as shown by Figure 60, is composed of four parts—England, Scotland, Wales, and Northern Ireland. It occupies all of Great Britain, the largest of the British Isles (88,745 square miles) and the Northern Ireland por-

---

[1] L. Dudley Stamp, *The Land of Britain—Its Use and Misuse*, London: Longmans, Green and Co., 1948, pp. 38, 67, 85, and 183.

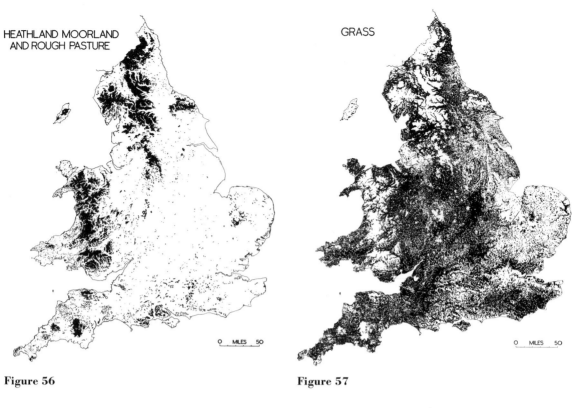

HEATHLAND MOORLAND AND ROUGH PASTURE

GRASS

Figure 56

Figure 57

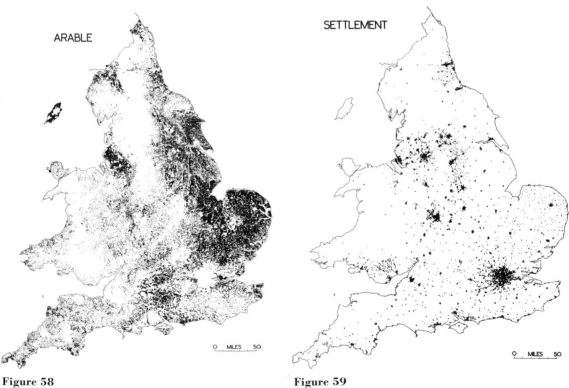

ARABLE

SETTLEMENT

Figure 58

Figure 59

The above illustrations courtesy of Longmans, Green and Co., Ltd., in conjunction with Geographical Publications, Ltd., taken from L. Dudley Stamp, The Land of Britain, Its Use and Misuse, *1948.*

tion (5,238 square miles) of the island of Ireland (32,375 square miles). These two largest islands and a large number of smaller islets comprise the British Isles, which lie in the Atlantic Ocean north of 50 degrees north latitude off the west coast of Europe midway between Gibraltar and northern Norway. Great Britain is an irregularly right triangular-shaped island some 550 miles from base to apex and 350 miles along the base. The altitude of the triangle tips westward nearly 30 degrees from a true north-south orientation. On the south Britain is bordered by the English Channel which separates England from France by 21 miles at its narrowest point. The islands form the western boundary of the North Sea on the east. On the west the Irish Sea separates Great Britain from Ireland. The United Kingdom was the mother country of the British Empire and remains the central country of the Commonwealth. Despite dependence on overseas areas over the past two centuries, the United Kingdom was built initially with materials found within her own borders.

In general, basic resources vary in kind and quality from northwest to southeast along an axis perpendicular to the trend of the Atlantic coast of Europe. Two of the world's three subsurface structural zones are found within the United Kingdom. An extension of the Scandinavian Shield occurs in the Precambrian rocks of northern Scotland. Eastern and southern England is an extension of the great Eurasian sedimentary plain across the shallow North Sea continental shelf into the English lowlands. Thus, as shown on the map in Figure 61 the west and north are highlands while the east and south are lowlands. The edges of the highlands are old sedimentary folded uplands—the English Pennine and the Welsh Cambrian Mountains. Along the eastern and southern slopes of these transitional uplands are the coal measures on which British industry has prospered. Iron-ore deposits have become concentrated in sediments adjacent to the coal measures in a band along the eastern margins of these folded highlands.

Maps in Figure 62 show resource associations important to agriculture—duration of the growing season, precipitation, and soils. The characteristics of these resources vary from northwest to southeast also. Considered in combination, an association of high precipitation (more than 80 inches per year), short growing season, and rocky upland forest soils occurs in the highlands on the Atlantic side of the country. In the southeastern plains the growing

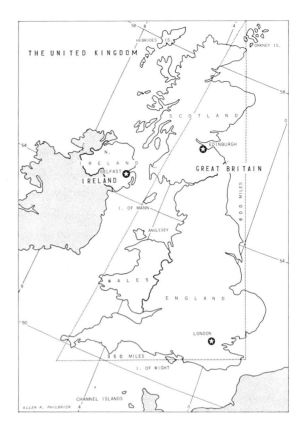

Figure 60

season is longer (more than 210 days per year), precipitation more moderate (25 inches and under, per year), and the lowland soils richer in plant humus. The rising of moisture-laden marine air masses over low mountains of Ireland, Wales, and Scotland along the Atlantic side dumps precipitation of more than 120 inches per year in some places. The growing season, except for the very highest elevations in northern Scotland, is more than 90 days everywhere in the United Kingdom; but in lowland Britain it lasts as long as 240 days in some places. Mildness of temperature, again, is the result of marine influences, particularly the warm ocean current called the North Atlantic Drift which warms the air masses moving eastward over the United Kingdom and western Europe.

The use of resources described above is reflected in the patterns of activities portrayed on the maps discussed previously in Figures 56 and 59. Arable land is concentrated in the east and south (see Figure 63A and B). Grassland is virtually everywhere, but occurs in the greatest proportion to total area in the center of England (Figure 64A and B) and in the western highlands. Heathland-moor-

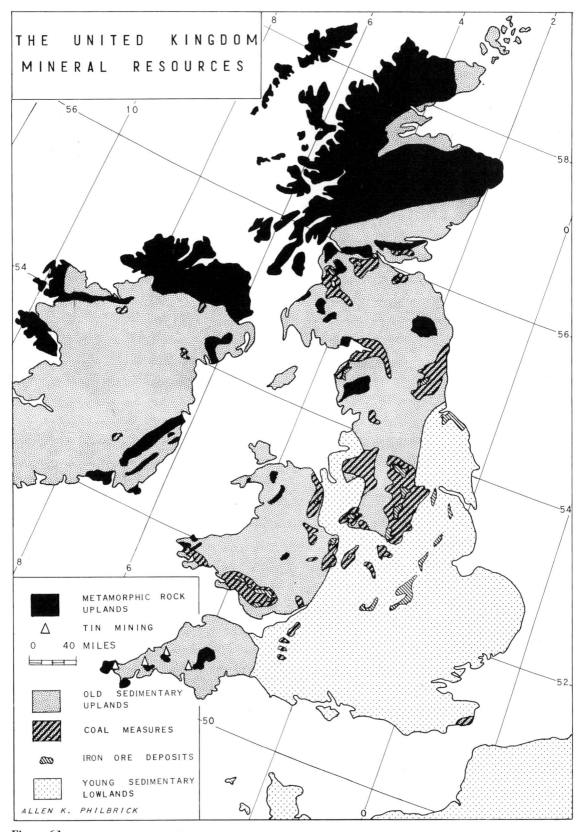

THE UNITED KINGDOM
MINERAL RESOURCES

METAMORPHIC ROCK
UPLANDS

TIN MINING

0   40 MILES

OLD SEDIMENTARY
UPLANDS

COAL MEASURES

IRON ORE DEPOSITS

YOUNG SEDIMENTARY
LOWLANDS

ALLEN K. PHILBRICK

Figure 61

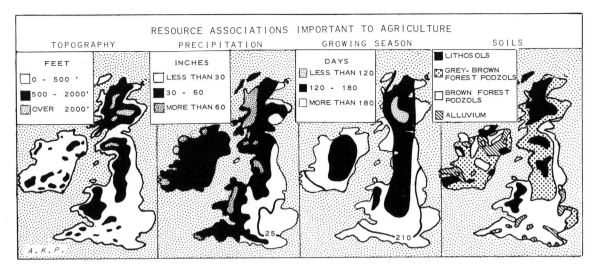

Figure 62

rough pasture is concentrated in the highlands along with forest-woodland. The most densely urbanized pattern of settlement, with the outstanding exception of London, occurs in relation to the distribution of coal fields. From these relationships it appears that the English have made consistently resource-oriented choices in locating their activities.

From the large-scale patterns of homogeneous land uses these activities also reflect a well-coordinated division of labor. The people who live in the cities do not raise their own cattle for meat or grow their own crops for food. The farmers in the countryside do not manufacture the consumer goods which they need, but, in fact, purchase them from the cities. The radial patterns of transportation lines symbolized on the map in Figure 65 suggest the many types of interconnections existing among the variety of establishments which are organized coherently in the industrial-commercial society of the United Kingdom. In addition, therefore, to the static patterns of the several uses of land by means of which it is possible to describe the land spaces of the country, it is equally valid to combine the many different kinds of activity into the units of *area organization* which are interconnected within the functioning regionality of the national economy. To visualize this economy is to examine the regional organization of the United Kingdom.

The Regional Organization of the United Kingdom

The entire country is one great nodal region composed of focal subregions, each of which is made up of many smaller communities and lesser units of area organization. As shown by the map in Figure 65, the center upon which all this hierarchical arrangement of areas and regions focuses is metropolitan London (*8,204,800* in 1959).[1] London is the largest city of the Commonwealth, its most important port (Figure 66), third largest city in the world, and the only large urban agglomeration in the United Kingdom not located on or adjacent to a coal field.

Regional Specialization. Each of the subregions has developed one or more product specialties for which it is world-famous. These are exported to world markets as well as from the local region to domestic markets within the country. Altogether they are combined into a kind of national division of labor, each operated locally, organized regionally, and coordinated nationally and internationally from London. Each subregion focuses on a major urban complex. Regions, their urban centers, and the major rail interconnections uniting them nationally, and focusing upon London, are shown on the map in Figure 65.

Coal, iron and steel, and shipbuilding industries are the specialties of Northeast England, centered on Newcastle (*852,210*) on the Tyne River. South Shields (108,700) and Sunderland (186,000) are other large industrial cities of this region. The great Cleveland iron ores in this part of England

---

[1] The population figure for cities over 100,000 is in each case the most recent given in the *United Nations Demographic Yearbook*, Table 7, pp. 285–348, New York, 1960. Figures printed in italics are the population of an urban agglomeration rather than the city proper.

Figure 63. (*Photographs courtesy of British Information Services.*)

(A) Cultivated land in the eastern lowlands, mostly in wheat and other grains. Fields surround individual farmsteads.

(B) Another common organizational form is the farm village such as Lydden village, Kent, located on the old coach road to Dover.

Figure 64. (*Photographs courtesy of British Information Services.*)

(A) Sheep grazing within wicker pens in Berkshire illustrates the extensive grassland agriculture in England on land which could be devoted to crops if preference were not given to commercial production of industrial raw materials such as wool.

(B) The use of stony upland hill country for grazing in Wales.

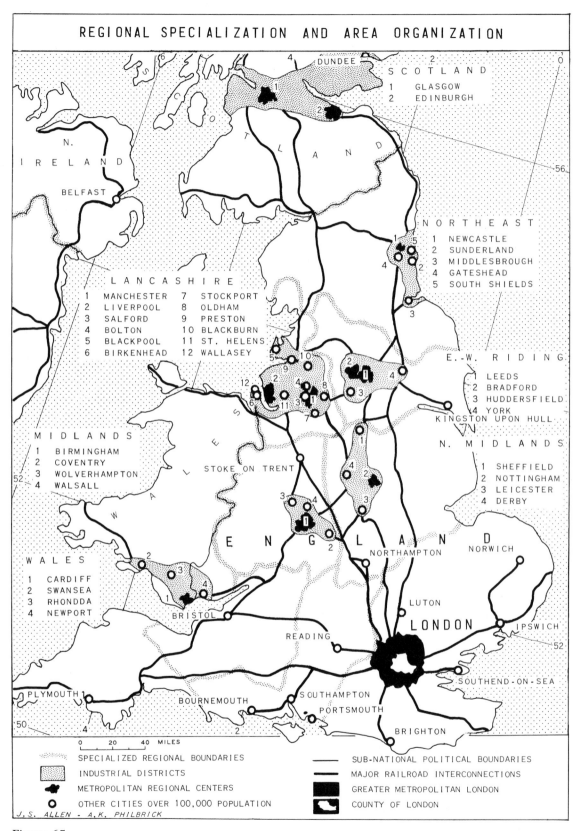

REGIONAL SPECIALIZATION AND AREA ORGANIZATION

SCOTLAND
1 GLASGOW
2 EDINBURGH

NORTHEAST
1 NEWCASTLE
2 SUNDERLAND
3 MIDDLESBROUGH
4 GATESHEAD
5 SOUTH SHIELDS

LANCASHIRE
1 MANCHESTER 7 STOCKPORT
2 LIVERPOOL 8 OLDHAM
3 SALFORD 9 PRESTON
4 BOLTON 10 BLACKBURN
5 BLACKPOOL 11 ST. HELENS
6 BIRKENHEAD 12 WALLASEY

E.-W. RIDING
1 LEEDS
2 BRADFORD
3 HUDDERSFIELD
4 YORK
KINGSTON UPON HULL

MIDLANDS
1 BIRMINGHAM
2 COVENTRY
3 WOLVERHAMPTON
4 WALSALL

N. MIDLANDS
1 SHEFFIELD
2 NOTTINGHAM
3 LEICESTER
4 DERBY

STOKE ON TRENT

WALES
1 CARDIFF
2 SWANSEA
3 RHONDDA
4 NEWPORT

BRISTOL

N. IRELAND
BELFAST

DUNDEE

NORTHAMPTON
NORWICH
LUTON
READING
LONDON
IPSWICH
SOUTHEND-ON-SEA
PLYMOUTH
BOURNEMOUTH
SOUTHAMPTON
PORTSMOUTH
BRIGHTON

0   20   40   MILES

SPECIALIZED REGIONAL BOUNDARIES
INDUSTRIAL DISTRICTS
METROPOLITAN REGIONAL CENTERS
OTHER CITIES OVER 100,000 POPULATION

SUB-NATIONAL POLITICAL BOUNDARIES
MAJOR RAILROAD INTERCONNECTIONS
GREATER METROPOLITAN LONDON
COUNTY OF LONDON

J.S. ALLEN - A.K. PHILBRICK

Figure 65

Figure 66. A large cargo ship entering the Royal Docks. The Port of London, with 69 miles of waterway and more than 4,000 acres of dock estate, is the second largest in the world, handling more tonnage annually than any other port except New York. From this port, more than 100 shipping companies operate to more than 300 overseas ports, and every month more than 700 ships on regular service leave for all parts of the world. Goods of every kind, from meat to marble, from plywood to perfume, pass through its docks. Imports are distributed all over the United Kingdom, though the port supplies primarily a population of 11.5 million people in Greater London and the Home Counties. (*Courtesy of British Information Services.*)

along with coal measures supply the main resources.

A great complex of wool-producing cities (Figure 67) focuses on Leeds and Bradford (*1,692,640*) and connects to the port of Hull as the regional outlet to the sea from the York subregion. Wool from sheep which graze upon central English grasslands along the eastern slopes of the Pennines is the traditional raw material in this region. Imports from Commonwealth members—Australia, New Zealand, and a former member, the Republic of South Africa—however, now far exceed the English production of raw wool.

There is an entire conurbation of cotton-manufacturing industrial cities (Figure 68A) focusing on Manchester (*2,419,150*) in the Lancashire subregion. Manchester is connected directly to the Irish Sea by the Manchester Ship Canal, but its port city (Figure 68B) traditionally has been Liverpool (*1,383,500*). Cotton from the American South,

from India and Egypt, as well as from many other parts of the world have made the Lancashire mills famous for their cotton-cloth products.

The Midlands subregion centers on Birmingham (*2,291,890*). Once a major iron- and steel-producing center, now that local iron ores are largely depleted production is specialized in metal fabricating and the manufacture of a wide variety of other consumer goods. Coventry (285,700), for example, located 18 miles east-southeast of Birmingham, specializes in automobiles, bicycles, and aircraft. Walsall (115,100), 10 miles north of Birmingham, is still a steel producer making use of local coal, limestone, and iron ore, although the amount produced is only a small fraction of the steel required for manufacturing within the subregion. Wolverhampton (146,100) which is northwest of Birmingham manufactures motors, machinery, and other hardware.

Figure 67. A typical layout of a wool factory in Yorkshire includes elements illustrated here—inland waterway, old brick multi-storied factory buildings, and the smoke from the burning of British coal. (*Courtesy of British Information Services.*)

Separated from the central Midlands by southern outliers of the Pennines, which are known locally as the Midland Plateau, is a second Midland subregion, the Northern Midlands. This subregion centers on Nottingham (313,300), a textile center specializing in lace and hosiery. The region is noted for diversified consumer goods. Leicester (279,400) is a center for the production of hosiery, shoes, textiles, paints, dyes, and pharmaceuticals. Derby (131,500) is the home of the Rolls Royce motor car, but is also noted for porcelains, silks, hosiery, electrical apparatus, varnishes, and chemicals. Sheffield (499,400) is a traditional steel center famous the world over for cutlery and armor plate.

North of England are the Scottish lowlands. Core of Scotland, these lowlands occupy a rift valley between the north and south Scottish highlands. Two famous rivers, the Firth of Forth from the north highlands and the Firth of Clyde from the south highlands drain into the North Sea and Irish Sea, respectively. They have been connected by a canal creating an inland water route between Scotland's two largest cities—Edinburgh (469,359), the

political capital on the south shore of the bay created by the Firth of Forth, and Glasgow which is located on the Firth of Clyde. Glasgow (*1,790,658*) is the largest city of Scotland, a deepwater port, and its labor force specializes in iron and steel production and the building of ships. Iron ores and coal measures outcrop along the lowland margins of the southern Scottish highlands.

West of central England is Wales. In the southern Wales subregion focused on Cardiff (254,200) coal mining, iron and steel, and shipbuilding are again the specialties.

Across the Irish Sea the Northern Ireland subregion has long been the scene of the ancient friction between the Irish and the English. The northern counties which are part of the United Kingdom have the port city of Belfast (436,200) as their capital. Northern Ireland is famous for Irish linens and shipbuilding (Figure 68C).

Each of the cities mentioned in the preceding thumbnail sketches is a major urban center with more than 100,000 population. In all there are seventy cities in the United Kingdom in this size

Figure 68. (*Photographs courtesy of British Information Services.*)

(A) Preston, one of the big cotton towns of Lancashire (114,200), is located about 30 miles northwest of Manchester.

(B) Wharves at Liverpool Docks, Lancashire.

(C) The Canberra at Belfast, March 1960.

category or larger. They are identified on the map in Figure 65. A very high proportion of these centers are clustered within short distances of one another in seven out of the nine subregions. Eleven of them are in the Lancashire cotton region; five within Northeast England. The Midlands, North Midlands, and southern Wales each have four large cities. The York subregion has three. The largest number, however, are in the vicinity of London, the central city of the nation. The London conurbation includes a cluster of twenty cities which exceed 100,000 in population. The total of fifty-one cities enumerated in clusters above represent a concentration of 73 per cent of all such cities within the United Kingdom, as specialized urban-core areas within the subregional organization of the country.

As previously mentioned the nodal organization displayed by the United Kingdom is focused on London, the center of a metropolitan region having southeastern England as its immediate hinterland. As the focus and capital city of the country, the overseas possessions, and the Commonwealth, the subregion of London is the political, economic, and social nexus of the entire British world.

The regional organization of Britain has previously been described as *hierarchical*. Only two of many steps in a hierarchy of organized areas are shown on the map in Figure 65. These are the steps between regional centers and their tributary subregions, and those between the subregions and the principal core area of metropolitan London.

Regional Interconnections. Every establishment has its own focus. From there linkages reach outward to each locality, and from hamlet and villages through small cities to subregional centers. From here the final step is to the nation. As explained in Chapter 2, all area units of organization, small and big, from the single establishment to the nation as a whole, are both internally and externally interconnected. The pattern of railroad lines between London and outlying subregions was selected to symbolize this fact. Highways and airways would reveal essentially the same pattern.

Less tangible kinds of interconnections also focus the organized activities of people onto the primary centers. The centralized functions of London are partly expressed in terms of this type of interconnection. London is the headquarters for British trade and finance. Not only the tangible movement of goods, but the control in the conduct of trading activities, which involve most other English ports,

focuses here to a great degree. This is because the great financial houses, trading companies, and governmental agencies have their central offices and policy-making bodies located in London. Dominance of London in this respect developed over a long period of time. It grew with the nation and the empire. London's proximity to Europe was undoubtedly encouraging from an early date to the development of trade with the continent. The crown-chartered companies which carried the name of England throughout the world became located in London. As the center of royal and civilian political and administrative control, all sorts of nonvisible contacts and interconnections came to a focus there, ranging from loyalty to opposition, from following to leadership. The Bank of England was formed in 1694 as a means of keeping the Royal Treasury balanced. In the development of the industrial revolution from which the present pattern of organization stems, London became the center of the accumulation of capital and its management. Although this function has now been somewhat decentralized in terms of the locating of banking facilities in other large cities, London is still the financial capital of the Commonwealth and of all areas financially geared to the pound sterling, which is known generally as the Sterling Bloc.

External Organization of the United Kingdom—Dependence on Foreign Trade. The external relations of such a concentration of productive activity must be taken into account if we are to understand the United Kingdom. As a direct result of British leadership in exploration, in naval and shipping advances, and because of innovations in economic production, there soon developed a dependence on areas not directly accessible to Britain for more and more food and raw materials. As these developments occurred the United Kingdom became the core of the regional organization of first an empire and now the Commonwealth. This type of relationship still characterizes the United Kingdom, although competition in world trade is forcing England to consider joining the European Common Market, which in turn would force adjustment in her Commonwealth commitments.

In the 1955 Handbook of Britain, the following official statement is made.[1]

The national economy of the United Kingdom

[1]Central Office of Information, *Britain, An Official Handbook,* London: Her Majesty's Stationery Office, 1955, p. 107.

offers to the rest of the world one of its most concentrated markets, particularly for food and the raw materials for industry. There are some 540 people to every square mile—eleven times as many as in the United States—and their standard of living is among the world's highest. But about half of their food is imported. They grow no cotton, rubber, or jute, possess little or no economically workable deposits of aluminum, lead, copper, tin, or zinc, and import four-fifths of their wood and their wool. The nation that invented steel can now supply only half its needs of iron ore, and the pioneer of the jet engine buys virtually all of its crude oil from abroad.

So much for imports! The statement of the British Handbook continues:

Yet the national economy of Britain, using, as it does, mainly imported supplies, is itself the second largest supplier of the world's needs: of machinery, electrical apparatus and vehicles; of fine quality textiles and pottery, of coal, chemicals, and cutlery; of whiskey, jet aircraft and fertilizers. About half the world's trade is conducted in its currency; and in London are held the gold and dollar reserves of the sterling Commonwealth and other sterling countries.

It is this external "breathing" of the economy of Britain which enables the functional organization *within* the United Kingdom to operate. Specific trade relations will be discussed in Chapter 11. It is sufficient to point out here that there are several outlying producing regions of raw materials and food stuffs in the peripheral countries of the Commonwealth which look to the United Kingdom as a dependable market.

Cultural Evolution of the Patterns of Occupancy

The patterns of human occupancy within the United Kingdom, both static and dynamic, have had a long and well-documented cultural evolution. The static patterns are represented by the discussion of homogeneous areas of predominant activity expressed by the land-use maps in Figures 56 to 59. The dynamic patterns are represented by the regional organization of the country expressed on the map in Figure 65.

Understanding the United Kingdom geographically and appreciating its significance requires awareness of the processes by which the English people combined resources and their transmitted and innovated culture in building their occupancy of their part of the British Isles. The importance of an accounting of this cultural evolution in the United Kingdom lies in its special significance to the main theme of the regional sections in this book.

The early pattern of occupancy in the United Kingdom was characterized by *subsistence organization of area*. The cultural evolution by which the present regional organization was built involved the origin and spread of *exchange organization of area* over most of the world.

Cultural Origins of Subsistence Agriculture in the United Kingdom. The beginnings of English culture are shrouded in unrecorded prehistory. England and the island of Great Britain were settled by successive waves of population from mainland Europe over a very long period. The organization of area by the early folk was undoubtedly based on extensive subsistence livelihood—hunting and gathering. Then a gradual change occurred in the visual appearance of the countryside, covering a period of the last thousand years—a change from an almost universally forested land to a land virtually cleared of forest. The clearing of forest to make room for sedentary agricultural occupancy was the first step in the cultural evolution of the United Kingdom of today. The two maps in Figure 69A and B[1] show the generalized patterns of land and vegetation which reflect agricultural resource conditions in Roman times. The generalized pattern of soils conforms to distinctions among highland and lowland areas of Britain. They also follow the bedrock and structure patterns of the subsurface from northwest to southeast. The soil pattern in the lowlands is that of alternate bands of glacial drift, heavy clay lands, and soils derived from low limestone ridges. The limestone ridges are associated with escarpments separating sediments of different geologic ages. Forest cover appears to have been heaviest on drift and less dense on the heavy clay and limestone uplands. Relatively unforested rough uplands early afforded grazing lands which needed no clearing; the unforested areas of Roman Britain are mostly such highlands of the west and north. Within the English Lowlands the unforested areas were usually low limestone ridges, poorly drained swamps, or sandy and gravelly areas.

Various peoples settling Britain had different backgrounds and apparently sought different

[1] J. M. Houston, *A Social Geography of Europe*, London: Gerved Duckworth & Co. Ltd., 1953, p. 67.

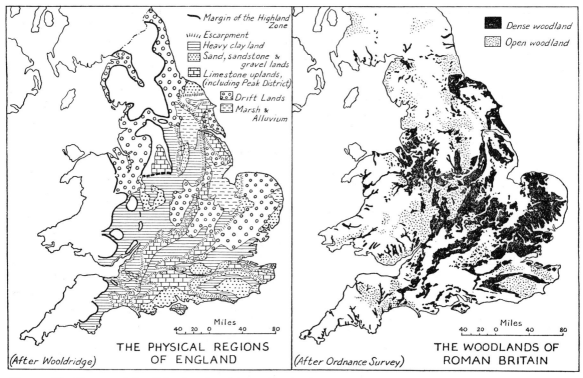

THE PHYSICAL REGIONS OF ENGLAND

Margin of the Highland Zone
Escarpment
Heavy clay land
Sand, sandstone & gravel lands
Limestone uplands, (including Peak District)
Drift Lands
Marsh & Alluvium

Miles
40 20 0 40 80

(After Wooldridge)

THE WOODLANDS OF ROMAN BRITAIN

Dense woodland
Open woodland

Miles
40 20 0 40 80

(After Ordnance Survey)

Figure 69. (*Courtesy of Gerald Duckworth and Co., Ltd., taken from J. M. Houston,* A Social Geography of Europe.)

natural resources with which to work. J. B. Mitchell, in his *Historical Geography*,[1] writes as follows.

It is probable that the majority of the migrants who arrived in Britain in the Neolithic and Bronze Ages were primarily herdsmen though they cultivated a little grain. . . .

The pre-Roman settlers sought dry pastures . . . and soils easily worked with hoes and digging sticks and light ploughs. . . .

In lowland Britain Neolithic and Bronze Age finds are most abundant on light soil uplands. Salisbury Plain, the Dorset Downs, the Cotswold Hills, Northampton Heights, Lincoln Edge and the Yorkshire Moors and the Berkshire Downs, the Chilterns, the Lincoln and Yorkshire Wolds show relatively high density of finds in this period.

These place names refer to the low uplands of southeastern England which had the lightest and most easily worked soils. Later a people familiar with a type of plow capable of turning heavier land learned to prefer the heavier soils. Such were the Anglo-Saxon farmers (*Angles* from Schleswig-Holstein, a province of Germany, and *Saxons* from

[1] J. B. Mitchell, *Historical Geography*, London: English Universities Press, Ltd., 1954, p. 107.

Saxony, another German province, who came with the *Jutes* from Jutland, Germany, during the fifth and sixth centuries). If they did not bring the moldboard plow to England, they certainly spread its use throughout the nation.

The moldboard plow was different from the simple hand or stick plow in that it had a board to turn aside the earth cut into by the plowshare, thus producing a furrow of turned-over earth. The plows used were the product of local craftsmen and were heavy, cumbersome pieces of farm equipment, requiring a team of several oxen to pull one. The turning of the plow after a furrow was a burdensome part of the plowing process. Hence, it became the practice to plow long strips with a few turnings as possible. The plowing created a series of ridges topped along the center by one passing of the plow back and forth. The traditional furrow was 220 yards long (a furlong). Plowing continued around and around such a central ridge to create a field strip 220 yards by 22 yards in size. These dimensions give the origin of the acre, from the German word "acre" meaning field. Each field unit or acre, hence, had 4,840 square yards or 43,560 square feet. This unit of measure, originally one day's plowing, is still in use today as the basic unit of area in the American land-survey system, in which there are 640 acres per square mile. According to Mitchell,[1]

The mould-board fitted behind the share turns over the sod. . . . If the overturned sod is not to lie on an unploughed strip of earth the line of the first furrow must be ploughed twice, once in each direction, and then the plough driven round it to throw two sods in the center to form a "top." Ploughing is then round and round this top to form a ridge. . . .

Use of this plow and the drying out of the turned-over land led to a preference for the heavier soils, from which better yields could be derived than from lighter soils. The necessity for plow teams (many oxen required many owners) and the cumbersome nature of the plows made cooperative labor more profitable. Therefore, people settled in villages and worked the land in common in open fields. Various systems of open-field tillage characterized the subsistence agricultural villages of Britain. They were based upon simple rotation of crops. The two-field and the three-field systems were the most prevalent. The two-field system divided the land into cultivated and fallow land which were rotated in alternate years. The three-field system divided arable land into three great fields. One area was planted with winter grain, a second with spring grain, and the third left fallow. In this case the rotation cycle was completed every three years.

The basic unit of area organization for livelihood purposes became the agricultural village surrounded by its arable lands. Its pattern was varied by meadows (lowland subject to flooding along streams which was used to produce hay), pastures (year-round grazing land), and areas of wasteland and woodland. The focal organization of many small units of village territory took many forms, depending on the variety of physical features and the specific cultural habits of the farmers, but the essentially *local* nature of the area organization for *subsistence* was characteristic.

According to Curtler,[2] by the time of the Norman Conquest (A.D. 1066),

We have established in England the world-wide agricultural unit of the village, an enlarged patriarchal family, the members of which worked together in the fields, shared their meadowlands, and enjoyed the common use of the waste. . . . They were . . . self sufficing, and more or less isolated from the rest of the world.

H. C. Darby,[3] discussing the economic geography of England from A.D. 1000 to 1250, wrote,

The arable land was the most important and conspicuous part of the village territory. It lay in strips, and every holding consisted of a number of these strips scattered about in different places, each strip separated from those of other tenements by fringes of unploughed turf or by unsown furrows. Each cultivator thus held a number of strips, but not in a compact bundle; and the intermixture of strips in this manner meant that the rules and methods of cultivation were the concern not of any individual but of the community as a whole.

Under the *two-field* system, the arable was arranged in two fields; of the field under cultivation one half was sown in autumn with winter corn, wheat, or rye, and the other half in the beginning of the year with spring crops, barley or oats. . . . The fallow field was ploughed twice at the beginning of summer. . . .

Between seed-time and harvest, the land under crop was protected by temporary fences; when the harvest was over, the barriers were removed, and the village cattle were allowed graze upon the stubble of the open fields.

The map in Figure 70 diagrams the layout of a typical English village around the year A.D. 1000. It shows the open fields, their division into strips, and the village center. The strips cultivated by one farmer are shown in black. The manor, an additional element not yet discussed, is also shown.

The manor is the dwelling and central buildings of the landowner of the village, from which the manorial system of feudal political organization takes its name. The manorial system is the political shell encompassing the village system of area organization. Each village had one or more head families, upon whose shoulders rested the responsibility of defense and administration of the village operation as an organized unit. At the same time, theoretically in return for his leadership, to this individual and his entourage came the benefits of tax or tithe in return. With the conquest of England by William the Conqueror in 1066, the manors became fiscal units through which the political hierarchy of king in relation to his lords levied and collected taxes and exerted the authority of his kingdom. Some

[1] *Ibid.*, pp. 109–110.

[2] H. R. Curtler, *The Enclosure and Redistribution of Our Land*, Oxford, England: Clarendon Press, 1920, p. 9.

[3] H. C. Darby (Ed.), *Historical Geography of England before 1800*, Cambridge, England: Cambridge University Press, 1936, pp. 191–193.

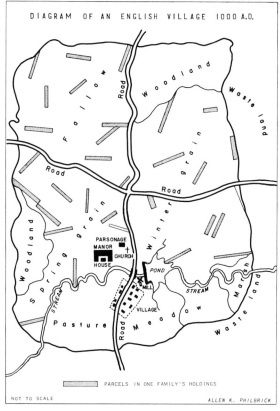

DIAGRAM OF AN ENGLISH VILLAGE 1000 A.D.

PARCELS IN ONE FAMILY'S HOLDINGS

NOT TO SCALE

ALLEN K. PHILBRICK

Figure 70

lords had many manors and grew rich upon the substance of many villages. The granting of royal patronage produced a wide disparity between the powerful and the petty, but, in principle, the relationship between lord of the manor and the people of the village or villages over which he wielded control was essentially simple. The villages remained the basis for subsistence and the unit of area organization upon which the livelihood of most of the population depended.

England at the Time of the Domesday Survey. Twenty years after the Norman Conquest, in 1086, King William caused an appraisal or survey to be made of his domain, which amounted to an economic census of England. The Domesday Book or Survey, one of the most remarkable documents of history, has been analyzed by the geographer, H. C. Darby.[1] His analysis reveals significant patterns of the society of the eleventh century. The even pattern of subsistence village organization found in the Domesday survey contrasts sharply with the present focal settlement pattern for the same area on the map in Figure 56. Based on the

Domesday Book information, there seems to have been a somewhat greater concentration of population in the English counties having the better agricultural land.

Seeds of Change. Seeds of change from subsistence to an exchange system of area organization may be noted in certain circumstances of the England of that time. There were beginnings of domestic and foreign trade, and beginnings of economic production for the specific purpose of trade. Again, the start is obscured. Commercial and manufacturing enterprises originated in political, administrative, and military centers. A series of focal points called boroughs, the administrative centers within the English counties, received official recognition from the Crown. These centers varied in prosperity and size; from available estimates it seems that they ranged from 500 to 5,000 persons. Their activities combined agricultural and trade functions.

Trade was primarily in corn, wool, and cloth, with some evidence for additional products such as iron, salt, lead, and tin. According to Darby,[2]

In summing up the commercial geography of medieval England before 1250, one point must be emphasized. When all is said, the fact remains that this expanding trade, this mining activity, this active manufacture, this rise of mercantile towns, were only the beginnings of things. They were simply hints of changes that were to come with the full tide of the "medieval renascence" in the thirteenth and fourteenth centuries.

Summary

This chapter has accomplished four things. After a brief reference to selected patterns of resources, the patterns of homogeneous activity involving use of the land were presented. These same static patterns of activity were then made dynamic by the portrayal of the regional organization of the United Kingdom. The chapter concludes with an introduction to the cultural evolution of the patterns of occupancy in the United Kingdom which establishes and characterizes the early subsistence agricultural organization of local village areas as a starting point for the chapter which follows. The next chapter deals with the geographic impact of the industrial revolution in England.

[1] H. C. Darby, *The Domesday Geography of Eastern England* and *The Domesday Geography of Midland England*, Cambridge, England: Cambridge University Press, 1952 and 1954.

[2] H. C. Darby (Ed.), *Historical Geography of England before 1800*, Cambridge, England: Cambridge University Press, 1936, pp. 228–229.

7 The Geographical Impact of the Industrial Revolution in England

The preceding chapter examined patterns of occupancy in the United Kingdom and sketched the beginning of their cultural evolution. It is the purpose of this chapter to outline additional circumstances which in combination account for the shift in England from subsistence to exchange organization of area.

From the middle of the eleventh to the middle of the eighteenth centuries the seeds of economic, political, and social transformation grew slowly. During that period most of the people lived in subsistence agricultural villages. The continuation of this mode of life is shown by the slow growth in population. From an estimated million and a quarter people at the time of the Domesday Book (1086), the total had grown only to an estimated 6 million persons by 1750. In nearly 700 years the population had only increased five-fold. In the space of the next 200 years, however, during the industrial revolution, the population increased much more rapidly from 6 to 50 million.

Within the first 80 years of these two centuries, from 1750 to 1830, the organization and use of the land was almost completely altered. It was as if slowly marshalling energies during a long period of preparation had been released suddenly and become directed to a common purpose, producing with almost explosive social upheaval a transformation into a new system of area organization.

Preparation for English Leadership in the Shift from Subsistence to Exchange Organization of Area

It was the industrial revolution in agriculture and manufacturing which brought about this change. The preparation for English leadership in the industrial revolution entailed a number of circumstances. (See Table IX for an outline of these circumstances.)

The Shift from Subsistence to Commercial Agriculture. The evolution of commercial agriculture began when people became aware that they could produce something from the land which they could sell. In England the product was wool. Its market was in the cities of the Low Countries and to a certain extent in England, where artisans were producing wool cloth. Already cleared lands could produce pasturage well suited to raising sheep. These animals, formerly shepherded on common lands could be better raised in enclosed fields, which gave rise to private ownership of both land and animals. Enclosure of land already under tillage represented a change both in ownership and in land management. The subsistence units held in common by the people of an entire village were now to be brought under individual control. These parcels of land were now used for commercial agriculture. Private control meant that one person could now decide how the land was to be used and could also reap the reward from his own acreage. Much land was shifted from cultivation to grazing.

During the early period of enclosure, the shift to grass and the resulting increased production of wool provided (1) a major basis for commercial agriculture and (2) the wool for export in the development of foreign trade, as well as (3) the basic raw material for domestic wool and textile manufacture. Hoskins stated[1]

> The most striking single aspect of the English landscape at the beginning of the sixteenth century was that there were about three sheep to every human being. There were only two and a half to three million people in the whole country, and possible eight million sheep. . . .
>
> By the end of the sixteenth century there was, for example, if not a continuous belt of grassland on the Liassic uplands of Northamptonshire and Leicestershire, at least something very near it, and tens of thousands of cattle and sheep grazed over what had been the arable lands of the medieval peasantry. And instead

[1]W. G. Hoskins, *The Making of the English Landscape*, London: Hadden and Stoughton, Ltd., 1956, pp. 108 and 117.

TABLE IX CIRCUMSTANCES OF ENGLISH LEADERSHIP IN
THE INDUSTRIAL REVOLUTION

1. *A Gradual Shift from Subsistence to Commercial Agriculture.*
   a. Enclosure of common lands into private fields and the shift from arable to grass land with an increase in wool production.
2. *Evolution of a Geographic Division of Labor and the Beginnings of Mechanization.*
   a. Development of cottage industries.
   b. Relocation of wool-cloth production in defiance of the jurisdiction of the city guilds, and in relation to the beginnings of mechanization.
   c. Beginnings of mechanization in mining related to innovations leading to the invention of the steam engine.
3. *Development of an External Orientation of the English Economy.*
   a. Shift from alien to English control of foreign trade.
   b. Emergence of British sea power.
4. *Development of Political and Social Freedoms.*
   a. Strength of Parliament and of Common law.
   b. Dissolution of monasteries and other types of ecclesiastical authority during reformation period strengthening both religious tolerance and the economic position of private interests related to production resources.
   c. Beginnings of intellectual leadership.

of a hundred peasants, the typical figure was that of John Isham. "The astute merchant turned squire," perambulating his newly-made enclosure at Lamport in 1586, lovingly counted his sheep and jotted down the totals in his account book. Piously he added, "God bless them all."

The wool produced was a vital factor in the preparation of England for the industrial revolution which was to follow. As the most important item in foreign trade it was an important creator of capital.

The transition from the common-control and open-field system of agriculture to private ownership of farm land occupied a very long period, from at least the beginning of the thirteenth to the end of the nineteenth centuries. Thus, the transition from an almost completely subsistence organization to a predominantly exchange organization of area, as expressed by the total development of the enclosure movement, covered a period of six centuries. This period may be divided into two parts, with regard both to the time and to the territory involved. The first is from the time of the Black Death (the plague) in mid-thirteenth century to the reign of Queen Elizabeth (1588–1603). The second part is from the beginning of the seventeenth to the middle of the eighteenth century, when the industrial revolution is said to have begun.

The first part is characterized by a great increase in the amount of land in pasture for sheep raising and in abandonment of much land under cultivation. This shift made many landlords wealthy from the profits derived in the wool trade. There can be no doubt that it also separated many hundreds of thousands of people from the relative security of common operation of open fields in a subsistence organization of livelihood. The second part is associated with a return to cultivation of arable land for grain and foodstuffs, which proved to be in its turn as profitable as was previously the case with the shift to sheep raising. It became a period of renaissance of agriculture, and, despite the continuing hue and cry against enclosure, it was also a period of widespread voluntary enclosure by a very large percentage of small land holders.

In terms of area, the first period was marked by enclosure in a series of counties around the periphery of England, in the southeast, the north, and the west. The idea has been advanced that the southeastern counties in the plains, because of their proximity to the largest city, London, and to the foreign markets of the continent, could scarcely be expected to resist for very long the larger profit to be derived from privately owned commercial farming. This was true of both sheep and grain land. The counties of the north and west were those in which arable land was only a small percentage of the total occupied. Here enclosure involved more the development of increased grassland from waste than transference of previously arable lands to grass. The area of enclosure in the second part of the enclosure period is primarily in the eastern counties —the heart of agricultural England. Here enclosure was accomplished with the support of Parliament, instead of previous parliamentary opposition. Some idea of the greatly increased rate of enclosure in the few short decades of the later eighteenth century may be gained from the number of enclosure acts passed by Parliament as shown in Table X.

Applying his comments to the start of the eighteenth century, some sixty years before the date

TABLE X NUMBER OF PARLIAMENTARY ACTS OF
ENCLOSURE[a]

COMMON FIELD AND SOME WASTE		WASTE ONLY	
Period	*No. acts*	*Acres*	*No. acts*	*Acres*
1700–1760	152	237,845	56	74,518
1761–1801	1,479	2,428,721	521	752,150
1802–1844	1,075	1,610,302	808	939,043
1845 on	164	187,321	508	334,906
Total	2,870	4,464,189	1,893	2,100,617

[a] W. H. R. Curtler, *The Enclosure and Redistribution of Our Land,* Oxford, England: Clarendon Press, 1920, p. 148.

considered to mark the beginning of the industrial revolution, Hoskins writes,[1]

It is impossible to say precisely how much of England still lay in open fields in 1700 or thereabouts, but one can make a rough estimate. We know that enclosures by parliamentary act and award dealt with about 4,500,000 acres of open field, leaving aside for one moment the enclosure of the common [pasture common] and other "wastes." Gregory King had estimated in 1688 that the arable land of England and Wales amounted to nine million acres in all. We shall not be far wrong then if we say that in 1700 about one-half of the arable land was already enclosed in the kind of fields that we see today, and that about one-half still lay in open field, a landscape which survives today only in patches. . . .

. . . in the great majority of the parishes it was a complete transformation, from the immemorial landscape of the open fields, with their complex pattern of narrow strips, their winding green balks, or cart-roads, their headlands, and grassy foot paths, into the modern chequer-board pattern of small, squarish fields, enclosed by hedgerows of hawthorn, with new roads running more or less straight and wide across the parish in all directions. It was a triumph of planning in so short a time for so complicated a matter, most of it carried through in most places within a year or two years of the passing of the act.

The conclusion is warranted that the transition to commercial agriculture, that is, to an exchange organization of area, was at least half completed by 1750. By the mid-eighteenth century preindustrial England was predominantly oriented toward exchange-type area organization. Furthermore, the rapidity of completion of enclosure after long struggle over the issue parallels both the revolution in industrial production and the rapid increase of population which is characteristic of the years from 1760–1840.

The Evolution of a Geographic Division of Labor and Beginnings of Mechanization.
Two important points of geographic significance occurred in the development of wool manufacturing. First, a geographic division of labor developed which corresponded generally to the steps in the processing of wool. Second, earlier concentrations of manufacturing had been in the larger towns and under strict control of the guilds. The power of the guilds became weakened by the competitive dispersal of industry into rural districts. By contrast the manufacture of cloth in Flanders and Italy remained con-

centrated in the cities by restrictions placed on innovations in the very name of the protection which the guilds attempted to exercise for its preservation.

The many specialized phases in the manufacture of wool cloth were accomplished by separate persons with different skills and tools, and these usually worked separately or independently in their own establishments. The processing of wool included:

1. Initial sorting and preparation of the raw wool by beating and washing.

2. Preparing the wool for spinning. (This was a matter of *carding* if short-staple, or *combing* if long-staple wool. The difference was in the length of the teeth on wooden instruments fashioned with short metal hooks or with long metal teeth.)

3. The spinning of the wool into thread. (This was accomplished by hand with the distaff and spindle or with the spinning wheel, itself a mechanical innovation probably of the thirteenth century.)

4. The dying of the wool thread. Or

5. The weaving of cloth and then dying the cloth. (Intermediate steps preparatory to weaving were performed by *warpers*, who made ready the looms by sizing and winding the warp threads on the loom, and by *spoolers*, who wound the bobbins for insertion in the shuttles. The actual *weaving* was a two-person operation for large cloths, called broadcloths.

6. The *fulling* of the wool cloth after weaving. (This was originally a heavy job performed by trampling the cloth, once woven, in a trough of water. The purpose of this process was both to cleanse the cloth and to thicken the fibers and induce it to "felt.")

7. The stretching of the cloth to the exact dimensions desired by attaching it with tenterhooks to a frame or tenter against which it was pulled tight upon shrinking.

8. And finally the raising of the nap of the cloth through a process known as *raising*, along with shearing, brushing, mending, and folding.

The wool-manufacturing processes were subdivided into many specialized steps, each accomplished by a different artisan working at home. This came to be called the *cottage industrial system.* The system was organized by various entrepreneurs and agents who passed the semifinished products on from artisan to artisan. Such entrepreneurs (derived from French, meaning "to take in hand, or to contract for") often controlled the materials all the way from the raw wool to the finished cloth. A

[1]Hoskins, *op. cit.*, pp. 138–139.

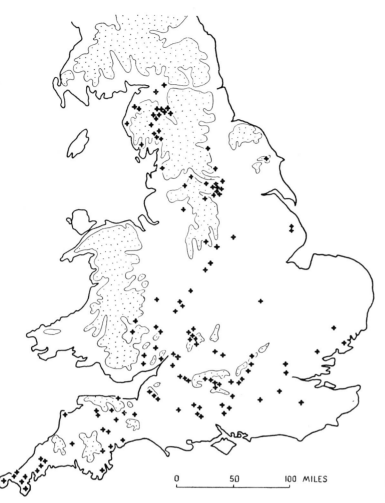

Figure 71. Distribution of fulling mills in documents before the time of Edward III. (*Courtesy of English Universities Press, Ltd., taken from J. B. Mitchell,* Historical Geography.)

wide degree of variation in the association of the different skills was possible. Some large establishments *did* develop in which many artisans worked in centralized premises which were provided for the purpose of housing the various stages in the manufacture of wool cloth. This anticipated the factory-type establishment but was not the manner in which production was usually organized during this period. Geographically distinct locations of different stages of production in close association over an area was both a beginning and a preparation or training period for more complicated and involved geographical division of labor to come.

The initial development of wool manufacturing in England had taken place under the protection of guilds in larger towns, such as Stamford, Lincoln, London, Oxford, Colchester, Norwich, Beverly, York, and Winchester; but unlike the situation in the Low Countries of Europe it did not remain there. One impetus to rural location, for example, was fulling. A simple machine constructed by combining heavy, wooden hammers, cams, and a water

wheel made it possible to beat wool cloths mechanically in a trough of water. The sites appropriate for such fulling mills were in the upper reaches of streams where small dams could readily be constructed in order to produce the power needed for the operation of the hammers. The map in Figure 71 shows the fulling mills mentioned in the literature prior to the time of Edward III (1327–1377).[1] There is a high correlation between the distribution of fulling mills and the extent of enclosure of the fifteenth century. There is a strong inference of association between enclosure of land for sheep grazing, the rural location of cloth manufacturing, and the location of fulling mills which developed over a period of time.

The discussion of the changes in cloth manufacturing in England during the Middle Ages contained in *The Cambridge Economic History of Europe* is appropriate here.[2]

[1]Mitchell, *op. cit.*, p. 238.
[2]M. Postan and E. E. Rich (Eds.), *The Cambridge Economic History of Europe.* Vol. II, 1952, pp. 421 ff.

. . . in one respect the fifteenth century "clothier" (as the English manufacturer now came to be called) differed radically from his predecessors the Flemish *drapier*, the English *draper*, and the Italian *lanaiuolo*. Not only in name was he a new and specifically English product. For he operated under what can only be described as conditions of free enterprise in contrast to the regimented control once common in England and still then customary abroad.

At the time that England's woolen industry outdistanced its rivals and won first place on the markets of Europe it was concentrated in no such vast urban agglomerations as were those of Flanders or Italy in their heyday. Nourished though it had once been in many an ancient borough behind whose walls weavers, dyers, and drapers could ply their trade in freedom and security, immune from the restraints and obligations which burdened the members of the feudal society without, the city had never gained a stranglehold upon it. For English cities had never assumed such large proportions or achieved so great a measure of autonomy as their Flemish or Italian counterparts, if only because England had been slower in developing an advanced industrial and commercial economy, and quicker in developing an effective central monarchy. And when England's industry reached maturity the relative advantages and disadvantages of doing business in borough or manor were very different from what they had once been. The feudal society was in dissolution; villeinage had all but disappeared; the borough with its battlemented walls was becoming as much an anachronism as the baronial castle; its liberties had become privileges for the few, and its economy was more rigidly regimented and more heavily taxed than that of the manor had ever been. The ancient proverb "city air maketh free" could have had little meaning for an Englishman of the late fifteenth century, least of all for an aspiring captain of industry.

The progressive manufacturer usually, though not invariably, *kept away from the city and developed his business unrestricted in the countryside,** making his headquarters in some small market town or village, which grew as the industry grew, in haphazard fashion, unregulated, under the aegis of the manor rather than the borough. With no walls to con-than the borough. With no walls to confine and limit it, it was a straggling growth, integrated only by its central market place and by the stately parish church which dominated it—built originally to serve a small rural parish, but now often wholly rebuilt to meet the needs of an industrial community and to witness its wealth. Wide open streets with low two-storey houses took the place of the narrow alleys and the tall close-packed houses with their projecting third and fourth storeys almost meeting overhead in which the city burgesses had mostly been content to live. . . . Moreover, *the new industrial township stood seldom in isolation but merged almost imperceptibly into neighboring townships;* a dozen such lay within a radius of seven miles in the clothing district of the West Riding which included Leeds, Bradford, Halifax and Wakefield; in Suffolk, Cavendish, Long Melford, Glemsford and Sudbury lie along a six mile stretch of the River Stour, and Dedham, Strafford and Bergholt are within a mile of each other. . . .

Freedom to experiment had always characterized the rural industry. In an age of expanding business the progressive manufacturer was very ready to welcome new methods of mechanisation which, for capital outlay, would enable him to reduce costs and increase production without increasing his labour force. By the early fifteenth century, if not before then, a means of mechanising the first finishing process, that of raising, had been invented, and west country clothiers were using the "gigmill" for their fine broadcloths. Instead of the tedious process of drawing teasels by hand over the surface of the cloth, the cloth was now passed over a roller set with teasels and kept whirling by being attached to the spindle of a water wheel—a device in all essentials similar to that used today. . . . *That its use was becoming general and giving rise to considerable opposition as the fulling mill had done, is shown by a petition to Parliament. . . .*

Few clothiers exported their own wares. Most of them sold either to the drapers, whose agents travelled up and down the country collecting cloth, or direct to merchants at the ports, to the Hanseatics, to the Italians, *but above all to the Merchant Adventurers.* For as the cloth trade had expanded, so in each of its principal ports the English merchants concerned in it had drawn together into fellowships of Merchant Adventurers, *"adventurers" in that they were engaged not in the regular old-established traffic to and from Calais with wool, but in seeking new outlets for England's manufactures.* Their wealth and influence at the close of the Middle Ages is itself eloquent witness to the growth of England's industry. In the great marts of the Low Countries where now they chiefly congregated, the Merchant Adventurers of England, who went in stately procession to their own richly furnished chapel at the opening of each mart, were then of as much consequence as once had been the merchants of the Flemish Hanse in London, for English cloth and English exporting firms were now second to none.

New solutions to problems of production and distribution in the textile industry were being found and tested in England. Such a trial period was the

*Italics by present author.

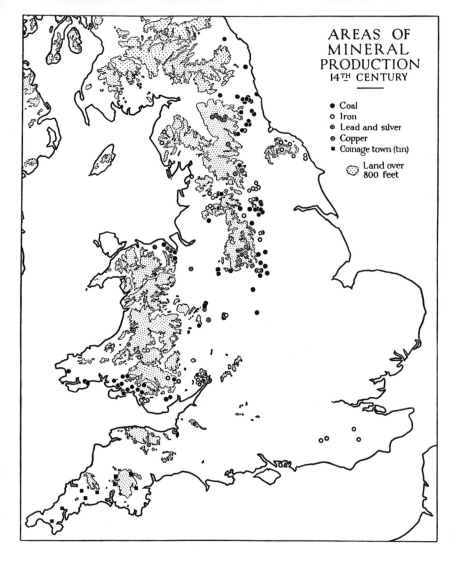

AREAS OF
MINERAL
PRODUCTION
14TH CENTURY

● Coal
○ Iron
◉ Lead and silver
⊕ Copper
■ Coinage town (tin)

◌ Land over
800 feet

Figure 72. (*Courtesy of Cambridge University Press, taken from H. C. Darby (Ed.),* Historical Geography of England before 1800.)

necessary preparation for the drama of industrialization and transformation in area organization which was soon to develop out of these circumstances.

Beginnings of mechanization were not confined to the textile industry's fulling and gigmills. In mining, the disposal of ground water had long presented a real problem. Any mining site which could not be drained to the outside by ditching was soon flooded and had to be abandoned. Toward the end of the seventeenth century experiments were made with steam to assist air pressure in activating pumps. More than one hundred such *atmospheric pumps* were put into use in English mines in the first half of the eighteenth century. The role of steam was to produce a partial vacuum by condensation thus activating the piston through atmospheric pressure. The prior innovation of the atmospheric engine made easier what A. P. Usher called[1] the "strategic innovation" made by James Watt in his invention

of the *steam engine*. Watt, when repairing one of these atmospheric engines, by an "act of insight" made a "critical revision" in the atmospheric engine—the substitution of steam instead of the atmosphere to drive the piston. The point of interest is the preparation for this innovation by others who set the stage for the invention of the rotary steam engine by widening the horizon of popular understanding, making it easier for the new principle to be appreciated and adopted.

The map in Figure 72, of Darby's historical geography,[2] shows fourteenth-century areas of mineral production. The pattern is strikingly similar to the present day one. After Roman times coal is first mentioned in mid-thirteenth century as "sea coal," where wave action had exposed seams outcropping

[1]Abbot Payson Usher, *A History of Mechanical Inventions,* Cambridge, Mass.: Harvard University Press, 1954, pp. 66–70, 342–357.
[2] H. C. Darby, *op. cit.,* p. 257.

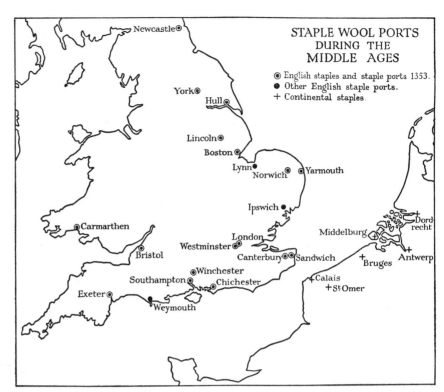

Figure 73. (*Courtesy of Cambridge University Press, taken from H. C. Darby (Ed.),* Historical Geography of England before 1800.)

near the water line. Later "sea coal" is mentioned as being mined inland. Coal was unsuitable for domestic consumption until the chimney came into common use in dwellings during the seventeenth century. A great expansion in domestic coal trade during the seventeenth century is traceable to the "multitude of chimneys recently erected."[1] In the time of Queen Elizabeth, as demand and price increased, coal mining expanded throughout the country.

The quantity of coal recoverable from any one pit was restricted by the possibility and cost of carrying it to the hoist. This inhibited the acreage underground which could be mined economically from any one shaft. Coal was initially carried by basket on men's backs, or on sledges hauled by men harnessed in chains. Solution to this problem contained the germ of later development in the railroad. First, where the floor of a mine would permit it, wheels supplanted sledges; then planks were laid down to facilitate movement over difficult places, and finally a double line of planks for four-wheeled wagons. According to Ashton,[2]

. . . A pin was made to project from the bottom of the waggon into the space between the rails so as to

[1] L. F. Salzman, *English Industries of the Middle Ages,* Oxford, England: Clarendon Press, 1931, pp. 1–20.

[2] T. S. Ashton and J. Sykes, *The Coal Industry of the 18th Century,* Manchester, England: University Press, 1929, p. 63.

prevent the waggon from leaving the track. . . . Such simple railways were used above ground at an early date; they existed at the collieries of the Willoughbys, near Nottingham, at least as early as 1610; . . . before the opening of the eighteenth century they were found in South Wales and about the Tyne, where they were carried over elaborate bridges and embankments to the shipping points. Early in the seventeenth century railroads had probably been constructed along the horizontal drifts of the Shropshire coalfield, but it is doubtful whether they were extensively used for underground transport until the following century; in 1756 their presence at pits in the north of England attracted the attention of a foreign engineer.

The many mechanical innovations made during the preparatory period before the industrial revolution had something in common. Each was a mechanism which awaited only the introduction of a more efficient source of power to revolutionize its application. Such a revolutionary change in prime mover was later to be introduced in the form of the steam engine.

External Orientation of the English Economy. England had begun as a colony of Rome. Even in the late thirteenth century England was primarily a supplier of raw wool for the artisans of Flanders and Italy. English merchants soon outdistanced earlier foreign interests in the conduct of English exports. The map in Figure 73 shows the principal wool ports of England from which trade was conducted during the fourteenth and fifteenth centuries.[1] The export of raw wool (sacks) and hides with the wool unshorn (fells) is the expression of England's role as the supplier of raw materials. The export of cloths, broadcloths, and worsteds is the expression of the change to an English-controlled export of domestically manufactured articles.

The building of ships and the development of establishments to handle the movement of goods presupposes the production of goods and the desire to trade or exchange them with others. A growing internal and external exchange of goods and the development of a monetary system by which such exchange was facilitated preceded and accompanied the development of external mobility by sea.

Ocean trade first developed in England under protection of chartered companies with monopoly rights granted by the Crown, and then by the Navigation Acts of Parliament. The Navigation Acts were of decisive importance from the time of the Restoration in 1660 until 1849, when *free trade* became the national policy. The Navigation Acts established a monopoly for English shipping. This encouraged English shipbuilding which, until the time of the iron and steel ship, suffered a competitive disadvantage because of the increasing scarcity of timber for shipbuilding. More important than this fact, however, was the fact that a *national purpose* was implied and accepted by the seventeenth-century Englishman. England, an island country, had to trade if she prospered; and if she traded she had to do it in ships. Accordingly, in the face of all other conflicts of interests, between landlord and tenant, artisan and manufacturer, merchant and feudal lord or king, the national interest in England's *success upon the seas was never sacrificed,* but, on the contrary, always had some small margin of encouragement.

England found herself, along with numerous other northern European countries, *centrally located with respect to overseas lands,* as the age of exploration and geographical discovery brought an increasing awareness of the centrality of Europe with respect to the rest of the world. The accepted view at the end of the fifteenth century had been one of three continents—Europe, Africa, and Asia. The idea of sailing west to reach the east coast of Asia occurred within the context of a belief that the world was smaller than it actually turned out to be.

No one dreamed that there were four additional continents. It took nearly a generation after 1492 for people to realize that the western lands contacted by sailing westward were *not* the eastern shores of the Eurasian land mass, but literally "Newfoundland."

When the true proportions of the world's lands became generally clear, Europeans discovered that their continent was truly central in position on the scale of the world as a whole. This position does not specially favor any individual part of Europe concerning access to the sea. Reference to the map in Figure 74 demonstrates this relationship. Note, for example, the lands within the bands five to six thousand miles distant from the estimated "geographic" center of gravity for Europe located near Nurnberg, Germany. All of Europe lies within a radius of one thousand miles of Nurnberg. South Africa, the east coast of virtually the entire continent of Asia from Ceylon to Kamchatka, the west coast of North America across the Atlantic, all lie within a distance of from four to six thousand miles from any point in Europe.

England was, therefore, only *one of many* countries in Europe which aspired to profit from the development of overseas trade. The basis of these desires was awareness of a certain "complementarity" existing between Europe and more tropical lands. Steps or stages in the development of this awareness occurred somewhat as follows. First, England exported raw wool, later the manufactured cloth. Such exports led to the development of an English trade in English ships under the control of English merchants. Exploration and widening overseas horizons introduced the procedure of importing, processing, and re-exporting new products from distant lands, such as sugar, tobacco, spices, coffee, tea, rum, porcelain, cotton fabrics, and many others. Contact with and use of such products, in turn, induced new domestic wants among Englishmen which brought about manufacturing based on imported raw materials to satisfy *both* domestic and foreign markets. In this way, the establishment and development of foreign trade quickened and intensified the development of interregional division of labor characteristic of an exchange-type organization of area. Events in the development of English freedom of the seas in competition with Portugal, Spain, Holland, and France during the century from 1660 to 1760 (marked by intensification of English commitment to a protectionist policy through the Navigation Acts) represent the final

---

[1] H. C. Darby (Ed.), *Historical Geography of England before 1800,* Cambridge, England: Cambridge University Press, 1936, p. 313.

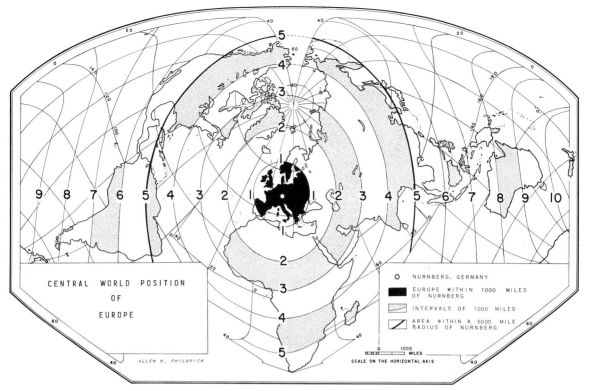

Figure 74

stages of that preparation for the transformation of England embodied in the events of the industrial revolution.

Political and Social Freedoms Associated with English Creativity. The last three circumstances in the preparation for the industrial revolution concerned *freedoms:* freedom of *control,* freedom of *faith,* and freedom of *thought.*

Surely it can*not* be said that the Englishman at the end of the Middle Ages possessed freedom in an absolute sense, either politically, religiously, or intellectually. The struggle for and the achievements toward independence both in *thought* and in action were greater in England than anywhere else in the world at this time.

The bloodless political revolution of 1688–1689 "decided the balance between Parliamentary and regal power in favour of Parliament."[1] This victory cleared the way for the development of private economic interests unfettered by abritrary centralized power.

At the same time religious toleration achieved a certain measure of observance. The Church of England remained "a body with exclusive political and educational privileges," but it ceased to be a persecuting arm of legal authority. The English historian, Trevelyan,[2] summarizes the situation.

In 1695 the censorship of the press was allowed to lapse, so that Milton's dream of "liberty of unlicensed printing" was realized in England. The even balance of the powerful Whig and Tory parties protected critics of government who spoke from either camp. The cessation of persecution under the Clarendon code put an end to a mass of continual suffering, hatred, and wrong. After a thousand years, religion was at length released from the obligation to practise cruelty on principle, by the admission that it is the incorrigible nature of man to hold different opinions on speculative subjects. On that stubborn fact the modern State, like the medieval Church, had broken its teeth in vain. The indirect consequences of this victory of the individual conscience were far-reaching and manifold, not to be revealed in the lifetime of the Whigs and Tories who worked out that curious patchwork of compromise, illogicality, and political good sense, the Toleration Act of 1689.

Intellectual leadership produced the phrase "The

[1] G. M. Trevelyan, *History of England*, Vol. II, Garden City, N. Y.: Longman Green and Company, 1929, p. 475.
[2] *Ibid.*, p. 476.

pen is mightier than the sword." This aphorism of Edward Bulwer Lytton (1803–1873) expresses the point of view made possible by relative religious and political freedom which had been achieved by Englishmen. This quality is perhaps best illustrated by reference to the intellectual leadership of Adam Smith, the author of *Wealth of Nations* (1776). Robert L. Heilbroner[1] in his introduction to *The Worldly Philosophers* observes for a number of "economic thinkers" starting with Adam Smith,

By all the rules of schoolboy history books, they were nonentities: they commanded no armies, sent no men to their deaths, ruled no empires, took little part in history-making decisions . . . yet what they did was more decisive for history than many acts of statesmen who basked in brighter glory, often more profoundly disturbing than the shuttling of armies back and forth across frontiers, more powerful for good and bad than the edicts of kings and legislatures. It was this: they shaped and swayed men's minds.

The point is that Adam Smith's book, *Wealth of Nations*, dealt with and expressed the *goals* to which the reorganization of England's economy on a market basis was directed. It does not matter whether his theoretical analysis was correct or not; his *intellectual leadership* gave conscious expression to the organizing concept of a national economy. In Adam Smith England possessed the first great intellectual leader—the first philosopher—of capitalism.

By the eighteenth century, agriculture had become reorganized on a commercial basis. Subsistence agriculture was disappearing; commercial production of industrial wool and food crops were increasing. Substantial beginnings had already been made in mechanization of some steps in both manufacturing and mining processes. These developments had from the very start a relationship to an expanding domestic and foreign trade. The foreign trade had rapidly passed from alien to English control and production for commerce had transferred the centers of manufacturing from urban guilds to manufacturing establishments in the rural towns and into thousands of participating peasant households. These changes were all possible because of new and developing freedoms in political, religious, and intellectual pursuits. Such internal developments were matched outside the country by English supremacy on the seas. By the beginning of the

eighteenth century, England was in a position to capitalize, as no country on earth had ever been before, on the inherent creative ingenuity of a relatively free people. Innovations were already in progress which only needed the discovery of the steam engine to transform patterns of human occupancy in completely unforeseen ways.

The English Industrial Revolution

The events of the industrial revolution may be generalized under three main headings. First, the *pattern of mechanical innovations* from 1700 to 1880 defines spatially the English culture hearth of the industrial revolution. Then the new prime mover, *steam*, comes into focus. From it stems the great concentration of energy in the factory system of production. The third element, the *interrelatedness* of the many innovations involved both spatially and technologically, transforms the industrial revolution from a series of separate events and places into a tremendous movement of people and materials within an organized region.

The Culture Hearth. The industrial revolution had its start in a number of separate points of origin within a region of England delimited on the map in Figure 75. These points define the extent of the English culture hearth of the industrial revolution. Eighteen innovations are presented as examples of the origins of the industrial revolution. Their places of origin are shown as black dots on the map in Figure 75; they are also listed with their dates in Table XI. From these points of origin the innovations became dispersed. The places to which they were initially spread are also plotted on the map, which shows their connection to the centers of origin by dotted lines. Dispersion to places hundreds of miles distant from point of origin took place very quickly. The resulting pattern, although only a sample, gives a definite idea of the concentration of inventiveness in the center of England. The map also indicates a wider dispersion outward from the culture hearth to other parts of England. The area of the culture hearth is bounded by Birmingham on the south, Coalbrookdale on the west, Handsworth which is near Sheffield to the northeast, and Preston-Bradley to the north.

Steam—the New Prime Mover. James Watt's "inversion" of Thomas Newcomen's atmospheric engine ushered in the age of steam. This new form of mechanical power immensely multiplied the effective force which could be concentrated at a

[1] R. L. Heilbroner, *The Worldly Philosophers*, New York: Simon and Schuster, 1953, p. 3. Copyright 1953, 1961 by Robert L. Heilbroner. By permission of Simon Schuster, Inc.

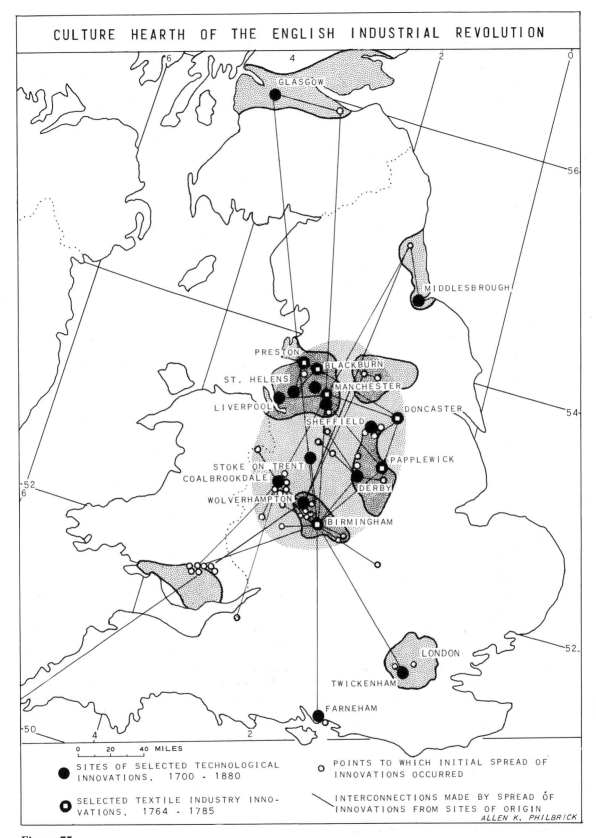

CULTURE HEARTH OF THE ENGLISH INDUSTRIAL REVOLUTION

GLASGOW

MIDDLESBROUGH

PRESTON
BLACKBURN
ST. HELENS
MANCHESTER
LIVERPOOL
DONCASTER
SHEFFIELD
PAPPLEWICK
STOKE ON TRENT
COALBROOKDALE
DERBY
WOLVERHAMPTON
BIRMINGHAM

LONDON
TWICKENHAM
FARNEHAM

0   20   40 MILES

● SITES OF SELECTED TECHNOLOGICAL
   INNOVATIONS, 1700 - 1880

◉ SELECTED TEXTILE INDUSTRY INNO-
   VATIONS, 1764 - 1785

○ POINTS TO WHICH INITIAL SPREAD OF
   INNOVATIONS OCCURRED

INTERCONNECTIONS MADE BY SPREAD OF
INNOVATIONS FROM SITES OF ORIGIN
ALLEN K. PHILBRICK

Figure 75

TABLE XI   EIGHTEEN SELECTED INNOVATIONS OF THE INDUSTRIAL REVOLUTION, 1700–1880

Innovation	Date	Place of origin
Iron reduction using coke instead of charcoal	1709	Coalbrookdale
Atmospheric engine	1712	Wolverhampton
Silk "throwing" machine	1717	Darby
Sulfuric acid in bulk quantities in lead containers for textile bleaching and metallurgy	1736–1746	Twickenham-Birmingham
Crucible cast steel	1747	Sheffield
Inland canal from St. Helens to the Mersey River	1757	St. Helens
Spinning jenny for weft threads	1764	Blackburn
Frame with rollers for warp threads	1768	Preston
Combined jenny and frame called "mule"	1779	Bolton
Low-pressure steam engine	1765–1788	Glasgow-Birmingham
Mechanized production of chinaware	1769	Stoke on Trent
Iron rails for moving coal at collieries	1768–1771	Coalbrookdale
Power loom for weaving	1786–1787	Doncaster
Puddled and rolled iron	1783–1784	Farneham
High-pressure steam engine	1802–1804	Coalbrookdale
Railroad locomotive, "The Rocket"	1829	Liverpool-Manchester
Bessemer converter, pig iron to steel	1860	Sheffield
Thomas liner of dolomite for using phosphoric ores in Bessemer converter	1879	Middlesbrough

given point to perform work. The steam engine, invented and improved in the period from 1765 to 1788, almost immediately had a concentrating effect on the geographic location of economic production. The first engines were low pressure machines of between 10 and 80 horsepower. According to Ashton,[1]

The introduction of the rotative engine was a momentous event. . . . After 1783, when the first of the new engines was erected—to work a hammer for John Wilkinson at Bradley—it became clear that a technological revolution was afoot in Britain. Before their patents expired in 1800, Boulton and Watt had built and put into operation about 500 engines, of both types, [to and fro, and rotative] at home and [in a few instances] abroad. The new form of power and, no less, the new transmitting mechanisms by which this was made to do work previously done by hand and muscle, were the pivot on which industry swung into the modern age.

Spatial and Technological Interrelatedness of Innovations.

It is the interrelatedness of these and many other innovations which gives them truly geographic character because it makes a regional pattern out of them instead of a series of isolated points on the map. How intricate the web of interconnections between the threads of cultural innovation which Englishmen during this period were "weaving" into the fabric of human society! T. S. Ashton[2] shows how

. . . discoveries in different fields of activity were linked together. Sometimes it was simply a case of *imitation*,* as when the principle of attenuating material by passing it through rollers was transferred from the iron to the textile industry, or when Wilkinson's method of boring cannon was turned to the making of steam-engine cylinders. Sometimes an advance in one sphere was a *condition of progress* in another, as when the development of coke ovens made possible the extraction of tar. Often two or more industries went *hand in hand*, each contributing to the forward movement of the other. Without the discovery of smelting with coke, which made is possible to supply larger and more intricate castings, Newcomen could not have perfected his engine; and without Newcomen's engine Darby could hardly have obtained the blast that was necessary to produce iron on the scale required. Both the atmospheric and the steam engine helped to increase the output of coal and metals, and the larger supply of these (and especially of copper and brass) reacted on the development of engineering. "Invention is the mother of necessity:" an improvement in one process frequently put *pressure* on those concerned with an earlier, parallel, or later process in the same industry. The invasion by the founders of the territory of the forge-masters made these look to new ways of reducing the cost of wrought iron; the introduction of the fly shuttle made it imperative for the spinners to seek out better methods of producing yarn; and the later improvements in spinning and weaving brought a new urgency to the search for quicker methods of bleaching and finishing. In all these ways *innovation bred innovation*.

The establishments at which each of the chief discoveries was first applied—Coalbrookdale, Cromford, Carron, Etruria, and Soho—*became centers from which ideas and enterprise radiated* to other parts of the land. . . .

[N. B. "Etruria" was Hanley near Stoke on Trent, and "Soho" refers to the Soho plant of Watt and Roebuck in Birmingham.]

[1]T. S. Ashton, *The Industrial Revolution*, Oxford, England: The Oxford University Press, 1948, p. 70.
[2] *Ibid*, p. 88 ff.
*Italics are the present author's.

The interconnections between the *jenny* the *frame* with rollers, and the *mule,* in turn, with the *power loom,* which mechanized the cotton-textile industry, is a classical example of interrelated ideas progressively evolving toward a common goal. The separate inventors did not approach their tasks as a conscious team; yet in the evolution of the technology the result over a period of years would appear almost as if a team of inventors had been engaged in coordinated effort. In Table XII the above four inventions and the steam engine are shown in time sequence from 1764 to 1785—21 years from the invention of the spinning jenny to the application of the steam engine to the spinning and weaving machine in the first mechanically powered factory in the world at Papplewick, England. The table amply illustrates the connections existing between these five separate acts of innovation. Papplewick may be identified on the map in Figure 75.

Another series of innovations led to railroad transportation. It began in the English coal mines with wooden planks and wooden rails and continued with the iron rails developed by Richard Reynolds at Ketley and Coalbrookdale which were based on the invention of puddled and rolled iron by Henry Cort. In 1802 the series of innovations picked up again with the improvement in the steam engine by Richard Trevithick represented by the development of the high-pressure boiler. This made it possible to reduce the size and weight of the steam engine while increasing its horsepower. Then, in 1829, George Stevenson combined with smooth-flanged wheel on a smooth rail with the steam engine to prove that a railroad locomotive could develop the necessary traction to run his engine, "The Rocket," from Liverpool to Manchester. This event ushered in the railroad era.

English leadership in the industrial revolution continued during the nineteenth century to produce innovations with far-reaching impact. The eighteenth century puddling process of steel production by Henry Cort was small scale and expensive. It was adequate for early stages of industrial mechanization, but the demand for steel outstripped production capacity by this method. It remained for two subsequent interrelated innovations to make *mass production* of steel from pig iron a reality. These originated in England during the second half of the nineteenth century, and made possible the modern patterns of industry in the age of steel. These innovations were the *Bessemer converter* by the metallurgist-inventor, Sir Henry Bessemer; and a *modifi-*

TABLE XII   INTERRELATEDNESS OF SELECTED INNOVATIONS IN ENGLAND, 1764–1785

Innovation, originator, place, and date	Relationship
Spinning jenny, for the weft threads, by James Hargreave at Blackburn, 1764–67	The weft and warp are the two directions of threads on a loom. The warp threads take more strain and are harder to spin mechanically than the weft.
Frame with Rollers, for spinning the warp threads, by Richard Arkwright at Preston, 1768–69	
"Mule," combining the jenny and the frame with rollers into one machine, by Samuel Crompton at Bolton, 1779–85	Harks back to earlier machines and looks forward to the power loom.
Power loom, to do for weaving what previous machines had done for spinning, by Edmund Cartwright at Doncaster, 1786–87	Makes use of mechanically spun thread in mechanically weaving cloth—awaits mechanical power.
Steam engine, by James Watt, first applied to factory production 1785 to drive mechanical textile production at Papplewick, England, 1765–85.	Makes the mechanization of cotton-textile manufacture complete.

cation of the lining in the converter by Sidney Gilchrist Thomas.

Bessemer's innovation was the discovery that pig-iron castings could be decarbonized by blowing air through the molten metal. The oxidation of the carbon in the metal is itself a heat-producing reaction, maintaining the metal in a molten state. The first Bessemer furnace "converted" more than a ton of steel on its first "blow" at Sheffield in 1860.

Thomas's invention consisted on the introduction of blocks of magnesian limestone (dolomite) as lining instead of silica blocks in the converter. The significance of the dolomitic lining is in the elimination of phosphorus from iron which it makes possible. It is known as a *basic* (limestone) as opposed to an *acid* (silica) process of conversion. The first successful trials of this modification were made in Middlesbrough in 1879. The "basic" converter lining transformed the iron ores of Europe, which are high in phosphorous, into a usable resource base for the European steel age.

Still another innovation was the development of the *open-hearth* method of converting pig iron into steel. This type converter is based on the principle of the regenerative gas furnace. Gas heat is em-

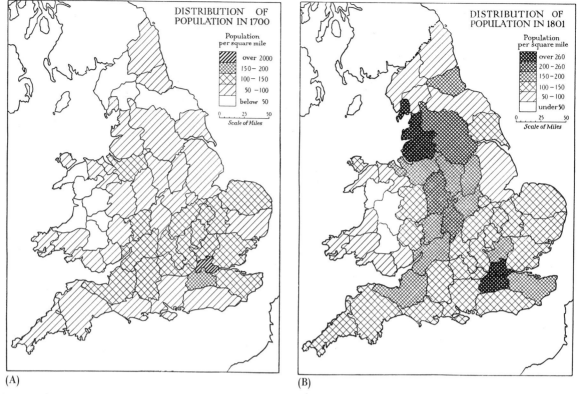

Figure 76. (*Courtesy of Cambridge University Press, taken from H. C. Darby (Ed.),* Historical Geography of England before 1800.)

ployed. The exhaust gases are used to heat brick-work which in turn preheats new gas and air before it is burned over a bath of molten iron being converted into steel. Open-hearth units are capable of making up to 300 tons of steel at one time. The process of decarbonization takes longer (8 to 10 hours) than in the Bessemer converter, but the precision with which it is possible to control the quality of the steel is much greater. The open hearth can be lined either with dolomitic limestone or with silica to handle either phosphoric or nonphosphoric ores. The open-hearth converter is now the most prevalent type used in modern steel mills.

Worldwide Dispersion of the Industrial Revolution

The industrial revolution, which originated in England, has spread exchange-type organization of area throughout the world during the past two centuries. Four stages are observable in the complex dissemination of this great social, economic, and geographic revolution. These stages, although somewhat overlapping in time, are geographically separate. They are:

1. The spread within Great Britain.

2. The dispersion to Europe and eastern North America.

3. The export of industrial revolution to secondary exchange-type regions in the Southern Hemisphere, such as southern South America, South Africa, Australia and New Zealand, and czarist Russia.

4. The present-day rush to develop the less well-developed areas of the world.

Modern offshoots of the continuing impetus of the industrial revolution are assisting the national aspirations of many peoples of the world in places still characterized by local subsistence-type area organization.

The dispersion of industrial know-how in the United Kingdom transformed that nation from a subsistence basis to an exchange basis of area organization. The transition is demonstrated by the redistribution of population shown by maps for 1700 and 1801 in Figure 76 A and B.[1] The relatively

[1] H. C. Darby (Ed.), *Historical Geography of England before 1800*, Cambridge, England: Cambridge University Press, 1936, pp. 524 and 525.

even population in 1700 contrasts with the emergence of a more densely populated region of manufacturing counties by 1801. Note that the counties having an average of more than 150 persons per square mile, correspond fairly closely to the area of the culture hearth of the industrial revolution defined by the map in Figure 75. There were only two counties with more than 150 persons per square mile in 1700; by 1801 there were fifteen. In more specific terms the pattern of regions specializing in certain types of production, shown on the map in Figure 65 of the preceding chapter, emerged from the culture hearth of the English industrial revolution. Each of the points of origin of specific innovations lies within and has had something to do with the evolving character of industry in one or another of these specialized regions. In other cases the early dispersion of innovations to other places from the culture hearth determined the direction in which regions outside the culture hearth have continued to develop to this day.

The evolution of the patterns of regional organization in the United Kingdom has been described in more detail than will be possible for other regions. This was done because the United Kingdom contains the culture hearth of the industrial revolution and pioneered the shift from subsistence to exchange organization of area. It is more appropriate to discuss the other stages in the dispersion of the industrial culture originating in England in the chapters pertaining to those regions.

This chapter has demonstrated how the cultural evolution of human values, ways of doing, and specific works of man can change the patterns of area organization. Attention now turns from the United Kingdom to the mainland of Europe.

8 Europe

Europe, the platform from which European culture has been carried throughout the world, is but a peninsula of Eurasia. It is a peninsula of peninsulas. The axis of the traditional body of Europe, which narrows rapidly from east to west, extends 2,500 miles from the southern Ural Mountains to the Bay of Biscay in France, as shown by the map in Figure 77. The distance from Leningrad (*3,300,000*) at the eastern end of the Gulf of Finland to Odessa on the Black Sea is 900 miles, while France is 440 miles wide from the Gulf of Lions on the Mediterranean to the English Channel at Le Havre (*173,287*). Just west of the Ural Mountains, which are the traditional eastern limit of Europe, the greatest north-south extent of nearly 1,500 miles reaches from the mouth of the Pechora River in north European Russia to the mouth of the Ural River on the Caspian Sea in the south. Europe is next to the smallest continent, the smallest being Australia (2,974,581 square miles). Europe's 3,850,000 square miles is approximately the size of Canada. If European Russia is excluded, non-Russian Europe is 1.9 million square miles, approximately equal in size to the area east of the Rocky Mountain states in the United States. Again, if the east European satellites of the Soviet Union are also excluded, West Europe shrinks in size to 1.3 million square miles, which is the equivalent of the loss of North and South Dakota, Minnesota, Iowa, Nebraska, Kansas, and Missouri.

Extending from the main body of Europe, the Scandinavian, Balkan, Danish, Italian, and Iberian peninsulas reach far outward into the water bodies bounding Europe on two sides. These smaller peninsulas produce extensive embayments of the Atlantic Ocean and the Mediterranean Sea. The map in Figure 77 identifies these waters. The whole region, excluding the Soviet Union, is in the shape of an irregular right triangle, with the *90-degree angle* pointing toward the Middle East, the *base* along the Mediterranean, the *altitude* separating Europe from European Russia, and the *hypote-*

nuse along the Atlantic shore from Norway to Spain. This diagrammatic arrangement of Europe gives some idea of the distances involved from the fact that it is approximately 2,000 miles north-south between the Dardanelles and North Cape, Norway, and the same distance east-west to Cape St. Vincent, Portugal. Along the hypotenuse from Cape St. Vincent to North Cape is approximately 2,500 miles.

Regions of Europe

Europe may be divided into regions on the basis of at least three sets of criteria. One basis of regional divisions is the historically evolved cultural similarities shared among peoples. A second basis is the homogeneity of common activities and product specialization. The third is organizational—that of a core and its peripheral regions. Using all three bases in combination, Europe is divided into five major regions, as shown by the map in Figure 78. Each one of the five is distinctive and possesses a degree of homogeneity. Four of the regions—Mediterranean or Southern Europe, Scandinavian or Northern Europe, Celtic or Atlantic fringe of Europe, and Slavic or Eastern Europe—are peripheral to the fifth region, the industrial core region of Europe as a whole.

The Mediterranean. The countries of the Mediterranean region share the common circumstances of ancient Greek and Roman cultural heritages which were based on early organization of the lands rimming the Mediterranean Sea. This region also possesses the similarity of climate associated with the name. A basically uniform type of agricultural use of land, water, and warmth resources prevails. Winter wheat (grown on the basis of winter moisture), olives, grapes, citrus fruits, and vegetable crops are found in parts of every Mediterranean country. The countries of this region are Spain, Portugal, southern France, peninsular Italy, and Greece. Small, irrigated coastal and river plains are intensively developed and support

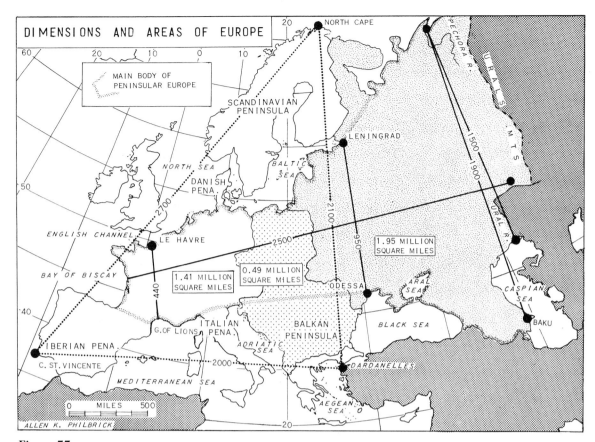

Figure 77

relatively large populations. A large part of the predominantly agricultural population is landless farm labor, living in circumstances of relative poverty. The average standard of living is low. A common Romance language base in Latin and a common religious heritage in Roman Catholicism are continuing elements of Mediterranean cultural similarity.

Scandinavia. The Scandinavian region of northern Europe contrasts sharply with the Mediterranean. Again, the region possesses common elements in the cultural heritage of its peoples. History finds them politically united or dominated by one another more often than by outsiders. Their languages have common Germanic roots and the Protestant Evangelical Lutheran Church is a religious preference which has the status of recognized state religion in all Scandinavian countries—Norway, Sweden, Iceland, Finland, and Denmark. These countries share ancient traditions concerning individual political rights which are the fundation of their modern democratic political organization.

Celtic or Atlantic Fringe. The third region is composed of remnants of countries, except for Ireland, which have been absorbed into other political units. Nevertheless, ancient Celtic cultures are still preserved in the fringes of the European continent along the North Atlantic. These peoples of upland fragments have a common heritage as minorities. They include the Irish, the Gaelic of northern Scotland, the Welsh, the Bretons of Brittany in France, and probably the Basques of northern Spain. They produce similar crop and livestock products from common agricultural resources. Products include meat, butter, cheese, and wool.

Slavic or Eastern Europe. The cultural unity of Slavic Europe is less uniform than that of the other regions. The essential character of the eastern region is that of a broad *buffer zone* between Germanic and Russian Slavic peoples. The primary resources and activities of the people, with few but important exceptions, have remained agricultural. Exceptions, based on coal and metallic ores, have been industrial subregions of East Germany, Bohemia, and Silesia.

The region historically has been a corridor,

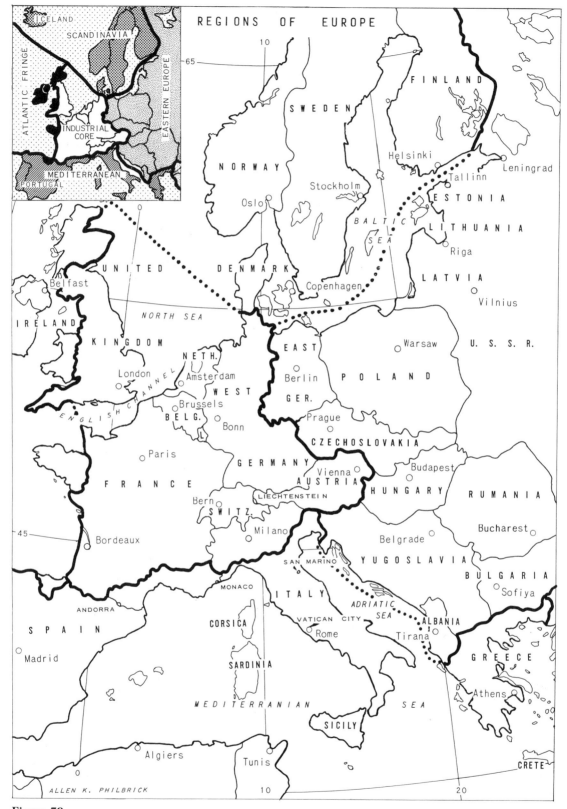

Figure 78

demonstrated by the existence of a series of east-west routes. From north to south these are: the Baltic Sea route, the widening of the North European Plain from west to east, the Moravian Gate, and the Danube Valley and Iron Gate south of the Carpathian Mountains.

In the same fashion religious differences are found in banded strips of population extending in an east-west direction. From north to south these are: Protestants in a narrow strip along the Baltic, Catholics in the center, and a Greek Orthodox portion in the south in which Mohammedan minorities are intermixed.

The basically Slavic language pattern is also broken into sections. From north to south there are: a belt of Baltic languages, giving way to north Slavic tongues (Polish, Czech, and Slovak). South of the center there are non-Slavic Magyars who speak Hungarian and Roumanians whose language is a Romance tongue. Again, in southeast Europe southern Slavic speech (Bulgarian, Serbian, Croation, and Slovenian) predominates.

On the east, Russian Slavic culture extends from north to south the entire distance from the Baltic to the Black Sea. Since the time of the early Christian era there has been a vigorous north-south trading contact along the Dnieper River to the Baltic. Kiev (1,104,000), Novgorod, and Moscow (5,032,000) figured prominently in the early control of different phases of the movement of goods and people.

The East European region between Russia and Western Europe has always been a buffer or a cordon. Eight new nations were created at Versailles by the dismemberment of Austria-Hungary. At the time they were an east European buffer between the then new Communist state in Russia and "the West." Today, after World War II, all of those countries except neutral Austria are behind the "Iron Curtain"—Poland, Czechoslovakia, Hungary, Roumania, Bulgaria, Yugoslavia, and Albania. The buffer against "the East" was turned into a buffer against "the West." In addition East Germany now is in the Communist orbit. Perhaps no single force is as strong in uniting eastern Europe as the organized Moscow orientation of new "democratic" Communist republics. Whether enforced organization of unity will long survive in eastern Europe only the future can tell, but the region today is part of the Communist Bloc.

Industrial Core Region. While each of the four peripheral regions of Europe, with the possible exception of East Europe, has significant unifying cultural attributes among its peoples, it must be recognized that the core region does not have such cultural uniformity. Quite the contrary! The very strong conflicts of economic interest among the countries of the core region have long fed on deep-seated differences in language, religion, customs, and points of view. The core region is composed of both Germanic- and Romance-language-speaking peoples. It is divided among populations of Catholic and various Protestant faiths. The cultural backgrounds of the people in the industrial heart of Europe are more diverse than those within any similar-sized region of the continent. This industrial core region consists of all or parts of nine nations—France, West Germany, Italy, Austria, Switzerland, Belgium, Luxemburg, the Netherlands, and the United Kingdom. The principal axis of the twentieth-century pattern of area organization in West Europe is the Thames-Rhine rivers-Alpine passes-Po Valley alignment. This generally north-south axis is paralleled on the west by the Paris-Dijon-Lyons-Marseilles route utilizing the valley of the Rhone River. On the east another parallel north-south route across the main stem of peninsular Europe is now cut off by the division of Germany into East and West Germany by the "Iron Curtain."

The European core region is a complex of important manufacturing districts served by the network of river-canal (Figure 79A, B, and C) and railroad interconnections of Europe which render their functioning possible. Here is one of the world's great concentrations of industrial activity. Essential raw materials for manufacturing must reach these industrial districts, but the ultimate goal of production is consumption which is dependent on the transportation and trading of the goods produced within the core region throughout Europe and the rest of the world.

Each of the industrial concentrations of the European core, as is the case in England, is a district of industrial specialization. In England, however, all have a common focus on the metropolitan hub of the Commonwealth, London. On the mainland, on the other hand, the industrial district of each country within the core region also focuses internally. This means that many of the industrial areas focus outward on the main service, political, and cultural centers of the countries to which they belong. The core of Europe is, therefore, a junction zone consisting of parts of four big powers and five small powers. The four big powers are France,

(A) The upstream harbor of Duisberg, Germany, is visited every day by barges from Belgium, France, Germany, the Netherlands, and Switzerland.

(B) The port facilities of Rotterdam at the canalized mouth of the Rhine River are almost due east of the mouth of the Thames River in England. Rotterdam serves as a transhipment and break-of-bulk point for the entire Rhine River region.

(C) The shifting of wheat from ocean freighter to river barge.

Figure 79. (*Photographs courtesy of United Nations.*)

Figure 80. Fiat cars come off the assembly lines at the Mirafiori plant in Turin, Italy. (*Courtesy of United Nations.*)

Germany, and Italy on the continent and the United Kingdom across the channel to the north. The five small powers are Belgium, the Netherlands, Luxemburg, Switzerland, and Austria. Each of the four major powers contributes only a part of its area to the common core of Europe. Virtually the entire area of the five small powers except Austria is within the core region.

Each of the nine nations of the European core has its own focus. In each national focus there is one major city. The core region of France is the Paris Basin, with the city of Paris (*4,823,252*) and its metropolitan region as the primary focus. The patterns of organization of Italy and Germany are more complex. Italy's most populous and productive industrial region is the Po River Valley (Figure 80), with its primary focus in the city of Milan (*1,450,359*); yet the capital of the nation and Italy's most important cultural center is Rome (*1,947,360*). Italy is politically an assemblage of relatively small separate units of organization reflecting its retarded unification and achievement of national status only in the late nineteenth century (1869). Germany, likewise, is a combination of many separate regions. In pre-World War II days Berlin became the political and cultural focus, after a late unification (1871), within a coreland of the North German Plain. The present captive position of Berlin, divided between "East" (1,085,000) and "West," (2,211,349) and the accompanying division

of Germany herself into Communist East Germany (German Democratic Republic) and non-Communist West Germany (Federal Republic of Germany) has required two separate political and economic orientations. East Germany focuses on Moscow and the Soviet system. West Germany is an independent unit of the community of free nations of western Europe. The core of West Germany is the Rhine Valley which focuses on the industrial complex of the Ruhr district (Figure 81A, B, and C). Just south of the Ruhr on the Rhine River lies the present political capital of the Federal Republic at Bonn (144,283). The Ruhr is the single most important industrial region of Western Europe today. Based on tremendous reserves of high-quality coking coal, scientific and managerial genius within Germany has developed Europe's largest iron and steel industry, chemical industries, and other diverse manufactures from the late nineteenth century to the present day. The spectacular bids for economic, political, and military supremacy in Europe which culminated in World Wars 1 (1914–1918) and II (1939–1945) were based by Germany on the production of this district integrated with other industrial areas of Germany and of Europe. In the postwar period West Germany, since 1945, has made a phenomenal comeback. The picture in Figure 82 shows part of an automatic steel wire-rolling operation in a mill near Duisberg which is typical of the modernization of techniques since

Figure 81. (*Photographs courtesy of United Nations.*)

(A) The production of ingots of pig iron involves the pouring of molten metal from huge ladles such as this one.

(B) A sense of the drama of steel making is portrayed as workers stoke the furnaces in a modern seamless-tube works in Dusseldorf, Germany.

(C) The finished product of this mill.

Figure 82. The white lines of heavy steel rods snaking through the automatic guides in the wire mill are not completely unattended: the workers stand by to service the machine. (*Courtesy of United Nations.*)

World War II. The Ruhr, the industrial district of the Rhineland, and the one focused on Stuttgart (626,075) in the upper Neckar Valley—all parts of the European coreland—are proving once again to be the basis of an integrated German national unit second to none in Europe.

A summary of the five regions and countries in each, by area and population, is given in Table XIII.

The English core focusing on London has the most strategically situated capital in Europe—directly in line and midway between the industrial districts of its own country to the north, northwest, and west, and the most important other industrial district of the continent, the German Ruhr. Of the four big-power capitals, London, Paris, Rome, and Berlin, London is the most centrally located within the core region of Europe. It is in the most accessible position for trade with more of the important industrial districts of Europe than any other major center, yet it is protected by the open waters of the English Channel, as by a moat, from ready military access in time of war. Neither Napoleon nor Hitler chose to try invasion by ship across the Channel.

Four of the small powers of the European core region lie between Germany and France. The focus of Holland is the regional conurbation of Rotterdam (*811,144*)-The Hague (*728,099*)-Haarlem (*215,003*)-Utrecht (252,892)-Amsterdam (*917,460*), with a primary focus on Amsterdam. The core of Belgium is the combined metropolitan regions of Antwerp (*584,395*) and Brussels (*955,929*), with primary focus in Brussels. The core region of Luxemburg is

the city of Luxemburg (71,612). The core of Switzerland is in the Swiss plateau, which has its primary focus at Zurich (*519,600*), although the political capital is located in Berne (*217,700*). Austria, a new neutral on the scene, focuses traditionally on Vienna (1,656,292).

The highly developed character of the core region. Three criteria will be used to demonstrate the advanced developments characteristic of the European core region, in contrast with the four peripheral regions.

1. Composite urban hinterlands of cities over 100,000 population.

2. Per cent production of European engineering exports.

3. Proportion of working population employed in industry.

A more precise idea of the urban pattern of Europe than that provided by urban-rural ratios by countries is given by the distribution of cities which have more than 100,000 inhabitants. The map in Figure 83 shows this pattern by means of the number of overlapping hinterlands of 100-miles radius drawn around each such large city. The north-south alignment of the European core region stands out from the pattern designating the overlapping of five or more urban hinterlands. The alignment extends from Scotland on the north end to north Italy on the south end. Another alignment, with one gap in Germany, extends from Calais, on the English Channel, to the Polish border on the east.

Within these alignments there are several specially concentrated urban areas. Outside of them almost

TABLE XIII REGIONS OF EUROPE, COUNTRIES, AREAS, AND POPULATIONS, 1950–1960

Regions	Rank in area, whole country	Rank in population, whole country	Country name, or part of country	Area, thousands of sq. mi.	Population, millions, 1950	Population, millions, 1960
Mediterranean or Southern Europe	1	4	Mediterranean France	20.5	4.2	4.5
	2	5	Spain, less Basques	192.3	27.3	28.8
	7	3	Italy, less Po Valley	85.9	34.8	36.0
	12	15	Greece	50.5	7.6	8.2
	18	14	Portugal	35.4	8.5	8.5
	27	30	Andorra	0.2	0.005	0.007
	29	29	San Marino	0.02	0.01	0.02
	30	27	Monaco	0.006	0.02	0.02
	31	31	Vatican	—	0.001	0.001
			Subtotal	384.826	82.436	86.048
Scandinavian or Northern Europe	3	17	Sweden	173.6	7.1	7.4
	4	21	Finland	130.1	4.1	4.1
	5	22	Norway	125.1	3.3	3.5
			Svalbard and Jan Mayen Is.	24.1	—	—
	16	26	Iceland	39.8	0.1	0.1
	21	20	Denmark	16.6	4.3	4.5
			Faeroe Is.	0.5	—	—
			Subtotal	509.8	18.9	19.6
Celtic Fringe or Atlantic Europe	10	2	Northern Scotland, Wales, Northern Ireland	33.7	4.7	5.5
	20	23	Ireland	27.1	2.8	2.8
	1	4	Brittany (Fr.)	13.6	3.7	4.0
	2	5	Basque (Sp.)	2.7	1.0	1.1
			Subtotal	77.1	12.2	13.4
Slavic or Eastern Europe	6	6	Poland	120.4	25.0	28.8
	8	8	Yugoslavia	98.8	16.9	18.6
	9	9	Rumania	91.7	16.1	18.1
	13	10	Czechoslovakia	49.4	12.3	13.5
	14	16	Bulgaria	42.8	7.2	7.8
	15	7	East Germany	41.9	18.1	17.4
	17	12	Hungary	35.9	9.3	9.9
	25	24	Albania	11.1	1.2	1.5
			Subtotal	492.0	106.1	115.6
Industrial Core of Europe	1	4	France, less Mediterranean Brittany	178.7	34.6	36.3
	7	3	West Central Po (It.)	30.4	12.2	12.7
	9	1	West Germany	95.5	51.8	54.4
	10	2	U. K. less Northern Scotland, etc.	60.5	45.5	46.3
	19	18	Austria	32.4	6.9	7.0
	22	19	Switzerland	15.9	4.8	5.2
	24	13	Belgium	11.8	8.7	9.1
	23	11	Netherlands	12.5	10.4	11.3
	26	25	Luxemburg	1.0	0.3	0.3
	28	28	Lichtenstein	0.06	0.01	0.01
			Subtotal	439.0	175.2	182.6
			Total	1,902.8	394.8	417.2

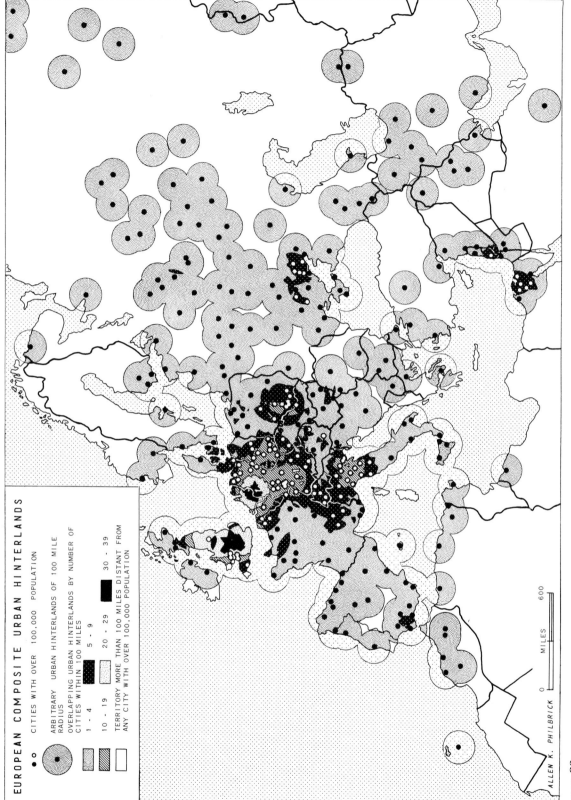

EUROPEAN COMPOSITE URBAN HINTERLANDS

- ● ○ CITIES WITH OVER 100,000 POPULATION

ARBITRARY URBAN HINTERLANDS OF 100 MILE
RADIUS

OVERLAPPING URBAN HINTERLANDS BY NUMBER OF
CITIES WITHIN 100 MILES

1 - 4   5 - 9

10 - 19   20 - 29   30 - 39

TERRITORY MORE THAN 100 MILES DISTANT FROM
ANY CITY WITH OVER 100,000 POPULATION

0   600
|——————————|
MILES

ALLEN K. PHILBRICK

Figure 83

143

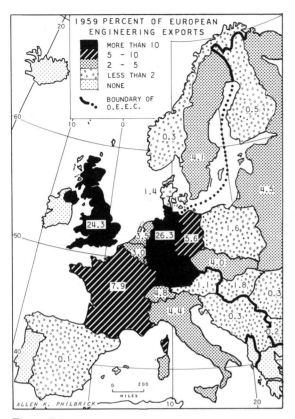

ALLEN K. PHILBRICK

Figure 84

the Silesian industrial district of Poland.

A second criterion of high development for the European core region is illustrated in the map in Figure 84. Here the core region is shown by the per cent of European engineering products exported.[1] Among engineering products are machine tools which produce the machines of production. The building of the *means of production* and engineering products generally are especially important criteria of industrial maturity and "know-how," for it is from the producers of the machinery of production and engineering that new developments of manufacturing capacity usually originate. West Germany and the United Kingdom lead in this respect. The map shows that seven of the countries of the core region—France, Switzerland, Italy, the Netherlands and Belgium, in addition to the first two —combined produce nearly 85 per cent of Europe's machine tools.

The third criterion of high development is the proportion of the work force engaged in industrial occupations. The map in Figure 85 is based on minor civil divisions of countries.[2] The data "around 1930" reflects conditions during a period when Europe was more united functionally than it is today. The present-day line of the "Iron Curtain" has been superimposed on this map, however. Population working in industry includes mining, handicrafts, and construction as well as those employed in factory-type production.

For purposes of discussing the pattern of industrial employment in relation to the core region of Europe, reference should be made to the diagrammatic shapes in the inset to the map in Figure 85. Europe is a right triangle in shape. A circle within the triangle encompasses the center of Europe from the southern tip of Scandinavia to the northern half of the Italian Peninsula. Outside the circle lie the European margins in which less than 15 per cent of the working population is engaged in industrial pursuits. Within the circle the proportion is more than 15 per cent. Only very small, scattered districts have an industrial labor force of more than 15 per cent of the working population outside this circle. Inside the circle in the diagram is an isosceles triangle. Its apex corresponds to Scotland on the northwest and its base is a line running diagonally from Marseilles (661,492) on the

[1]Organization of European Economic Cooperation, *The Engineering Industries in Europe,* New York, 1960, p. 105.

[2]U. S. Dept. of Agriculture, *Agricultural Geography of Europe and the Near East,* Misc. Pub. No. 665, Washington: U. S. Government Printing Office, p. 21.

any place in Europe is within 100 miles of from one to four cities of more than 100,000 in population. Only a few places in Europe are more than 100 miles distant from at least one large city. At the other extreme it can be seen from the map in Figure 83 that central England and the lower Rhine Valley, which includes the Ruhr district, are the most densely urbanized areas of the continent. They are also the most concentrated in this respect for the world as a whole. There is one area in the center of England which is within 100 miles of more than forty cities of more than 100,000 inhabitants. The lower Rhine valley approaches that concentration with more than thirty cities with overlapping hinterlands. The continuity of the urban alignment from the upper Rhine and Switzerland to north Italy is all the more remarkable, when it is remembered that the core region, thus defined, crosses the so-called "barrier" of the Alps.

East of the "Iron Curtain" there are enough large cities close enough to one onother to produce two areas comprising partial overlapping of more than twenty urban hinterlands of 100-miles radius. One of these areas is in East Germany; the other is

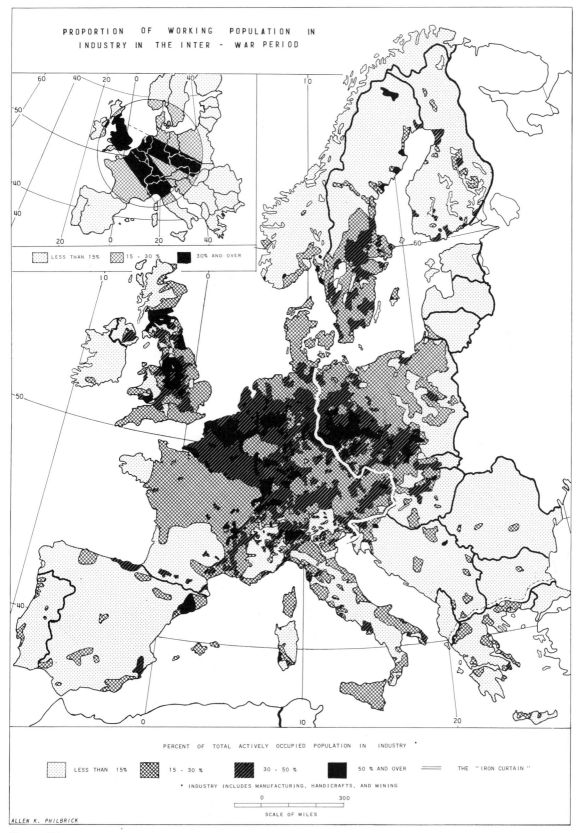

PROPORTION OF WORKING POPULATION IN INDUSTRY IN THE INTER - WAR PERIOD

LESS THAN 15%   15 - 30 %   30% AND OVER

PERCENT OF TOTAL ACTIVELY OCCUPIED POPULATION IN INDUSTRY *

LESS THAN 15%   15 - 30 %   30 - 50 %   50 % AND OVER   THE "IRON CURTAIN"

* INDUSTRY INCLUDES MANUFACTURING, HANDICRAFTS, AND MINING

0   300

SCALE OF MILES

ALLEN K. PHILBRICK

Figure 85

south to Breslau (now Wroclaw, 429,000) in Poland on the northeast. Within this triangle the proportion of the total working population engaged in industry rises to more than 30 per cent. A scattered pattern of urban industrial districts in which industrial employment accounted for more than half of the labor force during the 1930's is shown in white. The alignments of these more concentrated urban-industrial districts on the map in Figure 85 are the same as the overlapping hinterland alignments visualized on the map in Figure 83. The inner isosceles triangle can be viewed as having two "legs" which form an inverted "V." The western or left "leg" of the inverted "V" is the core region of Western Europe extending from Scotland to northern Italy. The other leg, which extends in a more southeasterly direction to Polish Silesia, represents the former eastern extension of Europe's industrial core region. It is now located in the Soviet zone of influence, cut off from Western Europe by the "Iron Curtain," and is oriented toward the Soviet economy.

The Resources Used to Build the Pattern of Occupancy

What are the resources with which Europeans have constructed this complex pattern of activities? How do they feed and clothe themselves? Whence come the resources which keep the industrial districts supplied with raw materials? These patterns of physical resources will be discussed under three main headings—subsurface structure and surface zones, resource associations for agriculture, and mineral resources.

Gross Pattern of Subsurface Structure and Surface Zones.

Four district zones extending irregularly from west to east characterize the subsurface and surface of Europe. From north to south, as shown on the map in Figure 86, they are:

1. The Scandinavian metamorphic shield with an outlier in northern Scotland.
2. The North European Plain, which is a portion of the largest sedimentary lowland on earth—the great Eurasian Plain extending and widening from England on the west across western Russia to the east.
3. A complex checkerboard of ancient metamorphic massives and intermontane plains which narrows eastward to the Black Sea.
4. The Alpine mountain system.

The first, second, and fourth zones above correspond to the three structural zone types discussed generally for the world as a whole in Chapter 4, and shown in Figure 36. The third zone may be regarded as transitional between the sedimentary lowlands and the European Alpine system, a portion of the world zone of crustal instability. Zones three and four, particularly, are divided into regional subdivisions which are important to understanding Europe. Both ancient massives and more recently folded mountains compartmentalize Europe into lowland regions interconnected by lowland gaps and highland passes through surrounding uplands.

The folded Alpine mountain system is a looping and twisting line of crustal weakness. From the Bay of Biscay on the Atlantic it may be traced along the crest of the Pyrenees. From the Mediterranean end of these mountains is plunges below the sea, appearing only as the peaks of submerged mountains in the islands of the Majorca group, emerging again in southern Spain as the Sierra Nevadas. Crossing at Gibraltar, the zone bends sharply eastward along the alignment of the Atlas Mountains of North Africa. It jumps the Mediterranean again to the Apennines of Italy by way of the island of Sicily. Looping around the basin of the western Mediterranean to the northwest up the center of Italy, the Alpine mountain zone bends sharply north and eastward in the Alps proper which surround the Po Valley. At the eastern end of the Austrian Alps the zones breaks into two branches. One branch forms the coastal ranges of the southern Balkans along the Adriatic Sea, leading to Greece and the islands of the Aegean Sea. The other loops northward and eastward around the Hungarian Plain as the Carpathian Mountains. Turning southward and westward to the Danube River as the Transylvanian Alps, the Alpine system, now known as the Balkan Range, disappears under the waters of the Black Sea. The zone emerges above the surface again as the Crimean Peninsula of southern Russia and continues as the Caucasus Mountains of the Soviet Union.

The subsurface regions of Europe are divided into two significant groups on the map in Figure 86. The categories will be called, for simplicity, *old* and *young*. The category marked *old* in the legend is itself subdivided into two parts. One of the two subdivisions consists of ancient metamorphic crystalline rocks; the other consists of the oldest sedimentary rocks—selected areas of Paleozoic sediments. Reasons for grouping ancient

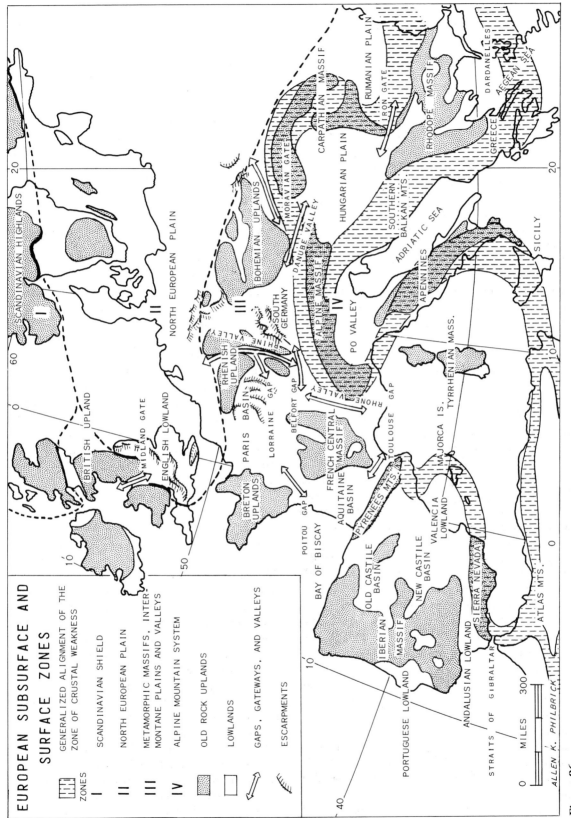

EUROPEAN SUBSURFACE AND SURFACE ZONES

GENERALIZED ALIGNMENT OF THE ZONE OF CRUSTAL WEAKNESS

ZONES

I   SCANDINAVIAN SHIELD

II   NORTH EUROPEAN PLAIN

III   METAMORPHIC MASSIFS, INTERMONTANE PLAINS AND VALLEYS

IV   ALPINE MOUNTAIN SYSTEM

OLD ROCK UPLANDS

LOWLANDS

GAPS, GATEWAYS, AND VALLEYS

ESCARPMENTS

ALLEN K. PHILBRICK

0   MILES   300

Figure 86

147

metamorphosed and old sedimentaries together will be apparent in the section of this chapter devoted to minerals. Both of the old-rock regions contain tougher rocks which form rough uplands. The second category, designated as *young*, consists of younger sedimentary areas which are less hardened and which underlie the lowland plains of Europe. This distinction between age and hardness and, therefore, resistance to erosion, is at least in part, responsible for the striking pattern of plains of young sedimentary origin surrounded by isolated old-rock uplands. Such a fragmented pattern seems to contradict the first interpretation of European subsurface structure as a series of east-to-west trending zones, yet the two are not incompatible. They are interpretations at different scales. It is readily apparent that the fragmented pattern is contained within the more general zonal one. Accordingly, north of the Alpine system but south of the great northern European Plain, an arc of alternately rough and level uplands and plains respectively, swings in a clockwise direction from the Pyrenees to the Balkans.

From the Mediterranean through the Toulouse-Carcassone Gap, a lowland route widens into the Aquitaine Basin in southwestern France. The basin lies between the Massif Central of France, the Pyrenees Mountains, and the Bay of Biscay. To the northeast the Poitou Gap between the Massif Central and the old-rock highlands of Brittany leads into the Paris Basin. Just east of the Toulouse Gap the north-south trending Rhone-Soane Valley begins. It, too, flanks the French Massif Central and the loop of the French-Italian Alps, which, in turn separates the Po Valley of Italy from France. To the north and between the Rhenish Upland and the Alps is the east-west trending Burgundian or Belfort Gap, which leads into the upper Rhine at Basel. From this pivot, routes are accessible eastward into south Germany, or east and then southward into the Swiss Plateau, or northward and down into the "graben" or rift valley of the middle Rhine.

The Rhenish Upland is split by the north-south trending Rhine Valley, which escapes through the Rhine Gorge into the Rhine delta marking the margin of the north European Plain on the North Sea. The middle Rhine Valley may be considered to extend from Cologne (770,715) to Basel (286,400). The Rhine Gorge covers that portion of the river from Cologne to the bend just west of Mainze (128,193). From Mainze to Basel the river course travels in a rift valley which comprises the upper-middle Rhine. Tributaries have eroded transverse gateways through the old-rock uplands on either side of the rift valley. One important opening into the Rhine Graben from France is the Lorraine Gap. Through it today, the Marne-Rhine Canal connects Paris with Strasbourg (238,749) on the Rhine River. On the northern slopes of the Rhenish upland, passage through the Ardennes forest is afforded by the valley of the Meuse River to the great northern plain into which the Rhine empties north of Cologne.

Access to the North European Plain is also afforded from south Germany between the Rhenish Upland and the Bohemian Massif through a region of complex low mountains which have been dissected and penetrated by the Weser River and its tributaries on the west and the Elbe River and its tributaries on the east. To the east the plain and plateau country of south Germany is drained by way of the valley of the Danube into the interior plains of Hungary. This flat alluvial floor of internal drainage surrounded by the Alps, the Carpathians, and the Transylvanian Alps possesses two additional gateways. One, the Moravian Gate—between the Bohemian upland and the Carpathians—leads into southern Poland. It is an ancient entry to Europe through which nomadic peoples from the plains of Russia have ever pressed into central Europe. The other is the famous Iron Gate, where the Danube escapes through a gorge in the Transylvanian Alps to flow eastward into the Black Sea.

The east-west direction of the Alpine alignment of mountain ranges, intermontane plains, and foot hills means that virtually no upland barrier is presented to marine air masses from the Atlantic Ocean—the Westerlies—which sweep moisture-laden air deep into the heart of Europe. This circumstance accounts for the deep penetration of warming marine air into the continental interior, and for the general trend from humid to less humid and finally dry conditions progressively from west to east in Europe.

An example of this warming influence is the fact that the ice during the last glaciation penetrated equatorward less far in Europe than it did in the corresponding glaciation of North America. The southward reach of the ice sheet crossed 50 degrees north latitude only in more continental Russia north of the Black Sea. In North America, as will be seen in Chapter 12, glaciation extended well south of the fortieth parallel. This line from the Netherlands to Russia marks the break of the North European Plain with higher land to the south, either hill country or low plateaus. Great quantities of wind-blown silt collected along and upon the south margins of the European Plain during the immediate postglacial period. This material, known by the German word "loess," forms a very important constituent of the soils where it has collected. Such loessial soils are among the world's most fertile. The aeolian soils later became stabilized in position through the growth of trees and grasses.

Resource Associations for Agriculture. In describing the resources important to agriculture, four elements which vary in quality from place to place within Europe as a whole are depicted in composite on a map in Figure 87. The criteria shown in maps in Figures 88, 89, and 90 are: amount of precipitation, duration of the growing season, surface configuration, and type of soil, respectively. Each of the criteria except soils is presented in terms of one selected measure. This cannot be accomplished for soils. Loess, alluvial-transported soils, and residual black-earth grasslands along with brown to gray-brown forested soils are combined as exhibiting the greatest natural fertility. All other soil groups are regarded as less fertile. With respect to moisture the 20-inch average annual isohyet was selected to separate dry from humid regions. Ninety days duration of the growing season was selected to separate short from moderate length of the frost-free period. Three months is regarded as the shortest time interval in which most grain crops may mature. The predominantly level surfaces characteristic of the major plains and plateau regions are assumed to distinguish them from the rough lands of hilly and mountainous areas.

The map in Figure 88 recording humid and dry conditions demonstrates that Europe is basically a *humid* continent. From Iceland on the north and in an irregularly clockwise circuit through northernmost Scandinavia to the north portion of the Ural Mountains in Russia, thence southwesterly to the Black Sea, the 20-inch precipitation line bends eastward almost as far as the Caspian Sea and around Turkey. From the northern Middle East the line approaches the east coast of the Mediterranean Sea. Thence it follows the basin of the Mediterranean between Africa and the islands of Crete, Sicily, and Corsica to the coast of Spain. This irregularly circuitous line, as may be seen on the

map, is the inner edge of the great Arid Crescent which virtually encircles the North Atlantic region of western Europe and eastern North America. (See also the map in Figure 31 of Chapter 3.)

The map in Figure 89 showing length of growing season has the most nearly latitudinal pattern. The line of ninety days growing season approximates the sixtieth parallel. Frost-free conditions prevail poleward as far as southern Spain, southern Greece, Sicily, Cyprus, and southern Turkey. Nearly frost-free conditions touch the north shore of the Mediterranean, except in the northernmost Aegean, Adriatic, and Ligurian embayments of that sea. But the pattern of growing-season duration also shows the effect of marine versus continental position to some extent. The category "nearly frost-free" extends on the Atlantic coast as far north along the Iberian Peninsula as 42 degrees north latitude. At the eastern end of the Mediterranean it reaches only 37 degrees north latitude. Still further to the east it dips markedly equatorward to 25 degrees north latitude east of the Persian Gulf. Duration of the growing season changes rapidly with differences in elevation, exposure, and certain other conditions.

Soils are the most complex association of physical circumstances. The map in Figure 90 shows loess soil accumulations along the foothills of the central and southern European highlands. Narrow ribbons of alluvial deposition occur in the many river valleys which thread their way toward the seas from a once primarily forested continent. Gray-brown and brown podzolic forest soils and black-earth grassland soils are the residual cover over most of the North European Plain and the lowlands and lower slopes of intervening old-rock uplands in plateau and hill country north of the Alpine system. North of the European Plain, podzolization has produced less fertile soils. To the south, rocky uplands are characterized by lithosols, which are the surface soils over rock and steep rocky slopes. They are mostly shallow and stony soils which are low in productivity. To the east of the black-earth regions, aridity reduces both natural organic content and productivity of the soils. Therefore, outward in all directions from a long east-west belt of medium to highly fertile forest soils, and very fertile black-earth grassland soils, productivity decreases—north, south, and east. It will readily be appreciated that this diminution of productivity corresponds also with shorter growing season poleward and with longer growing season, summer

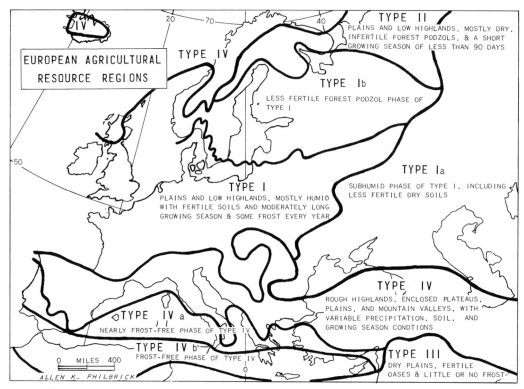

Figure 87

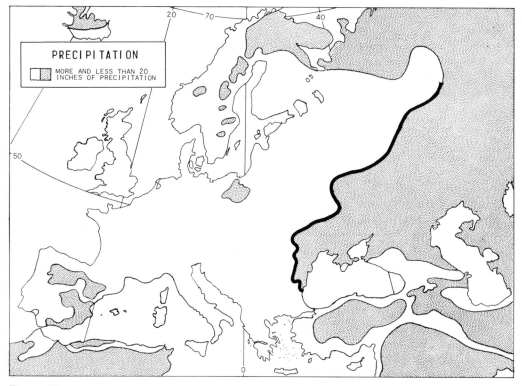

Figure 88

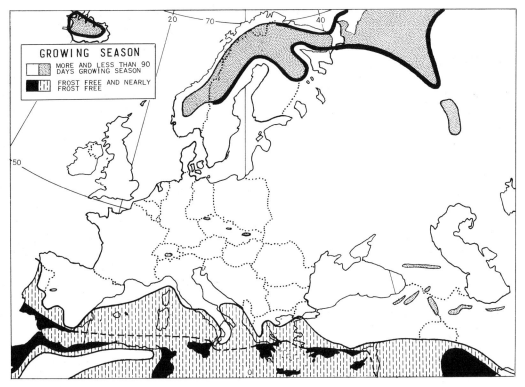

Figure 89

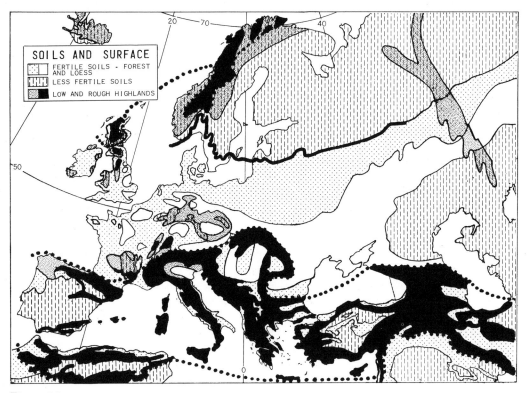

Figure 90

151

drought, and winter precipitation equatorward on the European side of the Sahara.

The composite map in Figure 87 shows that over a very high proportion of the total area of Europe, all four of a certain set of conditions prevail. There are very extensive areas where level land with medium to high soil fertility receives more than twenty inches of precipitation annually, and experiences warmth without frost for more than ninety consecutive days each year. The regions bordering this central region characterized by the above set of conditions are in marked contrast. To the north it is rougher, colder, and wetter. To the east it is considerably drier. To the south it is drier and hotter, particularly in the summer months, as the duration of the growing season lengthens. Across the Mediterranean, Europe is bounded on the south by the great expanse of the Sahara Desert, a land without winter or dependable water supply.

Agricultural-Producing Areas in National Economies. There is a tendency for each country to produce its own staples, such as bread grains, sugar, and root or grass crops for livestock. Agricultural products are sold within each country on the basis of the evolved division of labor between farm and city, and to a certain extent they also enter into international trade on the basis of a larger regional division of labor.

Each of the countries of Europe has a distinctive pattern of agricultural production which is characteristic for each of Europe's five regions. Each country, depending on the circumstances of its agricultural resources, has a "best agricultural region," which may be regarded as its "breadbasket" or agricultural heartland. These are shown on the map in Figure 91, and should be compared with the distribution of wheat production in Figure 92, sugar beets in Figure 93, and cattle in Figure 94. The best agricultural region in each country is not necessarily the equivalent in quality to that of its neighbors'. Each nation must do the best it can with the resources available.

In France, for example, it is the humid Paris Basin and the Rhone-Soane Valley which together connect it to the Mediterranean Sea. Wheat and other grains, sugar beets, dairy products, and livestock are produced in the Paris Basin. Near the great urban markets truck gardening is important. The great north-south interconnecting valley of the Rhone-Soane Rivers is particularly noted for wheat and vineyards. Spain's breadbasket is the semiarid central plateau region of pastoral livestock raising

and large-scale grain farming. In the Low Countries of Belgium and the Netherlands diversified truck farming and dairying predominate in the reclaimed polder lands, as well as in the sandy and loamy plains with loess deposits north of the forested Ardennes uplands. West Germany's best agricultural regions are the loess-soil southern margins of the North European Plain, the Rhine Valley and its bordering eastern uplands. The better land in East Germany is also along the southern margins of the North European Plain. The heart of Switzerland is the northern Swiss Plateau, while that of Italy is the Po River Valley and the eastern edge of the south Italian Peninsula around Foggia. In the Scandinavian countries, except for Denmark where the best land is on the east side of the peninsula, it is the southern tips of Norway, Sweden, and Finland which provide practically the only areas with suitable combinations of resources for agriculture. Dairying predominates, but wheat and other food crops are grown as extensively as possible.

In Eastern Europe, Poland's best farm land lies along the southern margins of the North European Plain, again, where loess soils are the most productive. The agricultural heart of Czechoslovakia is in the plains of Bohemia, which are surrounded by the uplands of the Bohemian Massif. In the south great alluvial plains of Hungary and Rumania are divided among Hungary, Yugoslavia, Rumania, and Bulgaria. The granary of Greece is along that country's eastern and northern margins. Each of the above districts is that part of the country where the staple crops for everyday existence are produced, rather than specialized crops for export. In the next sections one country from each of Europe's five regions will be discussed in more detail as a sample of the region.

France as an example of agriculture within the core region. Outside the agricultural heartland of France in the northeast, other parts of the country are more specialized. In the center and south vineyards produce the wine for which France is famous in such river valleys as the Loire, the Garonne, the Meuse, the Soane, and the Rhone. In the northwest uplands of the Breton Peninsula the farms have hedgerows and trees separating the fields. This type of country is known locally as the "Bocage" as opposed to the rolling, treeless farmland of the Paris basin—the "Champagne." The Bocage is less fertile, and as recently as the turn of the present century was still organized predominantly on a subsistence basis. With improved trans-

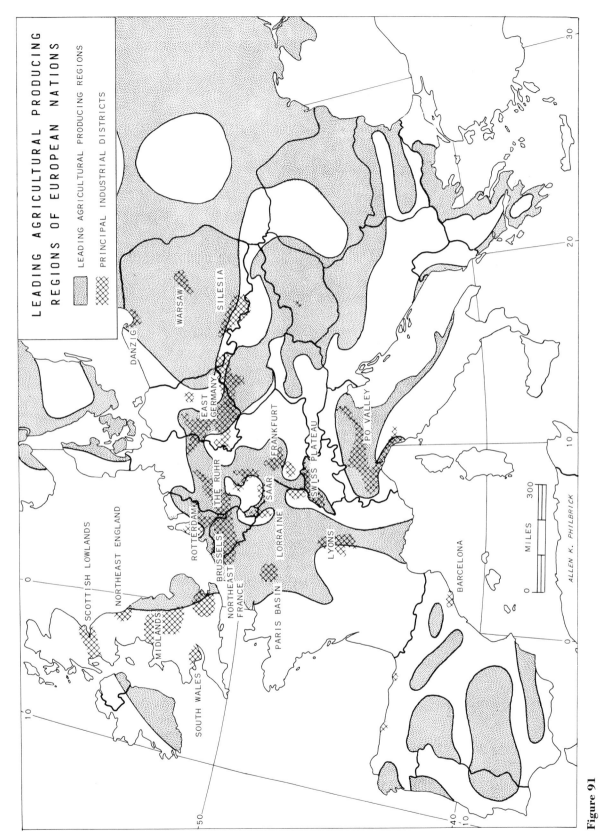

LEADING AGRICULTURAL PRODUCING
REGIONS OF EUROPEAN NATIONS

LEADING AGRICULTURAL PRODUCING REGIONS

PRINCIPAL INDUSTRIAL DISTRICTS

WARSAW

SILESIA

DANZIG

EAST
GERMANY

FRANKFURT

THE RUHR

SAAR

SWISS PLATEAU

PO VALLEY

ROTTERDAM

BRUSSELS

LORRAINE

LYONS

NORTHEAST
FRANCE

PARIS BASIN

BARCELONA

SCOTTISH LOWLANDS

NORTHEAST ENGLAND

MIDLANDS

SOUTH WALES

MILES

0   300

ALLEN K. PHILBRICK

Figure 91

153

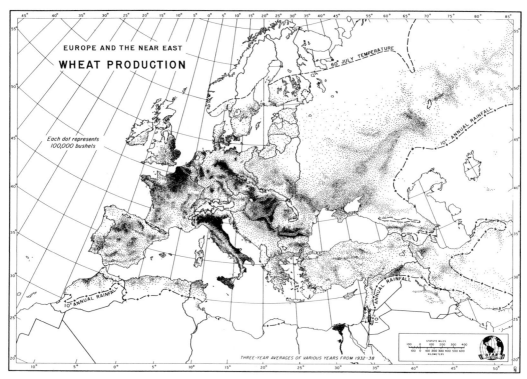

Figure 92. (*Courtesy of U. S. Dept. of Agriculture, taken from* Agricultural Geography of Europe and the Near East, *1948.*)

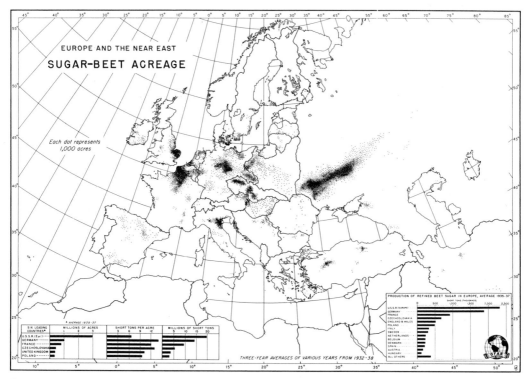

Figure 93. (*Courtesy of U. S. Dept. of Agriculture, taken from* Agricultural Geography of Europe and the Near East, *1948.*)

portation, however, the farmers specialize in milk, cheese, meat, and market produce for northeastern urban markets. In the southwest of France two regions are outstanding. The pine-planted sandy plains of the Landes coastal region south and west of Bordeaux is the region from which come forest products such as turpentine, mine pit props, and timber; while in the basin of Aquitaine, grains, tobacco, fruits, and early vegetables are produced. Between Aquitaine and the Rhone Valley is the Massif Central, which is divided between a northern half devoted to cattle grazing and only limited cultivation, and a pastoral southern half devoted primarily to sheep raising. East of the Rhone are the French Alps. Wheat, oats, corn, and cattle characterize a pre-Alpine section, while grazing of both cattle and sheep predominates in the Alps proper. In the extreme south of France, along the Riviera, the traditional Mediterranean crops of olives, grapes, and wheat have in recent years shared importance with citrus fruits, flowers, and early vegetables. Products of the southern specialty-crop zone are marketed throughout France, particularly in Paris. Each specialized production region is well-interconnected with principal markets by a well-developed pattern of road, rail, and canal routes.

Spain-Portugal as examples of agricultural production in the Mediterranean region of Europe. Surrounding the grazing and extensive grain region of the interior Meseta are three specialized agricultural regions. These are the northern mountain-pasture zone, a northern coastal hill-farming region, and a peripheral Mediterranean region. Both of these countries are primarily agricultural in their economies. Each represents to a considerable degree a survival of subsistence agricultural organization of area. Only two crops—olives and grapes—enter significantly into export trade. Agricultural practices are backward. Fallowing rather than fertilizing is used to restore soil fertility. Crops are grown to yield food for direct consumption. In the coastal hill-farming region of northern Spain products are corn, potatoes, root-forage crops, and cattle. Products of the Mediterranean belt are adapted to winter rain and summer drought. Vineyards and cold-susceptible, drought-resistant tree crops such as cork and olives are of primary importance in both Spain and Portugal. Citrus fruits are also grown. Subsistence farming prevails in the growing of

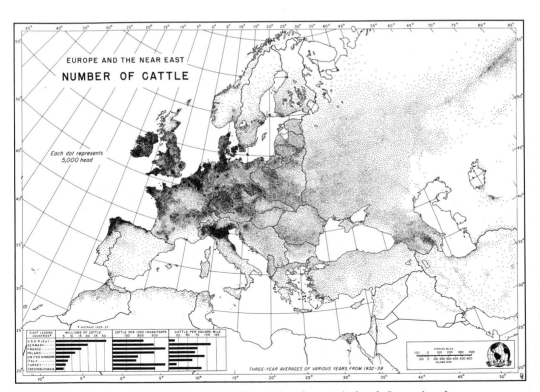

Figure 94. (*Courtesy of U. S. Dept. of Agriculture, taken from* Agricultural Geography of Europe and the Near East, *1948.*)

wheat, vegetables, and barley, with or without irrigation, along with sheep, goats, and cattle. These characteristics of a primarily agricultural economy which yields a generally low-level subsistence living standard fit all the countries of the Mediterranean region.

Sweden, an example of agriculture in the Scandinavian region. A century ago Sweden's agriculture was principally one of local subsistence. Now, however, a primarily commercial dairy economy has developed. Southern Sweden produces enough wheat, potatoes, and garden vegetables to contribute substantially toward Sweden's growing commercial and industrial economy. There are three agricultural zones from north to south in southern Sweden. These are the central lowland west of Stockholm, the Smaland Plateau, and the southern coastal plain. The Smaland Plateau, an ancient crystalline upland, is largely forested. There the people specialize in forest industries. The southern coastal plain is used to produce dairy products which are exported to Germany. Sweden's best agricultural land in the central lowland is also mainly a dairy region, but it is also used in more diversified grain and livestock production for the national market. Forestry and an emphasis on forest products, an agriculture primarily oriented toward dairy production for domestic consumption and export, and only partial fulfillment of the basic food requirements of the nation, is the pattern of characteristics substantially reproduced by the agriculture of each Scandinavian country. Denmark and Iceland are exceptions. Forests are unimportant in Denmark, where the emphasis is on production for export to the industrial districts of neighboring industrial countries. Iceland is treeless and is not primarily an agricultural country. Products of the sea supplant the products of the land in Iceland's economy.

Hungary, an example of agricultural production in Eastern Europe. Hungary, part of the former Austrian-Hungarian Empire, is mainly a plains country, with small parts of its area in hill land. The plains are composed of loess grassland soils, one of the more fertile black-earth regions of the world. The Hungarian Plain consists of two parts called the *Little Alfold* and the *Great Alfold,* separated by the Bakoney Forest which occupies a low, limestone ridgeland between them. Southwest Hungary is hilly land. The two-thirds of Hungary which is plain provides wheat, rye, oats, and corn. Sugar beets and grapes are also grown. Formerly much of the land was in large estates, but land reform both before and since the communizing of Hungary has reduced the amount of land in private estates. Collectivization has not been completed in Hungary. More than 10 per cent of the arable land is in model state farms patterned after those of the Soviet Union, and possibly half of the agricultural land has been brought into the collectives; but too many of Hungary's farmers are passionately devoted to the idea of owning their own land and have resisted collectivization. The trend, however, is toward larger units of farm management and the cooperative use of machinery. The granary characteristics of the Hungarian Plain fit the agricultural patterns of Eastern Europe generally, particularly Rumania, Bulgaria, and northern Yugoslavia. In Poland rye and potatoes are a larger part of total production than is wheat. In all of the countries of Eastern Europe the balance between urban and industrial development and agriculture is changing in favor of manufactures; yet the region is still agricultural in emphasis.

Ireland, an example of agricultural production in Europe's Atlantic Fringe region. The west coast of Europe is the most humid region of the continent —and also the cloudiest. Only two relatively small regions of eastern Ireland may be called crop land: the northeastern and the northwestern corners of the island, which are somewhat sunnier and less humid than the rest. Flax, potatoes, oats, some wheat, barley, and sugar beets are grown in both of these districts. In the north flax is the basis of Northern Ireland's linen industry. Root crops, supplementing the grazing of livestock in the central plains, are emphasized in the southern region of Ireland. Meat and dairy products are the largest exports from Ireland, and are shipped primarily to the United Kingdom. The importance of livestock and dairy products is typical of the "Atlantic Fringe" region.

In each of the examples presented above, individual national production of agriculture has a double orientation. On one hand, each is principally directed toward the service of the national economy of which it is a part. On the other hand, each agricultural sector contributes to the functioning of other national economies through international trade. This is particularly true of the trade by countries of the European peripheral regions with countries of the core and represents a significant part of the functional unity of the continental economy as a whole.

Mineral Resources. The evolution of a more

than local geographical division of labor accompanied the development of commercial agriculture in Europe. The evolution of patterns of trade and the manufacturing of articles for trade is in part based on the mineral resources of the earth's subsurface. As observed in Chapter 4, they may be classified into three principal categories—*mineral fuels, metals,* and *nonmetals.* The distribution of the occurrence of exploitable minerals in each of the above categories is associated with the patterns of metamorphic and sedimentary rocks. The map in Figure 95 repeats the pattern of two categories of subsurface regions shown earlier in Figure 86. These two categories were called *old* and *young.* Within the areas marked as "old" a dividing line between metamorphic or crystalline rocks and old sediments is also shown. The major old-rock districts of Europe are listed in Table XIV and are classified according to the subsurface zones to which they belong. Each of these specific blocks of old sedimentary and still older metamorphic rocks is a relatively compact, generally oval or triangular-shaped territory. Each is also a highland area of mountainous, hilly, or rough terrain.

The map in Figure 95 shows the proximity of coal and iron-ore deposits to one another in the vicinity of parts of each of the older rock regions listed in the table. Three of the old-rock uplands which combine ancient metamorphic rocks and the oldest sediments are particularly rich in a number of large coal measures, and, at not a great distance, in iron-ore deposits as well. These three are the British Uplands, the Rhenish Uplands, and the Bohemian or Upper Silesian Uplands. Coal and iron deposits are also located relatively adjacent to each other in other of the old-rock areas; but they are smaller and less important occurrences. In the development of present-day manufacturing enterprises, large quantities of raw materials sufficient for production over a period of many years are required before the investment of the necessarily large amounts of capital in plants and facilities can be justified.

While these three regions are the basis of European heavy industry, other mineral-producing regions are important in supplying other metallic ores. As the manufacturing industries have developed and technological innovations have multiplied, the need for copper, lead, zinc, the steel alloy metals, aluminum, and many others has increased. The patterns of other principal metallic ores are also shown on the map in Figure 95. The relation-

TABLE XIV	REGIONS OF ANCIENT METAMORPHIC AND PALEOZOIC SEDIMENTARY ROCKS	
Major zone		*Major uplands of "old" rocks*
I. North European highlands		1. Scandinavian Highlands
		2. British Highlands
II. Central European plains and hill country		3. Brittany
		4. Iberian Massif
		5. French Massif Central
		6. Rhenish Upland
		7. Bohemian Upland
III. Alpine cordilleran region		8. Pyrenees Mountains
		9. Sierra Nevada Ranges
		10. Tyrrhenian Massif
		11. Alps Massif
		12. Carpathian Massif
		13. Rhodope Massif

ships of these patterns to metamorphic rock regions is strikingly apparent. In addition to metals, a variety of nonmetallic minerals, such as building stone, salt, sulfur, and other chemicals are also important. The pattern of "other" minerals spreads out more than that of the metallic ores; and it is clear that the majority of nonmetallic ores are of sedimentary origin.

Functional European Unity

The patterns of occupancy have evolved in European regions from the use of mineral resources for industry and the use of agricultural resources for the production of food. Despite the political division of Europe into thirty-one independent units, there is considerable functional unity within Europe as a whole because of the common focus which all the countries of peripheral regions have on the countries of the core region.

The Focus of Intra-West European Trade among Five European Regions. This common focus of European countries is expressed in terms of international trade and demonstrated in Table XV and the map in Figure 78. Both the table and the map show the division of the traditional continent of Europe into *two* separate functional units —free Europe and the Soviet Union, with East European satellites. Within each of these units the table shows the existence of a separate focusing of trade.

In the "West," for example, more than two-thirds of the imports of Scandinavian countries are derived from the countries of the industrial core (69 per cent). Imports of the Mediterranean region and the "Atlantic Fringe" region are also predominantly from the highly industrialized countries of the core region (76 and 90 per cent, respectively). In the

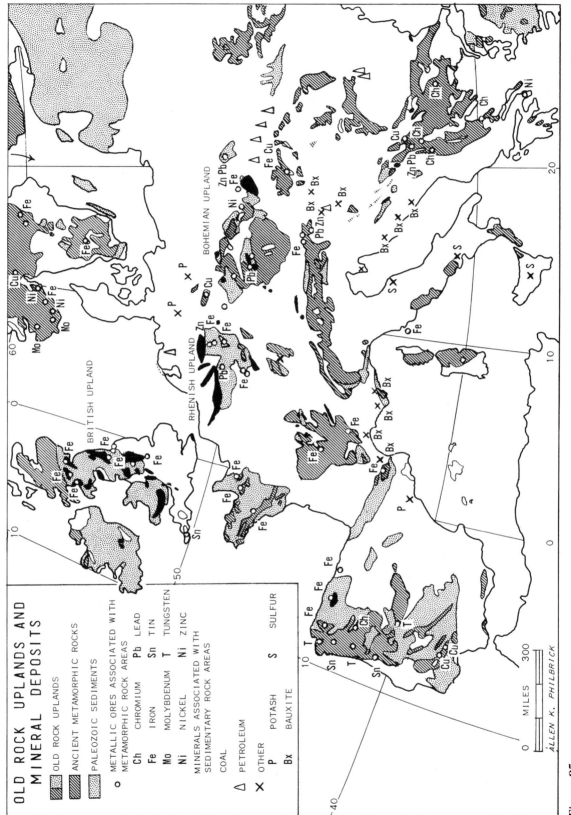

OLD ROCK UPLANDS AND
MINERAL DEPOSITS

☐ OLD ROCK UPLANDS
▨ ANCIENT METAMORPHIC ROCKS
▧ PALEOZOIC SEDIMENTS

METALLIC ORES ASSOCIATED WITH
○ METAMORPHIC ROCK AREAS

Ch CHROMIUM   Pb LEAD
Fe IRON   Sn TIN
Mo MOLYBDENUM T   TUNGSTEN
Ni NICKEL   Ni ZINC

MINERALS ASSOCIATED WITH
SEDIMENTARY ROCK AREAS

△ COAL
✕ OTHER   S   SULFUR
      P   POTASH
      Bx BAUXITE

MILES
0   300

ÁLLEN K. PHILBRICK

BRITISH UPLAND

RHENISH UPLAND

BOHEMIAN UPLAND

Figure 95

TABLE XV PER CENT OF IMPORTS AS A MEASURE OF THE DIRECTION OF TRADE AMONG FIVE EUROPEAN REGIONS, 1956[a]

Importing region	Core	Scandinavia	Atlantic fringe	Mediterranean	Total, west	Slavic, east	U.S.S.R.	Total, east	Total
Core	64	16	2	11	93	5	2	7	100
Scandinavia	69	16	...	4	89	6	5	11	100
Atlantic fringe	90	7	...	3	100	...	...	...	100
Mediterranean	76	11	...	6	93	6	1	7	100
Slavic, east	16	6	...	2	24	48	28	76	100
U.S.S.R.	14	9	...	2	25	75	...	75[b]	100

[a] Sources for the data for the countries of the "West" are: United Nations, *Direction of International Trade*, New York: 1957; for eastern Europe and the Soviet Union: United Nations, *Economic Survey of Europe*, Geneva: 1958.

[b] If the unspecified internal trade of the Soviet Union's republics with the R.S.F.S.R. were added to the total, percentages for this line of the table would be more in line in comparison with the core region of the "West."

"East," by contrast, the Slavic region and the Soviet Union are developing as a separate unit which focuses on Moscow and comprises a second core region. It is important to note that the countries of the core region are their own best markets. In terms of volume, considerably more than half of the trade of Europe as a whole passes between member nations of the core.

The focus of internal European international trade is even more meaningful when the kinds of commodities which move in exchange are considered. A group of maps in Figure 96 (A through G) shows the movement of selected commodities in intra-West European trade.[1] Map A shows the imports of timber from Scandinavia into the countries of the core. This movement represents saw timber and pit props for mining, but no pulp. Map B shows the movement of iron ore. Large amounts of iron ore from Sweden represent exports from the Kiruna district of northern Sweden to the principal iron- and steel-producing districts of England, Belgium, and Germany. France uses primarily the Lorraine ore within its own borders. Smaller amounts of iron ore from the north of Spain represent shipments of high-grade ores into England from Bilbao.

Map C shows the all-important mineral fuel, coal. Exports of coal from England and the Ruhr as well as from the Belgian coal fields are in two categories. One is the supply of coking coal for steel production and industrial coal to the manufacturing enterprises of the core countries. The second category is the supply of power and fuel to

[1] Lois Grotewold, *Intra-West European Trade*, unpublished M.S. thesis, Dept. of Geography, University of Chicago, Chicago, Illinois, 1954.

peripheral regions. The core receives needed iron ores and other metals from production points in peripheral regions. It, in turn, supplies mineral fuels for heat and power to the countries of the peripheral regions of Europe.

The remaining four maps represent the movements of specialized food products: fruit (D), vegetables (E), meat (F), and livestock (G). The map of the movement of fruit illustrates the complementary trade in citrus and other fruits from subtropical Mediterranean farms to northern urban markets. The same is true for vegetables. Products from specialized meat, and dairy-producing agricultural areas of the Low Countries, Denmark, and Ireland are represented by the maps of meat and livestock movements. These maps are a sample drawn from diversified trade in industrial raw materials and foods which flows between the parts of the continental economy considered as a unit of separate and competing parts. They are a one-sided sample, however. In addition to imported raw materials, fuels, and foods, European trade among countries of the continent is heavily committed to finished products of manufacture. Textiles, metal goods, machinery of all types, both producer goods and consumer items, move in large quantities as exports of the countries of the core region to each other and the nations of the European periphery.

A United Europe? One of the great driving ideas in Europe since Roman times has been that of uniting Europeans under one common, organized leadership. Efforts to accomplish this end have always seemed to be doomed to failure of disruptive cultural, political, and economic reasons.

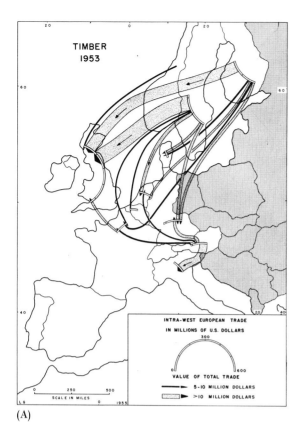

(A)

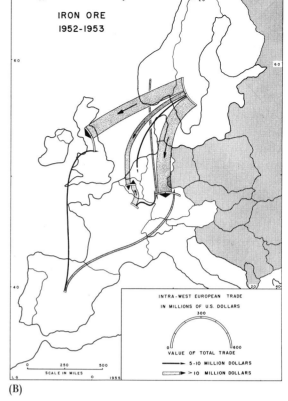

(B)

Figure 96. The common focus of European regions on the core region of Europe is illustrated by selected commodity flows in intra-West European trade. (*Courtesy of Lois Grotewold,* Intra-West European Trade.)

Politically it has proven impossible to accomplish European unity from the top, either voluntarily or by force of arms. The balance of power has long been maintained in the arena of international politics, whose chief architect in the past has been the United Kingdom. England's past interests have been to prevent the domination of Europe by Germany. Since World War II, it has become the "West's" purpose to prevent the domination of Western Europe by the U.S.S.R.

In the past there have been several formal expressions of partial economic unity. These are particularly important because they concern primarily the countries of the core region. In 1814 the first treaty of Paris after the defeat of Napoleon declared that "navigation on the Rhine shall be free in that it can be forbidden to no one." The 1918 treaty of Versailles, after World War I, recognized the same principle. It is interesting to note the names of the countries which were repre-

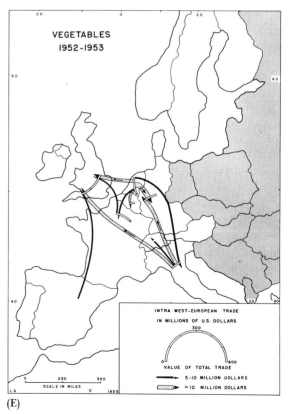

(E)

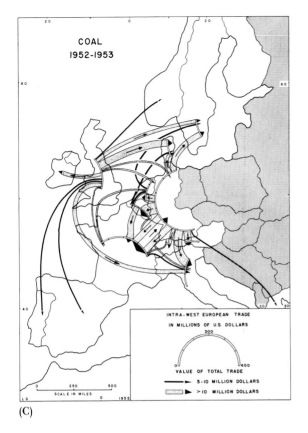

(C)

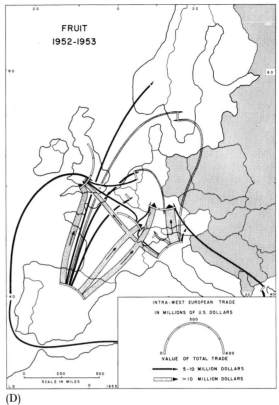

(D)

(F)

(G)

161

sented on the international commission for regulating the use of the Rhine. They were the countries of the core region—The Netherlands, Germany, France, Switzerland, Belgium, Italy, and Great Britain (Article 355 of the Treaty of Versailles).

As early as 1949 plans for the creation of an economic union of the three countries—Belgium, Netherlands, and Luxembourg—were being put into effect. The purpose was to accomplish unification by stages, through the creation of a partial customs union which could gradually be extended if all conflicting interests could be brought into agreement. The title "Benelux" does not yet apply to a completely united economic unit; but the governments of these three nations are moving steadily in this direction.

The European Economic Community (EEC). Benelux had been a "trial balloon" for more extensive efforts and expressions of operational unity. In 1951 the governments of six nations —the three countries of Benelux and West Germany, France, and Italy—established the Coal-Steel Community. This common market region for coal and steel has the objective of removing tariffs and import quotas on these two specific commodities, coal and steel. The agreement vests the control of trade in these basic items in a supranational "high authority" of the "Community." The plan links the coal and steel industries across national frontiers into a single regionally organized unit governed by a single set of policies. Since this initial step toward functional unification was taken, the plan which originally bore the name of Robert Schuman of France has been extended by formal treaties in 1957, setting up and establishing procedures for the achievement of the European Economic Community (Euromarket) and the Atomic Energy Community (Euratom). Since that time, beginning in 1958, machinery has been organized for the gradual reduction in tariffs on all industrial commodities. So powerful is the competitive leverage of this movement toward unification that repercussions have been felt throughout world trading circles. The United Kingdom is applying for membership in the European Common Market. Other alignments of states with similar purposes are springing up. The United States is moving in the direction of similar modification of its tariff laws in anticipation of meeting the challenge of European competition.

It is not to be supposed that these efforts toward more unified operation of the regional economy of the European coreland are proceding without problems and setbacks. Nevertheless, the concept of gradual unification by stages and by the negotiation of differences on specific issues, taken up one at a time, is bringing about a partial integration of important sectors of the economy.

The fact that machinery for the functioning of this supranational organization is operating is of the greatest significance. Complex checks and balances between its principal organs are provided for. A council, commissions, an assembly, and a court of justice have been set up. If it continues to function and to solve problems as they arise, and if it is able to withstand disruptive internal and external pressures, the Common Market may prove to be a transitional stage toward even more fundamental unification among European nations within the twentieth century.

Summary

This chapter has demonstrated the regional organization of the European continent. It has portrayed the basic resources on the basis of which selected fundamental activities of food production and manufacturing proceed. Important evidences of continental functional unity have been sketched which seem to point to still further integration of the European economy as a whole. The next chapter will deal with the disruptive elements which have in the past made a paradox of Europe.

EXERCISE   Reconstructing the Composite Map of European Agricultural Resource Regions

1. Place a piece of onion-skin typing paper over the map of precipitation in Figure 88 and trace the coastline of Europe. Then trace those portions of the precipitation lines representing 20 inches of water which are indicated in the heaviest black line. These parts of the precipitation pattern are the boundaries on the composite map contributed by the 20-inch isohyet of precipitation shown in Figure 88.

2. Next place the onion-skin overlay started in step one over the map showing duration of the growing season in Figure 89. Trace the most heavily lined parts of the growing-season pattern. Perform this task for both continuous heavy lines and heavy dashed lines. These parts of the duration of the growing-season pattern are the boundaries on the composite map contributed by the subject-matter distinction of the map in Figure 89.

3. Now place the same overlay over the third map in Figure 90 dealing with surface configuration and type of soil. Trace in the heavy boundaries of topographic regions shown on this map. These, in turn, are the boundaries of the composite map contributed by distinctions as to type of surface configuration.

4. Now compare the resulting outlines which you have constructed with the composite map of agricultural resource regions in Figure 87. Note the role of each measure of distinction in the respective subject-matter maps. From each one some part of the composite map is derived in formulating the regional associations of agricultural resources which are contained in the legend of the map in Figure 87.

Note, also, the additional subregions which the soil distinctions on the map in Figure 90 make it possible to define. In interpreting the significance of the associations of agricultural resources shown, be sure to think in terms of specific opportunities and problems rather than deterministically of environment limitations or responses. Remember that it is the understanding of potentialities and the nature of difficulties to be surmounted which represent the actual meaning to different persons in different cultures of the circumstances which these resource conditions describe.

9 *The Paradox of European Regional Organization*

In this chapter the geographical evolution of European regional organization will be examined. Presentation will focus attention on the paradoxical situation of Europe's simultaneous functional unity and political fragmentation among thirty-one different national states. The geographical impact of European culture on the rest of the world will also be introduced in terms of the tide and ebb tide of European colonization.

Six out of the seven world regions characterized by exchange-type area organization are occupied by peoples of European cultural background. The map of world regions in Figure 20 shows that three of the seven regions comprise the tripart regional core of the world today. In order to understand the emergence of a world core and the spreading of exchange-type area organization generally throughout the world, it will be useful to examine the development of exchange organization within Europe itself.

Evolution of the European Core Region

The evolution of nodal organization of the occupancy of Europe started from a base of prior village organization. When the regional organization of the Roman Empire collapsed, subsistence agriculture remained as the principal way of life. W. Gordon East has described Europe in the Middle Ages.[1]

In short, despite the variations in field patterns, in settlement types and in agricultural emphasis, medieval village folk engaged in essentially unspecialized farming. The potentialities of different regions on the basis of their peculiar conditions of soil, climate, aspect and relief, remained to a large extent unexploited in an age of small-scale internal trade. . . . The village derived from its fields, its meadows, and its wastes the main essentials of food, drink, and clothing. Only a few articles, like millstones, salt, pepper, and fine vestments, the production of which was geographically restricted, had to be brought in from outside.

The only centers of more than local significance were those of the organized Church and of multiple petty feudal kingdoms into which political power had become dispersed.

Emergence of Local-Regional Cultural Centers. Keeping the background of subsistence agriculture in mind, observe the map in Figure 97 which shows the most important cultural centers of Latin Christendom in the twelfth century.[2] The boundaries of the former Western and Eastern Roman Empires and the dividing line between the Western and Eastern Christian Churches are also shown. Note the general correspondence in shape of the present region of Western Christianity to the former extent of the Western Roman Empire. In the east, toward the Elbe River in Germany, some new centers are located beyond the old Roman Rhine frontier, but these are a relatively minor extension of European settlement in the twelfth century. Each dot on the map represents the site of a monastery, cathedral, university, or other center of culture. Each was a center of social or political life for a number of surrounding subsistence agricultural villages.

Only in the Christian Church did a form of the previous *regional* Roman organization of Europe survive. This was the result of the development of the Roman Catholic hierarchy and its area organization by the Church, the focus of which was the papacy at Rome. Although the unifying and hierarchical rule of the Church was primarily religious in character, through its secular organization as a great cultural force it became in many ways political and economic as well. In the Middle Ages the dominant *political* organization of area was *feudal* and *local*. The dominant *economic* organization was agricultural subsistence which was also local. Only in the *cultural* force of the Church was there still truly a regional organization of area.

[1] W. Gordon East, *An Historical Geography of Europe,* London; Methuen and Co., 1943, p. 106.
[2] R. R. Palmer, *Atlas of World History,* Chicago: Rand McNally and Co., 1957, pp. 54–55.

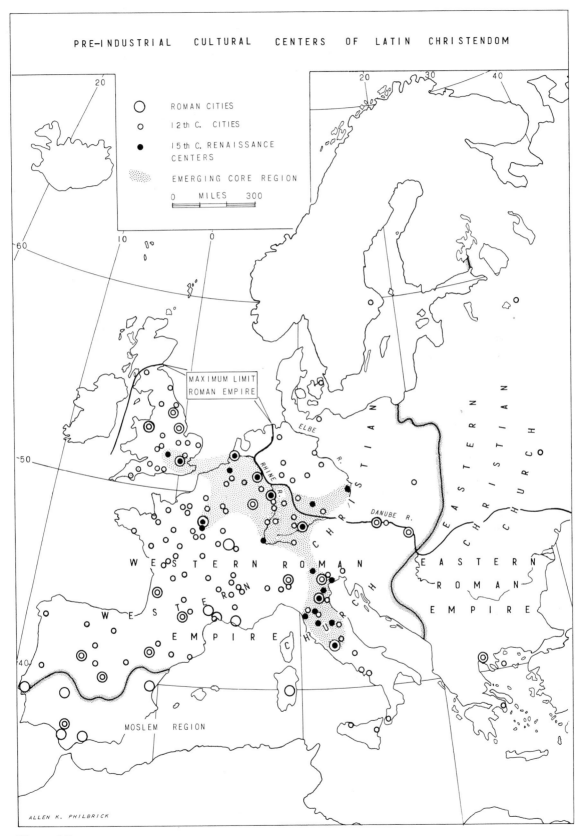

PRE-INDUSTRIAL CULTURAL CENTERS OF LATIN CHRISTENDOM

○ ROMAN CITIES
○ 12th C. CITIES
● 15th C. RENAISSANCE CENTERS
EMERGING CORE REGION

0 MILES 300

MAXIMUM LIMIT ROMAN EMPIRE

ELBE

RHINE R.

DANUBE R.

CHRISTIAN

EASTERN CHRISTIAN CHURCH

WESTERN ROMAN

EASTERN ROMAN EMPIRE

WESTE

RO N

EMPIRE

MOSLEM REGION

ALLEN K. PHILBRICK

Figure 97

165

Population Growth and the Transition from Subsistence to Exchange Area Organization. The long-range stability of the subsistence village organization of Europe is reflected in the virtual stagnation of population growth until the eighteenth century. Then a marked change occurred which corresponds to the revival of commerce and the continuing evolution of the production of commodities for trade. Population growth in Europe may be divided into two parts and a period for each one—slow and rapid growth. Population estimates and percentages of change by fifty-year intervals are given in Table XVI, which illustrates these two categories. Before 1700, as shown by the table, the average rate of growth per fifty-year period was about 5 per cent. After 1700, however, this rate increased to an average of 35 per cent per fifty years. While such estimates before census data were collected nationally are fragmentary as to details, they are undoubtedly correct in showing the great spurt in population after 1700 when commercial development was becoming important.

Development of Towns. Beginning in the twelfth century there was a thickening of the pattern of small regional centers within what is the present core region of Europe. While this region at that time in no way functioned as a core, the quickening of the tempo of commercial activity represented by this growth of towns was the harbinger of things to come. It is recorded on the map in Figure 97 with the cultural centers covered by a stippled pattern.

Against the background of the main overland trade routes of the thirteenth century, the expanding pattern of artisan manufacturing cities in the Low Countries and in the Po Valley of Italy are shown on the map in Figure 98. The trade routes of the thirteenth century interconnected commercial centers which had developed in each of Europe's lowlands. The routes followed valleys between the isolated old-rock uplands referred to earlier by Figures 86 and 95. Three main north-to-south routes connected centers of the North Sea region with centers of the Mediterranean. Marked A, B, and C on the map in Figure 98, they traversed a region bounded by Calais, Marseilles, Venice, and Lubeck at its four corners, which cut a wide swath across the long axis of the main body of peninsular Europe. This same region today contains Europe's industrial coreland.

For a number of reasons these three routes across Europe and the cities through which they passed very soon became the most important on the continent. First, they interconnected complementary resource regions. Second, they intersected the north and south coast of Europe at approximately the middle where port cities could conveniently tap coastal trade in at least three directions—two by sea, and one by land. At the north end was the principal east-west coastal trade route via the English Channel and the North and Baltic Seas. At the south end Genoa and Venice at either side of the base of the Italian Peninsula commanded the hinge positions midway in the east-west traffic of the Mediterranean. Both of the above reasons are as important today as they were in the beginning. Third, from the thirteenth century on handicraft manufacturing for trade began developing vigorously in both the Low Countries and in the Po Valley at either end of these routes.

On the map in Figure 98 the clustering of manufacturing towns and cities is shown where rapid growth resulted from the manufacturing of wool cloth. Some thirty cities owed their early growth and prosperity in northern France and Flanders (now Belgium) to this activity. Here was a preindustrial-era emergence of more than local geographical division of labor. Raw wool was imported from England, Spain, and Germany. Other raw materials for the manufacture of wool came from

TABLE **XVI**   THE CHANGING POPULATION OF EUROPE

Period (A.D.)	Population, millions	Change, millions	Percentage change per 50 years
14[a]	23	(32 pds.)	. . .
1600[b]	74	51	7
1650[c]	78	4	5
1700[b]	82	4	5
1750[c]ff.	115	33	40
1800	150	35	30
1850	206	56	37
1900	290	84	29
1950	396	106	37

[a] Julius Beloch, *Die Bevolkerung der griechisch-romische Welt*, Leipzig: Dunker und Humblatt, 1886, p. 507.

[b] A. P. Usher, "The History of Population and Settlement in Eurasia," *Geographical Review*, **20**: 121, 1930.

[c] Woytinsky and Woytinsky, *World Population and Production*, New York: Twentieth Century Fund, 1953, p. 34. Modified by subtraction of estimated population for Soviet Union and Russia as follows (European portion): 1950, 163 million; 1940, 142 million; 1900, 111 million; 1850, 66 million; 1800, 37 million; 1750, 25 million; 1650, 22 million.

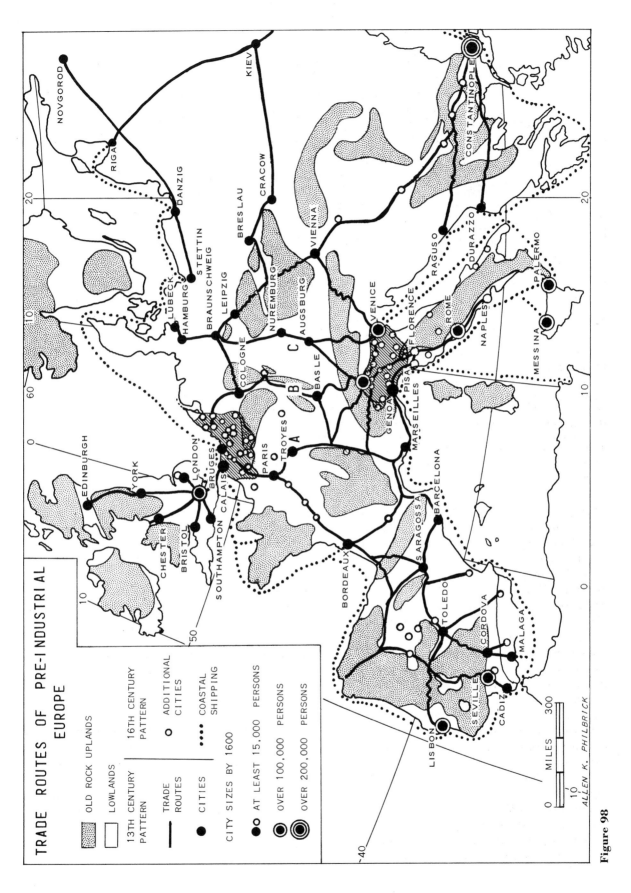

TRADE ROUTES OF PRE-INDUSTRIAL
EUROPE

OLD ROCK UPLANDS

LOWLANDS

13TH CENTURY   16TH CENTURY
PATTERN   PATTERN

TRADE   ADDITIONAL
ROUTES   CITIES

CITIES   COASTAL
                              SHIPPING

CITY SIZES BY 1600

AT LEAST 15,000 PERSONS

OVER 100,000 PERSONS

OVER 200,000 PERSONS

MILES

0   10
0   300

ALLEN K. PHILBRICK

Figure 98

NOVGOROD
RIGA
DANZIG
STETTIN
LUBECK
HAMBURG
BRAUNSCHWEIG
LEIPZIG
BRESLAU
CRACOW
KIEV
VIENNA
NUREMBURG
AUGSBURG
COLOGNE
BASLE
VENICE
FLORENCE
RAGUSO
DURAZZO
ROME
NAPLES
PALERMO
MESSINA
CONSTANTINOPLE
PISA
GENOA
MARSEILLES
TROYES
PARIS
BRUGES
CALAIS
SOUTHAMPTON
LONDON
YORK
EDINBURGH
CHESTER
BRISTOL
BORDEAUX
SARAGOSSA
BARCELONA
TOLEDO
CORDOVA
MALAGA
SEVILLE
CADIZ
LISBON

A   B   C

167

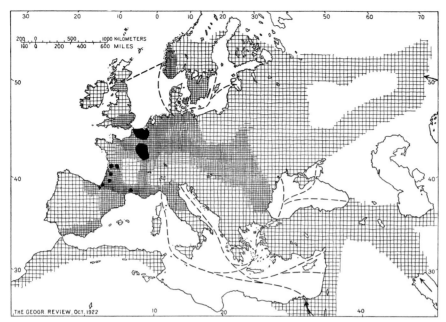

Figure 99. The economic sphere of the most important commodity fairs of Europe in the twelfth to fifteenth centuries—the fairs of Champagne and Flanders. The large black patches represent the territory over which the fairs were held, Champagne to the south, Flanders to the north. The hachures represent the regions having regular relations with the fairs, the depth of shading corresponding approximately to the degree of relative importance. Broken lines show the principal routes of maritime traffic, and arrows indicate the direction of imports brought from the Far East by Arab navigators and by Russo-Chinese caravans. (*Courtesy of The American Geographical Society of New York, taken from André Allix, "The Geography of Fairs," Geographical Review.*)

other parts of the continent. The people of the cities who were engaged in wool manufacture required food imports. Grain from the Paris Basin, fish from the North Sea, wine from Poitou, Gascony, Burgundy, and the Moselle are outstanding examples of the movement of staple items in trade which were linked to cloth-manufacturing activities. The cloth itself was moved and sold throughout Europe. Much of it was sent over these same three main routes southward to the Italian centers of commerce, whence it was shipped via the Mediterranean routes, both westward and eastward. Italian city-states which grew wealthy on the revival of trade also were centers of cloth manufacture, although their roles were more concentrated on the finishing processes of production. A clustered pattern of fifteen principal trading and manufacturing cities of north Italy are also shown on the map in Figure 98.

The Commodity Fairs. Commodity fairs in Europe provided a primary place and occasion for the retailing of commodities in the Middle Ages. Their pattern is prima facie evidence of the begin-

nings of commercial focality. Trade fairs associated with the early Champagne region in northern France and with Flanders in what is now Belgium drew people and goods from all parts of Europe. In the fifteenth century European commerce was primarily focused in the two rival fairs at Lyons and Geneva.

Those of Champagne were held in four towns, Provins, Troyes, Bar-sur Aube, and Lagny-sur-Marne; those of Flanders in several places but more particularly at Thourout, Bruges, Ypres, Lille, and later at Ghent and Antwerp. The chief advantage of this subdivision was that, passing on from one center to another, the fairs were distributed throughout the year and thus in fact constituted a permanent market.[1]

The chief centers for medieval fairs are indicated on the map in Figure 99. These places became centers of manufacturing and trade, points of focus which in the aggregate define Europe's emerging core region which now extends from England to Italy.

[1]André Allix, "The Geography of Fairs," *Geographical Review,* Vol. 22, Oct., 1922, pp. 533–536.

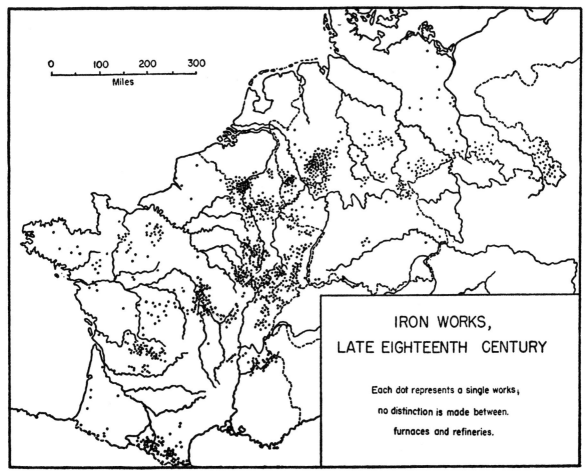

Figure 100. (*Courtesy of Indiana University Press, taken from N. J. G. Pounds and W. N. Parker,* Coal and Steel in Western Europe.)

While textile manufacturing and trade were concentrating economic growth along the major routes and at the two ends of the north-south axis of Europe, economic life was still primarily local in character and in organization of area. Evidence of this may be seen in the map by Pounds, shown in Figure 100, of the iron works during the late eighteenth century. The map shows that production of iron was remarkably localized throughout Europe. Its uses were as local as its production—for domestic utensils, agricultural implements, and ornamental wrought iron. Iron as a local raw material, when converted to steel, was used locally for

. . . the manufacture of knives and cutlery, of swords, saws, files, and other tools, of watch and clock springs and of such personal armour as continued to be worn. But of those uses which today consume the greater part of the iron made—railway

lines, naval construction, bridges, machinery, and ferro-concrete buildings there was scarcely a trace.[1]

The Paradox of Europe

While the development of commerce and the emergence of exchange organization of area were initiating the functions of the core region of Europe, other cultural and political developments were taking place which effectively prevented development on a unified basis. These circumstances were the emergence of separate cultures and group consciousness which resulted in the organization of separate national areas. This is the paradox of Europe—a contradiction between unity and disunity. It is paradoxical that the people in the world who have accomplished so much toward the evolu-

[1] N. J. G. Pounds and W. N. Parker, *Coal and Steel in Western Europe,* Bloomington, Ind.: Indiana University Press, 1957, p. 28.

tion of technology which has united the world should themselves have remained so divided. Europe, which is less than two million square miles in area, is yet divided among thirty-one national units. The continent has been the center of conflict in two recent world wars which have basically accomplished nothing but to bring disaster to millions of people. Despite this almost explosive social evidence of disunity there has emerged from Europe a common industrial culture which is distinctive and unique!

Cultural Fragmentation. The national areas of Europe are the result of cultural processes in accordance with which people have maintained separate ethnic identity. They have evolved and preserved separate languages and differ concerning their organized religious preferences. These and other cultural differences cannot be interpreted as the result of either physical or social environmental conditions, but rather are the result of continuing evolution along directions set at critical points by deliberate and conscious choices.

One such line of development is that of national consciousness which has resulted in separate political units. There have been many of these in Europe. The map in Figure 101 shows a zone of boundary shifting in the evolution of political units in Europe from the Roman Empire to the present time. It covers roughly 2,000 years from 60 B.C. to A.D. 1940 and clearly shows the disunity of the core of Europe throughout its history—from the Low Countries to northern Italy. The zone of conflict comprising shifting national boundaries widens at the ends and constricts in the middle. At the northern end it extends from Calais to the present Dutch German border. The middle lies between the Soane and the Rhine rivers. At the southern end it extends from the mouth of the Rhone River west of Marseilles to Venice or Trieste at the head of the Adriatic Sea. Note that the present national units are both small and numerous within this zone. In addition to countries, three other territories, the Saar, Alsace, and the Lorraine, have changed hands several times between France and Germany. The traditional neutrality of Switzerland is also indicative of the buffer character of the frontier zone between France and Germany.

Other elements within the development of national consciousness have been languages and religious faiths. Fragmentation of the core region by language and religious differences in addition to political boundaries is recorded on the map in Figure 101. Perhaps the most direct and clear-cut difference separating national cultures and the greatest barrier to familiarity and communication among peoples of different backgrounds is *language*. The boundary between the Romance-language family and that of German tongues extends through the very heart of the core zone of maximum political fragmentation.

A more detailed map in Figure 102 shows that European peoples may be grouped into three major families by languages which they write and speak.[1] Each family grouping is subdivided into the particular languages of the separate countries. The Romance languages—Spanish, Portuguese, French, Italian, etc.—trace their origins to Roman times in the south of Europe and have a common basis in Latin. Germanic languages are represented among the peoples of Scandinavia, Germany, the Low Countries, and England. The Slavic tongues are spoken among Polish, Slovakian, Russian, Ukrainian, and other eastern European peoples. Greek stands between ancient Greek and modern Slavic languages to which it gave the Cyrillic or Greek-Russian alphabet. Other basically different language roots occur among Celtic peoples who speak Irish, Gaelic, Welsh, and Breton dialects; the Baltic affords us Lettish and Lithuanian; and some other of more obscure origin are the languages of the Basques, Hungarians, Finns, and Albanians.

Language and political boundaries are not identical. A number of European countries are bi- or trilingual. Switzerland, for example, has no single national language. Distinct population groups occupy areas within the country where German, French, or Italian speech predominates. Belgium is divided into a French-Walloon-speaking and a Flemish-French-speaking region. Finland has two official languages, Swedish and Finnish, each of which is very different from the other. In most cases, however, one basic language tends to be spoken by the majority of the population in each country. There are also a great many local variations or dialects of speech which are noticeably characteristic of specific parts of individual countries. The map in Figure 102 shows the degree of correspondence of the major languages within individual and grouped political states.

The boundaries of the schism of Western Christianity into several Protestant regions and Catholic

---

[1]Lucille Carlson, *The Geography of World Politics*, New York: Prentice-Hall, Inc., 1957, p. 188.

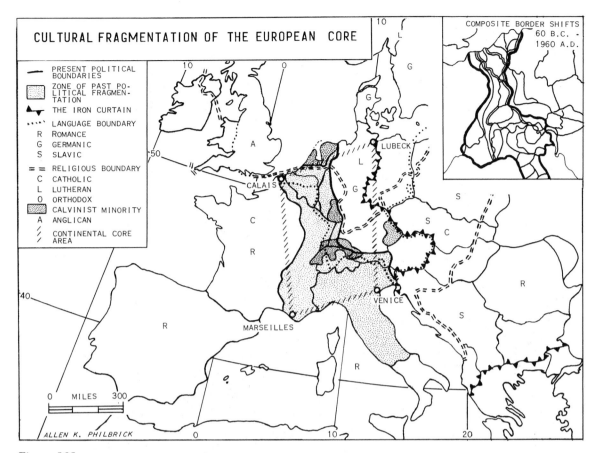

Figure 101

Europe also lie within the fragmented linguistic and political pattern of the European coreland. England is Anglican. Across the channel are Catholic Belgium and France. East of Belgium is the Lutheran region of Germany. Between France and Germany are several smaller regions of another Protestant division, the followers of Calvin. While the two principal divisions in Western Europe are Catholic and Protestant, a third, in Eastern Europe is the Orthodox or Greek Orthodox Church. Moslem and Jewish—particularly the latter—are significant minorities in Europe. Moslems predominate only in Albania, although parts of Yugoslavia and Bulgaria possess Mohammedan concentrations. The Jews, although a much persecuted and segregated, primarily urban minority, have contributed far out of proportion to their numbers to the development of almost every European country.

The map in Figure 103 shows the principal division by areas of dominant faiths. Such religious differences, along with barriers in speech, are abiding cultural characteristics of peoples. National status reflects and in many ways combines into a single expression through the organization of territory the several cultural strands—economic, political, and other cultural attributes and activities of a people. In the north England has possessed the unity of the southern half of the island of Britain since the Norman Conquest of 1066. To the west France, except for its northeastern and eastern borders, has been a political unit virtually unchanged in form since the mid-fourteenth century. To the east Germany did not emerge as a formally unified political unit until Bismarck's time in 1871. The hundreds of petty kingdoms into which the region of German speech was divided, however, have been united, even if weakly, as the Holy Roman Empire, since the tenth century.

Individual boundaries shown on the map in Figure 101 are not important in themselves. The salient point is the fact that the core of Europe has been for a long time and still is today a zone of transition. It is a zone of intense cultural fragmentation which is expressed in political, language, and

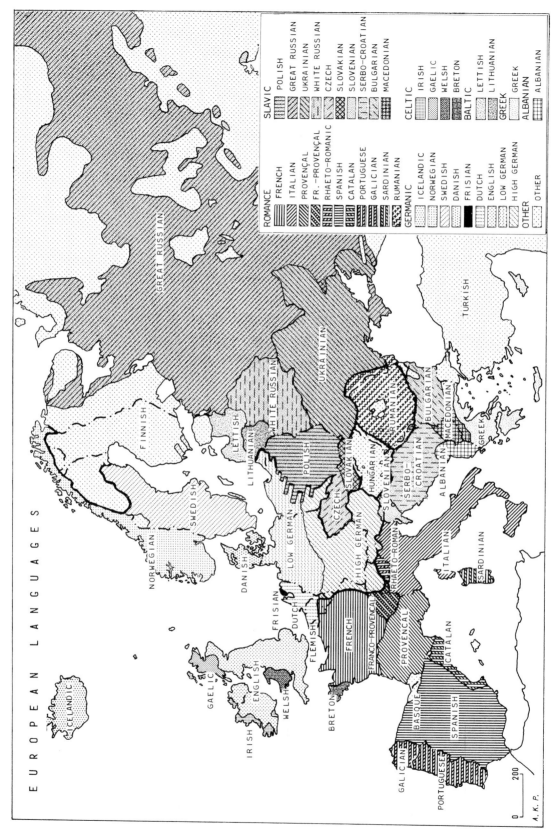

Figure 102. (*Courtesy of Prentice-Hall, Inc., taken from Lucille Carlson, The Geography of World Politics, 1957.*)

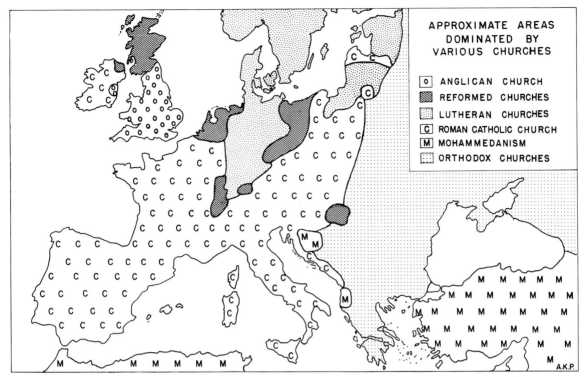

Figure 103. (*Courtesy of the University of Chicago Press, taken from William McNeill,* History Handbook.)

religious boundaries. These facts render even more understandable the circumstances of competitive territorial organization in *economic* affairs which has been characteristic of Europe's emerging core region. By contrast these same facts give significance to the much greater degree of uniformity evident among the countries of the Mediterranean, Scandinavian, and Slavic eastern Europe.

The Perpetuation of a Divided Europe.
The industrial revolution in Europe, measured in terms of the mechanization of production, was delayed one hundred years after that of England. Probably the single most important reason for this delay was the disunity, not only of Europe as a whole, but the disunity within individual nations. France was superficially a united political region during the entire eighteenth century; but actually it was a patchwork of separate states shifting in outlines through time in accordance with the maneuverings and machinations of the royal family. Each of several separate parts had different laws. There even were customs duties to be paid upon shipment of goods from one part of France to another. Privileges, such as certain exemptions from taxes, were enjoyed by the nobility and the

higher clergy. The position of privileged minorities survived from previous feudal relationships long after the transfer of local power had been made to central authority. Not until the French Revolution of 1789 were many of these inequalities erased.

The same situation prevailed, but without a development of national political unity, until 1871 in Germany. The struggle between central authority and sectional interests which was decided in England by victory of Parliament in 1688 was not decided in France and Germany until a century or more had passed. From 1789 until the defeat of Napoleon in 1814, Europe was in a turmoil. The unifying effects of the Napoleonic era, such as the unification of the legal code and the reorganization of many European economies were not evident until the second decade of the nineteenth century.

A second set of reasons for Europe's tardiness in following in the footsteps of the English industrial revolution lies in basic resources and their use. Attempts to substitute coke for charcoal which had become scarce and more expensive were at first unsuccessful in the iron and steel industry on the continent. This lack of success is explainable partly as a misunderstanding of the coking process. The

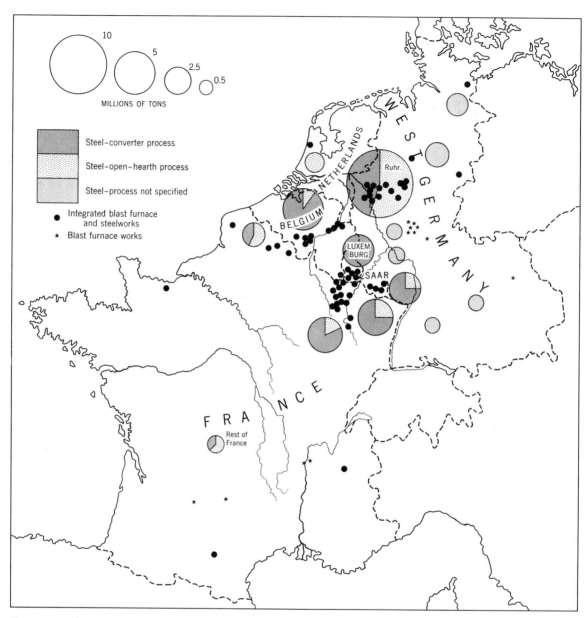

Figure 104. Blast-furnace works and crude-steel production of Western Europe, 1954. (*Courtesy of Indiana University Press, taken from N. J. G. Pounds and W. N. Parker,* Coal and Steel in Western Europe.)

reduction of iron ore using coke rather than charcoal required a larger furnace than that used by charcoal-furnace operators. Simply replacing charcoal with coke in charcoal-sized furnaces met with unsatisfactory results. Consequently the use of charcoal persisted and the dispersed small-scale production of iron continued to mark the European pattern of iron making well into the nineteenth century. Failures were also partly due to the fact that the coal used for coking was at first of poor quality. The rich reserves of coking-quality coal in Europe were the deep underground coal measures. The shallower measures first exploited were generally not of coking quality. Use of bigger furnaces and the employment of the deeper, better-grade coals did not take place until the second half of the nineteenth century. According to Pounds,[1]

Everywhere in Western Europe coke smelting came

[1]*Ibid.,* p. 110.

slowly. For this there were two reasons. Iron workers were distrustful—and often with reason—of the quality of the pig-iron produced; it did not work well either in the refinery or on the puddling hearth, and these fears were not dispelled until the Bessemer converter and the open hearth replaced the older methods.

When the refining of iron with coal did gradually spread in Europe it had an important effect in relocating the iron industry. Use of coal brought about the same shift of the iron industry to the coal fields of Europe that it had earlier brought about in England. When this transformation became marked in the mid-nineteenth century, the distribution of European manufacturing began to assume the modern pattern of concentration within the Rhine Valley and around the resources—particularly coal—of the Ardennes-Rhenish old-rock upland. This is the pattern of the blast-furnace works in 1954, reproduced from Pounds' and Parker's *Coal and Steel in Western Europe* in Figure 104.[1]

For the first two decades of the age of steel, after the invention of the Bessemer converter in 1860, Europe was dependent on imported pig iron. As previously noted it was not until the dolomite lining of the furnace invented by Thomas Gilchrist made it possible to use ores with phosphoric content that European iron ores could be developed. The Thomas innovation by its seemingly small change in the chemistry of steel conversion transformed the relative resource picture almost overnight.

The hitherto despised "minette" of Lorraine and Luxembourg became at once the most important ore deposit in western Europe. The Normandy ores and bedded ores of North Germany and English Midlands, all highly phosphoric, also came into prominence. Only the lack of railways stood in the way of using the vast deposits of high-grade ore in Northern Sweden. The low-phosphorus iron from Cumberland, Siegerland, and Spain ceased to dominate the market.[2]

The transformed resource picture of the steel industry in Europe was divided, however, among the three largest powers—the United Kingdom, Germany, and France. It was not long until the steel output of the industry on the continent had outstripped that of the originator of steel, the United Kingdom; and by the beginning of the twentieth century Germany alone had a greater

[1]*Ibid.*, p. 266.
[2]*Ibid.*, p. 120.

annual production of steel than that of Britain. The continent's major producers, France, Belgium, and Germany, combined make the relative shift appear even more marked. The production figures in Table XVII tell this competitive story.

The coincidence of the pattern of northern Europe's industrial cities with the extent of the North European Plain from the old-rock uplands northwestward to the North Sea is shown on the map in Figure 105. The resource orientation of the coal-producing cities aligned along the coal beds at the line of contact between the plain and the old-rock Ardennes and Rhenish Uplands is striking. From the French coal fields, through the Belgian Mons-Charleroi-Liege industrial districts and the southern Netherland Limburg district to the German Ruhr, the same type subsurface structure supplies coal for politically separated units of the same types of industry.

South of the old-rock upland, iron ores from Lorraine and coal from the Saar have obvious orientations to numerous industrial cities in those districts. Metz and Nancy are cities of major importance in France. Saarbrucken is the primary

TABLE **XVII**   CHANGES IN STEEL PRODUCTION FOR SELECTED EUROPEAN COUNTRIES FROM THE NINETEENTH TO THE TWENTIETH CENTURIES[a]

| | PRODUCTION IN MILLIONS OF METRIC TONS | | |
Date	United Kingdom	West Germany	Combined production West Germany, France, Belgium
1880	1.3	0.7	1.2
1890	3.6	2.2	3.1
1900	5.0	6.6	8.9
1910	6.5	13.7	19.0
1913	7.8	18.9	26.1
1923	8.6	6.3	13.9
1929	9.8	16.2	30.0
1930	7.4	11.5	24.3
1939	13.3	22.4	33.4
1945	12.0	0.3	2.7
1950	16.6	12.1	24.6
1956[b]	23.1	29.3	47.9

[a] Woytinsky and Woytinsky, *World Population and Production*, New York: Twentieth Century Fund, 1953, p. 1118.

[b] Supplemented by *Mineral Trade Notes*, Vol. 49, No. 2, Washington: U. S. Dept. of the Interior, Bureau of Mines, August 1959, pp. 24–25.

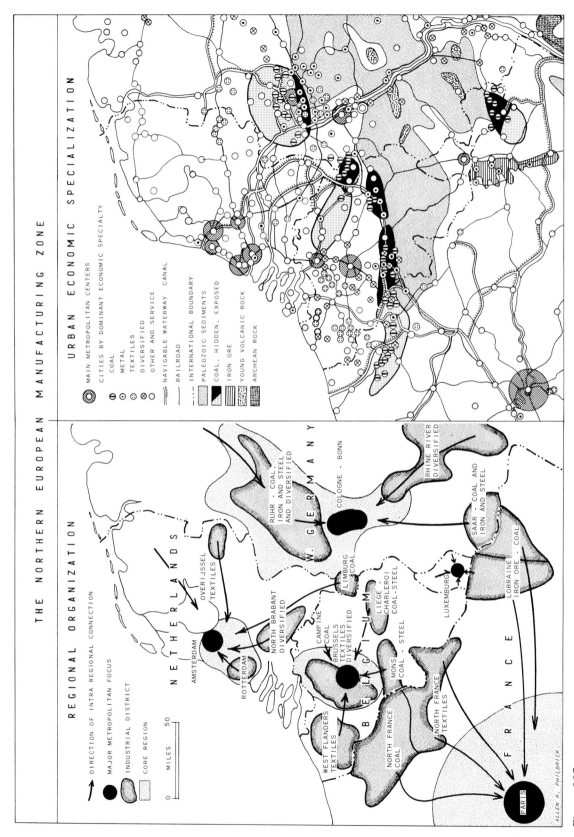

THE NORTHERN EUROPEAN MANUFACTURING ZONE

REGIONAL ORGANIZATION

DIRECTION OF INTRA REGIONAL CONNECTION
MAJOR METROPOLITAN FOCUS
INDUSTRIAL DISTRICT
CORE REGION

0   MILES   50

URBAN ECONOMIC SPECIALIZATION

MAIN METROPOLITAN CENTERS
CITIES BY DOMINANT ECONOMIC SPECIALTY
COAL
METAL
TEXTILES
DIVERSIFIED
OTHER AND SERVICE
NAVIGABLE WATERWAY CANAL
RAILROAD
INTERNATIONAL BOUNDARY
PALEOZOIC SEDIMENTS
COAL, HIDDEN, EXPOSED
IRON ORE
YOUNG VOLCANIC ROCK
ARCHEAN ROCK

N E T H E R L A N D S

OVERIJSSEL
TEXTILES

AMSTERDAM

ROTTERDAM

NORTH BRABANT
DIVERSIFIED

RUHR - COAL,
IRON AND STEEL
AND DIVERSIFIED

W   G E R M A N Y

COLOGNE - BONN

RHINE RIVER
DIVERSIFIED

LIMBURG
COAL

CAMPINE
COAL

B E L G I U M

BRUSSELS
TEXTILES
DIVERSIFIED

LIEGE
CHARLEROI
COAL-STEEL

SAAR - COAL AND
IRON AND STEEL

LUXEMBURG

MONS
COAL - STEEL

LORRAINE
IRON ORE - COAL

WEST FLANDERS
TEXTILES

NORTH FRANCE
COAL

NORTH FRANCE
TEXTILES

F R A N C E

PARIS

ALLEN K. PHILBRICK

Figure 105

176

focus of the Saarland. The iron ores of Lorraine and the Thomas process of steel production started Germany on the way to industrial power after the Franco-Prussian war of 1871 saw Alsace and Lorraine become German territory. Since World War I when Germany lost Lorraine, German steel production had to be reorganized on the basis of other German iron-ore deposits and the heavy importation of high-quality Swedish ores from Kiruna.

In this manner the political divisions of the earlier formative period were perpetuated and intensified by the competition for industrial leadership emerging after the industrial revolution. Only now and by complex negotiations over a long period of time are some of the specific problems which have resulted from the cultural fragmentation of the European core being re-examined. Possibly the paradox of European disunity despite her great contributions to industrial know-how will now be resolved, but only the future of a more unified core region for Europe will be able to answer the question: "How much more influential could Europe be if it were unified?"

The Tide and Ebb Tide of European Colonialism

Despite the results of and partly because of the disunity of Europe, her people have been exploring, colonizing, and attempting to control the rest of the world's land surfaces. This has been a process of geographical dispersion of peoples and cultures during the past four and one-half centuries. It is the flood tide and ebb tide of European colonialism, only now coming to a close, shown on the two world maps in Figures 106 and 107. The first map, "The Flood Tide of European Colonialism," is a composite showing the overlapping patterns of European political hegemony since the age of discovery. Twelve European countries have contributed to this impressive pattern—Portugal, Spain, England, France, Belgium, Italy, Germany, Norway, Sweden, Denmark, the Netherlands, and European Russia.

Explorations by Portuguese around the rim of Africa before Columbus's discovery of America established way stations on the way to and away from India, Burma, Malaya, the East Indies, and the Philippine Islands. These way stations represented the earliest examples of European colonialism. The goal of all initial overseas explorations was re-establishment of contact and trade with the Orient—specifically with India and the islands

of the East Indies—which had been disrupted by the capture of Constantinople by the Turks in 1453. The goal was first achieved by the Portuguese. They were followed in their route around Africa by the Spanish, Dutch, French, and English. Each of these country's nationals maintained supply stations and trading posts along the way to the Orient. These early supply points are reflected on the map in Figure 106 in the fringes of Africa and South Asia where early Portuguese, Spanish, and Dutch colonial occupation is generalized. Early coastal colonial patterns in Africa and Asia show the fundamental difference between these initial coastal routes around Africa which skirted the Old-World side of the enclosed Atlantic-Indian Oceans, and the bolder transoceanic routes of exploration which sailed westward around the world. The westward sailings initiated the Columbian era of trans-Atlantic worldwide exploration.

The earliest large-scale colonies of Europeans were those of the Spanish and Portuguese in Latin America. These acquisitions followed hard upon the heels of the great voyages of discovery by such figures as Columbus, Vasco de Gama, and Magellan in the late fifteenth and early sixteenth centuries. Somewhat later north of these initial discoveries, French and English interests in the New World came into major conflict in the present territories of the United States and Canada, as expressed by the overlapping patterns on the map in Figure 106. After the French and Indian Wars of the eighteenth century, French loss of her first overseas empire was sealed by the treaty of Paris with the British in 1763.

At about the same time that overseas exploration and colonial acquisitions started, eastward expansion by the Russian people also began. The eastward overland sweep of the Russian branch of European culture was carried to the Pacific and across the Bering Strait into Alaska by 1741.

While these events were taking place in the Americas and across the steppes and forests of Russia, colonial penetration continued around Africa to the Far East. The Dutch expanded their control of the island archipelagoes of Southeastern Asia, which became the Netherlands Indies. The English occupied and controlled Ceylon, India, and Burma, the southern end of the Malay Peninsula, Singapore, and parts of Borneo. They also occupied and began colonizing Australia and New Zealand. The French began the development of a second overseas empire which numbered Indo-

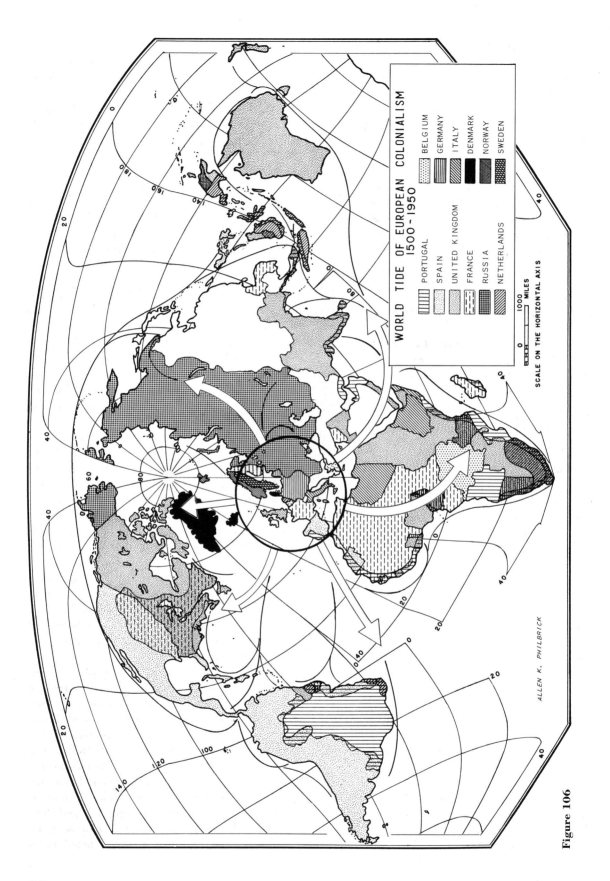

WORLD TIDE OF EUROPEAN COLONIALISM
1500-1950

PORTUGAL SPAIN UNITED KINGDOM FRANCE RUSSIA NETHERLANDS
BELGIUM GERMANY ITALY DENMARK NORWAY SWEDEN

SCALE ON THE HORIZONTAL AXIS

0   1000
MILES

ALLEN K. PHILBRICK

Figure 106

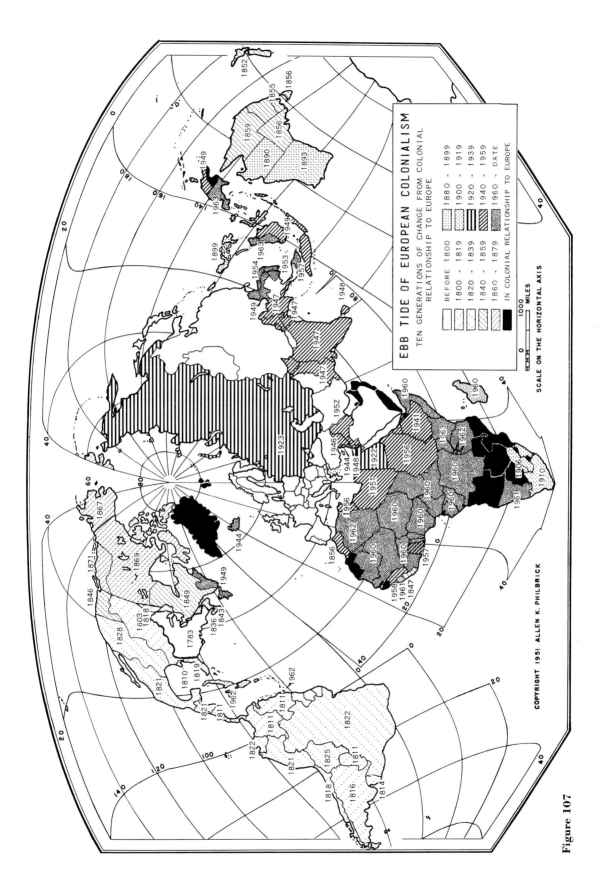

EBB TIDE OF EUROPEAN COLONIALISM

TEN GENERATIONS OF CHANGE FROM COLONIAL
RELATIONSHIP TO EUROPE

	BEFORE 1800	1880 - 1899
	1800 - 1819	1900 - 1919
	1820 - 1839	1920 - 1939
	1840 - 1859	1940 - 1959
	1860 - 1879	1960 - DATE

IN COLONIAL RELATIONSHIP TO EUROPE

SCALE ON THE HORIZONTAL AXIS

0   1000
MILES

COPYRIGHT 1951 ALLEN K. PHILBRICK

Figure 107

179

china and nearly one-third of the continent of Africa among its prizes. Portugal maintained footholds along the earlier route to the Indies by way of the African coast, and Spain controlled the Philippine Islands.

At the same time the ebbing of the colonial tide began to occur. Activities of independent national development soon started as the cultural forces set in motion by the dispersion of European ways of life began to operate. America, with the Declaration of Independence in 1776 and the founding of the United States in 1783, holds the proud position of first in the parade of ten successive generations of nationalist liberation from European political control. The geographical distribution of the ebbing of colonialism, generalized through nearly two hundred years, is shown on the map in Figure 107. Independence was completed for nearly all portions of the Americas and Australia-New Zealand during the nineteenth century. The only large exceptions are Newfoundland which changed status from a crown colony to province of the Dominion of Canada in 1949, the Federation of the West Indies, which assumed Commonwealth status as an independent country in 1959, and the three Guianas of northern South America, which remain colonial possessions of France, the Netherlands, and the United Kingdom, respectively. Additional small territories, such as British Honduras, Bermuda (United Kingdom), St. Pierre and Miguelon Islands (France), the islands of the Netherlands Antilles north of Venezuela, and a few others remain under the control of European countries in the Western Hemisphere. By contrast, among the territories of the Old World only the Union of South Africa had gained national independence from a colonial status before the turn of the century. Note the resurgence of nationalism particularly since World War II. After a generation of stability preceding World War I and the Russian Revolution which marked the only significant shift in status during the interwar generation from 1920 to 1939, no less than forty-two new nations have appeared on the scene since 1945.

With the emergence of Communist satellite territories a new kind of Communist colonialism may be said to have developed. This new phenomenon is not included on the maps in Figures 106 and 107 which were designed to visualize only the flood and ebb tides of the traditional form of European colonialism.

If special concessions and spheres of influence were considered in addition to outright political control, European colonialism has been literally a worldwide phenomenon. The maps in Figures 106 and 107 show how little of the world's total land area has escaped outright political control from Europe at some time within the past 450 years. The map in Figure 107, in turn, shows how little of the world yet remains under the colonial control of any European power. The flood tide and ebb tide of European colonialism readily demonstrates the geographical extent of European *cultural impact*. Of the twelve European colonial powers, half were part of the core region of Europe; three were Scandinavian, two Mediterranean, and one Slavic.

At no time during the previous history of the human race has the culture of any single continental region so dispersed its impact over the entire world. The events of European cultural expansion are therefore a fundamental geographic phenomenon. Understanding the world's regions cannot be achieved without taking into account the many ramifications of the impact of Europeans on the world's peoples.

Summary

This chapter has presented the paradoxical situation of Europe's disunity within the context of its great unifying contribution as the culture hearth from which European civilization has spread throughout the world. The last four chapters have initiated regional analysis of the world. They have demonstrated how the three aspects of geography—physical, cultural, and organization of area—are united in the lives of the people within a continental region. Taken broadly, the chapters on the United Kingdom and Europe have described the resources for and the spread of European ways of life.

It can be appreciated how the resources of the subsurface, surface, and atmosphere have been used, how the creative genius which made use of these resources produced innovations of the industrial revolution in England and extended their application to the mainland. The patterns of regional organization characterized by complex regional divisions of labor have been visualized for Europe as a whole. The paradox of the unity and disunity of Europe has been examined in terms of evolution of European regional organization.

There is a unique mingling of the ancient and the atomic in the European region. From the crumbling walls of the ancient Romans to the most modern structures of scientific industrial society, all stages in the evolutionary process of the exchange world are represented. Great urban centers, blackened coal-grimed manufacturing neighborhoods, nucleated agricultural villages of a subsistence-organized past, modern diesel-electric-powered railroads, ribbons of autobahn-type expressways which traverse the same traditional gaps between the old-rock uplands by which Caesar's legions passed—all move before the mind's eye in review. They represent the accumulated cultural experience and expression of human society in Europe which has created modern society's pattern of occupancy—evolving it day by day, year by year, and century by century on the same stage using the materials of the earth available for the taking. The materials of the earth have contributed their own unity to the process of development; the thread of human creativity has endowed the process of development with a continuity of effort. Described and analyzed from the viewpoint of geographical distribution, Europe has organized pattern, focus, and function. These have been made understandable in terms of physical materials and "know-how" organized in area by the leadership and following from many generations of Europeans.

10 *Africa South of the Sahara*

European partitioning of Africa marked the closing decade of the nineteenth century, and now, seventy years later, African nationalism is marking the final stages of European colonialism. In contrast to the long tradition of independent development and power characteristic of European nationalism, the independent nations of Africa south of the Sahara, with few exceptions, are fledglings on the world scene. Comparison of the European homelands with the territories of their former African colonies reveals profound differences which make it appropriate to follow the chapters on Europe with an examination of "Africa south of the Sahara."

Europe, including European Russia, is one-fourth the size of Africa. Exclusive of European Russia, it is one-sixth the size of the African continent (1.9 compared to 11.6 million square miles), and one-fourth the size of Africa south of the Sahara. In contrast to Europe, which was described as a peninsula of peninsulas, Africa presents a block-like appearance on the map and is to be characterized as the "plateau" continent. It is a huge tableland elevated on the east and south and inclined toward the north and west. While Europe is primarily temperate and relatively humid throughout, Africa is a huge, tropical plateau which ranges from absolute aridity to extreme wetness in equatorial latitudes. Europe is one of the three most compactly populated continental regions with an average density per square mile of more than 200 persons. Africa is one of the least densely populated of the continents with only an average of 18 persons per square mile. The predominantly Negro population and primarily agricultural livelihood of Africa south of the Sahara are distinct from the Caucasian population and dominantly industrial activities of Europe. The region, Africa south of the Sahara, will be discussed in terms of the cultural attributes of population, material resources, and the types of area organization evolved within its subregions.

The African Continent

The map of world regions in Figure 20 of Chapter 2 shows Africa divided into three main parts, referred to as North (Saharan) Africa, Africa south of the Sahara, and South Africa. These names are neither descriptive of the areas of human occupance to which they refer nor do they reveal the cultural distinctions and differences in area organization which make this division of the continent significant.

Cultural Regions. Regional divisions on a cultural basis are difficult to formulate in Africa because any one region is multicultural and contains overlapping elements of indigenous, European, and other peoples. The map in Figure 108 (using Murdock[1]) shows the principal indigenous African culture provinces arranged according to major language divisions. The two main cultural regions are defined by the Hamitic and Nigritic-Bantu language stocks which correspond roughly to Saharan and sub-Saharan Africa. They also correspond to the distinction between Caucasian and Negroid races and between Arab-Moslem culture in the Saharan north as opposed to tribal animistic cultures south of the Sahara. Multiplicity of tribal cultures at the time of European partitioning of Africa is demonstrated by the 700 different languages spoken among 6,500 tribal groups.[2] European conquest of Africa took almost no cognizance of indigenous African cultures or of the variations in material resources. The partitioning was a "grab-bag" affair accomplished "in absentia" in the chancelleries of the major European powers.

Now that European control is coming to an end in Africa it is only fitting that cognizance *be* taken of the cultural backgrounds of indigenous peoples

[1] G. P. Murdock, *Africa--Its Peoples and Their Cultural History*, New York: McGraw-Hill Co., 1959, p. 15.

[2] *Ibid.,* pp. 64–76, 89, 222, and 273, and map "Tribal Africa" in pocket on back cover.

of Africa in both the Saharan region and south of the Sahara. Africans themselves are looking back to the original patterns of their own cultures, re-establishing the continuity of their independent existence and actions—interrupted by less than a century of European colonialism. The map in Figure 109 outlines the location of principal culture hearths in Africa and the movements of cultural diffusion from them which are important to an understanding of the division of Africa into three great regions—not only Saharan and sub-Saharan Africa, but the third multicultural region demarcated by the political unit, the Republic of South Africa.

The arrow into Egypt from Iraq refers to the entry into the Nile Valley of neolithic people who possessed knowledge of crop cultivation. This entry established subsistence village agriculture in the oases of the desert. The largest oasis was the Nile Valley itself, which has been settled from 4500 B.C. until today and represents perhaps the longest continuity of sedentary agricultural occupancy anywhere in the world. The arrow across North Africa represents the movement of both people and knowledge—the cultural borrowing of a people known as the Berbers in northwest Africa from the people of the Nile. These two arrows also symbolize the later conquest of North Africa by Moslems. The southward-pointing arrows represent Moslem influences which have been carried by nomadic people and traders across the Sahara to the region south of the Sahara.

South of the Sahara, anthropological findings have demonstrated the existence of an African culture hearth where certain tubers and root crops were first cultivated. Agricultural innovations were carried outward from this territory of the upper Niger River. The arrows eastward from the Niger headwaters and westward from the upper Nile signify a thousand-year-long exchange of farm and pastoral know-how. On the basis of this cultural interchange the subsistence technology of agriculture and pastoral economies developed in the transitional zone between the Sahara and the equatorial rainforest regions.

Introduction of still other forest agricultural crops from Malaysia also occurred by way of Madagascar. The arrow arching equatorward from Madagascar through Uganda and westward to the Guinea coast of west Africa records Murdock's hypothesis of a diffusion corridor through which knowledge of

Figure 108. African languages about A.D. 1500 (1—Furian; 2—Hamitic; 3—Khoisan; 4—Kordofanian.) (*Courtesy of McGraw-Hill Book Co., Inc., taken from G. P. Murdock, Africa, Its Peoples and Their Culture History,* © *1959.*)

bananas, taro, and possibly of the yam reached west Africa. These crops were essential to the expansion of the Bantu people from their place of origin in the Cameroons uplands. The southeastward-trending arrows from the great bend of Africa at the Gulf of Guinea symbolize the pathways of forest agricultural diffusion produced by the migration of the Bantu peoples into central and south Africa. Beginnings of the Bantu migration preceded the start of European colonialism; but the later phases of it, including the reaching of the southern end of the continent, coincided almost exactly with the initial settlement of the Dutch in Capetown, South Africa.

The penetration by the Dutch and the English into the southern tip of Africa resulted in the evolution of the present Republic of South Africa. This country has the largest European population in Africa. While the three million persons of European descent in the Republic are a minority of the fifteen million total in the country, they represent the only example in Africa south of the Sahara where a sizable European minority has organized an independent national state. For this reason the

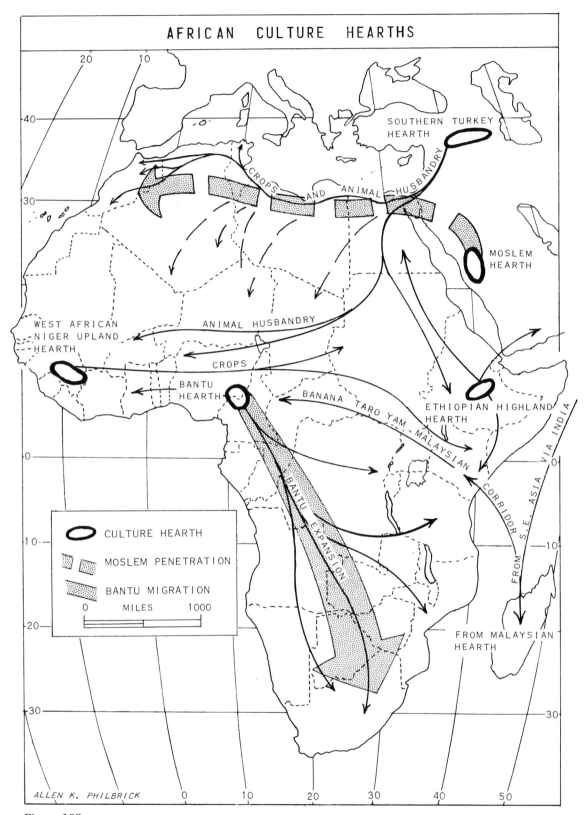

AFRICAN CULTURE HEARTHS

SOUTHERN TURKEY
HEARTH

MOSLEM
HEARTH

CROPS AND ANIMAL HUSBANDRY

WEST AFRICAN
NIGER UPLAND
HEARTH

ANIMAL HUSBANDRY

CROPS

BANTU
HEARTH

BANANA TARO YAM MALAYSIAN

ETHIOPIAN HIGHLAND
HEARTH

FROM S.E. ASIA VIA INDIA

CORRIDOR

BANTU EXPANSION

CULTURE HEARTH

MOSLEM PENETRATION

BANTU MIGRATION

0   MILES   1000

FROM MALAYSIAN
HEARTH

ALLEN K. PHILBRICK

Figure 109

184

complex English, Afrikaner, Bantu, Colored,[1] and Indian-occupied region of the Republic of South Africa is classified as a third major division of the continent as a whole, which will be part of the subject matter of Chapter 11.

European culture was superimposed on all parts of the indigenous African landscape. As a result of colonial economic development a number of urban centers for administrative and economic control and development purposes have grown up throughout Africa. The cities on any atlas map of Africa are the centers of importation and diffusion of European culture in Africa. Accra (491,060), Brazzaville (93,500), Leopoldville (402,492), Lagos (364,000), and others have become important bases from which new nations of Africa are operating in their efforts to construct coherent patterns of occupancy today.

Habitats. From the standpoint of outstanding combinations of resources, the definition of three main habitats (Figure 110) is significant for Africa as a whole. These are the *Dry Habitat,* where lack of water is a primary characteristic; the *Wet Habitat,* where the abundance of water is outstanding; and *The Highland Habitat,* where elevation has an important directly modifying effect on temperature, and indirectly on available moisture. Stippled areas between and surrounding the three habitats on the map are transitional with respect to the circumstances which make each one outstanding. Africa south of the Sahara shares two of the three habitats (rainforest and highlands) and the transitional zones bordering them.

Surface drainage condition shown on the map in Figure 111 is a convenient means of further characterizing the differences between habitats. The three principal types of surface drainage include regions without surface runoff or with drainage which evaporates before it can reach the sea. This type is characteristic of the Saharan region, but is also true of the desert areas of southwestern Africa. A second type is the major river systems which form shallow basins within the surface of the interior plateaus. Six separate river basins occupy most of the surface of Africa south of the Sahara. Last, there are the relatively narrow continental margins characterized by steep slopes and narrow coastal plains which are drained by many small streams and short rivers.

---

[1]In South Africa the word "colored" refers only to persons of mixed European and Negro ancestry.

The four largest streams which have incised the surface of the interior tableland are among the world's largest rivers in drainage area and stream length; yet in navigable distance from the coast inland they are among the shortest for their size. The 2,900-mile Congo is blocked initially only 80 miles from the Atlantic coast by falls above Matadi. The Zambezi is navigable in its lower reaches for some 300 miles; but this distance is small in proportion to the 1,600-mile total length of the river. Of the Nile's 4,000-mile length only a little more than 600 miles are below the first cataract. Of the Niger's 2,600-mile length only a little more than 400 miles are below rapids. The Nile, Niger, and Congo source regions correspond substantially to the wet-tropical habitat. The Zambezi and the Orange and Limpopo drainage basins to the south are almost entirely within the Highland Habitat. Each of the major drainage systems, except for the Niger, has cut deeply into the plateau in establishing a route to the sea from an elevated basin-like interior. These interior basins drain alternately to opposite sides of the continent. In the south the Orange River flows from east to west. The Zambezi north of the Orange drains from west to east into the Indian Ocean. In central Africa the Congo system escapes its plateau basin rim from east to west into the Atlantic. The two great river systems of northern Africa also flow in opposite directions—the Nile draining northward into the Mediterranean, the Niger first north, then south into the Gulf of Guinea.

Resources for Human Occupancy

Before examining results of the processes of cultural evolution, it is necessary to set down additional information concerning the diversity and wealth of material resources on which human activity in Africa south of the Sahara is based.

Warmth. Reference should first be made to the world map of warmth regions in Figure 28 of Chapter 3. Temperatures present small to moderate average annual ranges except in the central Sahara, where the range is greater than 30 but less than 50 degrees. Seasonal cycles of average daily temperatures are almost entirely hot or warm-hot. The only exception occurs in the south where elevations reduce daily average temperatures below 50 degrees but still above freezing. Frost is a rarity in Africa and occurs only in the high plateau country of the Republic of South Africa and in certain situations at high elevations elsewhere. Growing season is

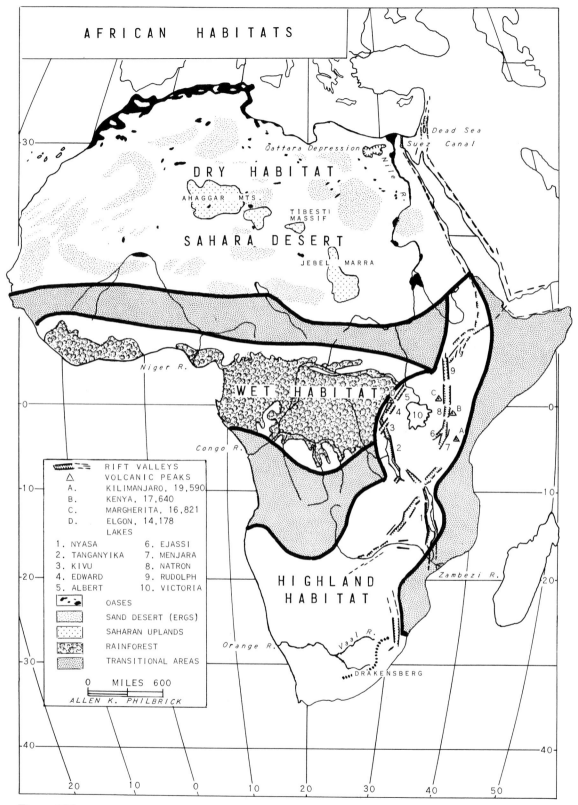

AFRICAN HABITATS

DRY HABITAT

Qattara Depression

Dead Sea

Suez Canal

Nile R.

AHAGGAR MTS.

TIBESTI
MASSIF

SAHARA DESERT

JEBEL MARRA

Niger R.

WET HABITAT

Congo R.

RIFT VALLEYS
VOLCANIC PEAKS
A. KILIMANJARO, 19,590
B. KENYA, 17,640
C. MARGHERITA, 16,821
D. ELGON, 14,178
LAKES
1. NYASA   6. EJASSI
2. TANGANYIKA   7. MENJARA
3. KIVU   8. NATRON
4. EDWARD   9. RUDOLPH
5. ALBERT   10. VICTORIA

OASES
SAND DESERT (ERGS)
SAHARAN UPLANDS
RAINFOREST
TRANSITIONAL AREAS

0   MILES 600

ALLEN K. PHILBRICK

HIGHLAND
HABITAT

Zambezi R.

Orange R.

Vaal R.

DRAKENSBERG

Figure 110

186

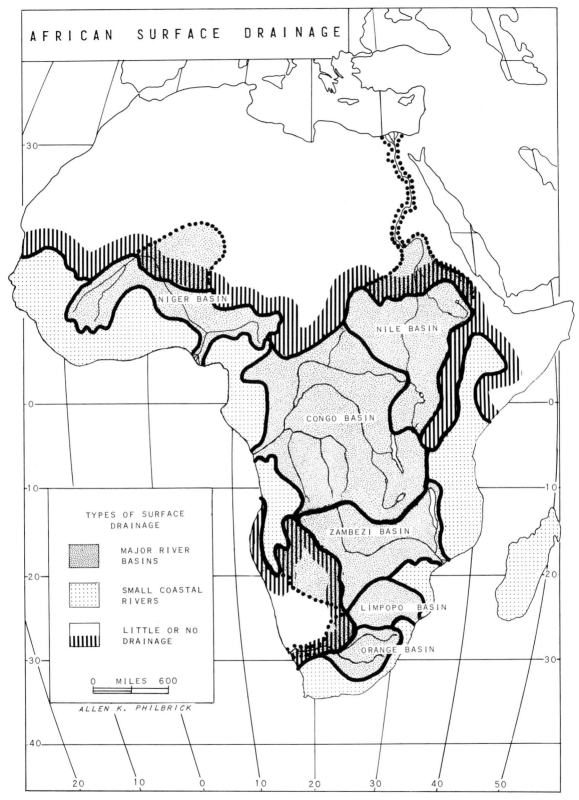

AFRICAN SURFACE DRAINAGE

NIGER BASIN

NILE BASIN

CONGO BASIN

ZAMBEZI BASIN

LIMPOPO BASIN

ORANGE BASIN

TYPES OF SURFACE
DRAINAGE

MAJOR RIVER
BASINS

SMALL COASTAL
RIVERS

LITTLE OR NO
DRAINAGE

0   MILES   600

ALLEN K. PHILBRICK

Figure 111

187

year-round, except for the high interior of the Republic of South Africa. In most of Africa south of the Sahara limitation on plant growth comes from drought rather than from frost. The most important modification of warmth characteristics is the result of elevation illustrated by the map in Figure 112. Spot average annual temperatures and the average annual isotherm of 70 degrees on the map show 7- to 15-degree differences in temperature between highlands over 3,000 feet and corresponding coastal lowlands at equivalent latitudes. Similar differences also obtain between minimum and maximum temperatures of the highlands and lowlands.

Water. Africa south of the Sahara, as shown by the map in Figure 31 of Chapter 3, is humid to wet. Precipitation is moderately dependable with a maximum in the summer. Saharan Africa is dry, variable, with seasonal maxima in the winter for the most part. Along the equatorward margins seasonal maximum precipitation occurs in the summer. The eastern third of southern Africa is humid with a summer maximum. Drought increases westward with maximum amounts shifting to the winter months. The southernmost margin of the continent east of Capetown is humid with precipitation reasonably well-distributed throughout the year.

Because the restrictions on plant growth by drought are more significant than by cold in Africa, seasonality of precipitation has special importance. Lines on the map in Figure 113 show the average duration of the longest dry season for the region south of the Sahara. The area with no dry season characteristic of tropical rainforest vegetation is restricted to the Guinea coast of Africa and a relatively narrow territory from approximately 2 degrees south to 2 degrees north of the Equator and from the eastern highlands westward to the Atlantic. Length of the dry season increases in a concentric pattern with distance north, east, and south of the all-year-round precipitation region. A dry season is measured in terms of the number of consecutive months with total average precipitation less than one inch per month. All the rest of frost-free Africa outside of the year-round precipitation region experiences a season of drought varying from a few weeks to year-round desert conditions as in the Sahara of northern Africa and the Kalahari desert in the southwest.

Relatively high tropical temperatures reduce the effectiveness of precipitation for vegetation and agriculture because of higher rates of evaporation.

Impact on natural vegetation is profound. Rainforest quickly gives way to mixed forest, scrub woodland, and tall, coarse grasses. A wide range of vegetational mixtures are collectively known as savanna. Poleward the association of vegetation changes to more grass and more widely spaced and fewer trees, until trees disappear altogether with ever-decreasing total amounts of precipitation and greater duration of the dry season. Still further poleward grasses continue to become sparser and shorter until vegetation virtually disappears in the hearts of the deserts.

Soil. Under conditions of constantly warm to hot temperatures which average approximately 80 degrees in equatorial lands, alternate wetness and drought produce distinctive soils. The soils are lateritic red loams and laterites. Rock materials steeped in warm water below the surface of the permanent water table undergo chemical transformation. One of the results is the occurrence of a deep layer of bleached hydrous silicate of alumina in which iron salts have been dissolved. Above this, in the zone of surface materials which are alternately wetted and dried, iron and other chemicals rise by capillary action and are deposited upon evaporation of the moisture. Thus, a zone of iron concentration occurs near the surface. Upon exposure at the surface, red or yellow-red hydrated iron oxides and aluminum hydroxide harden into bricklike masses of rock. Soils formed, in turn, by erosion of this lateritic rock formed at the surface by chemical action from other rock differ very little from the parent lateritic material, with the exception of added humus.

All the equatorial and tropical red soils agree in being reddish, in being leached . . . to the extent of having lost their lime. The minerals of the parent rock have been almost completely changed so that the soils consist of quartz fragments (sand, often angular), hydrous aluminum silicates and aluminum hydroxides (clay or clay-like substances), and hydrated iron oxides (giving red or red-brown colors). The organic content is low except where decomposition of vegetation accumulated in swamps and hollows has been slowed down. The downward washing by rain of the fine particles in the soil has often left a sandy surface layer—a hungry sand which easily dries out—over a heavier impervious or "clay-pan" layer.[1]

[1]L. Dudley Stamp, *Africa: A Study in Tropical Development*, New York: John Wiley and Sons, 1953, p. 107.

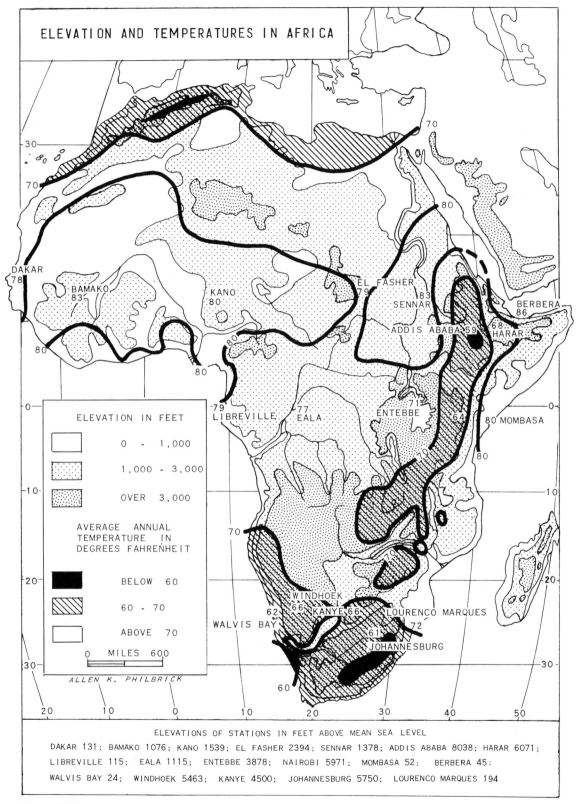

ELEVATION AND TEMPERATURES IN AFRICA

ELEVATION IN FEET

- 0 - 1,000
- 1,000 - 3,000
- OVER 3,000

AVERAGE ANNUAL TEMPERATURE IN DEGREES FAHRENHEIT

- BELOW 60
- 60 - 70
- ABOVE 70

0 MILES 600

ALLEN K. PHILBRICK

ELEVATIONS OF STATIONS IN FEET ABOVE MEAN SEA LEVEL

DAKAR 131; BAMAKO 1076; KANO 1539; EL FASHER 2394; SENNAR 1378; ADDIS ABABA 8038; HARAR 6071;
LIBREVILLE 115; EALA 1115; ENTEBBE 3878; NAIROBI 5971; MOMBASA 52; BERBERA 45;
WALVIS BAY 24; WINDHOEK 5463; KANYE 4500; JOHANNESBURG 5750; LOURENCO MARQUES 194

Figure 112

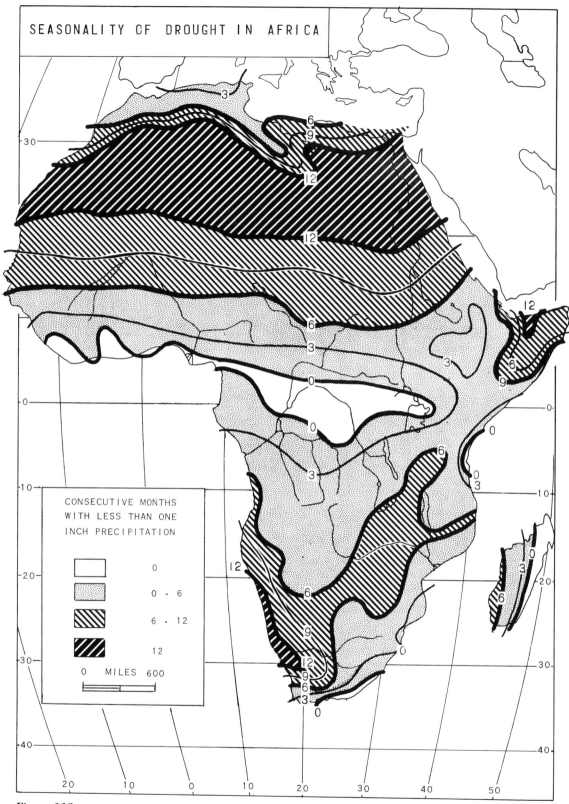

Figure 113

As shown in the generalized soils map in Figure 114[1] there is a marked coincidence of soils with the pattern of rainfall, shown in Figure 115,[2] as well as with the pattern of vegetation described in preceding paragraphs. Lateritic loams of varying reddish hues occupy the lowland wet and dry tropics. On the subhumid margins and in the eastern and southern African highlands, where grassland vegetation grows in response to small amounts of precipitation and long periods of drought, a darker chernozem-like group of soils has been formed. The red lateritic tropical soils are relatively infertile and require frequent fallowing to recover after tillage. Highland grassland soils are more fertile, but they are not as fertile as middle-latitude grassland soils. The single factor of higher temperatures even in the relatively cooler highlands dissipates critical nitrogen content of the soil faster than in corresponding middle-latitude grasslands.

These circumstances of moisture, drought, leached lateritic tropical soils, and unlimited growing season as far as warmth is concerned, indicate that *conservation* of agricultural resources will be increasingly necessary if food and commercial crop production in Africa are to maintain their present levels, to say nothing of further expansion of production.

It is suggested that the patterns of temperature, precipitation, vegetation, and soils be compared with that of generalized subsistence agriculture shown in Figure 116. The general conformity of tropical rainforest with shifting subsistence agriculture, of drier wet-and-dry savanna with mixed agriculture and pastoral subsistence economies (particularly in the highlands of eastern Africa), and last, the subhumid grasslands with a purely pastoral economy is striking. The conformity attests to the perception on the part of subsistence agriculturists of the appropriateness of certain kinds of agricultural techniques to particular combinations of resources. The same environments have been put to different uses by people operating from the technological standpoint of different cultures—African and European.

Subsurface Structure and Minerals. The map in Figure 117 shows the subsurface structure of the African continent. It is evident why the region of Africa south of the Sahara gives the name "plateau continent" to Africa. A very large proportion of the total subsurface is metamorphic rock, crystalline in nature. The block-like crystalline rock structure of the region gives it stability and

resistance to change. Structural breaks in the continental block are the rift valleys of the eastern highlands and the volcanic Cameroon Mountains—with an offshore island chain at the corner of the Gulf of Guinea. At opposite ends of the continent are two folded sedimentary highlands, the Atlas Mountains of North Africa and the eroded remnants of folded mountains in coastal sections of the extreme south of the Republic of South Africa.

The principal tableland of plateau Africa slopes from southeast to northwest from a general elevation of more than 6,000 feet in the eastern highlands of South Africa to a prevailing average elevation between 500 and 1,500 feet in the Sahara. The sedimentary strata of the Sahara are interrupted by central highlands which rise in excess of 10,000 feet. Despite these mountainous areas, the Sahara is primarily an extensive sedimentary plain. Narrow sedimentary coastal plains characterize Africa's east coast. In the center of the crystalline interior tableland the shallow Congo and Zambesi basins are also thinly covered with sedimentary bedrock. With these exceptions, the largest part of the subsurface of Africa is metamorphic crystalline rock.

The East African rift valleys are one of the world's great topographic features. The rifts or grabens extend intermittently from northern Syria in the Middle East to the southern end of the African continent. Extensive faulting occurred in association with the general uplifting of the continental plateau to form the alignment of linear trenches or rifts shown diagrammatically on the map in Figure 110. Some of these trenches contain extensive and deep fresh-water lakes. The alignment beginning is clearly evident in Lake Nyasa, although there is some evidence of rift faulting as far south as Natal.[3] From Nyasaland northward the rifts soon divide into an eastern and a western branch. The western belt is occupied from south to north by Lakes Tanganyika, Mweru, Kivu, Edward, and Albert which together mark the eastern border of the Republic of the Congo. The eastern rift belt is similarly occupied from south to north by a series of smaller lakes, Ejassi, Menjara, Gelai, and the larger Lake Rudolph.

The two branches of the rift topography and associated highlands rim a plateau basin which is divided between two drainage systems. The south-

[1] *Ibid.*, p. 94.

[2] *Ibid.*, p. 70.

[3] Rift faulting shown on the map in Figure 110 south of Lake Nyasa is based upon original field observation by Dr. Harm De Blij of Michigan State University.

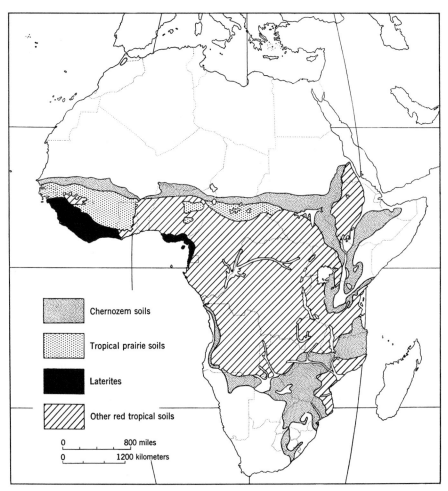

Figure 114. Simplified soil map of Africa (*after Marbut*). (*Courtesy of John Wiley and Sons, Inc., taken from L. Dudley Stamp,* Africa, A Study in Tropical Development.)

ern half of the oval-shaped region drains into the Congo by way of Lake Tanganyika. The northern half contains shallow Lake Victoria—elevation 3,720 feet. Lake Victoria spills northward over Owen Falls into the Victoria Nile. It is the second largest fresh-water lake in the world with an area of 26,640 square miles, exceeded only by Lake Superior in North America. From Lake Rudolph the eastern rift belt continues northeastward splitting the Ethiopian highlands into two sections. The Gulf of Aden-Red Sea depression is a continuation of rift-valley structure through the Gulf of Aqaba still further northward through the Jordan River Valley occupied by the Dead Sea. The rift alignment ends in northern Syria after having traversed more than 3,500 miles, a distance greater than that across the entire continental United States. Mountains of volcanic origin were also formed in asso-

ciation with rift faulting. Among these Mount Kilimanjaro (19,317 feet), Mount Kenya (17,040), and Mount Ruwenzori (16,795 feet) are the three highest in Africa.

In keeping with the relationship of economic mineral types to major bedrock types, the map in Figure 117 also shows location of the most important mineral-producing districts. Petroleum and coal occur in older sedimentary rocks. Metallic minerals are mined from the main body of the metamorphic continental block. Organization of African mineral production will be discussed later.

Three Africas

There are three Africas superimposed one upon the other—alien European Africa, tribal "African" Africa, and the new nationalist African republics. The cultural mixture is a result of European con-

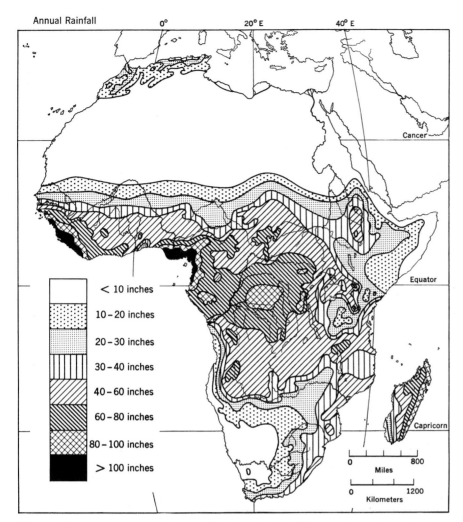

Figure 115. Average annual rainfall. (*Courtesy of John Wiley and Sons, Inc., taken from L. Dudley Stamp, Africa, A Study in Tropical Development.*)

quest of Africa and reaction to colonialism. Forced participation of tribal Africans in production of food and raw materials for export to Europe introduced a veneer of European culture into tribal "African" Africa. Now that political freedom is being won by country after country new aspirations of Africans are finding expression. A third culture is evolving as Africans make use of what they have absorbed from European culture and combine it with their own traditional values and ways of doing things in the building of the new African republics.

South of the Sahara the majority of the population is Negro. Europeans, except in the Republic of South Africa, are a tiny minority. This minority of Europeans, however, has had a tremendous impact everywhere on indigenous tribal African society. Under colonialism black Africans lived primarily by local subsistence agriculture, although they worked elsewhere for European enterprises. In the colonialist period Europeans were the masters, overseers, administrative officials, missionaries, technical developers, and imported workers. Very few, except in South Africa, and in parts of east Africa, were permanent settlers.

Types of Area Organization. When the patterns of tribal areas in Africa are compared with the political map illustrating European partition, it is very evident that the colonial territories were set up in complete ignorance of the distribution of African peoples themselves. Patterns of African area organization reflect a complex mixture of

AFRICA SOUTH OF THE SAHARA 193

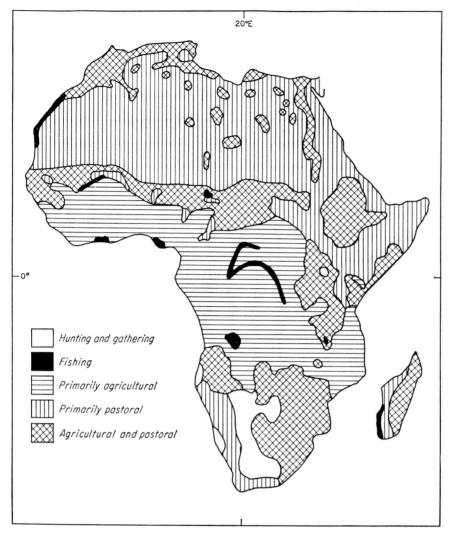

Figure 116. Distribution of types of subsistence economy. (*Courtesy of McGraw-Hill Book Co., Inc., taken from G. P. Murdock,* Africa, Its Peoples and Their Culture History, © *1959.*)

local subsistence area organization and regional exchange organization which resulted from the overlapping occupancies of Africans and people of European cultures. Saharan Africa is characterized by indigenous pastoral subsistence and oasis agriculture. These livelihood patterns are overlaid by a system of urban points of focus and transportation linkages created by European exchange organizers of area. In a similar fashion Africa south of the Sahara exhibits dual patterns of indigenous forest, field and livestock-oriented local subsistence livelihood, and externally oriented commercial plantation and mining enterprises linked with foreign areas in world trade. In only one region of the entire continent has *exchange organization of area* developed to the point of such prominence that the

existence of a coherently organized national economy is recognizable. This region is the Republic of South Africa, which is classified and discussed in Chapter 11 as a secondary core region of exchange organization important on a world scale.

The political impact of Europeans on Africa may be visualized by examining the two maps in Figure 118 and 119 in comparison with that dealing with indigenous African cultures in Figure 109. The first two maps of African colonialism and of African nationalism show the tide of colonial partition of the continent from 1884 to 1914[1] and the corresponding ebbing of colonialism on the world map in Figure 107, particularly after World War II.

[1] Stamp, *op. cit.*, pp. 27 and 31.

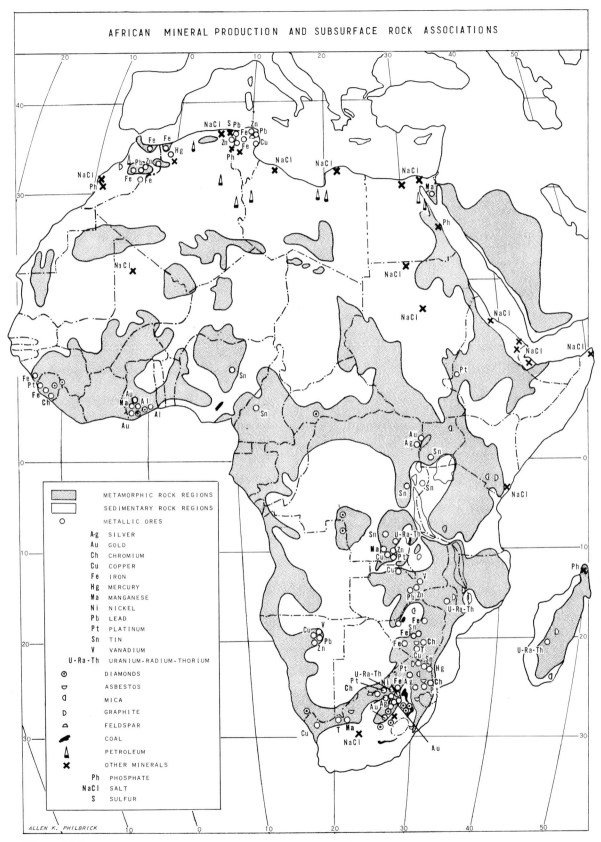

AFRICAN MINERAL PRODUCTION AND SUBSURFACE ROCK ASSOCIATIONS

METAMORPHIC ROCK REGIONS
SEDIMENTARY ROCK REGIONS
○ METALLIC ORES

Ag SILVER
Au GOLD
Ch CHROMIUM
Cu COPPER
Fe IRON
Hg MERCURY
Ma MANGANESE
Ni NICKEL
Pb LEAD
Pt PLATINUM
Sn TIN
V VANADIUM
U-Ra-Th URANIUM-RADIUM-THORIUM

DIAMONDS
ASBESTOS
MICA
GRAPHITE
FELDSPAR
COAL
PETROLEUM
OTHER MINERALS
Ph PHOSPHATE
NaCl SALT
S SULFUR

ALLEN K. PHILBRICK

Figure 117

195

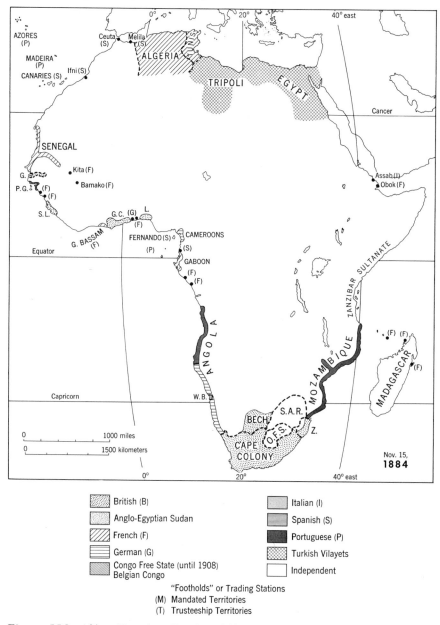

Figure 118. Africa, November 15, 1884. This map shows the spheres of influence of the various European powers prior to the Berlin Conference. It indicates also the footholds or trading stations. With the exception of two French trading stations in Senegal, influences were entirely restricted to the coast. (*Courtesy of John Wiley and Sons, Inc., taken from L. Dudley Stamp, Africa, A Study in Tropical Development.*)

These three maps should be examined in conjunction with the world map on the tide of colonialism in Figure 106 in Chapter 9.

The pattern of European penetration has been expanded inward from many points on the coastal fringes. The partitioning has been compared to the cutting of a cake. In Africa the central dividing line is irregular and near the middle of the continent. Arbitrary "bites" into the body of Africa were often immense segments of territory extending from the sea deep into the interior. Others were small coastal enclaves surrounded on three sides by the colonial territory of some other power.

For many decades the political map of Africa

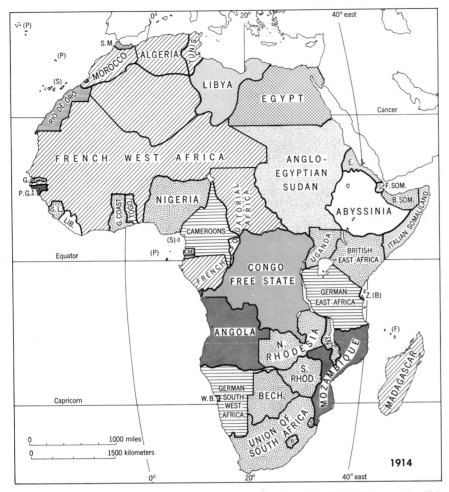

Figure 119. Africa in 1914. This was at the outbreak of the First World War, and it will be noted that the Germans had so far extended their territory of the Cameroons as to split French Equatorial Africa into two separated portions. (*Courtesy of John Wiley and Sons, Inc., taken from L. Dudley Stamp,* Africa, A Study in Tropical Development.)

was relatively stable. Within the artificially created boundaries it was not surprising that peoples of a common tribal language group often found themselves "belonging" to different European "mother countries" which spoke entirely different languages, with different currencies, customs, and conflicting economic interests. Political boundaries and private property meant very little to tribal Africans. These were concepts of European but not of African culture. Individual Africans owed allegiance to a tribe and to a tribal headman rather than to a particular territory. The abstract idea of patriotism attached to land did not originally exist among Africans. The idea of a national state was learned from Europeans. It must be remembered, also, that each tribe originally existed in relative isolation

from even nearby tribes. The spoken language could only be understood locally. Subsistence agricultural and pastoral local economies still further subdivided each tribal area into small groups of people which also often moved from one place to another within the tribal region. When these facts are borne in mind it can be imagined what misconceptions existed on both sides when Europeans began imposing their will upon Africans.

The complex of cultures arbitrarily combined under one colonial administration can be appreciated by the case of former French Equatorial Africa. That arbitrary political unit, composed of Bantu, Negrito, Sara Borgo, Sudanese, and Semite peoples, encompassed a great many different local language groups. Local Africans were actually less known to one another than are the nationals of one European country to those of any other country in Europe.

That the domination of nearly 200 million people in Africa as a whole by less than five million Europeans could have continued for 70 years underscores the multiple division, local isolation, and rudimentary level of organization originally characterizing indigenous Africa. Only three of the approximately 700 independent languages *spoken* in Africa ever achieved *written* form before the coming of Europeans. Lack of education retarded African nationalism more than any single factor. As education of a rudimentary level was achieved and political experience began to be acquired, it became a foregone conclusion that a unified will toward independence would develop. The political map of Africa can become more fragmented although it will continue to reflect the former pattern of European control to a large extent.

Political Patterns. For the present political division of Africa, a current atlas should be consulted and compared with the colonial pattern of Africa in Figure 119. The partitioning of Africa was originally dominated by France and the United Kingdom. The French acquired the bulk of the northwest third and the British at one time controlled virtually the entire eastern third of the continent from Egypt to Capetown. French territory is now reduced to a small portion of its former 3.8 million square miles. Algeria, which until 1962 was still considered an integral part of metropolitan France, is now an independent, predominantly Moslem country.

The British have fared little better. Cecil Rhodes's unattained dream of a "Cape to Cairo" railroad symbolized the imperial concept of British Africa. In the northern half of this great strip of territories, Egypt and Sudan are now independent. These countries are flanked on the west by independent Libya and Tunisia, formerly Italian and French, respectively, and on the east by the ancient kingdom of Ethiopia. South of the Sudan the former Belgian Congo, west of British East Africa, is now independent. Tanganyika was made independent in 1961. It is only a question of time before Uganda, Kenya, and the recently federated North and South Rhodesias and Nyasaland will also become national states. British and Italian Somaliland were combined as the Somali Republic in 1960, which is flanked on the north by French Somaliland. In southern Africa the English and Afrikaner-con-

trolled territory and ex-Commonwealth member, the Republic of South Africa, separates the two largest Portuguese colonies of Angola on the west coast and Mozambique on the east coast.

North of the Equator the west coast of Africa is marked by relatively numerous small colonial penetrations by Spain, Portugal, and former colonies of the United Kingdom. From south to north these are —Cabinda, adjacent to the narrow corridor of the Congo Republic (Portuguese and administered by Angola); the small Spanish colony of Rio Muni, or Spanish Guinea (surrounded by former French Equatorial Africa); four islands in the Gulf of Guinea (two of them Portuguese—Principé and Sao Thomé—and two of them Spanish—Fernando Po and Annobon); the largest former British colony, Nigeria, which gained its independence in 1960; the former British Gold Coast, now Ghana; the independent Ivory Coast; Liberia (independent since 1834); bordered on the west by the new republic of Sierra Leone; and two remaining colonial areas, Portuguese Guinea and British Gambia. Proceeding around the western bulge of the continent toward Gibraltar are the Spanish colony of Sahara, or Rio de Oro, and the recently freed country of Morocco, which includes the international city of Tangier (*200,000*).

All of these smaller mainland colonies and former colonies used to be enclaves, that is, territory surrounded on two or three sides by territory of another power—either French West Africa or French Equatorial Africa. The first French colonies to gain independence were the Moslem states in north Africa, Tunisia and Morocco, in 1956. In 1959 French Guinea, which was part of French West Africa south of the Sahara, automatically gained independence by refusing to ratify the De Gaulle French constitution of that year. In 1960 this fledgling was joined by the Mali Federation, a union of the former colonial provinces of Senegal and Sudan. Another group of countries which are named the Council of the Entente, became independent that same year. They are Dahomey, Ivory Coast, Upper Volta, and Niger. A third loose federation consists of the Chad, Congo Republic, and the Central African Republic. These three form the Union of Central African Republics from territory of former French Equatorial Africa. Four other French territories in northwest Africa also became independent in 1960. These were Mauritania, north of Senegal in the western Sahara, Togoland, east of Ghana, Cameroun, east of Nigeria, and

Gabon, west of the Congo Republic. These names complete the roster of sixteen independent countries which have emerged from French Africa, including Algeria. One more territory, the former French island of Madagascar, southeast of Africa in the Indian Ocean, is now the Malagasy Republic.

It is clear, therefore, that Africa, which had been partitioned and partially Europeanized since the end of the nineteenth century, has since 1945 substantially won its independence from Europe. The nationalist movement has introduced the third Africa, that of the new African republics. All three Africas, tribal subsistence, European-oriented participation in economic colonialism, and the striving toward coherent national area organization are elements in varying degrees on the African scene. Colonialism and the evolution of coherent national organization represent the penetration and development of exchange-type area organization in Africa.

Subsistence Agricultural Area Organization. The majority of subsistence agricultural units referred to earlier on the map in Figure 116 are in village or hamlet form (Figure 120A). Tillage is by hoe in areas of permanently cultivated land, as well as in the shifting slash of burn-type cultivation in forested areas and savanna. Use of the plow had not penetrated south of the Sahara before the introduction of European culture (Figure 120B). Lack of domesticated animals because of the tsetse fly prevented use of the plow in non-mechanized farming practices. Outside the tsetse fly areas, according to Murdock,[1]

Animal husbandry plays varying roles in the economies of different parts of Africa. It may make a negligible contribution to subsistence, as in the tropical-forest zone. It may provide a significant, though subsidiary, supplement to the products of tillage, as in many agricultural areas. It may combine with cultivation in a balanced economy with approximately equal dependence upon both activities, as in many societies that are commonly regarded as "pastoral," e.g., among the majority of the Berbers, Galla, Nilotes and cattle Bantu. Or it may be in large measure detached from agriculture, becoming the basis of an independent nomadic mode of pastoral life in which subsistence depends primarily upon milk and other animal products.

Independent pastoralism of this type has existed from the dawn of recorded history among the Beja peoples between the Nile Valley and the Red Sea, deriving presumably from the neighboring Bedouin Arabs to the east. Elsewhere in Africa, however, it did not develop until a surprisingly late date, probably nowhere much earlier than A.D. 1000. It has never the less spread very widely among the Afar and Somalis of the Eastern Horn, most North African Arabs, the Taureg of the Sahara, the Fulani of the western and central Sudan, and the Herero and Hottentot of southwestern Africa. Pastoralism may center on sheep and goats, on camels, or on cattle. Primary dependence upon small livestock characterizes the Arab nomads in the hinterland of the Mediterranean coast in North Africa. The camel assumes first place among the Beja, the Afar, and Somali, and the Arab and Berber tribes of the Sahara. Cattle play the dominant role among the Galla, the Baggara Arabs of the eastern Sudan, the Fulani, the Hottentot, and all Negro pastoralists.

From the above quotation it should become clear that pastoral activity in Africa south of the Sahara is usually in combination with cultivation. Two exceptions are the Nilotes of northeastern highlands on the margins of Ethiopia and the Hottentots in the desert and semiarid regions of southwest Africa. Long-horned cattle of the Watusi in Ruanda Urundi are one of the chief forms of wealth, as shown in Figure 120C.

The wet and dry savanna regions have a system of agriculture best described as "shifting cultivation, land rotation, or bush fallowing." According to Stamp,[2]

In a given year the villagers working together as a community will clear a part of . . . village land, cutting and burning the woodland or scrub and then planting the crops appropriate to the climate and soils of the area. In due course the crops are harvested communally and the land used for a second and perhaps a third year. It is then abandoned, and a fresh tract of the village land is cleared. The abandoned land quickly becomes covered with a second-growth woodland or scrub. In due course the clearings reach a full cycle, and if a given tract has been allowed to "lie" fallow for about fifteen years, it may be regarded as fully rested. Bush clearing is largely man's work. There is also surrounding the village itself, often as a series of enclosed gardens or "compounds" attached to individual huts, the "women's land," cultivated regularly to afford a supply of vegetables of the pot—often kokyams, peppers, beans, melons, bananas, etc. The women's land is enriched by house sweepings, ashes, refuse, and manure afforded by chickens, goats, and human beings.

The system has often been condemned as wasteful of natural forest, of land and of labor. But it has many good points. The natural forest is probably

[1] Murdock, *op. cit.*, p. 20–21.
[2] Stamp, *op. cit.*, pp. 150–151.

Figure 120

(A) The adult is Sho Fai Yuwar, a subchief, with his children in a subsistence village compound.

(B) The irregular appearance of subsistence cultivation is illustrated by this farm in a village near Lama-Kara, Togoland.

(C) The people of Ruanda and Urundi, especially the Watusi, attach great value to cattle, and the entire social system is built around the ownership and care of this livestock.

Photographs courtesy of United Nations

second growth of little value anyway. The land cleared in small patches protected by surrounding woodland escapes the evils of soil erosion, and its nutrient status temporarily enhanced by the ashes of the burnt bush is maintained by the fallowing, the soil not being exposed to the atmosphere long enough for serious oxidation. Expenditure of labor is minimized by burning and no attempt is made to remove large stumps. The cultivation is by hand—by hoeing—so the stumps do not constitute the obstacles there would be if the plow were used. We may accordingly agree with Lord Hailey when he says that shifting cultivation is "less a device of barbarism than a concession to the character of a soil which needs long periods for recovery and regeneration."

The map in Figure 121 shows the regions infested with the tsetse fly.[1] This pest carries the diseases of sleeping sickness among humans and nagana disease among domesticated animals. Modern medicine can successfully prevent and cure them, but their eradication in cattle will be a long and involved struggle of disease control. The so-called "fly belt" overlaps livestock-raising regions. Overlap represents areas in which cattle are raised with difficulty and where the diseases carried by the tsetse fly are endemic. Extension of livestock herding to all Africa would greatly benefit African agriculture by supplying motive power, a source of fertilizer, and a more widely distributed source of protein for the human diet.

Commercial Agriculture. The principal areas of specialized cash-crop production in Africa south of the Sahara are much the same after political independence as they were before. Management remains European for the most part, although it has changed hats. That is to say, management of commercial ventures is under the control of new national governments, but nationals of the same European countries which formerly ran these properties as colonial enterprises are now performing virtually the same tasks under contract for the new masters.

The map in Figure 122 shows the principal areas of continuing specialized commercial farming enterprises in their context with subsistence livelihood. The areas on the map are elongated and linear in shape because each one in the pattern of such territories is located with reference to transportation and accessibility to coastal ports.[2] Consequently lands developed for the exportable crops are near transportation lines by which tropical and subtropical industrial and food crops such as cotton, cacao, coffee, peanuts, coconuts, bananas, sisal, copal resin, rubber, hemp, and sugar cane

can most readily reach the sea (Figure 123A–D). It should be remembered that the introduction of such commercial farming represents the initial impact of European culture on African ways of life. Along with the crops came the exchange economy which dislocated and tended to replace the subsistence or self-sufficient organization of the African local scene.

Each of the relatively isolated patches of commercial agriculture on the map comes to a focus in towns and small cities which have been constructed in order to handle the products funneled through them (Figure 124A–B). These small centers and railhead and river ports at which materials are transhipped to coastal ports became centers for the dissemination of European ways of doing things. In a word, such commercial farming areas supported centers of the spread of European culture. The commercial economy introduced was specialized. It had as its purpose to obtain a few particular products with which to supplement the diversity within each European country's domestic economy. While these products complemented those of Europe, they tended to create a lopsided economy in the African territories from which they came. Manpower, soil, and water thus devoted to a few commercial products were withdrawn from the respective African domestic food-production lands. Last, replacement of traditional tribal organization by only partially understood and incompletely assimilated European ideas and a wage economy was often both disruptive and demoralizing.

On the other hand, Europeans brought religious instruction, improved health measures, and some education into the lives of many Africans. The impact of even partial Europeanization has been tremendous. The processes of area development set in motion by the introduction of exchange organization of area will continue to evolve under African aegis and with Afro-European cooperation in the new republics.

The land-use map[3] of a farm in Buganda, Uganda (Figure 125) by Hans Carol shows an

---

[1] Stamp, *op. cit.,* p. 170.

[2] Commercial agriculture locations in the tropical portion of the map in Figure 122 are based on data taken from William A. Hance, Vincent Kotschar, and Richard J. Peterec, "Source Areas of Export Production in Tropical Africa," map, plate IV, in pocket *Geographical Review.*

[3] Field map made and reproduced by permission of Prof. Hans Carol from field studies in Uganda. Prof. Carol, originally from the Department of Geography, University of Zurich, is now professor of Geography at York University, Toronto, Canada.

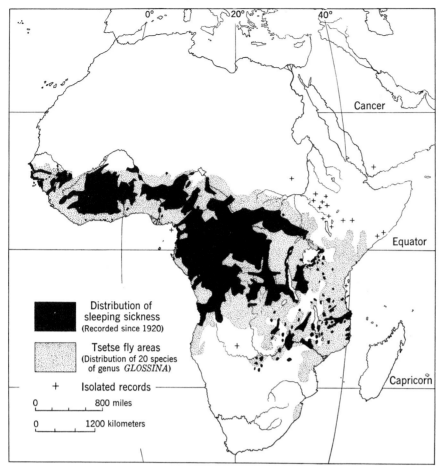

Figure 121. Sleeping sickness and tsetse fly areas. (*Compiled from information supplied by P. A. Buxton and H. S. Leeson.*) (*Courtesy of John Wiley and Sons, Inc., taken from L. Dudley Stamp,* Africa, A Study in Tropical Development.)

African farm which is transitional in nature, since it exhibits characteristics of both tribal and European field agriculture. The farm is small—7.5 acres. Fields are irregular and small, less than one acre, and they are evenly divided between subsistence and commercial crops. The main subsistence staple is plantain which is a member of the banana family. Principal cash crops are coffee and cotton. From the amount of area devoted to them by the African farmer it can readily be appreciated that production is nonmechanized and on a very small scale. Yet, in the aggregate, such farmers produced 134,000 metric tons of cotton in 1956 in Uganda. When integrated by a system of centers for collection, processing, storage, and shipment which are in turn connected by roads to a rail line operating between the commercial farming areas and a deepwater port, the production and movement of cotton

represents the beginning of an exchange organization of area. The operation of the cotton-producing enterprises of Uganda has been a training ground for Africans in the operation of a specialized exchange economy. Points of focus and lines of movement characteristic of the cotton producers of Uganda in the early 1950s are shown on the map in Figure 126.[1] The small-dot symbols signify the ginneries to which individual farmers, such as the one operating the farm depicted by Hans Carol, bring raw cotton. From these points of initial processing the cotton proceeds to less numerous local cotton markets, whence it travels to the railhead. The railroad from Uganda carries the cotton to Mombasa for export. Centers for handling the

[1]William Senteza Kajubi, "Cotton in Uganda," unpublished M.S. thesis, University of Chicago, 1954, p. 88.

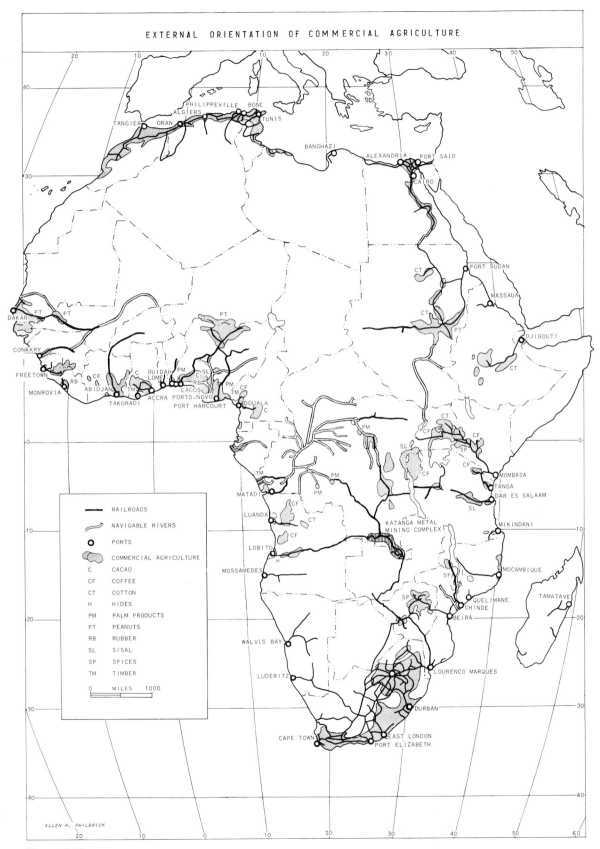

EXTERNAL ORIENTATION OF COMMERCIAL AGRICULTURE

RAILROADS
NAVIGABLE RIVERS
PORTS
COMMERCIAL AGRICULTURE
C   CACAO
CF   COFFEE
CT   COTTON
H   HIDES
PM   PALM PRODUCTS
PT   PEANUTS
RB   RUBBER
SL   SISAL
SP   SPICES
TM   TIMBER

0   MILES   1000

ALLEN K. PHILBRICK

Figure 122

203

Figure 123. Food, fibre, and wood illustrate the products of commercial agriculture and forest exploitation destined for export from externally oriented African participation in the European exchange economy. (*Photographs courtesy of United Nations.*)

(A) Above, a train load of cut sisal enroute to the rail head from the Yungi estate near Morogoro, chief city of the eastern province of Tanganyika.

(B) An African laborer cuts a bunch of fresh bananas at the Tiko plantation in the former British Cameroons.

(C) The principal industry and largest export of Liberia is natural rubber.

(D) Timber is being sorted and graded at Kumasi, Ghana, before being shipped by rail to Takoradi for export. Some idea of the size of these tropical woods can be gained by comparison with the people walking past the logs shown in the picture.

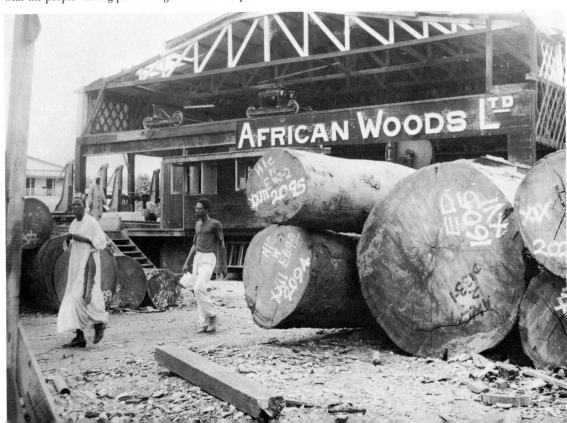

Figure 124. (A) Above, the unloading of crates of Dutch beer over the surf at Accra, Ghana. At least 30,000 tons of cargo comes in monthly by surf boat, an operation that is both difficult and costly. A new harbor is under construction at Tema, 16 miles from Accra.
(B) Below, logs floating in the harbor at Takoradi, Ghana's only modern deep-water harbor.
Photographs courtesy of United Nations

LAND USE ON A BUGANDA FARM - UGANDA

SUBSISTENCE
CROPS

FIG
TREES

PAPAYA
TREES

CORN

SUGAR

CASSAVA

SORGHUM

SWEET
POTATOES

YOUNG
PLANTAIN

PLANTAIN
FOR BEER

PLANTAIN

ELEPHANT
GRASS

COMMERCIAL
CROPS

COTTON

COFFEE

0   FEET   100

ALLEN K. PHILBRICK   from an original field survey by DR. HANS CAROL

HOUSE   KITCHEN   TOILET

Figure 125. (*After a field map by Prof. Hans Carol.*)

207

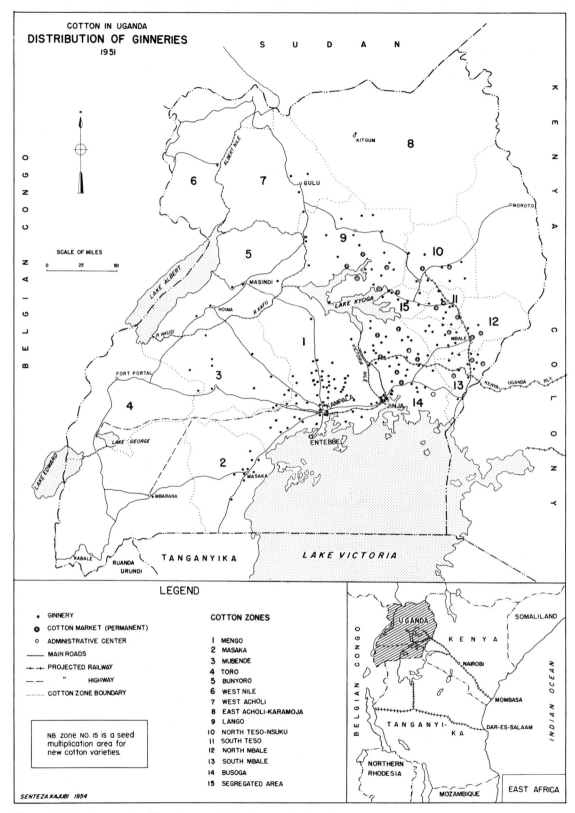

Figure 126. (*Courtesy of William Senteza Kajubi,* The Introduction of Cotton in Uganda.)

Figure 127. A view of the Wankie Colliery in Southern Rhodesia. At the left are the by-product coke ovens, with the "bench" on which the coke is quenched with water before being graded and loaded into railway hopper cars. The large tank in the right foreground contains crude tar recovered from the coke oven gases. (*Courtesy of Federal Information Department, Southern Rhodesia.*)

administration and control of the cotton trade are located in Kampala and Jinja. Brokerage aspects of trade management are focused at the port of Mombasa and overall management and control is localized in London.

Development of Mineral Resources. Mineral extraction is principally for export, as is commercial agriculture. Coal, of course, is mined for use in power generation and for smelting in connection with mining metals for export. Each colonial power's efforts have been directed toward finding those mineral deposits which would be most economical to develop from the many standpoints of demand, distance, quality, reserves, and ease of recovery. The ability of minerals mined in Africa to compete on the world market depends on these variables. Since development has not been directed toward use of the minerals within integrated African economies, the benefits to Africans from mining

were indirect under colonialism. They were measurable in job opportunities, side benefits such as medical facilities, markets for food and service supplied to miners in some areas, and a host of good and bad informal "educational" experiences.

Only in the Republic of South Africa and in the Rhodesias was there anything approaching integrated domestic use of the products of mining within Africa itself. These are the only two regions south of the Sahara which produce iron and steel in Africa. At Wankie, Southern Rhodesia, coal is mined from the edges of the interior basin's sedimentary beds. Some of it is moved north to the Katanga copper mines where it is used for electrical power generation and for smelting copper. More is used on the railroads to provide transportation, while additional amounts are made into coke, as shown in the picture of the coking mill in Figure 127, and used in the iron and steel works at Que-

Figure 128. The copper belt of Northern Rhodesia is one of the world's chief sources of copper, the largest in the Commonwealth and the third in the world. There are four producing mines at present and more are being developed. Shown here is the Roan Antelope Copper Mine in Northern Rhodesia. (*Courtesy of Federal Information Department, Southern Rhodesia.*)

que, Southern Rhodesia. Even in this latter use, however, the iron and steel from the mills is absorbed primarily in products used in the mining industry. The Rhodesian mining industry is the chief economic base of European settlement in both Rhodesias and is mainly export oriented. The same picture will be described for the Republic of South Africa in the next chapter.

The Katanga copper districts of the southern Republic of the Congo and Northern Rhodesia symbolize African mining, although because of their large size they are not typical. The battle over the secession of the Katanga district from the former Belgian Congo when it became independent in 1960 attested to the economic value set by conflicting interests on these mining properties. The metamorphic rock region in which the copper formation is located is divided by political boundary between former Belgian and British interests followed the continental drainage divide between the

Congo and the Zambesi river systems. The rail lines carry the copper in opposite directions on either side of the border. From one side copper is carried westward to the Atlantic at the port of Benguela on Lobito Bay, or moves by rail and river to Matadi on the River Congo. On the Rhodesian side copper journeys southward to the rail system of South Africa to Beira, Mozambique. It is well to remember that all this activity which is jeopardized but not stopped by civil war is controlled by the Union Miniere du Haut Katanga, an Anglo-American Corporation of Johannesburg and American Metals of New York. It involves financial control from centers at London, Brussels, Johannesburg, and New York. Operation in the Katanga districts involves both open-pit and shift mining and smelting at strategic points along the rail lines which interconnect the mines. The view in Figure 128 shows African miners drilling charge holes for blasting copper ore from a mine face. Refer to the maps in Figures 117 and 122. In addition to dependence on Wankie coal, electrolytic smelting makes use of extensive electrification from power plants on the Lufira River. Figure 129 shows an African workman stacking copper "pigs" at the smelter in Elisabethville (183,711) in the Congo Republic.

In addition to copper, cobalt, tin, radium, and uranium, among other minerals, are produced in Katanga. Belgian control of uranium in Katanga was important in the American development of the atomic bomb, and the Congo is still an important source for pitchblende, one of the principal minerals from which uranium is extracted.

While the specifics vary from mineral to mineral and from country to country, each one comes from a widely separate producing district isolated from the others, as, for example, the hydraulic mining of tin in Ruanda Urundi in Figure 130. Movement of the products of mining is controlled from and oriented toward the industrial centers of Europe and the Americas. Mineral extraction, therefore, gives further substance to the picture of external orientation and domination of European area organization over Africa. Political independence will not change this orientation immediately. Economic independence will only appear with the building of coherent national economies possessing increasing economic diversity. To be free they must be able to produce a larger share of their own peoples' needs within their own territories. This construction, indeed, if it is a possibility, will take time, capital, planning, hard work, and integration among groups of the new republics of Africa.

The present pattern of railroads, cities, and ports against the background of the emerging national map of Africa expresses the past *external* organization of commercial agricultural and mining economies south of the Sahara (see Figure 122). It is a linear pattern within the continent as a whole in which separate rail lines lead individually from the coast to productive interior hinterlands. The separate lines are linked in relatively few places. In north Africa the French have linked the lines penetrating into the interior by a transverse railroad paralleling the coast. Such a tie-up represents the beginning of a *network*. Most of the rail mileage examined country by country is a series of unconnected lines, except for the network in the Republic of South Africa.

Minimal transcontinental connections have been established across Africa south of the Sahara. By

Figure 129. The copper of the Union Miniere du Haut-Katanga, Elisabethville, Republic of the Congo, comes from the same copper belt referred to in the caption to Figure 128. (*Courtesy of United Nations.*)

combining rail-river-lake-rail transportation it is possible to move from the mouth of the Congo on the Atlantic to the east coast port of Dar es Salaam (128,742); but this transcontinental route is two separate systems facing outward, each backing up to opposite shores of Lake Tanganyika. Steamers on Lake Tanganyika connect the two systems over a distance of eighty miles. Coast-to-coast movement is the exception. From Beira, Mozambique, a second rather devious transcontinental connection exists through the Rhodesias to the Katanga mineral district of the southern Congo. The route then follows the southern edge of the Congo westward to and through the colony of Angola to Benguela on the Atlantic. Also, from Bulawayo (*190,000*), in southern Rhodesia routes connect with the better-developed rail network of the Republic of South Africa; but again inward- and outward-bound traffic is more important than cross-continental movements.

Up to the present time European national policies

Figure 130. An open cast mine in the Katumba area of the former Trust Territory, Ruanda Urundi. The tin ore is sluiced out of the hillside by water under high pressure. Other minerals from this site include wolfram, columbite, and beryllium. (*Courtesy of United Nations.*)

have directed the piecemeal development of transportation. Each power built to serve its own trade within its own colonial territories and only, if possible, to attract some business from its foreign neighbor did it connect its transportation to that of a neighboring colony. Under these circumstances the contrast between the rail-transportation pattern of Africa and of Europe may be compared to the difference between two wheels—one with a rim and spokes but without a hub (Africa), and the other complete with hub, spokes, and a rim (Europe). In this analogy the rim represents the sea; the spokes are the radial transport lines forming a network leading to the hub, which represents the core region of primary activity within the coherent regional organization of exchange. Africa has no core region for any major region, except South Africa. The external orientation of the former European African colonies was peripheral to the core region of Europe.

European Orientation of African Foreign Trade. The world is divided into core and peripheral regions which are organized in a complex arrangement of conflicting political, economic, and strategic blocs of power. Africa south of the Sahara

until now has been basically peripheral to Europe. Export and import data for African countries show conclusively how complementary has been the trade of Africa with European economies. Tropical African territories have *supplied food and raw materials,* and in turn have *consumed manufactured products.* This situation is duplicated in many other parts of the world and is not peculiar, of course, to Africa. The items of this complementary trade are subject to certain general observations. Exports from African territories reflect *resource-oriented* production of either commercial agriculture or of mining. For example the five largest exports of the new country, Ghana, are, in order of their value, cocoa, tropical woods, diamonds, manganese ore, and palm kernels. Figures covering these exports and other imports into Ghana are given in Table XVIII. Note that the first item in importance, cocoa, accounts for two-thirds of the entire export trade. The first five items represent 98 per cent of the total value of all exports. The entire commercial economy depends on a few specialized resources, in contrast to the diversified economies of the countries of the European and American corelands. These same points can be

TABLE XVIII   THE DIRECTION OF TRADE TO AND FROM THE TERRITORIES OF AFRICA SOUTH OF THE SAHARA EXCLUDING THE UNION OF SOUTH AFRICA, 1956[a]

Territory, capital	First 5 export items, millions of dollars	Per cent of total	First 5 import items, millions of dollars	Per cent of total	First 5 countries, destination	Per cent of total	First 5 countries, source	Per cent of total
French West Africa Dakar	Groundnuts	27	Cotton fab.	12	France	61	France	66
	Coffee, raw	25	Motor vehicles	9	U.S.	9	Morocco	5
	Cocoa	21	Machinery	6	Netherlands	6	U.S.	5
	Palm oil	5	Petroleum prod.	5	Algeria	5	W. Germany	3
	Cotton, raw	4	Rice prod.	4	W. Germany	3	Cambodia	3
		82		36		86		82
French Equatorial Africa Brazzaville	Tropical woods	37	Machinery, parts	17	France	64	France	57
	Cotton, raw	34	Motor vehicles	7	W. Germany	11	U.S.	9
	Coffee, green	5	Gasoline	5	Fr. Cameroons	4	Neth. Antilles	6
	Diamonds	4	Cotton fab.	4	U.S.	3	W. Germany	4
	Groundnuts	3	Beer, wine	4	Nigeria	3	Belg. Congo	3
		83		37		85		79
French Cameroons Yaoundé	Cocoa beans	34	Machinery, non-elect.	10	France	57	France	63
	Coffee beans	20	Elect. machinery	6	Netherlands	11	U.S.	7
	Bananas, fresh	8	Petroleum prod.	4	U.S.	7	W. Germany	4
	Tropical woods	6	Motor vehicles	4	Fr. W. Africa	6	U.K.	3
	Cotton, raw	6	Alcoholic bev.	4	W. Germany	5	Netherlands	2
		74		28		86		79
Tanganyika Dar es Salaam	Sisal	25	Motor vehicles	11	U.K.	31	U.K.	45
	Coffee	21	Petroleum prod.	9	W. Germany	12	Japan	8
	Cotton, raw	17	Cotton prod.	9	U.S.	8	W. Germany	7
	Diamonds, unset	6	Machinery	6	Belgium	8	India	7
	Oil seeds	3	Iron, steel	6	Netherlands	7	Netherlands	4
		72		41		66		71
Rhodesia-Nyasaland Federation Salisbury	Copper	63	Machinery	10	U.K.	59	U.K.	41
	Tobacco	16	Motor vehicles	10	U. of S. Africa	9	U. of S. Africa	33
	Asbestos	5	Elect. machinery	7	U.S.	7	U.S.	6
	Chromium ore	2	Iron, steel	7	W. Germany	5	W. Germany	2
	Tea, maté	2	Clothing	5	Italy	3	Canada	2
		88		39		83		84
Kenya-Uganda Nairobi	Coffee	42	Petroleum prod.	11	U.K.	24	U.K.	44
	Cotton, raw	32	Motor vehicles	10	India	19	W. Germany	6
	Tea, maté	5	Machinery	7	W. Germany	14	India	5
	Sisal	3	Postal pck.	7	U.S.	12	Bahrain	4
	Soda ash	2	Iron, steel	7	Japan	4	Iran	4
		84		42		73		63

TABLE XVIII (CONTINUED)

Territory, capital	First 5 export items, millions of dollars	Per cent of total	First 5 import items, millions of dollars	Per cent of total	First 5 countries, destination	Per cent of total	First 5 countries, source	Per cent of total
Belgian Congo Leopoldville	Copper	42	Machine tools	10	Belgium-Luxemburg	53	Belgium-Luxemburg	36
	Coffee	8	Motor vehicles	8	U.S.	14	U.S.	21
	Cotton, raw	8	Steel prod.	8	France	8	W. Germany	8
	Palm oil	8	Mineral oils	6	U.K.	8	U.K.	7
	Cobalt ore	7	Cotton goods	4	Italy	4	U. of S. Africa	4
		73		36		87		76
Angola (Port.) Luanda	Coffee	45	Wines	9	U.S.	23	Portugal	47
	Diamonds	12	Cotton prod.	9	Portugal	22	U.S.	14
	Fish	10	Motor vehicles	9	U.K.	14	U.K.	11
	Sisal	7	Petroleum prod.	5	Netherlands	9	W. Germany	10
	Cotton prod.	4	Tractors	2	W. Germany	8	Belgium-Luxemburg	4
		78		34		76		86
Mozambique (Port.) Lourence Marques	Cotton, raw	28	Cotton prod.	14	Portugal	44	Portugal	29
	Sugar	14	Motor vehicles	7	India	8	U.K.	15
	Tea	10	Rail roll. stock	6	U.K.	8	W. Germany	14
	Copra	9	Alcoholic bev.	5	U. of S. Africa	6	U.S.	9
	Cashew nuts	8	Indust. machinery	4	France	6	U. of S. Africa	8
		69		36		72		75
Madagascar (Fr.) Tananarive	Coffee	43	Cotton prod.	9	France	62	France	72
	Rice	8	Textile prod.	7	U.S.	15	U.S.	4
	Cloves	6	Machinery	7	Réunion	4	Algeria	3
	Tobacco	6	Motor vehicles	5	Algeria	4	W. Germany	2
	Raffin	3	Alcoholic bev.	5	U.K.	1	U.K.	2
		66		33		86		83
Nigeria Lagos	Palm oil prod.	27	Textile prod.	24	U.K.	64	U.K.	45
	Groundnuts	23	Motor vehicles	8	Netherlands	10	Japan	13
	Cocoa beans	18	Metal fab.	6	U.S.	10	W. Germany	8
	Cotton prod.	6	Basic metals	6	Italy	5	India	5
	Tin ores, conc.	6	Petroleum prod.	5	W. Germany	4	Netherlands	4
		80		49		93		75
Sierra Leone Freetown	Iron ore, conc.	38	Cotton prod.	12	U.K.	71	U.K.	60
	Palm oil	25	Metal fab.	6	W. Germany	12	India	5
	Diamonds	14	Rice	6	U.S.	7	Hong Kong	4
	Cocoa beans	7	Motor vehicles	5	Netherlands	6	Neth. Antilles	3
	Coffee	5	Petroleum prod.	4	Gambia	2	Netherlands	3
		89		33		98		75

TABLE XVIII (CONTINUED)

Territory, capital	No. export items = 1%	No. import items = 1%	First 5 export items, millions of dollars	Per cent of total	First 5 import items, millions of dollars	Per cent of total	First 5 countries, destination	Per cent of total	First 5 countries, source	Per cent of total
Gambia / Bathurst	12	21	Groundnuts	77	Cotton prod.	25	U.K.	96	U.K.	50
			Palm kernels	3	Kola nuts	9			Sierra Leone	9
			Oils, veg., anim.	3	Mineral fuels	5			India	8
			Oilseeds, meal	1	Medicines	3			Japan	6
					Elect. machinery	3			Neth. Antilles	3
				84		45		96		76
Ghana / Accra	13	23	Cocoa	66	Cotton prod.	11	U.K.	28	U.K.	47
			Tropical woods	12	Motor vehicles	9	U.S.	20	Japan	10
			Diamonds	10	Misc. mfctrd. gds.	6	W. Germany	18	Netherlands	8
			Manganese	9	Petroleum prod.	5	Netherlands	12	W. Germany	5
			Palm kernels	1	Metal prod.	5	Italy	3	U.S.	4
				98		36		81		74
Liberia / Monrovia	8	20	Rubber, raw	77	Motor vehicles	17	U.S.	87	U.S.	62
			Iron ore, conc.	16	Machinery, non-elect.	9	Netherlands	5	W. Germany	11
			Palm kernels	2	Textile prod.	9	W. Germany	4	U.K.	11
			Indust. diamonds	1	Cereal prod.	7	U.K.	2	Netherlands	7
			Cocoa	1	Clothing	6	Belgium	1	Italy	1
				97		48		99		92

[a] Source: United Nations, *Yearbook of International Trade Statistics, 1956*, Vol. 1, New York, 1957.

Territory	No. export items = 1%	No. import items = 1%	Territory	No. export items = 1%	No. import items = 1%
Fr. W. Africa	12	21	Mozambique	8	15
Fr. Eq. Africa	13	23	Madagascar	16	17
Fr. Cameroons	8	20	Nigeria	10	21
Tanganyika	14	22	Sierra Leone	9	26
Rhod. Nyas. Fed.	6	24	Cambia	4	13
Kenya-Uganda	11	21	Ghana	5	24
Belgian Congo	13	26	Liberia	4	26
Angola	13	14		146	313

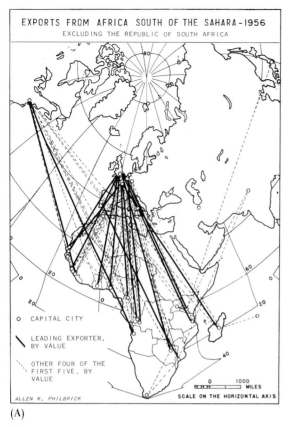

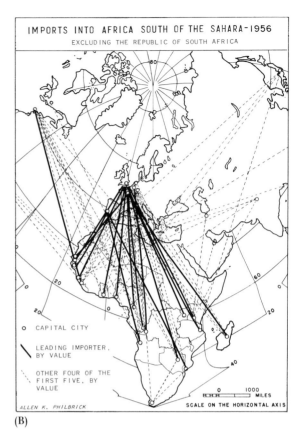

Figure 131

appreciated in connection with all the territories of Africa by reference to Table XVIII. An example selected from east Africa is the Rhodesian-Nyasaland Federation. Copper, tobacco, asbestos, chromium ore, and tea or maté are the first five items in importance by value of total exports. Copper leads the list with 63 per cent of total export value. From Portuguese Angola, coffee, diamonds, fish, sisal, and cotton lead in that order. Again, the first item, coffee, represents a sizable 45 per cent of total value of all exports. In the largest single former colonial region, French West Africa, 82 per cent of total exports in 1956 were four foods and one fiber—groundnuts, coffee, cocoa, palm oil, and cotton. The first three were exported in the ratio of 27-25-21 per cent, respectively.

Imports are a different story. Instead of being concentrated in a few large items, they are spread in smaller amounts over a much wider range of manufactured commodities. Former French West Africa serves as an example. Its first import by value was cotton fabrics in 1956, as shown by Table XVIII, but first place amounted to only 12

per cent of import values. The first five items of importance included, in addition to cotton, motor cars, machinery, petroleum products, and rice; yet together they comprised only 36 per cent of the total value of all imports. With an additional ten items the total swells only to 59 per cent. The second ten items are refined sugar, other metal work, electrical machinery, hardware and implements, flour, tires and tubes, paper products, condensed milk, cycles and motorcycles, and ceramics.

The five most valuable imports into Angola in 1956 were wines, cotton goods, motor vehicles, petroleum products, and tractors; yet the largest single item, wine, amounted only to 9 per cent. The total of the first five items was only 34 per cent as compared with 78 per cent represented by the first five exports.

In the Rhodesian-Nyasaland Federation, the first five imports were machinery, motor vehicles, electrical machinery, iron and steel, and clothing. They amounted to 39 per cent of total imports by value. The largest import was machinery which accounted for 10 per cent as contrasted with the 63 per cent of exports by value represented by copper.

Returning once again to the example of Ghana, the first five imports in 1956 were 36 per cent of total imports—cotton fabrics, motor vehicles, miscellaneous fabrics, petroleum products and metal-fabricated products. The first, cotton fabrics, was only 11 per cent of the total imports by value. The evidence confirms the statement that the interconnections between African economies under European leadership were indeed complementary. Little has happened to change this economic picture since 1956.

What of the direction of the trade? Does it interconnect Africa south of the Sahara with Europe significantly? Ghana's exports go first to the United Kingdom, then the United States, West Germany, the Netherlands, and Italy. The first five recipients of Ghana's exports accounted for 81 per cent of all exports. The four European recipients represented 60 per cent of total exports. In the case of imports, nearly three-fourths (74 per cent) came from five countries—the United Kingdom (47 per cent) followed by Japan, the Netherlands, West Germany, and the United States. The non-European countries' share in the first five imports was 14 per cent. It seems clear from an examination of Table XVIII, therefore, that the trade ties of Africa south of the Sahara are first with the European countries which now control or recently controlled them. Second in importance is the United States. The pattern of this interconnection of Europe with Africa south of the Sahara is expressed visually in maps A and B of Figure 131. On these maps the first-ranking importers and exporters to and from each African country are shown by a solid line, and each of the other first five by a dashed line. Truly such lines of movement in foreign trade make Africa south of the Sahara seem to hang like a pendant from the neck of Europe. Note that both imports and exports show fundamentally similar patterns. Note also the secondary but important role of the North American coreland as both receiver and supplier in substantial trade with countries of tropical Africa.

With remarkable consistency exports from tropical Africa are resource-oriented food and industrial raw materials; while imports represent not only capital goods for development, but a wide variety of manufactured consumer goods for which the standards of living introduced by Europeans have created an ever-increasing demand. Local African economies are not in a position to supply themselves with such goods, nor are they soon likely to become equipped to supply them. This fact underscores the important difference between Africa and Europe. It is the difference between a region with a well-developed geographical division of labor—Europe—and a series of regions in which such areal patterns of organized facilities for the production of manufactured goods do not exist—Africa. It also emphasizes the difference between the *development* of resources in Europe and in Africa. The European developer of African resources selected those which complemented the diversification of European needs. The impact of such development on Africa was completely incidental to the European. To the African, however, continuation of this dependent circumstance is onerous; and as African peoples aspire to and achieve political independence they may be expected to strive to plan and develop more diversified uses of their own resources in the future. Despite such eventual changes in the area organization of Africa, and the greater diversification of its economies, fundamental geographical differences in material resources will yet remain as the basis for interregional trade.

Cities as Agents of Cultural Dispersion. The cities of Africa are important centers of cultural conflict and agents of cultural dispersion. As might be expected the economic base of African cities is centered in activities having strong external orientation. Each has tended to gain economic prominence through production, processing, or handling of commodities, or by the administration and control of other areas performing these tasks. This has required the localization of sizable numbers of people; and the composition of this population has always included two or more cultures and a multiple number of ethnic groups. African cities have been the "schools" in which Africans have learned the Europeans' ways of doing things. Examples are listed in Table XIX.

Labor was supplied by Africans, supplemented by Asians. Local and regional commerce was controlled primarily by Asian tradespeople, supplemented by rudimentary development of retail trading by Africans. Foreign trade under the colonial system, of course, was in the hands of the Europeans. Accordingly, the distinctly different populations, each with different languages, attitudes, and cultural values, and ways of doing things had their closest contact in cities. The groups often had nothing more in common with each other than the fact of their location in a given city and a division of labor focused on the production, handling, or

TABLE XIX   COMPOSITION OF POPULATION IN SELECTED AFRICAN CITIES SOUTH OF THE SAHARA, EXCLUDING THE REPUBLIC OF SOUTH AFRICA[a]

City, country	POPULATION COMPOSITION					
	African	European	Asian	Arab	Mixed	Total
Ibadan, Nigeria	495,000	2,000	. . .	3,000	. . .	497,000
Leopoldville, Congo	359,332	20,982	. . .	. . .	. . .	380,314
Salisbury, S. Rhodesia	125,000	61,850	3,700	. . .	. . .	190,550
Nairobi, Kenya	115,000	11,000	38,000	. . .	. . .	164,000
Bulawayo, S. Rhodesia	94,000	42,000	3,700	. . .	. . .	139,700
Accra, Ghana	135,926	3,000	. . .	. . .	. . .	138,926
Dar es Salaam, Tanganyika	93,000	4,478	24,981	1,545	2,460	126,464
Mombasa, Kenya	65,000	3,500	37,000	3,500	. . .	109,000
Broken Hill, N. Rhodesia	40,000	4,200	. . .	. . .	. . .	44,200
Jinja, Uganda[b]	18,000	1,000	8,000	. . .	. . .	25,000

[a] Table based, except for Jinja, on Owens, *African and Middle Eastern Travel and Commerce Guide*, London, 1959, p. 1126.

[b] Data for Jinja taken from A. E. Larimore, *The Alien Town*, Chicago: University of Chicago Press, August 1958, p. 54.

administration which formed the economic justification for the city's existence (Figure 132). Economic stratification and racial segregation tended to keep each culture in its "place." It is not surprising, therefore, that clashes of interests arose immediately and found expression in social, political, and economic conflict within such centers as were provided by African cities.

In Jinja, Uganda, for example, the city is typically divided into different sections along cultural and racial lines. There are separate sections for Africans, Europeans, and Asians. Each section is the center for a complexly interwoven pattern of area organization. Their interrelationships form a multicultural example of the organization of area and overlapping tributary hinterlands. Such separation implies buried possibilities for conflict, but it also suggests the concentration of multicultural contact. The latter organized and unorganized contact constitutes the basis for cities to be centers of cultural dispersion and mixing.

Through African Eyes

A final means of seeking insight into the nature of Africa is to examine through the eyes of Africans the differences between their own African homeland and Europe or the rest of the world. This dramatizes the differences in cultural background of the two peoples—African and European—revealing as it does how far apart mutual understanding of the separate ways of life can be. For this purpose words by Dr. Albert Schweitzer will be used, taken from this missionary surgeon's *African Notebook*, written

in 1938. The final pages record the impressions of several tribal Africans who accompanied their European masters to Europe on a visit.[1]

A planter from above Samkita had taken his faithful cook, N'Gema, whom I knew well, with him to Europe. . . . On the first evening after their return, N'Gema's friends gathered in front of the kitchen to hear what he would tell them about Europe. His master, who had a good knowledge of their language, extinguished the light and listened from the dark veranda. N'Gema described the voyage on the big steamer, the storm at sea, the railway journey, the white men's large huts, the splendid plantations which needed no protection against elephants. And further he told of the forests in Europe where one can walk about without cutting one's way with a machette, of the plantations which produce flour and wine, of the villages in which so many people dwell that they don't all know each others' names, and of more besides. At each item the listeners uttered an astonished "Ah!" and asked to hear more. Then he told them about submarines and airplanes. But as the most wonderful thing of all he concluded with, *"In Europe the people work entirely by themselves. There's no need for overseers to stand beside them."* . . .

Two boys who had accompanied their employers from a timber concession in the jungle to their country estate in Europe also had to tell their acquaintances all about the remarkable things they had seen. They related that the most extraordinary thing of all is that in Europe *even animals work.* To satisfy the curiosity

[1] Albert Schweitzer, *An African Notebook*, translated by Mrs. C. E. B. Russell, Bloomington, Ind.: Indiana University Press, 1958. pp. 142–144. (Italics by present author.)

Figure 132. The central portion of the city of Salisbury, Southern Rhodesia (271,000), reflects its European culture. It looks like any modern city, but resembles American more than European urban forms. (*Courtesy of the Federal Information Department, Southern Rhodesia.*)

they had aroused by saying this, they had to describe again and again how when they left the ship they climbed into a big carriage to which were attached two animals larger than buffalo, and how the white man had spoken with these creatures as if they were human beings and then they had run now quickly, now slowly, or had stopped. As there are no horses here they did not find it easy to describe these animals to their listeners. They had great difficulty also in explaining *the work of oxen when plowing.*

In all the accounts given by natives who have returned from Europe, I have always noticed that it is not the railways and airplanes, *but the cultivation of the soil that makes the greatest impression.* My own experience on my way home is the same. The city, the hotel, the railway all seem at once familiar again. *But then to travel across the country where field follows field—that* is so unusual and seems to me so grand a thing that I am stirred to the very depths of my being.

In Europe man is lord over the earth. In the primeval forest of Equatorial Africa he is a creature that with difficulty wrests a bit of land from the wilderness. His plantation is always surrounded by forest and sooner or later the forest will swallow it up again. . . .

Contrast in ways of doing things, a central difference in human culture, is responsible for the geographical significance of these comments by Africans and Albert Schweitzer. What more con-

clusive evidence is possible of the essentially *local* nature of the organization of area in Africa than the amazement of Africans at the *continuity* of farm land in Europe?

The observations of Africans quoted above reflect the attitudes and understanding of unsophisticated tribal Africans. Nothing is static, and new nationalists of Africa today have a more sophisticated view of the world. Perhaps the most outspoken leadership comes from Dr. Kwame Nkrumah, president of Ghana, who spoke in the following trenchant terms before the General Assembly of the United Nations in 1960.[1]

Cast your eyes across Africa: the colonialist and imperialist are still there. In this twentieth century of enlightenment, some nations still extol the vainglories of colonialism and imperialism. . . . In my view possession of colonies is now quite incompatible with membership in the United Nations. This is a new day in Africa and as I speak now, thirteen new African nations have taken their seats this year in this august assembly as independent soverign states. . . . There are now twenty two of us in the Assembly and there are yet more to come. . . .

[1]Kwame Nkrumah, "Africa in the World Forum," excerpts from a speech to the United Nations General Assembly, New York, September 23, 1960, in Peter R. Gould, *Africa Continent of Change,* Belmont, Calif: Wadsworth Publishing Co., 1961, pp. 12–16.

Out of a total African population of over two hundred and thirty million people, some three percent are of non-African origin. To suppose that such a small minority could in any other continent produce acute political difficulties would be unthinkable. Yet such is the subconscious feeling of certain European settlers in Africa that to them the paramount issue in Africa is not the walfare of the ninety-seven percent but rather the entrenchment of the rights of the three percent and only considers the rights of the ninety-seven percent within the framework which is acceptable to the rest.

The world must begin at last to look at African problems in the light of the needs of the African people and not only of the needs of the minority settlers. Colonialism, imperialism, and racialism are doomed in Africa, and the sooner the colonial powers recognize this fact the better it will be for them and the world.

Paralleling forthright recognition of political purpose is the emergence of coherent exchange area organization. This includes the development of production and transportation facilities for the operation of the domestic economies of Africa. The African landscape is changing as the same cycle of the transition from subsistence to exchange economy and area organization which remade Europe is now taking place. In the words of C. W. Barwell concerning a part of Kenya,[1]

The traditional economy, as in so many other areas, was based on a cycle of activity involving marriage and agriculture. As soon as a man had sufficient cattle, sheep, or goats for the bride price he acquired a wife. Having done so it became the wife's job to assist her husband in accumulating sufficient wealth in cattle to buy a second wife and at the same time to produce sons and daughters by him. Daughters were very popular acquisitions to the family, because, in their teens they could be disposed of as brides and the family herds of cattle and small stock augmented as a result of the aquisition of the bride price stock accruing to the bride's father. Indeed the whole life and economy of the tribe hinged upon stock. . . .

Today, however, the scene is very different and

[1]C. W. Barwell, "A Changing African Economy," quoted from *Journal of African Administration*, Vol. VIII, No. 2, April 1956, in Gould, *op. cit.*, pp. 164–169. (Italics by present author.)

some significant changes have taken place. Perhaps the first and most impressive thing that strikes a visitor to the Kipsigis tribal area today is its resemblance in many ways to certain parts of England. This resemblance is largely due to the existence of the many small *enclosed fields* which are demarcated with hedgerows and are interspersed with small plantations of trees. Almost every square inch of land is now individually, as opposed to communally owned. . . .

Early in the last war the government introduced a policy of increasing the maize acreage in Kenya as a contribution to the war effort and, after a slow start, the Kipsigis readily accepted this food production drive. . . . the younger generation began a process of systematic land grabbing, accompanied by a mutual respect for each others' boundaries. It is interesting to note that although initially enclosure was practised with the sole idea of bringing about the permanent demarcation of the individual holdings, as the practice gradually became more general it was not difficult to persuade the more intelligent land holders that subdivision of their farms into areas of arable and pasture was needed in order to afford protection to the crops.

Private enclosure of land from subsistence to private farms in England was a preparatory step toward the industrial revolution. The impact of the spread of exchange organization of area is now increasing in Africa south of the Sahara.

Summary

Africa south of the Sahara has been examined in the context of the African continent as a whole. Its multicultural background and different resources compared with those of Europe are in striking contrast to the materials presented in the previous chapters. The "three Africas," indigenous tribal, European colonial, and African nationalist, were briefly examined in their spatial relations within the region. The continuing orientation of the economies of the new African republics to Europe was pointed out and the major contrasts of Europe and Africa were viewed through African eyes. The continuation of the spread of exchange organization of area which is rapidly changing the African landscape is predicted as the region of Africa south of the Sahara begins a period of rapid development.

11 Australia, New Zealand, and the Republic of South Africa

Australia, New Zealand, and the Republic of South Africa are examples of the emergence of secondary regions of exchange-type area organization started by Europeans in these parts of the world. They represent the independent evolution of transplanted European culture. The three countries are sufficiently similar in background and alike in their patterns of development to be discussed as one regional type; and yet each is individually different from the other. Although the Republic of South Africa has now left the Commonwealth, the fact that each of these units originally developed primarily under the leadership of the English as parts of the Empire and later the Commonwealth has been a unifying factor.

Similarities and Contrasts among Three Secondary Exchange-Type Regions

The exchange-type area organization introduced into each of the three countries from Europe is still in the formative stages of development. In Australia and the Republic of South Africa there are huge hinterland territories linked to more thickly settled core regions. The hinterland of New Zealand is limited by the relatively small sizes of the two main islands comprising that country.

Regional Similarities. Economic production in each of the countries has made use of a similar resource base. Each produces raw-material surpluses in both agriculture and mining. Wool is the leading export item from each—in 1956 in Australia, 45 per cent; Republic of South Africa, 17 per cent; and New Zealand, 33 per cent. In cumulative totals gold has been the largest mineral export, although other minerals are now more important as exports from New Zealand and Australia. In 1956 the proportion of total trade with the United Kingdom was 33 per cent for Australia, 29 per cent for the Republic of South Africa, and nearly two-thirds for New Zealand.

The three countries are located in the Southern Hemisphere and are therefore a great distance from the important ports of the Northern Hemisphere. Capetown (*731,484*), South Africa is 7,000 steamship miles from Liverpool, England; Melbourne (*1,777,700*), Australia, is 12,764; and Wellington (*142,300*), New Zealand, is 12,778 miles away. Southern Hemisphere position also means that their growing seasons are reversed from those of the Northern Hemisphere. All three occupy somewhat similar positions as the end of the road in migrations of aboriginal populations. Persons of European descent represent the meeting of permanent white settlement with indigenous peoples of strikingly different cultures and more primitive technological stages of development. The regions were similar in their historical development as colonies. The independence and Commonwealth status came to each at about the same time—Australia in 1901, New Zealand in 1907, and the Union of South Africa in 1910.

Regional Differences. The three countries also differ in many ways. Outstanding are differences in racial and ethnic composition of their populations. Of the Republic of South Africa's 14,673,000 people in 1959, only slightly more than 3 million —3,067,000—were people of European origin. This represents slightly more than one-fifth (20.9 per cent) of the total. The great majority of the population is Negro, of Bantu stock (estimated at more than 9,751,000). A second substantial minority is the Colored population (more than one million) which in South Africa is the name applied to a wide range of mulattoes (mixture of European blood with Negro); while a third minority is the Indian population of 450,000. By contrast virtually all of Australia's 10,166,173 people are of European stock. From an estimated 300,000 at the time of European discovery, Australia's aborigenes have dwindled until today a scant 20,000 remain. A

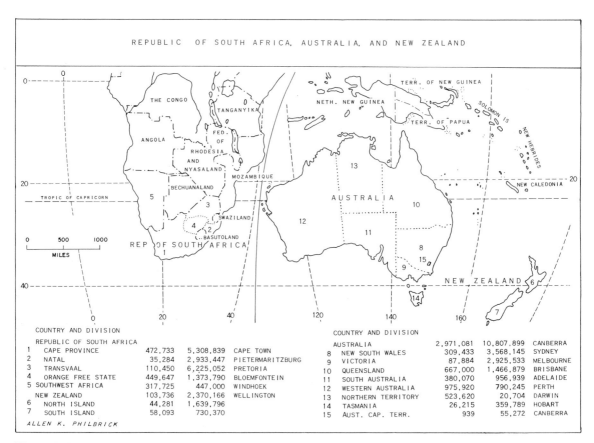

COUNTRY AND DIVISION			
REPUBLIC OF SOUTH AFRICA			
1 CAPE PROVINCE	472,733	5,308,839	CAPE TOWN
2 NATAL	35,284	2,933,447	PIETERMARITZBURG
3 TRANSVAAL	110,450	6,225,052	PRETORIA
4 ORANGE FREE STATE	449,647	1,373,790	BLOEMFONTEIN
5 SOUTHWEST AFRICA	317,725	447,000	WINDHOEK
NEW ZEALAND	103,736	2,370,166	WELLINGTON
6 NORTH ISLAND	44,281	1,639,796	
7 SOUTH ISLAND	58,093	730,370	

ALLEN K. PHILBRICK

COUNTRY AND DIVISION			
AUSTRALIA	2,971,081	10,807,899	CANBERRA
8 NEW SOUTH WALES	309,433	3,568,145	SYDNEY
9 VICTORIA	87,884	2,925,533	MELBOURNE
10 QUEENSLAND	667,000	1,466,879	BRISBANE
11 SOUTH AUSTRALIA	380,070	956,939	ADELAIDE
12 WESTERN AUSTRALIA	975,920	790,245	PERTH
13 NORTHERN TERRITORY	523,620	20,704	DARWIN
14 TASMANIA	26,215	359,789	HOBART
15 AUST. CAP. TERR.	939	55,272	CANBERRA

Figure 133

similar situation prevails in New Zealand. Total population is 2,381,000, of which less than 150,000 are Maoris, the original Polynesian inhabitants of the islands whose ancestors migrated there from the eastern Pacific several centuries ago. These differences in population composition accompany striking differences in policies affecting race relations, as will become evident later in the chapter. The roles of indigenous population differ markedly. In the Republic of South Africa the Negro majority is the bulk of the labor force in the mines, on the farms, and in the factories. By contrast the Aborigines of Australia occupy isolated interior "bush" lands on a subsistence basis; while the proud Maoris of New Zealand, once nearing extinction, now are given real opportunity to maintain their own culture and participate as respected individuals in the life of New Zealand.

New Zealand is a series of islands, only two of which are large. The two large islands, along with the several smaller ones, have a combined area of 103,736 square miles. Australia is the largest of the three countries with 2,974,481 square miles, while the Republic of South Africa is the southern 472,733 square miles of the world's second largest continent, Africa. The principal territorial divisions, their total areas and populations are given on the map in Figure 133.

Livelihood Resource Base and Economy

The economies of the three countries are based on similar resources.

Resources for Agriculture. The same selected resource criteria important for agricultural production in Europe will be examined separately and compositely for all three countries in Figure 134: *precipitation* (20-inch isohyet), *duration of the growing season* (240 frost-free days), *level versus rough surface*, and *soils*.

New Zealand is far enough south to be in the westerly wind circulation of Southern Hemisphere middle latitudes. Since the islands are comparatively small and have interior mountain ranges, the Westerlies bring moisture in relatively large amounts.

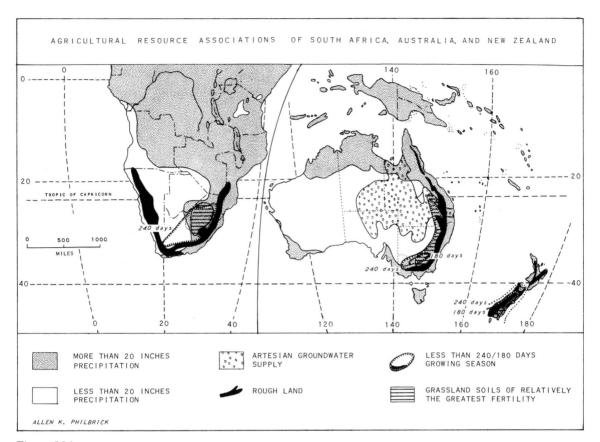

MORE THAN 20 INCHES PRECIPITATION

ARTESIAN GROUNDWATER SUPPLY

LESS THAN 240/180 DAYS GROWING SEASON

LESS THAN 20 INCHES PRECIPITATION

ROUGH LAND

GRASSLAND SOILS OF RELATIVELY THE GREATEST FERTILITY

ALLEN K. PHILBRICK

Figure 134

Although the eastern slopes are drier than the windward side, all portions of New Zealand experience more than twenty inches of precipitation annually. The wet tropic zone lies equatorward, to the north of both Australia and the Republic of South Africa. A dry interior and western continental dry region is surrounded on the north, east, and south by relatively narrow humid zones in each land. The twenty-inch rainfall line passes from north to south through nearly the center of the southern portion of the African continent. Drought increases rapidly in intensity westward from the humid east and becomes desert condition in southwest Africa. The same is true of western Australia. East-central Australia is almost equally dry, but receives the benefit of large underground water supplies. Artesian waters seep westward into the interior along underground rock surfaces from the well-watered low highlands of the more moist tropical northeast coast.

Except in New Zealand, which among all three countries lies farthest poleward, the regions of a winter-frost season are significantly related to high elevation. It is the High Veld in the interior and the higher escarpment region of the eastern part of the Republic where the area with less than 240-days growing season lies closest to tht tropics. In Australia less than 240-days growing season occurs on the interior slopes of the mountains and the higher portions of the interior plains adjacent to the Great Dividing Ranges. In New Zealand, all of South Island has less than 240-days frost free. In the interior highlands the length of the growing season falls below 180 days from the combined effects of latitudinal position and elevation above sea level.

The greater part of the Republic of South Africa is a generally level tableland which slopes from southeast toward the northwest. It is rimmed on its seaward margins by rough land associated with a great continental escarpment which rises to a general level of 5,000 feet, and in some places reaches heights of 9-10,000 feet behind a narrow coastal plain. Australia has the least highland of any continent. Only 5 per cent of its total area is over

2,000 feet in elevation. The highest point on the continent rises only 7,316 feet—Mt. Kosciusko in New South Wales, part of the eastern highlands. These highlands stretch as a rough dissected hill zone and low mountain barrier behind the coastal territory of the east and southeast coast. They extend from Brisbane (567,000) to Melbourne and are known as the Great Dividing Ranges, representative of old and worn mountain surfaces. The great central sedimentary lowlands and the ancient metamorphic (crystalline) plateau are essentially level land.

By contrast the higher and geologically more recent mountains of New Zealand are vigorously folded and alpine in character. Mount Cook—12,349 feet in elevation—dominates a range of mountains which covers half of South Island. East-coast ranges cover about one-third of North Island.

The southeastern coastal plains on each of the main islands have a longer growing season than the interior highlands. They also are less humid as they are sheltered from prevailing westerly winds by mountains. These circumstances account for grassland soils of the southeastern interior in each continent. The rain-shadow effect east of the mountains of New Zealand's South Island, in particular, is undoubtedly related to eastern coastal grassland soils. Natural grass covers the eastern plains and slopes of South Island, New Zealand, the southeast plains on the inland sides of the southeastern highlands in Australia, and the region known as the High Veld in the Republic of South Africa. It is particularly in these regions that the agricultural-resource association of grassland soils, moderate precipitation, frost every year, and predominantly level land are combined.

Agricultural Land Use in the Three Countries. The significance of the coincidence of these circumstances which represent resources of agriculture may be seen by comparing the map in Figure 134 with the map of cultivated land in Figure 47. The greatest proportion of agricultural land in relation to total land area has developed where the above combination of resources exists. The degree of farm activity is measurable by the fact that, except for smaller areas of intensive specialized farming elsewhere, these regions are the three largest blocks of agricultural land in each country. It is also clear from the maps of combined resources of agriculture and of cultivated land that the areas devoted to farming in each country are more nearly the same size than would be anticipated from the great differences in their total areas.

In each country the major agricultural area is backed on one side by rough land and on another by either the sea or the desert. In the Republic of South Africa and in Australia the agricultural heartlands are interior tracts separated from the sea by highlands to the southeast and demarcated by transition to drier lands on the west and northwest. In New Zealand the agricultural lowlands lie between northwest highlands and the sea. In the two continental countries the drier interior lands are occupied by sheep and cattle in decreasing densities paralleling the decreasing precipitation and grass cover to the west and north. Insular New Zealand has no such vast interior open spaces. There are other important specialized agricultural districts in addition to the agricultural heartland in each country.

Farming districts of the Republic of South Africa. The coreland of farm production is the *High Veld* in the southern Transvaal and eastern Orange Free State, a region corresponding roughly to the resource association just discussed. (See Figure 135.) The most diversified commercial crop and livestock association is located here. The principal crop is corn, a staple item in the diet for Africans, and also used for animal feed and silage. Diversity of crops in the High Veld reflects the division of labor between farming and urban activities of the industrial and mining district which focuses on Johannesburg in the Witwatersrand gold fields. Outward from the more diversified agricultural-producing region, cattle and particularly sheep raising extends over the eastern third of the country wherever there is more than twenty inches of precipitation.

On the east coast of Natal and the southern tip of the south coast in the Cape Province there are specialized crop districts. The Natal coast is a sugar-producing subtropical coastal strip. It has been compared to Florida or Cuba (pre-Castro) in relation to the United States. Its farmers are specialized producers of winter vegetables and citrus fruit for northern interior markets. Behind the coast in the hill country of Natal, cattle are important. This fact is also analogous to Florida in the United States, where livestock ranching has become increasingly important in recent decades. Behind the hill country lies the Drakensberg Range, the Republic's highest escarpment edge and roughest terrain, which rises at some points to elevations

Figure 135. Two "natives" plow a field which has been fallowed. This flat land is in the High Veld east of Kimberley. Mechanization has reduced the number of laborers required in South Africa. Note the cluster of trees around the farmstead in the distance. (*Courtesy of South African Information Service.*)

over 10,000 feet. The British Crown Colony of Basutoland contains the highest plateau country of South Africa which is surrounded by Natal, the Orange Free State, and Cape Province. Wheat lands of South Africa lie toward the higher plateau bordering Basutoland on the south. These are part of the diversified agricultural coreland of the High Veld. The southern edge of the Cape Province is the oldest settled portion of the country and also has a distinctive farming pattern, rather like that of California. With characteristic Mediterranean winter rains, it is not surprising to find Cape agriculture growing winter wheat in amounts up to half of the Republic's entire wheat crop. Appropriately, too, the Cape is the region of grape and wine products (Figure 136A–B), as well as of citrus and deciduous fruits. Fruit crops are irrigated largely as in Australia.

Farming districts of Australia. Agricultural-producing districts of Australia, shown on the map in Figure 137, will be mentioned in a clockwise direction around the coast from north to south on the east and from east to west on the south. In the tropical northeast, coastal farmers specialize in sugar, bananas, pineapples, and some dairying. Along the coastal fringes of New South Wales and Victoria, farmers concentrate in dairy products and vegetables for urban markets. There is some specialization under natural rainfall conditions, where

the incidence of frost is not severe, in citrus fruits along the coast north of Sidney. In South Australia, wheat, sheep, and fruits are major agricultural products, as they are in West Australia. The agricultural heartland is the Australian wheat belt of Queensland-Victoria-New South Wales. (Figure 138A and B). It also has specialized areas of grapes and citrus fruits, in the Murray River Valley and the Barossa Valley of South Australia (Figure 139). Irrigated areas are shown on the map in Figure 137. The relative importance of the core agricultural region in Victoria-New South Wales may be inferred from production figures by states in Table XX.

Wool is the most important item in the primary economy. The clip from more than 100,000,000 sheep (Figure 140) regularly accounts for nearly half the value of total exports. The main sheep zone forms an arc of territory along the inland side of the eastern highlands. The greatest concentrations of sheep occur in the zone receiving between fifteen and twenty-five inches of precipitation annually, which is also the heart of the wheat belt; about one-third of Australia's sheep graze on farms which also grow wheat. The Victoria-New South Wales agricultural core region is the largest sheep-producing area. Sixty-five per cent of the flocks are in these two states. It should be remembered, of course, that sheep production is also exceedingly

Figure 136. (A) Above, grapes are being harvested against a background of the rougher lands of the escarpment in Cape Province. (B) Below, this oblique air view shows a factory where much of the wine for Cape Province is collected. (*Courtesy of South African Information Service.*)

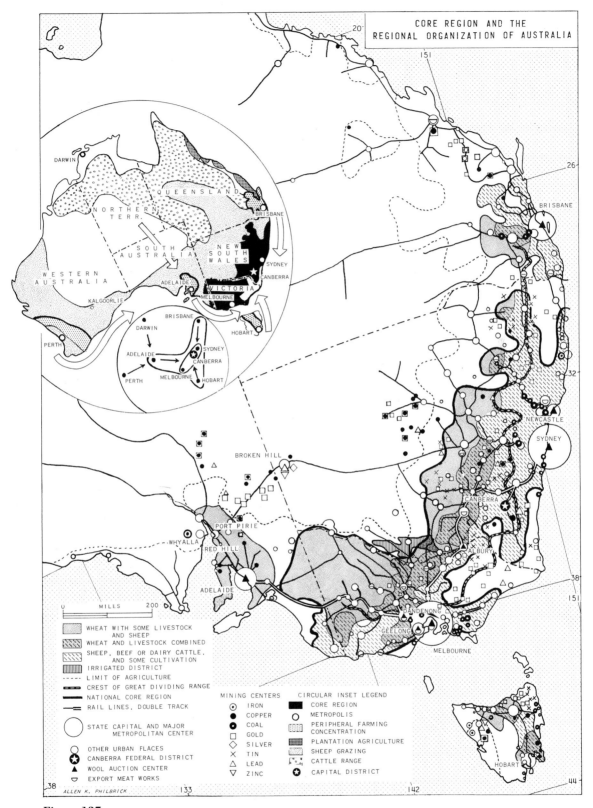

QUEENSLAND

NORTHERN
TERR.

DARWIN

SOUTH
AUSTRALIA

WESTERN
AUSTRALIA

KALGOORLIE

PERTH

NEW
SOUTH
WALES

BRISBANE

SYDNEY
CANBERRA

VICTORIA
MELBOURNE

ADELAIDE

HOBART

BRISBANE

DARWIN

ADELAIDE

SYDNEY
CANBERRA

PERTH

MELBOURNE

HOBART

BRISBANE

NEWCASTLE

SYDNEY

CANBERRA

BROKEN HILL

ALBURY

PORT PIRIE

WHYALLA

RED HILL

ADELAIDE

DANDENONG

GEELONG

MELBOURNE

HOBART

MILES   200

WHEAT WITH SOME LIVESTOCK
  AND SHEEP
WHEAT AND LIVESTOCK COMBINED
SHEEP, BEEF OR DAIRY CATTLE,
  AND SOME CULTIVATION
IRRIGATED DISTRICT
LIMIT OF AGRICULTURE
CREST OF GREAT DIVIDING RANGE
NATIONAL CORE REGION
RAIL LINES, DOUBLE TRACK

◯ STATE CAPITAL AND MAJOR
     METROPOLITAN CENTER

◦ OTHER URBAN PLACES
✪ CANBERRA FEDERAL DISTRICT
▲ WOOL AUCTION CENTER
▽ EXPORT MEAT WORKS

MINING CENTERS
⊙ IRON
● COPPER
◉ COAL
☐ GOLD
◇ SILVER
✕ TIN
△ LEAD
▽ ZINC

CIRCULAR INSET LEGEND
■ CORE REGION
◯ METROPOLIS
▦ PERIPHERAL FARMING
     CONCENTRATION
▦ PLANTATION AGRICULTURE
▦ SHEEP GRAZING
     CATTLE RANGE
✪ CAPITAL DISTRICT

ALLEN K. PHILBRICK

Figure 137

Figure 138. (A) Above, in southern Queensland west of the Great Dividing Rance is an extensive granary known as the Darling Downs. This air photo shows wheatlands of the region. (B) Below, the harvesting of wheat by modern "bulk" handling methods. On a farm in the Wimmera wheat belt, Victoria, where such methods are the most advanced in Australia, units such as these, popularly known as "field artillery," speed up the harvest. Toothed "headers" harvest the grain, and as the tractor-drawn unit moves through the crop, a screw auger forces the grain up the pipe and pours it into the grain box moving alongside it. Then the wheat is loaded into trucks by the same method. (*Courtesy of Australian News and Information Bureau.*)

Figure 139. These vineyards surround a winery in South Australia's Barossa Valley. Near Adelaide, the capital and only large city of the state, much of Australia's wine is produced in this sunny and fertile area. (*Courtesy of Australian News and Information Bureau.*)

dispersed over a wide range of circumstances and resources in regions where the density of sheep per square mile decreases rapidly with the decline of precipitation, as in the interior.

Cattle ranching, an important livestock activity, is an adjunct of sheep raising in the better-watered country of the southeast. Cattle receive major emphasis in subtropical northern and interior grasslands where sheep do not thrive, that is, in Queensland and the Northern Territory. Cattle country on the whole, is relatively poor water-resource territory. Carrying capacities are low and cattle stations are

correspondingly huge in area. Some of them cover thousands of square miles. Cattle densities per square mile, like those of sheep, decrease "drought-ward" into the interior (Figure 141). Examples range from as high as one beast per ten acres in the moist conditions of eastern Queensland to less than ten animals per square mile in the northern part of the continental interior. Even the carrying capacities in the interior are only possible as the result of artesian water supplies, which are fed from the precipitation on the subtropical and tropical western slopes of the Great Dividing Ranges in the

TABLE XX ACREAGE[a] OF WHEAT AND SELECTED FRUITS BY STATES, AUSTRALIA

Crop	Years	Victoria-New South Wales	Per cent	South Australia	Per cent	Western Australia	Per cent	Queensland	Per cent	Other	Per cent	Total
Wheat	1949–50	6,840	55	1,896	16	2,894	24	600	5	10	...	12,240
Vineyards	1949–50	62	46	60	44	10	7	3	3	...	...	135
Citrus fruit	1949–50	40	69	7	10	5	9	7	12	...	...	59

[a] Acreage in thousands. Department of National Development, *Atlas of Australian Resources*, Agricultural Supplement, Canberra, 1953.

Figure 140. A drove of sheep on the 8,000-acre Uriarra Station, 18 miles from Canberra, Australia's national capital. In the background is the station homestead. (*Courtesy of Australian News and Information Bureau.*)

northeast. Boundaries of interior artesian water supply and the region of flowing bores were recorded on the earlier map of agricultural resources in Figure 134.

Farming districts of New Zealand. Grass is the key resource in New Zealand; and again, wool is the chief product on which until recently export trade and the overall livelihood of the country has depended. The dairy industry is now a close second and increasing rapidly in relative importance. The dairy industry, of course, is also based on grassland, of both natural and cultivated varieties.

Dairy districts lie on the moister northern and western sides of North Island, New Zealand, primarily in the plains (Figure 142A). Sheep occupy less moist, generally east-facing highland slopes and the east coastal plains on both islands. The eastern half of South Island is the most diversified in agricultural production—characterized by wheat, sheep, and dairying. Wheat is the principal crop of the Canterbury plain, and is produced primarily for New Zealand consumption. The livestock portion of the mixed-farming east-coast districts of South Island is devoted to sheep raising, sown

grass—a feed crop for sheep—and some dairying. On the slopes of the New Zealand Alps, the nearest approach to Australian "out-back" country appears in the very large high-country sheep runs. A high proportion of these occupy Crown leaseholds.

On North Island, it is worthy of note that approximately twelve million acres of sown grass in hill country replaced the forests which were cut down and burned in the course of a giant transformation from natural forest vegetation to man-made grassland. This area is devoted primarily to sheep grazing. In dairy districts nearly five million acres of grassland are fertilized and used in rotation for heavy grazing rather than feed production. The New Zealand dairy industry represents a union of rural and urban phases of life within a single industry (Figure 142B)—an industrialized dairy farming-factory processing of butter, cheese, and condensed milk—in a very efficiently managed commercial portion of the nation's export economy. New Zealand has a small region of subtropical production on the northernmost warm coasts of North Island.

In summary, these three independent countries of the Southern Hemisphere possess the full gamut

Figure 141. A herd of cattle waters at a government bore on the main north-south stock route near Alice Springs. Water pumped from underground sources by windmill is stored in a large ground tank and piped to troughing as required. (*Courtesy of Australian News and Information Bureau.*)

of middle-latitude farm resources from subtropical forest to grassland steppes, from year-round growth to winter frost. They likewise have similar agricultural patterns of land use which are oriented toward production of mutton and beef, supplemented by subtropical and Mediterranean products, wheat, vegetables, and other fruits.

Mineral Resources in the Three Countries. The map in Figure 40 Chapter 3, shows the correlation between old metamorphic and old sedimentary rocks at the surface and the occurrence of particular types of mineral deposits.

Mining in South Africa. The oval pattern of the metamorphic uplands which are the backbone for the southern peninsula of Africa is distinctive. A shallow basin of younger sediments occupies its center. Small regions of old paleozoic sediments which are coal-bearing in places account for the coal measures of Rhodesia and of the Transvaal and Cape Provinces. The diamonds of Kimberley are located in old volcanic necks in the region between the Vaal and the Orange Rivers. The gold of the "Rand"—short for "Witwatersrand" (meaning, in Afrikaans, "white waters' ridge")—is found in

a steeply plunging Precambrian quartzite. Gold in southern Africa is in scattered concentrations from the Lake Victoria fields to the "Rand." Hematite iron ores have been developed to serve the gold fields. These ores are concentrations in sediments of the original iron content of metamorphic rocks, which with coal nearby are the basis of south African iron and steel industry. Copper is also found in direct association with metamorphic rocks, particularly in the Katanga district of the Congo and Rhodesia, but also in southern Africa.

Gold is still the primary mineral by value produced in the Republic of South Africa. Until very recently gold has been synonymous with the Witwatersrand and Johannesburg, but new gold finds southwest of the Rand in the Orange Free State give promise of equaling the Rand's riches, where more than 3 billion dollars' worth of bullion is still believed to be awaiting removal from the ground. Cumulatively, gold has accounted for 81 per cent of total mineral production from the time of earliest record until 1952 in the Republic of South Africa (Figure 143).

Of leading minerals produced, gold still holds

Figure 142. (A) Above, dairy cattle graze in the western Taranaki District of North Island, with the symmetrical cone of Mt. Egmont in the background. (B) Below, freshly churned butter in a New Zealand dairy factory demonstrates the union of farming and processing of food products. (*Courtesy of New Zealand National Publicity Studios.*)

Figure 143. An aerial view of Rand gold mine. (*Courtesy of South African Information Service.*)

the spotlight, although not to quite the same degree as in the past. It still accounts for two-thirds or more of total production today. The production of coal, iron, and limestone, the three basic raw materials of the steel industry which were originally subsidiary to the gold-mining industry are the foundation for a widening of the economic base of the country. While precious minerals such as gold, diamonds, and platinum are more than three-fourths of all mineral production, one additional mineral should be mentioned. Production of uranium extracted from gold-bearing ores was begun in state-controlled plants in 1952.

Gold mining is controlled by the Transvaal Chamber of Mines founded in 1889—an association of sixty-seven gold-mining companies, twelve financial companies, and twenty-two coal-mining companies in both the Transvaal and Orange Free State. This centralized private authority is responsible for 96 per cent of gold production as well as 70 per cent of coal production in the Republic. The diagram in Figure 144 shows the angle or line of strike of the gold-bearing conglomerate or reef which dips deeply into the earth from the line of outcropping in the Witwatersrand. Mining to a

depth of 10,000 feet is now considered practicable.

Mining in Australia. The subsurface pattern of Australia is divided into three major bedrock regions. From east to west these are old sedimentaries with very important scattered outcrops of Precambrian metamorphic rocks, more recent sedimentary lowlands, and a western metamorphic shield of Precambrian age.

According to the Department of National Development,[1]

Australian mineral deposits occur within two broad regions; in the west, a region of Pre-Cambrian rocks, geologically the oldest part of the continent; and in the east, one of Paleozoic rocks, much younger than the Pre-Cambrian, but nevertheless ancient. The rocks are intruded in places by masses (batholiths) of granite and kindred rocks, which are of the utmost importance, in that nearly all of the metalliferous deposits are associated with them. . . .

The areas of exposed Pre-Cambrian rocks include much of Western Australia, South Australia, and the Northern Territory, and portions of western Queens-

[1] Dept. of National Development, Commonwealth of Australia, *Atlas of Australian Resources, Mineral Deposits,* Supplement, Canberra, 1953, p. 5.

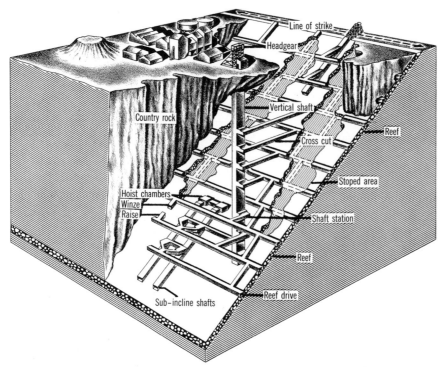

Country rock

Line of strike

Headgear

Vertical shaft

Cross cut

Reef

Stoped area

Hoist chambers

Winze

Raise

Shaft station

Reef

Sub–incline shafts

Reef drive

Figure 144. Diagram of the underground workings of a gold mine. This diagram shows the dip of the quartzite with which the gold is associated. From the relatively small extent of this plunging wedge of gold-bearing material and its reach far down into the surface zone of the earth's crust, some idea of the underground structures and mining engineering required to recover the gold can be derived. The demand for steel created by the requirements of gold mining is readily apparent. (*Courtesy of Transvaal and Orange Free State Chamber of Mines, taken from* Year and Guide Book to Southern Africa, 1961.)

land and western New South Wales. Their mineral provinces contain deposits of lead-zinc-silver, gold, iron, and copper, and they are by far the most important of the present day producers of these metals, apart from copper. . . .

The metalliferous Paleozoic rocks extend around the eastern portion of the continent from Western Victoria to northern Queensland, and form much of Tasmania. They are the host rocks of major deposits of gold, copper, lead-zinc-silver, tin and tungsten. . . .

Cumulatively, as in the Republic of South Africa, gold has been the most important mineral export from Australia. Gold was more important earlier than now, however. Coal, for use within the country, is now the most important mineral product. This shift serves to mark the change from colonial to independent economic status in Australia.

In all-time production, Queensland, Victoria, Western Australia, and the Northern Territory have produced far more gold than any other mineral.

For New South Wales it has been coal; in Tasmania, copper, and in South Australia, iron (Figure 145). At present gold leads in production only in West Australia and in the Northern Territory. These states, farthest from the core of the country, have the least diversity and produce mainly gold for export. By contrast, those states neighboring or containing the agricultural core, produce the most coal and the iron which are basic to a more industrial society and a wider division of labor regionally. The southern and eastern states of Australia have in general, therefore, the more diversified mineral production.

Mining in New Zealand. While the mineral resources of New Zealand are less important than those of Australia and the Republic of South Africa, that country repeats the same pattern of development. In total mineral production since 1853 gold surpasses all other minerals by representing 75 per cent of all minerals produced by value. In the post-World War II period, however, coal has surpassed gold by 66 to 21 per cent of total

Figure 145. Iron Monarch, South Australia, the source of some of the world's best iron ore and Australia's main supply. The ore is hauled 34 miles by rail to Whyalla, whence it is shipped to the blast furnaces at Newcastle and Port Kembla on the east coast more than 1,100 miles away. (*Courtesy of Australian News and Information Bureau.*)

mineral production. The gold in New Zealand comes chiefly from the dredging of alluvial gravels (Figure 146). Coal occurs in sedimentary beds on the west coast of both main islands. The shift from precious metals typical of the colonial period to more diversified production within an internally organized economy is part of the development of a secondary core region of exchange-type organization in New Zealand.

Patterns of Area Organization in the Three Countries

An examination of the organization of area within each country shows that each has a core on which internal organization is focused. At the same time, continued dependence on Commonwealth and other world markets demonstrates that each of these countries is in a transitional stage in the development of its economic independence. The pattern of geographical division of labor between city and countryside, and between specialized producing districts tells a story of evolving internal coherency of area organization. Lines of movement bringing the many different parts into a common focus in the core of each country renders this internal organization visible.

The Republic of South Africa. The pattern of organization in the Republic is shown by the map in Figure 147. The core region which focuses in the "Rand" is delimited by its surrounding agricultural hinterland. The economic capital is Johannesburg (*1,096,541*). A tripartite division of leadership among Pretoria (*415,989*), the administrative capital and capital of the Transvaal; Capetown, the parliamentary capital (*731,484*) and capital of the Cape Province; and Bloemfontein, the judicial capital (*140,924*) and capital of the Orange Free State, is an expression of the split within the Europeans between the English and the Afrikaners. The Afrikaners are the Boers, farmers of Dutch origin, who made the trek from the coast to escape further conflict with the British. They are Dutch Reformed in faith (Calvinist) and still primarily farmers. The English, concentrated in the coastal provinces, the Cape and Natal, are primarily urban. The Union of South Africa was formed after the Boer War be-

Figure 146. A gold dredge at work at Loburn, near Cromwell, on the South Island of New Zealand. (*Courtesy of New Zealand National Publicity Studios.*)

tween the Dutch and English elements ended in defeat for the Afrikaners. Seventy-five per cent of the Europeans, half of whom are English and half of whom are Afrikaners, live in cities. The remaining 25 per cent of the Europeans are farmers, 82 per cent of whom speak Afrikaans.

South Africa was declared a republic in 1961 by the Afrikaner Nationalist Party government which has been in power since 1948 and which voted to leave the Commonwealth in October 1960. Johannesburg (Figure 148) is the hub of the Republic of South Africa. It is the focus of rail, road, and air transportation. Specialized farming areas on the coasts of Natal and Cape Provinces are linked by these radial lines to the interior core area of the High Veld. The extensive grazing lands of the interior plateau and the intensively farmed maize-sheep-wheat areas of the High Veld are the economic base for rural Afrikaans-speaking Europeans of Dutch background. Bloemfontein, Kroonstadt (28,652), and Bethlehem (19,484) are important processing and farm collection centers. Each is a railroad center, and focus of grain elevators and agriculturally oriented industries. The principal urban markets are in the country's largest conurbation, which con-

sists of the many mining cities of the Witwatersrand, totaling in the aggregate more than 1.6 million persons out of the total of 3.8 million in cities of more than 20,000 people. Heavy industries in support of gold mining—coal, iron, and limestone mining, and the iron and steel industry—are located in a number of centers on the immediate periphery of the "Rand." As shown on the map in Figure 147, coking coal moves from Witbank 72 miles west to the Pretoria works of the South African Iron and Steel Industrial Corporation, Ltd. (ISCOR). There it is made into coke and combined with iron ore from Thabazimbi, 160 miles to the north, and limestone from Marble Hall, 145 miles to the north and east, to make steel. At Vereeniging (*216,000*), 36 miles south of Johannesburg, a second group of steel works has developed on a coal field which is close to still another coal supply of coking quality from the Newcastle coal fields of Natal.

While the primary purpose of the iron and steel industry has been service to the gold mines, it has had the additional effect of supplying increasingly diverse manufacturing of other types as well. In the Rand, in addition to gold mining, diamond

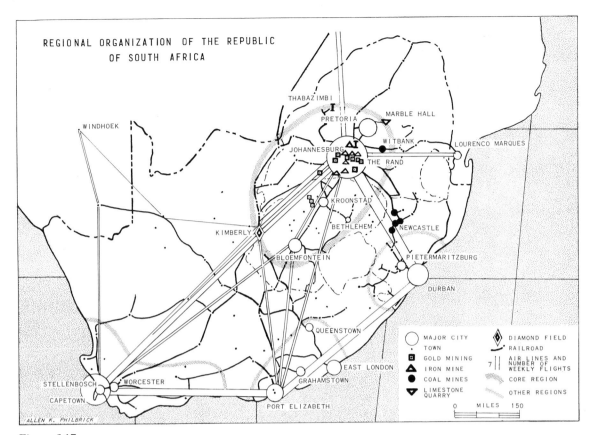

ALLEN K. PHILBRICK

Figure 147

cutting, and basic iron and steel production, a listing of manufactures in Johannesburg includes food, drink, clothing, textiles, drugs, chemicals, leather, metal fabricating, and many others. Capital accumulated from gold and diamond mining originally developed the Union of South Africa industrially. The story of diamonds began earlier than that of gold. The first diamond was discovered in 1866. Gold was not discovered in the Rand until 1884. The focus for diamonds is Kimberley, equivalent to Johannesburg as the focus of gold mining. The head offices of the Diamond Corporation, Ltd., the Diamond Producers Association, and the Diamond Trading Company and Industrial Distributors, Ltd., with offices also in London, are all in Kimberley. World production, distribution, and sale of diamonds is controlled by the DeBeers Consolidated Mines Ltd., which was founded by Cecil Rhodes in 1888 and based on Kimberley Mines. The Kimberley Open Mine, known as "the big hole," now closed and gradually filling with water, is thought to be the greatest man-made hole on earth. From it over 21,000,000 tons of diamond-

bearing "blue rock" were brought to the surface over the period of 44 years during which the mine was in operation. From this mass 15,000,000 carats —about three tons—of diamonds were recovered.

Surrounding this central region—roughly oval in shape and encompassing diamond, gold, coal, iron mining, and sheep-cattle-corn and wheat production of the High Veld—are three peripheral regions of importance. Their interconnections with the core region point up the fact that the people of the peripheral regions both serve and are served by the activities on the High Veld. The subregions are the Natal coast, with its principal center at Durban; the east coast of Cape Province, with its main center in Port Elizabeth and a second important center at East London; and the oldest region of South Africa, the southwest coast and hinterland of Capetown. The port cities of these three regions are the main outlets for the interior coreland. Harbors are government owned and are operated by the Railways Administration. Durban is the closest outlet to the veld and is the leading port both for the interior and the country

Figure 148. Johannesburg dates from 1886 when gold was discovered in what is known as the Main Reef. Within a year the Witwatersrand became world famous and a gold-rush camp sprang up where South Africa's largest city now stands. The reefs, which have been the means of creating this large city on a hitherto almost useless tract, run east and west of the town for a distance of over 120 miles, and the undulating country is dotted in all directions with great tailing heaps and buildings connected with the working of the mines. (*Courtesy of South African Railways.*)

as a whole. It is followed in importance by Capetown, Port Elizabeth, and East London. In general South Africa imports more than it exports, but exports exceed imports at Durban (*655,370*), where two-thirds of all exports leave the country.

The radial pattern of the nationally owned railroads which interconnect the coastal centers and interior points are the lines along which specialized products, in addition to imports and exports, move inland to the country's major market. These are agricultural products such as those already enumerated: sugar, winter vegetables, citrus fruits, and livestock from Natal; wheat, vine products, citrus and deciduous fruits from the Cape. Further discussion of special circumstances and problems within the apparent unity of the Republic of South Africa will be mentioned after consideration of the patterns of human organization of area in Australia and New Zealand.

Australia. Australia is the only country in the world which occupies an entire continent. The pattern of regional organization focuses on six separate metropolitan core areas first, and only secondarily on a core region for the country as a whole. Each of the six political states of Australia focuses primarily in a single metropolis.[1] In Western Australia over half (54 per cent) of the population lives in the capital at Perth. The same is true for Melbourne in Victoria. Approximately half (49.7 per cent) of the people of New South Wales live in Sydney. Only Tasmania (30 per cent in Hobart) and Queensland (36 per cent in Brisbane) have less than half their people in their respective state capitals. The Northern Territory is relatively uninhabited. In Australia as a whole, therefore, well over

[1] Elaine M. Bjorklund, *Focus on Adelaide,* Chicago, The University of Chicago, Dept. of Geography, Research Paper No. 41, 1955, map frontispiece.

half the total population lives in cities over 100,000 in population size. Eighty-five per cent of all inhabitants live in cities of over 20,000 persons. Canberra, the national capital (*43,973*) is located in a small neutral capital territory within the state of New South Wales.

As shown on the map in Figure 137 earlier in this chapter, the country as a whole comes to a focus in a core region for Australia. This core region consists of two great metropolitan areas— Melbourne (*1,777,700*) and Sydney (*2,054,800*) (Figure 149A and B)—and the core agricultural region landward from the southeast Dividing Range. The agricultural coreland is connected by a network of railroads to the dual metropolitan core cities for which it is the hinterland. These also interconnect a concentration of smaller cities, particularly on the west slopes of the eastern highlands. Overlapping of wheat lands and grazing lands for livestock in the higher and better-watered parts of the rolling uplands coincides with the axis of land connections by rail between Sidney and Melbourne, as may be seen by the map. The locational pattern of meat-export works in meat-producing areas and of wool auctions in principal ports is evidence of the focus and movement of Australia's primary product, livestock. In every one of its many forms—as meat, wool, hides, and dairy products— direction of movement is from producing area to collection points (railheads), to processing centers (meat works), and thence through ports to world markets. Australia's commitment to Commonwealth international organization is demonstrated by the fact that the United Kingdom absorbs the greatest portion of these products.

While the supply of foods and raw materials exported continues to rise, the diversity and amount of manufactured goods produced for domestic markets and exported in competition with the United Kingdom is also steadily expanding. The map in Figure 150 which is reproduced from an official source[1] shows the extreme concentration of manufacturing in the great metropolitan capitals, particularly those in the core region (Figure 151). It also shows the concentration there of twenty-five secondary manufacturing cities. The diagrammatic inset to the map of the core regions reveals a radial pattern in the distribution of peripheral regions. There are three inner peripheral regions around the

core to the northeast, west, and south, respectively, Queensland, South Australia, and Tasmania. Each has its own main metropolitan center within it. An outer periphery to the far north and far west is connected to the core region through Adelaide (*562,500*), South Australia, by transcontinental railroad from Perth (*389,000*), Western Australia, and by road from Darwin, Northern Territory.

The single greatest concentration of economic power in Australia, just as in the Republic of South Africa, has origins and continuing strength in a particular mining property. Australia like South Africa based its mineral-industrial development on gold. Silver, lead, and zinc deposits were discovered later, almost by accident, from claims staked on a shrewd hunch on the part of an amateur prospector at a place descriptively named Broken Hill. A company, the Broken Hill Proprietary Co., Ltd., of New South Wales, was formed in 1885 in order to develop the rich silver-lead ore body. This company has become a legendary producer of capital, like the "Rand" companies of South Africa (Figure 152). It was found most practicable to smelt the silver and lead ores at Port Pirie, South Australia—200 miles to the west. In the process of smelting, a high-iron-content fluxing stone (limestone) from Wyalla, across Spencer Gulf from Adelaide, was used. In 1911, BHP, as the company was popularly known, began iron and steel production on the basis of this iron ore. The ore is moved to coal at Newcastle near Sydney where the steel is manufactured. Products of BHP steel mills built Australia's rail networks and continue to be the basis for modern industrial development. In both South Africa and Australia the development of primary steel occurred in conjunction with mining. In both cases the mining involved precious metals, gold or silver. In each the investment of capital derived from mineral wealth widened the economic basis for national development from a purely extractive-for-export orientation toward greater self-sufficiency. C. Hartley Grattan, describing the significance of the BHP in his book, *Introducing Australia,* points out that now

. . . the BHP is, first and foremost, Australian Steel, and since 1935, when it absorbed its last prospective competitor, it has had a monopoly. It is also deeply involved in controlling the materials it uses; it produces its own iron, limestone, dolomite, fluorspar, and coal. It has built a plant to handle the alloys needed in producing special steels. It owns the shipping necessary to move its materials to New-

[1]Department of National Development, Commonwealth of Australia, *The Structure and Capacity of Australian Manufacturing Industries,* Melbourne, 1952, p. viii.

Figure 149. (A) Above, an aerial view of Sydney, largest city in Australia, looking south across the harbor bridge and shipping wharves. The Pacific Ocean is in the distance. (B) Below, looking east along Bourke Street, Melbourne, the capital city of Victoria. This is the retail center of the city, where most of the department stores are located. At the top of Bourke Street, in the distance, can be seen the pillars of the State Parliament House, with the spires of St. Patrick's Roman Catholic Cathedral behind it. This section is still known as "the Golden Mile," in reference to the roaring days of Victoria's gold rushes, a hundred years ago, when miners paid for their purchases with nuggets and gold dust. (*Courtesy of Australian News and Information Bureau.*)

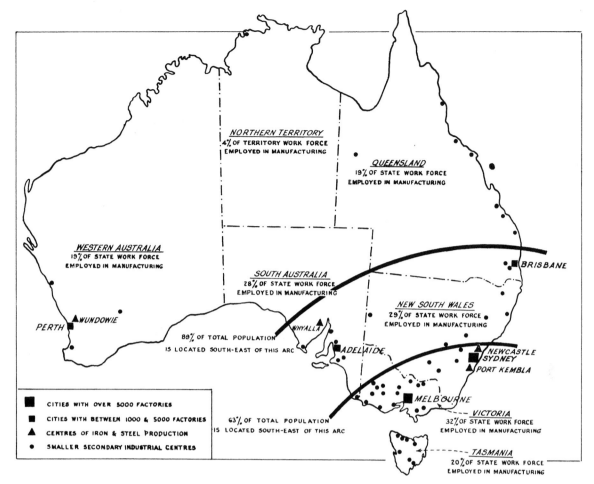

Figure 150. Australian manufacturing is concentrated in the south and east coastal areas. (*Courtesy of Dept. of National Development, Commonwealth of Australia, taken from* The Structure and Capacity of Australian Manufacturing Industries.)

castle, especially iron ore from South Australia. It is closely interlocked, either directly by shareholders, by directorships, or by being the sole supplier of the basic material of the industries, with shops producing black and galvanized sheets, plain and barbed wire, wire netting, fencing wire, wire rope, nails, steel wheels, tires, axles, and so on through the roll of steel processing industries. It usually succeeds in tying up with any concern whose activities have to do with steel as, for example, the American Rolling Mill Company which recently built a plant in Australia to produce steel sheets. It is directly or indirectly concerned, through the utilization of the by-products of various phases of its productive activities (e.g. the making of coke), in supplying the Australian market with sulphate of ammonia (used on the sugar fields of Queensland), benzol (used as motor fuel), napthalene, road tar, concentrated ammonia liquor, and so on. Naturally it is the principal Australian ally of Imperial Chemical Industries. It is interested in gold mining. In association with General Motors-Holden, Ltd., a

partly American concern, and the Broken Hill Associated Smelters, Pty. Ltd., of Port Pirie, it began in 1937 "the biggest aircraft development in the history of Australia."[1]

"BHP" has a London as well as an Australian board of directors. This situation underscores the continuing importance of the Commonwealth as an international and worldwide organization of area. Beyond and behind political independence of all the members of the Commonwealth lie a host of economic management interconnections which give its operation real hierarchical substance.

The railroad systems of Australia, unlike the railways of South Africa, grew up separately in the individual states, and function individually even though integrated into a national network. During the colonial period the idea was to have railroads

[1]C. Hartley Grattan, *Introducing Australia,* New York: The John Day Co., 1942, pp. 77–78.

Figure 151. General Motors-Holden's plant in Melbourne occupies a 50-acre site on the Yarra River in the Fishermen's Bend industrial zone. Here the first all-Australian car, the Holden, is mass produced with an employment of 3,500. (*Courtesy of Australian News and Information Bureau.*)

acting as feeders to the port cities, collecting the produce of the interior for export. Hence each of the separate rail nets focused on its colonial capital and certain other ports. Their competitive protection from "capture" by connecting lines from neighboring ports and states was guaranteed in practice by constructing each state's railways on a different gauge. Thus, the state-managed railways of Queensland operate on a 3-foot, 6-inch track; those of New South Wales run on a 4-foot, 8½-inch gauge; at Albury on the border of Victoria the gauge changes again to 5 feet, 3 inches. The Victoria gauge is partially integrated with that of South Australia, so that trains are able to proceed north of Adelaide to Red Hill, south of Port Pirie, before changing once more to the gauge of the Commonwealth-owned transcontinental line to Kalgoorlie, Western Australia. The transcontinental gauge is 4 feet, 8½ inches again. Once across the continent at Kalgoorlie, however, the rest of the way to Perth is traveled on the Western Australian gauge of 3 feet, 6 inches. Since late nineteenth century and increasingly since federation in 1901, there have been periods of agitation, conferences,

and even agreements on plans for unification of the Australian rail systems into one system with a common gauge. That a genuine unification has *not* been accomplished to date testifies to (a) the degree of competition between interest groups in the major regional centers, and (b) the development of other means of interconnection, by road, by sea, and by air. Conversion of only 253 miles of 3-foot, 6-inch rail line to the standard 4-foot, 8½-inch gauge between Port Pirie, South Australia, and Broken Hill would make uninterrupted rail travel possible without break of bulk from Brisbane (*567,000*) to Kalgoorlie—a total distance of 2,672 miles. The fact that South Australian opposition in favor of conversion to the 5-foot, 3-inch gauge of the bulk of that state's rail system has blocked even this plan serves to emphasize still further how important and powerful are the sectional interests of the Australian states over those of the nation as a whole.

Australia's population increased 20 per cent from 7.0 to 8.4 million between 1939 and 1951. While this remarkable increase was taking place the number of wage earners and salaried personnel grew 51.8 per cent, from 1.7 to 2.6 million; and manu-

Figure 152. The silved-lear-zinc mines at Broken Hill, New South Wales. (*Courtesy of Australian News and Information Bureau.*)

facturing employment rose nearly 60 per cent (59.5), from 563,866 to 917,661. An idea of the diversity and increasingly basic character of Australian manufacturers can be derived from the proportion of 1939 and 1951 manufacturing employment among the major categories of production shown in Table XXI.

The last five categories shown in the table—food, leather, textile, and clothing industries—are oriented toward agricultural and pastoral raw materials. They utilize for domestic markets some of the primary production which also supplies the major export trade of the country. These categories employed 42 per cent of those engaged in manufacturing before World War II, but only 36 per cent after the war. During the same period nonagricultural and nonpastoral-oriented manufactures increased their share of employment from 58 to 64 per cent. Basic manufacturing activities such as heavy metals are now a major component of Australian industry. Table XXI shows that the categories of *metal production, transportation equipment, machinery,* including plant and equipment, and *electrical or electronic products* accounted for one-third of manufacturing employment in 1939 and 40 per cent in 1951.

Most of the transportation equipment firms are American and English. Chrysler Australia, Ltd., is controlled by Chrysler Corporation of Detroit. The head offices of Australia's Ford organization, which is owned by the Canadian Ford Motor Company, is at Geelong, Victoria. General Motors-Holden Ltd., as does Chrysler, manufactures cars for sale in Australia. Its headquarters and plant are in Adelaide, South Australia. International Harvester of Australia, headquarters in Melbourne, manufactures trucks. It is wholly owned by the parent company at Chicago and has plants at Geelong and Dandenong, Victoria. There are also Australian branches of United Kingdom companies, including the Austin Company, Ltd., which makes the Austin-Healey automobile.

The category of machinery, plant equipment, and apparatus includes the all-important *machine-tool industry,* which is everywhere the mark of independent industrial organization. In Australia the subcategory of machine-tool industries employed 26,222 persons in 1939. By 1951 this number had increased 180 per cent to 73,331 people. Plant construction and machinery for woodworking, tobacco processing, textiles, tanning, soap, smelting and refining, rubber, pulp and paper, paperboard, plastics, printing, paint, mining, metal working, laundry, food production, chemicals, boots and shoes, as well as agricultural machinery will give some idea of the growing diversity of machinery

Category	PER CENT OF TOTAL MANUFACTURAL EMPLOYEES	
	1938	*1951*
Fuels	2	2
Nonmetallic minerals	4	4
Timber products	8	8
Pulp and paper	*	1
Paper products	7	5
Chemicals	3	3
Rubber	1	1
Subtotal, fuels to rubber	25	24
Metals	5	5
Transport equipment	13	15
Electrical products	3	4.4
Machinery, including plant equipment	12	15.6
Subtotal, metals to machinery	33	40
Food	15	14
Leather	2	2
Textiles	5	4
Clothing	19	15
Other textiles	1	1
Subtotal, food to textiles	42	36
Final total	100	100
Number	(563,866)	(917,661)

[a] Department of National Development, Commonwealth of Australia, *The Structure and Capacity of Australian Manufacturing Industries*, Melbourne, 1952.

*Less than 0.5 of 1 per cent.

production with which to make the goods so characteristic of a modern industrial society. Such evidence as this makes it reasonable to classify Australia as one of the four outlying regions of exchange-type area organization characterized by regional rather than local division of labor.

A final indication of the transformation from an organized supplier of raw materials and food to a status of internal self-sufficiency within a coherently organized domestic economy is the beginnings of an export trade in *consumer* goods. Approximately 10 per cent of total Australian exports are manufactured goods, in competition with the other industrial core regions of the exchange world. The percentage of total exports from the Republic of South Africa in manufactured items is about the same.

New Zealand. The patterns of area organization of New Zealand are shown on the map in Figure 153. There is little evidence of a single predominant core region for New Zealand. Instead there are four regions, each with a separate urban focus. No one of the four appears to dominate with respect to the other three. This pattern is in keeping with the characterization of New Zealand as "an outlying industrialized farm" of the United Kingdom. The core of New Zealand might, therefore, be said to be in London, England—the focus of the Commonwealth. This places New Zealand in the position of being an economically colonial dependency, even though politically independent. To so classify New Zealand is to ignore the beginnings of political and economic regional focus.

The political capital is Wellington (*142,300*) at the south end of the more populous North Island. This city is connected by air and coastal sea routes with each of the other major cities of the country. It is true that the largest air-freight shipments occur between the centrally located cities of Christchurch (*213,710*) and Wellington. Just as the Canterbury Plain focuses on Christchurch and is the "breadbasket" of New Zealand, so the combination of the southern region of North Island focusing on Wellington and the north region of South Island is the emerging core region of the country as a whole. There is potential for slowly increasing self-sufficiency within the country. New Zealand depends for steel and many other raw materials on imports from other Commonwealth countries, such as Australia and the United Kingdom. Manufactures are of two types—processing of New Zealand primary production for export, and manufacture of imported materials of domestic consumption. Less than 1 per cent of New Zealand's exports are manufactured consumer goods, such as those which characterize the exports of the United Kingdom.

Basic Contrasts between the Republic of South Africa and Australia and New Zealand

The characteristics of the population of the Republic differ from those of Australia and New Zealand. The Republic of South Africa is a plural society, that is, its population is divided among substantial numbers of five large groups—Europeans (subdivided between English and Afrikaners), Africans, Indians, and Coloreds. The composition

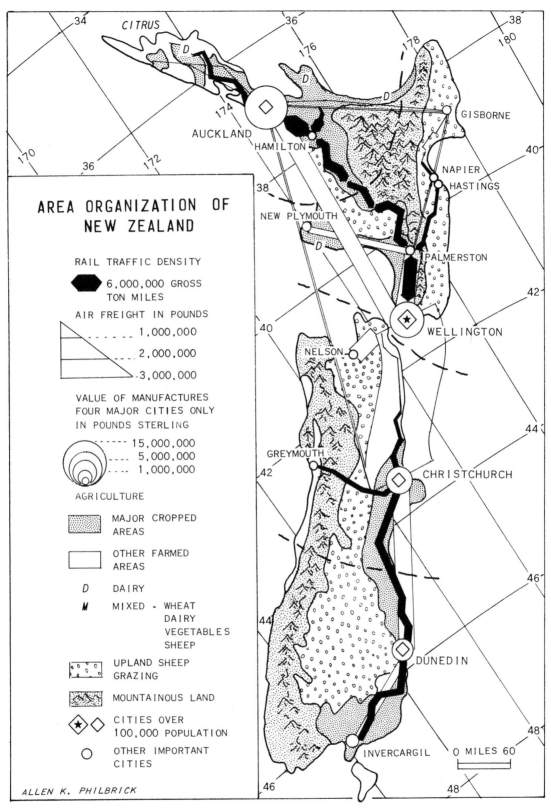

AREA ORGANIZATION OF NEW ZEALAND

RAIL TRAFFIC DENSITY

6,000,000 GROSS TON MILES

AIR FREIGHT IN POUNDS
- 1,000,000
- 2,000,000
- 3,000,000

VALUE OF MANUFACTURES
FOUR MAJOR CITIES ONLY
IN POUNDS STERLING
- 15,000,000
- 5,000,000
- 1,000,000

AGRICULTURE

MAJOR CROPPED AREAS

OTHER FARMED AREAS

D DAIRY

M MIXED - WHEAT DAIRY VEGETABLES SHEEP

UPLAND SHEEP GRAZING

MOUNTAINOUS LAND

CITIES OVER 100,000 POPULATION

OTHER IMPORTANT CITIES

ALLEN K. PHILBRICK

CITRUS

AUCKLAND
HAMILTON
GISBORNE
NAPIER
HASTINGS
NEW PLYMOUTH
PALMERSTON
WELLINGTON
NELSON
GREYMOUTH
CHRISTCHURCH
DUNEDIN
INVERCARGIL

0 MILES 60

Figure 153

of Australian and New Zealand population is less complex. The fundamental problem in the Republic of South Africa is the relationship between the African *majority* and the white European *controlling minority*. The current central policy of the Republic expresses the will of the Afrikaners and basically also that of the English in the word *apartheid*, which means the separation of the races. Ideological consistency would seem to require that apartheid mean the complete separation into independent countries of the African and the European, but this is not the intent. The Europeans require the labor of the African but are unwilling to pay the price which *economic* association with Africans implies in terms of social and political rights for Africans as human beings. Apartheid is for some Afrikaners a sincerely believed expression of Christian Reformed Church desire to maintain the cultural identity of Afrikaans-speaking people. In practice, however, it has become the instrument of a ruling minority to maintain its position by suppression, segregation, and exploitation of the African majority.

In 1946 42 per cent of the African population was living in Native Reserves under tribal organization; 28 per cent were farm laborers on farms owned by whites; an additional 24 per cent were urbanized in towns connected with mining compounds. The proportion of the Negro-African population in urban environments is rapidly increasing. It was 12.5 per cent in 1921 compared with 29 per cent in 1951, largely as the result of movement out of the Native Reserves. It may be estimated today that Africans are approximately evenly divided, one-third in each of three settings—the reserves, European-owned farms, and urban places. Apartheid has come to mean, therefore, segregation, socially and politically, with economic association primarily to the advantage of the European minority.

Division of this type cannot help but become an increasingly explosive issue with dangerous and unpredictable consequences for the future. In this situation time is on the side of the Africans because they and other *non*-Europeans are increasing at a faster rate than those of European descent. In fifty years it is estimated that the proportion of Europeans to the total population will have fallen to 15 per cent from its present ratio of 20 per cent.

Other fundamental divisions in the population of South Africa are those between English and Boer; the whites and Bantus in relation, respectively, to the Asiatics; and the position of the Coloreds. Within the basic conflict between Africans and Afri-

kaners, the problems of each subminority are intensified. The organization of area, accordingly, must be regarded as having a less stable social base than in Australia and New Zealand.

The Commonwealth

It should be clear that development of the three countries which are the subject of this chapter has been consistently entwined in the fortunes of the United Kingdom and the emergence from the British Empire of the Commonwealth. It is appropriate to end this chapter with a brief examination of the worldwide organization of the Commonwealth focusing on the United Kingdom. To do this serves not only as the larger context within a framework of total world trade for an appraisal of the Republic of South Africa, and Australia and New Zealand, but also serves as an introduction to the later consideration of other contrasting world regions both within and outside the Commonwealth. Regional analysis in this book began with the United Kingdom and then widened in scope to the European continent. Africa south of the Sahara demonstrated, by contrast, geographical differences which revolved around economic dependence on the United Kingdom and other European countries. Examination of secondary exchange-world core regions in South Africa, Australia, and New Zealand demonstrates the continuing expansion of European culture. Portrayal of the worldwide pattern of the Commonwealth will serve as a convenient bridge to other considerations. It will direct attention to other Commonwealth members, such as Canada in the New World and its great English-speaking neighbor to the south, the United States of America. At a point approximately midway in the regional portion of this book, a brief account of Commonwealth trade in relation to *world* trade serves as a reminder that all the world is bound together by interconnections between peoples of individual regions. Against the background of that idea examination of the Commonwealth will emphasize the great contrast between a far-flung interregional organization focusing on London and united by sea and the compact continental organization of area represented by the *Communist Bloc*.

The Commonwealth in International World Trade. Table XXII shows the leading nations of the world by rank in the value of their international trade for the two years 1938 and 1956. Each country listed contributed at least half of 1 per cent to total world trade in either or both 1938 and 1956.

TABLE XXII LEADING COUNTRIES IN WORLD TRADE 1938 AND 1956[a, b, c]

	1938				1956		
Rank	Name	Per cent	Cum. per cent	Rank	Name	Per cent	Cum. per cent
1.	United Kingdom	(16.28)	16.28	1.	United States	17.00	17.00
2.	United States	12.10	28.38	2.	United Kingdom	(10.77)	27.77
3.	Germany	10.73	39.11	3.	Germany	7.50	35.27
4.	France	5.03	44.14	4.	Canada	(5.75)	41.02
5.	Canada	(3.64)	47.78	5.	France	5.35	46.37
6.	Japan	3.50	51.28	6.	Netherlands	3.51	49.88
7.	Belgium-Luxemburg	3.47	54.78	7.	Belgium-Luxemburg	3.44	53.32
8.	Netherlands	3.20	57.95	8.	Japan	3.06	56.38
9.	India	(2.72)	60.67	9.	Italy	2.84	59.22
10.	Australia	(2.69)	63.36	10.	Sweden	2.21	61.43
11.	Italy	2.63	65.99	11.	Australia	(1.94)	63.37
12.	Sweden	2.36	68.35	12.	Switzerland	1.71	65.08
13.	Argentina	2.18	70.53	13.	Venezuela	1.69	66.77
14.	Denmark	1.58	72.11	14.	India	(1.58)	68.35
15.	Switzerland	1.53	73.64	15.	Malaya-Singapore	(1.45)	69.80
16.	Indonesia	1.48	75.12	16.	Brazil	1.40	71.20
17.	Malaya-Singapore	(1.48)	76.60	17.	Union of S. Africa	(1.36)	72.56
18.	Czechoslovakia*	1.48	78.08	18.	Denmark	1.29	73.85
19.	Union of S. Africa	(1.43)	79.51	19.	Argentina	1.11	74.96
20.	Brazil	1.34	80.85	20.	Norway	1.06	76.02
21.	U.S.S.R.	1.19	82.04	21.	Austria	.97	76.99
22.	China	1.15	83.19	22.	Indonesia	.93	77.92
23.	Poland*	1.08	84.27	23.	Mexico	.93	78.85
24.	New Zealand	(1.02)	85.29	24.	Neth. Antilles	.92	79.77
25.	Norway	1.01	86.30	25.	Finland	.89	80.66
26.	Neth. Antilles	.92	87.22	26.	U.S.S.R.	.84	81.50
27.	Finland	.83	88.05	27.	Br. Persian Gulf Sts.	(.83)	82.33
28.	Hong Kong	(.78)	88.83	28.	Hong Kong	(.78)	83.11
29.	Egypt*	(.76)	89.59	29.	New Zealand	(.76)	83.87
30.	Algeria	.70	90.29	30.	China	.74	84.61
31.	Mexico	.68	90.97	31.	Cuba	.70	85.31
32.	Rumania*	.64	91.61	32.	Spain	.64	85.95
33.	Philippines*	.64	92.25	33.	Algeria	.64	86.59
34.	Venezuela	.63	92.88	34.	Colombia*	.64	87.23
35.	Hungary*	.63	93.51	35.	Saudi Arabia	.54	87.77

[a] Compiled from United Nations, *Direction of International Trade*, Annual Data for the years 1938 and 1956.

[b] Starred countries in 1956 column not represented in 1938 column; in 1938 column not represented in 1956 column.

[c] Countries in italics, figures in parenthesis are members of the Commonwealth.

Commonwealth Countries		30.80	Commonwealth Countries		25.22
United States		12.10	United States		17.00
	Total	42.90		Total	42.22

While there are many shifts in relative ranking, of all countries contributing 1 per cent or more to world international trade in 1938, only six are not in this category in 1956. Of these only Czechoslovakia and Poland have dropped below half of 1 per cent. In the 1956 column, of all the countries contributing more than 1 per cent to total foreign trade, only Venezuela was not in that category in 1938.

It is evident from the table that world trade is somewhat less concentrated today than before the last world war. In 1956 only twenty countries participated in foreign trade at a rate exceeding 1 per cent of total international trade, as opposed to twenty-five countries in 1938. The first twenty account for slightly more than three-fourths of all foreign trade in the 1956 list, whereas in 1938 the first twenty trading countries accounted for nearly 81 per cent of the total foreign trade of all nations. In saying that foreign trade is less concentrated it should be noted that it took thirty-one countries to accumulate as much as 85 per cent of total foreign trade, whereas in 1938 this amount was achieved by the sum of the foreign trade by only twenty-four countries.

The shift in rank between the United States and the United Kingdom is the most dramatic change shown by the table. The two countries virtually changed places in both rank and in the proportion of total foreign trade which they conducted. In 1938 the United States, which was in second place in foreign trade, accounted for 12.1 per cent of the world's international trade. In 1956 the U.S. share rose to 17 per cent and occupied first place. The United Kingdom during the same period saw its share of total foreign trade fall from 16.3 per cent to slightly more than 10 per cent (10.77) and dropped from first to second place in total world foreign trade.

Nine of the first thirty-five countries by foreign trade in Table XXII were part of the British trading community—the Commonwealth—in both 1938 and 1956. These countries are italicized in the table. They accounted for 30.8 per cent in 1938 and 25.22 per cent of total foreign trade in 1956. In dollars each of the first thirty-five countries shown in the 1956 column of the table are in the billion class in foreign trade.

If the English-speaking United States is added to the Commonwealth total in both 1938 and 1956, the figures are nearly identical for each of the two years, 42.9 and 42.2 per cent, respectively. If the data of Table XXII are rearranged according to international trade among the world's major exchange world regions, the relative importance of the core regions is emphasized. These data are summarized in Table XXIII. The countries of the Commonwealth are distributed among four of the

TABLE XXIII   TRADE OF THE EXCHANGE WORLD, 1938 AND 1956

	1938		1956	
	Per cent	*Cumulative per cent*	*Per cent*	*Cumulative per cent*
Primary corelands				
European coreland[a]	42.87		36.09	
North American coreland[b]	15.74	58.61	22.75	58.84
U.S.S.R.	1.19	59.80	.84	59.68
Secondary corelands				
Japan	3.50		3.06	
Australia-New Zealand	3.71	7.21	2.70	5.76
Southern South America[c]	3.52	10.73	2.51	8.27
Union of South Africa	1.43	12.16	1.36	9.63
Total exchange-world cores		71.96		69.31
Additional Commonwealth countries[d]	5.74	77.70	4.64	73.95

[a] United Kingdom, Germany, France, Netherlands, Belgium-Luxemburg, Italy, Switzerland, and Austria.
[b] Canada and the United States.
[c] Argentina and Brazil (Chile and Uruguay, less than 0.5 per cent).
[d] India, Malaya-Singapore, British Persian Gulf States, and Hong Kong as well as Egypt in 1938.

seven core regions. Again, only countries trading at a level of a billion dollars or more in international trade in 1956 are included. From the previous table, the Commonwealth countries fitting this criterion had a total foreign trade in 1956 in excess of one-fourth of world foreign trade. This compares favorably with the world's major corelands in Western Europe and North America as summarized in Table XXIII. In a comparison of blocks of countries it is perhaps better to use only the international trade of the United Kingdom itself, which includes that country's trade with Commonwealth members as one nodally organized worldwide unit, with flow of materials and goods to and from a common focus. When this is done the *United Kingdom* ranks third (10.77 per cent), after the *European coreland* combination (25.32), and the *United States* (17.0). It is perhaps significant from the data in Table XXIII that the share of core regions in total foreign trade fell slightly from 1938 to 1956, which further indicates the trend of world international trade to become less concentrated than formerly.

Direction of United Kingdom Trade. The United Kingdom's foreign trade is perhaps the most striking example of an interregional division of labor in the world today. It has an irregularly concentric or wheel-form pattern on the map diagram in Figure 154. Based on countries with which the United Kingdom did 1 per cent or more of its international trade (with six exceptions) in 1956, the data in Table XXIV which are presented geographically on the map account for more than 83 per cent of the United Kingdom's foreign trade. The data in both table and map are arranged according to a classification into the four principal directions of the United Kingdom's foreign trade—North Atlantic, South Atlantic, Mediterranean-Suez, and English Channel-North Sea.

London's role in the financing of international trade demonstrates the centrality of the core city of the United Kingdom as the focus of the Commonwealth.[1]

In the financing of international trade, both visible and invisible, the part played by the City of London is of outstanding importance. By a process of evolution through the centuries, "the City" has developed an efficient and adaptable organization of *trade and financial services* capable of meeting the needs, not only of Britain, but of the world in general. The

[1]Central Office of Information, *Britain, An Official Handbook*, London: Her Majesty's Stationery Office, 1956, p. 308. (Italics are present author's.)

TABLE XXIV   1956 INTERNATIONAL TRADE OF THE UNITED KINGDOM[ab]

North Atlantic Route

	Per cent
The United States	9.30
Canada[c]	7.30
West Indies	1.92
Venezuela	1.01
	19.53

South Atlantic Route

Argentina	1.53
Ghana	.78
Nigeria	2.14
Union of South Africa	3.58
	8.03

Mediterranean and Suez

Australia	6.63
New Zealand	4.50
India	4.32
British Persian Gulf States	2.38
Rhodesian Federation	2.31
Malaya-Singapore	2.21
Ceylon	.91
Kenya-Uganda	.88
Pakistan	.77
Iraq[d]	.79
Hong Kong	.74
	26.45

English Channel-North Sea

Netherlands		3.68
West Germany		3.07
France		3.00
Belgium-Luxemburg		2.07
Italy		1.69
Switzerland		.91
(European core)		14.42
Denmark		2.87
Sweden		3.53
Norway		1.87
Finland		1.58
Spain		1.06
Ireland		2.76
(European periphery)		13.67
U.S.S.R.		1.54
Total Europe		29.63
Total trade shown		83.64

Total Commonwealth, including Sterling Bloc Non-Commonwealth Iraq	42.17
Commonwealth, Iraq and United States	51.47

[a] United Nations, *Direction of International Trade*, New York, 1960.

[b] With the exception of Ghana, Ceylon, Kenya-Uganda, Pakistan, Iraq, Hong Kong, and Switzerland, the data are restricted to countries with whom the average of exports and imports is 1 per cent or more of total foreign trade of the United Kingdom in 1956.

[c] Italicized names are members of the Commonwealth.

[d] Iraq is not part of the Commonwealth but is part of the Sterling Bloc.

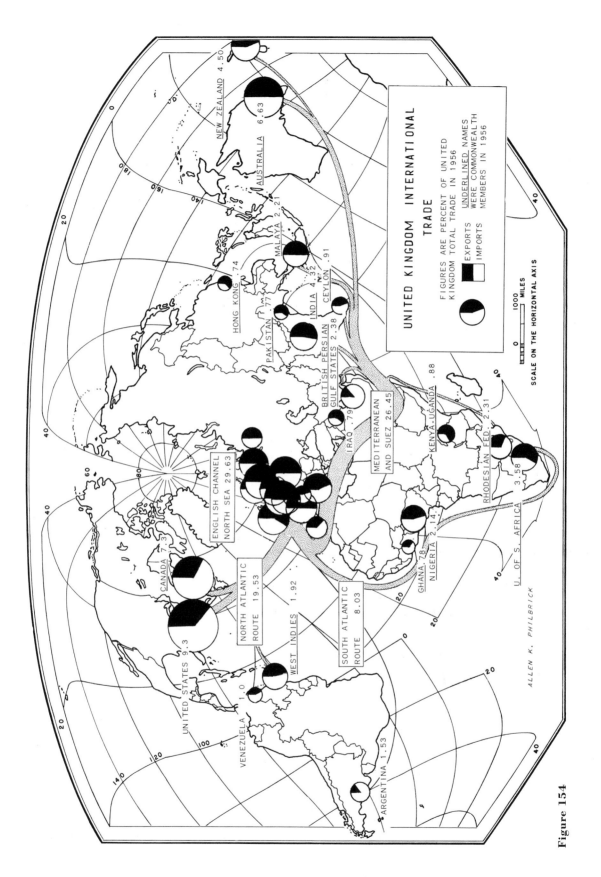

UNITED KINGDOM INTERNATIONAL TRADE

FIGURES ARE PERCENT OF UNITED KINGDOM TOTAL TRADE IN 1956

UNDERLINED NAMES WERE COMMONWEALTH MEMBERS IN 1956

EXPORTS IMPORTS

SCALE ON THE HORIZONTAL AXIS

0   1000   MILES

ALLEN K. PHILBRICK

NEW ZEALAND 4.50

AUSTRALIA 6.63

MALAYA 2.21

HONG KONG .74

PAKISTAN .77

INDIA 4.32

CEYLON .91

BRITISH PERSIAN GULF STATES 2.38

IRAQ .79

MEDITERRANEAN AND SUEZ 26.45

KENYA-UGANDA .88

RHODESIAN FED. 3.58

GHANA .78

NIGERIA 2.14

U. OF S. AFRICA 2.31

ENGLISH CHANNEL NORTH SEA 29.63

CANADA 7.3

NORTH ATLANTIC ROUTE 19.53

WEST INDIES 1.92

SOUTH ATLANTIC ROUTE 8.03

UNITED STATES 9.3

VENEZUELA 1.0

ARGENTINA 1.53

Figure 154

supremacy of London in this respect derives from a number of factors—historical, geographical, and economic—as well as the technical efficiency and low costs of its services. In the nineteenth century the rapid growth of British industry, commerce, and shipping under the stimulus of the industrial revolution made Britain the market as well as the workshop of the world. It became the site for the chief world markets in raw materials, freight, insurance, and precious metals. At the same time British capital was invested in overseas countries to assist in their development, increase their output and exports, and provide markets for manufactured goods. London became the *chief supplier of capital for many Commonwealth and foreign governments* and a centre for entrepot trade proceeding to and from the growing industrial areas on the continent of Europe and in North America. In the course of time the pound sterling and the sterling bill of exchange developed into the principal form of money for transactions between one country and another in all parts of the world. Britain is now the banker for the sterling area and *sterling is used in the finance of nearly half the world's transactions.*

Side by side with these developments a sound commercial banking system and a flexible system of central bank control have been built up, while specialized institutions such as discount houses, merchant banks, accepting houses, the Stock Exchange, investment trusts and finance corporations have evolved to satisfy particular needs of short- or long-term finance. The facilities provided by merchant banks and accepting houses, for example, have long been used to finance shipments of goods not only to and from Britain, but between any two outside countries.

Reference to the earlier map of the area organization of the United Kingdom and the map in Figure 65 enables us to draw a clear picture of both internal and external organization of the country. British dependence on foreign trade is traditional. The diagram in Figure 154 demonstrates the geographical division of labor involved. The controlling nerve center of leadership is London. Internally within the United Kingdom are the specialized manufacturing districts which make what the English have to sell. Overseas, which is the primary subject of the diagram, the specialized raw-material and food-producing regions are radially distributed

throughout the world and are connected to the United Kingdom by major world sea lanes.

Exports represented 46 per cent of the United Kingdom's foreign trade in 1956. Imports were 54 per cent. With some variations in proportions in each direction for different parts of the diagram, the United Kingdom had an over all unfavorable balance of trade in 1956. For example, from the Persian Gulf oil-producing countries, imports are 87 per cent of their total trade with the United Kingdom; imports are only 13 per cent. With other countries the balance is the other way. In 1956 the Union of South Africa received more exports from the United Kingdom than it supplied imports by a ratio of 61 to 39. Still others have almost a balanced trade. The imbalance of imports over exports has been true of British foreign trade for over a century. The balance is usually made good in normal years by net invisible exports, in terms of dividends, profits, insurance charges, and payment for services accruing to Britain in her role as the world's banker. But in recent years it has become increasingly difficult to balance the books and show a net profit for the country as an internationally operating national economy. This explains the austerity programs which Englishmen have been forced to bear and England's desire to improve her position by entering the European Common Market.

The countries which are the subject of this chapter represent approximately 15 per cent of all United Kingdom foreign trade and 4 per cent of total world international trade. As examples of the spread of exchange organization of area and the industrial revolution carried overseas by Englishmen and the nationals of other European countries, the Republic of South Africa, and Australia and New Zealand are secondary core regions which have maintained strong ties with the Europe from which they derived their culture.

Attention now turns to the Americas which in their regional organization of divisions of labor, evolved from European cultures by peoples of European descent, have developed a completely independent regional focus which is parallel to Europe in its world significance.

12 Resources of the Americas

After the initial success of the Portuguese in reaching the Far East by sailing around Africa, it was only a question of time before someone would try to get there by crossing the Atlantic. In the fifteenth century the double continent of the Americas between Europe and Asia was unknown. Columbus failed in 1492 in his true objective to sail across the Atlantic to the Far East, but he found the "New World" instead.

The New World

Conquest and settlement of the New World soon became more important than the search for a passage to the East by going west. Yet, from the time of discovery in 1492 and even after passage of the first ship through the Panama Canal Zone in 1914 (see Figure 155), the quest for passage across, through, or around the continental barriers has been persistently if intermittently pressed for more than 400 years. A northwest route by surface vessel was achieved through the Canadian Arctic via Bellot Straits in 1958. More dramatic was the first under-ice passage across the North Pole by atomic submarine: the Nautilus sailed from the Bering Strait under ice to England also in 1958.

Size, Shape, and Position of the American Continents. Each of the two continents is basically triangular in shape. As may be seen from the map diagram in Figure 156, the long side of each triangle faces the Pacific Ocean. The opposite angles and the shorter sides of the triangles protrude into the Arctic-Atlantic waters of the land-water realm. North America (9,435,000 square miles) is somewhat larger than South America (6,860,000 square miles). Latitudinal position of the two continents is significant. North America has its broadest east-west extent in temperate latitudes, while South America is most extensive in the tropics.

An idea of the relative sizes of the continents may be gained by comparing distances from the corners. Nome, Alaska, is nearly 4,000 miles from St. John's, Newfoundland. The other two sides of the North American triangle are represented by the shortest side, which is 3,100 miles from St. John's to Salinas Cruz, a point on the Tehuantepec Gulf coast of southern Mexico, and the longest coast along the Pacific. It is 4,500 miles from Nome to Salinas Cruz. The dimensions of South America are about the same magnitude. Along the Caribbean coast it is 3,100 miles from Panama City, which is the southeastern and Pacific terminus of the Panama Canal, to Natal, Brazil. Natal is the point on the American mainland closest to Africa—only 1,850 miles away. Cape Horn at the southern end of South America is 3,800 miles from Natal along the South Atlantic coast of the continent, while it is 4,400 miles from Panama along the Pacific side to Cape Horn. The two continents are connected by the Central American Isthmus which is 1,200 miles in length from northern Mexico to western Colombia. The Panama Canal which artificially separates the two continents links the Atlantic and Pacific Oceans across 40.3 miles of the Isthmus of Panama. Continuous land stretches from Point Barrow, Alaska, at 71° 20′ North to Cape Horn at 55° 59′ South Latitude—a total distance of nearly 10,000 miles. Polar ice nearly fills the Arctic Ocean, inhibiting surface passage around the north side of North America. At the southern end the land barrier is breached in upper-middle latitudes by the 630-mile-wide Drake Passage between Cape Horn and the Palmer Peninsula of Antarctica. This gap provides all-year-round access by water between the Atlantic and Pacific Oceans. "Rounding the Horn," as passing from east to west around Cape Horn was called in the days of the sailing vessel, was famous for the difficulties presented in beating a westward passage through this gap against strong prevailing westerly gales in these latitudes. The only alternative is to circumnavigate Antarctica by way of the Indian Ocean.

Imagine setting out to sail to China from Lisbon, Portugal, across the Atlantic and literally not knowing the existence of nearly 20 million square miles

Figure 155. The Panama Canal, a man-made strait joining the Atlantic and Pacific Oceans, serves as an immense funnel for ships moving from one ocean to the other. About 50 million tons of cargo each year pass through the Canal which was built by the United States between 1904 and 1914 at a net cost of $380,000,000. It takes ships, which come from every maritime country in the world, about eight hours to make the 50-mile trip through the locks. Once the gates are closed, the flow of water starts to raise the ship. Here, two ships are being raised to the level of Gatun Lake, from where they go on their own power to Gatun Locks. The Gatun Locks form one continuous flight of three steps which raise or lower ships 85 feet. This set of locks is 1⅙ miles long. (*Courtesy of United Nations.*)

of land and ice blocking your way virtually from pole to pole! The early navigators who followed Columbus did not know, of course, how extensive the land barrier which Columbus had discovered would turn out to be. What was the New World like? What resources did it contain—resources either of an agricultural or of a mineral nature? Further exploration presented to millions of Europeans the opportunity to develop and to use the resources of two entire continents. What did successive generations of Europeans inherit who were thus to participate, along with other millions from Africa, in the most dramatic of all migrations in history?

It is the task of the present chapter to describe the resources of the Americas. The following chapter describes the emergent patterns of area organization in the Americas, with special attention on the United States. A third chapter on the Americas analyzes and describes the role of culture in evolving the patterns of settlement as regions in the Americas began to develop divergently. First the initial migrations of peoples from Europe and Africa, which set the pace of cultural evolution, are discussed. Then, the geographical development of

the patterns of settlement and of regional organization are traced with particular emphasis, again, on the background for understanding the United States.

Patterns of Resources in the Americas. The patterns of resources to be discussed for the Americas are of the same types discussed in other regions. They are the resources needed in the production of food, and the manufacture of goods, as well as the sources of energy by which people have learned to extend through mechanical means the power of the human mind and body.

The basic patterns of agricultural and mineral resources in the Americas repeat the triangular shapes of the continents. They reflect the distribution of subsurface zones and rock associations, as modified by the complex processes resulting from interaction of forces within the earth's surface zone. The configuration of the land, the patterns of drainage, and to some extent even the amounts of precipitation and warmth available, as well as the characteristics of the soil, are all indirectly related to subsurface conditions.

As was true for the world pattern as a whole, the subsurface structure of the Americas is also divided into three categories. These create a relatively sim-

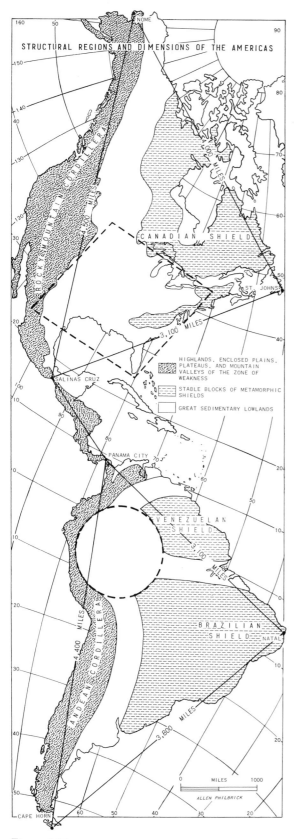

STRUCTURAL REGIONS AND DIMENSIONS OF THE AMERICAS

ROCKY MOUNTAIN CORDILLERA

CANADIAN SHIELD

ST. JOHNS

SALINAS CRUZ

PANAMA CITY

VENEZUELAN SHIELD

BRAZILIAN SHIELD

NATAL

ANDEAN CORDILLERA

CAPE HORN

NOME

HIGHLANDS, ENCLOSED PLAINS, PLATEAUS, AND MOUNTAIN VALLEYS OF THE ZONE OF WEAKNESS

STABLE BLOCKS OF METAMORPHIC SHIELDS

GREAT SEDIMENTARY LOWLANDS

0   MILES   1000

ALLEN PHILBRICK

Figure 156

ple repeated pattern of metamorphic crystalline shields, sedimentary lowlands, and a cordilleran zone of geologically recent mountain building. The principal rock associations characteristic of these three zones are shown in Figure 156. They should be compared with those on the map of European rock associations in Figures 86 and 95. The European pattern was subdivided into thirteen separate regions of old rock combining in many the relatively close proximity of both coal-bearing sediments and ancient mineralized ore-bearing metamorphic rocks. The patterns in both American continents show extensive interior sedimentary lowlands surrounded on three sides by mineralized highlands of metamorphic and other rock types. Mining takes place within many parts of each of these marginal regions on all three sides of each continent. In North America such mineral production is integrated with farming, mineral-fuel production, and manufacturing in the interior lowlands. In South America such mineral-producing districts are externally oriented through coastal ports to markets outside the continent. A similar external orientation also marks the direction of flow of agricultural production. The fundamental difference in trends of continental development has characterized the geographical patterns of occupancy in the two American continents from the beginning of European settlement. The eastern third of the interior lowlands of North America not only holds a storehouse of energy in the form of coal, petroleum, and natural gas beneath the surface, but also in and on the surface itself possesses the highest quality combination of resources and conditions favorable for agriculture. On the three margins of this same central land association of farmland and subsurface energy fuels, iron, copper, nickel, and other resources are located which serve as the sinews of modern manufacturing production.

No such common focus on food and power-producing interior lowlands links the tropical interior of South America with the coastal areas. Instead a series of peripheral concentrations of productive activity in both agriculture and mining are externally linked primarily with North American but also with European and other world markets overseas.

In addition to the basic similarity in subsurface structural patterns between North and South America, three important differences are evident. Carboniferous sedimentary regions in North America are extensive but in Central and South America they are scanty. This fact accounts for the much larger amount of coal in North America than is found in South America. A second contrast is the comparative width of the sedimentary lowlands. They are relatively narrow in the southern continent and wide in the northern continent. The interior lowlands of South America are narrow near the sea and widen into the interior. Three river basins converge upstream into the upper Amazon Basin— the Orinoco, the Amazon, and the Paraguay-Parana. The upper Amazon basin is roughly circular in shape but has a diameter of less than a thousand miles. By contrast in North America, as can be seen from the map in Figure 156, the interior lowland region is generally rectangular in shape and opens outward toward the Atlantic Ocean and Gulf of Mexico. The region is 1,500 miles on a side, and 2,000 miles on the diagonal from Miami, Florida, to Bismarck, North Dakota, and the same distance from Chihuahua, Mexico, to New York City. The accessibility of the interior to the sea in North America is in marked contrast to the inaccessibility of the upper Amazon. Last, the major lowland of North America is temperate, while the largest lowland of South America is tropical.

Continental Divides and Drainage Regions. Surface drainage patterns represent the results of long periods of interaction between subsurface forms and structure and hydrologic conditions. Surface drainage also provides a convenient basis for defining regional subdivisions of continental land surfaces, expressed in major river systems and continental divides. The great drainage divides and drainage regions of the Americas are shown on the map in Figure 157. The most important continental divide is the crest of the cordilleran mountain system which stretches from one end of the double continent to the other. The larger portions of the two continents lie east of this north-south trending divide. The larger eastern portion is, in turn, divided into approximately equal northern and southern halves by low, often imperceptible, east-west trending divides. In North America the northern half, mostly Canadian, drains northward into the Arctic Ocean. Such drainage is dominated by two river systems. The Mackenzie, second only to the Mississippi River of the southern half of the continent, flows generally north and empties beyond the Arctic Circle. The Nelson-Saskatchewan drains eastward into Hudson Bay. The south half likewise consists of two major drainage basins. The Great Lakes-St. Lawrence system, which contains the world's largest sources of fresh water, empties northeastward

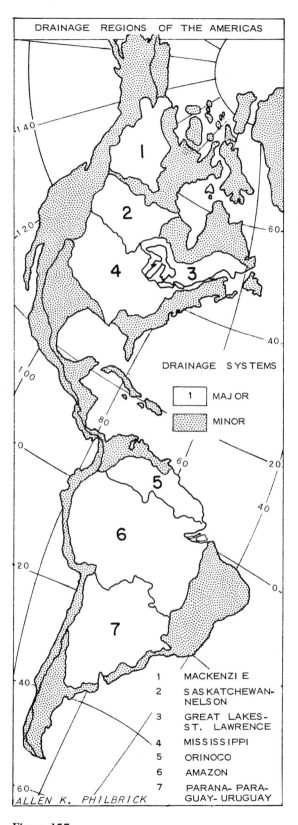

Figure 157

into the North Atlantic. The huge Missouri-Mississippi River system flows generally southward to empty into the Gulf of Mexico.

South America east of the Andean divide also has a northern and southern half. The tropical northern half is drained by the mighty Amazon River and the much smaller Orinoco. The Amazon has its headwaters within 100 miles of the Pacific and flows eastward into equatorial Atlantic waters, as does the Orinoco. The southern portion of the continent is drained by a single system, which is the Parana-Paraguay-Uruguay system emptying into the estuary-like Rio de la Plata. The Plate, as it is called, widens into the South Atlantic. Relative lengths and areas of drainage for each of these systems and their main channels are given in Table XXV.

From this table it is apparent that the seven main river systems of the two continents occupy nearly half of their total combined mainland areas, one-third of North America and almost 60 per cent of South America.

Agricultural Resource Regions of the Americas

Again, four particular resources or conditions of agriculture are to be used in composite to define and characterize the agricultural resource regions of the two continents. As in other regions the measures used are surface configuration, precipitation, growing season, and soils. Each will be examined briefly and then in composite arrangement.

Surface Configuration. The main surface features of the Americas are shown on the map in Figure 158. They are classified according to major land-form regions. Plains and plateau surfaces are essentially level as opposed to mountain and hill regions which are moderately or steeply sloping. Low highlands that are rough and stony are included within the category of hill country. It is not the function of this discussion to deal with physiographic features in themselves, but instead to group regions of similar surface character together. Clearly the great interior sedimentary lowlands provide the

TABLE **XXV**   LENGTHS AND DRAINAGE AREAS OF MAJOR RIVERS IN THE AMERICAS

Continent and region	River basin	Length of named river channel	Drainage[a] area, sq. mi.	Per cent of each cont.	Per cent total area
Total area of double continent (excluding islands)			15,343,626		100
North America			8,483,626	100	
North	Mackenzie	2,525	640,000	7.5	4.2
	Nelson-Saskatchewan	1,660	417,000	4.9	2.7
South	Great Lakes-St. Lawrence	2,100	482,000	5.7	3.1
	Mississippi-Missouri	3,875	1,253,000	14.8	8.2
	Total		2,792,000	32.9	18.2
South America			6,860,000	100	
North	Amazon	3,900	2,700,000	39.4	17.6
	Orinoco	1,500	100,000	1.2	0.6
South	Parana-Paraguay-Uruguay	2,720	1,200,000	17.6	7.8
	Total		4,000,000	58.2	26.0
	Final Total		6,792,000		44.2

[a] Includes large portion not in sedimentary lowlands.

largest extents of level land, followed closely by large intermontane basins and plateaus, and last by the continent-rimming coastal plains of varying widths between highlands and the seas.

Precipitation. Like a giant tongue the western "horn" of the Northern Hemisphere arid crescent reaches out of the Arctic down across western Canada and into southwestern North America. A similar, less extensive dry region cuts diagonally across South America from northern Peru on the Pacific side of the Andes into southern Argentina to the Atlantic. Precipitation characteristics of the double continent vary through a wide range. Isohyets for 20 and 60 inches of precipitation are shown on the map in Figure 159, which distinguishes *wet, dry,* and *humid* regions.

Growing Season. The map in Figure 160 divides the Americas into regions according to the duration of frost-free periods. Except for variations due to elevation, growing season regions tend to follow latitude lines more nearly than do iso-lines of precipitation. Growing season categories are defined as *long* (frost free), with a subcategory of nearly frost free (up to five days of frost); *moderate* (frost from 5 to 275 days); and *short* (less than 90 days free from frost). North America is fairly evenly divided between regions of short and moderate growing season. The 90-day growing season line follows an east-to-west path only a short distance north of the Canadian border, dips into the United States in the Rocky Mountain region, but bends far northward along the western shore of the Pacific coast all the way to the Aleutian Islands of south and western Alaska. Latin America is predominantly frost free; but the narrowing middle latitude region of southern South America, primarily in the Andean highlands and in the southernmost tip of the continent, has less than 90 days growing season. The transitional territory with occasional frost is a wide band across southern Brazil, all of Paraguay, and portions of northern Argentina, southern Bolivia, and southern Peru. In the Caribbean the transitional zone between temperate North America and tropical Central America and the Caribbean islands is a narrow band from southern Florida which crosses the Gulf of Mexico into Central Mexico and skirts the Sierra Madre mountains northwestward to Baja California.

Soils. The most fertile of the grassland and forest soil categories are the chernozem and prairie grassland great soil groups and the gray-brown podzolic forest soils. These three great soil groups are shown on the world map of soil in Figure 46 of Chapter 4, surrounded by all the other great soil groups. This concentric pattern of the fertile triangle in the center of the North American interior lowlands has already been cited in Chapter 4. It should be pointed out again that soils appear to be the most restricting resource among the measures to be combined in the composite designed to define agricultural resource regions.

None of the separate resources such as growing season and precipitation are equivalent. When they are superimposed, therefore, the comparative measures of the different resources and conditions can only be significant in illustrating the existence of differing practical problems for the successful conduct of agriculture, rather than an absolute measure of any kind. The boundaries of the most fertile soil groups are shown superimposed on the composite map of agricultural resource regions, but have not been incorporated in the definition of resource regions themselves.

Composite Agricultural Resource Regions. The map in Figure 161 shows the composite regions made by combining three of the four primary resources and conditions of agricultural significance. Their spatial combinations define four great agricultural resource regional types which are named in terms of the resource combinations. In addition to the four major types there are a number of transitional zones between them which are important subtypes. The four principal agricultural resource associations in the Americas are:

1. Plains and low highlands, mainly humid, with moderate to long growing season, but some frost every year.

2. Plains and low highlands, mostly dry, with less than 90 days without frost.

3. Rainy tropics with no frost over plains and low highlands.

4. Mountainous highlands, including intermontane basins, plateaus, and mountain valleys.

Humid plains with moderate growing season. Comparison of the resource regions with the present pattern of farmland use in Figure 162 and arable land in Figure 47 shows that the lion's share of cultivated land is in the region of this first category. In these regions there is an unusually large proportion of total area devoted to farming over great stretches of territory uninterrupted except for small areas of woodland, marsh, wasteland, and land occupied by villages, towns, and cities with the

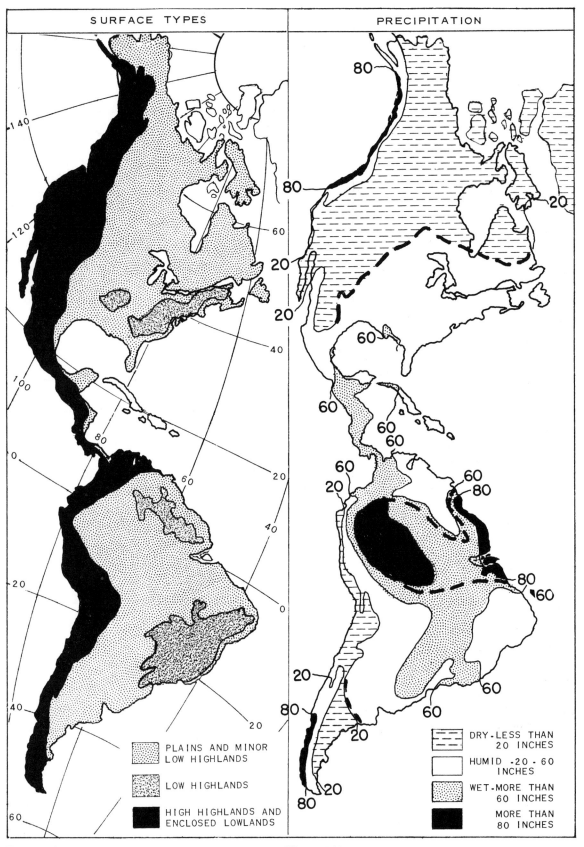

SURFACE TYPES

PRECIPITATION

PLAINS AND MINOR
LOW HIGHLANDS

LOW HIGHLANDS

HIGH HIGHLANDS AND
ENCLOSED LOWLANDS

DRY-LESS THAN
20 INCHES

HUMID -20 - 60
INCHES

WET-MORE THAN
60 INCHES

MORE THAN
80 INCHES

Figure 158

Figure 159

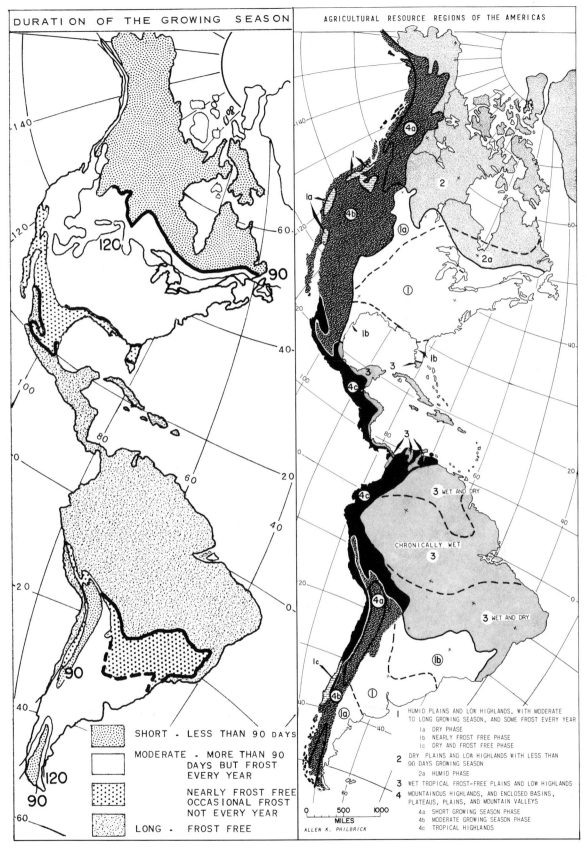

DURATION OF THE GROWING SEASON

AGRICULTURAL RESOURCE REGIONS OF THE AMERICAS

SHORT - LESS THAN 90 DAYS

MODERATE - MORE THAN 90 DAYS BUT FROST EVERY YEAR

NEARLY FROST FREE OCCASIONAL FROST NOT EVERY YEAR

LONG - FROST FREE

1 HUMID PLAINS AND LOW HIGHLANDS, WITH MODERATE TO LONG GROWING SEASON, AND SOME FROST EVERY YEAR

   1a DRY PHASE
   1b NEARLY FROST FREE PHASE
   1c DRY AND FROST FREE PHASE

2 DRY PLAINS AND LOW HIGHLANDS WITH LESS THAN 90 DAYS GROWING SEASON

   2a HUMID PHASE

3 WET TROPICAL FROST-FREE PLAINS AND LOW HIGHLANDS

4 MOUNTAINOUS HIGHLANDS, AND ENCLOSED BASINS, PLATEAUS, PLAINS, AND MOUNTAIN VALLEYS

   4a SHORT GROWING SEASON PHASE
   4b MODERATE GROWING SEASON PHASE
   4c TROPICAL HIGHLANDS

0   500   1000
MILES

ALLEN K. PHILBRICK

Figure 160

Figure 161

259

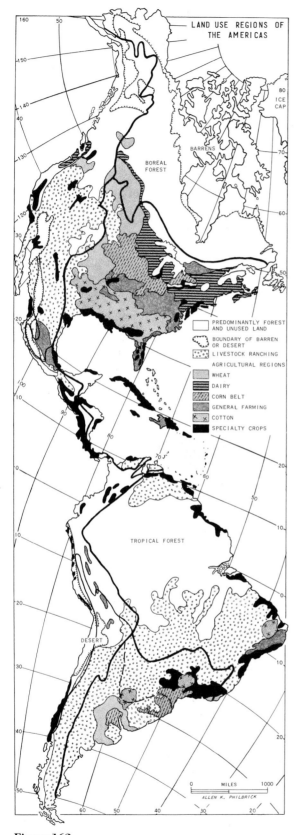

Figure 162

means of communication and transportation between them.

That portion of farmland (first category in above list) occupied by the chernozem-prairie grassland and gray-brown forest soils represents inherently superior agricultural land, although other portions may be only slightly less good for farming. Farm management has rebuilt many different soils, fitting requirements of individual crops by specific fertilization and other management practices. The regions which represent the first resource association are found in the southeast quarter of North America, in the Pacific Northwest, in the Argentine Pampas and surrounding territory of Uruguay, southern Brazil, and northern interior Argentina. Another area is in south central Chile.

Dry plains which have less than 20 inches of precipitation and moderate to long growing season are important regional variants of this first agricultural resource association, and when irrigated have become important areas of specialized crop production. Examples are the Central Valley and southern coast plains of California, the Imperial Valley of the Colorado delta plain, the lower Rio Grande region of southern Texas and northern Mexico, and irrigated river valleys of the Great Plains of North America. The same is true of north central or "Mediterranean" Chile on the west side of the Andes and of dry western Argentina in the "rain shadow" east of the Andes.

The nearly frost-free humid plains and low highlands (designated as type Ib on the map in Figure 161) are located on the equatorward margins of winter-frost regions. These regions, which are transitional to the true tropics where there is never any frost, experience occasional frost, but not necessarily every year. Farmers must take the calculated frost risk which offsets the advantage of double and even triple cropping afforded by the length of the growing season. Increase in soil laterization equatorward creates problems of soil fertilization, such as the absence of trace elements[1] which assure adequate nutritive values in products grown in the soil. Soils on the equatorward margins of the first resource association have this problem, as in Florida and the Gulf Coast of the United States, where trace elements have to be added. Other regions designated as type Ib are quite extensive in northeast Argentina, Paraguay, and southern Brazil. Cattle

[1] A trace element is one such as cobalt, iron, or copper, needed in small amounts to prevent deficiency diseases in plants, grazing animals, and in man.

grazing is expanding into these frontiers, where the industry faces problems of clearing the savanna scrub and brush vegetation, control of insect pests and cattle diseases, the necessity of breeding heat-resistant strains of cattle, to say nothing of creating transportation and marketing facilities. It appears to be difficult in these regions to produce meat of comparable quality to meat produced in more temperate regions.

A third variant of type I in the list of agricultural resource associations is both dry and frost free. Tropical deserts are of type Ic, as exemplified in Lower California and the rainless coasts of southern Peru and northern Chile.

Plains and low highlands, mostly dry, with less than 90 days growing season. This second type of plains and low highlands has less precipitation and more frost and is characteristic of the north central plains of North America, as well as the great shield region of northern and eastern Canada. One advantage in this type of resource combination is that cooler temperatures reduce evaporation and increase the efficiency of scanty precipitation. The great extent of fertile grassland soils in the prairie provinces of Canada assures that region of a high productivity in grain as long as minimum requirements of moisture are met. The low highlands and plains of the crystalline shield region of Canada, however, were largely denuded of soil by several successive glaciations. In addition, therefore, to shortness of growing season and the small quantity of annual precipitation, soil deficiencies and rough stony surfaces reduce the efficiency of agricultural resources in northeastern Canada below an operable minimum.

Rainy tropics with no frost over plains and low highlands. At the opposite extreme is the resource combination of the wet tropics, which has a much greater amount of available moisture and a complete absence of a winter-frost season. Regions of the wet and humid plains without frost are of two sub-types. These are the winterless plains with chronic rainfall characteristic of the Amazon Basin, and the winterless plains with seasonal rainfall characteristic of savanna vegetation on the poleward margins of the Amazon in Venezuela and south central Brazil.

Highlands. The major highlands and associated intermontane basins, plateaus, and mountain valleys are the fourth major category of agricultural resource combinations. This category consists essentially of the great cordilleran region of mountain ranges from Alaska to Tierra del Fuego—the 10,000-mile-long Pacific rimland of subsurface weakness through the Americas. As may be imagined the resource variations within any highland region, particularly one across the length of two continents, is very complex. From the standpoint of agricultural resources, however, the great western highland zone of the Americas may be divided into three parts:

1. The virtually nonagricultural region (marked IVa on the map in Figure 161) is *continuously frost-bound more than 275 days each year* because of a combination of high altitude and latitudinal position.

2. The second highland variant, in middle-latitude highlands, is *mainly dry with some winter frost but a growing season longer than 90 days.* Within this category are the great plateaus and basin and range regions of the United States which are utilized primarily for cattle grazing.

3. The third highland variant is the *tropical highland,* which may be *wet, humid, or dry, but without frost* (except at every high, spot elevations in limited Alpine-type areas). It is within this category that the *vertical* zonation of agricultural resources achieves its greatest range and significance. It is possible to move vertically through successive zones from tropical to alpine conditions within a quite short horizontal distance. The analogous contrast from tropical to alpine climatic conditions at sea level is achieved only by travelling thousands of miles.

Tropical highlands. The cooling effect of elevation which produces an irregular pattern of temperate atmospheric resource conditions in tropical latitudes. Extensive areas of relatively uniform water, warmth, and surface conditions do *not* occur in highlands as they do in lowland plains. Temperate conditions known as *tierra templada* lie between hot, wet lowlands which are *tierra caliente* on the one hand, and, at higher elevations still, the cold dry conditions of *tierra fria* on the other hand. It is difficult to define such zones accurately by a single set of elevations because of variations at different latitudes and because of prevailing winds. Average data for the three major altitude zones are given in Table XXVI.

Comparison of the maps in Figures 158 and 161 with that of cultivated land in Figure 162 shows that a high proportion of cultivated land in the tropics is in highland regions. There are also, however, considerable areas of cultivation in tropical low-

TABLE XXVI   MAJOR ZONES OF TROPICAL HIGHLANDS

Zone	Average elevation, feet	Vegetation	Crop associations
Tierra caliente (hot)	Sea level to 3,000	Desert, savanna, tropical evergreen rain forest	Cacao, corn, sugar, tobacco, rice, bananas, yams, melons, casava
Tierra templada (temperate)	3,000–6,000	Subtropical evergreen rain or semideciduous forest	Coffee, corn, (up to 7,500 feet in some areas)
Tierra fria (cold)	6,000–10,000	Tree line at upper limit	Potatoes, barley, wheat
Tierra paremos (frigid)	10,000–15,000	Snow line upper limit, treeless alpine vegetation	Alpine meadow grazing
Ice cap (frozen)	Above 15,000	None	None

lands. The resulting wide variation in temperature conditions, as well as other resources of agricultural production within short distances between tropical lowlands and highland areas accounts for a large part of the relatively high degree of crop diversity within the regions defined as tropical highlands. The maps of individual crops in Figure 163 and 164 show rice, sugar, coffee, tobacco, cotton, and cocoa production in two of the major resource associations within the tropics—*winterless rainy tropics in plains and low highlands* and *tropical highlands*. The maps show characteristically scattered and patchy distribution for each crop. Production is isolated and concentrated in many small districts and the patterns of crop specialization do not show striking duplication in locality. If all the separate crop maps were combined, the results would demonstrate crop *diversity*. Partial overlapping of crop patterns in some localities produces the greatest diversity in the lower levels of tropical highlands, above 1,000 feet but below 6,000. By contrast, poleward in the temperate plains of the middle latitudes, dominance of one or two crops over great areas is prevalent.

A second feature of the diversity of patchwork agriculture in tropical lands is its specialization. Coffee, sugar, tobacco, cacao, and bananas are produced for export rather than for either subsistence or for local domestic or national markets. This is not to deny that internal markets exist, but only to indicate that intercontinental trade between complementary temperate and tropical environments is the most important underlying motivation for tropical highland production. Middle-latitude agricultural production in southern South America competes in South American and Caribbean, as well as European markets with similar production from North America. Grains and livestock are the principal products in competition.

The Broad Patterns of the "Agricultural" Uses of Land. The term "agricultural" is here extended to mean forest and range uses of the land as well as farming. Crops, livestock, and forests occupy the most extensive territory in the course of human activities making use of the resources of the land. A generalization of these three patterns of "agricultural" uses of land, water, and air resources of the Americas is shown on the map in Figure 162. Comparison of this map with the patterns of resources shown in Figures 156 to 161 demonstrate a basic harmony between the particular associations of resources and the patterns of land use. This is a matter of human perceptivity and action based on understanding. The map in Figure 162 may also be thought of as showing the stages to which the agricultural resource association in the Americas have been developed up to the present by the descendants of the Europeans who migrated to the New World.

The correspondence of the patterns of farm land use and arable land with humid plains and low highlands with moderate growing season (designated

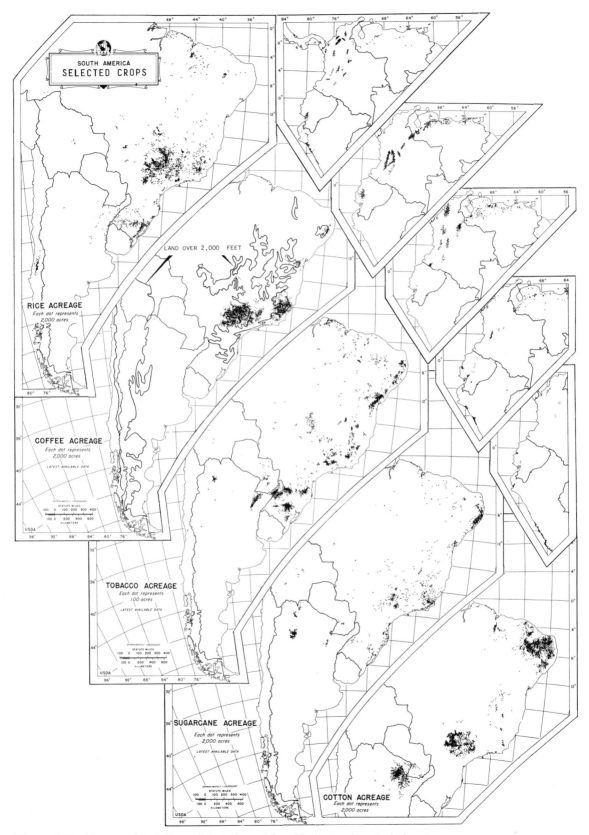

Figure 163. (*Courtesy of U. S. Dept. of Agriculture,* Atlas of Latin American Agriculture.)

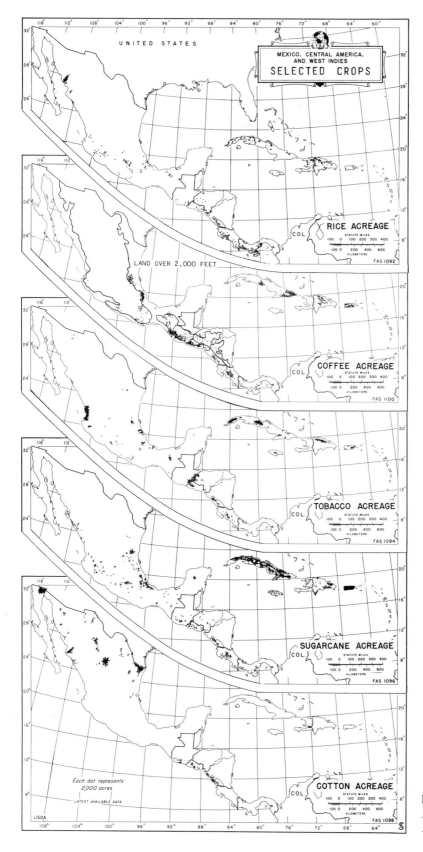

Figure 164. (*Courtesy of U. S. Dept. of Agriculture,* Atlas of Latin American Agriculture.)

type I on the map in Figure 161) has already been pointed out. This region in North America and the Eurasian Plain of Western Europe and the Soviet Union combined are the two greatest agricultural regions of the earth. Basically triangular in shape, the interior lowlands of North America repeat the contour of the continent. Bounded on the north by subarctic forest lands, and on the west by the great western highland, its third margin is *accessible to the sea* on the southeast. On the east the region is interrupted to some extent by the relatively low highlands of the older Appalachian system of mountains, but picks up as a coastal plain which narrows northeastward along the Atlantic from a width of 150 miles in Georgia to end at New York on the north. Inland from the Gulf of Mexico, coastal plain and interior lowland merge almost imperceptibly so that from the tip of southern Florida south of Miami to the Peace River in Alberta, Canada, a straight line can be drawn for nearly 3,000 miles across almost continuous agricultural lands. The width of this agriculturally developed triangle, which opens outward from its Canadian apex to the sea on its southeast margin, is some 1,600 miles from Corpus Christi, Texas, to New York.

These are the plains and low highlands of type I, mostly humid with some frost every year, but at least 90 days growing season. Within this great realm the forests which were originally present at the time of European colonization have been cut down, partly regrown, and cut down again. The original grasslands and prairies have been put to the plow. The days of exploration and initial settlement by the pioneer are now mere memories. The present generations of population within this great region regard with surprise any region which is not under continuously extended cultivation from horizon to wherever they stand, so accustomed have they become to the agricultural continuity about them. (See Figures 165A, B, and C.) When persons who have always lived in this region leave it for the first time, traveling northward into the forested areas or westward across the great plains into ranching country, they are overwhelmed by the strangeness of movement through seemingly "empty land"—forest or grass—as the highway carries them as on a bridge from town to town. The region in which they feel "at home" is characterized by continuous dispersed farm settlement, focused on thousands of farm-service towns, villages, and cities distributed relatively uniformly throughout virtually its entire extent.

Conversely people coming into such agricultural zones from forest and range lands are at first amazed by the uninterrupted extent of cultivated land. As they move north from the transitional borders of the region they first meet cut-over lands and intermittent forest, and then the great relatively untouched coniferous forests of the subarctic. On the western transitional border of this region lie the wheatlands of the high plains (Figure 166). Here mountain-fed rivers have created steep slopes and grazing supercedes grain farming. Wheat still occupies level tops between the stream valleys and slopes. Then almost abruptly appear forested mountains, intermontane basins and plateaus of a predominantly livestock economy (Figure 167A and B). This is the cordilleran region of the Rocky Mountains—Columbia and Colorado plateaus—and the basin and range country. The cordilleran region is bounded on the east by the Rocky Mountain Front Ranges in the central United States, in front of which lie Denver, Colorado, and Cheyenne, Wyoming. Nine hundred miles to the west the region is bounded by the Sierra Nevada and Cascade ranges. In Mexico and Canada the cordilleran region is narrower. Along the northern border of the United States it narrows to 400 miles in width. Along the Mexican border the comparable distance across is approximately 500 miles.

Beyond the mountain region lies another world —the Pacific coast of North America, from Alaska to Baja California. Its regional subdivisions are small in area only by comparison with the continental dimensions of the humid eastern half of the United States. Important among those subdivisions are the Puget Sound area, the Willamette Valley, Southern California, the Central Valley of California, and the Imperial Valley of the Colorado River delta in Arizona, California, and Mexico.

As shown by the map in Figure 162, the humid east is divided into a number of large subregional crop associations or agricultural specialities. On the subhumid western margins of the humid east, from north to south, are the major winter and spring wheat regions of Canada and the United States, respectively. From north to south in the East four farming regions are stacked. These are the dairy belt, the corn belt, a general farming belt, and a southern and Gulf Coast diversified special crop zone. (Types of farming are illustrated in pictures A, B, and C, of Figure 168.)

The broad pattern of cultivated, forest, and range land in Latin America is fundamentally dif-

Figure 165. These three photographs illustrate the striking contrast between the three major types of land-use associations in the Americas.

(A) A segment of the extraordinary continuity of cropland which, in effect, extends for 3,000 miles by 1,500 miles in the great interior triangle of lowland North America. The strip cropping of these fields near Temple, Texas, emphasizes the organized variety in farm patterns today. (*Courtesy of U. S. Dept. of Agriculture.*)

(B) A different kind of continuity, that of the northern forests which take over from agriculture where the growing season is short and soils less fertile, so that the decision not to compete with other resource associations has long since been made. This view from a fire tower near Houghton Lake in central Michigan shows second growth forest cover as far as the eye can see. (*Courtesy of Allen K. Philbrick.*)

(C) A third great association, that of the range country to the west of continuous cropland where drought presents a major problem in land management. Here, in Wyoming, the organized grazing of animals represents the most significant solution by which the short grasses of the semi-arid range are converted into commercial products of animal agriculture. (*Courtesy of U. S. Dept. of Agriculture.*)

Figure 166. The combining of wheat in a field near Liberal, Kansas, in the southwest corner of the state near the Cimarron River. Note the great size of the field and the almost complete absence of trees or bushes except in the farmsteads in the far distance. (*Courtesy of U. S. Dept. of Agriculture.*)

ferent from that of North America. Isolated and separated agricultural areas prevail. They are relatively small and on or near to the coasts of the continent, forming a ring around the virtually empty grazing and forested tropical interior.

In middle-latitude Argentina, a continuously cultivated temperate region gives way to grazing land in all landward directions. This region is the Argentine Pampas, which is about 400 miles in diameter. Across the Andes to the west a narrow band of Mediterranean agriculture is found in Chile, which consists primarily of a narrow irrigated Central Valley in the north and a smaller unirrigated portion of the same valley in the south. This region averages 40 miles in width, but extends 600 miles from north to south.

Northeast of the Argentine Pampas is the subtropical and tropical coast of Brazil. One characteristic of Brazil is lack of extensive coastal plains, quite different from the southeast coast of the United States. In two separate agricultural regions of the Brazilian south Atlantic coast, plantation-type commercial agriculture extends several hundred miles into the interior behind coastal highlands. These subtropical southern Brazilian agricultural regions are somewhat tempered by elevation.

Much of the land is over 2,000 feet above sea level. Brazilian agriculture occupies primarily the former semideciduous forest areas corresponding generally to the southeastern highlands over 2,000 feet in elevation. In terms of the total amount of land ever brought under cultivation, subsistence agriculture in Brazil has far exceeded commercial agriculture in the course of four hundred and fifty years of settlement.

Brazilian subsistence agriculture involves a system of land rotation. Forest is cleared by tenants for a landowner. After several years of subsistence tenancy the landowner takes over the newly cleared tracts for cattle and the tenants must move on. After a few more years the newly created pasture land gives out and is allowed to go back to brush and forest. This process of clearing, cropping, pasturing, and abandonment has recurred again and again. Within the large region characterized by subsistence land rotation, minority areas of specialized crop developments shown on the maps in Figure 163 have occurred in successive periods up to the present pattern of diverse plantation farming.

Beyond the ends of rail and road pattern in the interior stretch wild tropical-savanna range lands (very unlike the cultivated uplands) which merge

Figure 167. Ewes and lambs grazing on the abundant and nutritious grasses of western Montana. (*Courtesy of Northern Pacific Railway.*)

gradually into the Amazon rain forest or selva. In South America the upper highlands are higher than in North America. The same is true of intermontane basins and plateaus. Some of these tablelands and basins in the high Andes of Bolivia and Peru provide the resources for a temperate subsistence Indian agriculture which is completely different from the livestock ranching and irrigated commercial agriculture of intermontane basins and plateaus in North America.

From the standpoint of similarity between the continents, it can be said that both possess great regions of cultivation, ranchland, and forest. Yet, differences far outweigh superficial similarities. Except for Argentina, which corresponds to the North American Middle West, or the Central Valley of Chile, which corresponds to central and southern California, the cultivated lands of South America are used either for subsistence farming or for specialized tropical and subtropical commercial agriculture. Except for high highland forests and those of middle-latitude southern Chile and Argentina,

the forested regions of Latin America are tropical rainforest or tropical savanna rather than the temperate deciduous and mixed forests of North America. The most significant difference, of course, is the much greater mixture of species in tropical forests, as opposed to great stands of uniform species or groups of a few kinds of trees. In the tropical selva of the Amazon as many as 3,000 species of trees per square mile have been identified where intensive study of the forest has been conducted. The uniformity of tree species is of great importance in the economic exploitation of the forest resources of temperate regions, which makes it possible to harvest large quantities of wood products of uniform type and quality in North American forests. The converse is true of tropical forests.

Latin American range lands are of indifferent quality in comparison with those of North America. Subtropical savanna range lands are much more extensive in South America than in the United States. Low soil fertility, cattle diseases, ticks, less nutritive grasses, the enervating effects of heat, all

Figure 168

(A) A herd coming from pasture for milking on the Ray White dairy farm in Bristol County, Massachusetts. (*Courtesy of U. S. Dept. of Agriculture.*)

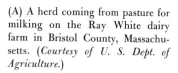

(B) A typical corn-belt field in Illinois. (*Courtesy of Corn Industries Research Foundation, Inc.*)

(C) The use of the sloping lands of limestone-karst-lake topography of Winter Garden, Florida, for citrus groves. (*Courtesy of U. S. Dept. of Agriculture.*)

plague the livestock in Latin America, and accordingly make life difficult for the livestock rancher.

In summary, many fundamental differences exist between North and Latin America in regard to agricultural resources and agricultural uses of land. North American agriculture is lowland and humid with a winter season. It is characterized primarily by grains, feed, and livestock associations, and secondarily by specialized food and industrial crops. It covers the second most extensive agricultural realm in the world. By contrast Latin American agriculture is tropical and wet in both lowland and highland. It is characterized by specialized plantation-type food and industrial crops more than by grains, feed, and livestock. Most significant of all is its fragmented coastal pattern instead of an extensive and uninterrupted continental pattern as in the United States and Canada.

Mineral Resources of the Americas

Discussion of the mineral resources of the Americas directly involves the subsurface materials classified at the beginning of this chapter. The two most basic associations of minerals distributed geographically with reference to rock types are, again, the *mineral fuels* within sedimentary lowlands and the *metallic minerals* in highly localized concentrations within metamorphic rock regions.

The maps in Figures 169 and 170 demonstrate these locational relationships in considerable detail. They show only the most important mineral-producing localities. Again it must be remembered that only those minerals of relatively high yield and greater accessibility to major concentrations of population in relation to their inherent value are in active production. There are many additional potential mineral resources not now economically feasible to mine which occur within the rock-association regions. These are not shown by the principal producing localities on the map. The number of mineral-producing sites is considerable nevertheless and their pattern is widely distributed among the regions of the double continent. Examination of the map reveals the specific location of minerals within the following regional categories: (1) the metallic minerals associated with the ancient Precambrian metamorphic rock regions on the continental margins and (2) the mineral fuels—coal in carboniferous strata of Paleozoic sediments and the natural gas and crude petroleum fields also of sedimentary origin—in the interior lowlands of North America primarily.

The geographical distribution of structural and rock-association regions divides the mineral resources of the Americas into seven main regions which follow the triangular shape of the paired continents. The metallic minerals are primarily located within six principal igneous-metamorphic upland regions, three of which mark approximately the margins of each of the triangular-shaped continents. The North American regions are the Canadian Shield, Appalachia, and the great Western Cordillera. In South America, they are the Venezuelan Shield, the eastern Brazilian Shield, and, again, the great Western Cordillera. In Latin America and the California coast of southwestern North America, narrow coastal sedimentary regions also include some mineral fuels, particularly oil. The seventh region is the interior sedimentary lowlands of North America which are amazingly rich in mineral fuels—coal, oil, and natural gas.

Mineral-Producing Districts of the Canadian Shield Region. Outstanding among specific mineral districts shown on the map are those on, near to, or connected to manufacturing users by transportation across the *contact line* of the Canadian Shield with the interior sedimentary region of North America. These districts extend in a great semicircle from Port Radium on Great Bear Lake, an important source of uranium, to the Labrador-Quebec border, where new iron-ore mines have in recent years been connected by rail to the improved St. Lawrence Seaway. In between are the important Flin Flon copper district of Canada, the Lake Superior iron district of Canada and the United States, (See Figure 171A), and the Sudbury-Noranda nickel, copper, and gold district.

Mineral-Producing Districts of the Appalachian Region. The Wabana iron-ore district of Newfoundland, together with coal and limestone of eastern Nova Scotia, provide the basis for steel production at Sydney, Nova Scotia. The latter district is the northernmost of those belonging to the second geographical grouping, the Appalachian highlands from Newfoundland, Canada, to Georgia in the United States. From north to south in this group important mineral-producing districts include the Adirondacks iron ore and Pennsylvania-New Jersey copper and iron-ore district, the Ducktown copper of east Tennessee, and the Birmingham iron and steel complex in Alabama.

Mineral-Producing Districts of the Western Cordilleran Region. The third alignment of mineral districts is that of the great western highlands.

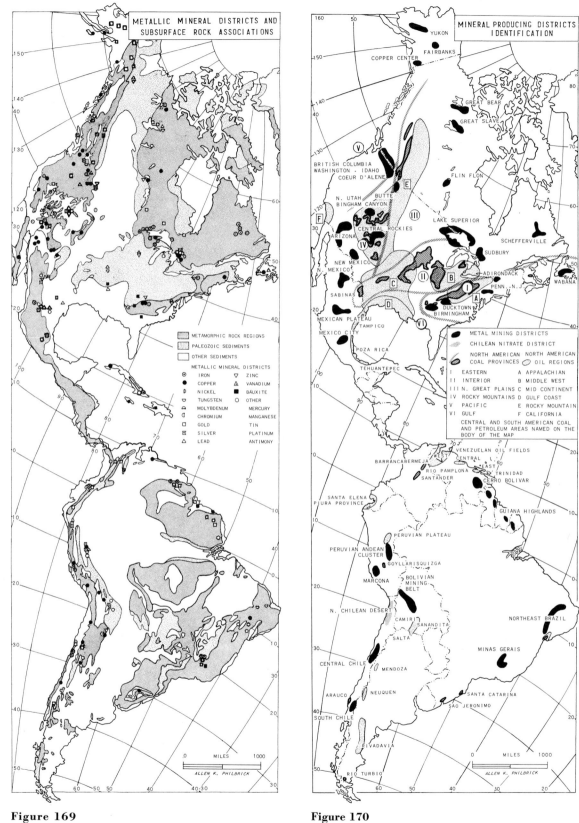

Figure 169

Figure 170

271

Figure 171. (A) Above, a view of the Hull-Rust-Mahoning open-pit iron-ore mine looking east from the edge of Mahoning toward North Hibbing. This pit is the largest iron-ore mine in the world. It has a total area of 1,275 acres, is three miles long, varies in width from one-half to one mile, and has a maximum depth of 435 feet. There are 55 miles of track in the pit, development of which started in 1895. (*Courtesy of Standard Oil Co. of New Jersey.*) (B) Below, a view of the open-pit copper mine at Bingham Canyon, Utah. New tunneling is visible at the bottom. The huge size of these mining enterprises gives a good idea of the commitment in capital investment and labor involved, and illustrates why only the largest and most productive mineral sites are selected for development. (*Courtesy of Kennecott Copper Corp.*)

Again, from north to south and associated with the igneous and metamorphic rocks of the cordilleran highland are such mineral districts as the gold mining in Alaska, focused on Fairbanks, and copper from the copper center district of the Wrangell range in southwestern Alaska. Across the international border in the Yukon Territory of Canada are the world-famous gold-mining areas with storied names such as Dawson and Klondike. In the United States-Canadian border region in southern British Columbia-northern Washington and Idaho is a mineral district of great importance which supplies copper, gold, silver, lead, and zinc from fifteen or more scattered mining localities. Among these, that of Coeur d'Alene in northern Idaho yields up to 25 per cent of the lead and zinc requirements of the United States. From the northern Utah district in the vicinity of Salt Lake City come copper from Bingham Canyon (See Figure 171B), and also gold, lead, zinc, and some iron from other mining localities. Other important mining districts are the Butte district in Montana with copper and the central Rockies district of Colorado, with scattered production of lead, gold, silver, and molybdenum. In the southwest are the copper mines of southern Arizona and New Mexico. Across the border in Mexico metallic minerals are mined in scattered locations throughout the Sierra Madre Occidental. The western highlands of Mexico are igneous rock. The Guadelupe Mountains on the east of the Rio Grande in southern New Mexico and west Texas are folded mountains of sedimentary origin. In them, lead, zinc, and mercury are mined. The Altiplano Mexicana, or central Mexican Plateau, lies between the western igneous-rock mountains and the eastern folded sediments and is also of recent sedimentary origin, from which lead and zinc are also derived.

In the latitude of Mexico City a range of recent volcanic origins contains most of Mexico's active volcanos. This range cuts across Mexico in nearly an east-west direction for some 650 miles from the Pacific to the Atlantic. Most of the population of Mexico lives directly north of the volcanic range in the intermontane plateau basins.

Mineral Fuels of the Interior Sedimentary Lowlands. The "hard-rock" minerals classified above surround the interior sedimentary lowlands. As already pointed out this triangular interior region of North America contains the second largest agricultural region on earth. In addition below the surface it possesses the world's most important mineral-fuel-producing regions within rocks of

sedimentary origin. The map in Figure 170 demonstrates the great wealth of North American sediments in coal, petroleum, natural gas, chemical salts, limestone, and certain other minerals, which include some metals such as lead, zinc, and aluminum that have been chemically concentrated by ground water in sedimentary rocks. So widespread are the deposits of mineral fuels that reference to them in terms of individual mining sites is scarcely appropriate. Generalizations are made on the map and in later tabular classification by referring only to producing "provinces" in the case of coal, and "fields" in the case of petroleum and natural gas. The mineral fuels are identified separately rather than in combination. They are extracted at a great many individual locations over large areas, rather than in large amounts from a relatively few scattered localities. It must also be pointed out that many of the coal provinces, particularly in the western plains states, are of low-grade coal (lignite), and even the better coal (bituminous grade) of the western coal provinces is far less actively exploited than are the coals in the Middle West and in the East. Coal production from the less extensive, somewhat fragmented coal measures of the mountain states is now increasing as the steel industry gains momentum, which reflects growing western markets for steel.

The map in Figure 170 shows six coal provinces in North America. The two most important producers are the eastern and interior provinces. The eastern province contains three separate subregions: a small hard-coal region (meta-anthracite) in Rhode Island, and the famous Pennsylvania anthracite region and the very extensive Appalachian coal fields from northwestern Pennsylvania to western Alabama. The most important producing region of the interior province is the Illinois-southern Indiana-western Kentucky field. The other interior coal regions southwest, west, and north are negligible in production, although the western region which is very extensive from Iowa to southern Oklahoma averages approximately 15 million tons a year. The relative significance of production may be seen from the average figures given in Table XXVII.

Other provinces and subregions of coal production, as shown by the table, have importance beyond the small amounts which they contribute to total production in the size of the reserves they represent. North American coal production is close to 40 per cent of world production, and its reserves are the world's largest. By far the greatest part of this reserve lies within the northern great plains and

TABLE **XXVII**   AVERAGE PRODUCTION OF COAL BY REGIONS IN NORTH AMERICA[a]

Province	Region		Production in millions of metric tons	Per cent
Eastern	Maritime, Canada		6	1
	Pennsylvania, anthracite		56	10
	Appalachian (main)		335	61
	Appalachian, Alabama		16	3
		Subtotal	413	75
Interior	Eastern		89	16
	Western		14	2
	Northern		. . .	. . .
	Southwestern		. . .	. . .
		Subtotal	103	18
Northern great plains			11	2
Rocky Mountains			21	4
Pacific			5	1
Gulf			1	. . .
Northern Mexico			. . .	. . .
			554	100
		Total	554	100

[a] William Van Royen, *Atlas of World Resources, Mineral Resources*, Vol. II, New York: Prentice-Hall, 1952, p. 11. Average of 1929, 1937, and 1944 production.

Rocky Mountain provinces of North America and is divided between coals of both good and poor quality. Coal is not plentiful in Mexico and is mined only for use in Mexico's steel industry at Monterrey. Coal measures there are an extension of the southwestern coal region of Texas across the Rio Grande into Mexico. This coal is a seam only five feet thick in a measure some 34 miles long by 15 miles wide. This modest field is nevertheless one of the best sources of coal in all of Latin America. It is called the Sabinas region after a tributary river of the same name which flows into the Rio Grande.

The oil and gas-producing regions of North America can also be summarized in six major producing units. As shown by the map in Figure 170 these regions are: the midcontinent region of Texas, Oklahoma, Kansas, and parts of Arkansas, Louisiana, and Mississippi; the Gulf Coast of Louisiana, Texas, and Mexico; and the California region. Other regions, although of minor significance in total production, are the Appalachians, Middle West (including southern Ontario), and Rocky Mountain regions. Venezuela in South America ranks second in production in the Americas.

Since it was discovered in 1859 in Pennsylvania, and in Ontario, Canada, in 1858, the past hundred years has seen worldwide search for "liquid gold." The fortunes and statistics of production and of reserves have been ever changing, as region after region has entered upon the scene. In such a changing picture, definitive absolute figures are impossible. Two major groupings of producing regions, however, clearly dominate the world production of petroleum and natural gas. These are the fields in the Americas, as just outlined, and those in the Middle East. Data in Table XXVIII record the relative significance of these regional groupings in terms of 1958 production, and cumulative production of crude petroleum since the beginning. Note the great difference between North American and Latin American production, which is even more striking if the contrast is made between regions of the Northern and Southern Hemisphere. Production south of the Equator is a tiny fraction of that north of that line.

Mineral Fuels in Latin America. As shown by the preceding table, Latin America is better endowed with petroleum than with coal. Petroleum fields, however, are located on the periphery of the continent. Venezuela, which is one of the major producing fields in the world, exports rather than utilizes its oil. Colombia, Ecuador, Peru, Bolivia, and Argentina, however, cannot satisfy their own relatively modest means from their own domestic production of petroleum products.

Latin America is generally lacking in coal. Only a few small coal measures with very limited reserves are available for industrial use. As shown on the map in Figure 170, these are the Rio Pamplona and Santander fields in Colombia; the Goyllarisquizga fields of Peru; the Arauco field in Chile; the Rio Turbio field of Argentina; and the Santa Catarina and Sao Jeronimo fields of southern Brazil. South American coal reserves are less than 30 billion tons, compared with 2,800 billion tons in North America. The pattern of Latin American coal measures is within the small extent of Paleozoic sedimentary rocks bordering some of the ancient metamorphic highlands, which means that coal-producing regions are all on the margins of the continent. Younger noncoal-bearing sediments prevail in the interior.

Major Mineral-Producing Districts of Latin America. As shown by the maps in Figures 169 and 170, the major "hard-rock" mineral-producing districts in Latin America, again, are associated in the same triangular-type continental pattern as those of North America. On the north or Caribbean side in the crystalline uplands of Venezuela is the great iron-ore body Cerro Bolivar (south of the sedimentary Orinoco-lowland oilfields). To the east, continuing in the extension of these highlands into the Guianas, are numerous gold-mining activities. On the southeast, in the metamorphic Brazilian highland, the mining exclave of Brazil is the most important district. Iron ore, gold, and manganese are produced. On the west in South America's Andean portion of the great cordillera of the Americas, is the southern continent's greatest display of mineral districts. In the Peruvian highlands a cluster of mining activities yields copper, gold, lead, and zinc. The Bolivian tin, gold, and copper district is that country's most notable economic contribution. This mining belt is located on the edges of Bolivia's high plateau (Figure 172A and B). The metallic ores occur in veins of igneous intrusions, most of which are mined under the severely adverse condition of thin high-altitude atmosphere. They are above the timber line and require importation of all lumber and most food.

TABLE **XXVIII**   PETROLEUM PRODUCTION IN THE AMERICAS IN RELATION TO WORLD PRODUCTION, 1958[a]

Regions	Production, thousands of barrels	Per cent of world	Per cent of world, cumulative
World	6,607,373	100.00	100.00
Midcontinent	1,230,937	18.65	
Gulf Coast	521,837	7.90	
California	317,004	4.80	
Rocky Mountains	238,516	3.60	
Middle West	106,087	1.60	
Appalachian	33,696	0.50	
United States	2,448,077	37.05	55.35
Canada	165,236	2.50	1.03
North America	2,613,313	39.55	56.38
Venezuela	950,558	14.39	10.85
Mexico	92,453	1.40	2.90
Colombia	46,375	0.70	0.77
Trinidad	36,700	0.55	0.58
Caribbean	1,126,086	17.04	15.10
Argentina	34,231	0.52	0.64
Peru	19,000	0.29	0.49
Brazil	18,923	0.29	0.04
Chile	5,568	0.08	0.02
Bolivia	3,455	0.05	0.02
Ecuador	3,144	0.05	0.07
Other South America	84,321	1.28	1.28
Latin America	1,210,407	18.32	16.38
Western Hemisphere	3,823,720	57.87	72.76
U.S.S.R.	817,300	12.37	9.69
Middle East	1,564,786	23.68	11.63
USSR-Middle East	2,382,086	36.05	21.32
Other European	188,429	2.85	2.71
Africa	32,353	0.49	0.27
Far East	180,786	2.73	2.93
Other	401,568	6.07	5.91

[a] Source: *World Oil*, New York and Dallas, February 15, 1959, pp. 100, 108.

Mineral districts in Chile include the famous nitrates of the northern Chilean desert; the copper of Chuquicamate, Portrerillos, and El Teniente; and iron ores from El Tofo. The significant pattern is one of short feeder railroad lines from coastal ports to inland mining locations in the upland. The rail spurs carry the wealth of the subsurface out for export, which is in basic contrast to the organization of mineral production in North America. In Chile, Brazil, Venezuela, Colombia, Peru, and Mexico, as well as Argentina now, beginnings are being made in the development of metal manufac-

Figure 172. (A) Left, this mine at Oruro, Bolivia, was once worked by the Incas for its silver. The exterior view of the San Jose mine plant shows what is now one of the principle tin producers of Bolivia. (B) Right, the women in this picture are employed at the Hilluni mine 15,000 feet high in the Andes Mountains. (*Courtesy of United Nations.*)

tures based on domestically produced raw materials, which will be discussed in the chapter on the organization of area in the Americas.

This chapter has explained the major contrasts in the patterns of resources, both agricultural and mineral, which characterize the North and South American continents and the Central American Isthmus which connects them. It answers the question—what resources have been inherited by successive generations of European in-migrants who have participated, along with millions of Africans and the original Indian population of the Americas, in the development of a new world on the western side of the Atlantic.

EXERCISE   Reconstructing the Agricultural Resource Regions of the Americas

1. Place a piece of onion-skin typing paper over the map of surface types in Figure 158 and trace the coastline of the Americas. Then draw in the inner border of the high highlands and enclosed lowlands shown in solid black. This line is the portion of the surface-pattern map which contributes a major distinction on the composite map of agricultural resource regions shown in Figure 161.

2. Next place the onion-skin overlay started in step one over the map showing precipitation. Trace the heavy dashed lines representing 20 and 60 inches of precipitation, respectively, east of the great western cordilleran region. These parts of the precipitation pattern are the boundaries on the composite map contributed by the use of the map in Figure 159.

3. Next place the same overlay over the third map dealing with duration of the growing season. Trace in the heavy solid and dashed-line boundaries shown on this map, representing 90 days duration of the growing season, nearly frost-free conditions and frost-free or unlimited growing season as far as frost is concerned, respectively. These lines, in turn, are the boundaries on the composite map contributed by the subject-matter distinctions of the map in Figure 160.

4. Now compare the resulting outlines which you have constructed with the composite map of agricultural resource regions in Figure 161. Note the role of each measure of distinction in the individual subject-matter maps from which the composite map is derived in formulating the regional associations of agricultural resources which are contained in the legend of the map in Figure 161.

Compare, also, the pattern of residual soil fertility shown for the Americas on the world map of that name in Figure 46. Note the additional subregions which these soil distinctions makes it possible to define.

In interpreting the significance of such associations of physical phenomena, be sure to think in terms of specific opportunities and problems rather than deterministic environmental responses. Remember that it is the understanding of potentialities and the nature of difficulties to be surmounted which represent what actual conditions mean to different persons attempting to understand and make use of these resources.

13 *The Area Organization of the Americas*

The general outline of the uses of land in the Americas has been described by the patterns of "agriculture" and of mining in Figures 162, 169, and 170 of the preceding chapter. It is the purpose of this chapter to show how these same resources and activities representing their uses are *functionally organized* into the nodal regions of the two continents. The people in North America have linked the fuel and food-rich interior lowlands with the minerals from the surrounding metamorphic highland regions in fashioning the regional organization of twin national economies—the United States of America and the Dominion of Canada. The core regions on which each economy focuses are adjacent to one another and extend inland from the central eastern seaboard of the continent.

By contrast in Latin America there is no such continental unity among twenty-one independent countries and a number of *colonial* territories. In addition to the larger number of political divisions reflecting separate functional organization of territory, *external orientation* of productive activities destined for export outside Latin America in both agriculture and mining contrasts sharply with the primarily internal orientation of regional organization in North America.

Area Organization of the Americas as a Whole in a World Setting

Emphasis in this chapter will be on the countries of Anglo-American culture, but the regions of specialized agricultural and mineral production in Latin America will be discussed in relation to the area organization of the Americas as a whole in a world setting.

Focus of the Americas on the North American Coreland. The map in Figure 173 shows the overall pattern of area organization of the Americas focused on the North American core region. In this view specialized producing regions in Latin American republics are similar in principle to subregions within the United States and Canada in having a common focus on the major coreland of the double continent. On the map each subregion which trades principally with the United States is connected by a continuous straight line between its major city and New York—the largest metropolitan center in the world. Within North America dotted lines are used to show connections of internal subregional centers with New York. Similar lines connect the principal focus of the Canadian core region at Montreal with subregional centers in Canada.

Economic evidence of the focality of the countries of the Americas on the core region of the United States is detailed in Table XXIX. The table shows the direction of international trade to and from nations of the Americas in 1956. Comparison may also be made between the United States and Western Europe as a whole with respect to trade with each country of the Americas. In this comparison, for example, it can be seen that Argentina and Uruguay, which possess the Latin American equivalent in agricultural resources of the Middle West and Great Plains of the United States, are not part of the focus on New York. In the case of Argentina, trade with the United States-Canada is only 17 per cent, while that to Western Europe accounts for nearly half of the total trade (48 per cent). For Uruguay the figures are 15 per cent of total trade with the United States, and 53 per cent with Europe. Certain Caribbean possessions of the United Kingdom focus on London rather than on New York. These exceptions are shown on the map by dashed lines from Jamaica, Trinidad, Tobago, and from British Guiana to London in the United Kingdom. Countries trading more with Europe than the United States are connected by straight continuous lines to the North Sea-English Channel area, as from Buenos Aires and Montevideo.

The dominance of total trade with the United States by the bulk of Latin American countries is very pronounced. The following data taken from Table XXIX make an impressive array of product specializations primarily focused on the United

States. Proceeding alphabetically, the figure in each example is the per cent of that country's *total* exports devoted to that product. Not all of it but a large proportion must go to the United States, since in each case the United States is the largest importer: Bolivian tin, 55 per cent; Brazilian coffee, 61 per cent; Chilean copper, 38 per cent; Colombian coffee, 77 per cent; Costa Rican coffee, 49 per cent; Dominican Republican sugar, 80 per cent; Ecuadorian bananas, 35 per cent; the coffee of El Salvador, 82 per cent; Guatemalan coffee, 79 per cent; Haitian coffee, 61 per cent; Honduran bananas, 53 per cent; Nicaraguan coffee, 44 per cent; Panamanian bananas, 60 per cent; Venezualan petroleum, 92 per cent.

The table also shows the first five export and import products in order of their importance for each country and territory. From these lists it is apparent that mineral and agricultural raw materials dominate the export picture from Latin America. In twelve out of the twenty Latin American republics in 1956, 90 per cent or more of their exports were accounted for by the largest five items. By contrast no single item dominates the total imports of any Latin American country. Most items are less than 10 per cent of the total imports and the proportions of the first five items to total imports ranges from 25 to 50 per cent. The character of the imports are primarily manufactured goods, petroleum products, machinery, motor vehicles, and food products.

A high degree of specialization in export trade is indicated when the percentage of the first five items *exported*, by value, is a large share of the total. If the largest five *import* items by value are a small part of the total, it indicates that imports are widely spread among a large number of items. From the table it is apparent that Latin American export trade is narrowly and relatively insecurely based on a large volume within a narrow band of commodities. The corollary is also true. The lack of diversified domestic production is reflected in an import trade divided among the many items of consumers goods on which the standard of living is based.

On the other hand, countries whose exports are manufactured goods, while their imports are raw materials and specialized foods, probably possess diversified domestic economies. Both sides of this comparison are represented in the Americas. The United States is undoubtedly the country in the Americas, if not in the world, with the greatest diversity in industrial production. The figures in Table XXIX for the United States show an almost evenly matched proportion between the five most important import and export items and total imports and exports—32.5 and 31.2 per cent, respectively. Four of the export items listed for the United States are *manufactured* products. Only the fifth ranked item, cotton, is a raw material. All five of the most important items imported, by value, are either specialized *food* products or industrial *raw materials*. It is indeed significant that the largest import which amounts to 11.5 per cent of the total import budget of nearly 13 billion dollars is devoted to a single specialized *luxury* item—coffee. High rates of consumption of petroleum, paper, alloy metals for steel production, and copper within the United States necessitate supplemental imports. Such imports come mainly from raw material producers in the Western Hemisphere and are represented by the next four of the first five items by value in the import column of the table. In possessing such a diversified domestic economy the United States is almost alone. Canada and Argentina more nearly resemble the United States in this respect than any other country in the Americas. Both of these countries export raw materials and food products and import manufactured goods, but their dependence on single items or a relatively few commodities is not as extreme as is the case for the others. Canada's single largest export commodity in 1956 was paper and paperboard—a manufactured or semiprocessed item—but it accounted for only 15 per cent of total exports. From Argentina the single largest export item, wheat, was only 16 per cent of total exports in 1956. Argentina is also the only country in Latin America with which another country in the Americas conducted a higher percentage of its total trade than it did with the United States. Paraguay exported more to Argentina, as shown by Table XXIX than to either the United States or western Europe.

World Trade Setting of American Regional Organization. The regional organization of the Americas as a whole can best be understood in relation to the pattern of *world* trade. The main line of world trade is a great-circle alignment across the world's land-water realm from the east coast of North America over the North Atlantic to England and the north coast of Europe. Thence the main line follows the alignment of the core region of Europe to and through the eastern Mediterranean to the Suez Canal-Red Sea route between Asia and Africa to the Indian Ocean. (See Figure 17 in Chapter 2.) Shipping, of course, uses the coastal

TABLE XXIX   THE DIRECTION OF TRADE TO AND FROM THE TERRITORIES OF THE AMERICAS[a]

Territory, capital	First 5 export items, millions of $	Per cent of total	First 5 import items, millions of $	Per cent of total	Per cent of total trade with first, second countries and U.S.-Canada, and W. Europe			
					First territory	Second territory	U.S.-Canada	W. Europe
Argentina Buenos Aires	Wheat	16	Petroleum, crude	13	U.S. 17	U.K. 13	17.3	48.2
	Beef, frozen (chilled)	11	Trucks, vans	8				
	Wool, greasy	9	Machinery, motors	7				
	Meat, preserved	7	Chem. pharmaceut.	6				
	Maize	5	Iron and steel prod.	6				
		48		40				
Bolivia La Paz	Tin ore	55	Mining mach.	9	U.S. 51	U.K. 24	51.4	35.4
	Wolframite	13	Agric. mach.	6				
	Lead ore	7	Cattle	6				
	Silver ore	6	Motor vehicles	6				
	Zinc ore	5	Sugar, white	5				
		86		32				
Brazil Rio de Janeiro	Coffee, unroasted	61	Petroleum, crude	8	U.S. 40	W. Germany 6.4	41.0	32.8
	Cocoa	5	Wheat	7				
	Pine lumber	5	Fuel, dies. oil	5				
	Iron ore, conc.	3	Car chassis	3				
	Sugar	3	Tractors, parts	3				
		77		26				
British Guiana Georgetown	Cane sugar	45	Machinery, other	14	U.K. 39	Canada 19	29.1	47.0
	Bauxite, conc.	32	Petroleum prod.	8				
	Rice, unhusked	11	Motor vehicles	4				
	Rum	4	Elect. machinery, other	3				
	Wood, unshaped	2	Wheat, meal, flour	4				
		94		33				
Canada Ottawa	Paper, paperboard	15	Machinery, other	11	U.S. 67	U.K. 12	66.8	19.6
	Wheat, unmilled	11	Motor vehicles	8				
	Wood, shaped	7	Iron, steel	7				
	Pulp, waste paper	6	Metal mfg., other	5				
	Aluminum	5	Petroleum, crude	5				
		44		36				
Chile Santiago	Copper, elect.	37	Machinery, other	12	U.S. 45	U.K. 12	45.6	38.6
	Copper, blister	36	Cotton, raw	6				
	Saltpeter	9	Automobiles	5				
	Iron ore	2	Petroleum, crude	5				
	Other ores	2	Railtrans. equip.	4				
		86		32				

TABLE XXIX (CONTINUED)

Country / City	Exports	%		Imports	%		Partner 1	%	Partner 2	%		
Colombia Bogotá	Coffee, unroasted Petroleum, crude Bananas, plantain Sugar, refined Tobacco, raw	77 13 5 1 1	97	Machinery, other Elect. machinery Iron, steel Motor vehicles Metals, mfg. other	12 10 8 7 5	42	U.S.	67	W. Germany	9	69.5	22.5
Costa Rica San José	Coffee Bananas, plantain Cocoa Livestock, for food Manila fiber	49 40 5 2 1	97	Petroleum prod. Motor vehicles Iron, steel Machinery, other Elect. machinery	6 6 6 6 5	29	U.S.	53	W. Germany	18	57.0	32.8
Cuba Habana	Sugar, raw, refnd. Tobacco, raw, proc. Molasses Nickel ore Copper ore	78 6 3 3 1	91	Indust. machinery, parts Motor car, parts Machinery, other Petroleum, crude Iron, steel mfg.	7 6 4 4 4	25	U.S.	70	U.K.	4	71.6	17.6
Santo Domingo Santo Domingo	Sugar, raw, refnd. Coffee, unroasted Cocoa Chocolate Tobacco, raw	60 16 8 3 3	90	Machinery, apparatus Chem. pharmaceut. Iron, steel struct. Elect. machinery Other iron, steel	7 6 6 5 4	28	U.S.	56	U.K.	15	58.0	30.8
Ecuador Quito	Bananas, plantain Coffee, unroasted Cocoa beans Rice, husked Saw, veneer logs	35 30 19 5 2	91	Machinery, non-elect. Transport equip. Textile yarn Base metals Elect. machinery appl.	13 11 7 7 6	44	U.S.	56	W. Germany	12	57.7	31.8
El Salvador San Salvador	Coffee Cotton (others less than 0.5%)	82 11	93	Motor vehicles Machinery, other Cotton fab. Petroleum prod. Iron, steel	9 6 6 5 4	30	U.S.	48	W. Germany	19	49.4	33.2
Guatemala Guatemala City	Coffee Bananas Veg. oils Chicle . . .	79 8 2 1	90	Iron, steel manufs. Tractors, parts Textiles Gasoline Paper prod.	9 5 4 4 3	25	U.S.	69	W. Germany	8	69.2	20.7

TABLE XXIX (CONTINUED)

Territory, capital	First 5 export items, millions of $	Per cent of total	First 5 import items, millions of $	Per cent of total	Per cent of total trade with first, second countries and U.S.-Canada, and W. Europe			
					First territory	Second territory	U.S.-Canada	W. Europe
Haiti Port au Prince	Coffee Sisal Sugar, crude Cocoa Molasses	61 18 8 2 2 91	Cotton fab. Wheat flour Motor vehicles Gasoline Iron, steel manufs.	15 13 4 4 4 40	U.S. 48	Belgium-Luxemburg 12	51.7	39.0
Honduras Teguchigalpa	Bananas, plantain Coffee, unroasted Wood, shaped Livestock, food Abaca	53 19 8 4 2 86	Motor vehicles Petroleum prod. Machinery, other Cotton fab. Manufs., other	7 7 6 6 5 31	U.S. 66	W. Germany 6	71.2	12.0
Jamaica Kingston	Bauxite Sugar, and prod. Bananas Rum Spices	44 28 11 3 3 89	Machinery, non-elect. Transport equip. Textile fab. Base metals Manuf. metals, other	12 7 7 6 6 38	U.K. 42	U.S. 22	39.5	47.7
Mexico Mexico City	Cotton raw, Coffee, unroasted Lead, unwrought Petroleum prod. Copper	16 16 8 6 6 54	Machinery, non-elect. Motor vehicles Iron, steel Petroleum prod. Maize, umilled	22 10 7 5 5 49	U.S. 75	W. Germany 5	77.4	15.3
Netherlands Antilles Willemsted	Petroleum prod. ..	96 96	Petroleum prod. ..	74 74	Venezuela 38	U.S. 18	20.2	20.3
Nicaragua Managua	Coffee Cotton Cottonseed Lumber Cattle	44 34 5 4 3 90	Petroleum prod. Insecticides Cotton fabrics Iron, steel Motor vehicles	8 6 5 4 4 27	U.S. 51	W. Germany 4	52.2	32.0
Panama Panama City	Bananas, plantain Fish Cocoa Sugar ..	60 28 4 2 94	Machinery, non-elect. Transport equip. Textile yarn Petroleum prod. Iron, steel prod.	9 8 7 7 4 35	U.S. 65	U.K. 4	67.0	12.8

TABLE XXIX (CONTINUED)

Country / City	First five exports		First five imports		Trade direction					
Paraguay Asunción	Wood, shaped Quebracho Cotton Canned meat Hides, raw	33 16 16 7 4 — 76	No data		Argentina	33	U.S.	16	16.0	28.7
Peru Lima	Cotton, raw Sugar, cane Lead products Copper prod. Iron ore	21 15 11 8 7 — 62	Other mech. apparatus Iron, steel manufs. Vehicles, parts Elect. mach. parts Chem. pharmaceut.	19 8 12 7 6 — 51	U.S.	44	U.K.	10	45.8	35.0
Trinidad and Tobago Port au Spain	Petroleum prod. Sugar Cocoa	83 9 2 .. .. — 94	Petroleum prod. Machinery, other Iron, steel Motor vehicles Wheat flour	25 8 7 4 3 — 47	U.K.	36	Venezuela	11	15.7	43.7
United States Washington	Mach., n. e. s. Motor vehicles Aircraft Iron, steel Cotton	11 8 6 4 4 — 33	Coffee, raw Petroleum, crude Paper, paperboard Nonferrous ores Copper	12 7 6 4 3 — 32	Canada	22	U.K.	5	21.8	25.0
Uruguay Montevideo	Wool prod. Beef prod. Agric. prod. crude Cattle, hides Linseed oils	50 17 7 6 5 — 85	Sugar, raw Petroleum, crude Industrial mach. Motor vehicles Iron, unmanuf.	6 4 4 4 3 — 21	U.S.	14	Netherlands	13	14.8	53.0
Venezuela Caracas	Petroleum prod. Iron ore Coffee Sugar Cocoa	92 5 1 1 .. — 99	Mech. apparatus Iron, Steel, pipe Motor vehicles Chem. pharmaceut. Iron, steel semimanuf.	21 14 7 4 4 — 50	U.S.	46	Neth. Antilles	20	48.4	20.7

[a] Sources: First five exports and first five imports, *Yearbook of International Trade Statistics*, Vol. 1, United Nations, New York, 1958, Tables 2 and 3 for each country; first and second countries with which given territories traded and the comparison of the direction of trade to U.S.-Canada and to Western Europe, *Direction of International Trade*, United Nations, International Monetary Fund, and International Bank for Reconstruction and Development, New York, 1958, tables of individual countries.

routes to Gibraltar and runs the length of the Mediterranean from the English Channel to Suez. Continuing in the same great-circle direction, the main line can be extended across the Indian Ocean to India, the Far East, or to Australia and New Zealand. It is clear from the map that the two major core regions of North America and Western Europe not only face one another across the North Atlantic but also align in such positions on the globe that their major axes of industrial districts become a series of points on a straight-line artery of global trade.

At right angles to this main artery of trade from America to New Zealand, several supplementary shipping lanes collect the ocean traffic of the world and bring it to points on the main line. These trunk-line routes are shown on the map in Figure 17 of Chapter 2.

The Caribbean-South Atlantic route. This route connects the interior inland waterway system of the Mississippi River basin through the port of New Orleans across the Gulf of Mexico and down the length of the Caribbean region. It rounds the eastern corner of South America and continues along the South Atlantic coast of that continent. It makes contact with the main line along the southeast coast of the United States, at the Ohio River's confluence with the Mississippi, and at the port of Chicago (*6,220,913*) in the Middle West of the United States' interior lowland.

The Pacific Basin coastal routes. These routes connect in what is virtually a great-circle alignment at right angles to the main line along the Pacific sides of North and South America to East Asia and the corner of the Eurasian land mass in Southeast Asia at Singapore. This encompasses a total distance more than half way around the earth of nearly 16,000 miles. This longest world trunk-line feeder is connected to the main line by the Panama Canal in Central America. Trade between North and South America has been greatly facilitated since the completion of the Panama Canal. (Figure 155). This canal, which has shortened routes from Pacific coast points to the ports of the United States-Canadian core region since 1914, accomplishes for the Americas what the Suez Canal makes possible for Europe—the direct linkage of the main line of world trade with the Pacific Basin without going around either the continents of South America or Africa.

The Arctic-West European or Baltic and West African route. This route cuts at right angles across the main line through the North Sea and the English Channel. It connects points over a distance of 10,000 miles from Murmansk (226,000) and the Soviet Arctic down the Atlantic coast of Western Europe past Gibraltar to Dakar (*230,887*), Senegal, and thence around the great western bulge of Africa to the Guinea Coast and down to South Atlantic side of Africa to Capetown.

Indian Ocean route. The last major trunk line cuts across the main line from Capetown to Singapore (*992,500*) and beyond to Tokyo (*9,504,997*), a distance of 9,000 miles. It connects the ports of East Africa with the main line at Aden at the south end of the Red Sea. From Singapore it overlaps the Pacific Basin route.

The distance from Chicago to London is 4,000 miles; to Aden is an additional 3,700 miles; and from Aden to Wellington, New Zealand, is yet another 9,000 miles. These air-route distances total nearly 17,000 miles, in almost a perfect great circle. Ocean trade, of course, varies at will to ports some distance either side of this "straight" line. The four trunk lines which cut across it at right angles to act as feeders to the "main line" are 6,000, 13,500, 10,000, and 9,000 miles long, respectively, for a total of 38,500. Adding the main line and trunk lines together gives a total of first-order, ocean-route connections of more than 55,000 miles.

It should be noted how the Western Hemisphere trunk lines which interconnect from peripheral regions of the Americas to the United States-Canadian core region serve to put most of the Americas into direct contact with the main line of world trade. The fundamental geographic position and the inherent centrality of the North American coreland lies in its being the common focus of movement from all of the Americas. This functional focusing on the North American coreland simultaneously brings all of the subregions of the Americas into effective contact with the rest of the world. The Panama Canal is the key to making the trunk-line system effective for the Pacific coast countries and regions.

Advanced and Emerging Core Regions. The trend of development within human society is toward more complex competitive units of area organization. A natural desire to improve themselves on the part of people within every locality is responsible for this trend, along with increasing independence within economic areas which develops even as the mutual interdependence of the geographic division of labor is itself evolving. One index of growing competitive economic independence within the Americas is the decentralization of the iron and steel industry. The steel industry in the United States originated in the East and migrated westward to Chicago, southward to Birmingham (*629,248*) and Houston (*1,243,158*), and more recently still further westward to Provo, Utah (*106,777*), and Fontana, near Los Angeles (*6,742,696*), California. In recent years, especially since World War II, basic steel production has also spread to countries in Latin America. Despite so-called "handicaps" of relative lack of large quantities of good-quality coking coal in Latin America, working with what resources are at their disposal, the people are making the effort to build constructively toward a greater measure of local regional independence. There are now basic steel plants in Latin America, as shown on the map in Figure 174, in Mexico at Monclava, Monterrey (600,609), and Eagle Pass; in Venezuela at El Pao near the delta of the Orinoco; in interior Colombia at Belencito; in Peru at Chimbota on the coast; in Chile near Concepcion at San Vicente; at Volta Redondo and Itbara in Brazil; and in Argentina at San Nicolas on the Parana River. Of these the Brazilian integrated mill at Volta Redondo is the largest with a capacity of 1,250,000 tons which is one-hundredth of the production of the United States. Most of the Latin American steel mills, it is true, measure their production in hundreds of *thousands* of tons, while the great producing centers of the United States measure theirs in tens of *millions* of tons of steel. Nevertheless, this should not detract from the significance of the Latin American decentralization of steel production, particularly with respect to the future development of more integrated and diversified independent economies in these countries and regions. The map in Figure 174 shows the position of known sources of coking-quality coal in Latin America. By lines from the symbols representing the steel mills, the principal sources of raw materials focused on these mills are indicated. From the patterns it can be appreciated that the development of separate, national steel production in these cases makes the national economies and subregions of the United States and Canada involved less dependent on the major centers of North American production. At the same time it in no way changes the basic pattern of the double continental organization as a whole. (Pictures in Figure 175 show selected examples of these new mills.) Latin America's pattern of regional organization remains scattered and peripheral in nature, focusing on the primary core region of the United States-Canada.

The core regions of the United States and Canada are the primary manufacturing concentrations of the Americas. The great assemblages of resources for the steel industry, which include the fresh water of the Great Lakes, are also shown on the map in Figure 174. There are no less than fifteen heavy industrial steel centers using these resources. The most important of the producing centers are located at Chicago, Gary, Detroit, Cleveland, Buffalo, Pittsburgh, and Sparrows Point, Maryland, in the United States; and at Sault Ste. Marie and Hamilton in Canada. The location of the steel industry is perhaps the most important industrial anchor for the location of the core region of the Americas. The core region of North America, shown on the map in Figure 173, contains less than 10 per cent of the total area of the United States-Canada, but contains half the total population and nearly three-fourths of the industrial employment. Less advanced subcore regions in the Americas (each having an iron and steel industry) are shown by a special dot symbol on the map in Figure 174, in both North and Latin America.

The Regional Organization of the United States

A basic radial pattern of present area organization in the United States is the composite result of historical evolution from patterns of previous American societies. From the processes of American cultural evolution, as will be discussed in the next chapter, four major regions have emerged: the Eastern Seaboard, the Middle West, the South, and the West. The central portions of the Seaboard and the Middle West have combined in forming the national *core* region. The outer margins of the Middle West may be divided among a series of *gateway* regions through which the core region is linked with outer peripheral regions in the South and the West. These outer peripheral regions are partly the result of the expansion of the Middle West and the South well into the Great Plains to the limit of arable land. Islands of settlement in the central Mountain West have multiplied and become interconnected into regional groupings of mining, forestry, irrigated and dry farming, and ranching operations. These regions cover many parts of the several mountain states. In the Pacific West, north, middle, and south divisions center on the Willa-

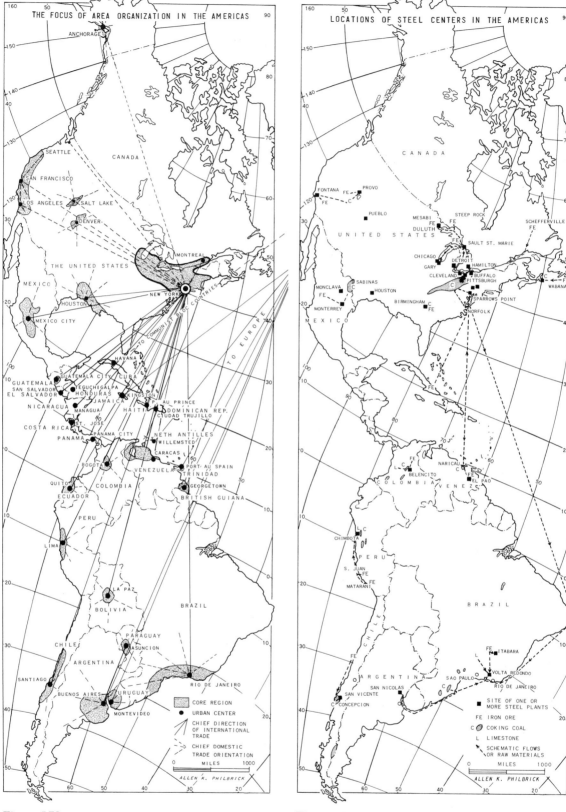

Figure 173

Figure 174

Figure 175

(A) Argentina's new National Steel Works, the nation's first large-scale plant, rises from the pampas at San Nicolas, on the Parana River. At present it is operated entirely with imported raw materials. United Nations technical assistance for the government's steel program has been concerned with the study of Argentine raw materials—iron ore, coal, and manganese. It is expected in the future that it will become possible to use larger and larger proportions of local materials. (*Courtesy of United Nations.*)

(B) Brazil's national steel plant at Volta Redonda is at present the largest in capacity in Latin America. Its principal markets are industrial users in Rio de Janeiro and Sao Paulo. (*Courtesy of Brazilian Government Trade Bureau.*)

(C) Bottom, the West in the United States is also coming into its own in the development of basic steel production. The West's largest integrated steel works, near Provo, Utah, appears against the background of Wasatch Range and Utah Lake. (*Courtesy of United States Steel Corp.*)

mette and Puget Sound areas, the great Central Valley of California, and Southern California, respectively.

In all, seventeen functional subregions may be distinguished within the four main culture regions of the United States. They are arranged in such a manner on the map in Figure 176 to demonstrate their radial focusing on the northeastern urban-core region of the country. The companion map in Figure 177 by Edward Ullman demonstrates the linkages between the core through gateway regions to the regions of the American periphery. The regions will be discussed briefly under headings of the four principal cultural divisions of the United States.

Eastern Seaboard. The Eastern Seaboard region is the oldest and most complexly developed area of the United States. It contains the eastern third of the present-day core region of the country, the world's largest port, the nation's most populous city and metropolitan area, and greatest urban concentration anywhere on the globe. (See Figure 178.) This is a continuous belt of urban concentrations which extends from Boston, Massachusetts, through New York, Philadelphia, and Baltimore to the nation's capital at Washington, D.C.

Subregions of the East are (1) northern New England which focuses on Boston through local-regional centers at Portland, Maine, and Manchester, New Hampshire; (2) the Middle-Atlantic core region which focuses on New York; and (3) the Tidewater-Piedmont region which focuses on Washington, D.C.

The four standard metropolitan areas of the coastal core region—Boston, New York, Philadelphia, and Baltimore—total 13.4 per cent of the national population, perform 15 per cent of the country's retail trade, 31 per cent of the wholesale trade, and over 41 per cent of the nation's brokerage business. Shipping from New York ranks first in tonnage nationally; Philadelphia ranks fourth and Baltimore fifth. Each of these leading trans-shipping centers has a developed hinterland which is tapped by a major railroad system. The port of New York is served by the New York Central Railroad system, Philadelphia by the Pennsylvania, and the port of Baltimore by the Baltimore and Ohio Railroad system. All three of these eastern systems join forces at Chicago to tap, along with some nineteen other major railroad companies, the services and supplies of the nation through the greatest combined radial network of rail, road, air, and inland waterway transport routes in the world.

The Middle West. With the growing importance of such metropolitan areas as Chicago (6,220,913), Detroit (3,762,360), Cleveland (1,786,740), and Pittsburgh (2,405,435), the western end of the manufacturing belt became the control centers for an expanding and increasingly diversified Middle West. (See Figure 179.) Chicago, the Middle West's central city, ranks second in the United States in many respects. Its metropolitan area population is 3.6 per cent of the nation's 185 million; it transacts 4.6 per cent of the nation's retail trade and 7.4 per cent of the wholesale trade; and it transacts 11.9 per cent of the nations brokerage business. In all these respects it is second to New York. It is also the world's largest railroad center, is served by one of the world's busiest international airports, and is the nation's largest lake port. In these and many other respects Chicago is the primary focus for the interior sedimentary lowlands of the United States which are concentrated mainly in the Middle West. The western end of the American Manufacturing Belt thus joins with the Northeastern Seaboard to form the core region of the United States.

Manufacturing production of the Middle West is based first on the steel industry. Iron ores from the metamorphic rocks of the upper peninsula of Michigan, from Steep Rock, Ontario, and the Quebec-Labrador iron district, as well as from the Mesabi range of Minnesota, are transported by water to the major mill sites, as shown by flow lines on the map in Figure 174. There are also less important iron-ore bodies in the metamorphic Appalachian highlands, with the principal sources of coking coal in the sedimentary interior coal fields of the same area. Note on the map of railway traffic in Figure 177 the heavy tonnage lines representing coal movement from the interior West Virginia coal fields to Toledo (454,472) and from the central Pennsylvanian fields to the mills of the Pittsburgh district. The world's largest fully integrated steel mill is located at Gary (573,548), Indiana. Extensive use of steel in the automobile industry, which is centered in Detroit, is shown on the map also. Steel production and uses are examples of the concentration of manufacturing industries in the Middle West as the mineral fuels of the interior are brought together with the metallic ores of the surrounding metamorphic highlands. Reference should be made at this point to the mineral distribution maps in Figures 169 and 170 in the preceding chapter.

The agricultural patterns of the Middle West are equally striking in their focus on Chicago and the western end of the American core region. Overlapping patterns depicting the regions of high-value farm property, the corn belt, and the hog and cattle feeding by livestock farmers overlie the western end of the manufacturing belt of the United States. Chicago is the major commercial and food-processing center which is common to both patterns. Over 90 per cent of the grain trade of the country is transacted on the trading floors of the Chicago Board of Trade. The Chicago Stockyards, which once dominated the processing of meat before competition of the truck for the transportation of cattle decentralized the industry, is still a major center of this activity.

•To the northwest and southwest of the main concentration of the corn belt lie the major spring and winter-wheat-producing regions in the Dakotas and Kansas, respectively. Focusing on major regional gateway railroad centers, storage, processing, and trading in wheat is actively participated in by important cities as indicated by the relative storage capacities of their grain elevators; yet the trade in grain is dominated by the Chicago Board of Trade grain pits. The railroads, inland waterways, and Great Lakes shippers handle huge quantities of grain as it moves from gateway storage and processing centers through Chicago to domestic markets in the east and to foreign consumers.

Overlapping the manufacturing belt on the northern margins of the corn belt and east of the northwestern wheat region is the dairy belt. From northern Minnesota, across northern Wisconsin and Michigan into upstate New York and northern New England, corn for silage and hay crops are fed to dairy cattle for the production of fluid milk and processed dairy products destined for the major urban markets immediately to the south.

The Middle West as a whole is subdivided into seven subregions. Two of these subregions, the central and eastern Middle West, when combined with the middle-Atlantic core region of the eastern seaboard, are the national core region. Surrounding the manufacturing belt and acting as gate-ways between the principal manufacturing centers of the nation and the outlying peripheral regions of the South and West and of Canada to the north, are five additional subregions of the Middle West. Each of these regions has a different set of specializations which focus through its major cities on the national core region. The general boundaries of these regions

on the map in Figure 176 compared with the maps of agricultural regions and mineral-producing districts in Figures 161, 162, 169, and 170 can be used to visualize the important activities of primary production of food and raw materials which each contributes to the national economy.

The central Middle West. The central Middle West focuses on Chicago, which, along with the region, is the core for the entire Middle West. To a degree the central Middle West is the focus of a still larger region including the South and West of the United States, but in this capacity it is serving a subordinate role as the western nexus of the *national* core region. The central Middle West covers portions of the corn and dairy belts and along the east shore of Lake Michigan a fruit and vegetable belt. The corn belt includes a high proportion of cash corn-oriented farmers, but it includes, also, many steer and hog feeders as well as dairy men. All of the agricultural production focuses on the primary urban market at Chicago in one way or another.

The eastern Middle West. There are three major cities in the eastern Middle West. These metropolitan areas form an alignment of specialized industries at Pittsburgh (steel and glass), Detroit (the Motor City), and Cleveland (diversified in steel, electrical machinery, and automotive industries). In agriculture the eastern region combines fruit, corn, dairy, and general farming areas.

The southeast Middle West. This region specializes in mining and shipping coal from the West Virginia Appalachians. It is oriented in two directions. Coal moves in huge quantities by rail into the interior through Columbus to Toledo, which is the largest coal-shipping port on the Great Lakes. Outward through tidewater Virginia coal moves first by rail to the ports of Norfolk (*541,494*) and Newport News-Hampton Roads (*223,029*). Thence it is shipped all along the eastern seaboard region from Newport to eastern Maine.

The southern Middle West. This subregion consists of the states of Kentucky and Tennessee and small parts of southern Indiana-southwest Ohio. Its major focus is the rail gateway across the Ohio River through Cincinnati (*1,067,669*), as demonstrated by the quantity of freight movement on the map in Figure 177. The southern Middle West is a transitional zone between the North and the South. It is predominantly a region of general farming, containing a small portion of the corn belt and areas of specialized tobacco farming.

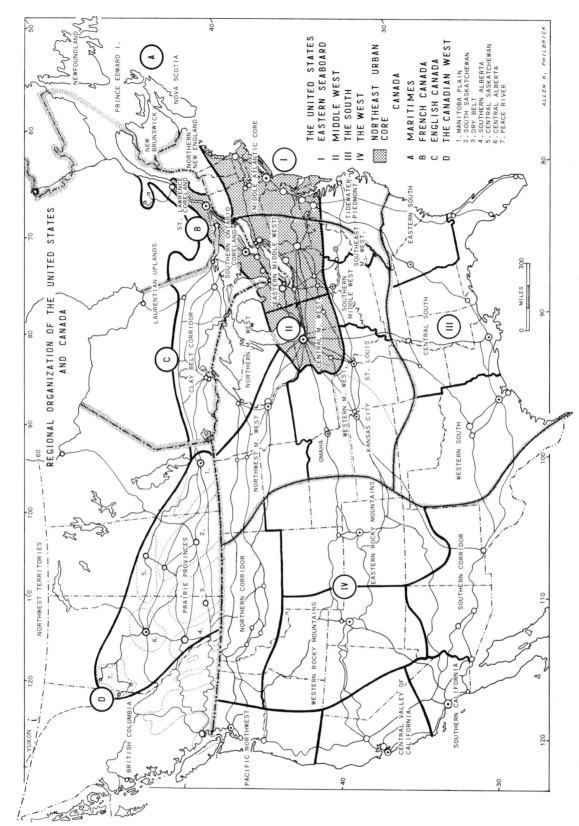

REGIONAL ORGANIZATION OF THE UNITED STATES AND CANADA

THE UNITED STATES

I   EASTERN SEABOARD
II   MIDDLE WEST
III THE SOUTH
IV   THE WEST

NORTHEAST URBAN CORE

CANADA

A   MARITIMES
B   FRENCH CANADA
C   ENGLISH CANADA
D   THE CANADIAN WEST

1. MANITOBA PLAIN
2. SOUTH SASKATCHEWAN
3. DRY BELT
4. SOUTHERN ALBERTA
5. CENTRAL SASKATCHEWAN
6. CENTRAL ALBERTA
7. PEACE RIVER

ALLEN K. PHILBRICK

Figure 176

290

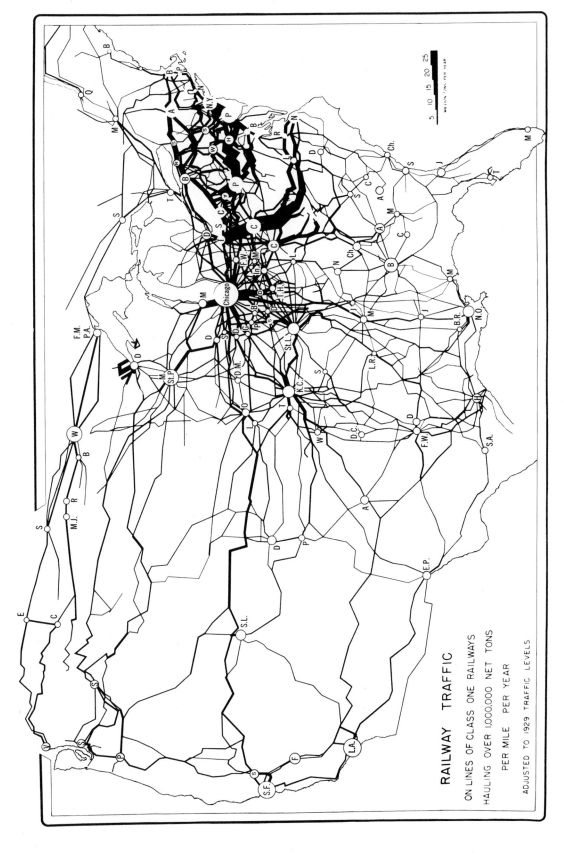

Figure 177. (*Courtesy of University of Washington Press, taken from Edward L. Ullman, American Commodity Flow, 1956.*)

(A) Midtown Manhattan today is dominated by two structures, the Empire State Building and the headquarters of the United Nations. This view is looking southwest across the island toward the Hudson River.

Figure 178

(B) Downtown Philadelphia, overlooking the skyscrapers and surrounding older sections of town.

(C) The port of Baltimore in the foreground with the downtown area at its head.

(D) The national capital surrounded by a city of public buildings is a show place for the entire country. In this city, established as the capital in 1805, there is scarcely a time when some major building is not under construction.

Figure 179

(A) This high, oblique view shows a great deal of the nation's second largest city's central portion. In the center is the vertically developed skyscraper "Loop" district. Here the skyscraper was created. (*Courtesy of Chicago Aerial Survey.*)

(B) The world's largest integrated steel mill, constructed in 1905 in Gary, Indiana. To the upper left from the main slip are tiers of plant facility from which raw materials enter blast furnaces to become "pig" iron, and move to the diagonally placed tiers of open-hearth furnaces to be made into steel. Thence steel is shunted before it has had a chance to cool to the rolling mills, the wire mills, and the structural steel mills. In the distance is the Buffington cement plant which is also owned by the U. S. Steel Corporation and is located here to make use of slag from the steel mill. (*Courtesy of Chicago Aerial Survey.*)

(C) The Detroit skyline is topped by the Penobscot Building in this view from the Detroit River looking northwest. In the foreground is Detroit's new convention facility, Cobo Hall. (*Courtesy of Detroit Chamber of Commerce.*)

The map in Figure 180, by Patton, shows the inland waterways developed and maintained by the U.S. Corps of Army Engineers. The treelike pattern of navigable tributaries of the Mississippi River is one of the most important inland-waterway systems in the world. It consists of the Ohio, Illinois, the upper Mississippi, the lower Missouri, the Tennessee, and the main stem of the Mississippi River. Along the base of the "tree" is the Gulf Coast intracoastal waterway. Major cities, such as Cincinnati, on the outer "limbs" and extremities of the system are the principal gateways into the American Manufacturing Belt. The bridging of these great rivers in the railroad-building era gave the points of easy access across the rivers gateway status. In a counterclockwise direction this is true for the important cities of Cincinnati, Louisville (*718,685*), Memphis (*619,722*), St. Louis (*2,060,103*), Kansas City (*1,039,493*), Omaha (*456,164*), and Minneapolis-St. Paul (*1,474,149*).

The western Middle West. St. Louis, Missouri, Kansas City, Kansas-Kansas City, Missouri, and Omaha, Nebraska, are the three major metropolitan areas of the western Middle West. The region covers a large portion of the western corn belt, part of the spring-wheat region, the fruit-producing tri-state area—common corners of Missouri, Arkansas, and Oklahoma—and the general-farming section of southern Missouri and northern Arkansas, known as the Ozarks. The main body of the region is the four states of Iowa, Missouri, Nebraska, and Kansas.

The northwest Middle West. This subregion combines the winter-wheat belt and parts of the dairy and northern corn belts. It covers the Dakotas, the southern half of Minnesota, and a part of western Wisconsin primarily tributary to the focus of the region in the twin cities of Minneapolis and St. Paul. All of Minnesota focuses on the state capital, St. Paul, and the twin cities as the largest metropolitan area of the state; but the flow of iron ore across Lake Superior indicates so strong an orientation toward the core region via the Great Lakes which is shared by other parts of the northern Middle West, that northern Minnesota, Wisconsin, and Michigan are combined as the northern Middle West.

The northern Middle West. A number of smaller centers are the decentralized gateways through the Great Lakes to the manufacturing belt. These are Duluth-Superior (*272,674*), Ashland, Marquette, Escanaba, and Sault Ste. Marie. All of these are lake ports important in the shipments of iron ore from the northern Middle West to the steel plants of the core region.

Each gateway subregion is in its own way a producing region which focuses on its own urban centers and through one or more of them on the national core region. In addition the gateway function underscores the manner in which these particular subregions link the core region with peripheral regions still farther away from the national core in the South, the West, and in Canada to the north. The focal relation of peripheral regions to the core operates in the reverse direction, too; for the manufactured goods of the cities in the urban northeast are distributed through the nation by means of these same gateway cities and their subregions.

The South. The most important products of the South are cotton, petroleum, cattle, and fruits and vegetables.

The western and central South. The oil fields of

(D) An aerial view of the extensive coal and ore docks at the port of Toledo. In the foreground are the facilities of the Toledo Lakefront Dock and Terminal Railroad Company, operated jointly by the New York Central and the Baltimore and Ohio Railroads. There are three single-car coal loaders, with a capacity of 3,000 tons per hour, at this facility, in addition to four Hulett iron-ore unloaders. In the background are the three single-car and one double-car loaders, plus three Huletts, of the Chesapeake and Ohio Railway Company. These facilities jointly ship from Toledo some 27 to 28 million tons of coal per year, receive some five million tons of iron ore, and ship close to 10,000 tons of petroleum coke annually. They have an ultimate handling capacity of about 60 million tons annually. These facts illustrate why Toledo is the Great Lakes' leading coal-shipping port, occupying a significance for the Middle West that the east coast port of Norfolk occupies for the eastern seaboard. (*Courtesy of Toledo-Lucas County Port Authority.*)

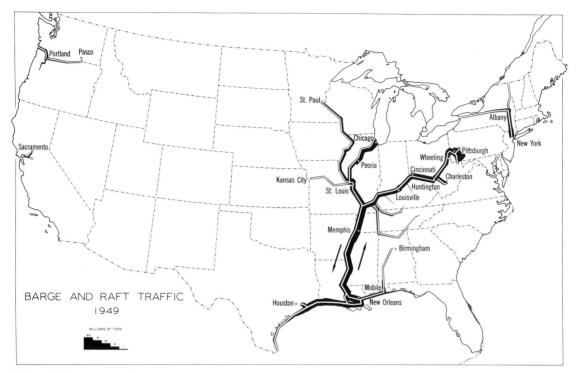

BARGE AND RAFT TRAFFIC
1949

MILLIONS OF TONS

Figure 180. (*Courtesy of* Economic Geography, *taken from Donald Patton, "The Traffic Pattern on American Inland Waterways."*)

the Gulf Coast of Louisiana and Texas and the interior fields of Texas and Oklahoma are the major producers in the United States. Based on petroleum and petro-chemicals, recent developments indicate the emergence of a Gulf Coast core region comprising parts of both the western and central South (Figure 176). Manufacturing districts comprise a belt from Dallas (*1,083,601*)-Fort Worth (*573,215*) to New Orleans (*861,299*). The market for steel pipe in connection with the oil industry has encouraged the development of basic steel production in Texas at Houston (*1,243,158*). This additional capacity augments the earlier production from steel plants at Birmingham, Alabama. Cattle and specialized production of vegetables and fruits, as well as irrigated cotton as an industrial crop are additional important contributions of the western South.

The Deep South. The central Deep South combined with the eastern South is the traditional antebellum cotton south of the pre-Civil War era. Cotton is definitely no longer "king" in the Deep South. Diversification including forest products, dairying, cattle, specialized fruit and vegetable crops now supplement the still important production of cotton. The region has no single focus.

Several candidates for this role and centers for different parts of the Deep South are Atlanta (*1,010,577*), New Orleans, Birmingham (*629,248*), and Memphis (*619,722*).

The West. The West is subdivided into seven subregions, each quite different from any of the regions in the eastern two-thirds of the country. This difference lies in the *intermittent pattern* of occupancy in the West as opposed to the *continuity* of occupancy in the East. The boundary separating the East (comprised of the Middle West, the eastern seaboard, and the South) from the West is the approximate line of continuous agricultural occupancy from range and oasis-type intermittent agricultural land to the west. The subregions of the West are divided into two categories—the interior central mountain regions and the border regions facing Canada, Mexico, and the Pacific Ocean.

Central mountain regions. These are two interior mountain regions outlined on the map in Figure 176. The eastern Rocky Mountain region focuses on Denver (*925,569*). Intermittent agricultural areas of the West are well illustrated by the irrigated valleys of the North and South Platt and Arkansas Rivers, and locally irrigated valleys behind the Front

Ranges. In addition both irrigated and dry farming along the Great Plains margins of the Rocky Mountain Front Range are important. Forests, forested rangeland, and open grassland range occupy higher mountain and lower slopes. (This is referred to again in the next chapter.) As may be appreciated by reference to the mineral map once again, in Figures 169 and 170, all of the western regions, including this one, have numerous examples of the metallic ores found in metamorphic rock within the cordilleran zone of crustal weakness. Basic steel production is located at Pueblo (*117,547*), Colorado, south of Denver, and is based on iron-ore deposits within Colorado. Local sedimentary rocks of Carboniferous age yield coking-quality coal. Copper, gold, silver, vanadium, and uranium are metallic ores that are also mined within this region.

The western Rocky Mountain subregion focuses on the Mormon capital at Salt Lake City (*381,961*), Utah (roughly the same combination of activities are developed here). Irrigable land in the Salt Lake area represented the "promised land" to the Mormons who crossed the continent by covered wagon in the 1840s. An iron and steel industry has been developed at Provo, Utah, based on local resources. The famous copper mine at Bingham Canyon, near Salt Lake, is the largest producer of copper in the world. Many additional metallic ores are mined in the region, in smaller amounts. As may be seen on the map, both of the interior mountain subregions are waystations and gateways in transcontinental transportation. Both Denver and the Salt Lake center are outer gateways of the Middle West, consolidating in the interior mountain region the central, northern, and southern transcontinental routes leading to and from the three subregions of the Pacific Coast. This is clearly demonstrated by the railway freight-flow map in Figure 177. Border regions of the western United States are five in number. There is a northern corridor region through Montana and Idaho which links the Pacific Northwest, focusing on Seattle (*1,098,741*), with the northwestern Middle West; and a southern corridor region which links Southern California with western Texas, from the major focus of the Pacific Coast regions at Los Angeles (*6,742,696*), California to San Antonio, (*687,151*), Texas by way of Phoenix (*657,688*), Arizona and El Paso (*314,070*), Texas. The fifth subregion is the Central Valley of California which focuses at San Francisco-Oakland (*2,783,359*).

Northern corridor. This subregion possesses wheat, grazing land, and metallic mineral districts, and is marked by a series of small centers which serve as waystations along its principal east-west routes. These are cities such as Spokane (*277,261*) in eastern Washington, Helena, capital of Montana, Great Falls and Billings, Montana. Copper, lead, zinc, gold, and manganese are among the important mineral products which flow eastward from mining and smelting centers in Idaho and Montana toward the manufacturing core zone of the urban northeast.

Southern corridor. This subregion takes in dry year-round range country from western Texas to the rich, irrigated, crop producing area of Southern California. Cattle and mining activities characterize it. Copper, lead, zinc, uranium, mercury, gold, and silver are among the important mineral products which flow eastward along the southern routes into the core region from the Southwest.

Pacific Northwest. The Pacific Northwest, focused on Seattle, combines the best remaining forest region in the country with the dairy and general farming of the Willamette Valley and specialized wheat production of the Palouse region in the Columbia River Plateau. Development of the Grand Coulee Dam for irrigation and power has brought the electricity-using aluminum reduction and radio-active-materials-producing industries into the Pacific Northwest.

Central Valley of California. The Central Valley focuses on San Francisco-Oakland metropolitan area. From the north, east, and southeast of the valley a wealth of farm crops are produced. Large parts of this production feed and supply the fast-increasing population of California, but much of it is also specialized under irrigation for national markets. For example, more than 80 per cent of the nation's grapes, nectarines, figs, and almonds are produced in the Central Valley. Cotton, cattle, and grapes are the most important products from the valley.

Southern California. This region focuses on Los Angeles, capital of the West. In addition to the nationally and internationally prominent movie industry, it possesses a steel industry at Fontana, near San Bernadino (*809,782*), for which most of the coal and some of the iron ore come from Utah by rail. Oil fields in the sedimentary-rock region along the coast are important producers of petroleum products; and specialized irrigated citrus and other Mediterranean-type crops are sold on a national scale.

Though small in production relative to the steel producers in the East, the fact that there are steel industries in three of the western subregions and the two southern subregions indicates the development of regional self-sufficiency within the United States. Nevertheless, at the present time all of the subregions focus primarily on the urban core region of the country in the traditional centers of the Northeast and Middle West.

Pacific Outliers of the United States— Alaska and Hawaii.

In 1959 two new states were added to the United States of America, bringing the total to an even fifty. The two new states are the first regions to achieve statehood which are non-contiguous with the main body of the country.

Alaska is the nation's largest state, with 586,400 square miles. It is more than twice the size of Texas. Little Diomede Island off the Seward Peninsula in the Bering Strait is 2.4 miles from the Soviet island, Big Diomede, which is the closest territory of the Americas to any point of the "Old World." Alaska is the most northerly land in the nation. Point Barrow, Alaska, referred to earlier as the northernmost point of mainland North America, lies well north of the seventieth parallel.

Despite its northerly position, Alaska possesses in a number of regions resource combinations capable of agricultural use. These are levelness of surface, more than three months growing season with adequate precipitation in relation to evaporation, and adequate fertility of soil. In mineral wealth Alaska represents very considerable reserves of strategic metals such as antimony, chromium, manganese, nickel, platinum, mercury, tin, and tungsten, and of gold, silver, copper, coal, and petroleum. The new state has no single dominant focus. The capital, Juneau, is in the southern panhandle section. The largest city and most important port is Anchorage at the head of Cook Inlet in south central Alaska. It is connected by rail to Fairbanks, the largest inland city. Fairbanks, which is the most northerly airport of North America, is a strategically located control point in North America's air-defense system. It is also the Alaskan Highway terminal point. This highway joins the state by road to the main continental body of the United States across Canada.

Peripheral position, which has inhibited Alaskan development because of its great distance from major markets in the United States or in other parts of the world, does not affect the region's strategic significance. This importance stems from its position on the great-circle route to the Far East. The shortest distance from United States west-east ports to Japan and other Asian countries is in a northwesterly direction skirting the Aleutian Islands off Alaska.

Hawaii is the nation's first island state. It is 2,100 miles west-southwest of San Francisco. The twentieth parallel of latitude passes through the main island of the chain comprising the Hawaiian island group. The fiftieth state is, accordingly, the most southerly land area of the United States. The Hawaiian island group has approximately the same latitudinal range as Cuba. The islands are our tropical outpost in the mid-Pacific, occupying an equally strategic position in terms of American sea and air defense west of the continental mainland as does Alaska to the north of it. While the population of Alaska, the largest state in area, is less than 150,000 people, that of Hawaii is nearly one million. The total area of the islands is 6,423 square miles. Of the total population more than 60 per cent is in the one metropolitan county of Honolulu (*488,822*), capital of Hawaii, on the island of Oahu.

The islands are volcanic in origin. In fact, of two volcanic peaks on the island of Hawaii, Mauna Loa, 13,680 feet high, is the world's largest active volcano. Its twin Mauna Kea, at 13,784 feet, is no longer active, but is the highest point in the state. Of all tropical Pacific islands, the Hawaiian Islands have experienced the most intensive commercial agricultural development. Sugar cane and pineapples are the primary products, accounting for 95 per cent of production. The United States is the primary national market for Hawaiian pineapples and sugar. This means that the Islands' population is integrated within the exchange system of economic area organization of the United States mainland. The former subsistence agricultural and fishing economy has all but completely disappeared. Scientific farming under the control and leadership of large corporate interests has applied mechanization, modern engineering, and the results of research to tropical insect, virus, and fungus problems with marked success. As might be expected the Islands are an ideal territory for the development of a recreation industry.

Back again on the mainland adjacent to the urban coreland of the United States is the gateway to that fourth great culture region of North America—the Dominion of Canada. Between the southern and the eastern shores of Lake Huron and the north shores of Lakes Ontario and Erie and the United

States-Canadian border on the St. Lawrence River is southern Ontario, Canada. This subregion is not only part of the core region of Canada, contiguous to the core region of the United States, but also is a vital *gateway region* between the two countries. This relationship is marked by the twin border cities—Detroit-Windsor (*185,865*). Niagara Falls Canada-Niagara Falls U.S. (102,394), and Port Huron, U.S.-Sarnia, Canada. The internal focus of Ontario is Toronto (*1,358,028*).

The Regional Organization of Canada

The United States and Canada are joined along an east-west international border which is like a seam, both stitching together and at the same time separating the heart and limbs of dual national economies. Of the two great areas created in North America by this line, Canada is the larger with 3,845,774 square miles. The United States, including Alaska and Hawaii, has an area of 3,615,210 square miles. Even though Canada is larger in total area, because of its northern location and the rocky nature of a high proportion of surface within the Canadian Shield, the total settled area of the country is much smaller than the settled area of the United States. Approximately 3 per cent of Canada is arable land, while the corresponding figure for the United States is 33 per cent. The occupied area of Canada, for the most part, is arranged in a relatively narrow belt along its southern international boundary.

Canadian regional organization is also the composite result of previous Canadian societies and the processes of their cultural evolution. From somewhat parallel processes of development to those of the United States—as will be discussed in the next chapter—four general regions of Canada have emerged which are analogous to the major divisions of the United States. These are the Maritime Provinces, French Canada, English Canada, and the Canadian West. Southern portions of Quebec and Ontario—French and English Canada—combined have become the core region of the country. A strip of Ontario just north of the Great Lakes is a gateway and corridor, as has been indicated above, which links the core region of Canada with the United States. Within Canada this part of southern Ontario is also the link between the core region and western Canada.

The northern half of the continent in Canada is regionally organized on a *linear* rather than on a radial basis. As shown on the map in Figure 176,

it is in the shape of a huge arc, extending from Newfoundland to British Columbia, and from Alberta northwestward along the Mackenzie Valley to the Arctic. A dozen subregions may be distinguished within the four main culture regions of the Dominion of Canada. They are arranged on the map in such a manner as to demonstrate their alignment with respect to the eastern core region in the Great Lakes-St. Lawrence region. Evidence of the twin-like character of United States and Canada is the common border of their corelands, respectively. From one end of a line beginning at Port Huron-Sarnia to the end of the New York State-Ontario border on the St. Lawrence River, a 700 mile-long water boundary connects the core regions of each country. Part of the immense significance of the improvement of the St. Lawrence Seaway for deep-sea vessel access into the Great Lakes is the fact that this waterway serves both core regions, as a highway down the middle between them.

The Maritimes. The Maritime Provinces of Canada are Newfoundland (including Labrador), Prince Edward Island, Nova Scotia, and New Brunswick. They surround the entrance to the St. Lawrence River, and comprise the eastern approaches to the coreland of Canada, which extends in almost a straight line from Quebec to Windsor.

Newfoundland. Named so by its discoverer, John Cabot, in 1497, it only joined the Canadian Confederation in 1949. Its principal products come from fisheries, forests, and mines. Iron ore represents more than half its mineral production and is shipped to the steel mills at Sydney (*108,347*), Nova Scotia, from Wabana. About half the ore, also, moves to the United Kingdom.

Nova Scotia. The coal to make iron and steel out of the ores from Wabana iron comes from Cape Breton Island, Nova Scotia. Coal represents more than two-thirds of Nova Scotia's mineral production. Other manufactures are fish, pulp and paper, and ship building. Both Newfoundland and Nova Scotia are heavily forested. The port of Halifax (*164,200*) is the principal wholesaling and transhipment center.

New Brunswick. Forest products and fish are the specialties produced in New Brunswick. The port of St. John is the principal focus, from whence these products are exported.

Prince Edward Island. This island is the smallest province of Canada. Nearly half the population (47 per cent) is agricultural, whereas in the other subregions of the Maritimes a much smaller proportion of the total is so engaged—28 per cent in New Brunswick, 17 per cent in Nova Scotia, and 4 per cent in Newfoundland. Dairy products and fish are the primary exports.

French Canada. The Province of Quebec is the home of French Canada. Physically, Quebec is divided between the sedimentary lowlands of the St. Lawrence and Ottawa River Valleys—the St. Lawrence coreland—and the metamorphic-shield region of the Labrador Peninsula—the Laurentian uplands.

The St. Lawrence coreland. The sedimentary valleys are part of the core region of Canada. Here urban population predominates over rural (66 to 34 per cent), although in area most of the valley lands are in farms. Montreal is Canada's largest city with more than a million and a half persons (*1,620,758*) (Figure 181A and B). In French Canada most of the population lives in the St. Lawrence coreland. Nearly two-thirds of them (64 per cent) are engaged in manufacturing occupations. The city of Quebec—meaning "where the water narrows"—was the starting point of French settlement in North America (Champlain in 1608). It is now the capital of the province (*309,959*) and the oldest Roman Catholic center in North America. Forty per cent or more of the economically active population is engaged in services and office work, 30 per cent in manufacturing, and 20 per cent in trade. The Chateau Frontenac hotel, symbol of French Canada, which is copied architecturally in at least one major structure in most large cities of Canada, is located in Quebec. From Quebec upriver past Montreal, all the way to the Ontario-New York border, the valley plains on both sides of the river are intensively farmed. The field patterns follow the old French lot lines, which run perpendicularly to the river, emphasizing the value of frontage on the only initial means of transport and communication—the river (Figure 181C). Beyond lies English Canada in Ontario. The change is marked by the rectangular agricultural land pattern of the "hundred"—more nearly square but still rectangular plots of one hundred acres each per farm (Figure 181D).

The Laurentian uplands of Quebec. The Laurentian uplands in Quebec are the Labrador Peninsula, a glaciated plateau surface of Precambrian rocks. Forestry and mining are the principal economic occupations, but in recent years an outstanding iron-ore deposit has been developed deep in the interior on the Labrador-Quebec border. This iron district at Schefferville is 300 miles north of the St. Lawrence River. Ore now moves by rail to Sept-Iles on the St. Lawrence estuary whence it is shipped by large ore carriers upriver via the newly expanded seaway to steel-producing centers in both Canada and the United States.

English Canada. The English took over control of French Canada in 1763, but French Canadians continued to live in and develop the pattern of occupancy which they had begun in Quebec. The English preferred to settle in a different place and so began the penetration of Ontario.

Southern Ontario coreland. Southern Ontario continues the alignment of the St. Lawrence coreland to the southwest into the Great Lakes region of the American Middle West. The sedimentary plains in a large peninsular area between southern Georgian Bay of Lake Huron on the northwest and Lakes Erie-Ontario on the southeast continue the coreland of Canada begun at Quebec in French Canada. A line of cities continues the urban concentration of the coreland in Ontario. Toronto, the second largest metropolis in Canada (*1,358,028*), is the primary focus of southern Ontario. Hamilton (*327,831*), London (*154,453*), and Windsor (*185,865*) continue the alignment of the six principal metropolitan areas in the core region. Their total population exceeded four million in 1956 which was one-fourth of the entire country's population. The total number of people in the two provinces of Ontario and Quebec was over ten million (10,033,311), which is nearly two-thirds (62.4 per cent) of the national total. With such a concentration of urban population it is not surprising that the core region is the major manufacturing zone as well as the largest consumer market in Canada.

Southern Ontario is the most southerly region of Canada. Its farm lands resemble those of central Michigan in the United States. In response to the markets represented by the urban population of the core, this Ontario farming belt is subdivided into farming areas of specialized production. The extreme southern tip of the Ontario Peninsula between Lakes St. Clair and Erie corresponds in agricultural resources and occupancy to the U.S. corn belt. The north shores of Lakes Erie and Ontario are specialized tobacco, fruit, and vegetable growing areas. Dairy farming prevails in an elongated belt paralleling but north of the urban belt and vegetable and fruit-farming districts along the shores. This dairy belt extends all the way from the St. Lawrence-New York border around Lake Ontario to the vicinity of London, Ontario. The remainder of the coreland, back from Lake Huron shores, is devoted to general farming. Urban and peripherally related agricultural activities complement one another in the Canadian region in accordance with the above geographical patterns.

Clay belt and corridor subregion. Northward and westward around Lakes Huron and Superior, away from the southern Ontario coreland, is the clay belt and corridor subregion. It is a 200-300-mile-wide band of metamorphic upland occupied by forest and mineralized districts and a lacustrine clay belt through which the eastern coreland is linked to western Canada. In this corridor the clay belt is the bed of a glacial lake on the otherwise uninterrupted rock-outcrop region of the Canadian Shield. Main transportation routes link the agricultural, forestry, and mining settlements of the clay belt across the corridor region. There are four main focal areas between the Ontario coreland and Manitoba, the beginning of western Canada. One is the railroad and mining-service community at Sudbury, where nickel mining is the economic base (Figure 182). Another is represented by a group of mining and paper-industry centers associated locally with clay-belt lands, which are interconnected by the Canadian National Railway. A third center is the Canadian Sault Ste. Marie at the Soo locks, which by-pass the rapids of the St. Marys River between Lakes Superior and Huron. This point is a key transhipment center in North America, controlling the interchange of ore-boat traffic on the three largest of the Great Lakes—Superior, Michigan, and Huron. The fourth focal area is the twin center at Port Arthur-Fort William, the western termini for prairie grain trade from western Canada by way of the Lakes and the St. Lawrence Seaway to European and world markets. These ports also tap the hinterland mineral district of western Ontario, which contains the reserves of iron ore in the Steep Rock mining property. Since this property is owned by the Inland Steel Company of Chicago, the ore moves primarily to the United States.

The Canadian West. The next major region in the wide arc is the West of Canada, corresponding to the West of the United States. It is the top of the triangular interior lowlands and the cordilleran region of North America. The lowland interior extends all the way to the Arctic Ocean through the Mackenzie Valley, but the settled portion narrows rapidly north of the United States border and terminates in the Peace River district.

The Prairie Provinces. There are seven subregions in the Prairie Provinces, as shown by the map in Figure 176. They are in many ways part of one large region focusing on Winnipeg (*409,121*), the gateway to the Canadian West. Historically the city has been both node of development for initial prairie settlement and nucleus from which railroad building pushed westward and northwestward to help settle and then serve the northwestern interior plains. The subregions of the Prairie Provinces (Manitoba, Saskatchewan, and Alberta) can be characterized briefly.

1. The eastern Manitoba Plain is the farming territory immediately contributary to Winnipeg, as well as the Manitoba Lake country to the north.

2. The Assiniboine River basin in southern Saskatchewan, with Regina, Brandon, and Saskatoon as local-regional centers is due west of the first subregion. Wheat is the major crop of both regions.

3. Still farther west a drier subregion on both sides of the border of Saskatchewan and Alberta and without a major urban center is known as the "dry belt." This is ranch country.

4. The latter subregion merges with high plains and rolling foot hills of the Rockies in southern Alberta, and focuses on the subregional center at Calgary (*200,449*). Proximity to the Rocky Mountains makes irrigation feasible. Coal, oil, and gas are the basis, also, of industrial development in this region. There are three additional subregions in a second more northerly tier.

5. Central Saskatchewan is transitional between the prairie, parklands, and woodlands of northern Saskatchewan. It has a mixed agricultural economy with wheat in the southern margins and a farming pioneer fringe along the north edge which gives way to forests. The principal focus is Prince Albert.

6. Central Alberta or the Edmonton region is the gateway to the north. Its future bears the same relationship to the opening of the northland in western Canada that Winnipeg has had in the past in the development of the West as a whole. The rail line toward the Peace River district reaches a railhead at Dawson Creek. Motor vehicles may go farther north on the Alaska Highway, which joins Alaska to the main body of the United States through Canadian territory as already mentioned. From a second railhead at the northern end of the

(A) A view of a section of downtown Montreal showing the Sun Life Building on the right and the St. Lawrence River in the background. Note the huge grain elevator along the river bank, indicating the major importance of Montreal as head of navigation below the rapids which the St. Lawrence Seaway now circumvents. Simpson's is the Canadian partner of Sears and Roebuck in the United States. (*Courtesy of Imperial Oil.*)

Figure 181

(B) A view of the St. Lawrence River from the ramparts of Quebec City. The city in the background, reached by ferry boat across the river, is Levis. Due to the damming of the Great Lakes by the falls at Niagara, the level of the St. Lawrence River seldom varies more than a few inches. (*Courtesy of Imperial Oil.*)

(C) A view of French long lots on the St. Lawrence River northeast of Montreal. (*Courtesy of Royal Canadian Air Force.*)

(D) A view of English rectangular lots at Brampton, Ontario. (*Courtesy of Royal Canadian Air Force.*)

Figure 182. The Falconbridge Nickel Mines Limited in the Sudbury Nickel Basin is one of Canada's major nickel producers. The buildings here are only part of a considerably larger layout of structures in which nickel is smelted. (*Courtesy of Canadian Consulate General.*)

Peace River settlement, the Hay River road extends to Great Slave Lake and the navigable portions of the Mackenzie River to the Arctic Ocean.

Edmonton is strategically situated within the coal, gas, and oil fields of Alberta. Tapping fields to the north, west, south, and east, the Alberta capital city is the refinery, petro-chemical, and gas-processing plant headquarters for one of the most significant petroleum-producing regions of the Americas (Figure 183). The Alberta pipe line carries crude and refined petroleum products southeastward across the Prairie Provinces, passing through Regina (with feeders to Saskatoon and Winnipeg) to the United States border west of the Red River. From this point the pipe line crosses United States territory through the northern Midwest gateway region to Sarnia, Ontario, by way of Mackinac Straits between the upper and lower peninsulas of Michigan. Near Sarnia, at the western end of the Canadian core region, is located the largest refining capacity in eastern Canada, serving the largest eastern Canadian market.

The Edmonton subregion is also one of mixed farming—grains, dairying, and hog raising. With the exceptions of Winnipeg (*409,121*) and Vancou-ver (*665,017*), the city of Edmonton (*251,004*) is the largest one west of Hamilton, Ontario. The two plains cities, Edmonton and Winnipeg, toward either end of the triangle of interior lowland settlement, represent the main axis of area organization in western interior Canada. Winnipeg joins the entire West to the main body of eastern Canada; Edmonton serves as the intermediate focus binding the North and Pacific West of Canada through the Prairie Provinces to the nation as a whole.

7. The last subregion of the Prairie Provinces is the northwestern corner of the agriculturally occupied portion of the interior sedimentary lowlands in the valley of the Peace River. This area focuses on Edmonton rather than on any major subregional center of its own. It is a region of pioneer farming, mixed grain and livestock raising.

Northwest territories. Canadians are turning increasingly to the northland. The mining of uranium ores in the Canadian Shield near Great Bear Lake, at Port Radium, and, decreasingly now, on Lake Athabasca at Uranium City, represented a northern boom during and just after World War II. This has tapered off with competition from less-distant uranium discoveries elsewhere in the United States

Figure 183. This aerial view of Imperial Oil's Edmonton refinery, which has a capacity of 28,500 Canadian barrels per day, shows only one of many such facilities. In addition, the scene shows the apparently unending continuity of cropland. The river bend on the left is the North Saskatchewan. (*Courtesy of Imperial Oil.*)

since the war. But other minerals, primarily gold, have long been exploited in the region; and the fly-in fisherman tourist trade is developing rapidly. There are potential coal and petroleum resources in the Mackenzie Valley, of which the oil field developed at Norman Wells is an example.

The Mountain West. The northwest-southeast trending Rocky Mountain cordillera bounds the Prairie Provinces on the west. Subdivided into a northern and southern portion—the Yukon Territory and British Columbia—the Mountain West consists of three broad mountainous territories. These are the coastal ranges, the central upland, and the inter-Rocky Mountain ranges which border the Prairie Provinces. The latter is a rugged region accessible from east to west through narrow passes across the northwest-southeast grain of mountain alignments. One of the access routes follows the Fraser River southward from the interior Fraser Plateau and is a large cattle and sheep-ranching territory. The Fraser Valley leads to the Canadian West's largest metropolis at Vancouver, which has more than half a million in its metropolitan area (*655,017*), making it the third largest city in Canada. This city occupies a relative status among Canadian cities analogous to Los Angeles in the United States.

Located at the head of a structural trench between the island mountains of Vancouver Island, Queen Charlotte Island, and other offshore islands of southern Alaska, Vancouver is Canada's west-coast transhipment port. Northwest along the inland waterway provided by the trench referred to, contact is maintained with forest and fishing activities both along the Canadian coast and beyond in Alaska. Products of the forest and mine outstrip in value those of the soil in British Columbia. Gold, copper, lead, and coal are produced in important amounts. The salmon catch, based on the annual return of that species of fish to fresh water for spawning, is 60-70 per cent of the fishing industry's activity. The other 30-40 per cent consists of halibut, herring, and shell fish.

A second outlet overland to the west coast, terminating at Prince Rupert, was created early in the twentieth century by constructing the Canadian National Railroad from Edmonton across the mountains. The expectation that the fishing village at the end of the line would blossom into a second major Pacific seaport has not been fulfilled. Fifty

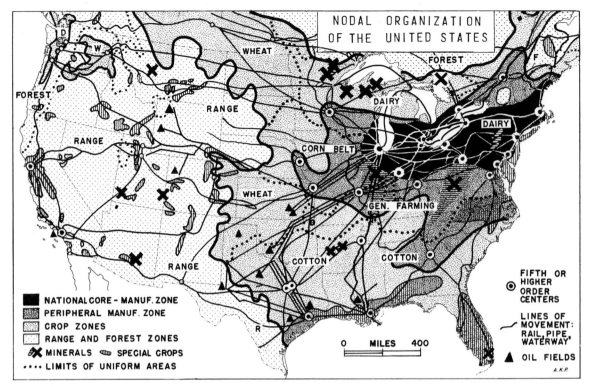

Figure 184. (*Courtesy of* Economic Geography, *taken from Allen K. Philbrick, "Principles of Areal Functional Organization in Regional Human Geography."*)

miles south of Prince Rupert, however, a large power project at Kitimat is the basis for aluminum reduction from imported ores.

Summary

This chapter has presented the areal organization of the Americas as a whole in a world setting, with special emphasis on the United States and Canada. The linear pattern of Canada's regional organization must be viewed on a continental scale as part of the radial organization of the United States. Both nations as a unit are organized around a common core region which spills over from the eastern seaboard regions of each country into the central lowlands. Coreland gateway regions link the core with the peripheral subregions of the North, the South, and the West. Specialized resource regions are tapped for fish and forest products, food, fiber, and minerals with which to make things, and for energy fuels with which to do the work. These items, in a diverse profusion of commodities, flow to the manufacturing establishments of the core region. They move by rail, highway, or air, by barge on inland waterways, by coastal ship, and

by pipe line. The radial arrangement of the means of transportation expresses the nodality of organization. The map in Figure 184, without subregional boundaries, shows the nodal organization of the United States and southern Canada today. Such interconnections as those referred to are symbolized by selected and generalized rail patterns, inland waterways, and pipelines. Primarily within the industrial complexes of the coreland, raw and semi-processed raw materials are made into steel, metal manufactures, electrical goods, chemicals, machinery, equipment, and a host of consumer-oriented products, which are then distributed using the same system of linkages previously employed in collecting the materials before manufacture.

This immense pattern of exchange organization in North America has emerged from the use of the resources of the Americas discussed in the previous chapter. The complex radial pattern of regional organization of the continent reflects the resource pattern of a great interior lowland rich in mineral fuel and food resources backed up on each of three highland sides by the resources of the mineral industries. The core region within this pattern is European oriented in its geographical position which confirms cultural development as a main instrument in the evolution of the present pattern of regional organization. In the regional organization of North America a basic similarity with that of Europe may be seen in the *four* great cultural regions which surround the continental coreland—the Eastern Seaboard, the South, the West, and north of the coreland, Canada.

It will be the task of the next chapter to contrast North American cultural evolution with that of Latin America and to discuss the cultural origins of North America, the most populous of the continents of the New World.

14 *The Peopling of the Americas*

At the time of the discovery of the Americas there were approximately 10 million indigenous occupants of the two continents. By 1962 there were 400 million primarily nonindigenous occupants. The latter figure is forty times the former; but the two represent nearly completely different statistical populations, also. The 10 million in 1492 were the successors of prehistoric migrants who moved *eastward* by way of the Bering Strait from Asia. From a few individuals the natural increase and infiltration of American Indian and Eskimo indigenes into all parts of the double continent occurred over a span of some 30,000 years. The 400 million today are the successors of a second migration mainly from Europe and Africa within the past 500 years. Generalized routes of the flow of population into the Americas in the second migration are shown on the map in Figure 185. Never before did so many people move so far within so short a period as in this *great migration*.

The age of discovery, exploration, settlement, and construction ushered in by immigration to the Americas has been the period of greatest change in the entire course of geographic evolution by human society. The cultures of the indigenous population and of Europeans and Africans who came or were brought to the Americas have mingled to some extent; but to a much greater extent European culture replaced indigenous cultures. The peopling of the Americas affords a striking example and opportunity for analysis of the impact of evolving cultures within new patterns of occupancy. The purpose of this chapter is to examine the geographical evolution of the patterns of human organization which evolved in the Americas. The present patterns of organization, it has been observed, are very different between Latin America and North America, partly because of differences in cultural values and ways of doing things which characterized the people who migrated to each region. It is only possible through understanding the differences in cultural development and uses of local resources to explain the outstanding differences between Latin and North American patterns of occupancy.

Contrasts between Latin and North American Settlement

The background of contrasts between Latin and North American settlement can be characterized under five main headings.

1. Already developed differences among peoples and their cultures in their places of origin.

2. The distinction between conquest and colonization.

3. The contrast in aims between landed aristocracy and the homesteader.

4. The difference in degrees of racial mingling or of racial separation.

5. The contrast in orientation between industrial diversity and raw materials and food-product specialization.

The geographical impact of the development of society in the Americas with respect to each of the above five points will be briefly reviewed.

Developed Differences among Peoples in Their Places of Origin. The map in Figure 185 shows by bands of varying widths and identity the source areas and destinations of the largest components of the great migration into the Americas. Total quantity of the immigrant population is estimated to have been 80 million people. Forty-five million of these entered the United States-Canadian regions from Europe; twenty million entered Central and South America from Europe; and 15 million Africans were involuntarily brought to Latin America and one million of these were imported into North America. Accurate data covering the entire period of the migration are, of course, not available. Some records of intercontinental migration have been compiled for immigration into the Americas from 1821 to 1932 and for emigration from Europe from 1846 to 1932. They are shown in Table XXX. The predominance of those whose destination was the Americas—91 per cent—is very evident. Of the total, two-thirds entered North America, one-fourth Latin America, while less than one-tenth went to other continents. Equally impressive is the proportion—97.0 per cent—of the emigrants supplied from Europe since the mid-nineteenth century. Although the quantities and periods are only partial, relationships undoubtedly reflect a true picture of the great migration.

Relative contributions of individual countries and of regions of Europe to intercontinental migration are indicated by the data in Table XXXI. Countries of the European core region accounted for nearly half of the total of 50 million emigrants. Nearly one-third—31 per cent—came from a single country, the United Kingdom. Well over one-third came from the British Isles, if the Irish are included with emigrants from the United Kingdom. The predominance of English emigrants is even more striking because of the fact that partly through numbers they became the dominant group in North America, fixing English culture on both Canada and the United States. The second largest group to emigrate from Europe was from the Mediterranean region—southern Italy, Spain, and Portugal. Spanish and Portuguese nationals immigrated primarily to Latin America and early gave to that territory a characteristic Latin culture. It should be noted that Italian emigration, shown in Table XXXI, has been divided between north Italy and south Italy in a ratio of 1 to 2. Of the 11.5 million persons from Italy, the majority went to the United States from both parts of Italy. The Portuguese predominated in Brazil, while the Spanish dominated in almost all of the rest of Latin America.

Certain patterns of movement characterize the flows of migration shown on the map. Spanish control centered first in the Caribbean but rapidly penetrated to the Pacific side of the Central American Isthmus and branched to the south and north into tropical highlands. The arrows representing Portuguese movement reach across the Atlantic to the northeast and southeast coasts of Brazil. In North America the French used the St. Lawrence River into the Great Lakes Region and thence down the Mississippi. They also followed rivers and lakes northward into Canada. The English also approached North America from the Caribbean, following the traditional route of sailing vessels, which was clockwise around the North Atlantic. The circuit used the Northeast Trade Winds from Europe to the West Indies. From there northward

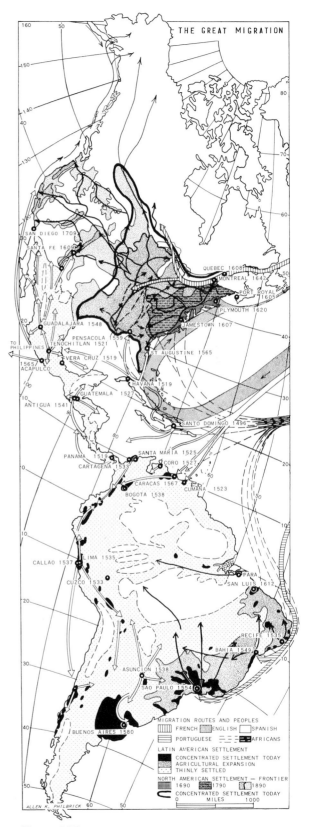

Figure 185

TABLE XXX   INTERCONTINENTAL IMMIGRATION AND EMIGRATION[a]

IMMIGRATION 1821–1932			EMIGRATION 1846–1932		
Continent	Number of immigrants	Per cent	Continent	Number of emigrants	Per cent
The Americas	53,826	91.0	Europe	51,696	97.0
North America	39,470	66.6			
United States	34,244	57.5			
Canada	5,226	8.8	Non-European continents	1,756	3.0
Latin America	14,356	24.4			
Non-American continents	5,361	9.0			
Total	59,187	100.0	Total	53,450	100.0

[a] Woytinsky and Woytinsky, *World Population and Production*, New York: the Twentieth Century Fund, 1953, p. 72. Only voluntary migration is recorded.

along the east coast of North America passage was aided by the Gulf Stream.

The slave trade from Africa became part of this North Atlantic circuit. Slaves were captured or bought for trinkets in Africa and were then shipped across the Atlantic to the West Indies. Here most of them were sold for sugar, molasses, rum, or other products which were taken on for shipment to North American coastal ports. Raw materials shipped from the American colonies to Europe completed the circuit. It was in such trade that many a New Englander made his fortune. Export-oriented production of foods and other raw materials also became fixed in this way in many localities of both continents. Furs from the St. Lawrence, timber and fish from New England, tobacco from Virginia, indigo and sea-island cotton from the Carolinas, are all examples of early export trade from North America. Sugar was a staple export from Spanish Caribbean and Portuguese Brazilian plantations. Indian and Negro slavery became an integral part of the productive system and commerce of the Atlantic between Europe, Africa, and the Americas. It was centered in the Caribbean whence it spread throughout tropical and subtropical plantation economies from the North American South to southern Brazil.

The Distinction between Conquest and Colonization. Whether or not Europeans were motivated by aims of conquest or colonization depended in part on their social origin and sense of values. The degree of emphasis between the two alternatives was also affected by the opportunity for conquest or settlement. The original motivation behind exploration in both continents was to acquire riches

of any sort with as little expenditure of effort as possible. At first no one was looking for land to colonize. Large grants of land were made by the kings of Spain, Portugal, France, or England to noblemen leading expeditions of exploration; but this practice represented the extension of feudal relationships into the New World and not necessarily a basis for colonization. In practice, however, differences soon began to emerge which were to be of lasting importance.

The Spanish conquistadores interposed themselves at the top of sedentary Indian societies which they conquered. The Portuguese also conquered and enslaved Indian populations for work on plantations. On the map in Figure 185 Spanish conquest of highland Latin America can be traced by examining the dates after the place names. Santo Domingo, was founded on the island of Hispaniola in 1496. Occupation of the mainland followed soon after with settlements at Darien (1510, no longer in existence) and Panama (1519). Mexico City, then called by its Aztec name, Tenochtlan, was captured in 1521. The capital of the Inca Indian Empire at Cuzco, Peru, was taken in 1533. (See Figure 186.) Lima was founded in 1535 and its port city, Callao, (population 1960, 135,244) in 1537. In little more than a third of a century after discovery, the Caribbean coast of Latin America had been explored, the Isthmus of Panama had been crossed to the Pacific Ocean by Balboa, its discoverer in 1513, and three major highland Indian civilizations—the Aztecs, Incas, and the Chibchas—had been conquered by Spain. From a base on the Colombian coast founded at Cartagena in 1533, the third sedentary Indian civilization, the

Chibchas, was conquered in highland Colombia, marked by the occupation of Bogotá in 1538. That same year Asunción, Paraguay, was founded by Spaniards moving up the Parana River from what initially proved to be an unsuccessful settlement at Buenos Aires. Permanent settlement at Buenos Aires dates from 1580. The sedentary highland Indian societies possessed a well-developed agriculture capable of producing food surpluses, and a technology which included gold and silver mining. Conquest by the Spanish meant the diversion of gold and silver to Spain and set the pattern for garrison-type settlements by the Spanish generally in the Americas.

The Portuguese, while they at first found no gold or sedentary Indian civilization on which to levy tribute, developed plantation-type agricultural production of sugar along the northeast coast of Brazil. Gold discovered in the interior at Cuiabá in 1719, and near Goias in 1725, replaced sugar as the primary basis of wealth in the eighteenth century. Gold exports developed Rio de Janeiro (3,123,984) as the major city of Brazil. In the nineteenth century coffee planting in the tropical highlands continued the external orientation of agricultural specialization which has persisted until the present day.

In North America, Indian population was less numerous and less concentrated. There were no advanced sedentary Indian cultures to conquer and no gold or silver to ship home. Despite this, according to Sauer,[1]

The early Englishmen who came to America, came to seek a northern way to the Orient, to bar the way of Spanish or French expansion, to seek wealth in furs, and in codfish, herring, and mackerel, to find precious metals like those of Mexico and Peru, or at least to secure profitable cargoes of medicines, spices, dyewoods, or naval stores. . . . The fact that any group of overseas colonists needed above all else to sustain themselves by the products of their agriculture was understood very slowly.

After a time, however, American colonists learned from the Indians land-clearing practices of tree girdling and planting seeds in "hills," rather than in cleared, plowed fields, and acquired the use of Indian crops such as corn, beans, and squash. In the South, following the pattern introduced from Latin America, a plantation-type economy based on tobacco, sugar cane, indigo, cotton, and rice developed early. It was the Middle Colonies, however, which held the key to the difference between

TABLE **XXXI**   EUROPEAN CONTRIBUTIONS TO INTERNATIONAL MIGRATION, 1846–1932[a]

Country and region of emigration	Emigrants	Per cent
Total Europe	51,695	100
United Kingdom[b]	16,191	31.3
Germany	4,889	9.5
Italy[c] (North)	3,364	6.4
France	519	1.0
Belgium, Netherlands, and Switzerland	749	1.5
European core region	25,712	49.7
Italy[c] (Mediterranean)	6,728	13.0
Spain	4,653	9.0
Portugal	1,805	3.5
Mediterranean Europe	13,186	25.5
Austria-Hungary[d]	5,196	10.0
Russia	2,253	4.4
Poland	642	1.2
Slavic East Europe	8,091	15.6
Sweden	1,203	2.3
Norway	854	1.7
Denmark	387	0.7
Finland	371	0.7
Scandinavian Europe	2,815	5.4
Ireland	1,892	3.7
Atlantic fringe of Europe[e]	1,892	3.7

[a] *Loc. cit.*

[b] Includes Malta.

[c] Italian data divided one-third to core region, two thirds to Mediterranean Europe.

[d] Austria-Hungary after 1919 Austria, Hungary, and Czechoslovakia; Austrian data not excluded from east Europe.

[e] Atlantic fringe region should have parts of French, Spanish, and United Kingdom population, not excluded from France, Spain, and United Kingdom.

conquest and colonization. According to Sauer, again,[2]

The basic pattern of the American farm is derived chiefly from the Middle Colonies, and thus from a continental European as well as from an English background. It was to the Middle Colonies that the greatest number of people came who were by birth and training tillers of the soil. Their coming was delayed sufficiently so that they brought with them some of the new agriculture that changed Western Europe so greatly in the eighteenth century.

[1] Carl O. Sauer, "The Settlement of the Humid East," *Climate and Man*, Yearbook of Agriculture, Washington, D.C., 1941, p. 161.
[2] *Ibid.*, p. 164.

Figure 186. These ruins of an old Inca fortress town called Machupicchu (High Mountain) are located northwest of Cuzco, Peru. Ruins include a temple and citadel surrounded by terraced gardens. The Inca Empire, established in the late eleventh or twelfth century, comprised a large area now part of Bolivia, Ecuador, Chile, and Peru. It united all the inhabitants in a common social, political, and religious community headed by the Inca emperors. (*Courtesy of United Nations.*)

Unlike New England, the Middle Colonies were not generally settled as closely knit township communities but as single farmsteads. Unlike the owners of plantations on the southern seaboard, the land operators to the north were themselves the tillers of the soil, occupants of single-family farms.

The most striking pattern contrast between North America and Latin America results from this difference, the continuity of settlement in North America described as the *frontier,* which was largely absent from Latin America. The line representing the concept of the frontier, which could be drawn on a map, had almost tangible meaning to the people of that day. Its meaning was in terms of relative security against Indian attack and in the relative degree of civilization represented by the attributes and amenities of settled existence. Nowhere in the Americas outside of Canada and the United States has this phenomenon been repeated,

except intermittently and on a small scale. Isochronic lines of settlement in the United States and Canada are shown on the map in Figure 185, indicating the steady westward march of the frontier from 1690 to 1890. In these two centuries, several million immigrant Europeans virtually replaced the American Indians in the central lowlands of North America. In over four centuries, by contrast, the settlement patterns of Latin American highlands have remained virtually stationary within the general territories of the conquered sedentary Indians. In the rest of Latin America expansion of settled area, while substantial, has been rather narrowly limited. It has consistently remained within a few hundred miles of continental margins. This distinction is the product of both greater numbers of settlers in North America than in Latin America and the difference between a motivation of conquest and one of colonization.

The Contrast in Aims between Landed Aristocracy and Homesteader. Despite the existence of the plantation system of production in the South of North America, the basic unit of farm settlement in the United States became the *single-family farm.* After beginnings rooted in the crown-granted land holdings to landed aristocrats during colonial days, westward settlement and the opening of frontier lands by settlers was dominated by the Jeffersonian ideal of a "nation of homesteaders."

By contrast the basic unit of European farm settlement in Latin America remained the *feudal estate.* The Portuguese and Spanish families who were awarded title to landed estates in Portuguese and Spanish America by the crowns of their respective countries transferred to America the land-tenure systems of Portugal and Spain. Indian and Negro slave labor did the work of producing commercial crops for export. This labor was expected also to be self-sustaining on a subsistence basis. The profits from the sale of products from the *hacienda* (Spanish) or *fazenda* (Portuguese) belonged to the landed aristocracy. Sale of products was accomplished by export through the nearest effective port and shipment to Spain, Portugal, or elsewhere in Europe.

The local economy within the hacienda or fazenda was virtually a closed unit. For the Indian and Negro population there was no necessity of market town or village, since they and their families were self-sustaining through subsistence agriculture. Village or town life, if it existed at all for the people of the countryside, was focused on the church. The market centers were the port cities where the landed aristocracy or their agents concentrated their own social life. They also disposed of their products in these port cities.

In North America the more numerous farm settlers were former landless peasantry from Europe. These people aspired to independent existence in the New World. The opportunity to acquire land and develop it into something through their own efforts brought about an entirely different attitude toward life than that characteristic of the landed aristocracy. The homesteader, beginning as a subsistence pioneer, became a commercial farmer as soon as patterns of commercial and manufacturing activities requiring a commercial agriculture began to evolve within regionally integrated national economies of Canada and the United States.

One of the geographical results of the difference in aims of the homesteader and landed aristocracy in North and Latin America survives today in the sizes of farms typical of the two regions. The impact of the system of landed estates and plantation agriculture in Latin America may be seen in the great range in size of farm holdings in country after country. The great majority of individual farm holdings are tiny, while at the same time a relative handful of people own a very large percentage of the total farmland. By contrast, in North America the very small and very large farm holdings are not as numerous as those of a medium-size range. Medium-sized holdings are most numerous—50–80 per cent—in the United States, Canada, and Uruguay. Countries in which small-size holdings are most numerous but more than half of the total farm area is in very large holdings are represented by Mexico, Guatemala, Ecuador, Brazil, and Chile. Other countries with small-size holdings most numerous but less than half of the total farm area in large holdings are Costa Rica, El Salvador, Panama, Cuba, the Dominican Republic, and Honduras. Small farms generally are less than 50 acres, whereas "large" means 1,000 acres or more. Data are unavailable for many countries, as, for example, Argentina.

The fact that so many of the farm holdings in Latin American countries are of small size reflects the great emphasis in former times on subsistence farming within the plantation system of production which reflects the relatively large proportion of total land area in large units of production. The concentration of very large amounts of land in the hands of a few large landowners reflects the continuing importance of a landed aristocracy. Such contrast of poverty and wealth with respect to land as the basis of livelihood within primarily agricultural countries has produced equally basic conflicts of interests in other spheres of life.

Mexico, the "New Spain" of the Americas, is the classic example of such conflict. It has experienced the struggle between two opposing systems of the organization of area in the *hacienda* and the *ejido*. The hacienda is the large, privately owned, landed estate, typical among descendants of the original Spanish landed aristocracy. The ejido is a landholding agrarian community, typical among descendants of the original Indians. By the end of the dictatorship of Profirio Diaz in 1910, concentration of land ownership in the hands of the large landowners had reached a maximum. Since the Mexican Revolution (1910–1915) there has been a continuing program of land expropriation and redistribution into ejido tenure involving at least 90 million acres. That land reform is still a burning social and political issue in Latin America and is not an issue north of the Rio Grande reflects the present-day consequences of the difference in aims of the landed aristocracy and the homesteader.

Differences in Degrees of Racial Mingling or Racial Separation.
Differences in racial mingling or racial separation within Latin America and North America depended on the numbers and social circumstances of early migrants. Since most of the explorer-soldiers of the early migration were without families, marriage with Indian women was frequent in Latin America. In North America, although there was an initial shortage of women settlers, and the union of European men with Indian women was not unheard of, the balance between the sexes among colonizers was much more nearly equal than in Latin America. There is a major difference between North and Latin America in population composition. North America's population is relatively unmixed racially, while that of Latin America is a series of complex amalgams of peoples. Exceptions to this generalization are Argentina, Paraguay, and Uruguay in the southern end of South America, and Costa Rica and Haiti in Caribbean America. Argentina, Uruguay, and Costa Rica are predominantly of unmixed European stock. Paraguay, on the contrary, is almost entirely Indian, while a majority of the population of Haiti is Negro. The original settlers of Argentina and Uruguay faced sparsely distributed and highly mobile plains Indians rather than sedentary agri-

cultural tribes which could be mobilized for agri-cultural labor. Therefore, very little intermarriage with Indians took place. By contrast, the early Spanish and Portuguese soldiers who married Indian women set a pattern for the present national and racial composition of most of Latin America. The offspring of the union of European and Indian persons are called *mestizos*. Mixtures of Negro and European persons occurred to a lesser extent and are called *mulattoes*. A still less common occurrence are persons, called *zambos*, resulting from the union of Negro with Indian blood.

The proportion of pure-blooded Negro and the proportion of mixed Negro-European population to the total people of the United States is impossi-ble to estimate accurately, although it is a minority. Similar mixture in Canada is negligible. Cross-mating between Europeans and North American Indians has always been of minor numerical importance.

Contrast in Orientation between Industrial Diversity and Raw Material and Food-Prod-uct Specialization. The results of the preceding differences in development within North America and Latin America were divergent paths of regional organization. In North America continuity between diverse elements began to emerge very soon after the beginning of sedentary settlement; in Latin America areas of specialized production remained isolated from one another. These two trends have ultimately produced the basic contrast in occupance patterns already noted in the previous chapter. In North America a basically unified and coherent inter-regional organization of production exists within twin national economies—the United States and Canada—characterized by great industrial diversity. These national economies focus internally on their primary core regions which possess a common boundary along one side. In Latin America, by contrast, specialized agricultural and mining activi-ties originally externally oriented during the colonial period, have persisted in that orientation under conditions of political independence. Long-con-tinued preoccupation with external markets for specialized production has delayed in Latin Amer-ica, until quite recently, the development of fully independent internally integrated industrial econ-omies. No single factor is responsible for this situa-tion, but very different results were brought about by a combination of the original differences in peoples themselves, in their motivation for conquest or for colonization flowing from attitudes inherent in different cultures and in social groups such as the landed aristocracy and the land-hungry peas-antry of Europe.

The difference between racial mingling and racial separation certainly can only be said to have con-tributed indirectly to the difference in patterns of organization. The presence of a large dominant culture group in North America—the large popu-lation of European origin—represented a broad base on which leadership could develop. By con-trast, the majority of population in Latin America, with certain exceptions already noted, was of mixed culture based in part on mixed racial origin; and the societies of Latin American republics tended to be much more unevenly stratified socially with leadership drawn from a much smaller segment of total population. In both Spanish and Portuguese Latin America, therefore, a *minority* of Europeans controlled a majority of either Indians or imported Negro slaves in the operation of economies which were externally commercially oriented, and based primarily on subsistence agriculture for the support of laboring classes within each country. These circumstances set a pattern of development which even after the abolition of slavery was not condu-cive to the evolution of diversified integrated indus-trialized economies. Even now, long after the achievement of political independence, Latin Amer-ica has not completely freed herself from economic colonialism.

Emergence of Regional Organization in the United States

The transformation of the thirteen original col-onies into a nation was the remarkable achievement of the revolutionary period. This creative change rested on the ability of the people in three regions of the eastern seaboard to submerge their differences in a common cause. The characters of the three regions, in turn, set the trends of cultural evolution of the United States.

Three Regions of the Colonial Eastern Sea-board. The three regions which set the pace of national development were the Virginia Tide-water, New England, and the Middle Colonies from the Hudson into the eastern Piedmont.

Tidewater Virginia. The settlers of the London Company coasted southward to the Canary Islands. They then followed the trade winds southwestward to the West Indies and northward beyond the Hat-teras coast of North Carolina to the protected waters of Chesapeake Bay. Jamestown, which they founded in 1607 on the banks of the James River in Tidewater Virginia, nearly ended in disaster. So deeply imbued were the settlers with the desire to find gold and silver or the "western" ocean which they thought must be just a few day's journey inland that most of them spent the precious growing season for several successive years in fruitless digging and exploration instead of securing the necessities of life as urged by Captain John Smith.

When gold and a water route to the west proved elusive they turned to experiments with oranges, vines, mulberry trees for silk-worm production, and cotton in efforts to find a commercial crop to sell profitably in Europe. Tobacco, which was to become the first big money crop, was developed by accident. A certain John Rolfe experimented in 1612 with tobacco to supply himself from his personal garden. He was so successful that by 1619 20,000 pounds of tobacco were exported; by 1626 this export had risen to half-a-million pounds. Tobacco became the staple Virginia crop in response to a rapidly increasing English and European market, and its success had a profound influence on the way of life along the tidewater. It is believed the tobacco plants were originally imported from Trinidad, following the example of the Spanish in the West Indies. Negro slaves, too, were soon imported to do the work of clearing the land and caring for the crops. Despite efforts of the leaders to increase needed food production, all land not absolutely needed for subsistence wheat, corn, and vegetables was put into tobacco.

The relatively wide Virginia coastal plain and the many, though short, navigable rivers which empty into protected waters of Chesapeake Bay provided direct accessibility to the individual plantations. Since tobacco cultivation quickly depleted soil fertility, plantations spread quickly upstream to and then beyond the limit of navigation.

As in Latin America the aristocratic slave-plantation economy developed few towns. Each plantation on tidewater tended to be directly and individually connected by sea to the London tobacco market. The population of early tidewater settlement may be divided among several categories. First were the officers of the colony who were the plantation owners. These men were English gentlemen, men of old-world property status. Below them and doing most of the normal work of the colony were English farmers or renters, laborers, and bonded servants. The latter were a category of unfree English labor under contract. Such contracts

had a termination date (usually a number of years) after which such individuals became free. The importation of Negro slaves began as the introduction of unfree servants. The idea of their perpetual servitude did not become legally recognized until after the 1660s. The social structure rooted in the ownership of land in Tidewater Virginia, however, was that of a landed aristocracy.

Inland from the tidewater, and unlike Latin America, European farm settlement took the form of subsistence farming by persons without prior background of landed-property status. There early appeared the opportunity, through the existence of free land in the interior, for individuals to advance their own fortunes by turning their backs on the aristocratic society of the tidewater. At the same time the importance of the plantation system in the tidewater lay in what was to favor its extension inland, also. For cotton as a cash crop and the plantation system of production were to carry the institution of slavery throughout the Southern states from the last decade of the eighteenth century until the end of the American Civil War.

Initially the plantation system spread northward into Maryland on the basis of tobacco culture. Initial spread southward occurred along the North and South Carolina and Georgia coasts and was based on commercial rice, indigo, and sea-island cotton production. South of Virginia, offshore sand bars and shallows prevented direct access to plantations, although inland water transportation by flat-bottomed barges was easily accomplished. Port cities—Savannah, supplemented by Darien and Sundbury in Georgia, and Charleston, supplemented by Georgetown and Beaufort in South Carolina—were developed to handle exports. Aside from the plantation establishments themselves, which were virtually self-sustaining, the ports mentioned, and a few administrative centers such as Williamsburg, Virginia, there were few if any towns or villages in the colonial South.

New England. The pattern of settlement in New England contrasted sharply with that of the plantation coast from Maryland and Virginia to the south. For New England settlement consisted of rural "towns," each with one or more villages or town nuclei. The pattern, as shown by the map in Figure 187,[1] is therefore a compact one of relatively con-

[1] The map is based on four maps in Charles O. Paullin, *Atlas of the Historical Geography of the United States,* New York: Carnegie Institute of Washington and the American Geographical Society of New York, 1932, plate 61 A-D.

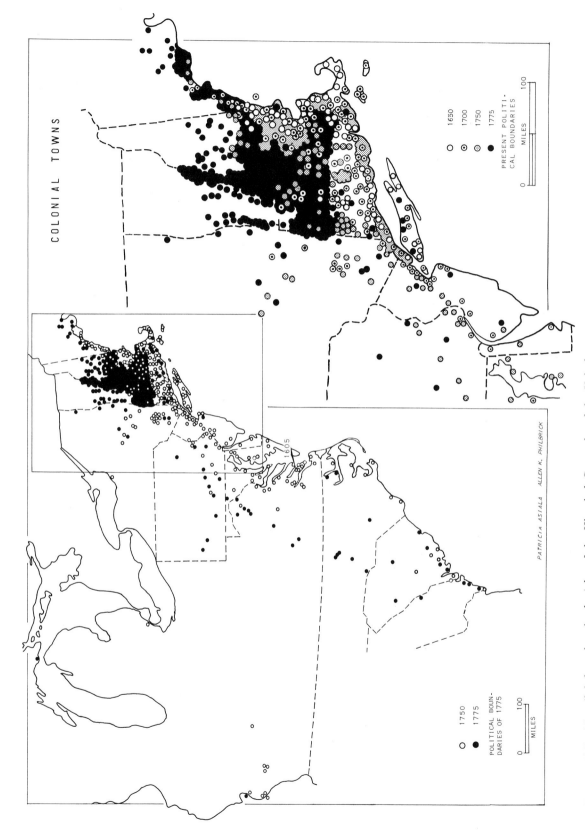

Figure 187. *(Compiled from data in the Atlas of the Historical Geography of the United States, by Charles O. Paullin, published jointly by The Carnegie Institution and The American Geographical Society.)*

PATRICIA ASIALA   ALLEN K. PHILBRICK

COLONIAL TOWNS

1650
1700
1750
1775

PRESENT POLITICAL BOUNDARIES

MILES

0   100   MILES

1750
1775

POLITICAL BOUNDARIES OF 1775

0   100   MILES

1605

centrated village settlement. The map covers the period from 1607 to the eve of the American Revolution. It shows a rapid increase in number and dispersion of the villages organized on this basis in New England, particularly in Massachusetts. What are the bases for this contrast between the tidewater area of Virginia, which was conspicuous for the slow development of towns, and New England in which town life was a major characteristic?

The unique mixture which may be called New England culture was a combined outgrowth of ways of life in the English countryside and the struggle of religious separatists escaping from harrassment by the established Church of England. Two principles of *old* English land tenure were combined in the land-tenure system of New England. First was the principle of *individual* ownership of land, expressive of the idea which was extending private land enclosure in England at that very time. Simultaneously the ancient principle of *common* ownership was carried over from the English village system of land tenure which had been characteristic of the subsistence organization of peasant agriculture. In the well-ordered arrangement of every New England village and town, division of land among the members of the community was conspicuous. Each family unit was responsible for clearing and cultivating private lands; at the same time all had a share in and use of the common forest and pasture land, as well as the central commons around which clustered the social and political institutions of *church* and *town meeting* upon which the life of the whole community focused. The attitude of the Puritans in religious matters provided a common ideological bond in the struggle to survive. Accordingly they built *together* at the same that they built *individually* their productive agricultural establishments around the village commons.

On the basis of the multiplication of such units throughout the region of New England, as shown in Figure 187, a concentrated pattern of nucleated settlements and interconnections among them developed. This pattern of settlement later became the basis of commerce and industry which expanded rapidly when the United States became independent of England.

The Middle Colonies. Reference has already been made to the fact that the eastern coastal plain of the United States narrows progressively to the northeast. The eastern low highlands which separate the great interior plains from the Atlantic seaboard are the Appalachians. The coastal plain ends at New York, as shown by the map in Figure 188. Behind the coastal plain is the Piedmont, the "foot hills" of the Blue Ridge Mountains which are constructed of metamorphic as well as more recent intrusive igneous rocks. Behind and paralleling the Blue Ridge is a region of folded sedimentary ridges and valleys along the western edge of which lies the uplifted edge of the Allegheny Plateau. Within the Ridge and Valley Province are many longitudinal valleys, the largest of which is known as the Great Valley and extends in a southwest to northeast direction. In western Virginia this valley is only separated by a low divide from the upstream limits of the Shenandoah, a tributary stream of the Potomac River.

Settlement spread from tidewater points at a relatively early date into the Piedmont region all the way from New York to the Carolinas, as well as in the long intermontane valleys of the Appalachians behind both the Piedmont and the Blue Ridge. The Middle Colonies and eastern Piedmont, accordingly, contain the starting line for the American "frontier." On its eastern edge the region is marked by an alignment of rapids and falls which are collectively called the "fall line," where the heads of navigation of the larger tidewater rivers occur. The Piedmont, accordingly, was the first settled region south of interior New England which was *not* directly accessible to the sea. The north end of the fall line, however, was extremely accessible to the sea. From the very start of settlement it contained the most important ports and urban centers at New York, Philadelphia, and Baltimore. Their sites are at the mouth of the Hudson, at the head of navigation of the Delaware, and at the head of Chesapeake Bay, respectively. The line of contact between the Piedmont and the narrowed northern end of the North American coastal plain became a zone of access between other parts of the country and the rest of the world. It was in this region that the homestead type of single-family subsistence farm originated as opposed to either the compact town-settlement pattern of rural New England or the commercial plantation-type landed estate of the Tidewater. The two hundred-year advance of the frontier began in this region and was extended first by the homesteader and later by other forms of the same phenomenon from the Atlantic to the Pacific. Its progress from 1690 to 1890 is recorded in generalized terms on the map in Figure 185. The lines of movement show the major routes of westward settlement. Carl Sauer has already said that the single farm of the Middle Colonies provided the prototype of the westward march of the homestead across the face of America.

The American historian Frederick Jackson Turner long ago pointed out that it was the Middle Colonies from New York and Pennsylvania to the western parts of Virginia and the Carolinas which became the country's first "melting pot," absorbing English, German, Scotch, and Irish, as well as emigrants from Tidewater and New England. The routes of the dispersion of the homestead-type farm into the interior are shown by the more detailed map in Figure 188. The principal avenues were the Hudson-Mohawk River Valley into western New York state and the combined Shenandoah-Great Valley to the southwest behind the Blue Ridge Mountains into Tennessee, Kentucky, and the lower Ohio River country.

Names such as Hudson, Rensselaer, and Amsterdam attest to the early Dutch settlement of lower New York. The particularly large estates of the *patroon* land-tenure system established by the Dutch and confirmed by the English left very large areas in manorial grants, most of which went undeveloped for a long time. Such commitment of acreage along the Hudson River Valley had a lasting influence on the development of New York state, for it encouraged new settlement to by-pass the lower Hudson and reach out toward the new lands in the interior along the Mohawk. After the American Revolution such settlement took place rapidly by Yankee New Englanders who moved into upper New York state. Scotch-Irish and Germans from Pennsylvania to western Virginia and North Carolina advanced through the Shenandoah route and were thus poised for continued migration across the Appalachians. In transmountain migration Scotch-Irish people by the tens of thousands poured through the Kentucky Cumberland Gap along Daniel Boone's Wilderness Road. Germans, Scotch-Irish, and others also pushed westward up the Susquehanna and its west branch into western Pennsylvania. These two flows of population met again in the lower Ohio.

Maps showing the distribution of the major religious denominations at the time of the American Revolution reflect the different national backgrounds of the several sections of colonial peoples. The Puritans of New England are clearly marked by the distribution of Congregational Churches. The planters of the Tidewater region are revealed by the area dominated by Episcopalians. Similarly the Dutch Reformed Churches of the Hudson Valley stand out, as well as the Presbyterian Churches of the Scotch-Irish in the Piedmont. The "melting pot" character of eastern Pennsylvania and lower New York is demonstrated by the map in Figure 189.[1] This map of the areas within which people of diversified religious backgrounds lived shows the degree of mixture by means of the overlapping areas of one or more religious denominations.

Continuing from Sauer's discussion of the settlement of the humid East,

The contributions of Europeans to the Colonies from the Hudson to the upper Chesapeake were varied. The Swedes and Finns are credited in particular with the introduction of the *log cabin*, which became the standard house of the frontier until the sod house of the western prairies took its place. The Dutch contributed better *breeds of livestock* and interest in *dairying*, and played a role in introduction of European *grasses and clovers*. The Scotch-Irish, under which term Irish and Scots are also included, provided a large proportion of the intrepid *backwoodsmen* who first ventured into the wilderness. It is also probable that they established the culture of the *potato*.

The German settlers as a group were most preoccupied with becoming permanently established as farmers wherever they settled. They were less mobile than the Scotch-Irish and so are often considered as forming a second wave of settlement behind the latter, who constituted an advance guard in the movement inland. The Germans were general farmers, accustomed to animal husbandry. They practiced *manuring* and, largely, *crop rotation*. Notable improvements in grain growing and stock breeding are credited to them. Architecturally they were the creators of the basic *American barn*, combining barn, stable, granary, and wagon shed under one commodious roof in the so-called Swiss, Mennonite, or bank barn. In contrast to the English colonists, they stabled animals in bad weather and were accustomed to *stall feeding*. Other items of importance to American farm settlement credited to the colonists from the Rhine are the introduction of the rifle, the *conestoga wagon* and the *stove* to replace the English fireplace.

From all northwestern Europe, farmers poured into the Colonies during the eighteenth century, settling from the Mohawk Valley to Pennsylvania and in the back country of Maryland. Here lay the largest bodies of rich land, with a familiar climate, convenient to the seaboard. All the accustomed crops and livestock of Europe thrived here. The Old World pattern of *general farming*, with emphasis on the

[1] Paullin, *op. cit.*, Plate 82, maps A-H.

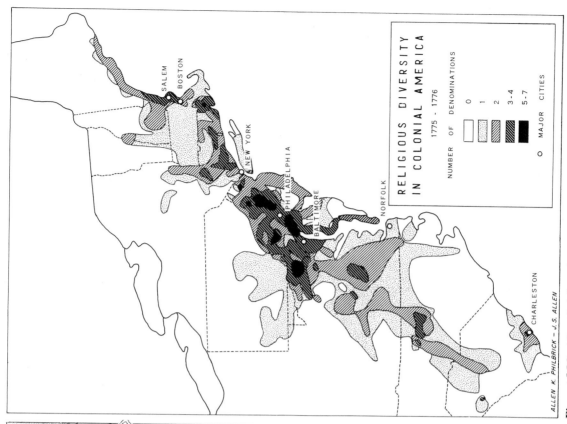

Figure 189. (*Compiled from data in the Atlas of the Historical Geography of the United States, by Charles O. Paullin, published jointly by The Carnegie Institution and The American Geographical Society.*)

RELIGIOUS DIVERSITY
IN COLONIAL AMERICA

1775 - 1776

NUMBER OF DENOMINATIONS

- 0
- 1
- 2
- 3-4
- 5-7

○ MAJOR CITIES

ALLEN K. PHILBRICK – J.S. ALLEN

SALEM
BOSTON
NEW YORK
PHILADELPHIA
BALTIMORE
NORFOLK
CHARLESTON

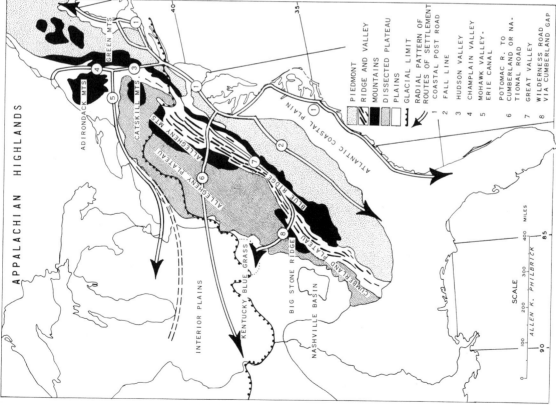

APPALACHIAN HIGHLANDS

PIEDMONT
RIDGE AND VALLEY
MOUNTAINS
DISSECTED PLATEAU
PLAINS
GLACIAL LIMIT
RADIAL PATTERN OF
ROUTES OF SETTLEMENT

1 COASTAL POST ROAD
2 FALL LINE
3 HUDSON VALLEY
4 CHAMPLAIN VALLEY
5 MOHAWK VALLEY-
ERIE CANAL
6 POTOMAC R. TO
CUMBERLAND OR NA-
TIONAL ROAD
7 GREAT VALLEY
8 WILDERNESS ROAD
VIA CUMBERLAND GAP

GREEN MTS
ADIRONDACK MTS
CATSKILL MTS
ALLEGHENY MTS
ALLEGHENY PLATEAU
BLUE RIDGE
CUMBERLAND PLATEAU
BIG STONE RIDGE
KENTUCKY BLUE GRASS
NASHVILLE BASIN
INTERIOR PLAINS
ATLANTIC COASTAL PLAIN

40
35

SCALE
0   100   200   300   400
MILES
90   85

ALLEN K. PHILBRICK

Figure 188

319

feeding of livestock was transferred here to the New World with one major modification—*Indian corn* was fitted quickly into the agricultural economy and greatly increased the livestock capacity of the farms. Maize was found to be a stock feed superior to anything known then or now in northern Europe. Corn, oats, wheat, rye, clover, and European grains formed a crop combination that provided the means of keeping more livestock and of obtaining and sustaining high yields. In late colonial and post-colonial time, these general crop and stock farmers spread this basic American way of farming westward and southwestward. . . .[1]

Regional Organization of the United States in 1790.

The tendency of the people in the former colonies, with their separate sectional backgrounds, was to continue locally along lines of economic development which had been characteristic of them before national union. The problem of developing and maintaining the unity of the new nation was of the greatest importance. Practically all of the people in 1790—94.9 per cent—were engaged in agriculture and the nature of farm life was primarily a matter of local subsistence organization. Philadelphia, the largest city in 1775, had no more than 35,000 persons, including its surrounding village suburbs. What, then, comprised the regional organization of the United States in about 1800?

The map in Figure 190 shows the area organization of the nation within the first generation of its existence. The limits of settlement are those of 1790, while the town and city pattern is that of 1800. The major post roads are taken from an 1804 map in Paullin's *Atlas of the Historical Geography of the United States.* The major migration routes show a basically radial pattern, within which they focus on the Baltimore-to-New-York region, the heart of the middle colonial "melting pot" previously discussed. To the northeast lies Boston and the post road into Maine. To the north is the Connecticut Valley of New England. In New York are the north-south Hudson Valley route and the Yankee-settled Mohawk Valley route west from Albany. The Susquehanna and Juniata Valley routes to Pittsburgh extend west of Philadelphia. From Pittsburgh a route northwestward reaches Lake Erie at Cleveland. The site of Cleveland had already been surveyed by Moses Cleaveland for the Connecticut Land Company in 1796. The major tidewater route connecting the original coastal settlements goes south from Baltimore toward a future Florida. Fall-line settlements are interconnected by

a route along the back edge of the coastal plain. To the west and southwest the Piedmont and the Blue Ridge Mountains are breached by the Cumberland Gap from the Great Valley and the valley of the Shenandoah. This is the route of Boone's road which lead to the Kentucky-Ohio River country.

There is a vast difference, however, between the *appearance* of radial interconnections from the central to the peripheral parts of the country indicated by these routes in the year 1800 and the *actual* movement of people and goods between these same and other parts of the country at that time. Land travel by wagon or stage could only be described as "very rough" along all but the best-developed routes, such as that from Boston south through New York to Philadelphia and Baltimore. No large quantity of material goods moved over land.[2] The carrying of letters over the post-road system by established stage lines and on horseback represented the maximum in transportation of items any great distance between overland points. The importance of livestock in the otherwise subsistence farm economy lay in the fact that cattle could be driven to market—a product which provided its own transportation. There was a close-in limit to the "reach" of any economic activities which involved more than local division of labor. The tendency was for people in each local economy first to develop exchange among producers and consumers within their own immediate territories.

Certainly, therefore, we must say that the United States in the beginning was economically characterized by local *subsistence* area organization. The overwhelming number of the citizenry lived by their own efforts, within the territory of their own homesteads, estates, or plantations. In the beginning

[1] Sauer, *op. cit.,* p. 165. (Italics are the present author's.)

[2] Wilbert Lee Anderson, in *Country Town,* p. 20, quoted by Bureau of the Census in *A Century of Population Growth,* Washington, 1909, p. 26, said: "Merchandise and produce that could not stand a freight charge of $15.00 per ton could not be carried overland to a consumer 150 miles from the point of production; as roads were, a distance of 50 miles from market often made industrial independence expedient. Where the produce of the farm could not be sold, where wood and lumber were not marketable, the people had no recourse but to raise their own wool and flax, and spin and weave and make their own clothing. Other crafts felt these influences, although the working of wood and metals and leather fell to skilled artisans in the villages rather than to the household. The local store had a small traffic in articles that could not be produced, and in luxuries. Salt fish was widely distributed; rum went everywhere, salt was a universal necessity; tools and utensils and furniture were imported; a few articles of dress carried the style of the city to the hamlet, so insignificant was the traffic uniting the country town to the great world."

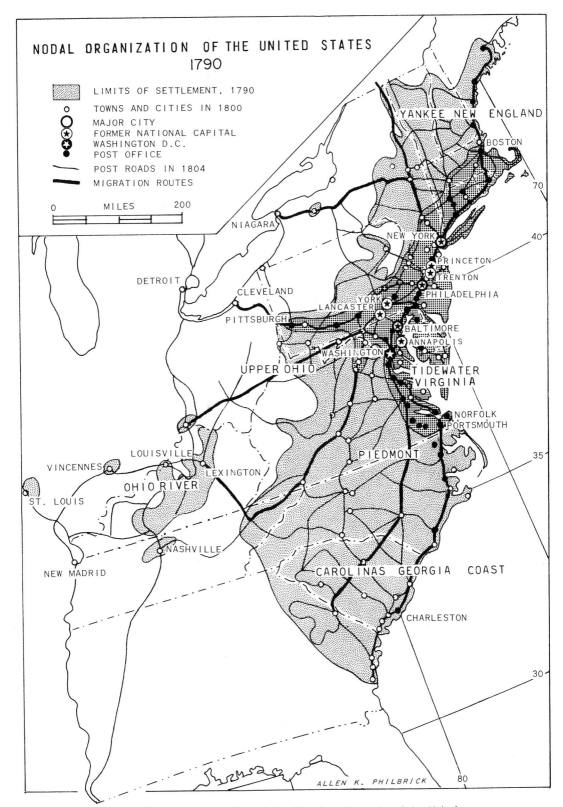

Figure 190. (*Compiled from data in the* Atlas of the Historical Geography of the United States, *by Charles O. Paullin, published jointly by the Carnegie Institution and the American Geographical Society.*)

organization of area beyond the ordering of the establishment within the communities and local regions was more in the *social* and *political* spheres than in *economic* functions. The focus on town meeting and church, for example, in the Puritan townships provided the initial functional organization of area beyond that of the individual farm. In Virginia the focus of the tidewater plantation life on the social and political functions of a center such as Williamsburg was the first step of internal area organization larger than that of the individual plantation. The development of the retail business districts in villages and small cities, as places where farmers and townspeople alike could be supplied with most of the necessities of life, as is the case today, was a later development.

The first regional focuses were on colonial capitals and port cities. The most important economic centers were ports, because through them external connections were maintained. The seven largest were Boston, Philadelphia, New York, Baltimore, Norfolk, Salem, and Charleston. Fifteen ports accounted for practically all of the shipping in 1790. The two Massachusetts ports of Boston and Salem alone received 26 per cent of the total tonnage entering American ports, did 35 per cent of the total United States export trade, and 53 per cent of the coastal shipping. Those two ports, along with New York, Philadelphia, Norfolk, Alexandria, and Baltimore accounted for 76 per cent of the tonnage entering American ports in 1790. It has been estimated that exports from Philadelphia at this time exceeded in value those from any other port, on the basis of the quantities of flour and wheat exported to the West Indies.[1]

The first national focus was political and came in connection with revolutionary unity and action against the British. The focus of political area organization was in Philadelphia which had been seat of the Continental Congress of 1774–1775 and 1776. There were only twenty-four places with more than 2,500 people in the entire country at the time of the first census in 1790. Of these, seven cities of over 8,000 people accounted for more than two-thirds of the country's entire urban population. New York, Boston, and Philadelphia accounted for nearly half (46 per cent) of the urban population. They were also the three largest port cities and contained the only banks in the nation, one in each city. The political capital shifted a number of times

between July 4, 1776, and 1800 when Washington, D.C., became the national capital. It is significant that the nine separate locations within a quarter of a century were all within the Middle Colonies. They were Philadelphia; Trenton and Princeton, New Jersey; Annapolis, Maryland; York and Lancaster in Pennsylvania; Baltimore; New York; and Washington, D.C. Since political area organization dominated national function, the national core region has been defined on the map in Figure 190 in terms of the series of capital cities from New York to Washington. This very same alignment persists within the larger national core region today.

The focus of subregions on the core region was primarily political, in that former colonies, now states with sectional interests, sought support from the national government. Five major sections of the country were politically united by leadership from the core, which consisted of the former Middle colonies and southern New England colonies as shown by the map. The peripheral regions were the Yankee region of upper New England and upper New York, Tidewater Virginia, the shallow-water coasts of the Carolinas and Georgia, the Piedmont from North Carolina through Georgia, and the trans-Appalachian region of the upper Ohio, mostly in Kentucky, from Pittsburgh, Pennsylvania, to New Madrid at the mouth of the Ohio River on the Mississippi.

An estimate of the value of the total real and personal property in the United States in 1805, which was politically organized and controlled from Philadelphia, is shown in Table XXXII. Study of the table shows that the small proportion of the total population living in cities (5.1 per cent in 1790) must have functioned through local or at most local-regional rather than national economic organization of area. Functional organization on a national scale was primarily political and in only a small degree economic. The single largest economic item in the national economy was the *public domain*. More than one-third of the total national wealth lay in potentially developable land beyond the frontier, under the control and direction of the federal government. At the same time, by far the greatest proportion of the already developed assets of the country fell within the subsistence category of area organization.

In the early period, as can be seen from the map in Figure 190, the basic pattern and some of the facilities (such as roads and a pattern of governmental postal service, leading cities, and ports) had

---

[1] U. S. Bureau of the Census, *op. cit.*, p. 30.

already assumed the basic importance which they have in the highly developed national economic organization of area today; but the development of this national *economic* area organization did not commence until after 1820.

Evolution of Settlement in the Forested Continental Interior

Daniel Boone's wilderness road tempted frontiersmen from the first frontier region which was east of the Appalachian highlands in the Piedmont through the Cumberland Gap into Kentucky. The trans-Appalachian migration began before the American Revolution and continued through the hostilities in the face of Indian attack. The geographic significance of the evolution of settlement in the forested interior will be discussed under four main headings: territorial acquisitions, cultural replacement, emergence of three new regions, and the pattern of area organization in 1860.

United States Territorial Acquisition. Acquisition of territories brought the area of the United States to the Rocky Mountains on the west by 1845 and to the Pacific coast a year later. The largest area, that of the Louisiana Purchase, was acquired in 1803 from France. Motivation of the purchase was to secure for the United States the mouth of the Mississippi. Trans-Appalachian settlement early demonstrated the importance of the Mississippi River system in providing avenues of transportation. Spain had previously ceded the Louisiana Territory to France in an effort to block expansion of the United States of America toward the west. Sale of the Louisiana territory to the United States by France brought about the purchase of Florida from Spain in 1821, and led ultimately to the acquisition of Texas in 1845. Three years later Mexico sold to the United States the southwestern territory including California. In 1846 the United States and England compromised on the forty-ninth parallel as the boundary from Lake of the Woods, Minnesota, to the Pacific coast, which extinguished English claims to the Oregon Territory. The Gadsden Purchase in 1853 and the Alaska purchase from Russia in 1867 completed the continental territory of the United States. Long before the Civil War the present territorial extent of the United States, except for Hawaii in 1898 and Alaska in 1867, had been established.

The Louisiana Purchase of 1803 set the pattern for the future. Emphasis shifted from the Atlantic seaboard to the interior lowlands. The steady west-

TABLE **XXXII**   AN ESTIMATE OF ALL THE REAL AND PERSONAL PROPERTY IN THE UNITED STATES (EXCLUSIVE OF LOUISIANA TERRITORY), 1805[a]

Item	Millions of dollars	Per cent
Total valuation for 1805	2,505.5	100
Items involved in primarily *subsistence organization* of family establishments:		
1 million of habitations and apparel for 6 million persons with shops, barns, implements, tools, furniture, etc., each $360	360.0	14.3
39 million acres of lands, averaged at $6	234.0	9.3
150 million acres adjoining and near the cultivated lands averaged at $3.50	525.0	20.9
1 million slaves, average value $200	200.0	8.0
Carriages and all livestock at $70 each family	70.0	2.8
Subtotal	1,389.0	55.3
Items involved primarily in local or regional *exchange* organization at the community or city level:		
Stock in trade: 1 million tons shipping; European, India merchandise, etc. specie, bank stock, insurance stock, and all incorporated funds	150.0	6.0
Country produce on hand for export, manufacturing, etc.	26.0	1.0
10,000 flour, grist, saw, iron, and other mills, value no less than $400 each	4.0	0.2
Turnpike, canal, and toll bridge stock	15.0	0.6
Subtotal	195.0	7.8
Items involved primarily in *national political and social area organization*		
Public buildings, churches, Washington city lots, arsenals, naval and military stores, arms, ammunition, frigates dock yards, timber, etc.	19.5	0.8
451 million acres, the residue of all lands in the United States, averaged at $2 per acre	902.0	36.0
Subtotal	921.5	36.8
Total	2,505.5	100.0

[a] This table is modified from one by Samuel Blodget, *Economica: A Statistical Manual for the United States of America*, 1806, p. 196, quoted in Bureau of the Census, *Historical Statistics of the United States, 1789–1945*, Washington: U. S. Government Printing Office, 1949, p. 1.

ward withdrawal of the American Indians in the face of the advancing frontier of settlement demonstrates the transfer of *control* in one hundred years from the American Indian to the descendants of those revolutionaries who founded the new nation in 1783.

Cultural Replacement. Basic differences in values and ways of life induced early settlement of the piedmont frontier and then migration across the Appalachians south of the Ohio River in the Kentucky part of Virginia. These differences included value differences between landed aristocracy and backwoods democracy, and also a struggle for land. The land struggle occurred between two systems of occupancy—plantation production for a money crop, and homestead subsistence farming. As long as there was free land to the west there was little doubt of the outcome. The homesteaders endlessly moved on. They were continually beckoned by their perception of the inherent qualities of western lands. They were attracted, for example, by the wild game of the Kentucky Bluegrass region and of the Nashville Basin in what was later to become Tennessee—game which was supported by the rich limestone soils. Before European settlement these areas had no permanent human occupants, for Indian culture found in these same resources the advantages of common hunting grounds for a number of tribes. In terms of game, therefore, both areas mentioned proved attractive to Indian and Virginia hunters alike. In the ensuing struggle between those two cultures, the Virginia backwoodsman drove away the Indian and settled the land to homestead farms.

Up to the time of their separation from Virginia the life of Kentucky's pioneers was in a certain way exceedingly rude; the greater part of the population was packed into the rustic castles . . . termed stations, of which there were two or three hundred within the State. Each of these places contained one or more dwelling houses and a "corral" so arranged with stockades and loopholes as to make a stronghold good against Indian assaults. There were usually from ten to fifty men at each station,—enough to make a good defense until succor could arrive. This rendered a certain crowding of the population necessary, which endured until it became safe to trust to the separate farm house, so dear to the English heart. It is surprising that the fortified station did not lead to some desire for village life such as we find in Europe; but as soon as the Indian depredations became even a little slackened, the people isolated themselves, as it had been their wont in Virginia. A lonely house in the middle of a great farm was their ideal, and they attained it even before it could be had with safety.[1]

The first step of cultural replacement was the subsistence homesteader who replaced the subsistence Indian hunter. This was followed, in turn, by the replacement of the homesteader by the planter and the commercial-crop economy which soon occupied the better land. North and south of the Ohio Valley a single rather than double replacement was typical, that of Indian culture by European culture.

The Growth of Three New Regions. The result of cultural replacement west of the Appalachians brought into being three new regions—the Middle West, the Middle South, and the Deep South. Migration into the upper Ohio through Pennsylvania to Fort Duquesne, later called Pittsburgh, involved homesteaders from the Middle Colonies. The Ohio country soon came to serve one of the functions previously performed by the seaboard Middle Colonies, that of meeting ground between the western extension of the plantation system of the south and the western extension of the Yankees from New England with their rapid development of commercialism.

The westward expansion of settlement types from New England and the Plantation South began the evolution of two modern regions, the Middle West and the Deep South. These two very important territories lay north and south, respectively, of the westward extension of population which was first to cross the Appalachians into the Ohio River country. The map in Figure 191 shows the limits of the Yankee North, the plantation South, and a middle ground which can be called the Middle South located in the Ohio Valley, as their respective frontiers were moved westward.

Double cultural replacement continued in the Ohio country or Middle South. As tobacco culture was brought across the Appalachians into Kentucky and Tennessee, the frontiersmen moved across the river into southern parts of Ohio, Indiana, and Illinois. Concurrently, northern parts of Ohio, Indiana, Illinois, and southern Michigan and Wisconsin were receiving a similar stream of Yankee settlers from New England by way of upper New York state. The two streams of culture, homestead frontiersmen of the southern Piedmont and to some extent of the western South and the Yankee townsmen of New

[1] N. S. Shaler, *Kentucky*, Boston: Houghton Mifflin and Co., 1915, p. 116.

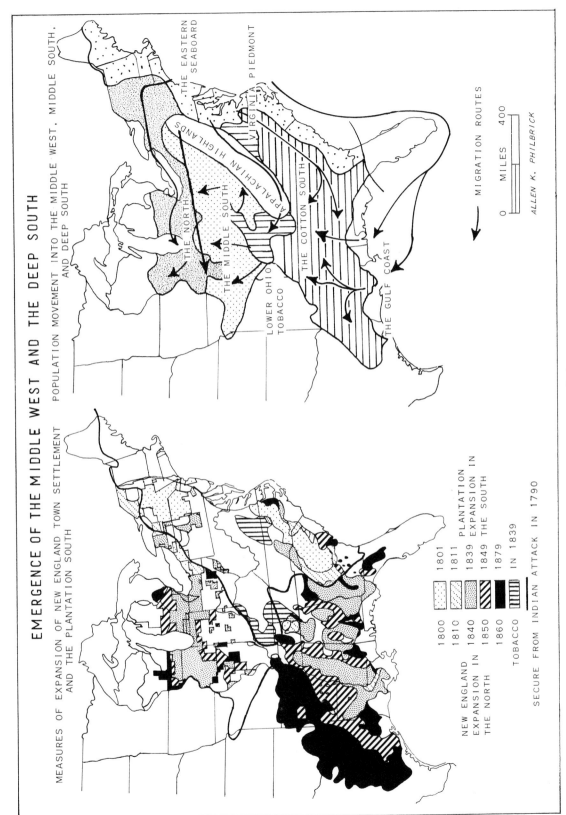

Figure 191. *(Compiled from data in the* Atlas of the Historical Geography of the United States, *by Charles O. Paullin, published jointly by* The Carnegie Institution *and* The American Geographical Society.*)*

England, met in the Middle West. Although they at first distrusted one another, the frontiersman and the Yankee eventually proved closer to one another in ideals and ways of life than either independently were to the ideals and interests of the southern planters.

In the North the first phase of settlement in the Middle West was also the subsistence homestead. A farm garden was wrested from the forest and followed as rapidly as possible by production of surplus wheat, corn, and livestock. As soon as transportation could be devised the surplus was sold outside the region.

In the South, gangs of Negro slaves cleared forests for new plantation lands during the mild winters, and planted, hoed, and worked cotton during the long growing seasons of the summer. The resource bases for cotton production—growing season, rainfall, and the better soils areas within the South—have proven to be important historically in the evolving pattern of cotton, which may be selected as the single most important item of production in understanding the initial settlement of the Deep South. Cotton is a long-growing-season crop, which uses from 200–260 frost-free days. Moisture requirements are reasonably flexible as to amounts for the year, but seasonal distribution is more critical for the life cycle of the plant. Light rains after planting, moderate showers-type rainfall during growth of the cotton bush to maturity, with a maximum of sunshine during the day time, and a cool, dry ripening and harvest period are optimal conditions. Within this description totals of precipitation may vary from as little as 20 to as much as 60 inches per year. The crop does very well under controlled moisture conditions of irrigation in the Southwest. Within these resource conditions a particular series of soils proved to be especially attractive to cotton planters. By 1860 these fertile alluviums as well as the better-drained upland soils districts had all been cleared and occupied for cotton production. The Gulf Coast margins are outside the cotton belt, as precipitation and humidity are excessive. Also wind damage and lack of a prolonged winter frost to kill or check insect pests proved to be disadvantages.

While it would be misleading to think of the plantation system and cotton as completely representing the economy of the antebellum South, the system of production based on leadership in these regards certainly set the direction of development. Multiple criteria of the map in Figure 191 shows

the extension of the plantation system in the South in terms of cotton and the expansion of the New England Yankee in the North. The map in Figure 191 also shows a similar progression of the tobacco plantation acreage in the Ohio Valley country of Kentucky and Tennessee. Similarly, the map in Figure 192 shows the emergence of wheat and corn belts in the Middle West north of the Ohio. From the overlapping patterns of corn and wheat production in the years 1839 and 1859, it is evident that the opening of new lands to production extended wheat and corn westward to the Mississippi River by 1860. Wheat production is shown to be generally located northward of the emerging outlines of the corn belt.

According to Everett E. Edwards,[1]

Until the prairies of western Indiana and Illinois were reached, the farming in pioneer communities west of the Alleghenies was essentially a repetition of the experience along the Atlantic seaboard during the two centuries of the colonial period. The frontiersman cleared 1–3 acres by girdling and grubbing and then planted the field to vegetables and corn. At this stage the family depended on game and other wild products to supplement the food raised. With more land cleared, additional corn and some wheat were added. Gradually a farm capable of producing surpluses for outside markets was developed.

The responsiveness of wheat to new lands is patent to students of agricultural tendencies, and its development in the region northwest of the Ohio River is an excellent illustration. . . . By 1860 the five states of the Old Northwest were supplying about half of the wheat produced in the entire United States. Within the region, the hilly counties of Ohio and the prairies and oak openings of Indiana, Michigan, Illinois, and Wisconsin were the areas of concentration. . . .

Corn production, like that of wheat, responded, though less quickly to the pull of the new lands of the Northwest. In general it tended to occupy a belt directly south of the wheat region, but prior to the end of the sixties a corn belt was not clearly delimited except for special areas, such as the rich bottom lands along the Scioto River and the limestone basins of Kentucky and Tennessee. The census of 1840 revealed Kentucky, Tennessee, and Virginia as the leading corn states, but within two decades the center of concentration had shifted northwestward to Illinois, Ohio, Missouri, and Indiana, with Kentucky and Tennessee in fifth and sixth place. . . .

[1] Everett E. Edwards, "American Agriculture—The First 300 Years," *Farmers in a Changing World*, United States Dept. of Agriculture, Washington, D.C.: U. S. Government Printing Office, 1940, pp. 202–205.

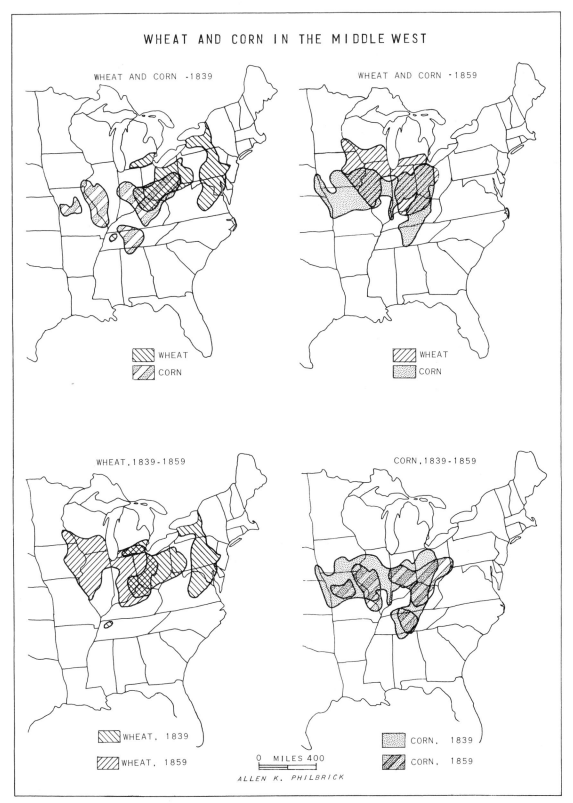

WHEAT AND CORN IN THE MIDDLE WEST

WHEAT AND CORN - 1839

WHEAT AND CORN - 1859

⬜ WHEAT
⬜ CORN

⬜ WHEAT
⬜ CORN

WHEAT, 1839-1859

CORN, 1839-1859

⬜ WHEAT, 1839
⬜ WHEAT, 1859

⬜ CORN, 1839
⬜ CORN, 1859

0   MILES   400

ALLEN K. PHILBRICK

Figure 192. (*Compiled from data in the* Atlas of the Historical Geography of the United States, *by Charles O. Paullin, published jointly by The Carnegie Institution and The American Geographical Society.*)

The corn of this northwestward-moving belt was marketed in the form of whiskey and hogs, the first because it was valuable in proportion to bulk and the second because hogs furnished their own motive power. The hogs of the frontier were a special type, essentially a product of the rigors of life in the open and were known aptly as "wind splitters," or razor backs. Many pioneers raised several hundred hogs a year. If they were left to feed on the forest mast alone, however, besides putting on flesh that was soft and difficult to preserve, they became untractable and without the stamina to survive the rigors of severe winters. It was therefore essential to supplement the mast with corn, and eventually, as markets developed, corn-feeding and marketing hogs became the basic activities of agriculture in the Old Northwest.

In the early nineteenth century the hogs were taken down the rivers on boats to be sold to the plantations in the South or driven overland to eastern markets. At first the farmers drove their own hogs eastward, but gradually a profession of drovers developed and the trade became standardized. Some herds numbered as many as 5,000 and moved eastward at the rate of 8 or 10 miles a day. Although the ultimate destination was usually Philadelphia, Baltimore, or New York, many herds were taken to the plantation of Tennessee, Virginia, and the Carolinas. This method of marketing declined with the development of meat packing along the Ohio, especially centering upon Cincinnati, which became known as "Porkopolis." The coming of the railroads was the final factor ending this trade.

A similar evolution occurred in the range-cattle industry. . . . The Bluegrass region of Kentucky and the Scioto Valley were the centers for corn feeding, and many of the leaders in this development were former Virginians who had known of similar methods on the banks of the Potomac in the days of Washington. Eventually these feeders reached out for additional stock from the prairies of Illinois, Iowa, and Missouri and from the wheat farmers to the northward. Before large-scale refrigeration, it was difficult to preserve beef in a palatable form, and beef packing did not develop on a scale comparable with that of pork. The eastern cattle drives, therefore, continued long after the hog drives had ceased. The advent of rail roads after 1850 brought an end to the drives, and the cattle feeding industry pushed westward to the Corn Belt.

The Pattern of Regional Organization of the United States in 1860.

The 1790 pattern of regional organization was political and its radial appearance was more potential than actual. As the nation developed, a basic conflict between the commercial-industrial Northeast and the plantation-slave system of agricultural production in the South emerged. The two sections of the country complemented one another but were also set against each other.

As already indicated the two extremes represented by New England and the southern tidewater regions overlapped in the Middle Colonies; and counterparts for each of the three seaboard regions developed in the forested interior. The geographical stage was being set for the Civil War between the North and the South. Before this took place, however, a triangular relationship developed which was transitional between the initial political regional organization of the country and the radial political-economic organization of the present day. This triangular regional organization was based on three paired relationships among the country's three most important sections—the Northeast, the Middle West, and the South. The evolving pattern of regional organization in the United States by 1860 can best be understood by portraying the complementary regional relationships between these three sections of the country.

The developing core region. The spread of the English industrial revolution to the New World, as might be expected, took root in New England and in the former Middle Colonies. It was not accident that one Samuel Slater, a mechanic with experience in the spinning factory of Sir Richard Arkwright in England, brought the "know how" for the construction of spinning machinery to New England. In 1789 he built from memory the machines to equip the first machine-operated cotton mill in North America. The factory was constructed with the capital of a rich Quaker merchant in Providence, Rhode Island. The invention by another New Englander, Eli Whitney, in 1793 made it economically feasible to process the short-fibered cotton of the American upland South. The cotton gin was thus indirectly responsible for the spread of slavery westward in the South. The institution of slavery, in order to be profitable, required the growing of a commercial crop with a steady market as well as cheap land and labor for its success. Cotton, western virgin soils of the South, and the Negro slave provided these three prerequisites. Cotton became more important as a commercial plantation crop for export than tobacco had proven to be in Tidewater Virginia during the colonial and postcolonial period. Cotton from the American upland South made the English Lancashire mills the most important in the world. It also supplied the expanding cotton-milling industry of New England.

Manufacturing based on American innovations as

well as the spread of the ideas of the English industrial revolution developed rapidly after the War of 1812. The most active manufacturing and commercial region of the country by 1860 was considerably extended from the political core region of 1790. The map in Figure 193 shows a new pattern of regional organization which had developed by the end of the Civil War in 1860. From a coastal core in 1790, the core region by 1860 stretched west to Lakes Ontario and Erie. This growth was largely the result of the opening of the Erie Canal through the Mohawk Valley of upper central New York state in 1825. New York and Philadelphia were still the two largest cities as well as the most important centers of manufacturing. However, the number of important smaller manufacturing centers had increased from seven in 1839 to twenty-two in 1859. One of two insets to the map in Figure 193 shows that the cotton-spinning industry by 1840 had begun to spread from the New England states into the Mohawk Valley and along the urban axis of the country from New York to Baltimore. The beginning concentration of the iron and steel industry in Pennsylvania and the upper Ohio by 1857 is shown by the second inset to Figure 193.

Accessibility, all important in the development of an exchange economy, is another index of the expansion of the core region of the United States by 1860. Two lines on the map show the increase between 1830 and 1857 in one day's travel distance possible from New York. By 1857 it was possible in a single day to travel from New York to Bangor, Maine, in the northeast; to Washington, D.C., on the south, or to Cleveland, Ohio, on the west. The core region, defined on the basis of the railroad pattern of 1850, extended from Bath, Maine, on the north, Buffalo on the west, and Washington, D.C., on the south. Water and road transportation routes were also developed. The Erie Canal connecting the Hudson River with Lake Erie by way of the Mohawk Valley was completed through New York state in 1825 (Figure 194). A great overland road, named the Cumberland Road, was surfaced by 1840. The name was derived from the town of that name on the Potomac River in western Maryland and is not to be confused with Daniel Boone's route. The road connected Vandalia, Illinois, with Baltimore, Philadelphia, and New York.

The development of transportation in peripheral regions. The development of cities and manufacturing in the Northeast affected the evolution of agriculture in the continental interior. Both the plantation agriculture of the South and the urban centers of the North increasingly became markets for grain and livestock products from the trans-Appalachian Middle West (Figure 195). Settlers in the interior found transport near at hand in the form of the great rivers of the Mississippi drainage system. The Ohio, the Mississippi, and other tributaries became avenues of traffic down which immense quantities of corn, pork, and other staples moved to the plantation South, and up which came manufactured good transhipped from the Northeast by way of east-coast shipping. The success of Fulton's steamboat on the Hudson River in 1810 was followed immediately by its introduction in 1811 on the Ohio River. The generally north-south alignment of the Mississippi and the northeast-southwest alignment of the Ohio implemented the emergence of new axes of trade and the rise of river cities such as Cincinnati and Louisville on the Ohio, and St. Louis, Memphis, and New Orleans on the Mississippi.

In addition to the railroad pattern of the national core region, other railroad networks were developed regionally by 1860 which focused traffic within peripheral regions. In the Southeast, for example, a rail network served the Virginian and North Carolina Piedmont, and a connection by rail was in operation from Charleston-Savannah to Atlanta, Chattanooga, and Memphis. River orientation of traffic is indicated by the existence of east-to-west feeder lines to the Mississippi at Vicksburg and New Orleans. As early as 1850 the Ohio Valley region showed rail feeders to Cincinnati from Sandusky and Cleveland on Lake Erie, and to the Ohio River from Indianapolis. The decade from 1850 to 1860 saw the Middle West emerge with a rail network second to none in the country. In 1850 rail connection from Detroit had reached New Buffalo on Lake Michigan. A rail line extended half-way across southern Michigan from Toledo. The first railroad out of Chicago was built west of the city to tap the Illinois River farm country in 1850; but by 1860 Chicago had become the dominant hub of a rail network with connections to New Orleans and to New York. The net effectively blanketed the region between the Mississippi and Ohio Rivers south of a line from Milwaukee to Detroit.

Triangular interregional trade. A three-fold inter-regional trade developed between the Northeast, the South, and the Middle West, which clearly expresses the regional organization of the United

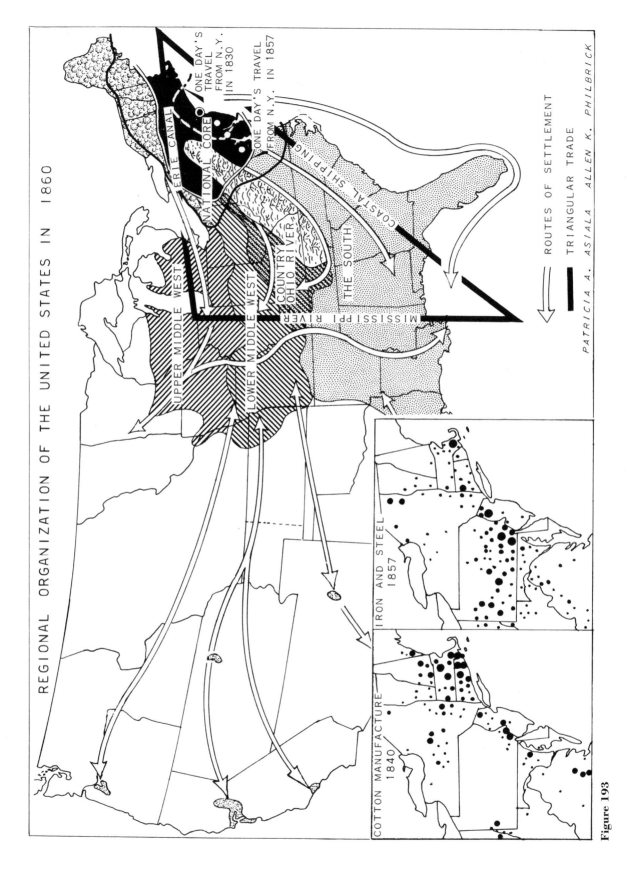

REGIONAL ORGANIZATION OF THE UNITED STATES IN 1860

ONE DAY'S TRAVEL FROM N.Y. IN 1830

ONE DAY'S TRAVEL FROM N.Y. IN 1857

ERIE CANAL

NATIONAL CORE

COASTAL SHIPPING

UPPER MIDDLE WEST

LOWER MIDDLE WEST

OHIO RIVER COUNTRY

THE SOUTH

MISSISSIPPI RIVER

ROUTES OF SETTLEMENT

TRIANGULAR TRADE

PATRICIA A. ASIALA   ALLEN K. PHILBRICK

IRON AND STEEL 1857

COTTON MANUFACTURE 1840

Figure 193

Figure 194. From the time of Washington's first term in 1789, the idea of a canal linking New York via the Hudson and Mohawk Valleys was thought of as a means of linking the trans-Appalachian "West" with the Eastern Seaboard. Completed in 1825, this project was nearly two generations in the realization. To this day, the route of the canal is the main line of the nation's core region, occupied by the New York Central Railway, the New York Throughway, the New York State Barge Canal (successor to the Erie Canal) and an alignment of upstate New York cities from Buffalo, Rochester, Syracuse, Utica, Rome, Schenectady-Albany-Troy, to New York City. (*Courtesy of Culver Pictures, Inc.*)

States in 1860. Cotton moved to New England from the South, while manufactured goods moved to the South from the Northeast. Coastal shipping was the traditional axis of this trade. The agricultural surplus of the Middle West moved partly to the South and partly to the urban Northeast. In return, manufactured goods moved westward and imports were transhipped northward on the Mississippi from New Orleans (Figure 196).

In addition to the complementary three-way trade pattern, of course, the fatal flaw in this transitional situation lay in unsettled issues of cultural value between the "commercialism" of the North and the "plantation system" of the South. The cultural replacement which drove the Southern frontiersman into the arms of the Yankee Middle Westerners may well have been the decisive underlying balance of forces in the victory of the North in the Civil War. The geographical significance of

the pattern of regional organization of 1860 lies in its background for the present regional organization of the country. By 1860, as well, the trans-Mississippian West contained the frontier of westward settlement in a different kind of environment. This huge territory, more than half of the continental United States, was largely uninhabited, but already contained nuclei of five important present-day regions. These were the Pacific Northwest, the San Francisco Bay area, the Los Angeles area, the Salt Lake oasis, and the Denver-Santa Fe region.

The Settlement of the Grasslands

By 1850 the settlement of the interior plains had reached the western margins of the virgin forest lands of North America. The maps in Figure 197 show the extent of virgin timber in 1620, 1850, and the extent of improved land in 1850.[1] The

[1] Paullin, *op. cit.*, Plates 3A–B and 144C.

Figure 195. This American farm scene, from a Currier and Ives print of 1853, shows the kind of farm which was both self-sufficient and a source of commerical livestock and grain. (*Courtesy of the Harry T. Peters Collection, Museum of the City of New York.*)

Figure 196. The Queen of the West, "rounding the bend," illustrates the great flotilla of Mississippi river boats which carried freight and passengers on America's great interior-plains river system between the North and the South. (*Courtesy of the Harry T. Peters Collection, Museum of the City of New York.*)

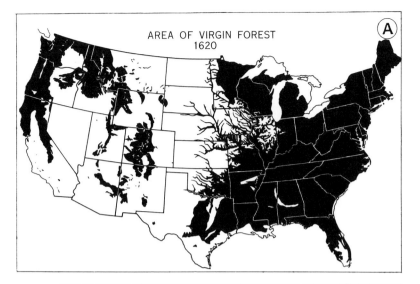

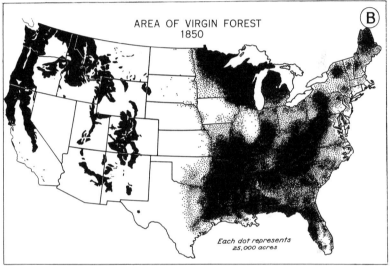

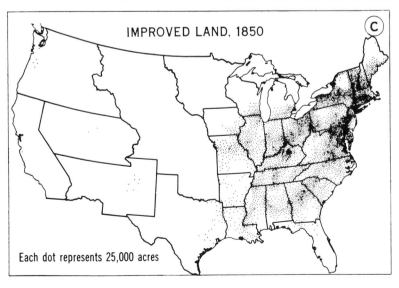

latter two maps of Figure 197 are comparable. (Each dot equals 25,000 acres.) It is readily apparent that nearly everywhere except in the older settled portions of the country along the eastern seaboard, along the upper Ohio near the Pennsylvania border, and in the Kentucky Bluegrass, the total land area in forests still exceeded the area in improved agricultural land. The composite map in Figure 198A shows, however, the great westward extension of improved land by decades from 1850 to 1920 after the end of World War I.

Important Differences between Forest and Grassland Phases of Settlement. The grassland phase of the settlement of the interior plains of North America was quite different from the forest phase. The first phase, from the Revolution to the eve of the American Civil War, occurred in the humid East. It saw the transplanting of the three major cultural groups—New England Yankees, the Middle Colonial and Piedmont homesteader, and the Southern planters—into the interior of the country. It detailed the emergence of the basic struggle between the capitalism of the Yankee North with the feudal economy of the South. The westward push of settlement always preceded the development of means of transportation to tie them to previously settled areas of the East.

The second phase of the settlement of the interior plains of North America was different in at least *three* important respects. First, it involved the less humid and arid western half of the country which was characterized by grass rather than forest vegetation, an environment to which Americans of European origin were totally strange. Settlers, accordingly, clung to the forested land. Forests were prized because it was believed such lands were more fertile than grasslands. Forest provided building materials, partial cover from wind and strong sun or bitter winters. Once the timber was even partially removed, forest soils were relatively easy to plow. By contrast the heavy grasses and thick sod of the wetter prairies adjacent to the forest were almost impossible to penetrate with the wooden plow, and were very difficult to turn even with the cast-iron plow. The main obstacle to early settlement of the grassland was the negative attitude of people toward such resources. The potentially rich fertile grasslands were considered to be the "great American desert."

Second, by the time settlement of the humid prairie grasslands of the Middle West was fairly started (1850–1860), the Civil War intervened and

the great issue of the *unity* of America over the question of slavery and the fundamental direction of national development was settled in favor of the North. In the westward sweep of settlement regional divisions of the country had taken the form of east-west trending strips in rows from north to south, representing the westward expansion of cultures of New England, the Middle Colonies, and the plantation South. This pattern ended at approximately the one-hundredth meridian in the middle of the Great Plains states from North Dakota to Oklahoma and Texas.

Third, by the time settlement of the grasslands began, population had leap-frogged both the grasslands and the mountains to the Pacific coast. They went to prospect for gold in California during the Gold Rush after 1848 and to settle in the forested lands of Oregon after the 1846 treaty with England which settled on the forty-ninth parallel as the United States' northern border, west to the Pacific. Pioneer trails overland were followed by the Pony Express, overland stagecoaches, and the transcontinental railroad in the short space of twenty-one years from 1848 to 1869, the year which saw the completion of the Union Pacific Railroad (Figure 198B), binding the west coast more firmly to the East. The success of the first transcontinental railroad was soon followed by four similar lines. The trans-Mississippian West had facilities for relatively rapid and dependable transportation *before* rather than *after* the beginning of intensive settlement, which was different from the situation which had earlier prevailed in the East.

Patterns of improved agricultural land by decades from 1850 to 1920, shown by the map in Figure 198A, demonstrate strong relationship to the pattern of transcontinental railroads. The heavy line marking the edge of the eastern forested lands corresponds closely to the frontier of improved land at the beginning of this period in 1850. The easternmost bulge of the grasslands into the forested East in Iowa and northern and central Illinois, as shown by the map, recorded the greatest increases in agricultural settlement during the decade 1850–1860, that is, to the eve of the Civil War; and also during the decade from 1860–1870, which may be termed the Civil War decade. Thereafter, except for the state of Oklahoma, which remained Indian Territory until 1890, the westward frontier of improved agricultural land each decade was roughly a straight alignment from north to south. The final decade shown on the map—1910 to 1920, which may be

Figure 198. (A) Above, this Currier and Ives artist's conception of the railroad crossing the continent in 1868 has three major ingredients: the wooded settlement on the frontier in the foreground, the flat grassland into which the railroad right of way disappears into the distance, and the mountains on the right. (*Courtesy of Harry T. Peters Collection, Museum of the City of New York.*) (B) Below, map showing increase in acreage and main lines of transcontinental railroads. (*Compiled from data in the* Atlas of Historical Geography of the United States, *by Charles O. Paullin, published jointly by The Carnegie Institution and The American Geographical Society.*)

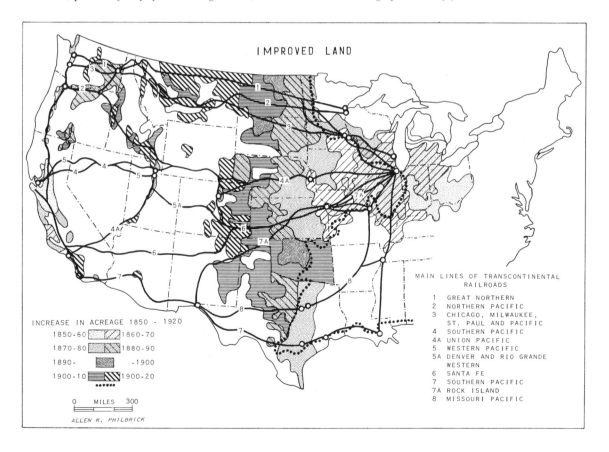

termed the World War I decade—saw the final expansion of acreage to the westward limits of the Great Plains at the very edges of the Rocky Mountain system of ranges from Idaho to western Texas. The map also emphasizes the emerging importance of Chicago at the southwest edge of Lake Michigan as the major railroad center of the continent.

The Middle West as a Staging Area for Settlement of the Western Ranges.
The geographical significance of the Middle West prairie states in the process of settlement lies in the fact that here for the first time settlers learned how to work with the resources of the grasslands. This learning process took place because prairie grasses reach far eastward across Iowa and Illinois to western Indiana, while forest extends throughout the same region along water courses. The intermingling of forest and grasslands provided an opportunity for initially forest-based settlers to become familiar with grassland conditions and to perceive and solve the problems of agricultural use of the prairies.

The invention and first manufacture of the *steel plow* by John Deere represents the technological innovation capable of subduing the thick, heavily matted, root system of the high grasses of the humid prairies. A second equally important technological innovation was, of course, the railroad, which made it possible to move supplies to the grassland farmer, as well as to give him access to markets for his crops. The construction of railroads throughout the western grasslands was subsidized by large land grants along projected rights of way. Such grants for both the construction of wagon roads and railroads from 1823–1871 are shown by the map in Figure 199.[1] A sample of the reaction of settlers to the access provided by projected as well as constructed rail lines is afforded by the map in Figure 200 of McLean County, Illinois.[2] The map demonstrates that before 1850 settlers cleaved to the forested lands. After 1850 the prairies were taken up with a rush of claims and only slightly more slowly were occupied by settlers and broken to the plow.

Features Characterizing Settlement of the West.
It is not possible fully to elaborate the geographical evolution of the pattern of settlement in the Americas in an introductory book. Long before

the western edges of the great interior lowlands of North America were initially occupied, the barrier of the "American desert" and mountain had been "leap-frogged" by the "forty-niners" of the Gold Rush and by other settlers. The map of the peopling of the Americas (Figure 185) demonstrates that the West of both the United States and Canada still has an intermittent pattern of permanent settlement which reflects great differences in character of the land and resources. A number of features can be summarized.

First, there were four major foci of settlement of critical importance as bases of supply and initial successes in achieving stable population, each associated with water as the most critical resource of the West. In order of their location from east to west, these foci are the Rocky Mountain Front Region, the Salt Lake Oasis Region of Utah, the Willamette and Columbia River Valleys of the Pacific Northwest, and the California coast and Central Valley.

Second, settlement in the Far West reflects the pattern of mining activities, as mineral prospecting early became a dominant element in western migration. The map in Figure 201, which shows population engaged in mining in the 1930s, demonstrates the impact of the distribution of mineral resources on the pattern of western population distribution.

Third, the predominant use of land west of the one-hundredth meridian in the United States is grazing. West of the wet prairies of the Middle West and the subhumid high-plains grain lands, precipitation diminishes in both quantity and reliability. Grassland vegetation is shorter and more intermittent west of the Great Plains than east of them. In the pre-European period of settlement, the western or dry plains were the home of the bison or American buffalo. These herds were exterminated in a period of intensive hunting when first Indians and then white men from the eastern half of the continent consumed the wild cattle. The Indian population increased as more and more of the eastern tribesmen were relocated and removed from the country east of the Mississippi. They found the buffalo a ready food resource. The literal decimation of the natural herds occurred, however, only when the white man, once more crowding the Indian out, wantonly and wastefully killed buffalo for hides at a rate far faster than that of the natural replacement of the herd. The period of destruction of the buffalo corresponds in general to the period of the crossing of the west by settlers and prospec-

---

[1] Paullin, *op. cit.* Plate 56D.
[2] Arthur W. Watterson, *Economy and Land Use Patterns of McLean County, Illinois,* Chicago: University of Chicago, 1950, pp. 31 and 49–57.

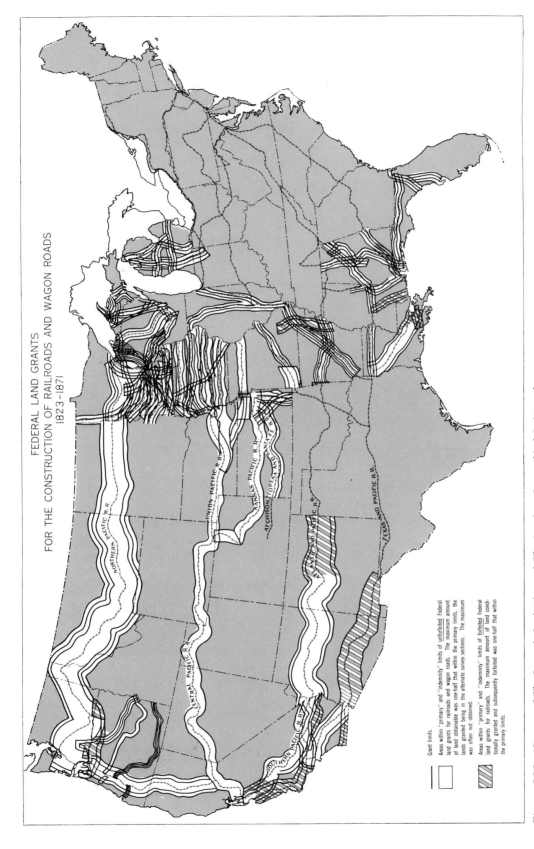

Figure 199. (*Courtesy of The Carnegie Institution and The American Geographical Society, taken from Charles O. Paullin, Atlas of the Historical Geography of the United States.*)

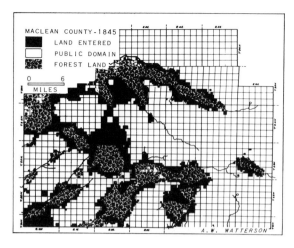

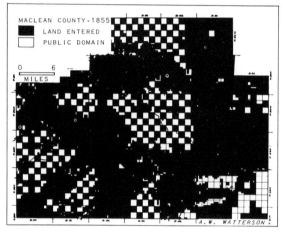

Figure 200. (*Courtesy of Arthur W. Watterson,* Economy and Land Use Patterns of McLean County.)

tors during the building of the railroads from 1848 to the immediate post-Civil War years.

Cattle replaced the buffalo grazing on government land which no one wished to occupy. By the late 1880s overgrazing had depleted the western grasslands to such a degree that huge losses by starvation began to plague cattlemen during severe winters. By a process of trial and error system and stability gradually evolved in use of the range. Resources of the range (map in Figure 202) can be classified by seasonal use of the resource. Summer range is either higher country or more northerly. Winter range is more southerly and at lower elevations. Some land in grazing districts is still largely in government ownership. It is grazed under the supervision of the Taylor Grazing Act, which controls the number of animals and regulates range practices on land with a limited capacity for the support of grazing animals.

The distribution of forests can be inferred from the pattern of summer range, and the map in Figure 202 also depicts the location of irrigated land. The patterns of these two types of land, when viewed in conjunction with the combined distribution of all grazing lands of any type, demonstrate a relationship between highlands and water. Highlands are the source of water for irrigation. They generally remain forested and provide summer range, also. In the vicinity of mountains, irrigated valleys show the use to which mountain runoff can be put. Drier plateaus and intermontane basins are devoted to low-density grazing. As might be expected, over half of the irrigated area is devoted to growing feed crops for livestock. Grains and specialty crops, such as sugar beets, fruits, and vegetables, account for the balance.

Emergence of National Regional Organization in Canada

Early French and later English occupancy in the St. Lawrence River Valley demonstrated a considerably slower development of settlement in what has become Canada than in the United States.

The St. Lawrence Valley. Quebec, at the first narrows, and Montreal, at the head of navigation of the St. Lawrence estuary, became important fortified points in the conduct of the early fur trade. Practically every stream and lake of the continental interior and the principal portages connecting them were routes of travel by the fur traders. These routes reveal the extent of the trading contact of the French and later the English with the Indians in the interior. Along the St. Lawrence River itself between Quebec and Montreal, the French king established the *seignorial* type of land tenure. The most conspicuous feature of this pattern of settlement was its long-lot character, with narrow frontage along the river and great length of narrow strips of land back from the river. This arrangement maximized the accessibility provided by the river. Less evident from the pattern is the fact that the system represented the transfer of feudal land tenure from France to North America. "Seignories" (long strips of land on a narrow frontage of river under the control of one gentleman) were to be settled by "habitants" analogous to vassals in the homeland. Once settlement became fairly started, toward the middle of the seventeenth century, the narrow seignorial tracts began to be

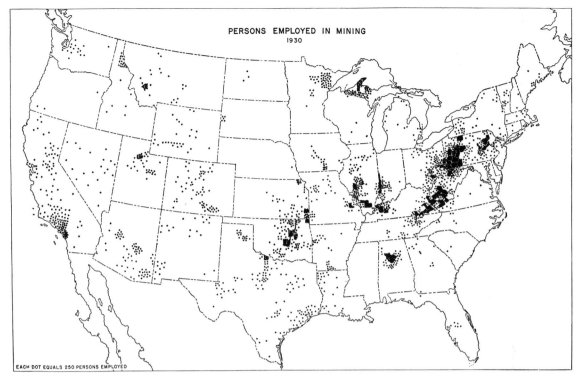

Figure 201. (*Courtesy of U. S. National Resources Committee.*)

subdivided into even narrower partitions called "concessions." According to Ralph Brown,[1]

Desire for frontage on the St. Lawrence River and its navigable tributaries obviously brought about this modification of the feudal system. The rivers furnished travel by water in summer and by ice in winter at a period and in an environment where other means of travel were either costly or wholly unobtainable. The natural result was a distribution of habitations like beads on a string, each one of which was within easy reach of the river, or to use habitant terminology, on the first "côte." Village life, a characteristic of the feudal system in France, was thus eliminated. Occasional small agglomerations developed around a parish church, but few trading communities evolved other than the larger ones of Quebec, Montreal, and Trois Rivières.

The partitioning process was aided also by the French practice of equal inheritance rights to sons. This pattern of settlement continued after the conquest of French Canada by the English in 1763, according to Brown.[2]

[1] Ralph H. Brown, *Historical Geography of the United States,* New York: Harcourt Brace and Company, 1948, p. 48.
[2] *Ibid.,* p. 171.

The report of one traveler, typical of many, states that the road from Quebec to Montreal . . . differs from all others I have seen, in this, that it may be said to be almost a continued street; one house succeeds another so quickly that I believe I may safely say there is not a mile without one. Except for the town of Trois Rivières, you have scarcely any place that deserves the name of a town: but every parish church has a village in its neighborhood and of these there are between Quebec and Montreal, upwards of 20.

The take-over by the English meant that the St. Lawrence Valley was to develop under a dual cultural leadership—French and English. The very fact of the persistence of the French cultural system as exemplified by the pattern of land tenure illustrates the contradiction. It was not until the English by-passed the Province of Quebec and moved foreward into Ontario that a typical rectangular-lot English system of land tenure with individual farmsteads could develop. This dual cultural nature of eastern Canada acted as a brake on the progress of settlement and development of the western interior.

For widely different reasons and on a quite widely varied resource basis the settlements built on fur trading and subsistence farming in the St.

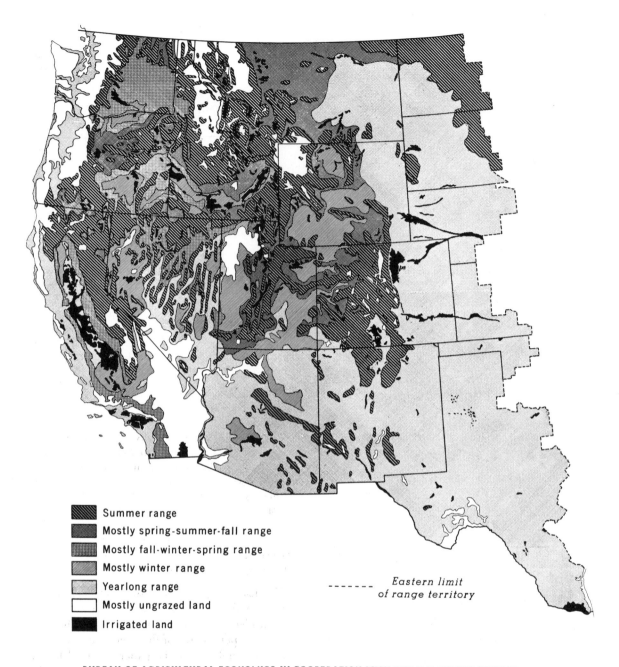

Summer range

Mostly spring-summer-fall range

Mostly fall-winter-spring range

Mostly winter range

Yearlong range

Mostly ungrazed land

Irrigated land

- - - - - - - *Eastern limit of range territory*

BUREAU OF AGRICULTURAL ECONOMICS IN COOPERATION WITH THE U. S. FOREST SERVICE

Figure 202. Seasonal use of Western range, 1947. (*Courtesy of U. S. Dept. of Agriculture.*)

Lawrence Valley resembled those of the plantation tidewater of Virginia in the United States. Both were linear and oriented toward navigable water, and they both came to a focus at only a few major points.

Comparison of Development of Canada and the United States. The evolution of the spread of settlement westward in the United States, previously described, was accompanied by a somewhat analogous development in Canada, paralleling in general but more slowly that of the United States. As in the United States, Canada was settled through the process of an expanding westward frontier from original points in the settled East.

Unlike the United States, however, Canada was developed by two major national groups, first French and then English. This means that within Canada's core region there are two distinct cultures. These cultures are represented by French-speaking Quebec and English-speaking Ontario. The union of these two major national groups has not always been harmonious. Efforts from both groups have been required to produce a union which is distinctively Canadian. Reference has already been made in the previous section to the French region of settlement. Conquest by the English brought no abrupt changes, for it was strategic in nature, intended to protect the northern flank of British colonies to the south in what is now the United States. Influx of settlers of English ancestry was very slow at first. Settlers came more from the colonies to the south than from England. The first major migration of English-speaking people into Quebec occurred during the American Revolution when Loyalist refugees from that conflict went north.

Once again a situation analogous to that discussed in the United States developed. As French people increased in number and the area of Roman Catholic farm settlement expanded in size from the original seignories in Quebec, English settlers in Quebec came into conflict with this natural expansion of French settlement. The conflict was resolved by the westward movement of settlers of English background into new lands in Ontario. This region in Canada corresponds, therefore, to the Ohio Valley and the Middle West in the United States. Early French settlement extended to the outer edge of the seignories in Quebec in 1765. English settlers increasingly moved into Ontario from 1760–1885. The pattern of English settlement then expanded westward into the Prairie Provinces and beyond to the British Columbian west-coast settlements.

Canada, like her southern neighbor, was formed originally within smaller borders than she later achieved. One important difference from the United States, however, was that cultural replacement in Canada did not lead to perpetuation of differences in ways of life which could only be resolved by civil war, as was the case between the plantation South and the manufactural and commercial North of the United States. Instead of a parallel advance in separate alignments north and south of one another, expanding settlement patterns in Canada passed through or over one another. That is, English settlement leap-frogged over or passed through French settlement into Ontario. From there expansion westward was on a rather narrow front, between the Laurentian upland on the north and the Great Lakes and the United States on the south. This circumstance had the effect of containing the expansion of French-speaking culture within the original Province of Quebec. Thereafter, Canadian expansion was a single line of predominantly English cultural background which spread westward.

Remnants of the impact of French and English cultures may be seen in the differences in landholding patterns established over the areas settled originally by the two groups within Quebec. French culture, dominated by the organized hierarchy of the Roman Catholic Church, reflects village organization within a long-lot system of land holdings fronting on the St. Lawrence and highways paralleling that river. The farms make a dispersed linear pattern, for, although they maintained cultural and social focus within them, farmers did not live in villages. By contrast the English township exhibits a rectangular-lot system and a pattern of dispersed farms. The farms focus on market towns or service centers, less dominated in Ontario by social organization led by a church and a faith as the way of life.

As the Canadian people moved westward the development of Canada shared another similarity. They both crossed the same successive continental land features and accompanying resource types in pushing their frontiers westward from the Atlantic to the Pacific. As in the United States, the construction of transcontinental rail connections both united and led to the further expansion of the nation. Railroads were principal agents in settling the Prairie Provinces of Canada. Thus, the same general sequence of specialized economic regions is observable in Canada as in the United States (Figure 162). There are forested Pacific coastal slopes, interior grasslands devoted to range use, and extensively farmed wheat lands in the northern great plains. There is a Great Lakes mineral-producing region, a small Middle Western corn belt, dairy and cattle-feeding agricultural belts merging with the urban eastern manufacturing core region in southern Ontario and the St. Lawrence Valley.

By contrast, however, rather than a wide expanse of national territory to the south of the core region as in the United States, the great expanse of Canada lies to the *north* of that narrow corridor-like belt of settled territory along the southern border of the country. This means forest rather than field for northern Canada. An association of relatively dry glaciated rocky terrain in a cold climate prevails to the north which differs sharply from the moist and richly soil-covered plains of the subtropical American South. On the other hand, the northern metamorphic shield of Canada is far larger than the metamorphic portions of the Appalachian regions within the United States. The difference in this respect means a far greater reserve of potential metallic mineral-producing areas in the Canadian north and east than in the south and southeast of the United States.

These circumstances explain the *linear* arc of regional organization in Canada, as opposed to the larger *radial* arrangement of the regions in the United States. In the larger continental setting, patterns of regions belonging to the two nations of North America fit rather well together in a single *radial* pattern focusing on dual cores on either side of the St. Lawrence River.

Summary

The peopling of the Americas must be summarized in terms of the striking contrast between the whole of North America, which is *Anglo-American* in culture, and Central and South America, which are *Latin American* in culture. The sweep of cultural replacement by people of European ancestry across North America has unified the diverse resources of the continent within a diversified economic productive system focusing primarily on a single core region shared by Canada and the United States.

The corresponding settlement of South and Central America was by conquest of peoples and by settlement within widely separated localities which have never been functionally united. The core regions of the many national states in Latin America have an almost "insular" character, regardless of whether they actually are islands or not. The perpetuation of externally oriented exporting economies based on initial colonial agricultural and mining activities even after political independence has long delayed the development of true economic independence and diversity for most Latin American countries. The gradual emergence of some Latin American regions from such one-sided development is now apparent in the trends toward greater diversity and the construction of basic iron and steel industries in Mexico, Venezuela, Colombia, Peru, Chile, Brazil, and Argentina. Despite these signs of growing maturity, however, overall functional nodality of the double continent remains focused on the core region of North America and the world leadership of the United States of America.

15 *The Regions and Peoples of Eurasia*

The majority of the human race lives in Eurasia. The importance of the world's largest continental land mass—the double continent of Asia and Europe—also rests in the fact that nearly two-thirds of its twenty million square miles is occupied by Communist Bloc countries. The Communist nations control nearly half (45 per cent) of the population of Eurasia within the single largest group of contiguous regions organized hierarchically under a common ideology in the world.

In creating a portrait of this human world regional analysis began with the discussion of an island country off the coast of Eurasia—the United Kingdom. This country was chosen because it was the culture hearth for much of human experience in the ages of exploration, and of the industrial revolution. The path of "travels" through discussion of world regions has carried us from Europe to Africa south of the Sahara, to the Republic of South Africa, the Commonwealth of Australia, and to New Zealand. After a brief examination of the Commonwealth focused on the United Kingdom, as an example of international interregional organization, attention shifted to the Americas. After seeing the impact of Europeans on the regions of Latin and Anglo-America, it is now appropriate to return once more to the Old World, to examine the impact of European culture on both relatively unpopulated lands and overpopulated lands in Eurasia.

Just as the English and other West Europeans migrated westward across the Atlantic primarily to North America, the Russian people expanded eastward in much lesser numbers, although on a comparable time table, to the Pacific and for a time even into part of North America across the North Pacific. Under the colonialism of the Czars this expansion eastward was conquest rather than settlement and development. There was no line of a frontier as in North America. The story was one of territorial expansion and garrison-type political control with little or no permanent settlement.

In southern and eastern Asia, however, several peoples had evolved to advanced stages of very different cultures long before European culture became important. At the time when European expansion took place during and particularly after the industrial revolution, Asia already had far more population than Europe.[1] The people of Asia and their cultures could not readily be conquered or pushed aside by Europeans. Peoples and cultures which Europeans could not replace by their emerging industrial culture could be manipulated and influenced, however. These circumstances blunted the impact of the European industrial revolution on the world majority of peoples living in Asia. Now, however, nationalist political revolutions have carried away all but the remnants of European colonialism in Asia; industrialization programs are underway throughout Asia against the competitive background of a struggle for leadership between the Communist and free enterprise societies. Eurasia is divided into the *Communist Bloc* in the center surrounded by the non-Communist countries and regions of the *Eurasian perimeter*.

The huge size of the Eurasian land mass can be appreciated by examination of its dimensions. From the Bering Strait at 65° 40′ North Latitude it is approximately 6,200 miles along the Pacific face of Eurasia to Singapore which is nearly on the equator at 1° 14′ N. The air distance from Singapore to Gibraltar along the south side of the double continent is the longest, nearly 7,500 miles, equivalent to nearly 110 degrees of longitude along the Equator. The shortest side is the Atlantic-Arctic face, which extends from Gibraltar to the Bering Strait 5,500 miles across the north pole.

Eurasia's more than twenty million square miles

---

[1] The estimated proportion of the world's population in Asia in 1650 was 60.6 per cent to Europe's 18.3 per cent. The same type of ratio in 1950 was 54.3 per cent for Asia to 23.3 per cent for Europe. W. S. Woytinsky and E. S. Woytinsky, *World Population and Production*, New York: The Twentieth Century Fund, 1953, pp. 34 and 36.

comprise 36 per cent of the world's total land area. In 1959, on slightly more than one-third of the world's land platform, more than two billion people lived (2,271,241,000). This figure represents more than three-fourths (77.6 per cent) of the human race. Old-world lands of Europe and Asia are thus comparatively crowded, while by contrast the rest of the world seems relatively underpopulated.

The purpose of this chapter is to introduce the final regional section of this book by defining the different kinds of regions into which Eurasia and its many peoples may be divided. For this purpose two distinctive kinds of regional divisions are necessary. The basis of regionalization to be discussed in the present chapter is primarily cultural. The second basis of regional division, that of resource associations—agricultural and mineral—will be the primary subject matter of the following chapter.

Cultural Regions of Eurasia and North Africa

The major regional division (shown on the map in Figure 203) from the standpoint of culture is that between the greater part of Eurasia, today controlled by the Communists, and the remainder of the continent. In the Communist territory of Eurasia a vigorous ideological culture is being actively dictated by a dedicated minority. Communist leadership strives consciously and deliberately to replace the previous culture of any population within which it achieves control by the ideas and program of Communism. The values, ways of doing, and works of the Communists are quite distinctive in their impact and differ sharply from the traditional cultures of the past.

Special Problems of Evaluation and Analysis. It is important to understand at the outset that there are special problems which render geographic analysis and evaluation of Communist regions difficult. Emotional bitterness stemming from the "cold war" make it difficult to be objective about the countries of the Communist Bloc. Also, reliable information concerning the Communist portions of the globe is both meager and difficult to interpret. It is often impossible to separate claims from facts, realistic plans from propaganda, and permanent achievements from wishful thinking. Because of the highly generalized form in which official statistics are published, it is usually impossible to get

accurate quantitative information for Communist countries. This is particularly true of subdivisions within the countries. Last, the rate of change in reorganization and development of both the Soviet Union and China presents its own problems. Russia in the past forty years and China in the past ten years have been undergoing thoroughly revolutionary developments politically, and socially, and economically. The full impact of revolutionary changes on culture and the organization of area is still developing. Construction and shifts in relative importance of different parts of the several national productive plants is difficult to keep up with when information about them is so meager.

Such limitations as these must be kept in mind when the facts selected to illustrate the patterns of occupancy within Communist Bloc countries are reviewed. The tendency on the part of some people, however, not to take the Communists seriously is a dangerous mistake. It would be just as dangerous, on the other hand, to assume that whatever they predict must come to pass.

The Communist portion of Eurasia is a single block of contiguous territory. Tiny Albania is the only exception on the coast of the Mediterranean; and the separation is due partly to the independent Communist policy of Yugoslavia which brings that country into conflict with Moscow. Similar patterns of dissidence seem to be affecting Albania's relations with Moscow also, but both countries will be treated here as part of the Communist Bloc.

By contrast, non-Communist Eurasia is a great strip of peripheral territory ringing the Communist Bloc from Scandinavia south and east to Singapore off the mainland and thence northeastward in island archipelagoes to northern Japan in Hokkaido. This encircling zone is composed of many regions. It is more than a thousand miles wide in places, yet its geographical characteristic is one of dispersion. One chapter will be devoted to the Communist Bloc and two chapters to the regions of the Eurasian perimeter. Each of these two divisions of Eurasia may be subdivided into six principal cultural units, as shown on the map in Figure 203.

Cultural Regions of the Communist Bloc. Within Communist Bloc countries live a billion persons (1,015,339,000 in 1959). Two countries, Russia and China, dominate the Communist world. Each is subdivisible into many subregions, but these may be generalized under three main cultural divisions for each country. For the Soviet Union these are the Russian coreland, the countries of

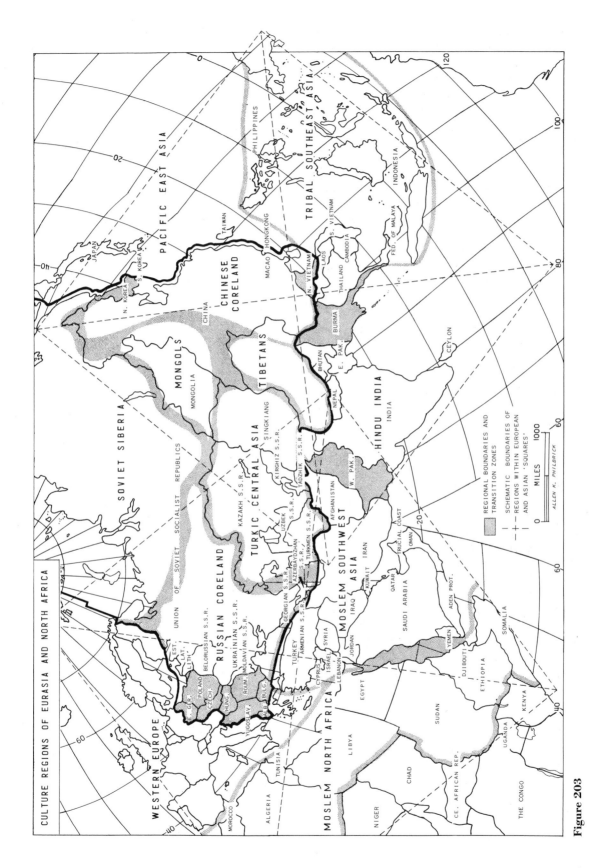

CULTURE REGIONS OF EURASIA AND NORTH AFRICA

WESTERN EUROPE

SOVIET SIBERIA

PACIFIC EAST ASIA

JAPAN

S. KOREA
N. KOREA

TAIWAN

MACAO HONGKONG

CHINESE CORELAND

CHINA

MONGOLS

MONGOLIA

UNION OF SOVIET SOCIALIST REPUBLICS

TIBETANS

TRIBAL SOUTHEAST ASIA

PHILIPPINES

INDONESIA

FED. OF MALAYA

S. VIETNAM
N. VIETNAM

LAOS

CAMBODIA

THAILAND

BURMA

SINGKIANG

BHUTAN

E. PAK.

NEPAL

CEYLON

HINDU INDIA

INDIA

TURKIC CENTRAL ASIA

KAZAKH S.S.R.

KIRGHIZ S.S.R.

TADZHIK S.S.R.

W. PAK.

UZBEK S.S.R.

TURKMEN S.S.R.

AFGHANISTAN

RUSSIAN CORELAND

BELORUSSIAN S.S.R.

EST.
LAT.
LITH.

POLAND

GER.
CZECH

HUNG.

UKRAINIAN S.S.R.

MOLDAVIAN S.S.R.

ROUM.

YUGOSLAV

ALB.
BULG.

GEORGIAN S.S.R.

AZERBAYDZHAN S.S.R.

ARMENIAN S.S.R.

TURKEY

CYPRUS

LEBANON

ISRAEL

SYRIA

JORDAN

MOSLEM SOUTHWEST ASIA

IRAQ

IRAN

KUWAIT

QATAR

SAUDI ARABIA

TRUCIAL COAST

OMAN

ADEN PROT.

YEMEN

MOSLEM NORTH AFRICA

MOROCCO

ALGERIA

TUNISIA

LIBYA

EGYPT

SUDAN

CHAD

NIGER

CE. AFRICAN REP.

THE CONGO

UGANDA

KENYA

ETHIOPIA

DJIBOUTI

SOMALIA

REGIONAL BOUNDARIES AND
TRANSITION ZONES

SCHEMATIC BOUNDARIES OF
REGIONS WITHIN EUROPEAN
AND ASIAN "SQUARES"

MILES   1000

0

ALLEN K. PHILBRICK

Figure 203

Soviet Central Asia, and the Soviet Arctic. The dominant people of the Russian coreland are the Great Russians. The cultural background of Soviet Central Asia is Turkic, while the Soviet Arctic consists of Samoyed and other Siberian tribal cultures. For China the three culture regions are the Chinese coreland, or eastern China, and two minority culture regions of western China, those of the Mongols and the Tibetans. Two groups of nations have emerged since World War II as appendages to regions of Russia and China. These are the East European Communist satellite countries and Asian satellite countries. These countries are undergoing a process of rapid cultural replacement.

Cultural Regions of the Eurasian Perimeter. Slightly more than a billion persons occupy the regions in Eurasia peripheral to the Communist Bloc. Including North Africa, which is culturally related to the Middle East, there are six regions here also. These are the nations of Western Europe, Moslem North Africa, Moslem Southwest Asia, the Hindu culture region of India, the numerous tribal cultures of peninsular Southeast Asia—including Moslem Indonesia—and the principally island nations of Pacific Asia. The last region also includes many separate tribal cultures, but the principal countries are Japan and the Philippines. (If North Africa is included, the population of the six peripheral regions is more than a billion and a quarter—1,343,913,000.) Major divisions, cultural regions, their populations and areas are shown in Table XXXIII.

Countries of the Communist and Perimeter Regions of Eurasia and North Africa. There are at least one hundred states and territories in the regions of Eurasia and Moslem North Africa, in both the central Communist Bloc and perimeter. Of these all but a handful are national states. A visual means by which to keep track of so numerous a group of countries within the dozen regions just referred to is presented in Figure 203. For purposes of visualizing the relationship of the countries in these regions, the device of two "squares" superimposed on the political map of Eurasia and North Africa provides a diagram which is simple to reproduce and remember. As can be seen, each of the two squares is subdivided into four parts by diagonals drawn from the corners. This gives four triangles for each square; and each triangle corresponds to a region or combination of regions. The squares are set on their corners and overlap slightly. Several regions also overlap to

some extent. The straight diagonal lines do not, of course, follow regional borders exactly. The two horizontal diagonals follow the alignment of the zone of weakness from the Mediterranean through the Caucasus and Himalayas to Southeast Asia. The vertical diagonal in the western square follows the border between the Soviet Union and Eastern Europe to the Mediterranean, and thence through the Suez Canal and Red Sea to the Indian Ocean. In the Asian square the vertical diagonal roughly parallels in its northern half the twenty-inch rainfall isohyet separating humid eastern China from the dry interior of China. The southern half of the line is taken as the Burma-Thailand border which separates South Asia from Southeast Asia.

The upper inside right and left triangles account for a large part of the Communist Bloc. The outer triangles are the six regions of the perimeter, although the outer top left and right triangles also contain the East European satellites and mainland China of the Communist Bloc, respectively. It is not intended that the square geometric shapes and their division into triangles be rigidly applied. Since anyone can easily draw a diagram of Eurasia with this device in mind, the geometrical pattern can supply guide lines for visualizing many worthwhile relationships. The countries of each region, their capitals, population, and area are given in Table XXXIII. European countries, however, will be found in Table XIII of Chapter 8.

The sweep of nationalism and the ebb tide of colonialism has already been dramatically illustrated by the map in Figure 107 in Chapter 9. With the exception of the countries of the Communist Bloc and Europe, almost all of the territories of North Africa, of Southwest, South, Southeast, and East Asia have won political freedom since World War II. The map shows the great change from the former predominance of Europe in the affairs of North Africa and Asia. Countries formerly politically controlled by European powers are shaded according to the generation of their achievement of political independence, and the dates of their political independence are written within their borders.

Eurasia's Two Humid Regions and the Arid Crescent

The map in Figure 204 and the data regrouped in Table XXXIV combine the twelve regions of the Communist Bloc and Eurasian perimeter and North Africa in a different way. Eurasia is divided

Name of region or country	Areas in sq. mi.	Population, 1959, thousands	Capital	Population, 1959
Total Eurasia and North Africa	**24,088,948**	**2,359,252**		
Total Eurasia	**20,102,199**	**2,271,241**		
Communist Bloc	**12,953,576**	**1,015,339**		
Eurasian Perimeter and North Africa	**11,135,372**	**1,343,913**		
West Europe[b]	**1,419,921**	**290,430**		
Moslem North Africa	**3,986,749**	**88,011**		
Algeria	919,591	10,930	Algiers	800,000[c]
Egypt	386,000	26,080	Cairo	2,852,000
Ethiopia	457,266	21,800	Addis Ababa	500,000
Djibouti (Fr.)	8,494	70	Djibouti	31,349
Libya	679,359	1,172	Tripoli	170,000
Morocco	171,305	10,550	Rabat	224,901
Somalia	246,201	1,990	Magadiscio	90,622
Spanish Sahara (Sp.)	102,702	25	Villa Cisneros	6,097
Sudan	967,499	11,459	Khartoum	245,736
Tunisia	48,332	3,935	Tunis	410,000
Moslem Southwest Asia	**2,297,455**	**88,495**		
Aden (Br.)	75	150		
Aden Protectorate (Br.)	112	660	Aden	99,285
Afghanistan	250,965	13,150	Kabul	310,000
Bahrain	231	143	Bahrain	61,726[c]
Cyprus	3,571	558	Nicosia	81,741
Israel	7,992	2,061	Jerusalem	160,000
Iran	636,293	20,149	Teheran	1,838,982
Iraq	171,599	6,952	Baghdad	656,399
Jordan	37,301	1,636	Amman	108,304
Kuwait	6,000	219	Kuwait City	125,929
Lebanon	4,000	1,550	Beirut	115,000
Oman	82,000	550	Muscat	5,000
Qatar	8,500	6,036	Doha	27,500
Saudi Arabia	617,760	40	Riyadh	150,000
Syria	71,227	4,539	Damascus	408,774
Trucial Coast	32,280	86	Dubia	40,000
Turkey[d]	292,259	25,516	Ankara	1,316,879
Yemen	75,290	4,500	Sana	60,000
Hindu India	**1,986,134**	**572,223**		
Bhutan	19,305	660	Punalcha and Tashi-cho-Dzong not available	
Burma[e]	261,789	20,457	Rangoon	774,676
Ceylon[e]	25,332	9,612	Colombo	778,291[c]
India	1,261,609	438,638	New Delhi	395,000[c]
Nepal[e]	54,362	9,044	Katmandu	106,579
Pakistan[f]	364,737	93,812	Rawalpindi	343,000
East	54,501	50,844		
West	310,236	42,968		
Tribal Southeast Asia	**1,250,682**	**173,583**		
Cambodia	66,607	4,845	Phnom-Penh	420,000[c]

TABLE **XXXIII** (CONTINUED)

Name of region or country	Areas in sq. mi.	Population, 1959, thousands	Capital	Population, 1959
Tribal Southeast Asia (cont.)				
Federation of Malaya[g]	130,879	9,426	Ipoh	125,759
Indonesia[f]	575,893	90,300	Djakarta	2,814,210
Laos	91,429	1,760	Vientiane	100,000
Philippines	115,707	27,456	Quezon	397,374
Portuguese Timor	5,763	496	Dili	43,589
South Vietnam	65,948	13,790	Saigon-Cholon	1,383,000
Thailand	198,456	25,520	Bangkok	1,330,153[c]
East Asia	**194,431**	**130,571**		
Hong Kong	391	2,857	Victoria	1,000,000
Japan	142,726	93,419	Tokyo	9,504,987[c]
Macao	6	215	Macao	181,908
South Korea	37,424	23,848	Seoul	1,646,000
Taiwan	13,884	10,232	Taipei	854,061
Communist Bloc	**12,953,576**	**1,015,339**		
Chinese Coreland Mongolia Tibetan and Chinese portion of Turkic Central Asia	3,805,315	690,890		
China	3,691,506	669,000	Peiping	4,010,000
North Korea	47,861	8,100		
North Vietnam	65,948	13,790		
Russian Coreland Soviet Turkic Central Asia and Soviet Siberia	9,148,261	324,449		
U.S.S.R.	8,656,370	210,500	Moscow	5,032,000
East European[h] Satellites	491,891	113,949		

[a] United Nations *Demographic Yearbook 1960*, New York, 1960, Table 1, pp. 99–117, and Table 7 pp. 285–348.

[b] From Table XIII plus European Turkey.

[c] Italics mean population is of agglomerated urban area rather than city proper.

[d] Asian Turkey.

[e] Primarily Buddhist.

[f] Moslem.

[g] Includes Brunei, North Borneo, Sarawak, and Singapore.

[h] For countries see Table XIII.

in a three-fold manner into two relatively densely peopled territories separated from each other by a wide zone of sparsely populated territory.

The three-fold division of Eurasia by population density on Figure 22 of Chapter 2 coincides with the pattern of humid lands in Figure 31 of Chapter 3. When the region experiencing less than twenty inches of annual precipitation is superimposed on the population map, it is immediately recognized that the sparsely populated zone is part of the nearly world-girdling Arid Crescent. This dry zone extends from the Sahara and Southwest Asia northeastward from the Red Sea coast of Saudi Arabia to the Bering Strait in easternmost Siberia. It separates humid Western Europe including part of European Russia from humid Southern, Southeastern, and East Asia.

Area and Population Relationships in Dry-Humid Regions of Eurasia. Important factual relations emerge from an examination of

Region	Area, sq. mi.	Per cent	Population, 1957	Per cent	Pop. per sq. mi.
I. Relatively densely populated humid regions of Western Eurasia	3,826,589	18.7	592,690,000	28.0	155
Western Europe and Turkey	1,713,090	8.4	325,641,000	15.4	190
Eastern European satellites	491,891	2.4	113,949,000	5.4	232
Western-Southern Soviet Union	1,621,608	7.9	153,100,000	7.2	95
Total Soviet portion	2,113,499	10.3	267,049,000	12.6	127
Total non-Soviet portion	1,713,090	8.4	325,641,000	15.4	190
II. Sparsely populated central Asian regions of the Arid Crescent	11,365,190	55.3	137,708,111	6.5	12
Moslem Asia without Turkey or W. Pakistan	2,077,757	10.1	62,856,000	3.0	31
Soviet Central Asia	1,541,133	7.5	20,900,000	1.0	14
Soviet Arctic, Siberia	5,436,300	26.5	26,200,000	1.2	5
Arid Western China	2,310,000	11.3	27,752,111[a]	1.3	12
Total Soviet portion	9,287,433	45.2	74,852,111	3.5	8
Total non-Soviet portion	2,077,757	10.1	62,856,000	3.0	31
III. Densely populated humid Eastern, Southeastern, and Southern Asia	5,343,343,	26.0	1,378,960,546	65.4	254
Island nations of Pacific Asia	1,181,977	5.8	244,145,000	11.6	207
Peninsular South Asia	2,107,712	10.5	517,339,000	24.5	245
West Pakistan	310,236	1.5	38,050,000	1.8	123
Asian satellites	107,748	.5	24,697,000	1.2	231
Humid East China	1,635,670	7.9	554,729,546[a]	26.3	340
Total Soviet portion	1,743,418	8.4	579,426,546	27.5	332
Total non-Soviet portion	3,599,925	17.6	799,534,000	37.9	222
Total	20,535,122	100.0	2,109,358,657	100.0	103

[a] Population figures for China are for 1953, Shabad T., *China's Changing Map*, New York: Praeger, 1956.

Table XXXIV, which gives numerical expression to the regional groupings recorded on the map in Figure 204. The relatively densely peopled humid European peninsula of Asia is less than one-fifth of the area of Eurasia. The densely populated Asian crescent of three regions occupies only a little more than one-fourth of the double continent, while the great dry interior portion of Eurasia comprises well over half of the total area (55 per cent).

Nearly 600 million people occupy the humid parts of western Eurasia, comprising 28 per cent of the total for the double continent. More than half of the dry continental interior supports less than 10

per cent of the people (6.5 per cent). Most dramatic of all, slightly more than one-fourth of the land area in the traditional regions of South, Southeast, and East Asia supports nearly *two-thirds* of Eurasia's population.

The division of Eurasia with respect to precipitation cuts across the boundaries created by the division of the double continent between Communist Bloc and non-Communist perimeter. The two humid zones and one arid zone of Eurasia are each divided into a Communist and a non-Communist portion. The map in Figure 204 and Table XXXIV show the relationship between these two separate

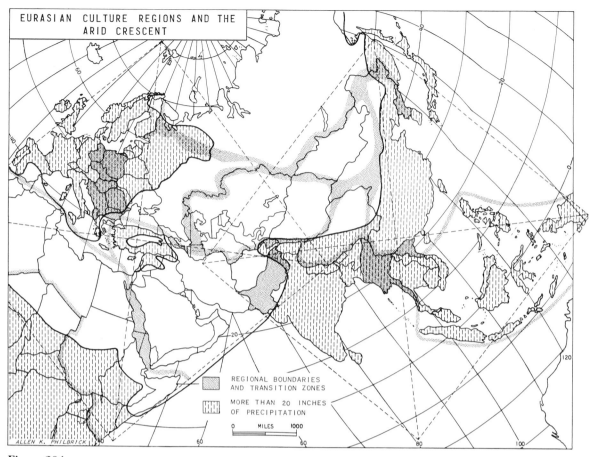

EURASIAN CULTURE REGIONS AND THE ARID CRESCENT

REGIONAL BOUNDARIES
AND TRANSITION ZONES

MORE THAN 20 INCHES
OF PRECIPITATION

0   MILES   1000

ALLEN K. PHILBRICK

Figure 204

categories of regions, making use of cultural regions and individual countries approximating the overlap between the two.

Humid western Eurasia approaches an even split in both area and population between Communist and non-Communist countries. Western Europe and Turkey total 1.7 million square miles (8.4 per cent of the Eurasian land mass); while European Russia, including the trans-Caucasian republics, are 2.1 million square miles (10.3 per cent of the *Eura*sian land mass). Western Europe and Turkey together have 325 million people (15.4 per cent of the total in Eurasia), while the corresponding region of the Communist Bloc numbers 267 million (12.6 per cent of the total). Within the interior, however, the part of the Arid Crescent which belongs to the Communist Bloc is compared to the part in the free countries by a ratio of 45 to 10. On these disproportionate land areas nearly the same number of people live—75 million in the Soviet portion to 63 million in the non-Soviet portion. In

percentages of the total population of Eurasia these figures represent 3.5 per cent to 3.0 per cent, respectively.

In the Far East the larger share of the humid lands of the Asian Crescent are still outside of the Communist Bloc by a ratio of more than two to one (3.6 to 1.7 million square miles). The populations, however, are more evenly divided (about 580 million to 800 million persons). The striking points in the Far East, however, are the high population densities in certain areas of both Communist Bloc countries and countries within the Eurasian perimeter.

Contrasts in Population Density per Square Mile. Average population densities per square mile within large regions are relatively meaningless in themselves because they include so wide a range in population densities among local regions within them. They give an overall quantitative expression of the combined differences of area and population, however, which is useful for large comparisons between regions. The average density per square mile of humid western Eurasia is 155 persons, while the corresponding figure for humid Asia is 254. By contrast the average density in persons per square mile for the dry interior is only 12. The highest average density per square mile for any comparably sized region of the world is that of humid east China. When it is remembered that the countryside of east China does include much rough land as well as plains, the average density of 340 persons per square mile over a region which is more than a million and a half square miles in size reflects local densities of population per square mile much larger than this figure. The North China Plains, for example, support a population of approximately 162 million people on only 237 thousand square miles of land—an average density of 683 persons per square mile. This is the equivalent in territory of a region comprising the combined areas of Illinois, Iowa, Indiana, and Missouri, with the addition of half of Ohio. The corresponding average density of persons per square mile in that area of the United States is actually 80—an area of 238 thousand square miles occupied in 1950 by 19 million persons.

Compare the average population density of 340 persons per square mile over a million and a half square miles with that of 12 persons per square mile within 11 million square miles! This comparison reflects the existence of many thousands of square miles in central Asia where virtually no one is living. One may travel hundreds of miles without seeing a single human habitation in many parts of this vast interior region.

The average population density in the European portion of Eurasia is less than half that of humid China (155 to 340), although it more nearly corresponds to the average figure for the non-Communist countries of South, Southeast, and East Asia of 222 persons, as compared with 190 persons, on the average, for Western Eurasia outside the Communist Bloc. Differences are correspondingly greater than this between the humid Communist portion of Western Eurasia (127 persons per square mile) and that of humid China and the Asian satellites of North Korea and North Vietnam combined (322 persons per square mile).

The lowest average population density for a large region of Eurasia is that of Siberia, including the Soviet Arctic, which has 5 persons per square mile. The total Soviet portion of the dry Eurasian interior has only 8 persons per square mile, as contrasted

with 31 persons for the non-Soviet portion of the Arid Crescent.

The average population density for the Eurasian land mass as a whole is 103 persons per square mile, compared with that of 50 for the world and 25 for the American double continent.

The Three Faces of Eurasia

Structurally Eurasia is divided into three "faces," back to back, so to speak, against triangularly arranged central highlands and their extensions to the three corners of the continent. The three great topographic divisions shown on the map in Figure 205 are (1) the northern Eurasian Plain, (2) southern subcontinental peninsulas, and (3) an eastern compartmentalized realm. The latter region of East Asia is composed of smaller plains separated by highlands, offshore-island archipelagoes, and partially enclosed seas.

Eurasian Highlands. The central Asian highlands and their corner extensions are the principal topographic divides of this double continent. They are located in zones of weakness of several geologic ages, in which the most recent mountain-building activity has produced the Alps, the Caucasus, and Himalayan mountain systems. From the eastern end of the Himalayas the most recent zone of weakness is marked by island archipelagoes which are the tops of submerged mountain chains that encircle Southeast Asia and East Asia in a giant loop all the way around to northern North America.

North of the Himalayas of northern India is the great mass of the central Asian highlands. This is a triangular-shaped region of high mountains, enclosed basins, and plateaus. The basins and plateaus are similar to the basins of the cordilleran region within the United States, but many of those within the central Asian highland region are at great heights above sea level. They are exceeded in elevation by towering ranges such as the mountains around them in Tibet. The floors of generally east-to-west-trending longitudinal valleys or basins in the Tibetan highlands, for example, all exceed 14,000 feet elevation, which means that the bottoms equal or exceed in elevation most of the mountain peaks of the United States, except Alaska. Before Mount McKinley, Alaska's 20,300-foot peak, was added to the United States by Alaskan statehood, the highest point was Mount Whitney in California which rises to 14,495 feet above sea level. Most of the peaks of the American Rockies are below 14,000 feet. North of Tibet, the Tsaidam Basin

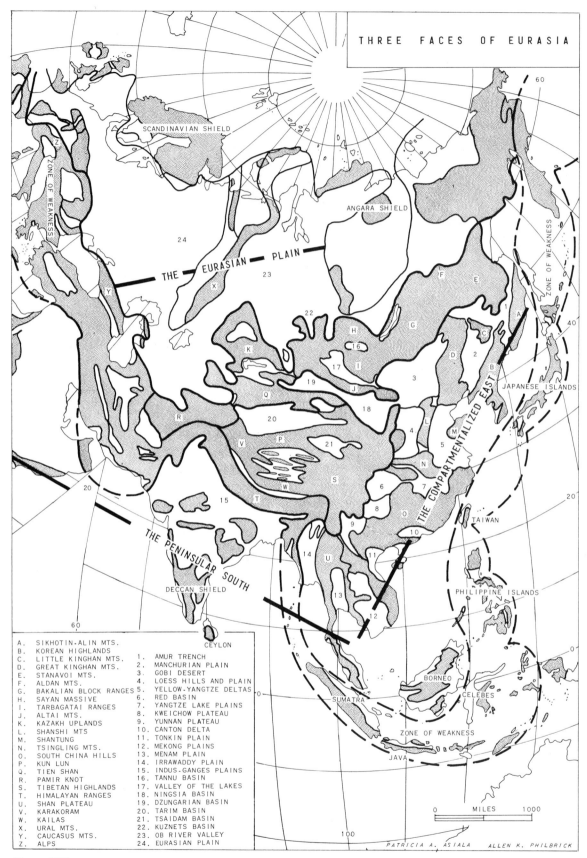

THREE FACES OF EURASIA

A. SIKHOTIN-ALIN MTS.
B. KOREAN HIGHLANDS
C. LITTLE KINGHAN MTS.
D. GREAT KINGHAN MTS.
E. STANAVOI MTS.
F. ALDAN MTS.
G. BAKALIAN BLOCK RANGES
H. SAYAN MASSIVE
I. TARBAGATAI RANGES
J. ALTAI MTS.
K. KAZAKH UPLANDS
L. SHANSHI MTS
M. SHANTUNG
N. TSINGLING MTS.
O. SOUTH CHINA HILLS
P. KUN LUN
Q. TIEN SHAN
R. PAMIR KNOT
S. TIBETAN HIGHLANDS
T. HIMALAYAN RANGES
U. SHAN PLATEAU
V. KARAKORAM
W. KAILAS
X. URAL MTS.
Y. CAUCASUS MTS.
Z. ALPS

1. AMUR TRENCH
2. MANCHURIAN PLAIN
3. GOBI DESERT
4. LOESS HILLS AND PLAIN
5. YELLOW-YANGTZE DELTAS
6. RED BASIN
7. YANGTZE LAKE PLAINS
8. KWEICHOW PLATEAU
9. YUNNAN PLATEAU
10. CANTON DELTA
11. TONKIN PLAIN
12. MEKONG PLAINS
13. MENAM PLAIN
14. IRRAWADDY PLAIN
15. INDUS-GANGES PLAINS
16. TANNU BASIN
17. VALLEY OF THE LAKES
18. NINGSIA BASIN
19. DZUNGARIAN BASIN
20. TARIM BASIN
21. TSAIDAM BASIN
22. KUZNETS BASIN
23. OB RIVER VALLEY
24. EURASIAN PLAIN

PATRICIA A. ASIALA   ALLEN K. PHILBRICK

Figure 205

352

stands at 9,000 feet. To the west the driest and most isolated desert of central Asia—the Takla Makan—occupies the center of the Tarim Basin, mostly at elevations over 3,000 feet above sea level. To the north there is a depression—Turfan—which is below sea level. Mount Everest, the highest mountain in the world, is precisely on the boundary of Nepal and Communist-held Tibet. Less than 500 miles south of Everest's 29,202 feet, the mouths of the Ganges' distributary channels empty into the Bay of Bengal. North of the Nepalese-Chinese border it is 3,000 miles to the mouth of the Yenisei River in the Soviet Arctic at approximately the same longitude as Everest; yet only 1,050 miles due north of Everest the Turfan Depression sinks below sea level in the interior of the world's largest land mass. Such are the ups and downs associated with mountain building in the zone of weakness. The border between the Soviet Union and China is marked by a series of faulted block-type mountain ranges which are the product of older mountain-building epochs than the Alpine-Himalayan orogeny. These older ranges, marking the northwestern flank of Asia's central highland, trend individually in a series of generally east-to-west alignments which are staggered in their positions from southwest to northeast. On the east the eastern highlands of China form the boundary between the series of coastal and river plains and the interior highland region. These plains and low highlands separating them are the product of erosion and alluvial deposition which characterize the compartmentalized eastern "face" of Eurasia.

The interior highland region of ranges and enclosed basins and plateaus occupies the triangular space between the three corner points of the central triangular mass, where the width of the highlands becomes pinched. On the west this narrowing is symbolized by the ancient Khyber Pass (Figure 206) on the route from Peshawar to Kabul in Afghanistan, and on to Samarkand in southern Russia. This route utilizes headwater valleys cut by western tributaries of the Indus River, and headwater valleys cut by the Amu or Oxus River draining to the Aral Sea on the Soviet side of the highlands. On the east corner 2,000 miles away, the narrowing, rugged highlands are not easily crossed. Deeply entrenched longitudinal valleys trending generally north to south are incised deeply into rugged plateau country over 3,000 feet in elevation which makes east to west communication very difficult. This bottleneck was the site during World

War II of the construction of the famous Burma Road from Lashio in Burma to Kunming and Chungking, capital of wartime China, on the upper Yangtze River (Figure 207). On the northeast corner, another 2,000 miles distant, the interior Asian highland triangle is marked by a third narrowing in the vicinity of Lake Baikal. Across this narrowing, communication from Soviet Irkutsk extends eastward through passes into northern Manchuria by way of Hulun and southward across the Republic of Outer Mongolia to Ulan Bator; and also across the Gobi Desert through the Kalgan Gap to Peiping in North China. The western side of the central highland mass from Irkutsk to Kabul, Afghanistan, or to the Khyber Pass, is also approximately 2,000 miles in length.

The major trend lines of the principal ranges along the three margins and within the central portion of the highland region are shown by the stippled pattern which generalizes rough land on the map in Figure 205. Each range is lettered and identified in the legend.

From the corners of the major highland region additional ranges extend outward to the three corners of the Eurasian continent. To the west these ranges are a continuation of the most recent zone of crustal instability. To the south, other older mainland highlands form the backbone of the Malay Peninsula and the Annam and Cambodian uplands in former French Indochina. Offshore archipelagoes of Southeast Asia continue as the tops of submerged mountain ranges already mentioned. In the northeast, the east Siberian highlands and island arcs of the zone of crustal weakness extend to the end of the continent and join across the strait from Alaska.

Distinctive Physical Regions Representative of the Faces of Eurasia. The three sides of the Eurasian land mass are separated by this radial system of high highlands. One of the three sides is a fully developed continental plain, the largest in the world, which extends with a minimum of interruption from the western edges of the Angara metamorphic shield of the central Siberian Plateau marked by the Yenisei River westward to the English Channel—a distance of nearly 4,000 (3,700) miles. (See Figure 208.) At its widest in central Russia the sedimentary lowland extends from the Arctic Ocean at the mouth of the Yenisei to the Afghanistan border 2,700 miles to the south-southwest. This immense continental lowland is comparable in significance to the 3,000-by-1,500-mile

Figure 206. A view of the famous Khyber Pass, the gateway to northern India. From the top of the Pass, the road snakes down into blistering defiles and wends westward toward Afghanistan. The constant vigilance and rigid security provided by mountainsides honeycombed with hidden gun emplacements, underground fortification, and observation posts used to be explained by the British Indian army as directed at unruly mountain tribesmen. The truth is, however, that the Khyber Pass is one of the strategic gateways between major world regions. In the days before the intercontinental ballistic missile and still today, the Pass controls the most direct and easiest over-land route between the Eurasian Plain of the north and the great lowlands of the Indian sub-continent. (*Courtesy of Wide World.*)

triangular lowland of North America. There are several major differences between them, however. The American triangular lowland has its narrow apex in the Arctic of Canada. Widening occurs along its longest axis where the American Plain achieves its broadest extent in a humid temperate region. The Eurasian Plain has its apex on the English lowlands and widens along its longest axis toward the east. Its broadest extent is in the sub-humid interior of the continent within the Arid Crescent. The open end of the triangular lowland in North America closely follows and almost parallels the major axis of world trade. It is approximately aligned with the "main line" of the great circle route across the Atlantic between New York and London and other North Sea ports of Europe (Figure 17). The open end of the great Eurasian Plain

faces the "dead" heart of the continent. The dead-end quality of the Eurasian Plain is a tremendous advantage in the defensive strategy of land warfare— the Russians have defended their country success-fully against both Napoleon and Hitler—but it has scarcely "contributed" to the participation of Russia in world trade. On the other hand, while it is true that the narrow end of the European Plain becomes a point on the Atlantic, the long sides of the triangle have remarkable access to the sea from Europe through North and Baltic Sea ports and through Mediterranean seaports. From northern interior lowland Russia, the Soviets have access to the sea through Black Sea ports, the Baltic, the White Sea, and for a limited season of the year through the long Arctic coast.

The second face of the continent is entirely

Figure 207. This aerial view of a section of the Ledo-Burma road shows one of the steep-sided eroded mountain valleys through which the highway was practically hewn. The road looks like a tiny ribbon, a contour scratched into the surface of the mountain side. (*Courtesy of Wide World.*)

different. On the east, facing the Pacific Ocean, no such extensive lowland plain spreads itself ocean-ward from the interior highlands. Instead, limited alluvial plains and other structurally level surfaces alternate with low mountains and hill country which subdivide the up-to-one-thousand-mile-wide continental margin of Asia into many relatively large lowlands. The southeast peninsula formerly referred to as Indochina is similarly subdivided. This peninsula is now divided among four national states—North and South Vietnam, Laos, and Cambodia. The map in Figure 205, showing level and rough surfaces, divides this eastern face of the continent into at least twenty-six physically discrete surface regions. Fourteen of them are predominantly level areas separated by a dozen distinctly rough-surface regions of mountains or hills. The identity of these subdivisions is given by number in the legend of the map in Figure 205.

The third face of the continent, to the west and south, consists of four great peninsulas. The first of these is Europe. The other three peninsulas shape the northern shores of the Indian Ocean. These are the Arabian Peninsula on the west, the Indian subcontinental peninsula in the center, and the Indochinese-Malayan Peninsula at the eastern corner of Asia. Between the four peninsulas are the Mediterranean-Red Sea, the Arabian Sea, and the Bay of Bengal. The Indochinese-Malayan Peninsula has already been included physiographically with Eastern Asia. It is set off from the Indian subcontinental peninsula by the eastern and southerly loop of the zone of crustal weakness which circles south, east, and then north through the island nations of the Pacific. To the west of India-Pakistan this same zone of recent geological stress dips southward to the coast of the continent before continuing west-northwestward toward Europe as the Iranian, Caucasian, and Turkish portions of the Alpine-Himalayan cordillera. At one point the zone of crustal instability touches the south coast of the continent and separates the Arabian Peninsula of Moslem Asia from the subcontinent of India.

The peninsular character of the southern-facing

Figure 208. The waving spears of wheat and the low bush height of the shelter belt "trees" wending their straight man-made path across the gently rolling expanse of the steppeland in the Ukraine illustrate two major aspects of the great Eurasian Plain: the great scale of the flat lands of the largest plains region on the globe, and the problem of periodic drought which plagues its use. (*Courtesy of Sovfoto.*)

borders of the continent extending outward into the Indian Ocean reflect a basic comparison with the immense north Eurasian lowlands. The Arabian and Indian peninsulas, particularly in their ocean-ward projections, are metamorphic crystalline shields of Archean age. Very considerable regions of recent sedimentary rock are also found between the southerly projections of these ancient plateaus and the crustal zones of instability to the north.

Summary

The present chapter has introduced various types of Eurasian regions. In a manner quite different from the Americas, the double continent of Eurasia is, so to speak, constructed "inside out." Its three faces extend from interior highlands to the three margins of the huge land mass, the world's largest plain on the north, plateaus and peninsulas pro-

truding from the south, and a complex compart-mentalized region on the east. The Americas have interior lowlands surrounded by marginal highland regions. Eurasia is also divided three ways into different and distinctive precipitation regions, a humid west and east and an arid center. People in the emergence of modern cultures have cut up the 20 million square miles of Eurasia in still other ways. Two groups—the Communist Bloc countries and the countries of the Eurasian perimeter—are the significant divisions of the human organization of the double continent. Each of these two concentric divisions are subdivided among six different cultural regions.

The next chapter examines in somewhat greater detail the resources of agriculture and the mineral resources of this, the largest and most heavily populated land platform of the world.

16 *The Resources of Eurasia*

The present chapter presents two resource associations which afford the people of Eurasia food, the materials with which to build and manufacture things, and the nonanimal energy with which to extend their capacity to perform work. As is true of other world regions discussed in previous chapters, these natural conditions and materials fall under the general headings of agricultural and mineral resources.

Agricultural Resource Associations

The several important physical circumstances which comprise the agricultural resource associations of Eurasia will be discussed individually and then selected ones will be put together to formulate agricultural resource regions of Eurasia. In the preceding chapter a three-fold division of Eurasia into "faces" was introduced. Each side of the continental triangle is set off from the other by the great central Asian highland extended linearly from the interior to the corners. This topographic division is in fundamental contrast to that observed in the Americas. Instead of a major lowland interior bounded by highlands on or near the margins, the arrangement of the continent is reversed. This distribution of surface divisions reflects subsurface structure.

Subsurface Structure. Subsurface structure underlies both agricultural and mineral resource associations. On the map in Figure 209 subsurface conditions are classified as in previous regions according to the same three types of earth structure—stable blocks, zones of weakness, and sedimentary lowlands.

The Precambrian metamorphic rock regions are shown in black and the shield areas are specially outlined on the map. They are the same stable blocks for Eurasia referred to on the world map in Chapter 15—the Scandinavian, Angara, Arab-African, Deccan, and Australian shields. Between these corner stones and the central zones of weakness which contain the highland alignments of Eurasia

lie most of the level sedimentary plains of the continent.

The circuitous alignment of the zone of weakness differs around the Southeast Asian Malay-Indochinese peninsulas and insular Borneo lowlands. The arcs of the Andaman and Nicobar Island chains off the coast of Malaya, the southwestern half of Sumatra, the chain of volcanic mountains of Java, and the rugged mountain peaks which form the Celebes and Philippine Island groups east and northeast of Borneo enclose a large shallow continental shelf which connects the sedimentary and tropical plains of Borneo with the subtropical and sedimentary mainland of Indochina. This is the southwestern third of the South China Sea which is less than 600 feet deep. From the Philippine Islands, north of which lies Formosa, a series of island arcs curve in great festoons all along the Pacific margins of Asia to Alaska. These are the Ryukyu chain southwest of Japan, the Japanese islands themselves, the Kurile chain of islands northeast of Japan, and the Aleutian chain which leads to the Alaskan mainland of North America. The ends of each of these separate arcs of islands and the mainland are marked by either a principal offshore island or peninsula. Formosa lies between the Philippines and the Ryukyus. It is Korea which is between southern Japan and Manchuria. Sakhalin Island separates Hokkaido from the Russian mainland. Between the Kurile chain and the Aleutian Islands is the Kamchatka Peninsula.

Between these principal island chains and the main islands and peninsulas which anchor them, so to speak, the Pacific coast of Asia is marked by five large enclosed seas which are shown on the map in Figure 205 of the previous chapter. These are the Bering Sea, the Sea of Okhotsk, the Sea of Japan, and the East China and South China Seas.

The Radial Pattern of Asian Drainage. The pattern of natural surface drainage reflects the radial arrangement of continental structure. Highlands (land above 1,000 meters, which is 3,280

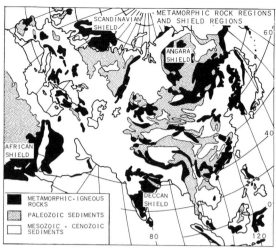

METAMORPHIC - IGNEOUS ROCKS

PALEOZOIC SEDIMENTS

MESOZOIC - CENOZOIC SEDIMENTS

Figure 209

feet) are shown by the territory enclosed by the 1,000-meter contour. This line is a measure of the central Asian highland and shows the radial alignment of mountain systems extending from it to the corners of Eurasia. The large drainage systems of Asia radiate outward from the central highlands to the Arctic, Pacific, and Indian Oceans, and internally within the principal interior basins of central Asia. These are the drainage regions for some of the longest and most extensive river systems in the world. Drainage in interior systems does not reach the sea. Water evaporates or is used faster than precipitation can supply it. Finally, there are all of the small rivers and coastal streams which have not yet created large basins by headward erosion. European drainage is included within the latter category on the map in Figure 210, on which the shaded area contrasts with the large territories occupied by major river basins and interior drainage which are left white. Drainage regions are outlined by a heavy black line, and identified by number.

The sources of the Indus, the Ganges, and the Brahmaputra rivers are all within a few hundred miles of one another behind the front ranges of the Himalayas. The Irrawaddy, the Salween, and the Mekong Rivers also flow south, but from the rugged highlands of the eastern corner of Asia's central mountainous mass. From the interior of the same highland region spring the waters which flow seaward to the east by such different routes as the Yangtze River of central China and the famous Huang Ho or Yellow River of North China. Between the drainage of the Yangtze to the east and the Mekong to the south, the smaller basins collect

waters which flow southeastward from the margins of the central mountain mass. These are the Hsi or West River of South China and the Yuan or Red River of North Vietnam. The northeast-flowing Amur River, which has its headwaters in the northern corner of the central mountain and plateau region of the continent in northern Outer Mongolia, forms the border between North China and the Soviet Union. From the north flank of the central highlands in eastern Siberia originate very extensive eastern Soviet river systems—the Lena, the Yenisei, and the Ob—which flow northward to the Arctic. Finally, west of the central highland region, surface waters descend into the interior basins of Soviet Central Asia. Principal rivers in this category are the Ili, which empties into Lake Balkhash, and the Syr and Amu (Oxus) rivers which drain into the Aral Sea within the arid lands of Kazakhstan. In this same category, but not starting from the central Asian highlands, is the Volga River system west of the Urals, which supplies the great inland Caspian Sea with water, and forms the western boundary separating Soviet Central Asia from southern European Russia. The eighteen river systems specifically mentioned are divided among the four radial directions—six to the south, five to the east, three to the north, and four which are involved in internal drainage.

As will be developed later, the radial drainage pattern of Asia is responsible for the pattern of alluvial plains on the coastal periphery of the continent. The larger of these plains are of key importance in the support of the large agricultural populations of most Asian countries.

Rough and Level Land. The map in Figure 205 in Chapter 15 has already been used to distinguish between the major surface features of Eurasia. The distinctions are the simplest possible—between essentially level surfaces and rough, uneven, or sloping surfaces. In this distinction the central idea remains the same as that used in previous continental descriptions of surface configuration, namely, that level-surfaced regions are those in which more than half of the total is level or even in character, while rough-surfaced regions are those in which more than half of the total is uneven, mountainous, hilly, or sloping in character. Discussion of the more important of the plains regions will be postponed until the section on specific agricultural resource regions in this chapter.

Precipitation and the Monsoons. The precipitation occurring over the land surfaces of

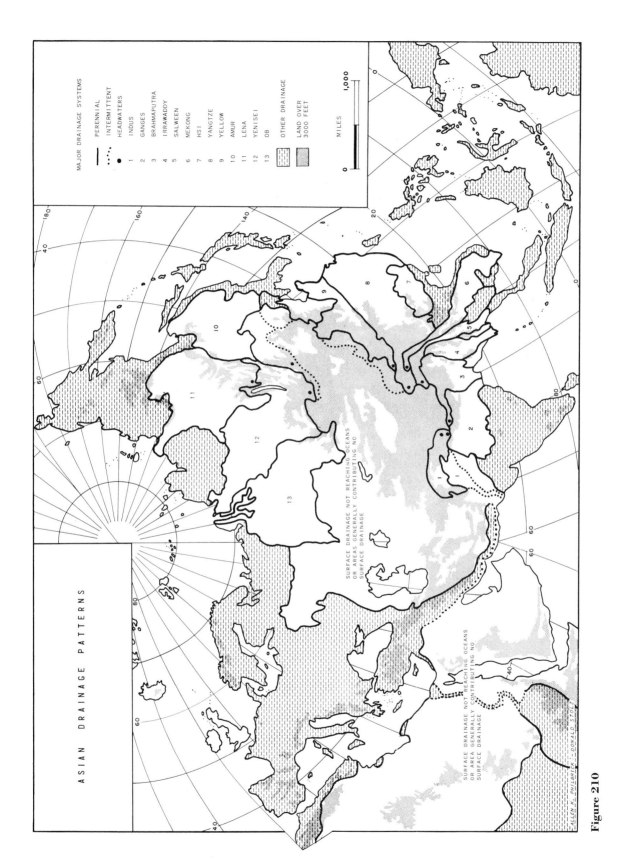

ASIAN DRAINAGE PATTERNS

MAJOR DRAINAGE SYSTEMS

PERENNIAL
INTERMITTENT
HEADWATERS

1 INDUS
2 GANGES
3 BRAHMAPUTRA
4 IRRAWADDY
5 SALWEEN
6 MEKONG
7 HSI
8 YANGTZE
9 YELLOW
10 AMUR
11 LENA
12 YENISEI
13 OB

OTHER DRAINAGE
LAND OVER 3000 FEET

MILES
0   1,000

SURFACE DRAINAGE NOT REACHING OCEANS OR AREAS GENERALLY CONTRIBUTING NO SURFACE DRAINAGE

SURFACE DRAINAGE NOT REACHING OCEANS OR AREA GENERALLY CONTRIBUTING NO SURFACE DRAINAGE

ALLEN K. PHILBRICK · DONALD STOLTMAN

Figure 210

Eurasia (Figure 211) is basically of two types, cyclonic and monsoon. Precipitation of western and northern, that is, European Eurasia has its primary origin in a series of cyclonic storms which move from west to east. Moisture-bearing air masses from the Atlantic and Arctic Oceans reach far to the east into the interior of the continent. They disgorge larger amounts of water nearer the west coastal margins than they do farther inland. Where storms rise over highlands precipitation is greater on the average than it is over continuously level lowlands. This means that cyclonic precipitation is increased by a secondary orographic effect. These two circumstances account both for the gradual diminution in the amount of average annual precipitation toward the continental interior, and the locally greater amounts which mark the western edges of the interior highland region along southern Soviet borderlands. The fortieth to sixtieth parallels on the map in Figure 211 indicate generalized paths of cyclonic storms from west to east across northern and western Eurasia.

The source regions of moisture-bearing air masses which move over the flanks of eastern and southern Asia are the tropical waters of the South Pacific and Indian Oceans. The processes which govern the average timing of air-mass migrations landward from the oceans and oceanwards from the continent explain a phenomenon called the *monsoon*. This effect has already been discussed in general terms in Chapter 3. Asia has two monsoons each of which has two phases—summer and winter. One monsoon effect comes in summer when air masses move into a general low-pressure area centered over the western end of Asia's central highland north of India. The opposite phase occurs in winter when air masses flow out of the corresponding high-pressure area similarly located. The monsoon operates because of land versus water temperature and pressure differentials which pull warm moist air from ocean to land in summer and reverse the direction for cool dry air to move from land to ocean in winter. The second monsoon occurs in response to low- and high-pressure areas centered over the northern end of Asia's tricornered central highlands in summer and winter, respectively. In effect, then, the movement of air masses induced at the surface by air-pressure differences over Asia is split into two parts by the height and mass of the central Asian topographic barriers which compartmentalize the monsoon effects into eastern and southern parts of Asia.

The impact of the monsoons on the supply of moisture to the agricultural population of Asia is so fundamental that some regional description of their operation in each of the two regions is warranted. The sources of maritime air masses are different, and the centers of low and high air pressure which localize the direction of air movement are in different places within Asia. During the winter, heat loss through radiation produces a persistent high pressure of atmosphere over much of Outer Mongolia and eastern Siberia. Cold dry air flows out of the continent and passes over much of China en route to the ocean. During the summer when heat input exceeds radiation, a corresponding low-pressure region develops in interior north and western China. Warm, moisture-laden air gradually pushes into China from the east, replacing the cold, dry air from the previous seasonal relationship. Over most of China, particularly northern and western China, the dry cold phase is predominant during a longer period of the year than is the inflow of warm maritime air. This means, therefore, a relatively short summer.

The reverse is true for India. After the spring sun begins to heat the Indus Valley region at a faster rate than radiation can dissipate the energy, the slight high-pressure ridge remaining from the previous season is erased and a summer low-pressure center starts developing over Southwest Asia. Air masses identified as the "southwest monsoon" are attracted to it. The shift from hot dry air flowing outward to incoming warm moist air is sudden in India. This is a gradual transition over eastern Asia where the "Pacific monsoon" operates. Once started the Indian or southwest monsoon may bring precipitation for as much as six months in the extreme south of India to as little as a few days in eastern Afghanistan.

Frequency and reliability of precipitation during the period of the monsoon varies with the number and strength of low-pressure centers which move from east to west with the progress of the monsoon into the interior of the Indian Peninsula. Relative position, elevation of the land, and the configuration of the surface are also locally important in affecting the amount of precipitation. The western slopes of peninsular India, known as the Western Ghats, as well as highland Ceylon and the mountains of the Burma frontier lie directly across the path of the monsoon when it first arrives across the Indian Ocean from the southwest. These regions, accordingly, experience heavy orographic precipitation.

The amounts vary with elevation and topographic exposure, from an average of 75 to as much as 200 inches. In some particularly exposed locations, as at Cherrapunji in eastern India, which is over 4,000 feet above sea level, the average precipitation exceeds 450 inches per year. This location is one of the wettest stations on record in the world. By contrast, the regions directly behind these southwestward-facing highlands are relatively dry since they experience a "rain-shadow" effect. Precipitation diminishes westward up the Ganges Plain toward western Pakistan from an average annual amount of 62.5 inches at Calcutta in the delta region to 19.6 inches at Lahore in northern West Pakistan.

The summer monsoon season lasts from June to October, followed by a cool dry season from November to February and a hot dry season from March to May, after which time the entire cycle is repeated. With certain relatively small regional exceptions, the cool and hot seasons are a period of the dry continental monsoon. During this period higher atmospheric pressure prevails over the subcontinent than over surrounding ocean areas. Cool dry continental air pushes away the remnants of the summer monsoon. During the retreat of the humid summer monsoon from November to January, the southeast coast of peninsular India and the west coast of Ceylon experience a second rainy season from what is called the "northeast monsoon."

During the two similar monsoon phases in eastern Asia, precipitation varies markedly from south to north. The subtropical coast and hill country of South China receives abundant precipitation from the rising of moist air over hill lands as it blows inland from south to north. The east-west barrier formed by the Ching Ling mountains of central China between the Yangtze and the Yellow Rivers marks the natural divide between warm and humid South China and cool, dry North China. In the south summer rains begin in April. By June they have reached their landward limit which provides moisture for orographic and convectional precipitation as far inland as Inner Mongolia. In northern Outer Mongolia, however, rainfall decreases from north to south. Moisture there is provided by cyclonic storms originating in the Atlantic and Arctic Oceans far beyond the reach of the Asian monsoon systems. By the end of October the dry winter monsoon is in full control of the continent.

In the equatorial regions and on the coasts of subtropical mainland Asia, precipitation may be described as chronic, although in most places there are marked variations in amount during different periods of the year. These variations are often described at wet and less wet rather than as wet and dry periods. East-facing coasts in southern Asia north of the equator are subject to orographic rainfall even when winds of continental origin, which have passed over large bodies of water, reach them from northeast directions during the fall and winter. This is true of the east coasts of Malaya, the Indochina Peninsula, and the Philippine Islands, as it is in southern India. In equatorial latitudes rainfall, while varying in amount, occurs throughout the year, except in certain protected and isolated topographic positions.

Growing Season. Growing season is no less important than moisture as an agricultural condition or resource. The combined indirect effects of latitudinal position, elevation, and humidity control the length of the frost-free season. The map in Figure 212 shows the regional distribution of three major categories in the duration of growing season: short (less than 90 days), moderate (frost every year but more than 90 consecutive days without frost), and long (frost free). An additional distinction of occasional frost not occurring every year is given by a line some distance poleward and generally paralleling the margins of frost-free regions.

From the map it can be seen that the southern rim of Asia is generally frost free from 25 degrees North Latitude southward. All but the northernmost fringe of the great western and northern Eurasian Plain has a growing season of longer duration than 90 days, but experiences some frost period. Winter ranges from severe in the north to quite mild in the south. In the interior of the Eurasian Plain, elevation of the highlands produces cooling such that a frost-free period of less than 90 days occurs in the Tibetan highlands as close to the equator as 28 degrees North Latitude. From this equatorward position shortness of growing season is characteristic over an intermittent zone to the northeastern corner of the continent, widening to include all of northeastern Siberia. An additional line, that of permanently frozen ground, demonstrates the grip of cold on central highlands and north and northeastern Eurasia from northern Scandinavia to the latitude of Lake Baikal and thence eastward to the Pacific.

Soils. A generalized pattern of soils is shown on the map in Figure 213, according to degrees of fertility. The greatest single highly fertile soils

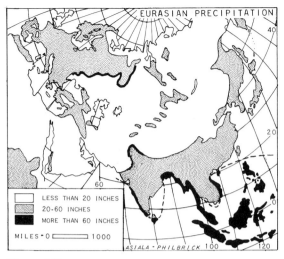

Figure 211

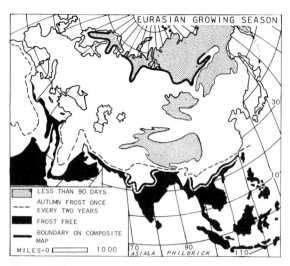

Figure 212

region is the loess and black-earth grassland soils region of southern and western Russia. These Russian grasslands suffer from drought because of their location on the drier margin of the humid lands of western Eurasia. North of the black-earth soils region soils of forest origin are less fertile. The principal areas of alluvial soils within eastern and southern Asia are located in conformity with the radial drainage pattern of Asia in the compartmentalized plains region referred to earlier. These are the important river valleys and deltas which receive transported silts from erosion within the interior. They will be discussed individually in the section on particular agricultural resource regions. The maps in Figures 210 and 213 of drainage basins and soil regions show that the sizes of alluvial valleys and deltas are roughly proportional to the sizes of drainage basins from which they are derived. This observation highlights the fact that alluvial plains are concentrated by erosion and deposition of soil originating in the interior. The larger the interior region from which such soils are derived and the greater the runoff supplied by precipitation, the larger can be the amounts of silt deposited in beds of alluvium which form flood plains and deltas along the margins of the continent. The gradient of land surfaces within the drainage basins, the character of vegetation land cover, and the degree to which land area has been disturbed by removal of natural vegetation through either natural or human agency have also had a great bearing on the amount of eroded material carried away by surface runoff.

Alluvial soils areas are among the most fertile,

particularly those subject to renewal by flooding. This is highly significant in regions of highly laterized residual tropical and subtropical soils as in Southern and Southeastern Asia. As already indicated in Chapter 4, laterization means rapid chemical decomposition and the removal by leaching of more soluble minerals and organic material. The process leaves behind relatively infertile concentrations of reddish alumina clays and iron oxides. Lush forests on tropical soils represent a balance of growth and return to the soil of organic materials supplied by the forest itself. Once the forest and the balance or cycle is destroyed, the infertile state of laterization quickly becomes established. A return to forest growth can gradually redevelop a more fertile soil by re-establishing the balance.

Alluvial soils, by contrast, often have been so recently deposited that they may be regarded as reservoirs of fertility transported from leached and eroded lateritic soils which are residual elsewhere. Concentrations of fertility by wind-blown collections of loess material repeat this same principal on the dry margins of the middle-latitude grasslands. One additional type of highly fertile soils is provided by certain highly mineralized volcanic parent material, as in particular locations of the highlands of Java and Sumatra.

From the map in Figure 213 it can be seen, therefore, that there are a number of alluvial and other highly fertile patches of small size which are of great local importance in supporting agricultural population. These areas in aggregate are an important part of the pattern of resources within the

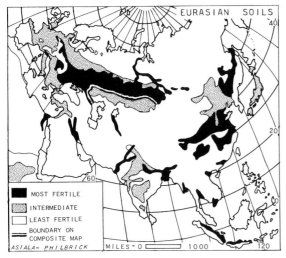

Figure 213

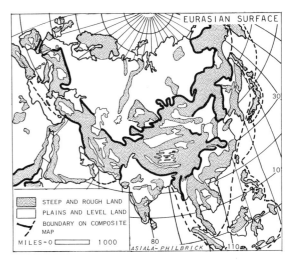

Figure 214

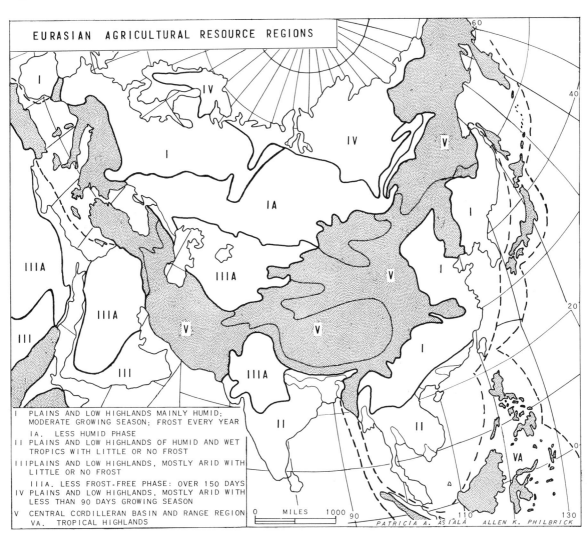

EURASIAN AGRICULTURAL RESOURCE REGIONS

I PLAINS AND LOW HIGHLANDS MAINLY HUMID;
   MODERATE GROWING SEASON; FROST EVERY YEAR

   IA. LESS HUMID PHASE

II PLAINS AND LOW HIGHLANDS OF HUMID AND WET
    TROPICS WITH LITTLE OR NO FROST

III PLAINS AND LOW HIGHLANDS, MOSTLY ARID WITH
    LITTLE OR NO FROST

    IIIA. LESS FROST-FREE PHASE: OVER 150 DAYS

IV PLAINS AND LOW HIGHLANDS, MOSTLY ARID WITH
    LESS THAN 90 DAYS GROWING SEASON

V   CENTRAL CORDILLERAN BASIN AND RANGE REGION
    VA. TROPICAL HIGHLANDS

Figure 215

broad regional classification, but they are difficult to show on a small-scale map. Thus, the northern and western Eurasian Plain presents the largest region of continuity in highly fertile soils. Next follows the compartmentalized or checkerboard pattern of large alluvial river and delta plains, wind-blown accumulations of loess, and structural basin-type residual soils. Soils regions of these types are the largest of high fertility in East, South, and Southeast Asia. Last, the fragmented pattern of relatively isolated small areas of high soil fertility must be noted within not only the cordilleran region, but also the many isolated areas within the island nations of Southeast and East Asia. Between regions and areas of highly fertile soils are extensive territories of less fertility.

The map in Figure 214 shows major surface condition at the same scale as precipitation, growing season, and generalized soils.

Agricultural Resource Regions of Eurasia

The map in Figure 215 shows the distribution of five primary associations of selected resources and natural conditions which are of significance to agriculture. They are given descriptive names in accordance with the selected criteria on the basis of which their boundaries are defined. The five associations in Eurasia are:

I. Plains and low highlands, mainly humid, with moderate to long growing season, but some frost every year.
   a. Less humid phase—not arid in view of reduced evaporation and precipitation concentration during the growing season.
II. Plains and low highlands of the humid and wet tropics, with little or no frost.
III. Plains and low highlands, mostly arid with little or no frost.
   a. Less frost-free phase, but with more than 150 days growing season.
IV. Plains and low highlands, mostly arid, with less than 90 days growing season—primarily permanently frozen ground.
V. Central cordilleran basin and range regions, composed of high highlands, including intermontane plains, basins, plateaus, and submerged mountain islands.
   a. Tropical highlands.

The categories include major regional variations as well. Study of the individual maps of resource conditions leads to the realization that there must be wide variations of the major associations within such large generalized categories and their regional distributions. Nevertheless, the generalizations serve the useful purpose of integrating the associated facts and focusing attention on the principal differences from place to place with respect to agricultural resources in Eurasia.

Before commenting on the regions and variants individually, it is appropriate to compare the major outline of resource combinations with the pattern of cultivated land in Eurasia shown by the world map in Figure 47 of Chapter 4. Such comparison reveals, again, that category I leads with respect to the amount of cultivated land. An important contrast with the Americas, however, is the much larger area of cultivated land within regions of the category defined as humid and wet tropics with little or no frost. Uninterrupted cultivation over great stretches of territory achieves its greatest extent in the regions of both categories I and II. Development of agriculture in other type resource areas requires special engineering or resource management. Application of human ingenuity to the problems of using available material resources includes such obvious means as irrigation within arid regions, terracing to create level land in hill country, and flood-control measures to protect the land from too much water, as well as to regulate the use of water. Fertilizing to restore soil nutrients used up or destroyed in the processes of farming is necessary wherever land is agriculturally used.

Often the areas which may be suitable for agricultural development by means of special measures are only a small portion of the total area. Cropland in such regions is accordingly limited in extent and becomes highly localized in those places where particular conditions favorable for development have been perceived. In large desert areas and permanently frozen tracts economical means of utilizing the existing resources and conditions for agriculture have not yet been found. Included among possible technological break-throughs which may well change the balance of resources are a cheap enough means of removing salt from sea water to make such water economically competitive with existing supplies of fresh water, the harnessing of nuclear and solar energy competitively with already existing sources of energy, and means of greatly increasing the quantity of fertilizers.

Until such time as additional technological

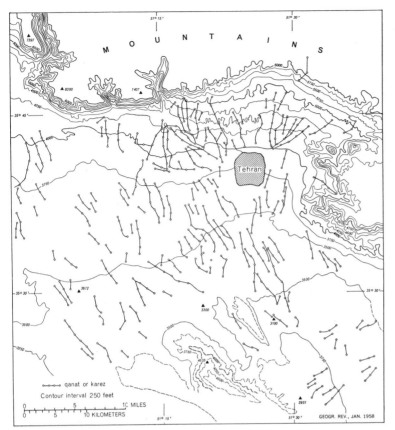

Figure 216. (A) Right, aerial photograph of qanats. Note that the ring of excavated earth around each well shaft is plainly visible from the air. (*Courtesy of the American Geographical Society, taken from George B. Cressey, "Qanats, Karez, and Foggaras," Geographical Review.*) (B) Left, qanats in the Tehran area, Iran. (*Courtesy of Army Map Service K501 (G. S. G. S. 3919), Sheet No. 9M, Tehran.*)

innovations are created and applied, however, the pattern of agricultural resources suitable for use in regions of categories III and IIIa—plains and low highlands, mostly arid, with little or no frost, including the less frost-free phase—will continue to be very spotty. The isolated oasis character or island-like settlement pattern in the dry lands of the Arid Crescent is a product of the distribution of water available for irrigation. Water has always been the critical resource in the alluvial valleys of the Nile, the Tigris and Euphrates, the Indus, and the Amu Rivers, as well as in many additional smaller stream valleys. Ground water from subsurface drainage made available by wells characterizes the sites of dry land agricultural village life in many places. Wells are located on alluvial fans which mark the lower edges of moisture-catching uplands in regions of internal drainage where surface runoff is intermittent or rare. Ancient designs of engineer-

ing works are still in use today which conduct underground drainage to the surface where it can sustain life. As shown by the picture referred to in Figure 216 many of these works from the Middle East would do credit to the engineers of any era. Access to underground channels is by rows of man-holes dug and kept clear without benefit of machinery, steel pipe, concrete, or mechanical energy. Such combinations of wells and tunnels are called *qanats* in Iran and *foggara* in North Africa. Advantages of these systems over surface drainage are the protection against contamination and the conservation of water against evaporation. In South Asia steep hillsides have been transformed into a series of step-like terraces. Water can be moved onto and off these pocket-sized fields by gravity. The engineering work involving modification of both surface and drainage for the purpose of moving water onto and away from the land are illustrated by paddy

Figure 217. Rice terracing in the Philippines. Water moves by gravity in this controlled engineering of land and water in Banawe Mountain Province. (*Courtesy of Charles Phelps Cushing.*)

fields in the Philippines, such as those shown in Figure 217.

Despite man's ingenuity, however, most of the land area in agricultural regions of categories III, IV, and V remains uncultivated.

The Northwest Eurasian Plain. The northwest Eurasian Plain is the largest predominantly level land surface on the planet. The resource associations combined within this region are generalized on maps in Figures 209 through 215 which indicate several reasons why it is not entirely used for crop agriculture. The great plain is divided primarily between regions of categories I, Ia, III, and IV. The distinction between categories I and Ia is primarily moisture. Each of the subregional categories, humid or subhumid, however, is also subdivided between a grassland and a forested soil portion, which means that region I–Ia is divided into four parts. The southern half of category I in the Soviet Union is the black-earth soils section. The northern half is characterized by forest soils. In the more humid western portion there are rela-

tively fertile gray-brown podzolic forest soils. In the south and west parts of less humid regional category Ia, drier steppe-grassland soils prevail. In the northeast part of region Ia, however, less humid coniferous and mixed forested soils are characteristic. The black-earth soils, both humid and subhumid, are the "bread basket" of the Soviet Union.

North of the regions of category I and Ia is the region of category IV. This northeastern portion of the Eurasian Plain and low highlands, the central Siberian Angara Shield region, is subarctic *taiga*, a forest of pine and fir mixed with larch, birch, and aspen. It thins gradually into the tundra along the Soviet Arctic coasts. Here, as farther east in eastern Siberia, the shortness of the growing season makes difficult the development of productive agriculture. Southeast of category I territory is a region of category IIIa—plains and low highlands, mostly arid, with frost every year but more than 150 days growing season. Development of agriculture here is dependent principally on the availability of water. It is a basin of internal drainage, which contains the

Caspian and Aral seas and numerous lakes of internal-drainage origin. The largest of these is Lake Balkhash. It is only 35 feet deep but covers more than 7,000 square miles. There have been several grandiose but as yet unfulfilled schemes to reverse the direction of major north-flowing rivers, such as the Ob, east of the Ural Mountains, in order to form a great inland sea which would enable irrigation to be greatly expanded.

The Caspian Sea, into which the Volga and Ural Rivers flow, is gradually silting up, evaporating, and being depleted by diversions for irrigation from the Volga. It remains, however, the world's largest inland body of water. The basin of the Volga River is its principal watershed and maintains Caspian Sea waters close to a mean level which is 85 feet below sea level. The waters are relatively fresh, at least in the shallower northern portion into which the Volga empties; but neither the Caspian nor the Aral seas can be used for irrigation directly because they are too brackish. The southern portion of the Caspian lies within a depressed basin which reaches a depth of more than 3,500 feet. The water in Lake Balkhash is fresh enough to be used for irrigation. The total area of Lake Balkhash (7,115 square miles), the Caspian Sea (169,383), and the Aral Sea (26,166), when combined (202,664 square miles), exceeds the total size of the five Great Lakes of North America (95,000 square miles) by a ratio of more than two to one. These three bodies of water within the steppe and desert regions of Soviet Central Asia approximate in their aggregate area the size of the whole state of Texas which is 267,339 square miles. Cotton is the most important subtropical crop in acreage which irrigation during the long growing season of Soviet Central Asia makes possible.

Humid Plains and Low Highlands in East, South, and Southeast Asia.

By contrast with the great extent of relatively uniform agricultural resources in the north and west Eurasian Plain, the humid plains and low highlands of East, Southeast, and South Asia are broken up into many smaller units. Some of these are important alluvial valleys and deltas of the drainage systems discussed earlier under the heading of the radial drainage pattern of Eurasia. A dozen of the more important ones are listed in Table XXXV. From the table, the map of population in Figure 22 (Chapter 2), and the soil map in Figure 213, it is apparent that great concentrations of agricultural population use the resources of these twelve plains areas. All but one of them are alluvial river and delta plains. The exception is the Red or Szechuan Basin of the upper Yangtze, a structural basin which derives its name "Red" from the color of the underlying sandstone. The total area of the twelve largest separate plains represents just over one-fifth of the territory of the humid lands of East, South, and Southeast Asia (not including the offshore islands of the Pacific). On this one-fifth of the area almost half of the total population gains its living. The largest uninterrupted plains are those of North China and the Ganges Plain of India, which are the most densely populated corelands of these two most populous nations of Asia and of the world. The views in Figure 218 show irrigated land in the Ganges Valley where irrigation is necessary to get a crop.

The plains of North China include the Manchurian Plain, the plain of the Huang Ho or Yellow River, and the lower Yangtze River delta. Here, on slightly more than one-tenth of the area of China, on plains which are adjacent to one another, is concentrated one-third of China's millions and one-tenth of the human race. Approximately one-third of India's 438 million persons live on the combined areas of the Ganges Plain and the Indian part of the Ganges Delta, both of which occupy part of the wet tropics of category II. Nearly 122 million persons in that plains region occupy an area of 175,000 square miles at an average density of 700 persons per square mile. By comparison the average density per square mile of the North China Plain, excluding the frontier region of the Manchurian Plain, is approximately 695 persons per square mile. The Ganges Plain represents only 14 per cent of the total area of India.

When densities of population are calculated in relation to cultivated area, many purely rural areas in North China have more than 2,000, and even 2,500, persons for every square mile of cultivated land. In the wetter eastern portions of the Ganges Delta many districts average more than 1,500 persons per square mile of cultivated land. The picture in Figure 219 shows the hand-labor involved in subsistence agricultural enterprise in Ceylon.

Population and Cultivated Land in Agricultural Resource Regions.

Comparison of the pattern of population in Eurasia shown by the map in Figure 22 with that of cultivated land in Figure 47 and with regional associations of agricultural resources in Figures 209 to 215 shows a high degree of correspondence of people, food production, and certain resource combinations. The cor-

Agricultural plain	Sq. mi.	Population	Pop. per sq. mi.	River System	Drainage area, sq mi.
Indus-Punjab	103,000	20,600,000	200	Indus	372,000
Ganges Plain including Indian Punjab	115,000 35,000	86,146,000 12,641,000	750	Ganges	350,000
Ganges-Brahmaputra Delta	80,000	65,000,000	810	Brahma- putra	361,000
Irrawaddy Delta	27,000	9,000,000	330	Irrawaddy	160,000
Menam Delta	12,000	7,000,000	580	Menam	61,800
Mekong Delta	14,000	5,600,000	400	Mekong	307,000
Red River Delta	6,000	6,000,000	1,000	Red	46,000
Hsi River, Canton Delta	18,000	30,000,000	600	Hsi	168,000
Yangtze Plain	103,000	75,000,000	730	Yangtze	706,000
Huang Ho, Yellow Plain	134,000	87,000,000	650	Huang Ho	287,000
Manchurian Plain	170,000	30,000,000	175	Amur	709,000
Szechuan Basin	75,000	50,00,000	658	. . .	. . .
Total	857,000	471,346,000	550	. . .	3,527,800

[a] Estimates from various sources; Norton Ginsburg et al., *The Pattern of Asia*, New York: Prentice-Hall, 1958; O. H. K. Spate, *India and Pakistan*, London: Methuen and Co., Ltd., 1954; George Cressey, *Land of the 500 Million*, New York: McGraw-Hill Co., 1955; and J. E. Spencer, *Asia, East by South*, New York: John Wiley and Sons, 1954.

respondence of people and cropland with soils regions of highest and moderate fertility, as opposed to soils regions of least fertility, is particularly striking. The classification of what constitutes good soils is based primarily on analysis of soils which duplicates human experience in the practice of agriculture by trial and error. Coincidence with water availability is just as striking.

Major agricultural resource regions embodied in categories I, Ia, II, and special areas of type IV account for the largest areas of agricultural development. The patterns of agriculture within regions of categories III and V are scattered and more fragmentary. Agriculture is least developed and most isolated within regions characterized by an extreme shortness of growing season. Following closely are those regions in other categories which have the least moisture, the most rugged terrain, particularly in areas isolated by distance from population concentrations which have already developed on the more easily exploited resource combinations. It will remain to be seen in the following chapters how people of differing cultures and creative ideas have used and organized the areas which have these agricultural resource associations and conditions.

Mineral Resources of Eurasia

Mineral resources will be considered in the two broad associations used in previous regions—those minerals associated primarily with *sedimentary* rocks, and those with *metamorphic-igneous* rocks. This means that the basic pattern of mineral distributions can be expected to follow the outlines of major divisions between these two great classes of rock associations of the earth's surface and subsurface. Discussion focuses on the two most important classes of minerals for modern industries, which are the mineral fuels from sedimentary rocks and the metallic minerals from mainly metamorphic and igneous rocks. The mineral fuels supply the energy to drive most of the machinery of modern industry, while the metallic minerals supply the chief ingredients of the manufactures produced by the application of that energy.

Mineral Patterns in Eurasia and the Americas. The association of rock types with mineral

Figure 218. (A) A part of the land surrounding the Tilaiya Dam and power station in Bihar Province west of Calcutta in northeast India. The Tilaiya is the first of seven multipurpose dams being constructed by the Damodar Valley Corporation as part of a gigantic project for the unified development of the Damodar River system. The project is designed to control the frequent devastating floods in the Damodar Valley brought by the monsoon rains, and to provide power for industry and permanent irrigation for more than a million acres, in addition to channels for navigation. (B) A traditional small-scale technique of single-purpose nature, the Persian wheel. It provides water in the age-old manner for wheat and corn, the principal crops in southeast Rajasthan. These lands are both fertile and heavily populated. (*Courtesy of United Nations.*)

Figure 219. The farmer sowing rice in a Ceylon field illustrates the hand labor of subsistence agriculture. The effortless grace of this individual belies the real labor which such painstaking placing of the seeds of rice in the soft mud actually represents. (*Courtesy of United Nations.*)

types is the same in Eurasia as in the Americas, but the patterns of their geographical distribution are very different—"inside out," by comparison. The reversed nature of the pattern of bedrock types, compared with that of the Americas, is observable in general terms from the map in Figure 205. The linear alignments of folded or block-type mountains are threaded between pivotal areas of the continental shields in Scandinavia, Africa, the Indian Deccan, Angara in northern Siberia, and Western Australia. These mountains have metamorphic and igneous rock cores. Sedimentary plains of more recent geological origins are located on the outer margins of these structural alignments of more ancient bedrock. Of course, not all ancient metamorphic rocks are located in the central highlands region, as shown in the geologic map in Figure 209; but, generally speaking, the ores of metallic minerals are located within or on the margins of the interior highlands and a minority are located within the shields and other crystalline uplands near the coasts. The mineral fuels are in more exterior lowland and seaward positions, although

many of these deposits are a good distance inland and away from the main line and major trunk lines of world trade.

Patterns of metallic mineral resources in North America are oriented toward the interior concentrations of mineral fuels where agricultural resources are also abundant. In Eurasia, as will be apparent in greater detail in the next three chapters, patterns of resource development and organization have evolved differently. Because the Eurasian continent is divided into three contrasting realms separated by arid and inaccessible highlands in Central Asia, both agricultural and mineral resource associations were originally organized by peoples of at least three separate and distinctive cultural backgrounds in relative isolation from one another. This cultural orientation may not necessarily continue indefinitely.

A geographical revolution in the orientation of Russian and Chinese peoples within two-thirds of the Eurasian continent is now taking place. This revolution in orientation accompanies the communization of two-thirds of Asia and is resulting in an *inward* facing of peoples of two formerly separate cultural backgrounds in the course of development of the interior of Eurasia. It may mark a revolutionary break with the historic past. In so breaking with the past the patterns of basic mineral resources are fundamental to an understanding of the revolution in geographical relationships between China and the Soviet Union since 1950.

Classification of Mineral Resources. The spatial association of mineral resources may be classified under four headings—complementary, noncomplementary, diversified, and specialized. Minerals are defined as "spatially economically associated" within a mineral resource region when they are located within a radius of 250 miles of one another. This somewhat arbitrary radius gives a diameter of 500 miles to the regions classified according to the above definition.[1]

---

[1] United Nations Secretariat, Department of Economic Affairs, *World Iron Ore Resources and their Utilization,* Lake Success, N.Y.: 1950, p. 33 and Table 13.

The radius of 250 miles was selected after examination of the distances by rail which it is estimated are the average transportation requirements for pig-iron production in Asia and the Far East. Estimates were averaged at 498 miles. Rounding to 500 and dividing by 2 yields the factor of 250 miles. This figure, in effect, is the average distance which coal and a metallic ore may be separated from each other at the mine head and be economically moved over land for smelting at a third place in relation to a market. The index is crude, but since it is proposed to define spatial limits of mineral resource complementarity, its use is perhaps justified.

Complementary minerals means the association within a 250-mile radius of both mineral fuels (coking coal) and metallic ores. Noncomplementary minerals are the association of either the mineral fuels or metallic minerals but not both. As the word complementary implies the advantage of relative close proximity of mineral fuels and metallic ores lies in the necessity of applying mechanical power in the mining and processing of metallic ores, and in the need for coking quality coal in the smelting process, particularly of iron.

Diversified means that there are within the resource association five or more major minerals, either mineral fuels or metallic ores. Specialized means that the mineral association is primarily confined to no more than four minerals. An example of the relatively isolated specialized mineral region is the Persian Gulf petroleum-producing region in the Middle East, and its counterpart in the Caucasus of the Soviet Union. They specialize in oil and produce little or nothing else of a mineral nature. Deposits of iron and copper in the Soviet portion of the Scandinavian Shield between the Baltic and the White seas exist and are produced in relative isolation. Production in such instances is externally oriented. An example of a diversified mineral resource region is the southern Ukraine, where the coal of the Donbas and the iron ore of Krivoi Rog are the basis of very large iron and steel industries. Nickel ores of Nikopol are important in making alloy steels. At least seven major minerals are produced.

Mineral Resource Regions

The most important mineral-producing regions in Eurasia, according to the above criteria, are shown on the map in Figure 220 against the background of their respective rock associations—igneous-metamorphic and sedimentary. Despite the antiquity of civilization in Eurasia, prospecting of the interior of Asia is still fragmentary and inconclusive in many regions. In Communist China, for example, a ministry for geology was established in 1952. It is pushing regional geological surveys throughout China, and particularly in the interior. Similar basic research was energetically pursued by Soviet geologists from the inception of the Communist regime and continues today in the U. S. S. R. The map in Figure 220 shows only the present known pattern of the mining of major mineral resources throughout Eurasia. It excludes Western Europe, which has been dealt with earlier.

Comparison of Mineral Resources of the Communist Bloc with Those of the Eurasian Perimeter. The map in Figure 220 should be studied in conjunction with the diagrammatic map in Figure 221, which serves as both summary and comparison of the number and mineral character of the mineral resource regions of the Communist Bloc and the Eurasian perimeter. The physical regional pattern of the continent may be reviewed from the diagram. It shows the tripronged central-highland system which separates northern plains from southern peninsulas, and in turn from the compartmentalized plains, highlands, and seas of the Far East. Three types of highland regions are distinguishable as the Alpine-Himalayan-island arc system, the central basin plateaus and ranges, and the older block-mountain ranges which separate Russia from China. The five pivotal Archean shields of Scandinavia, Africa, Northern Siberia, the Deccan Peninsula of India and Western Australia which are not specifically shown on the map, mark the outer limits of Eurasia, structurally.

Within this structural pattern the only political line shown is the boundary which separates the Communist Bloc from the Eurasian perimeter, and the Soviet Union from Communist China. Against this generalized background the twenty-nine mineral regions shown on the map in Figure 221 are plotted. Complementary mineral regions on Figure 221 have a horizontal dashed-line pattern over them; noncomplementary are left white. Those regions producing coal of coking quality are half stippled-in. More detailed information for each mineral resource region is given in Table XXXVI as well as on the map in Figure 220. The regions on the maps and in the table are divided among the four major regional divisions of Eurasia—west Eurasia, northern Eurasia, eastern Eurasia, and southern Eurasia. Each mineral region is classified according to its category as complementary or noncomplementary, and diversified or specialized. The major mineral fuels and metallic minerals produced in each region are listed in the table.

As may be found by counting the number of complementary mineral regions in Eurasia from either the table or the diagrammatic map, the noncomplementary regions are outnumbered in a ratio of 18 to 11. Obviously all of the regions which have complementary mineral resources are not of equal importance or degree of development. For example, south peninsular India is listed as possessing complementary resources. But the coals

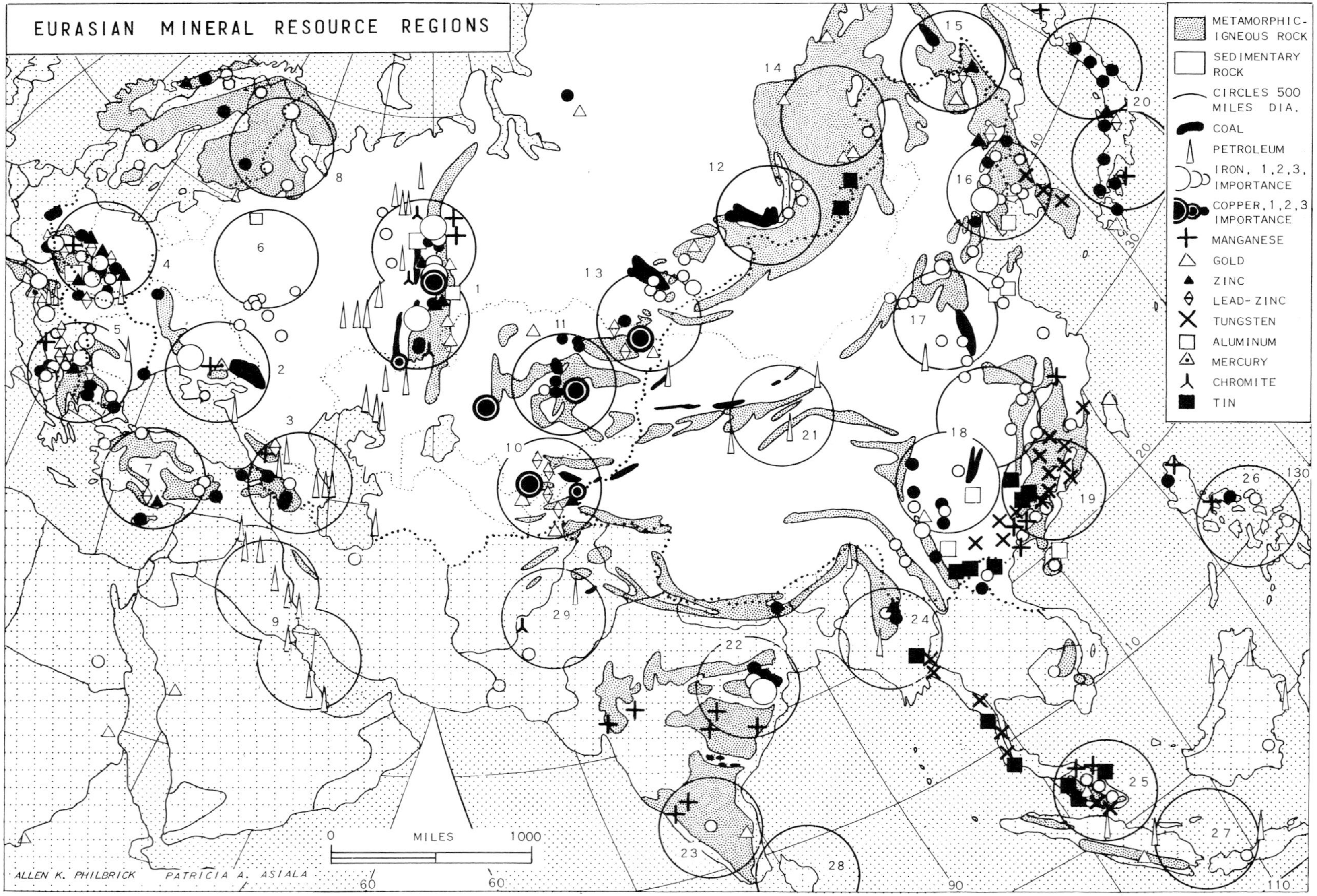
EURASIAN MINERAL RESOURCE REGIONS
METAMORPHIC-IGNEOUS ROCK
SEDIMENTARY ROCK
CIRCLES 500 MILES DIA.
COAL
PETROLEUM
IRON, 1,2,3, IMPORTANCE
COPPER, 1,2,3 IMPORTANCE
MANGANESE
GOLD
ZINC
LEAD-ZINC
TUNGSTEN
ALUMINUM
MERCURY
CHROMITE
TIN
0 MILES 1000
ALLEN K. PHILBRICK
PATRICIA A. ASIALA

Figure 220

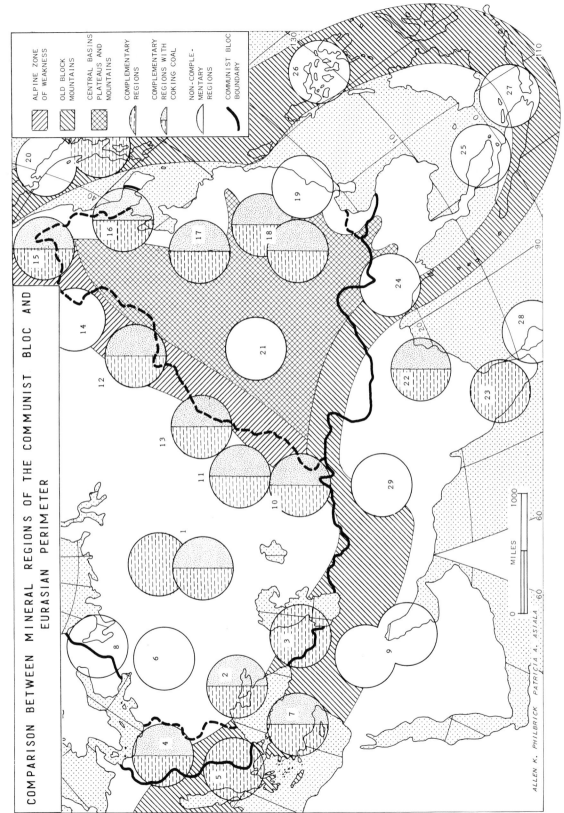

COMPARISON BETWEEN MINERAL REGIONS OF THE COMMUNIST BLOC AND EURASIAN PERIMETER

ALLEN K. PHILBRICK PATRICIA A. ASIALA

Legend:
- ALPINE ZONE OF WEAKNESS
- OLD BLOCK MOUNTAINS
- CENTRAL BASINS PLATEAUS AND MOUNTAINS
- COMPLEMENTARY REGIONS
- COMPLEMENTARY REGIONS WITH COKING COAL
- NON-COMPLE-MENTARY REGIONS
- COMMUNIST BLOC BOUNDARY

MILES
0   60   1000   60

Figure 221

TABLE **XXXVI** SPATIALLY, ECONOMICALLY ASSOCIATED MINERAL REGIONS OF EURASIA
(LESS WESTERN EUROPE)[a]

Map[b] key	Regional names	Total minerals	Mineral fuels	No.	Metallic minerals		No.
	West Eurasia		**Complementary diversified minerals**				
1	Urals	20	Oil Natural gas Coal[c] Lignite	4	Iron Chromium Nickel Manganese Copper Zinc Cobalt Titanium	Magnesium Gold Bauxite Platinum Columbium Tungsten Molybdenum Vanadium	16
2	Ukraine	7	Coal[c] Natural gas Oil	3	Iron Manganese Magnesium	Mercury	4
3	Caucasus	8	Oil Natural Gas	2	Manganese Molybdenum Lead	Copper Barium Bauxite	6
4	Central East Europe	15	Coal[c] Lignite Oil	3	Iron Manganese Cobalt Magnesium Tin Nickel	Uranium Copper Lead Zinc Antimony Barium	12
5	South East Europe	8	Natural Gas Oil	2	Uranium Iron Copper	Lead Mercury Bauxite	6
			Complementary limited minerals				
6	Moscow	3	Lignite	1	Iron	Bauxite	2
7	Turkey	4	Coal[c]	1	Iron Chromite	Copper	3
			Noncomplementary limited minerals				
8	Soviet Scandinavian Shield	3		0	Iron Copper	Columbium	3
9	Persian Gulf	1	Oil	1			0
	Northern Eurasia		**Complementary diversified minerals**				
10	Soviet Central Asia	10	Coal[c] Oil	2	Uranium Molybdenum Tungsten Copper	Zinc Lead Antimony Mercury	8
11	Kuzbas-Leninogorsk	7	Coal[c] Lignite	2	Iron Copper Lead	Zinc Barium	5
			Complementary limited minerals				
12	Irkutsk-Baikal	5	Coal[c]	1	Uranium Iron	Tungsten Molybdenum	4
13	Karaganda	3	Coal[c]	1	Copper	Antimony	2

TABLE XXXVI (CONTINUED)

Map key	Regional names	Total minerals	Mineral fuels	No.	Metallic minerals		No.
			Noncomplementary limited minerals				
14	East Siberian Highland	2		0	Gold	Tin	2
	Eastern Eurasia		**Complementary diversified minerals**				
15	Soviet Pacific High-lands	8	Coal[c] Oil	2	Iron Tungsten Molybdenum	Lead Zinc Tin	6
16	Southeast Manchuria-North Korea	7	Coal[c] Oil shale	2	Iron Copper Bauxite	Lead Zinc	5
17	North China	6	Coal[c]	1	Iron Lead Bauxite	Copper Gold	5
18	Yangtze	8	Coal[c]	1	Iron Manganese Antimony	Copper Lead Gold Zinc	7
19	South China	10	Coal[c]	1	Iron Manganese Tungsten Antimony	Copper Lead Zinc Tin Gold	9
20	Japanese Islands	10	Coal Oil	2	Iron Copper Manganese Chromite	Zinc Gold Tin Lead	8
			Noncomplementary limited minerals				
21	Western China	4	Oil	1	Iron Copper	Gold	3
	Southern Eurasia		**Complementary diversified minerals**				
22	Northeast Peninsular India	6	Coal[c]	1	Iron Copper Manganese	Aluminum Chromite	5
23	South Penin-sular India-Mysore	5	Coal	1	Iron Manganese	Chromite Gold	4
			Noncomplementary diverse minerals				
24	Burma	7		0	Iron Copper	Lead Zinc Tungsten Cobalt Nickel	7
25	Malaya	6		0	Iron Manganese Tungsten	Tin Bauxite Titanium	6

TABLE XXXVI (CONTINUED)

Map key	Regional names	Total minerals	Mineral fuels	No.	Metallic minerals		No.
			Noncomplementary diverse minerals (continued)				
26	Philippines	7	Coal	1	Iron Manganese Chromite	Copper Lead Zinc	6
			Complementary limited minerals				
27	Indonesian Islands	4	Oil Coal	2	Tin Iron		2
			Noncomplementary limited minerals				
28	Ceylon	1		0	Iron	(undeveloped)	1
			Noncomplementary limited minerals				
29	West Pakistan	4	Oil (minor) Coal[c] (minor)	2	Chromite Iron		2

[a] Sources: 1. *Oxford Regional Economic Atlas, the USSR and Eastern Europe*, London, Oxford University Press, 1956. 2. *Goode's World Atlas*, Chicago, Rand McNally Co., 1953. 3. United Nations, *Survey of World Iron Ore Resources*, New York, 1955. 4. United Nations, *World Iron Ore Resources and their Utilization*, Lake Success, New York, 1950. 5. Vei Chow Juan, "Mineral Resources of China," *Economic Geology*, June-July, 1946, pp. 399–474. 6. United Nations, *Proceedings of the Symposium on the Development of Petroleum Resources of Asia and the Far East*, Bangkok, 1959. 7. Theodore Shabad, *China's Changing Map*, New York, Frederick A. Praeger, 1956. 8. Cressey, George, *Land of the 500 Million*, New York, McGraw-Hill, 1955. 9. United Nations, *Non-Ferrous Metals in Underdeveloped Countries*, New York, 1956. 10. United Nations, *Coal and Iron Resources of Asia and the Far East*, Bangkok, 1952. 11. Ginsburg et al., *The Pattern of Asia*, New York, Prentice-Hall, Inc. 1958. 12. Edward A. Ackerman, *Japan's Natural Resources*, Chicago, University of Chicago Press, 1953. 13. Administration for Geology and Cartography, *Geographical Atlas*, MVD USSR, Moscow, 1955. 14. Alan M. Bateman, *Economic Mineral Deposits*, New York, John Wiley and Sons, 1950. 15. World Oil, *14th Annual International Outlook Issue of World Oil*, Houston, Texas, August 15, 1959. 16. William Van Royen, *Atlas of The Mineral Resources of the World*, New York, Prentice-Hall, 1952.

[b] Regions by number refer to maps in Figures 220 and 221.

[c] Coal of *coking* quality included.

of the central Deccan Peninsula in the valley of the Godavari River, which represent the mineral-fuel complement of metallic ores in the southern Deccan, are not of coking quality. Future development here is dependent on alternative methods of smelting which do not depend on coking coal. The same is true in many places throughout the Pacific island countries of East and Southeast Asia.

Identical limitations apply to some of the complementary mineral regions behind the "iron curtain," but not to the same extent. The Caucasus has petroleum but no coal; yet the Donbas coal of the southern Ukraine is not much more than 500 miles distant to the northwest, and cheap transportation is available on the Black Sea and navigable rivers for much of the distance. Southern central Soviet Asia has coal but no iron ore; yet a fledgling *Begovat* steel industry initiated during World War II in 1943, is supplied principally on a "diet" of scrap iron. The initial development of the magnifi-

cently rich iron ores of Magnitogrosk was linked with the production of coking coal in the Kuznets Basin. This meant steel production at both ends of a 1,000-mile rail haul of both coking coal and iron ore. Later, when coking coals of the Karaganda mineral district were discovered and developed, the land distance between coke and ore was reduced to 600 miles.

A simple comparison of complementary versus noncomplementary mineral resource regions between Communist and non-Communist portions of Eurasia is significant. Of the total of 29 mineral regions, 18 are in the Communist Bloc to 11 in the Eurasian perimeter. Of the 18 located in the Soviet sphere, 15 are *complementary* in their mineral representation. By contrast, of the 11 in the non-Communist portion of Eurasia (excluding Western Europe) only 4 are complementary: These are the northern Deccan of India and its companion in the south of India, Turkey, and Japan.

When the character of complementary representation is assessed in a little more detail with respect to coking coal and reserves, the comparison is even more unfavorable both actually and potentially for the countries of the Eurasian perimeter. Eleven of the 15 complementary mineral regions of the Communist Bloc have coking coal in significant amounts, while only 2 of the 4 outside the Communist countries do. Another rough measure of the mineral balance sheet between Communist and non-Communist Asia is the diversity of minerals represented in the various regions. There are a total of 178 mineral occurrences listed in Table XXXVI among all 29 mineral-producing regions. Of these 178 mineral occurrences, 127 of them are in regions of the Communist Bloc as opposed to 51 in the regions of the Eurasian perimeter. With the possible exception of the Indian subcontinent, the Communist mainland of Asia is much better endowed with both diversity and balance in mineral wealth than are the peripheral regions on the continental margins.

It will be the task of the next three chapters to reveal in what ways the peoples of the two major divisions of the continent—the Communist *center* and non-Communist *perimeter*—have organized the areas upon and from which they live.

EXERCISE   Reconstructing the Composite Map of Eurasian Agricultural Resource Regions

1. Place a piece of onion-skin typing paper over the map of Eurasian precipitation in Figure 211 and trace the coastline of Eurasia. Then trace those portions of the precipitation pattern representing 20 inches of water which are indicated in the heaviest black line. These small parts of the precipitation pattern as a whole are the boundaries on the composite map contributed by the 20-inch isohyet on the map in Figure 211.

2. Next place the onion-skin overlay started in step one over the map showing duration of the Eurasian growing season in Figure 212. Trace the most heavily lined parts of the growing-season pattern. These parts of the duration of the growing-season pattern are the boundaries on the composite map contributed by the subject-matter disinctions of the map in Figure 212.

3. Then place the same overlay over the third map, dealing with surface configuration. Trace the heavy boundaries of the topographic regions shown on this map. Note that these are the major alignments of subsurface regions which divide Eurasia into its three "faces"—the Eurasian Plain, the peninsular south, and the compartmentalized east. These surface distinctions are, in turn, the boundaries on the composite map contributed by the subject-matter distinctions shown on the map in Figure 214.

4. Now compare the resulting outlines which you have constructed with the composite map of agricultural resource regions in Figure 215. Note the role of each measure of distinction in the respective subject-matter maps. From each one some part of the composite map is derived in formulating the regional associations of agricultural resources which are contained in the legend of the map in Figure 215. The distinction between resource association labeled type Ia and IIIa in Asiatic Russia is labeled in terms of the 150-days duration of the growing season. Actually the border is drawn along the boundary between intermediate and least soil fertility north of the Caspian Sea, shown on the map in Figure 213. This particular soils distinction happens to approximate the 150-day growing-season line. Note the many additional subregions which the addition of soil distinctions makes it possible to define.

In interpreting the significance of the associations of agricultural resources shown, be sure to think in terms of specific opportunities and problems rather than deterministic environmental limitations or responses. Remember that it is the understanding of potentialities and the nature of difficulties to be surmounted which represent the actual meaning to different persons of the circumstances which describe these resources.

17 *Area Organization of Communist Bloc Countries*

Comparison of Communist Bloc countries with those of the Commonwealth was used in Chapter 1 to illustrate worldwide regional organization. In view of future relationships between Communist and non-Communist regions, it would be difficult to overemphasize the importance of understanding the Communist "world." The size and power of this international regional unit of organization may partly be expressed by the facts that China is the most populous and the Soviet Union has the largest area of any country in the world. In area China is third in size, and the Soviet Union is third in population. Only Canada and the Soviet Union are larger than China in area, and only the Republics of India and China have more people than the Soviet Union. These two countries with their satellites occupy virtually one contiguous block of territory comprising one-fourth of the world's land area which is occupied by more than one-third—36 per cent—of humanity. By contrast, the Commonwealth of Nations, focused on London, is scattered all over the world and accounts for less than one-fourth—23 per cent—of the land area which is occupied by about the same proportion—23 per cent—of the world's population.

Overview of the Communist Bloc

It is apparent from the political map in Figure 203 that there are two kinds of countries in both Russian and Chinese orbits within the Communist Bloc. Each power orbit consists of one major nation which predominates in population, area, and diversity of resources. Each is the political core in relation to several smaller nations which occupy peripheral locations.

Political Pattern of the Soviet Union. The Russian Soviet Federated Socialist Republic (R.S.F.S.R.) predominates in area and in population in the Soviet Union. The R.S.F.S.R. includes within its territory many autonomous national areas also. The Union of Soviet Socialist Republics consists of the R.S.F.S.R. and fourteen peripheral

Soviet Socialist republics, as shown by the map in Figure 203.

The R.S.F.S.R. The R.S.F.S.R. itself may be divided into two parts. One part is the core region of the Soviet Union, containing the most densely settled lands generally considered to be European Russia. The other part—northeast and east of the first—is the most sparsely populated region of the Union. The fourteen peripheral republics of the Soviet Union are located in three groups along the western and southern borders of the R.S.F.S.R. Arrangement of the less-populated portions of the R.S.F.S.R. to the east and the southern and western peripheral locations of the fourteen constituent republics of the U. S. S. R. is radial in pattern.

The European Soviet Socialist Republics. The Ukrainian Soviet Socialist Republic and the Belo- or White Russian Soviet Socialist Republic are the second and fifth largest republics of the Soviet Union in population, located between the Baltic republics and the Black Sea. Three Baltic republics, Latvia, Lithuania, and Estonia, were added to the Soviet Union during the first days of World War II, which the Russians call the *Great Patriotic War.* At the end of that war the Moldavian Republic was created from territory which was formerly part of Roumania.

Caucasian Soviet Socialist Republics. On the southern border of the Soviet Union, between the Black and the Caspian seas, are the three republics of the Caucasus region—Georgian, Armenian, and Azerbaijan republics. Efforts to expand their number by the addition of Kurdish national areas at the expense of Iran were defeated as a result of unfavorable public reaction abroad, and by great pressure brought to bear against the Soviet Union within the United Nations after World War II.

Central Asian Soviet Socialist Republics. Also, on the southern border of the country between the Caspian Sea and the western border of China, there are five republics of Soviet Central Asia. These are the Kazakh, Turkmen, Uzbek, Kirghiz, and Tadzhik republics. They occupy the arid basin of internal drainage bounded by the south end of the Urals on the north, the Hindu Kush Mountains of Persia on the south, the Caucasus Mountains on the west, and the Tien Shan of westernmost China on the east.

Political Pattern of Communist China. The political pattern within Communist China is also divided between two types of political areas. There is the main Chinese national area in humid Eastern China, which includes many small autonomous areas. There is also an emerging pattern of independent western republics. Only the Mongolian Peoples' Republic has achieved nominal independence and recognition, including membership (1961) in the United Nations. Two other regions which may ultimately achieve such status are Singkiang and Tibet.

The main national area of China is likewise divisible into two parts. The twenty-two provinces of China proper comprise the most densely populated portion; Inner Mongolia and Tsinghan—the most sparsely occupied areas—make up the other part. An extension of Kansu Province, known as the Kansu Corridor, crosses these sparsely occupied desert lands of Inner Mongolia and Tsinghan, sparsely occupied Singkiang, and the Mongolian Peoples' Republic to Eastern China by an alignment of oases. Settlement within these lands is dependent on water supplied by runoff from high mountains of Central Asia to the Eastern Tien Shan in the west.

Satellites. The roster of national political units of the Communist Bloc countries is completed by the addition of the East European satellites and the Asian Communist satellites. North Korea and North Vietnam, bordering China, fall in the latter category. East Germany, Poland, Czechoslovakia, Hungary, Rumania, Albania, and Bulgaria, all lying between Western Europe and the Soviet Union, have satellite status.

Perhaps the most important initial feature to point out from the political pattern of the map in Figure 203 is the concentration of coreland settlement at the two humid extremes, west and east in European Russia and in eastern China. A second important point is that the former isolation of Russia and China from one another across the intervening "dead" heart of Asia is undergoing considerable modification. Attention turns now to the two corelands of the Communist Bloc and their interconnections across the interior of Asia.

Corelands and Settled Regions of the U. S. S. R. and China. The pattern of Russian settlement narrows eastward from a broad western base between the Baltic and the Black seas (Figure 222). The main body of continuous settlement in Russia is a great triangular-shaped coreland region pointing directly toward China. This region is known as the fertile triangle. The east-west dimension from the Leningrad-Odessa line to the western border of the Mongolian Peoples' Republic is approximately 3,700 miles. At the Mongolian border the apex of the triangle meets the northwestward-facing slopes of the Central Asian highlands, which extend from the Khyber Pass along the southern border of the Soviet Union from Afghanistan to Lake Baikal. In addition to the coreland an alignment of intermittent settlement extends the length of the Russo-Chinese border. This line of settlement may be divided into three parts—the Caucasus, Central Asia, and Siberia. The junction of the two alignments of settlement occurs in the Kuznets Basin.

The pattern of settlement in China is less linear than in Russia. The pattern of agricultural plains in humid China, referred to in Table XXXV of Chapter 16, is compartmentalized into seven main parts. Four of these are of considerable size, and three of the largest merge to form the coreland and greatest extent of relatively uninterrupted settlement in China. These three, which form the North China Plain, are the lower river plains and delta regions of the Huang Ho and Yangtze rivers and the Manchurian Plains. The other large compartment is the Szechuan Basin. In each of these largest plains, with the exception of Manchuria, more than 60 per cent of the total land area is under cultivation. The central lowland of Manchuria, which has been under serious agricultural development only since 1900, is prairie analogous to the black-earth soil regions of the Ukraine, the Middle West of the United States, or the Argentine Pampas.

The *middle* valleys of the Huang Ho and Yangtze rivers and their tributaries are almost equally significant. The We and Fen Ho tributaries of the Huang Ho join the main river from opposite directions near the last great bend of the river where it changes direction from south to east. The Han, Kan, and Hsiang tributaries flow radially into the middle Yangtze district in central Eastern China, as shown on the map in Figure 223. The seventh main agricultural region is the Hsi (West) River of South China and its Canton delta region.

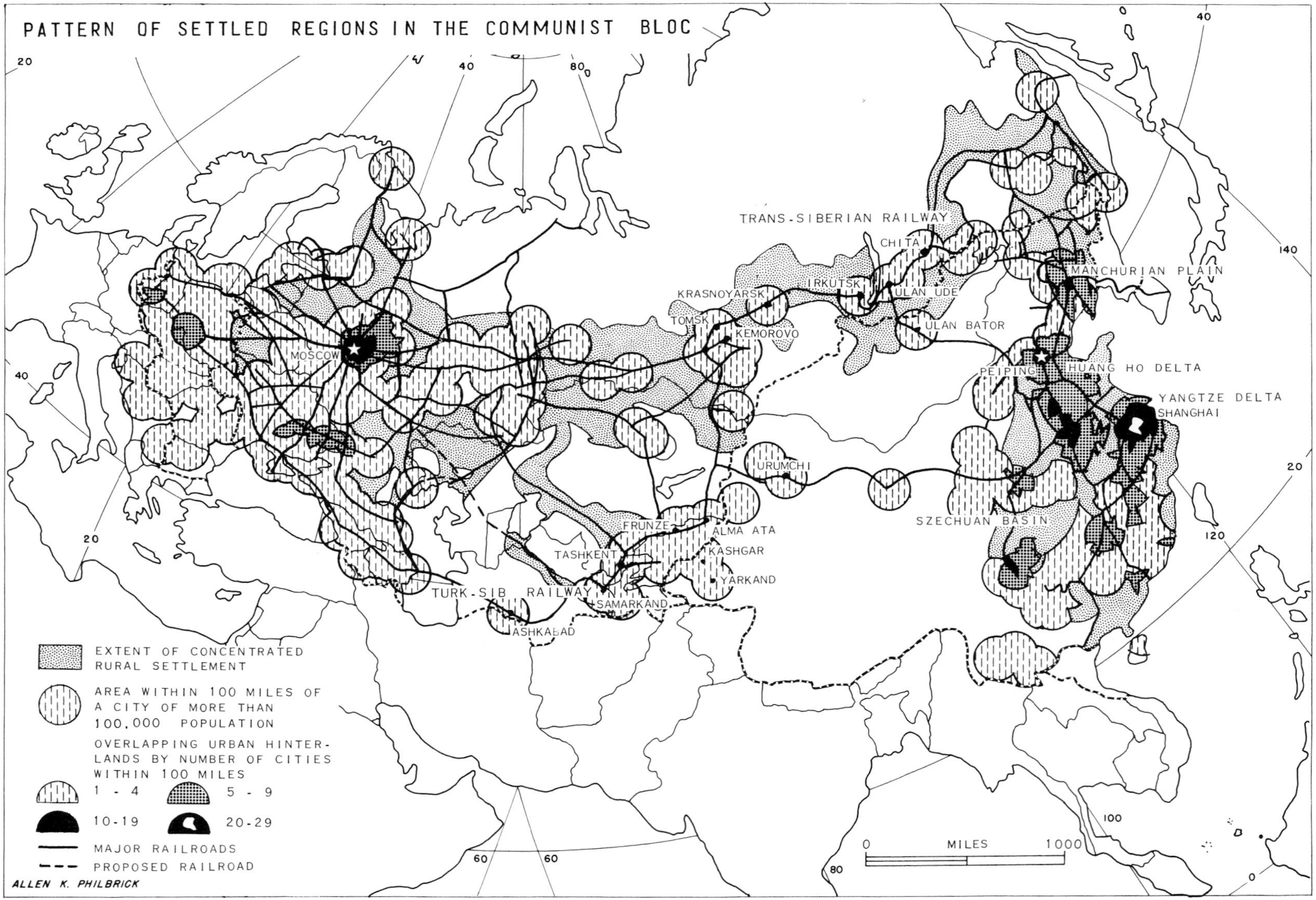
PATTERN OF SETTLED REGIONS IN THE COMMUNIST BLOC
TRANS-SIBERIAN RAILWAY
CHITA
IRKUTSK
ULAN UDE
ULAN BATOR
KRASNOYARSK
TOMSK
KEMOROVO
MANCHURIAN PLAIN
PEIPING
HUANG HO DELTA
YANGTZE DELTA
SHANGHAI
MOSCOW
URUMCHI
SZECHUAN BASIN
FRUNZE
ALMA ATA
KASHGAR
YARKAND
TASHKENT
TURK-SIB RAILWAY
SAMARKAND
ASHKABAD
EXTENT OF CONCENTRATED RURAL SETTLEMENT
AREA WITHIN 100 MILES OF A CITY OF MORE THAN 100,000 POPULATION
OVERLAPPING URBAN HINTERLANDS BY NUMBER OF CITIES WITHIN 100 MILES
1 - 4
5 - 9
10-19
20-29
MAJOR RAILROADS
PROPOSED RAILROAD
0 MILES 1000
ALLEN K. PHILBRICK

Figure 222

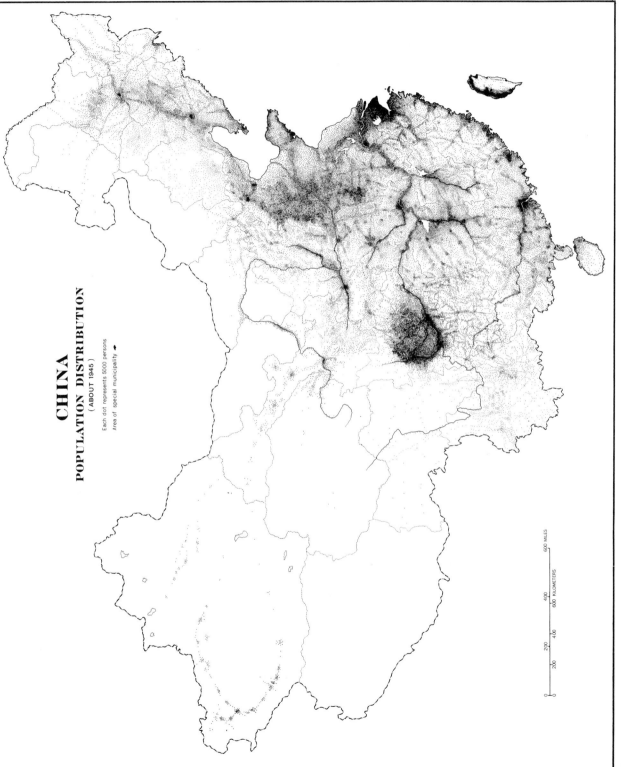

Figure 223. (*Courtesy of The American Geographical Society, taken from Glenn T. Trewartha, "New Maps of China's Population," Geographical Review.*)

The seven agricultural plains listed account for a high proportion of China's total population. The population map by Trewartha (Figure 223) shows the pattern in 1945 just before the Communists took over control of China.[1] The riverine pattern of population distribution outside of the large plains regions further indicates the agricultural orientation of China's subsistence economy at the end of World War II. In the evolution of the regional organization of a national economy since 1950, the North China Plains and the Manchurian Plain comprise the coreland of China. The lower Yangtze delta around Shanghai has the most concentrated population and concentrated pattern of cities, which reflects the former treaty-port status and commercial function of Shanghai in the pre-Communist period. Before World War II, Shanghai was the most important commercial city of mainland East Asia— gateway to the commerce of the great Yangtze River Basin. While the economic base of an emerging industrial China is now developing within a large number of widely separate centers—primarily within the region indicated as the coreland—it is difficult yet to identify one single predominating focus. To the west and south of the coreland region the pattern of compartmentalized agricultural plains is relatively widely spaced. In far-western China settlement is oasis patterned.

Both Russian and Chinese patterns of settlement are radial in form, as the transportation systems of each country demonstrates. Radial patterns of interconnection in each of the two countries are being integrated within the development of the Communist Bloc as a single unit.

Patterns of Interconnections within and between the Soviet Union and China. The

patterns of railroad interconnections show the developing integration of China and the Soviet Union. The Soviet Union has a well-developed pattern of radial and concentric railroads focusing on Moscow. Moscow is served by eleven trunk lines and a metropolitan belt-line interchange. Peiping, by contrast, has virtually a single rail crossing. It is served at present by only five trunk lines. The pre-Communist rail pattern was a criss-crossing of lines in the form of a somewhat rectangular grid which had no primary focus. Each line was developed to tap a separate hinterland and to bring

commodities to a coastal port. Before the Communists took over, individual Chinese railroad lines had never actually been operated as an integrated system. In China, today, Mukden and Peiping are the two most important centers in the emerging regional organization of the national economy. Mukden in southern Manchuria is the country's industrial capital, while Peiping in North China is the nation's ancient and modern cultural-political capital. From the region of these twin centers a realignment of rail and other interconnections is being constructed which is radial in pattern and nodal in function.

By contrast with pre-Communist China's rectilinear pattern of railroads, Russia's system has always been in the form of a giant wheel. At successive distances outward from Moscow as the hub of the wheel, a series of concentric belt lines interconnects the radial spokes of the wheel. Such circumferential belt lines are located 50, 500, 1,000, and from 1,500–2,000 miles from Moscow. The route farthest out toward the rim of the wheel is the "Turk-Sib" railroad. Certain navigable rivers, such as the Ob, the Yenisei, and the Lena from the Arctic Ocean to the Trans-Siberian railroad, represent continuations of the circuit. The Ob continues from Novosibirsk to the Ob estuary. In this fashion a radial and concentric network of railroads, supplemented by waterways, radiates outward like a giant fan from Moscow to all parts of the greatest plain on earth.

The map in Figure 222 illustrates how the Soviet Union's and China's radial patterns of transportation meet like the extended fingers of two hands at several important points in the interior of the continent. Let the right hand represent China and the left hand the Soviet Union. Hold the hands palms up so that the little and ring fingers of the right hand touch the index and middle fingers of the left hand. The two hands arranged in this manner represent the outlines of transcontinental railroad interconnections between China and the Soviet Union. Imagine a line connecting the extended ends of the fingers of the left hand continuing across the ends of the fingers of the right hand, not including the thumb on the left hand, and the resulting "S" curve describes a rail connection which crosses the ends of four major trunk lines radiating from Moscow linked with the ends of five major trunk lines radiating outward from the core of China. The portion of the "S" created by connecting four fingers of the left hand is the "Turk-

---

[1] Glenn T. Trewartha, "New Maps of China's Population," *Geographical Review*, April 1957, facing p. 235. In the construction of this population map of China, Trewartha had the help of Sen-Dou Chang as research assistant.

Sib" railroad. The Caspian Sea is bridged by a railroad ferry. The capitals of all the Soviet Central Asian republics are interconnected and joined at Novosibirsk to the Trans-Siberian railroad, which is the portion of the "S" curve on the right hand from that city to the Pacific at Vladivostok. On this hand diagram all five of the radial Chinese routes are interconnected by the Soviet transcontinental line. On the left hand the thumb represents the linkage of Moscow to Leningrad. The "ring" and little fingers projecting southeastward represent radial lines from Moscow to the Ukraine and the Central Asian republics. The two fingers of each hand which touch represent the two most direct transcontinental rail routes between the Soviet Union and China. The one represented by the middle finger on the left hand marks a new route from the Turk-Sib railway across western China through the Kansu Corridor to Lanchou, and thence by rail to the core of China. The second is the traditional Trans-Siberian route. From Irkutsk east of Lake Baikal, as can be seen from the map in Figure 222, four choices of interconnecting lines enter North China by way of Manchuria.

Although the distances are great and the supplies of life-giving water are intermittent and scanty, despite ideological differences, the Chinese and the Russians, from opposite humid ends of the Communist Bloc within Eurasia, are setting a basic pattern of regional international connections with which to draw closer to each other in the course of developing the available resources of the Asian continental interior. It is also significant that the main international air route connecting Moscow and Peiping, which has a flight frequency of from twenty to thirty trips per week, follows the principal rail route. It extends from Moscow, by way of Kazan, Sverdlovsk, Omsk, Novosibirsk, Krasnoyarsk, Irkutsk, and Ulan Bator, to Peiping.

The Patterns of Agriculture in Communist Bloc Countries

The map in Figure 224 shows the major agricultural regions of the Communist Bloc of Eurasia. Nineteen major regions and their crop and livestock associations are listed in Table XXXVII. Old distinctions between Europe and Asia are being reduced as China attempts to revolutionize her agriculture along Soviet lines, but many important differences will long remain and can be best understood by comparison.

TABLE XXXVII COMMUNIST BLOC AGRICULTURAL REGIONS[a]

Regions of the Russian coreland
1 Spring wheat, sunflower
2 Winter wheat, sugar beet, sunflower
3 Dairy, flax, winter wheat, potatoes
4 Potatoes, sugar beets, winter wheat

Regions of the Russian periphery
5 South central Asian livestock ranching
6 Irrigated cotton, specialty crops, and livestock
7 Northern and Siberian forest, local subsistence, and reindeer ranching

Regions of the Chinese coreland
1 Soybeans, spring wheat, kaoliang of Manchurian Plains
2 Winter wheat, rice of Lower Yangtze
3 Winter wheat, kaoliang of North China Plain

Regions of the Chinese periphery
4 Northwest spring wheat, millet
5 Wei and Fen Ho winter wheat, millet, cotton
6 Szechuan basin rice, sweet potatoes, field peas
7 South China hill rice, tea, tung
8 Southwestern rice of Yunnan Plateau
9 Southern double rice cropping
10 Western oasis agriculture and livestock ranching
11 Western mountain basin nomadic subsistence herding
12 Manchurian-Mongolian highland forests

[a] Numbers refer to regions on map in Figure 224.

Contrasting European and Asian Cultures within the Communist Bloc. Important differences between European and Asian cultures may be summarized as follows:

1. The Soviet Union's organization of area is characterized by *well-developed regional division of labor* between specialized producing regions. By contrast the characteristic pattern of Chinese life in the past has been one of extreme localization, with relatively little regional interdependence, except for external commercial orientation of certain specialized types of production in world trade.

2. The Soviet economy has become *highly mechanized.* Agricultural processes on collective farms are mechanized for a very high percentage of the total volume of work. The same is true of the mining industry and the timber industry. The opposite has until now been characteristic of production in China. Economic development plans call for mechanization at the fastest possible rate; but hand labor, hand tools, and handicraft manufactures still characterize a predominantly agricultural economy in

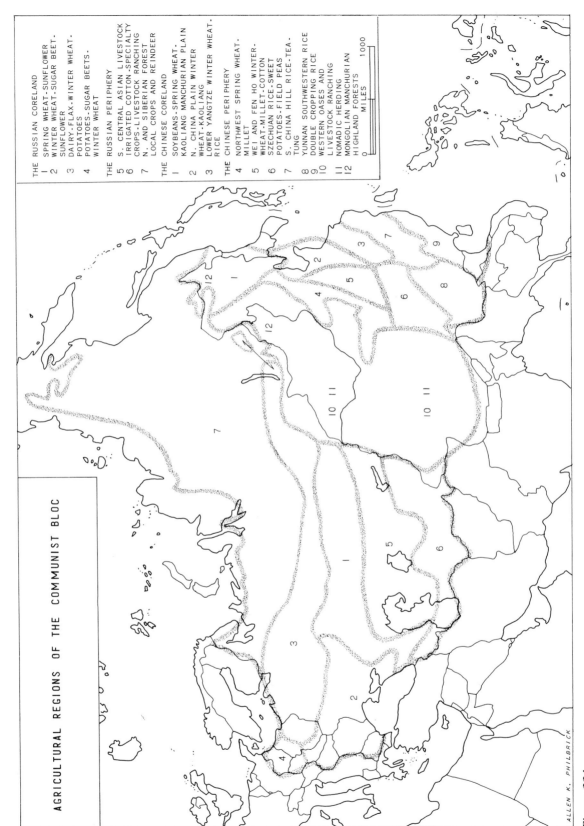

AGRICULTURAL REGIONS OF THE COMMUNIST BLOC

THE RUSSIAN CORELAND
 1 SPRING WHEAT-SUNFLOWER
 2 WINTER WHEAT-SUGAR BEET-
    SUNFLOWER
 3 DAIRY-FLAX-WINTER WHEAT-
    POTATOES
 4 POTATOES-SUGAR BEETS-
    WINTER WHEAT

THE RUSSIAN PERIPHERY
 5 S. CENTRAL ASIAN LIVESTOCK
    IRRIGATED COTTON-SPECIALTY
    CROPS-LIVESTOCK RANCHING
 6 N. AND SIBERIAN FOREST
 7 LOCAL CROPS AND REINDEER

THE CHINESE CORELAND
 1 SOYBEANS-SPRING WHEAT-
    KAOLIANG MANCHURIAN PLAIN
 2 N. CHINA PLAIN WINTER
    WHEAT-KAOLIANG
 3 LOWER YANGTZE WINTER WHEAT-
    RICE

THE CHINESE PERIPHERY
 4 NORTHWEST SPRING WHEAT-
    MILLET
 5 WEI AND FEN HO WINTER-
    WHEAT-MILLET-COTTON
 6 SZECHUAN RICE-SWEET
    POTATOES-FIELD PEAS
 7 S. CHINA HILL RICE-TEA-
    TUNG
 8 YUNNAN SOUTHWESTERN RICE
 9 DOUBLE CROPPING RICE
10 WESTERN OASES AND
    LIVESTOCK RANCHING
11 NOMADIC HERDING
    MONGOLIAN MANCHURIAN
12 HIGHLAND FORESTS

MILES
0   1000

ALLEN K. PHILBRICK

Figure 224

China. Even though collectivization is practically complete, mechanization of collective agriculture has lagged behind. A series of successive dry years has brought Communist China to the edge of disaster.

3. The Soviet Union's *urban population* is a much higher proportion of the total than is China's. Both Soviet and Chinese Communist societies began from a base which had a relatively high proportion of rural population. The population of czarist Russia in 1913, for example, was only 17.6 per cent urban. In 1925, at the time of the first Soviet census, this proportion was still less than 18 per cent (17.9). In 1953, as previously indicated, Communist China's first census showed the proportion of China's urban population was only 13.7 per cent of the total population. In 1956, however, the population of the Soviet Union was 43.4 per cent urban. In classifying the class structure of the population of the U.S.S.R., furthermore, official statistics of the national economy[1] list 58.3 per cent of the population under the category *factory, office, and other workers,* as compared with 41.2 per cent under the category *collective farmers and handicraftsmen.* There is within the Soviet Union, then, an approximate balance between workers and farmers—population organized in an urban as opposed to that in a rural setting. Such a balance has not yet been achieved in the much larger population of China. The traditionally agricultural nature of Chinese civilization still prevails.

4. *The basic unit of production* in the Soviet Union is factory, mine, or collective farm (Figure 225A and B). By contrast, until very recently the basic unit of production in Chinese society was the *family*—the peasant family organized within the agricultural village. Chinese Communists have taken bold revolutionary steps to reorganize their countryside. The agricultural patterns in each of the two countries will be discussed separately.

Russian Agriculture. The fertile area of Russia takes the form of an elongated triangle. Its main divisions follow the resource distinctions between black-earth soils in the south and gray-brown forest soils in the north. As the map in Figure 224 shows, wheat is the major crop of the great black-earth region of southern Russia. In the Ukraine, which occupies the more humid portion of this region, sugar beets are a second, so called, industrial crop.

[1] Central Statistical Board of the U. S. S. R., Council of Ministers, *National Economy of the U. S. S. R., Statistical Returns,* Moscow: Foreign Languages Publishing House, 1957.

Industrial crops are those associated with industrial processing without which consumption of the crop is not possible. The large sunflower crop is used for vegetable oil.

In the southern extension of the black-earth soils region, toward the Ural Mountains, great shelter belts have been constructed by planting trees. The purpose of the trees is to hold moisture in the soil and to effect "change" in the microclimatic conditions at the surface. The photograph in Figure 226 shows the ambitious modification of nature attempted by the Soviets in this region. Each of these belts are rows of trees 200 feet wide. The plan calls for some 3,500 miles of such rows of plantings in giant criss-crossings of the drought-prone portions of the black-earth soils region. By 1965 it is expected that the total area in farm shelter belts will exceed 23,000 square miles. It remains to be seen whether the effect on moisture content of the soil and general microclimatic improvement will be as projected. It will not be possible to assess the true worth of so large a program for some years after the entire project is completed.

In the northern half of the fertile triangle, crops are more diversified. This is in part a reflection of the presence of larger urban markets, but is is also because of a greater flexibility in the use of agriculture resources made possible by more humid conditions. Both wheat and rye are bread grains grown in the northern half of the agricultural triangle. The dairy, flax, rye, and potato-crop association of the gray-brown forest soil region east and west in the latitude of Moscow attests to a large urban market, as well as to the long tradition of textile manufacturing in northern European Russia.

An idea of the magnitude of the areas devoted to the various crop associations within the Soviet agricultural triangle may be derived from the figures in Table XXXVIII. This table lists the sizes in square miles and percentages of total cultivated area which are devoted to major crops in the Soviet Union. Between 1913 and 1955 some 260,000 square miles of land were added to the area under cultivation in the Soviet Union. The increase in cultivated land represents a territory greater in extent than the total area of the states of Michigan, Wisconsin, Illinois, Indiana, Iowa, Pennsylvania, and Ohio combined. In addition to greatly enlarging the total cultivated area, the ratio between various segments of the agriculture has been brought

TABLE XXXVIII CROP AREAS IN THE U.S.S.R.[a]

Category	Area, sq. mi. 1913	Per cent of total	Area, sq. mi. 1940	Per cent of total	Per cent change 1913–1940	Area, sq. mi. 1955	Per cent of total	Per cent change 1940–1955	Per cent change 1913–1955
Total all crop area	**456,363**	**100**	**580,694**	**100**	**27**	**717,374**	**100**	**24**	**57**
Grain crop:									
Wheat	127,413	27.9	155,598	26.8	22	233,591	32.6	50.0	83.3
Rye	108,880	23.9	89,189	15.4	−18	73,745	10.3	−17	−32.5
Wheat-rye	236,293	51.8	244,787	42.2	3.6	307,336	42.9	25.6	30.0
Other small grains	167,568	36.7	181,854	31.3	8.5	180,694	15.1	−0.6	7.8
Unspecified bal. in Soviet table	1,151	0.3	...	...	...	...	...	...	...
Totals	**403,861**	**88.5**	**426,641**	**73.5**	**6**	**488,030**	**68.0**	**14.4**	**21**
Industrial crops:									
Sunflower	3,783	0.8	13,668	2.4	264	16,371	2.3	19.8	332
Cotton	2,664	0.6	8,031	1.4	200	8,494	1.2	5.8	218
Flax	4,826	1.1	8,108	1.4	68	5,714	0.8	−29.6	18.4
Hemp	2,625	0.6	2,317	0.4	11.7	2,278	0.3	−1.0	−13.2
Sugar beet	2,625	0.6	4,749	0.8	81	6,795	0.9	43	155.0
Other industrial crops	2,396	0.4	8,687	1.4	262.0	7,838	1.1	−9.8	227.1
Totals	**18,919**	**4.1**	**45,560**	**7.8**	**141**	**47,490**	**6.6**	**4.2**	**151**
Vegetables and melon:									
Potatoes	16,216	3.6	29,730	5.1	83.4	33,590	4.6	13	107
Other vegetables	3,475	0.7	8,880	1.5	158	10,425	1.5	17	171
Totals	**19,691**	**4.3**	**38,610**	**6.6**	**96.5**	**44,015**	**6.1**	**14**	**124**
Fodder crops:									
Silage	...	...	3,089	0.5	...	22,008	3.1	613	...
Fodder root melons	...	...	3,861	0.7	...	6,178	0.9	60	...
Annual grass	3,089	0.7	16,216	2.8	425	56,757	7.9	250	1740
Perennial grasses	9,652	2.1	42,085	7.2	340	50,193	7.0	19	420
Other fodder crops	...	...	4,632	0.8	...	2,703	0.3	−42	...
Totals	**12,741**	**2.8**	**69,883**	**12.0**	**450**	**137,839**	**19.2**	**99**	**984**

[a] Central Statistical Board of the U.S.S.R., Council of Ministers, *National Economy of the U.S.S.R. Statistical Returns,* Moscow: Languages Publishing House, 1957, p. 96. In the case of other small grains, those specified were maize, spring barley, oats, buckwheat, millet, rice, and legumes.

Figure 225. (A) Above, women workers in a machine plant in Moscow. (*Courtesy of United Nations.*) (B) Below, the great size of the field units in Soviet collective farms is shown in the background of this view of mechanized agriculture on the north Caucasus steppes, Kuban district. (*Courtesy of Sovfoto.*)

Figure 226. This birds-eye view of forest shelter belts of the Voronezh steppe region in the Don River Valley shows some of the results of the drive to remake nature. (*Courtesy of Sovfoto.*)

into better balance. For example, as shown by Table XXXVIII, in 1913 the proportion of total crop area devoted to all grains approached 90 per cent. By 1955 this ratio was reduced to slightly more than two-thirds by the relative increases in industrial crops, vegetable, and fodder crops. The Soviets hope the latter will form the basis for future expansion in dairy and beef cattle components of the farm economy. The wheat acreage increase amounted to 106,000 square miles or 83 per cent over 1913—an area equivalent to nearly the entire acreage of the state of Colorado. At the same time rye, the former basis of black bread, which was a staple food of the Russian peasant, has been reduced in total acreage by approximately one-third. Taken together, these facts reflect a shift in the diet from black to white-bread standards. Wheat increases by 1955 placed that crop in possession of the largest single crop acreage—approximately one-third of the total cultivated land.

The second most important category is fodder crops. These are not specifically referred to in the crop associations shown on the map in Figure 224, except insofar as they are reflected in the designation of dairying in the dairy, flax, winter wheat, potato region of the northern half of the fertile triangle. However, the single largest increase in agricultural acreage—125,000 square miles—belongs to this category, which accounts for nearly half of the total increase (48 per cent) in agricultural acreage. The number of livestock in the Soviet Union does not reflect this increase in acreage devoted to fodder crops in anything like the degree which might be expected. Several special circumstances are involved: the *disruption* due to the resistance of the peasants to collectivization of agriculture during the 1930s when cattle were slaughtered in considerable numbers, and the *devastation* caused by the invasion of the Soviet Union by the Germans during World War II, when cattle were among the primary targets by foraging invaders as well as defenders. The scorched-earth policy of the Soviet Union during the war also resulted in the slaughter and destruction of millions of head of livestock to prevent them from falling into the hands of the enemy.

Unlike cultivated crops, it takes a number of years to grow herds of cattle, pigs, and sheep which represent the livestock population of a country. In 1928 there were within the present boundaries of the Soviet Union approximately 67 million head of cattle. By 1934 this number had been reduced by half to 33.5 million head. The decline of sheep and goats was even more catastrophic, from 114 million to 36.5 million, or more than two-thirds (68 per cent). Milk cows declined from 33.2 million to 19 million (43 per cent) by 1935. When World War II began in 1941, recovery had not yet brought livestock back to 1928 levels. Wartime devastation was not as destructive as the internal struggle over collectivization had been except with regard to pigs. The pig population of the Soviet Union hit an all-time low of 8.7 million shortly after the war in 1947. From low points immediately following World War II, numbers of livestock have climbed steadily with few setbacks, until finally in 1955 the Soviets had regained the 1928 level in numbers of cattle.

The Soviet Union has displayed great interest in increasing corn production after the model of the

United States. They would like to use greatly increased corn production to improve both the quantity and quality of beef production. Unfortunately the agricultural resource circumstances of the Soviet fertile triangle are not adapted to the requirements for high-yield corn production possessed by the humid American Middle West. Improvement of the relative position of Russian livestock production and also corn and other fodder crops in the Soviet Union can be expected to be small.

Of the increase in crop acreages recorded between 1913 and 1955 in Table XXXVIII, 11 per cent were devoted to industrial crops and 9 per cent to vegetables, including melons. Cotton and specialized subtropical fruits and vegetables are produced under intensive irrigation in the Trans-Caucasian and Soviet Central Asian republics. These specialized farming areas are resource oriented and also require engineering know-how and specialized management. In the nonirrigable steppes and desert

areas of Soviet Central Asia, large-scale ranching has been developed.

Pattern of functional farm units in the Soviet Union. Those who traveled by air used to be impressed by the marked difference in field patterns which showed dramatically on the two sides of the political border between the Soviet Union and Poland before World War II. This contrast was in the difference between the fragmented fields of peasant holdings in Poland and the continuity of large fields of collective farms in the Soviet Union.

At the present time there are about 19.7 million peasant families in the Soviet Union. These function within some 85,700 agricultural *artels* or *collective farms*. This means an average of 229 peasant households per collective farm. Table XXXIX shows the division and uses of land in the Soviet Union in 1955. From the table it can be seen that the total of 90,834 collective and state farms combined occupy and organize 3.7 million square miles of

TABLE **XXXIX**   TOTAL LAND AREA AND DISTRIBUTION OF AGRICULTURAL LAND AMONG LAND USERS IN THE U. S. S. R.[a]

	Area, sq. mi.		Per cent	Comment
Total land area	8,600,000		100	
Total agricultural area	3,655,100	(100.0)	43	
In collectives	3,122,000	(85.5)	32.5	Sectors of farm economy
In state farms	528,000	(14.4)	6.5	
Individual plots	5,000	(0.1)	. . .	
State forest fund	3,300,000		38	Corresponds to public domain
State land fund	1,234,000		14	in the United States
Other land users	410,000		5	Cities, reserves, etc.
Total peasant households collectivized				19,700,000
Total number of collective farms				85,700
Average number households per collective farm				229
Average gross area of agricultural land/collective farm				36.0 sq. mi.
Average area of agriculturally used land/collective farm				22.0 sq. mi.
Average arable land/collective farm				9.9 sq. mi.
Average cultivated land/collective farm				9.1 sq. mi.
Average crop land/collective farm				8.4 sq. mi.
Total number of state farms				5,134
Average gross area of land/state farm				103 sq. mi.

[a] Central Statistical Board of the U. S. S. R. Council of Ministers, *National Economy of the USSR, Statistical Returns,* Moscow: Foreign Languages Publishing House, 1957.

agricultural area. This makes the average size of the collective farm roughly equivalent to that of an American 36-square-mile township. With the collective farm the equivalent of an entire township, the 229 peasant households per collective farm approximately corresponds to the number of individual farm families which typically occupy individual farms in an American township (an average of 6.4 households per square mile). The term "collective" represents the entirely different manner of organizing the area of the farm within the much enlarged functional units (Figure 227A, B and C). State farms are even larger, approximately 100 square miles in average size. The average grain-growing state farm is 110 square miles. The size of the average Astrakhan sheep-breeding farm in the Kazakh Republic north of the Caspian Sea is over 700 square miles. By contrast, an average dairy state farm in the northern half of the fertile triangle is 38 square miles. It is evident from the categories that state farms are specialized producers of single or associated crops and livestock types, while collective farms are of more general purpose within the broader specializations of the regions in which they are located.

In mechanization, instead of duplicating tractors and other mechanized equipment for each farm, machinery is pooled in 9,009 machine tractor stations (MTS). Each MTS serves a number of collective farms. More than 90 per cent of the stations service four or more collectives; 41 per cent service six to ten farms; and slightly more than a third function for eleven to twenty and more farming units. In an economic hierarchy of agricultural units, peasant households are the most numerous and smallest geographical units. Villages are the next in order of complexity within the individual collective and state-farm units. Centers from which the MTS's operate in servicing a larger territory, comprising anywhere from two to twenty collective farms of a few to several hundred square miles, in an ever-enlarging series of nested area units, are a third step. Each larger-type unit contains many areas of the next lower subordinate-type unit. The descending numerical ratios are expressed by the census of establishments—19,700,000 peasant households, 90,834 state and collective farms, and 9,009 machine tractor stations. These numbers are matched inversely by an ascending order of progressively larger-sized units of area organized in the performance of the functions befitting a *household*, a *farm*, or a *machine tractor station*. The descrip-

tion sketched here of the hierarchy of operations and areas organized in a nested fashion to implement them is typical of the larger-than-local geographical division of labor of *exchange-type area organization*. It is identical in principle with exchange organization outside the Communist Bloc, although very different in specific pattern and political intent from the free-enterprise organization of area.

The greatest forest region on earth. The largest single region on the map of "agricultural" regional types is the northern forest. Soviet forests are the world's largest in area. According to Table XXXIX, the lands in the "state forest fund," as well as the portions of state forest assigned to collective and state farms for long term use, comprise well over 3.3 million square miles. This is a total forested territory greater in extent than that of the entire continental United States excluding Alaska. Trees are primarily coniferous, although along the borders of the agricultural triangle and in patches within it, there are deciduous and deciduous mixed with coniferous forest areas. Forest quality varies from south to north with moisture, cold, and wind. The treeless tundra of the subarctic is marked by the poleward limit of the forest region on the map in Figure 224. Species of trees are primarily larch, pine, spruce, and fir. Only a small proportion of the total is merchantable saw timber; a much larger proportion is potentially usable as pulp and raw materials for the chemical industry, which represents approximately one-third of the cellulose reserve supplies of the world. Mechanized timber cutting and hauling is done in the winter. In the spring, logs are floated down the tributaries of major navigable streams until great rafts of logs can be towed by steamer northward to the Arctic Ocean. Here at selected port cities, such as Archangelsk on the White Sea and Igarka on the Yenisei River, timber is sawed and stored for shipment overseas. Lumber is one of Russia's chief items of export. In recent years, however, more timber has moved into the industrial regions of the fertile triangle to the south than has been exported. Saw milling and pulp and paper-making centers have developed in the northern half of the Russian coreland to process wood resources from the forests of the north and east.

Chinese Agriculture. Chinese agriculture has been revolutionized during the short time since 1949. The basic subsistence-village pattern, referred to in defining subsistence organization of area in

Figure 227. These three views of agriculture in the Soviet Union are taken from widely separated points in the agricultural triangle. (*Courtesy of Sovfoto.*)

(A) The fields surrounded by shelter belts are large, and they are organized to focus on the collective farm buildings located in the foreground. This illustrates the larger scale of collective-farm organization than the corresponding groupings of individual farms within an American township. This collective is in the central black-earth region, like that in Figure 226 in the Voronezh area. For map comparison purposes, use 52 degrees north and 40 degrees east.

(B) The plowing of long-fallow land on the Znamya Kommunizma Collective Farm near Kulunda in the Altai territory. Note the huge size of this field and the three separate tractor-driven plow and drag-rake combinations. The headquarters of the collective is in the far distance on the left. For location comparison, use 52 degrees north, 74 degrees east.

(C) Reclaimed marsh lands of the Polessye district of White Russia. Note the large quantity of fodder crops collected from these huge fields. For location comparison, use 52 degrees north, 30 degrees east.

Chapter 2, has been collectivized and is now being communized. It is much too early to assess the results of collectivization, much less the development of the communes in Chinese agriculture. Claims of from 4 to 5 per cent increase in overall production per year and at a rate higher than the increase in population are difficult to substantiate. Inevitable differences in systems of accounting between Communist and pre-Communist periods, dislocation and disruption because of strangeness of new ways of organizing work, and resistance to change on the part of the peasantry must counterbalance spurts of labor which a people operating under the emotional "kick" of continuous campaigning could be expected to produce. Nor is it justifiable to predict complete failure in the face of natural disaster (drought) and the readily anticipated difficulties faced in so immense a task as the reorganization of a fragmented village agricultural economy into a large-scale collectivized one. Progress has undoubtedly been made. Disastrous setbacks have occurred. It will ultimately be possible to gauge the results, but to attempt it today is to speculate and to engage in argument rather than analysis.

The patterns of crop-association regions shown on the map in Figure 224 are based primarily on pre-Communist sources. It may be assumed that the basic crop associations remain similar even though the detailed pattern of organization is now different. Chinese agriculture is divided into three main regions: (1) a barely humid to subhumid north characterized by wheat, millet, and kaoliang (a grain sorghum); (2) a humid to wet south, which is the largest producing region of rice among the traditional rice economies of Asia; and (3) a dry and isolated western interior, developed on the basis of irrigated oases and sparsely populated nomadic herding.

It may be assumed that the crop-association regions in Figure 224 geographically locate the production indicated for 1955 in Table XL. The people of North China traditionally eat wheat, millet, and kaoliang. Millet is a grain which, like wheat, has its seeds in a tuft at the top of the stem. It grows up to twelve feet in height and is more

TABLE XL CROP AREA AND PRODUCTION OF MAJOR AGRICULTURAL PRODUCTS, 1955[a]

Crop	Crop area, sq. miles	Per cent total	Production thousands of metric tons	Per cent total 1955	Per cent total 1956
Total	**583,328**	**100.0**		**100.0**	**100.0**
Grains	457,131	78.3	174,812[b]	86.2	85.9
Rice	112,637	19.3	78,024	38.5	38.8
Wheat	103,239	17.7	22,965	11.3	11.7
Coarse	202,436	34.7	54,926	27.1	25.1
Potatoes	38,818	6.7	18,897	9.3	10.3
Soy beans	44,178	7.5	9,121	4.5	4.8
Cotton	22,289	3.8	1,518	0.8	0.7
Jute-hemp	459	0.07	257	0.12	0.1
Tobacco	973	0.16	298	0.15	0.1
Sugar cane	788	0.13	8,110	4.0	4.1
Sugar beets	444	0.07	1,596	0.8	0.8
Ground nuts	8,757	1.5	2,926	1.4	1.6
Rapeseed	9,027	1.5	969	0.5	0.1
Silk		. . .	131	0.1	0.1
Aquatic products		. . .	2,518	1.2	1.2
Tea leaves		. . .	108	0.1	0.1
Balance, unspecified	39,282	6.7			

[a] Table is adapted from two tables in Choh-Ming Li, *Economic Development of Communist China*, Berkeley and Los Angeles: University of California Press, 1959, pp. 245–246.

[b] The total and percentage figures are intended only as a rough gauge of proportional production. Obviously relative weights of cotton and wheat are scarcely of comparable significance.

drought resistant than wheat. Kaoliang is a coarse grain—a sorghum—which is resistant to both drought and flooding. It has found great favor as a subsistence food crop in the North China Plain, where alternate flood and drought occurs frequently. The crop is a form of insurance against the precariousness of the elements. Kaoliang is also used in making a Chinese whiskey—kaoliang chiu—analogous to corn whiskey. In this form it has the distinct commercial advantage of ease in transport in comparison with the bulkier grain itself. Stalks from all grains are used for building materials, thatch, fuel, and many other purposes.

The central mountains of eastern China divide wheat-eating North from rice-eating South China. From the table it is apparent that rice is the dominant food grain of China—it is the main food grain for the Szechuan Basin, the Yangtze River Basin and delta, and for all of South China. Supplementary food crops in the form of sweet potatoes and field peas are important in the Szechuan Basin, as are soybeans and sugar beets in Manchuria. Industrial crops figure prominently in the cotton of the sub-humid upper Yellow River and the tea and tung oil of South China.

Transformation of the countryside. Communization has changed the character and entire mode of area organization in China from a pattern of subsistence farm villages to collectivized farm land. Land which the peasant was promised belongs not to the individual but to everyone collectively. Such a fulfillment of a promise seems like an unusually cruel hoax in a western country where economies are based on the private organization of property. It is difficult to appreciate that the Communist does not think in that way. Individual holdings in land are virtually a thing of the past. The change to collectivized farm land means a form of area organization with a more than local division of labor, and hence carries China in a giant step toward the development of exchange-type area organization.

Even the family organization has been changed within the *commune,* which becomes the basic unit of agricultural production. Landlords have been replaced by the Communist hierarchy of state apparatus and bureaucracy.

. . . The average membership for the North China area seems to be about 7,000 families. Each commune absorbs the functions of one or several hsiang governments, the lowest formal administrative unit. In theory, at least, the communes are designed to fit natural geo-graphic formations, such as a watershed, and thereby facilitate efforts to make nature serve the new order. Like their comrades in other communes, the 43,265 Chinese in Wehsing are parts of a local "agro-industrial complex" managed by a Communist party elite that aims for self-sufficiency in manufacturing and tools, fertilizers, building materials, clothing, and other major requirements previously purchased outside, while producing even more in surplus farm products for delivery to the state. With its own nurseries to take the young, schools and "red universities" to educate them, mess halls to feed workers, and "happiness homes" providing for oldsters, the commune serves to supplant the family with a larger loyalty and an even tougher taskmaster.[1]

Pertinent to the geographical point is the fact that the commune means the breakup of the ancient local pattern of village life. With the collectivization of the land, fragmented patterns of fields can be eliminated. With the establishment of the commune, the last vestiges of family orientation on village life is submerged in the social organization of labor battalion, dormitory, mess hall, school, meeting hall, nursery, and old-folks home. New social establishments are substituted in the performance of old functions which traditionally have been centered in the patriarchical family units clustered within the villages. Combining several collective farms (former villages) into each commune makes possible still further enlargement and reallocation of blocks of agricultural land. The claim is that such "rationalization of production" will still further increase efficiency of agriculture and save many man and woman power units for other work.

The population problem. One may well ask, why raise the efficiency of production to save labor in an already overpopulated country like China? When the question of raising the standards of living in regions of high population density is posed, especially in subsistence agricultural regions, the first problem to appear is always the paradox of too many people. Of what use is it to produce more food when population increase keeps pace with that increased food supply? When viewed as a race to stay ahead of a natural increase in numbers of mouths to be fed, the question of raising living standards remains purely academic.

The Communists have not raised the controversial question of population control as their answer to this problem, although they are now freely dis-

[1] Albert Ravenholt, "Peoples Communes," *News Letter,* New York: American Universities Field Staff, October 23, 1958.

seminating both information and means to that end. Instead, they have launched a program for which the cornerstone of successful accomplishment is people. However many of them there may be, the people must work!

The engineering works to extend irrigation to more land, to drain more land, to dig wells, to put the silt from drainage and irrigation canals back onto the agricultural fields, to build the dams which can ultimately control the immemorial flooding of China's rivers, to put more fertilizer on the crops, to raise yields higher than an already efficient individual peasant agriculture had previously achieved— all these engineering works, if they are to be built in China, must still be constructed by battalions of men and women organized to do the work of machines. The regimentation, to which people in democratic societies in the West are most unsympathetic, is the possible key to the success of a gamble to escape the vicious circle of intensive subsistence agriculture's past tendency to keep pace merely with the birth rate. By accomplishing these kinds of engineering works and increasing agricultural productivity per person at the sacrifice of the former family-unit culture and area organization, the Communists expect to create, through the labor of the people, a surplus of population which can be redirected into mining, construction, and manufacturing industries in order to affect markedly the total production of food. It must, therefore, have come as an especially bitter shock to find that successive droughts in the interior of China have reduced the runoff of her great rivers to the vanishing point; for no amount of well digging and political exhortation can produce water beyond its actual amount of supply. Yet, when a normal cycle of precipitation resumes, it is this working labor force which will transform the national economy of China from one of subsistence agriculture to the Communist version of *exchange-type area organization*.

The pattern of functional farm units in Communist China. The Communists are determined to wipe out the previously fragmented field system, to introduce larger field units made possible by collectivization, and to proceed as rapidly as they may to acquire or build for themselves the machinery of mechanization. By the end of 1956, of the total of 121,480,000 farming households in China (compare 19,700,000 peasant households in the Soviet Union and 5,382,162 farms in the United States), 116,980,000 (96.3 per cent) had joined agricul-

tural producers' cooperatives. Of this number, 106,660,000 (87 per cent) were in collective farms.[1] From a single "highly developed" collective farm prototype and 18 less-developed ones in 1950, the number swelled to 746,000 highly developed and 14,000 less-developed collective farms by the end of 1956. Assuming collectivization is virtually completed this would make the average number of farming households per collective farm 141 as compared with 229 in the Soviet Union.

The development of specialized state farms and mechanization is also progressing, but has scarcely scratched the surface of the total problem. In 1956 there were 166 mechanized state-operated farms which cultivated 1,729 square miles of land. It is reasonable to assume that most of the mechanization thus far has taken place in the dry-land wheat country in the north. Cultivation by mechanized state farms in 1956 amounted to 1.6 per cent of 105,200 square miles devoted to wheat production in that year. This was only 0.6 per cent of a total estimated cultivated land area in 1956 of 282,000 square miles.

Similarly the development of state-operated tractor stations began to be reported as early as 1953. By 1956 there were 326 of these, after the model of the Soviet Union; but their machinery cultivated only 7,300 square miles, a fragment, less than 0.3 per cent of the cultivated area of China.

Industrial Regional Organization of the Communist Bloc

The key to understanding the regional organization of the Soviet system in both the U. S. S. R. and Communist China is the development of heavy industry and machine building. Without machine tools in an industrial society there can be no economic independence. The cornerstone of all economic policy in Communist Bloc countries, therefore, is the development of national and regional economic self-sufficiency. The patterns of activity reflecting this central policy will first be discussed for China, and then for the Soviet Union.

The basic revolutionary change which has occurred in the organization of the economy under the Chinese Communists is transformation of a subsistence agricultural economy, almost over night, into an exchange economy. From concern primarily with the provision of the local necessities of

[1] Choh-Ming Li, *Economic Development of Communist China*, Berkeley and Los Angeles: University of California Press, 1959, p. 243.

life within villages, the Chinese peasant finds himself now caught up within an industrial organization of the national economy as a whole. Agriculture, as everywhere in the world, is a base upon which population feeds itself. In exchange-type area organization, however, a regional division of labor is developed between food producers and the manufacturers of other goods. For this type of relationship to be "created" and given a push beyond the nascent beginnings in pre-Communist China, the central government had first to secure a firm grip on the food supply. This they acquired by the development of farmers' cooperatives and collectives, and now communes. Not only do these new forms of organization change the patterns of fields and functioning farm units, but they have a broader purpose as well. This is the organization of the *distribution* and *allocation* for distribution of the national food supply among the various sectors of the economy. Such control has been accomplished by the organization of wholesaling and retailing of commodities.

Beginning in 1950 the state set up a trading apparatus which deals in food and clothing, raw materials such as fuel, cotton, and industrial supplies, as well as controlling exports and imports. This apparatus consists of a network of state-operated agencies and marketing cooperatives. These took the form of "consumer's cooperatives" in urban areas, and "supply and selling" cooperatives in agricultural areas. Already existing private trading establishments were rapidly absorbed within the state system which greatly extended this form of control in the distribution of commodities. The creation of this system, of course, was a means to an end—guaranteeing adequate surpluses for the expansion of nonagricultural activities, particularly *manufacturing*, and within this category heavy or producers' goods manufacturing. Only on this basis could the industrialization of China proceed in the furtherance of the Communists' political, economic, and social blueprint to surpass in production first the United Kingdom and then the United States. The fact that they have thus far found the pace difficult in no way changes the fact of their intent.

Emerging Core Region of Communist China.

The map in Figure 228 shows the pattern of major agriculture and manufacturing activities in China. From the map it is evident that there are a number of distinct industrial districts. The three most important ones are in the Central Manchurian Plain focusing on Shenyang (Mukden, 2,411,000), in the North China Plain focusing on twin centers of Peiping (4,010,000) and Tientsin (3,220,000), and in the Lower Yangtze delta region comprising the Shanghai (6,900,000), Nanking (1,419,000), Wuhan (Hankow, 2,146,000) triangle and focusing on Shanghai. Together with additional cities in these three general areas, which are distributed throughout these most populous farming lands of China, the three industrial districts are the emerging coreland of an industrializing China.

The significance of the emergent nodal organization of China is not yet fully reflected in absolute amounts of production. Based on Soviet Russian experience, the projection of rates of development indicate that China will become increasingly important as an industrialized nation. In 1952 China produced only 1,350,000 metric tons of steel. In 1957 the figure was 5,240,000 metric tons. It is evident that a national effort will be made in the next fifteen years to take a leap forward in steel production and general industrial output. The first goal is to surpass the present rate of United Kingdom's steel production of 40 million tons per year.

The Chinese iron and steel industry. The centers where this greatly expanded production of steel and other heavy machinery industries will take place are at least the seventeen principal sites of the present pattern of the Chinese iron and steel industry, shown in Figure 229. These are arranged in six major districts—Manchuria, North China, Lower Yangtze, Middle Yangtze, Chungking, Shanshi, and Inner Mongolia. The first three are within the core region of the country. Approximately half of China's iron- and steel-producing capacity (2,500,000 tons) is located at Anshan (805,000), Manchuria. Other producing centers in Manchuria are all in the same vicinity. In addition to Shenyang (Mukden) the economic capital of the region, they include Penki (449,000), Fushun (985,000), and Dairen (1,508,000). The iron and steel industry of the North China region is localized at Tientsin, Shihkiachwang (598,000), which is an industrial suburb of Peiping, Tangshan (800,000), and Süanhwa (114,100). In the Lower Yangtze, steel mills operate in Shanghai and Maanahan. Production in each region is based on ores and coking coal available within a reasonably short distance. Facilities for marked expansion of present levels of production are under construction at inland sites in four other locations. One of these is at Haangshih near Wuhan (Hankow) on the Middle Yangtze, using local high-grade iron and coking coal from Pingsiang in

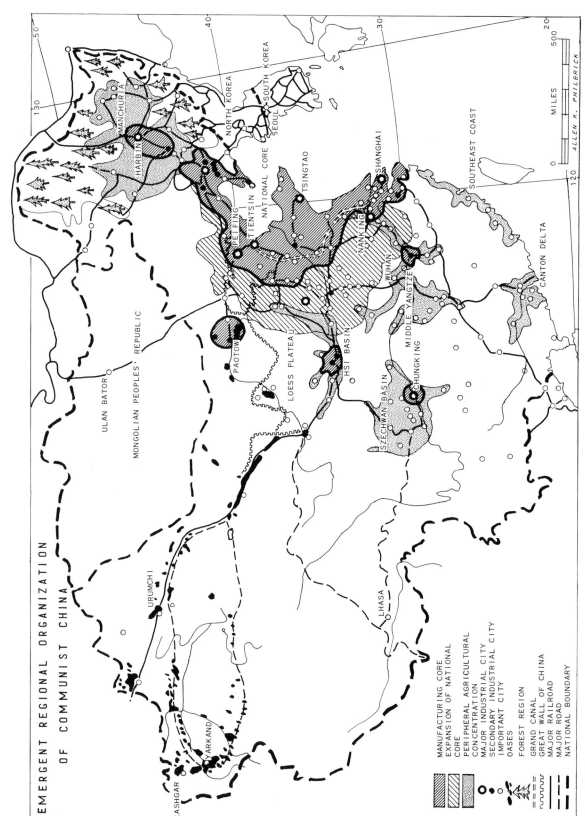

EMERGENT REGIONAL ORGANIZATION
OF COMMUNIST CHINA

MANUFACTURING CORE
EXPANSION OF NATIONAL
CORE
PERIPHERAL AGRICULTURAL
CONCENTRATION
MAJOR INDUSTRIAL CITY
SECONDARY INDUSTRIAL CITY
IMPORTANT CITY
OASES

FOREST REGION

GRAND CANAL
GREAT WALL OF CHINA
MAJOR RAILROAD
MAJOR ROAD
NATIONAL BOUNDARY

ALLEN K. PHILBRICK

MILES

500

Figure 228

396

Kiangsu Province. Another producing district is farther upstream on the Yangtze River at Chungking (2,121,000). Here in the wartime capital of China during World War II, iron and steel got its start with plant facilities transported upriver ahead of the invading Japanese troops. Rebuilding and construction of new facilities here will give Szechuan Province basic iron and steel production for the development of the regional economy. In the hill lands of Shansi Province iron and steel plants are being built at Taiyuan (1,020,000) and Yangchuan (177,400), while in the northwest in Inner Mongolia iron mining and blast furnaces at Paiyunopo and Paotou, north of the great bend in the Huang Ho River, which use coking coal from mines at Shihkaikow, are destined to swing the center of gravity of the iron and steel industry toward the interior and away from the coastal regions.

The pattern of *machinery* and *machine-tool* manufacture in China is shown also on the map in Figure 229. Such production follows closely the location of iron- and steel-producing centers in the Chinese core region. There are twelve major cities engaged in basic producers' goods manufacture—Harbin, Changchun (975,000), Mukden, Dairen, Peiping, Tientsin, Fushun (985,000), Shanghai, Taiyuan, Tsinan, Tsingtao (1,121,000), and Loyang (171,200). These centers, by their distribution, outline the shape of the core region.

If the present center of heavy industry is in northern Manchuria at Anshan and Mukden, that of light industry is in the Yangtze delta focused at Shanghai, and in the coastal provinces of North

China. Since the cotton crop is centered on the western and drier portions of the North China Plain, as shown on the map in Figure 224, new production facilities nearer the source of raw materials are being developed at Peiping (4,010,000), Shihkiachwang, Hantan, and in the tributary valleys of the Wei Ho at Sian and Sienyang. Even with such developments, however, the manufacture of cotton in the cities of the Shanghai-Nanking-Wuhan triangle represents the largest focus of cotton production in China.

Both military security and national development require a better balance of industrial development between coastal and inland geographical locations in China. In 1952 more than 80 per cent of the capacity of iron and steel production was in the coastal areas of the country, most of it, as already indicated, confined to the single producing center at Anshan. These facilities were constructed by the Japanese during their control of Manchuria after conquest in 1931. Since the Communists took power in 1949 the same shifts in emphasis can be noted. They are recorded in Table XLI for the period from 1952 to 1956. The table shows that inland cities have increased their share of industrial output from slightly more than a quarter to approximately one-third. Most of this shift is accounted for by developments in heavy industry. Since the manufacturing enterprises of the coastal provinces of South China are relatively minor, the figures in the table also show the importance of coreland provinces—Hopei, Shantung, Kiangsu, and Liaoning. The development of industrial cities in China

TABLE XLI   THE LOCATION OF FACTORY INDUSTRY ACCORDING TO VALUE OF PRODUCT AT 1952 PRICES, 1952 TO 1956, IN BILLIONS OF YUAN AND PER CENT[a]

Location	1952, billions of yuan	Per cent of total	1955, billions of yuan	Per cent of total	1956, billions of yuan	Per cent of total	Per cent change, 1952–1956
Inland[b]	7.3	26.9	14.3	32	18.8	32.1	258
Coastal[b]	19.7	73.1	30.5	68	39.8	67.9	201
Total	27.0	100.0	44.8	100.0	58.6	100.0	217
Shanghai	6.6	24.3	9.1	20.1	11.8	20.1	178
Tientsin	1.8	6.8	2.9	6.4	3.5	6.0	194
Peiping	0.8	2.8	1.4	3.1	1.9	3.2	400

[a] Sources: this table was compiled by Choh-Ming Li and "was computed from relative weights and index numbers given in (1) "Several Problems of China's Socialist Industrialization," *Hsin-Hua pan-yueh-k'an*, **1**:67–71, January 1957; and (2) Yang Ch'ing-wen, "Two Problems of Industrial Location," *Chi-hua ching-chi (Planned Economy)*, **8**:13–15, August 1957.

[b] The seven coastal provinces are Liaoning, Hopei, Shantung, Kiangsu, Chekiang, Fukien, and Kwantung. The inland provinces are Shensi, Honan, Hupei, Anwhei, and Shansi.

constitutes an industrial or manufacturing belt, comparable potentially to the industrial belts of Europe, the Soviet Union, and North America. The Chinese industrial belt lies within and characterizes the core region of the country.

The diagrammatic map in Figure 228 has shown the nodal organization of the Chinese national economy. A nodal pattern of regional organization is emerging against the background of the previously separate and scattered regions of China within which life was traditionally of a subsistence-type organization.

The core region of China comprises the four major provinces of the coastal region, in which two-thirds of the manufacturing industries of the country define the beginnings of a manufacturing belt. The 1953 population of the four provinces was 143 million, or one-fourth of the total population (24.6 per cent) of mainland China at that time. The provinces immediately to the west of the core region—Shansi, Honan, Hupei, and Anwhei—form a secondary ring around the primary core region. It is to this second ring that the term "inland" is primarily applied in Table XLI, with the possible addition of Shensi Province west of Shansi. These five additional provinces contain approximately another 140 million persons (22.3 per cent). These 275 million persons of the North China Plains and bordering loess plateau and hill country form the largest single concentration of agricultural population in the world. They also are the most urbanized portion of China.

The average population density for the 546,000 square miles of the nine-province region which comprises the core region and its western annex is more than 500 persons per square mile (508). The concentration within the four coastal provinces averages nearly 700 persons per square mile (680), and ranges from more than 1,000 persons per square mile in Kiangsu to as little as 360 in the southern Manchurian province of Liaoning. In Liaoning Province, where agricultural population has settled only during the past fifty years, and total population is no more than 20 million, there are nearly 9,000,000 persons dwelling in cities. Within the four-province core region the ratio of urban to total population in 1953 was approximately 27 per cent. This proportion is double the national average; and the nearly 39 million city dwellers within the coastal core were slightly more than half of the urban population of all China in

1953. As may be seen from the map in Figure 230, the proportion of urban population in all the rest of China, except for the other two provinces in Manchuria (23 and 24 per cent) and the coastal provinces of South China (11 per cent each), ranges from 4–7 per cent which is less than one-third to one-half of the national average.

The emergence of North China as the core of industrial Communist China continues a former trend. This region has long had the largest and most concentrated population and the largest cities. But development there of a nodally organized national economy with a manufacturing base radially interconnected with regions of specialized production elsewhere in China is new. Historic origins of Chinese civilization occurred from primitive subsistence beginnings in the loess areas of the Wei Ho and Fen Ho, tributaries of the Huang Ho at the "Great Bend" of the Yellow River in the third millenium B.C. The primary Chinese culture hearth lies directly west of the present core. Early civilization was based on perception of the fertility of loess soils and the ease of their cultivation under irrigation. Success here led to the second stage of development—the channeling of water for irrigated agriculture on the delta region.

The Huang Ho or Yellow River derives its color from the huge load of yellow loess soils which it has carried during the centuries from the interior to the Yellow Sea. As it has constructed the alluvial delta seaward, the channel and bed of the river has shifted on many occasions in historic times. The delta of the Huang Ho has filled the area between the Shansi or "Western Mountains" and the Shantung or "Eastern Mountains" with rich alluvium. The river has changed its course so many times that the "mouths" of the Huang Ho on both sides of the Shantung peninsula are separated by as much as 300 miles. The havoc wrought by floods when the Huang Ho has burst its man-made dikes has given the river another name also—"the River of China's Sorrow." One of the tasks of the new regime, to which it has perhaps overambitiously set itself, is that of constructing flood-control and irrigation works in order "finally" to bring under control and subject to their will the vagaries of the giant yellow stream. This has been the ambition of many in the long history of the dynasties of China's rulers.

The map in Figure 231 shows the probable foci and expansion from them by northern and

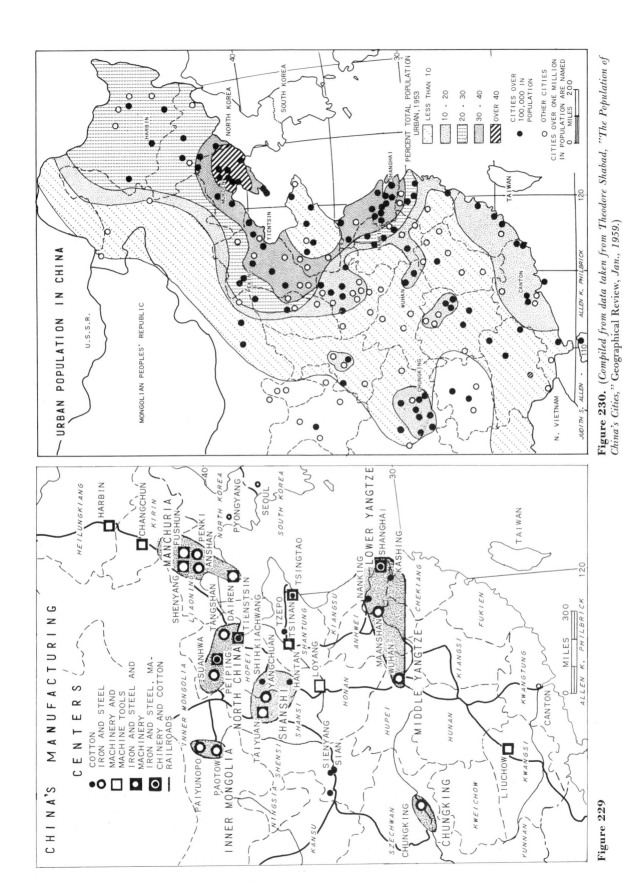

Figure 230. *(Compiled from data taken from Theodore Shabad, "The Population of China's Cities," Geographical Review, Jan., 1959.)*

Figure 229

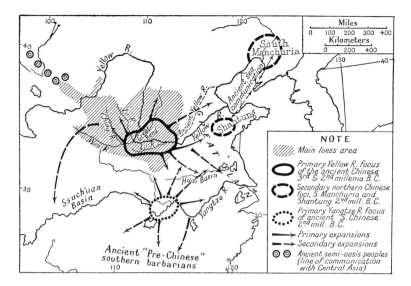

Figure 231. Foci and expansion of the northern and southern Chinese in third and second millennia B.C. (*Courtesy of The American Geographical Society, taken from Owen Lattimore, "Inner Asian Frontiers of China."*)

southern Chinese in the third and second millenia B.C. In the words of Owen Lattimore,[1]

There are only two focal areas for the origins of Chinese history: a primary focus in the middle Yellow River Valley and a secondary focus in the middle Yangtze Valley. In time the processes of diffusion from each of these foci began to overlap and interact. This raised the question whether the North or the South was to be dominant. In the upshot the North prevailed, partly because it had certain inherent advantages at the early level of development and partly because, as the general interplay of historical forces became more complex, it developed into the area in which equilibrium was to be sought between the history of agricultural China and the history of the Inner Asian steppes, with their marginal oasis, mountain, and forest zones.

When the sum of the forces at work had once taken this bias, the geographical spread of the Chinese became uneven. Toward the south their expansion was immense. The ancient South China, lying between the middle Yangtze and the Huai and Lower Han basins, became mid-China, as one primitive barbarian tract after another was occupied and incorporated beyond the Yangtze to form the new South China. On the north expansion was not only unequal but irregular and fluctuating. Periods of advance alternated with periods of retreat. The line of the Great Wall came to represent the mean of these fluctuations. . . .

As for the middle Yangtze, its heavier rainfall meant not only marshes but rank jungle. It was an elaborate technique of irrigated rice-growing that eventually made settled agriculture possible and profitable for large populations along the middle and lower Yangtze.

[1] Owen Lattimore, *Inner Asian Frontiers of China*, American Geographical Society, Research Series No. 21, New York, 1940, map p. 26 and pp. 27–29.

To assume the working out of such a technique at the earliest stage of cultural and social development implies the ability to take a second major step forward at a time when the first tentative step had barely become possible.

Therefore it was the loess region that became the primary focus of Chinese history. . . . in the general region of the great bend where the Yellow River, after running from north to south between what are now the provinces of Shanshi and Shenshi, turns to the east and enters the great Plain.

Dominance of the north in China and the early importance of the North China Plain as the core-land of China is indicated by two of the major works of man during the historic period of the evolution of Chinese culture shown on the map in Figure 228. The first of these great works is the famous "Great Wall of China." This artificial defense system, as indicated by Lattimore, represented the mean of advance and retreat between two cultures—Mongolian nomadic horsemen of the continental interior, and Chinese sedentary agriculturalists based on irrigation in the North China Plain. The wall was first united and connected into a single system as early as the third century B.C., which attests to the importance the Chinese attached to the North China Plain and loess-hill country as the major "ecumene" or living space even before that time. The second work was the "Grand Canal." It is the longest artificial waterway in the world, which originates near the city of Hangchow in Chekiang Province, and traverses the provinces of Kiangsu, Shantung, and Hopei to within a short distance of Peiping, traditional

Mongol capital of China. Completed in the thirteenth century, its primary purpose was to transport grain tribute from South China to the core region in North China, which contained the political focus of the empires of several dynasties of Chinese rulers. Alignment of this canal is geographic expression of unity between north and south and domination of the north. It also expresses the unity of the Lower Yangtze Delta and the North China Plain.

Peripheral Regions of China in Their Relationship to the Core. The radial arrangement of the regions which are peripheral to the Chinese coreland is shown by the map in Figure 228. To the north and east lies central and northern Manchuria with its principal focus at Harbin (1,552,000). Peripheral to this subregion are the main forested slopes of mountainous terrain in the border regions and some of the principal coal mines of industrial China. To the east, also, is the Korean Peninsula, which extends generally northwest-southeast. Except for the Korean Strait (130 miles wide), it is a land bridge connecting the Chinese mainland with the Japanese Islands. It was this unhappy country which felt the full brunt of the Chinese-American struggle during the Korean War (1950–1955) and which resulted in the partition of the peninsula into two parts—North Korea (Communist) and South Korea (non-Communist)—along a truce line approximating the thirty-eighth parallel of North Latitude.

To the northwest is the nominally independent country, the Mongolian Peoples' Republic. Through its capital city Ulan Bator extends one of the main rail routes to the Soviet Union. Between the Chinese coreland and Mongolia is Inner Mongolia, in which basic steel and other industrial developments at Paotou (149,400) and elsewhere are under construction.

To the west is the Kansu Corridor, gateway to the central Asian highlands and enclosed basins. From the far central-west, petroleum and other mineral products are being developed which, if volume turns out to be large, will be of decisive importance to the industrial complexes of the humid east. Westward routes first traverse the traditional culture hearth of China in the valley of the Wei Ho. Here, also, new manufacturing activities are being created in harmony with the existing basis of agriculture. The regional focus is the capital at Sian (1,310,000). From the lines of interconnection between the west and the core region two additional alignments extend to the northwest and southwest. To the northwest, the new rail line, sometimes reported as completed through oases to Yumen (150,000) and Urumchi (275,000), connects the core with Singkiang and the Soviet Central Asian republics. Yumen in western Kansu, is a center of petroleum production. Urumchi is the seat of the People's Council of the Singkiang Autonomous Region.

To the southwest a newly completed rail connection ties the most populous province of China, Szechuan, with the core region. By way of Chengtu (1,101,000), the capital of the province, the rail line links the upper Yangtze River to the middle Huang Ho. The traditional contact of Szechuan Province is the greatest navigable river of China—the Yangtze—which flows east to the sea and brings the focus of its entire basin region on the port of Shanghai. From both Lanchow (699,000) in Kansu and Chengtu in Szechuan Province, roads lead southwest to convergence at Lhasa in Tibet, joining that region under military control and closer contact with the main body of Communist China.

To the south the main line of the rail route extends to the Yangtze at Wuhan (Hankow, 2,146,000). For the first time bridges have been constructed across the Yangtze (Figure 232A and B). After crossing the Yangtze the rail line proceeds to the capital of Hunan Province, Changsha (703,000), regional capital of inland South China. South China rail connections divide between the south route leading to the lower Hsi and Canton Delta region and the southwest route which extends to the frontier and links China with the Communist satellite country of North Vietnam. South China contains the sites of a number of relatively isolated but important mineral-producing areas, both for foreign trade and for national supply of tungsten, antimony, tin, molybdenum, mercury, copper, lead, and zinc. The more important mining localities of each are shown on the map in Figure 220. China holds first place in world production of tungsten and antimony.

On the basis of reorganization of former subsistence areas of the country, China is rapidly being transformed from an intensive agricultural occupancy to an agricultural-industrial exchange-type society. Although classified on the world map in Chapter 2 as a region of subsistence type, it should be understood that China, a complex of many regions, is undergoing a rapid transitional development.

Figure 232. (A) Left, the Yangtze River bridge at Wuhan in central China handles a heavy volume of transport between China's northern and southern provinces. It was built with the help of the Soviet Union and employs the latest technique of building the piers' foundations by a tubular-column, concrete-pouring method. Note the two levels and the large volume of pedestrian traffic contrasted with total absence of trucks on the top highway level. (B) Below, the second steel bridge across the Yangtze at Chungking is a double-track railway bridge. It will facilitate the economic development of Szechuan. Note the width of the Yangtze at this inland point, more than 1,000 miles by air from Shanghai. Between 250 and 350 miles down river from Chungking, the river passes through the famous Yangtze Gorges which make navigation difficult. Below the rapids the river is 130 feet above sea level as it enters the more than 600 miles of wide alluvial river plains terminating in the delta region. It is navigable from Wuhan by large vessels of deep draft for 685 miles by river distance (about 430 miles by air) to Shanghai. (*Courtesy of China Photo Service.*)

Nodal Regional Organization of the Soviet Union. From transitional China, attention is now directed to the nodal regional organization of the Soviet Union, which is the more powerful industrial core of the two principal Communist Bloc countries. By contrast with China, the pattern of Russia's regional organization is more mature, compact and unified. From the map in Figure 233 it is readily apparent that well-developed manufacturing regions lie within the coreland agricultural triangle of the country. The map is after one by John Thompson[1] and shows the relative proportions of the total manufacturing production divided among eleven main subregions. Six of the eleven are arranged in symmetrical fashion within the triangular agricultural coreland of Russia. Their focus is the Moscow industrial center. To the northwest is the Leningrad district, which comprises the industrial city of Leningrad. To the south of Moscow is the complex of manufacturing cities in the Ukraine. To the east of Moscow the Volga River has been made navigable and connected to Moscow by the Moscow-Volga Canal and by a series of locks and dams. A third manufacturing region occupies the Volga at strategic sites. European Russian districts account for 42 per cent of the Soviet Union's manufacturing production. Farther to the east, like the tail of a kite, are the manufacturing districts of the Urals (11.75 per cent) and the Kuzbas or Kuznets Basin (4.05 per cent) which completes the list of six regions within the agricultural triangle. Two more industrial districts are along the Trans-Siberian route to the Pacific—the Lake Baikal districts (1.35 per cent) and the Far East (1.85 per cent).

From the Urals district west, the number of separate cities among the five industrial subregions shown on the map in Figure 233 justifies the definition of the entire region as the Soviet Manufacturing Belt. The Urals and the four European Russian subregions comprise 54 per cent of the total. With inclusion of manufacturing cities within the manufacturing belt, but outside the specific industrial-district territories, the proportion of total manufacturing which takes place within the belt rises to 72.3 per cent. Remaining subregions outside the manufacturing belt are in the Caucasus—north Caucasus (2.1 per cent) and the trans-Caucasus (4.0 per cent)—and the central Asian

[1] Richard E. Londsdale and John H. Thompson, "A Map of the U. S. S. R.'s Manufacturing," *Economic Geography*, Vol. 36, No. 1, January 1960, pp. 36–52.

subregion (2.65 per cent).

Another way of looking at the same pattern of districts is in concentric zones outward at successive distances from the industrial center of Moscow. In this arrangement, the first concentric ring of districts consists of Leningrad, the Ukraine, the Volga, and the Urals. A second concentric ring of districts is composed of the two Caucasus districts, Central Asia, and the Kuzbas. A partial third ring is attached in the form of the two eastern Siberian minor subregions. That this basic radial pattern is functionally sound is indicated by the radial and concentric interconnections provided by the Soviet rail network. In all, nearly 90 per cent (88.30 per cent) of Soviet manufactures are accounted for within the manufacturing belt or outlying subregional industrial concentrations. The remaining 11.7 per cent of manufacturing is distributed among isolated centers between and not included within either the belt or any one of the outlying districts.

Principles of Self-Sufficiency and Interdependence in the Communist Bloc. The functioning of the system of area organization in the Communist Bloc operates on the basis of two interrelated principles. The first of these complementary concepts is that every region strives to develop its locally available resources so that they complement one another to the maximum degree possible. The second principle is that the national economies of both China and the U. S. S. R. also function nationally on the basis of the *interdependence* of the parts within the whole. This applies particularly in the Soviet Union to the relationship of the industrial center at Moscow with the peripheral regions of the country. The result of these two complementary principles is the existence of a hierarchy of self-sufficient local areas nodally organized into regions, in turn, nodally organized to make up the national economy of the Union of Soviet Socialist Republics, which functions as a single unit.

The data in Table XLII describes the types of manufacturing characteristic of each of the subregions of the Soviet Union. Note how often the words machinery, food or agricultural-product processing, textiles, and chemicals occur in varying combinations with other specialized manufactures. The basic activities everywhere in the Soviet Union are (1) machine building with which to create the possibility of using raw materials in the manufacture of other goods, and (2) the production of food and raw materials with which to feed the two com-

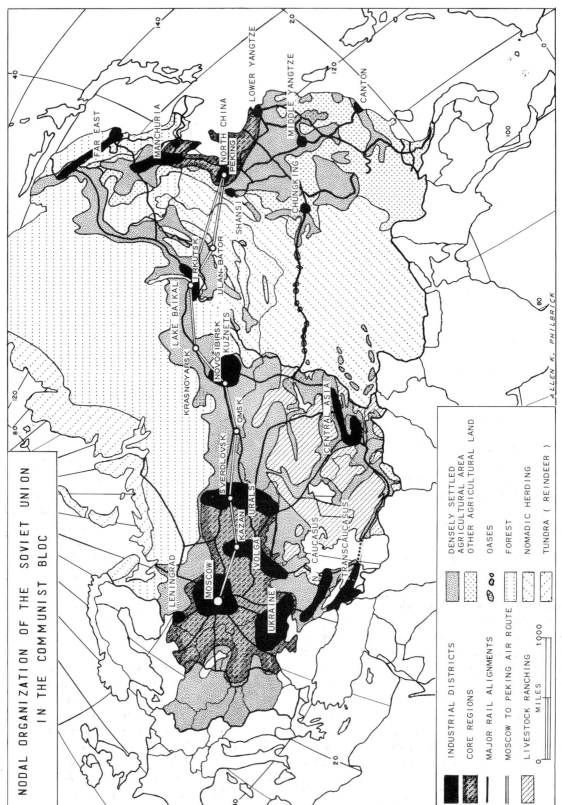

NODAL ORGANIZATION OF THE SOVIET UNION IN THE COMMUNIST BLOC

FAR EAST

MANCHURIA

NORTH CHINA

PEKING

LOWER YANGTZE

MIDDLE YANGTZE

CANTON

CHUNGKING

SHANSI

ULAN-BATOR

IRKUTSK

LAKE BAIKAL

KRASNOYARSK

NOVOSIBIRSK

KUZNETS

OMSK

SVERDLOVSK

URALS

CENTRAL ASIA

KAZAN

VOLGA

CAUCASUS

N. CAUCASUS

TRANSCAUCASUS

LENINGRAD

MOSCOW

UKRAINE

ALLEN K. PHILBRICK

INDUSTRIAL DISTRICTS

CORE REGIONS

MAJOR RAIL ALIGNMENTS

MOSCOW TO PEKING AIR ROUTE

LIVESTOCK RANCHING

DENSELY SETTLED
AGRICULTURAL AREA

OTHER AGRICULTURAL LAND

OASES

FOREST

NOMADIC HERDING

TUNDRA (REINDEER)

MILES

0   1000

Figure 233

404

Subregional name	Per cent nat. manuf.	Principal centers	Per cent nat. manuf.	Principal types of manufacture in the region
Moscow	18.10	Moscow	8.20	Machine production
		Gor'kiy	1.65	Precision equipment
		Yaroslavl'	0.65	Textiles
		Ivanovo	0.55	Clothing
		Tula	0.55	Chemicals
				Publishing
East Ukraine	14.00	Kharkov	1.65	Coal, iron, and manganese mining
		Stalino	1.30	Iron and steel
		Dnepernetrovsk	1.10	Machine building
		Rostov	0.85	Chemicals
		Zaporozh'ye	0.75	
		Makeyevka	0.65	
		Krivoy Rog	0.65	
		Lugansk	0.60	
Urals	11.75	Sverdlovsk	1.45	Processing iron, copper,
		Chelyabinsk	1.25	bauxite, chromium,
		Perm	1.10	potassium ores
		Ufa	0.95	Ferrous and nonferrous
		Magnitogorsk	0.65	metallurgy
		Niz Tagil	0.65	Machine building
				Chemicals
Volga	5.0	Kuybyshev	1.25	Machine building
		Kazan'	0.95	Oil refining, electric power
		Stalingrad	0.90	Food processing
		Saratov	0.80	Building materials
Leningrad	4.9	Leningrad	4.90	Quality goods, precision instruments
				Machines
				Electrical apparatus
				Chemicals, textiles
				Publishing
Trans-Caucasus	4.0	Baku	1.60	Processing agricultural products
		Tbilisi	0.75	Extraction, refining petroleum
		Yerevan	0.40	Machine building
North Caucasus	2.1	Krasnodar	0.60	Textiles
		Grozny	0.35	Metal working
Kuznets-Novosibirsk	4.05	Novosibirsk	1.10	Coking coal, ore processing
		Stalinsk	0.65	Iron and steel
		Prokop'yevsk	0.35	Heavy machinery
		Kemerovo	0.35	Chemicals, food processing
Central Asia	2.65	Tashkent	0.80	Processing agric. products
		Alma Ata	0.40	Processing mineral products
				Machine construction
				Textiles, metal working

TABLE **XLII**   (CONTINUED)

Subregional name	Per cent nat. manuf.	Principal centers	Per cent nat. manuf.	Principal types of manufacture in the region
Far East	1.85	Vladivostok	0.45	Processing local raw materials
		Komsomol'sk	0.35	Machinery, oil ref.
		Khabarovsk		Ferrous metallurgy
				Ship building, food
Lake Baikal	1.35	Irkutsk	0.60	Machinery, automobiles
		Ulan Ude	0.25	Mineral and agric. supplies
		Cheremkhovo	0.20	Lumber, food, coal
Notable dispersed centers		Kiev	1.60	Machine building
		Odessa	0.95	Chemical products
		Minsk	0.70	Food processing, clothing

[a]The proportions of manufacturing and definitions of manufacturing regions are taken from Richard E. Londsdale and John H. Thompson, "A Map of the U. S. S. R.'s Manufacturing," *Economic Geography*, Vol. 36, No. 1, January 1960, pp. 36–52.

ponents of the means of production—*people* and *machines.*

The map in Figure 234[1] shows the pattern of Soviet machine-building industries. Machine tools are the secret of the development of a manufacturing-based geographical division of labor in an exchange-type economy. The Soviet Union, since the consolidation of Communist political and military control of that country in the 1920s, has been engaged in a long-range program to produce the materials and the *machines* from their own iron and steel and other resources which would enable them to produce the plants and facilities of a modern industrial society. In the process of the operation of the many separately producing, relatively self-contained districts of the country, the economy as a whole exhibits flows of materials to and a focus on the heart of the country, which takes the form of the interdependence of the industrial center and peripheral regions of the entire economy. For Moscow is the economic, political, and social focus of the Soviet Union. Before World War II it was said of the "industrial center" that it comprised about 1 per cent of the total area, about 10 per cent of the total population, about 20 per cent of the total urban population, and about 30 per cent of the country's large-scale industry. Yet this most important of the country's regions possesses no coal (only lignite), no petroleum, virtually no iron ore, water power, or particular richness of soil. The circumstances which Moscow does possess above all others, however, is the continuity of a centralized position in the minds and activities of the Russian people, that is, a cultural-geographical centrality throughout the historical evolution of Russian and Soviet culture. As a result it has also possessed the nodality of existing radial transportation and communications between Moscow and all parts of the Communist Bloc territory.

The central industrial region, with Moscow as its focus, is centrally located within the east European Plain—European Russia. Relative isolation early ensured both maximum security from invasion and the development of communication radially by rivers flowing generally outward in all directions from this vicinity. By the thirteenth century the princes of Muscovy had assumed a dominating position as intermediaries between other outlying regions. Thus the nucleus of a Russian state originated. For comparison purposes, the maps in Figures 235 and 236 show this phenomenon of cultural nucleation for both the Soviet Union[2] and China.[3] The map in Figure 235 shows the territorial expansion of Russia (equated with expansion of Communism after 1917) from the thirteenth century to date. The map in Figure 236 reveals the advance and recession of Chinese historical claims to sovereignty in Eurasia. Certainly, the two great Communist powers of Eurasia have had historic

[1] N. N. Baransky, *Economic Geography of the U. S. S. R.*, Moscow: Foreign Language Publishing House, 1956, p. 45.

[2] Lucille Carlson, *Geography of World Politics*, New York: Prentice-Hall, Inc., 1957, map, p. 145.

[3] George B. Cressey, *Land of the 500 Million*, New York: McGraw-Hill Book Co., Inc., map, p. 40.

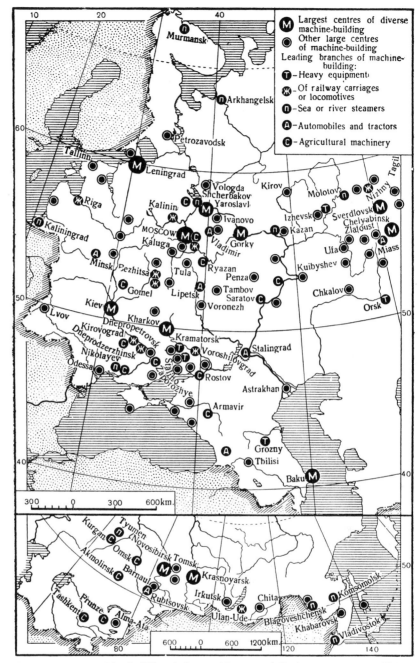

Figure 234. Machine-building industry. (*Courtesy of Foreign Languages Publishing House, taken from N. N. Baransky,* Economic Geography of the U.S.S.R.)

meeting ground in Central Asia! The core regions of each have exhibited a high degree of continuity.

N. N. Baransky, writing of the economic geography of the U. S. S. R., describes the national level of nodal organization of the Soviet Union in the following terms.[1]

As a result of railway construction in the second half of the last century and in the beginning of this century, the commodity exchange of the Industrial Center has developed in depth and in breadth; it extends now

[1] N. N. Baransky, *Economic Geography of the U. S. S. R.*, Moscow: Foreign Languages Publishing House, 1956, pp. 117, 118.

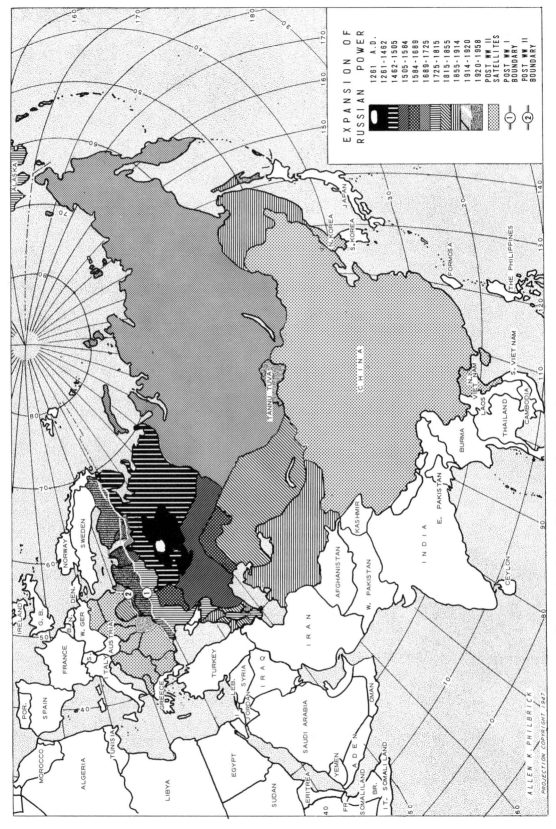

Figure 235. (*Courtesy of Prentice-Hall, Inc., taken from Lucille Carlson, Geography of World Politics.*)

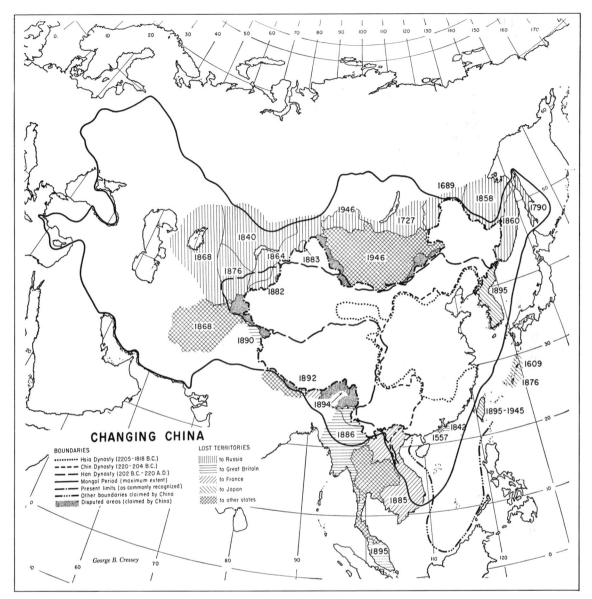

Figure 236. The shaded areas over which imperial China once claimed nominal sovereignty, now lost, total 1,547,500 square miles. Many of her present international boundaries are in dispute. (*Courtesy of McGraw-Hill Book Co., Inc., taken from George B. Cressey,* Land of the 500 Million: A Geography of China, © *1955.*)

to the entire vast territory of the country and is of exceptional significance for the national economy as a whole, and for the Industrial Center itself.

The external commodity exchange of the Industrial Center is distinguished for its extremely high volume. About 20 per cent of the country's total arrivals of mass freights by rail and water falls to the Industrial Center.

The second characteristic of the external commodity exchange of the Industrial Center is its wide territorial range; this exchange covers the whole territory stretch-

ing from the country's western border to the Pacific Ocean.

The third characteristic of the external commodity exchange is a pronounced predominance (especially in terms of weight) of receipts over shipments; this is due to the very structure of the exchange. The goods which *come to* the Industrial Center consist of *raw materials, fuel,* and *food-stuffs;** they are very bulky goods and include those which are very cheap per unit of weight, for example, coal, oil, timber, metal, grain,

* Italics by the present author.

salt, building materials, etc. On the other hand, the goods *shipped from* the Industrial Center consist almost fully of *manufactured articles,* which are expensive per unit of weight, for example *machines* (in particular the most complex and precision machines, and consequently the most expensive ones), fabrics, books, etc. The amount of goods received by the Industrial Center exceeds in weight almost threefold the amount of goods shipped from it. It must be borne in mind that this commodity exchange is of vital importance both for the Industrial Center and for other regions of the country.

The three systematic aspects of geography, *materials, culture,* and *organization,* are once more demonstrated as the basis by which people unite the parts into a whole. The resources of agriculture and of mining are perceived and woven into the fabric of the economy. The impetus of innovation and the transmission of culture have evolved and spread the impact of the original industrial revolution of eighteenth-century England half-way around the world. The emerging unity among Soviet and Chinese societies along with their satellites has produced in principle the same type of exchange organization of area characteristic of society in England, Europe, and in America.

What, then, distinguishes the Communist Bloc countries from the rest of the world? The Communist Bloc maintains a centralized and purposeful cultural leadership, dictating the planned and programmed economic, political, and social development of one-fourth of the earth's occupied land area and well over one-third (35 per cent) of the population of the earth.

18 *The Eurasian Perimeter*

Adjacent to the Communist Bloc is a second great division of Eurasia—the *Eurasian perimeter*—consisting of peninsulas and island archipelagoes. Its two subdivisions, east and west, were referred to in Chapter 15 by two squares superimposed over the political map in Figure 203. The western perimeter includes the free countries of Western Europe and the countries of North Africa and Southwest Asia; the eastern perimeter includes the countries and territories of South, Southeast, and the free countries of East Asia. Each of six regions of the Eurasian perimeter represents different combinations of cultures: in the west, the cultures of Western Europe and the Moslems of North Africa and Southwest Asia; in the east, the Hindu culture of the Indian subcontinent, tribal cultures of Southeast Asia, and diverse cultures, including Japanese, of the island countries of the Pacific.

Western Perimeter

Several chapters have been devoted to Western Europe already, so only a summary emphasizing certain ideas about Western Europe is appropriate at this point.

Western Europe. Several ideas about this region are important to emphasize. First, Europe has been the principal region of cultural origin and spread of the ideas and know-how of the industrial revolution in its beginning phases. This great series of innovations has changed the lives of people all over the world in the course of European exploration, expansion of commerce, and expansion of political control and settlement.

Second, the basis of the success of Western European exchange-organized industrial economies was perception and use of the natural resources of both Europe itself and much of the rest of the world—both agricultural and mineral. These developments have seen the evolution of a society based on a mutual division of labor between city and countryside, as well as between different regional locations. As the web of specialized producers grew with the integration of production within national and international units of economy, networks of transportation and communication were built to interconnect such activities.

Third, the resulting pattern of organized areas finds Europe today moving toward greater unity in the course of evolving more unified internal international organization in terms of the Common Market. Such economic integration, if it continues, will place Europe as a whole in a better position competitively with other regional economies which have now evolved in other parts of the world as the indirect result of the initial spread of historic innovations from Europe itself.

Finally, the paradox of Europe—power despite disunity—has spread throughout the world. The world is one, yet it is divided against itself: free enterprise against Communism; "have-not" against "have" nations; and the powerful against the powerless. The advanced scientific industrialism spawned by the English through their industrial revolution has grown through continuing technological evolution and geographical dispersion. Today the United States-Canadian joint region in North America and the Soviet Union in Eurasia represent two warring ideologies. Both are products of the same industrial culture. Europe, the culture ancestor of both, finds itself in the middle. Whoever controls Europe controls the most mature segment of the world know-how and resources in the balance of power within this "cold war."

The Moslem World. To the south of Europe lie two entirely different regions—North Africa and Southwest Asia. These two dry regions combined comprise the greater part of the Moslem world. Physical, cultural, and area organizational contrasts could hardly be greater than those existing between Western Europe and the Moslem regions. Discussion divided into four main parts will illustrate contrasts with Europe and at the same time characterize the Moslem world through cultural origins, organization of area in dry lands, the im-

411

portance of oil in the Middle East, and strategic position with respect to transportation and communication occupied by the Moslem regions between Europe and Asia.

Culture origins. The junctions of three continents—Africa, Europe, and Asia—occurs in the lands between the Mediterranean, the Red Sea, and the Persian Gulf. This region is one of important historic innovations. Not one but three of the world's great religions began within its limits—Judaism, Christianity, and Islam. Innovations in art, science, and letters, too numerous to mention individually at this time, had their origins within this region.

The spread of Christianity in the late Roman world, its split into two halves organized from twin centers of Rome and Constantinople, and the subsequent spread of Roman Catholic and Greek Orthodox branches throughout Western Europe and European Russia, link the ancient culture hearth of the Moslem world in the Middle East with western Eurasia. The acceptance of Christianity by Europeans laid the basis for the spread of Christianity in all its variations—Catholic, Protestant, and Orthodox—to the far corners of the earth.

The same outward dispersion from Judea characterizes the historically parallel dissemination of the Jewish faith through the wanderings of the Jewish people. Jewish settlement occurred primarily in urban places throughout the world. The return to Israel of so many of the Jews after World War II and the creation of the national state of Israel, accompanied by the conflict between Arabs and Jews in the Holy Land, represents a modern phase of an ancient problem.

The followers of Mohammedanism similarly spread the teachings of Mohammed throughout the Middle East and North Africa. The historic conflict between Christian and Moslem in the Middle Ages spelled final disintegration of the regional organization of human affairs which had been based on the Mediterranean Sea as the interconnecting linkage for many empires during classical times. Moslem armies marched northward into France in the west, and later the Turks threatened Vienna in the east after the fall of Constantinople in 1453. Contact between Europe and Asia was severed. Trade could no longer take place between the peoples of Europe and those of the Far East by means of the combined Mediterranean and overland routes to India and the Spice Islands. Re-establishment of such contact and trade with the Indies was a pri-

mary motive in the voyages of discovery made by Henry the Navigator of Portugal, and also of Columbus. There is a striking correspondence of Mohammedan culture to the limits of these two regions of North Africa and Southwest Asia. There are additional countries, beyond these regions, which are predominantly Mohammedan, such as Albania in the Balkan peninsula, Indonesia in Southwest Asia, and the province or autonomous region of Singkiang in west central China; but the great preponderance of Moslem population occupies a compact region from Turkey to Sudan, from West Pakistan to Gibraltar.

Area organization of dry regions. Countries of the Moslem world occupy arid lands, lying almost wholly within the "Arid Crescent." That same Arid Crescent which separates Western Europe from humid southern and eastern Asia in Figure 31 is shown in relation to the countries of Moslem Eurasia and north Africa on the map in Figure 237. The countries with predominantly Moslem populations occupy, for the most part, the drier tropical and subtropical parts of Africa and Asia. These countries are in grassland and desert regions which are mainly frost free or virtually so. More northerly and continental-interior dry regions of central China (Moslem Singkiang) and Soviet Central Asia which are also predominantly Moslem have frost seasons every year.

Patterns of occupancy in arid lands contrast sharply with those in Europe. The distribution of agriculture is oasis-like and insular instead of uninterrupted agricultural land. Oases of cultivated land where fresh water is available are separated by wide stretches of desert or steppe, within which there is little or no moisture. Fresh water is primarily dependent on runoff from moisture-catching highlands and not on general precipitation. Water sources in principal highlands, major river-drainage basins, and piedmont oases are shown on the map in Figure 237. Population-supporting "islands" of irrigated agriculture record the uses of such water resources. Most people in Moslem countries live by subsistence farming in which village organization of settlement is typical. Examples are the concentrated agricultural lands in the Nile, Tigris and Euphrates, and Indus valleys, of Egypt, Sudan, Iraq, and Pakistan, respectively. Other examples are piedmont oases such as those found in the Middle East's "Fertile Crescent." This piedmont region, famous since classical antiquity, is located south of the Turkish and west of the Iranian high-

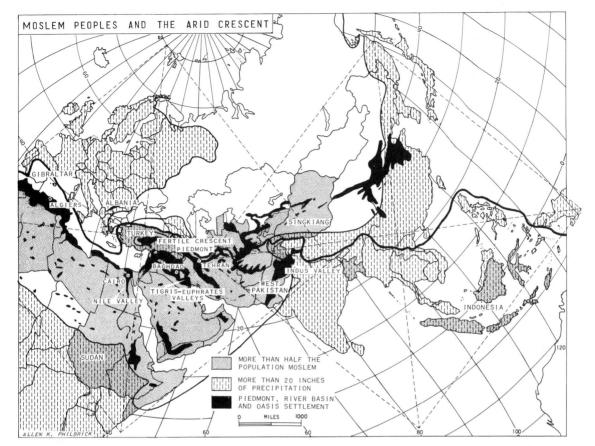

Figure 237

lands. It is an arc-shaped territory extending from northern Iraq by way of southern Turkey to northern Syria. Thence the Fertile Crescent meets the north end of the great rift valley through western Syria, Lebanon, and Israel, which extends southward through Africa to Nyasaland. The Fertile Crescent ends in the desert of the Negev in Israel and Jordan, and is bounded on the south by the Gulf of Aqaba at the north end of the Red Sea between Egypt and Jordan.

Still other agricultural areas are watered by winter cyclonic storms along the coasts of the southwestern Mediterranean in North Africa, and along the shore of the eastern Mediterranean on the seaward side of the hills of Lebanon and of Israel.

Oasis occupancy itself is of two types. While a majority of the population still lives an agricultural life, each principal agricultural island supports at least one relatively large city. Such cities are the centers of government, religious worship, and commerce. In them Europeanization has made the greatest progress. In cities such as Cairo

(2,993,000), Algiers (800,000), Baghdad (656,399), and Tehran (1,838,982), Western (European) quarters exist beside national (Moslem) areas of the respective countries. Urban areas have long been agencies of the spread of European customs and ideas. Commercial structures, hotels, and apartment buildings in the European quarters have a modern look; surrounding them, as exemplified in the Arab quarters of Cairo, are the mosques, bazaar-type commercial facilities, and crowded residential slums. In addition to city and subsistence-village agricultural-occupance types, tribes continue a traditional sparsely distributed nomadic-pastoral subsistence livelihood between densely settled agricultural "islands."

Middle East oil. With one outstanding exception mineral wealth is of minor importance in the Middle East. The exception is oil. Subsurface riches of "black gold" in the vicinity of the Persian Gulf are the largest known reserves of petroleum in the world. As already noted in the chapter on resources of the Americas, production in the Middle East accounts for almost one-fourth of world production. Almost all of the oil produced is exported, primarily to markets in Europe. Since World War II the refinery capacities of oil-importing Western European countries have been greatly expanded at their larger ports. These make use primarily of crude oil imported from the Middle East. Refineries have also been built in the Middle East. One of these, pictured in Figure 238, is at Abadan in southwest Iran, at the head of the Persian Gulf. The map in Figure 239 shows the locations of the principal producing fields, refineries, and oil pipelines.[1]

The modern technology of the refinery contrasts sharply with the ancient technologies of life surrounding them, and oil represents the most direct and dramatic impact of a delayed industrial revolution on the Moslem world. Royalties from the development of petroleum are paid by foreign oil companies—British, American, and Dutch—to the governments of the Middle Eastern kingdoms which are fortunate enough to have these riches in their subsurface sedimentary rocks. The incomes make possible long-range improvements which benefit their respective peoples. Unfortunately economic development policies are not invariably forthcoming.

Many other countries in the Moslem world, as may be seen from the map in Figures 169, 220, and 239, have no oil. Because of oil, already existing contrasts between "rags and riches" have been further intensified not only among countries but also within the oil kingdoms themselves.

Strategic position of the Middle East. Recent conflicts between Arab and European interests and between Arab and Israeli interests illustrate the age-old strategic position of the Middle East. The nationalization of the Suez Canal by Egypt interfered temporarily with tanker shipments to England by way of the Persian Gulf and the Mediterranean Sea. The Arab-Israeli conflict also involves a continuing threat to the flow of oil by pipelines overland between the Persian Gulf producing fields and the Mediterranean Sea. Through and above the Middle East traverse some of the most important routes of shipping, flight, and communication in the world. As has already been shown, the main line of world trade continues by way of the Suez Canal-Red Sea route to the Indian Ocean and beyond. Four principal types of access across the territory utilize way stations located within the Middle East.

[1] Norton Ginsburg (Ed.), *The Pattern of Asia*, New York: Prentice-Hall, Inc., 1958, map, p. 699.

These are canal, air, caravan, and pipeline transportation. The ancient caravan routes from Europe to Asia followed the shortest distances across the arid lands between oases, and avoided rough mountainous lands. Logical choices of routes were made with respect to the alignment of mountain systems to the north or south of them. The same choices apply today for the air routes from Europe to India and the Far East or to Australia-New Zealand. Today's air routes pass over the Middle East south of the main mountain systems because the routes north of the mountains are politically inaccessible since they pass over Communist territory. With the completion of the Suez Canal in 1869, cheap bulk shipment by water could by-pass the entire continent of Africa between parts of the North Atlantic and the western Pacific. The importance of such an all-water route to the Commonwealth of Nations with its primary focus in the United Kingdom needs no reminder!

In closing discussion of the western Eurasian perimeter emphasis today should be on the divergent pathways down which people have developed. The northwest is non-Communist industrialized Western Europe, and the two southern regions contain the subsistence and oil-producing non-industrial Moslem world. Smooth functioning of exchange-organized economies in Europe require some degree of coordination and coherency among these three regions of the western Eurasian perimeter. There is, however, no guarantee that such circumstances will continue or that improvements in that regard can be permanently achieved.

Eastern Perimeter

Equally striking changes have occurred within Asian regions. The diagrammatic map in Figure 240 shows three stages through which pairs of major regions of the Asian "square" have passed in recent years. During stage one, before World War II, the southern regions of South and Southeast Asia were predominantly European controlled. Only Afghanistan in South Asia and Thailand in Southeast Asia were not. During stage two, from the 1931 invasion of Manchuria by Japanese forces until the end of World War II thirteen years later, the eastern pair of triangles, East and Southeast Asia, were overrun by Japanese military conquerors. A third period continuing into the present was characterized in the northern two regions by the expansion of the Communists from the dry western into humid eastern China. In the 1930s Kuomintang Chinese forces under Chiang Kai-shek drove the Chinese Communists into western China. In 1949 the Chinese Communists defeated the Nationalist regime to take over all mainland China. Chiang Kai-shek and the Nationalists took refuge on Taiwan, which under occupation has become an island National Chinese Republic.

In one brief generation, colonialism in Asia has come to an end. The dates of independence for those nations achieving it since 1940 are written below their names on the political map in Figure 107. The upheaval which saw the formation of the Communist Bloc also produced the whole series of nationalist movements culminating in the appearance of a score of new nations within the Eurasian perimeter and North Africa. Twelve of them are in eastern Eurasia, as shown by Table XXXIII. Along with the year of their independence five of these, from west to east, are Pakistan (1947), India (1947), Nepal (1951), Ceylon (1948), and Burma (1948). These were all former colonies of the British Empire in the Indian subcontinental region. Burma is transitional with the Southeast Asian region, as West Pakistan is transitional, also, with the Southwest Asian region. Three other new countries were former French colonial territories of the Indo-Chinese peninsula which became independent in 1955—South Vietnam, Laos, and Cambodia. A fourth country, North Vietnam is now a Communist satellite. The border between North and South Vietnam is another "truce settlement" between the Communist Bloc and the "West." Similar to the border between North and South Korea, this one is along the seventeenth parallel, while the Korean "settlement" was along the thirty-eighth parallel. In addition two independent states are the new national Federation of Malayan States (1957) and the ancient independent kingdom of Siam or Thailand on the Malay Peninsula. Last, in the category of offshore Pacific island nations, there are Indonesia (1949) and the Philippines. The last named country was formerly a United States possession. Independence for the Philippine Islands was delayed by World War II until 1946.

Reference should again be made to the maps showing the expansion and ebb of colonialism in Figures 106 and 107 of Chapter 9; these maps place the independence movements of the post-World War II period in world geographical and historical perspective. It will be appreciated that remaining outposts of European colonialism, admittedly anachronisms today, were some of the earliest strategic points of contact between Europeans and Asians. For the most part they are small territories and involve comparatively small Asian populations, but are of great commercial and strategic importance.

The British are still in Hong Kong (1,000,000), which serves as a useful "window" into Communist China. It is a Crown Colony and was the first concession of territory made to the English by China in 1841. An important naval base, it is one of the great transhipment points for ocean trade in the Far East. The British also remain at Singapore (992,500), a strategic island Crown Colony and transhipment point at the tip of the Malay Peninsula. In the days when seapower meant physical control of territory, this outpost city and trading point could dominate the southeast corner of Asia by controlling the Straits of Malacca. In both Hong Kong and Singapore the English represent a fragment of the total population. Among the estimated 2.5 million persons in the Hong Kong Colony as a whole, a great many of whom are refugee Chinese from the Communist mainland, only 10,000 are English. Among the polyglot population of Singapore, 80 per cent is Chinese.

The Portuguese, likewise, occupy a small enclave in China and only in 1961 were forcibly ejected by India from Goa, on the west coast of India, which had been Portuguese since 1510. Macao, a small island and city of the same name (181,908) has been Portuguese since 1557. The Netherlands has lost (1962) possession of western Irian, which is the name of a large part of sparsely populated New Guinea. Their claim was disputed by Indonesia. The French relinquished their last territories in Asia in 1957 with the return to India of their commercial enclaves at Pondicherry, Mahe, Yanon, Kirkal, and Chandernagor on the Bay of Bengal.

The tide has turned against special privileges and extra territorial rights for Europeans and Americans. The high-water mark for extra territorial rights in China, short of outright political control, was represented by a series of treaty ports, some of them points far inland, to which China in the nineteenth century was forced to accede by major European powers and the United States.

Differences between East and West Eurasian Cultures. The principal differences between the European and Asian regions is cultural. The impact of industrialization on ancient cultures in Asia represents the most complex mixture of modern stages in the dispersion of the European indus-

(A) A view of the petroleum refinery at Abadan, Iran. (*Courtesy of United Nations.*)

Figure 238

(B) The sacking of potatoes in an oasis in Morocco. (*Courtesy of Charles Phelps Cushing.*)

(C) A diversified bazaar of the Casbah (old quarter) of Tunis. Many bazaars are specialized, but this one is general. On the left are a clothing store and a meat market; on the right, pots, pans, and bicycles are sold. (*Courtesy of Wide World.*)

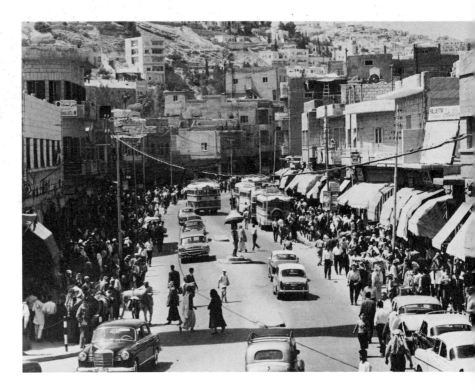

(D) Talal Street in Amman, capital of Jordan, gives some idea of the newer shopping centers growing under the influence of automobile technology. The street and the automobiles are new, but the awning-covered sidewalks are typical of the old bazaar. The throngs of people separated by streams of traffic represent an odd mixture of old and new. (*Courtesy of United Nations.*)

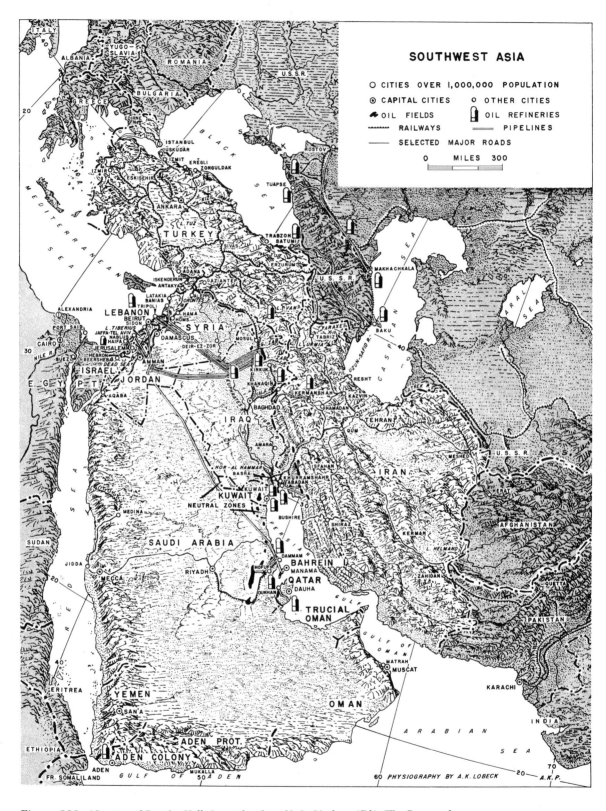

Figure 239. (*Courtesy of Prentice-Hall, Inc., taken from N. S. Ginsburg (Ed.), The Pattern of Asia, 1958.*)

trial revolution with the subsistence-livelihood practices of millions of Asians. One of the principal distinctions between cultures of western Eurasian and eastern Eurasian peoples is in food. *Wheat* is the most important grain crop in the West. The ancient concept of "bread as the staff of life" demonstrates how long wheat has represented at least a fundamental portion of the diet among the people of Southwestern Asia, North Africa, and Europe. By contrast, the most important food grain of Asia is *rice*. Intensive subsistence agriculture, organized on the basis of peasant villages was characteristic of all Asia until very recently. It gave rise to the descriptive name "rice economies," a term which reflects basic differences in farm practices between rice and other grains.

The agricultural resources on which wheat-based societies developed include humid to subhumid moisture conditions. In the rice areas, wet precipitation conditions prevail. Dry-field grain cultivation is more readily adaptable to mechanized techniques than is wet-rice cultivation. The systems of intensive cultivation evolved by the cultures belonging to the rice economies are based on irrigation. They more closely resemble garden horticulture than field agriculture. Rice cultivation is among the most efficient in the production of food per unit of area in the world; but it is also equally high in its labor requirements. Mechanization of agriculture tends to decrease production per unit of area, although it greatly increases production per man by the substitution of machinery for human hands. However, in countries under pressure from a huge and increasing population, the need is for greatly increased *total* production. Unless additional land and agricultural resources can be brought into production by the hands freed by mechanization, the introduction of machinery to agriculture may actually reduce total production. Increases in total food production are most likely to occur by application of additional fertilizers and better control of moisture than by the drastic reorganization of tillage practices involved in mechanization.

Rice Culture in Monsoon Asia—an Example of Cultural Persistence.

The cultivation of rice in Asia is so much a part of the culture in three regions of the eastern Eurasian perimeter that it has impressed its name on the culture as a whole. The broad geographical dispersion of this crop and the age-long persistence of the horticultural irrigation practices by which it has come to be known merit special attention as illustration of cultural stability.

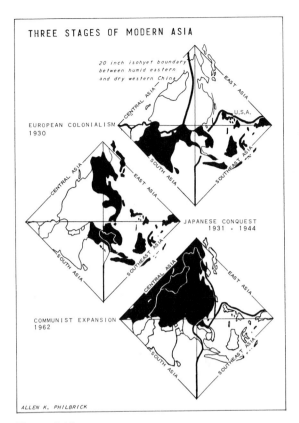

Figure 240

Attention is directed to the map of rice production in monsoon Asia[1] in Figure 241.

Resources and technology of rice production. Superimposed on the map of rice production are lines representing the 40-inch isohyet and the 180-day length of growing season. These two physical measures describe important resources for rice cultivation and show partially the physical limits within which most of the world's rice occurs. There are, of course, many kinds of rice, hence a relatively wide range of resources which may satisfy the needs of individual varieties.

In general, rice is a crop of lower river and delta regions of the wet tropics and subtropics. In such regions precipitation regimes are relatively high in amount and dependable in occurrence. Conditions for irrigation and drainage are excellent. Such sites provide level land with fairly heavy compact soils and good water retention capacities, which can be readily dyked for ponding without investment of

[1] William Van Royen, *The Agricultural Resources of the World*, New York: Prentice-Hall, Inc., 1954, map, p. 87.

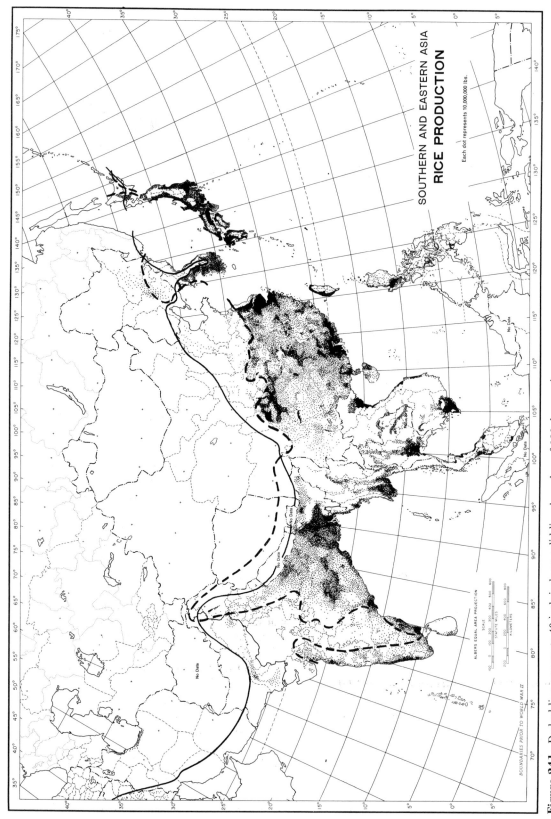

Figure 241. Dashed line represents 40-inch isohyet; solid line, boundary of 180-day growing season. (*Courtesy of Prentice-Hall, Inc., taken from William Van Royen, The Agricultural Resources of the World, 1954.*)

SOUTHERN AND EASTERN ASIA
RICE PRODUCTION

Each dot represents 10,000,000 lbs.

ALBERS EQUAL AREA PROJECTION

SCALE

STATUTE MILES

KILOMETERS

BOUNDARIES PRIOR TO WORLD WAR II

great expense and labor for terracing. Upland rice is the name which designates both location and varieties of rice grown under nonirrigated conditions. Upland production seldom accounts for more than 10 per cent of the total crop within any of the major rice-growing regions of Asia.

The occurrence of rice-environment complexes follows closely the outer extremities of the radial drainage pattern of monsoon Asia discussed earlier. They fit logically within the three different regional triangles of the Asian "square" and face outward in the three directions lending their names to East, Southeast, and South Asia. (See the map in Figure 203.)

The origins of rice as a domesticated grain are lost in antiquity. Rice was very probably known in India and China at least 5,000 years ago. The fact that in many Asian tongues the word for rice and for food are synonymous may be taken as an indication of the very early importance of the grain. The crop was probably first domesticated from a wild state in swampy terrain. Cultivation is comparatively easy as compared with dry farming, and can be accomplished with no tools at a primitive level.

Even today there are localities where the rice field is neither plowed, spaded, nor hoed. The soil may be thoroughly puddled and all the weeds destroyed merely by driving a caribou around in the flooded field, or the farmer and his family may accomplish the same purpose by splashing around in their bare feet.[1]

The double series of pictures in Figures 242 and 243[2] are designed to demonstrate the extraordinary dispersion and persistence of nearly identical cultivation practices in the system of rice production making intensive use of human labor in Asia. The steps in the cultivation of rice shown in Figure 242 are reproduced from wood cuts dating from the seventeenth century and even earlier times. Identical modern procedures are shown in the photographs in Figure 243, which demonstrate the persistence of these practices over a period of hun-

dreds of years. These very same farming practices extend, with only minor variations, throughout the regions shown as major rice-producing territory on the map in Figure 241. Although the points of origin and the movements of people carrying these practices throughout the length and breadth of monsoon Asia are now obscured, the geographical extent of their use attests to their dispersion within historic time, since completely independent invention would appear to have been most unlikely.

Importance of rice. The relative importance and dominance of rice among food grains within the regions and countries of the eastern Eurasian perimeter is shown by the data in Table XLIII. A number of significant comparisons and generalizations may be derived from this table. Measured in tons of rice in relation to amount of arable land, East Asia is the leading rice-producing region. East Asia has a little more than one-third of the arable land in the eastern perimeter, yet its rice production is well over half. South Asia, by contrast, with well over half the arable land of the eastern perimeter, produces only one-third of the rice. Southeast Asia's share of land and production of rice are about balanced at 10 and 13 per cent, respectively. In the Far East as a whole more than 60 per cent of all grain produced is rice. The range from the country-by-country statistics is from just over half in China (51.5 per cent) to virtually 100 per cent in the Malay Federation (99.5 per cent). In area the proportion of all land devoted to grains which is rice land varies from one-third (34.4 per cent) in China to virtually all in such countries as Thailand (98.6 per cent), Malay Federation (99.4 per cent), and Nepal (100 per cent). In production, again, it is significant that rice is more than 90 per cent of all grain production in at least ten countries. Rice culture is particularly dominant in the countries of Southeast Asia. There the lowest percentage (85 per cent) is in Indonesia.

Only two countries of the eastern Eurasian perimeter do not have a majority of their grain *acreage* in rice production, but they are the two largest—China and India. China extends northward beyond the resource conditions on which rice cultivation depends, and India, similarly, extends westward of such limits. Agricultural regions of China have already been examined in the preceding chapter. Wheat, grain sorghum, and cotton characterize the less-wet northern and western agricultural regions of China. Similarly, these same crops appear in the western and central drier parts of the Indian sub-

[1] V. D. Wickizer and M. K. Bennet, *The Rice Economy of Monsoon Asia,* Stanford, Calif.: Food Research Institute, Stanford University, 1941, p. 15.

[2] Both sets of pictures were supplied by L. A. Peter Gosling, Director, Center for South Asian studies, University of Michigan, Ann Arbor. The Chinese illustrations are wood blocks of the seventeenth century, reputedly based on other illustrations of the thirteenth century, reproduced in: Paul Pelliot, "A Propos du Keng Tche T'ou," in *Memoires Concernant L'Asie Orientale,* Tome Premier, Paris: L'Academie des Inscriptions et Belles-Lettres, 1913. The modern photographs, for comparison purposes, were taken in Malaya by L. A. Peter Gosling.

TABLE XLIII   AREA AND PRODUCTION OF RICE IN RELATION TO TOTAL ARABLE AND TOTAL LAND IN ALL GRAINS BY REGIONS AND COUNTRIES IN THE FAR EAST AND THE WORLD TOTAL[a]

Area name	Arable land, sq. mi.	Per cent of area	Area of all grains as per cent of total arable	Per cent rice area of all grains	Rice prod., thousands of metric tons	Per cent rice of all grain prod.	Per cent rice prod., Far East
World	**5,366,790**	**100**	**54.9**	**15.3**	**215,700**	**25.1**	. . .
Far East	**1,387,079**	**35.9**	**70.1**	**41.8**	**195,188**	**61.9**	**100**
East Asia	**481,207**	**34.7**	**99.3**[b]	**33.2**	**104,227**	**55.3**	**55.3**
Southeast Asia	**144,359**	**10.3**	**52.9**	**87.4**	**26,066**	**91.8**	**13.3**
South Asia	**761,513**	**55.0**	**55.0**	**43.3**	**64,895**	**66.1**	**33.4**
Countries		per cent F. East					
Humid China	368,293	26.6	101.3[b]	34.4	82,480	51.3	42.0
India	611,355	44.1	54.7	37.1	43,104	60.1	22.0
Pakistan	95,467	6.8	63.9	57.5	13,723	74.9	7.0
Indonesia	68,266	4.9	50.5	75.0	11,403	85.3	5.8
Japan	19,490	1.4	100.9[b]	63.7	13,623	77.0	7.0
Cumulative total		83.8			Total more than 5% prod.		83.8
Thailand	30,088	2.2	75.0	98.6	8,297	98.6	4.3
Burma	33,135	2.4	50.1	94.1	6,464	98.9	3.3
Philippines	28,170	2.0	62.4	60.8	3,346	78.9	1.7
Vietnam	11,730	0.8	84.5	98.9	3,443	99.1	1.7
S. Korea	7,741	0.6	111.5[b]	49.1	2,506	69.6	1.3
Taiwan	3,370	0.2	93.7	95.9	2,226	97.9	1.1
Cumulative total		92.0			Total more than 1% prod.		97.2
Laos	3,938	0.3	55.2	97.6	550	97.5	0.3
Cambodia	7,722	0.5	70.5	90.8	528	91.6	0.8
Malaya Federation	8,583	0.6	16.3	99.4	786	99.5	0.4
Sarawak	13,012	0.9	. . .	. . .	. . .	. . .	. . .
North Borneo	819	0.1	14.6	93.3	53	98.1	trace
Nepal	15,000	1.1	33.5	100.0	1,043	100.0	0.5
Ceylon	5,880	0.4	31.8	88.0	562	96.4	0.3
Cumulative total		95.9			Cumulative total		99.5

[a] Food and Agricultural Organization of the United Nations, *Production Yearbook*, 1958, Vol. 12, Rome.

[b] Double cropping raises significantly the percentage of all grains areas in relation to total arable in most cases, and becomes obvious only when per cent approaches or equals 100 per cent.

continent. In a great arc, therefore, from eastern India to middle China the traditional way of life within the rice economies has been the intensive subsistence cultivation of rice within the common base of area organization—the subsistence agricultural village.

In addition to subsistence crops, the peoples of these countries, under the impact of European leadership and the attraction of European markets during the past century, have developed the cultivation of certain commercial crops. The *tea* of China, Ceylon, and the Assam hills of India, the *rubber* of Malaya and Indonesia, the *jute* of India and Bengal (now East Pakistan), the *silk* cocoons of Japan and China, *abaca* for manila rope from the Philippine Islands, the *cotton* of India and China, *coffee* in the tropical highlands and *copra* in the tropical lowlands of South and Southeast Asia, all these and many more commercial crops were developed or extended in acreage within Asia during the past century of European colonialism, from 1840 to World War II.

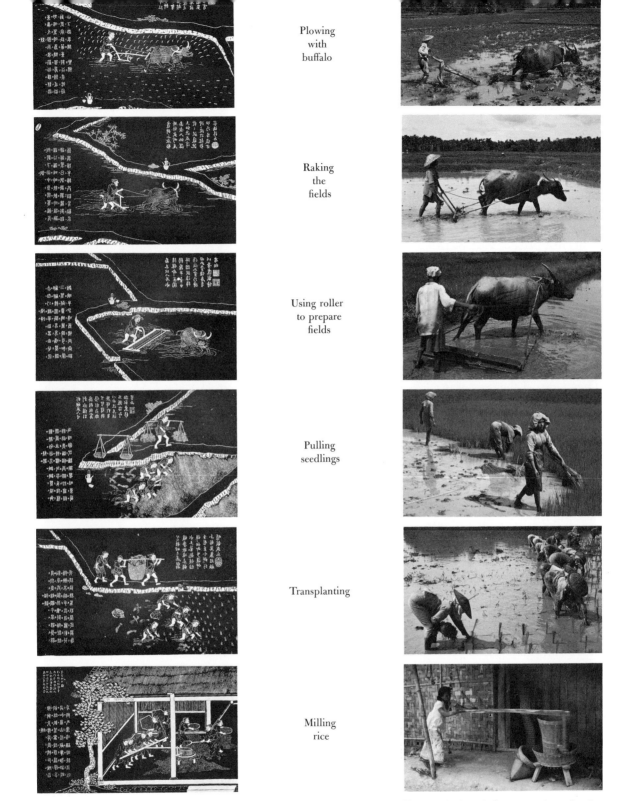

Plowing
with
buffalo

Raking
the
fields

Using roller
to prepare
fields

Pulling
seedlings

Transplanting

Milling
rice

Figure 242. Ancient procedures in rice production. (*Courtesy of L. A. Peter Gosling, taken from Paul Pelliot, "A Propos du Keng Tche T'oi" in* Memoires Concernant L'Asie Orientale, *Paris: L'Academie des Inscriptions et Belles-Lettres.*)

Figure 243. Modern procedures in rice production. (*Courtesy of Dr. L. A. Peter Gosling.*)

Such commercial plantation-agricultural developments were paralleled by mineral concessions in favorable localities. These include such items as *tin* from Malaya and the *tungsten* of China. The economic and political penetration of European capital into Asia, preceding the present period of successful nationalism, represents that same combination of domestic subsistence organization of area and external participation in the exchange world which is also characteristic of Africa and Latin America.

As attention is turned to examination of selected individual parts of the eastern Eurasian perimeter in the next chapter, it should be with a certain awareness that the new nations of the Asian periphery aspire to new relationships with the rest of the world. Not only is the raising of the standards of living important, but of even greater importance is the acquisition and maintenance of that dignity of economic diversity which alone will free them from the commercial counterpart of political colonialism. They must be able to win freedom from dependence on specialized production oriented toward foreign trade. These countries do not wish to buy their standards of living at the expense of perpetuating economic colonialism. They wish rather to build toward a greater diversity of economic development which will allow them to broaden the base on which they hope to *construct* rather than buy their own future higher standards of life. It is within the context of the national emergence of peoples and new states within the Asian perimeter that the greatest challenge of competition between the non-Communist and Communist Bloc countries exists. The size of the challenge is in proportion to the sizes of the populations involved in the struggle for leadership in the continuing expansion of the industrial revolution during the second half of the twentieth century.

Foreign Trade of the Eurasian Perimeter

Table XLIV is a country-by-country comparison of the major export and import items in 1956 and the principal directions of international trade for the six regions of the Eurasian perimeter, including North Africa. The purpose of the table is twofold. It serves as the basis of comparison between the countries of each region and for each region as a whole, and it affords an opportunity to indicate the continuing character of the "economic colonialism" which much of the foreign trade of the Eurasian perimeter continues to reflect.

Leading Exports and Imports. The table indicates that surplus rice is exported from Southeast Asia. Burma and Thailand exported 1.8 and 1.2 million tons of rice, respectively, in 1956. Both Cambodia and South Vietnam exported rice among their first five items of export by value in 1956, and rice has risen in importance since that time. Other territories of Southeast Asia are significant importers of rice, such as Malaya, Singapore, Indonesia, and the British colonies of Sarawak and North Borneo. There is a considerable net surplus of rice from Southeast Asia which moves to Japan, Ceylon, and India in adjacent rice-economy regions of monsoon Asia.

The data in Table XLIV, however, show a striking similarity in most cases between the countries of the Eurasian perimeter and those of Africa south of the Sahara with respect to exports and imports. Almost without exception a few principal raw materials or foods form a majority of total exports by value. The major imports, in turn, are in much smaller percentages, which indicates the greater diversity of imports over exports. The latter are primarily manufactured goods.

The *phosphate* of Morocco, *wine* from Algeria, *cotton* from Egypt and the Sudan, *coffee* from Ethiopia, and *bananas* from Italian Somaliland (now part of Somalia) tend to dominate the export trade of the countries representative of North Africa. From Moslem Southwest Asia Turkish *tobacco*, Syrian *raw cotton*, Israeli *oranges*, and the *petroleum* of Iraq, Arabia, and Iran similarly outstrip in importance the next most valuable export item for each of those countries named. Pakistan *jute*, Indian *tea* and *jute*, and the *tea* of Ceylon, continue, after independence, to be as important in the trade of those countries as they were during the British occupation.

With the exception of *rice* from Burma and Thailand, *rubber* is the most important export from the independent countries of Southeast Asia. *Petroleum* from British possessions in North Borneo's sedimentary basins exceeds by far any other product exported from those territories. The leading Philippine export is *copra* or *sugar* and from Taiwan, *sugar*. From South Korea, nonferrous ore concentrates, primarily *tungsten*, dominate the export trade with 41 per cent; second in importance is the 8 per cent of total exports in *graphite*.

Only in Japan, of all countries of the Eurasian

TABLE XLIV THE DIRECTION OF TRADE TO AND FROM THE TERRITORIES OF PERIPHERAL EURASIA (AND NORTH AFRICA) AND THE REST OF THE MAJOR COUNTRIES OF THE WORLD, 1956[a]

Territory and capital	First 5 export items, millions of dollars	% of total export	First 5 import items, millions of dollars	% of total imports	First 5 countries, dest.	% of total	First 5 countries, source	% of total
North Africa:								
Morocco Rabat	**Calcium phosphate**	**19.8**	**Sugar**	**9.2**	**France**	**53**	**France**	**48**
	Barley	6.8	Pass. motor vehicles	4.3	W. Germany	7	W. Germany	5
	Fish, preserved	6.7	Tea	3.9	Italy	6	China	4
	Citrus fruit	5.7	Gasoline	3.5	U.K.	6	Netherlands	3
	Wheat	5.2	Rayon fabric	3.1	Algeria	4	U.K.	3
		44.2		24.0		76		63
Algeria Algiers	**Wine**	**37.9**	**Other metal fab.**	**4.6**	**France**	**76**	**France**	**79**
	Iron ore	6.1	Sugar	4.5	U.K.	6	U.S.	5
	Figs, fresh, dry	6.0	Other textile prod.	3.8	W. Germany	3	Fr. W. Africa	3
	Other fresh veg.	3.8	Motor vehicles	3.3	Italy	3	Morocco	2
	Spiritous liquors	2.7	Other elect. app.	3.4	Fr. W. Africa	1	Sweden	1
		56.8		19.8		89		90
Tunisia Tunis	**Phosphate, natural**	**15.6**	**Cotton piece gds.**	**3.8**	**France**	**55.1**	**France**	**69.1**
	Iron ore	10.8	Wheat	6.6	U.K.	11.1	U.S.	4.6
	Olive Oil	9.9	Sugar	6.1	Italy	9.8	Italy	3.0
	Lead, L. alloys	7.7	Cars, passenger	2.5	Algeria	5.7	Algeria	2.7
	Alcoholic bevs.	7.4	Tea	2.4	W. Germany	1.8	Morocco	2.6
		51.5		21.7		83.5		82.1
Libya Tripoli	**Peanuts n.e.s.**	**21.5**	**Wheat, meal, flour**	**8.7**	**Italy**	**38.8**	**Italy**	**29.9**
	Anim.-veg. crudes	16.5	Tea and maté	5.2	U.K.	20.7	U.K.	21.9
	Iron, steel scrap	12.1	Petroleum prod.	4.5	Egypt	12.9	W. Germany	10.2
	Sheep, lambs	8.1	Cotton prod.	4.5	W. Germany	6.9	France	6.0
	Hides, skins, undr.	5.9	Cane sugar, refined	3.4	Netherlands	3.4	Egypt	6.0
		63.7		26.3		82.8		74.1
Egypt Cairo	**Cotton, ginned**	**70.3**	**Iron, steel**	**7.4**	**Czechoslovakia**	**14.6**	**U.S.**	**13.4**
	Rice	6.3	Machinery, other	7.1	Japan	7.5	U.K.	11.8
	Vegetables	4.0	Petroleum prod.	6.7	France	7.2	W. Germany	11.2
	Cotton thread	3.2	Elect. machinery, appl.	5.7	Sudan	6.5	Italy	6.4
	Cotton fab.	2.6	Motor vehicles	4.1	India	6.3	France	5.1
		86.4		31.1		42.1		47.9
Sudan Khartoum	**Cotton, ginned**	**63.6**	**Sugar, refined**	**10.2**	**U.K.**	**32.9**	**U.K.**	**28.2**
	Gum arabic	8.1	Cotton, piece gds.	6.4	India	13.2	Egypt	13.8
	Cotton prod.	7.2	Coffee, raw	4.2	Egypt	11.1	India	12.1
	Peanuts	5.8	Tea	3.7	Italy	8.9	Italy	5.5
	Sesame	3.0	Artif. silk piece gds.	5.0	W. Germany	7.0	W. Germany	3.8
		87.7		29.5		73.1		63.4

TABLE XLIV (CONTINUED)

Territory and capital	First 5 export items, millions of dollars	% of total export	First 5 import items, millions of dollars	% of total imports	First 5 countries, dest.	% of total	First 5 countries, source	% of total
Ethiopia Addis Ababa	**Coffee**	**53.8**	**Motor vehicles**	**7.8**	**U.S.**	**27.4**	**Italy**	**15.5**
	Goat skins	4.7	Gasoline, naphtha	7.3	Aden	19.2	India	14.3
	Chat, (mildly alk. leaves)	4.2	Cotton piece gds.	6.0	Italy	16.9	U.S.	10.9
	Linseed	4.0	Cotton, piece, gray	5.0	Fr. n.e.s.	8.7	Japan	9.5
	Sheep skins	3.2	Cotton manuf.	5.7	Saudi-Arabia	6.4	U.K.	9.5
		69.9		31.8		78.6		59.7
It. Somaliland Mogadiscio	**Banana, plantain**	**58.6**	**Machinery, other**	**15.5**	No data		No data	
	Hides, skins	10.4	Petroleum prod.	11.6				
	Cotton	6.9	Cotton fab.	8.0				
	Fuelwood, charcoal	4.8	motor cars	5.4				
	Fish, preparations	4.0	Rice	4.0				
		84.7		44.5				
S. W. Moslem Asia:								
Turkey Ankara	**Tobacco, unmanuf.**	**30.6**	**Machinery, other**	**13.7**	**U.S.**	**19.6**	**W. Germany**	**23.6**
	Cotton	8.6	Ships and boats	7.8	W. Germany	16.6	Czechoslovakia, U.S.	21.1
	Nonfer. ores (conc.)	8.7	Iron, steel	6.8	Italy	10.0	U.K.	8.2
	Dried fruit	6.5	Petroleum prod.	7.1	U.K.	7.7	Italy	6.4
	Wheat, unmilled	5.8	Elect. machinery, appl.	6.0	Czechoslovakia	5.6	Czechoslovakia	4.9
		60.3		41.4		59.5		64.2
Syria Damascus	**Cotton, raw**	**29.6**	**Diesel, fuel oil**	**8.3**	**Lebanon**	**23.4**	**U.K.**	**11.8**
	Barley	13.0	Artif. silk thread	3.6	France	12.3	U.S.	10.6
	Wheat	11.3	Automobiles, chassis	4.6	Italy	11.5	W. Germany	9.6
	Wool, raw	6.7	Gasoline	2.9	W. Germany	5.9	Lebanon	9.0
	Sheep	4.9	Chem. pharmaceut.	2.9	Iraq	5.6	France	8.0
		65.5		22.3		58.6		49.0
Israel Jerusalem	**Oranges**	**30.3**	**Wheat**	**7.3**	**U.K.**	**22.1**	**U.S.**	**31.8**
	Diamonds, cut and pol.	23.8	Crude, diesel, oil	6.1	U.S.	18.1	W. Germany	17.6
	Grapefruit	4.9	Diamonds, rough	5.8	Belgium-Luxemburg	6.3	U.K.	9.8
	Rubber tires, tubes	3.6	Other iron, steel	5.7	Finland	5.8	Netherlands	3.2
	Cement	2.9	Comm. drugs, dyes	5.2	France	4.0	France	2.8
		67.4		29.1		56.3		65.2
Jordan Amman	**Olive oil**	**18.8**	**Wheat flour**	**6.1**	**Lebanon**	**39.9**	**U.K.**	**19.3**
	Fertilizer	15.8	Iron, steel manuf.	5.7	Syria	26.0	Lebanon	14.9
	Tomatoes	10.3	Sugar, refined	4.7	Iraq	9.8	W. Germany	9.0
	Watermelon	7.1	Cotton piece gds.	4.7	Czechoslovakia	6.5	U.S.	6.7
	Lentils	5.5	Mech. equip, appar.	4.4	Yugoslavia	4.9	Syria-U.A.R.	6.0
		57.5		26.6		87.0		55.9

TABLE XLIV (CONTINUED)

Territory and capital	First 5 export items, millions of dollars	% of total export	First 5 import items, millions of dollars	% of total imports	First 5 countries, dest.	% of total	First 5 countries, source	% of total
Iraq Baghdad	**Petroleum**	**92.3**	**Boilers and parts**	**16.1**	**France**	**31.3**	**U.K.**	**27.6**
	Barley	2.9	Iron, steel	12.5	Italy	16.2	U.S.	13.6
	Dates	1.5	Autos, parts	7.8	U.K.	6.9	Germany	8.9
	Wool, raw	.9	Elect. machinery	7.4	W. Germany	6.8	Japan	6.1
	Cotton	.5	Tea	6.2	U.S.	4.4	Ceylon	6.0
		98.1		50.0		65.6		62.2
Saudi Arabia Tiyadh-Mecca	No data		No data		**Japan**	**17.4**	**U.S.**	**34.0**
					Italy	13.4	U.K.	11.3
					U.S.	9.6	W. Germany	6.9
					W. Germany	9.3	India	5.0
					France	8.1	Italy	4.9
						57.8		62.1
Iran Tehran	**Crude Oil**	**28.8**	**Beet, Cane sugar**	**11.9**	**U.K.**	**16.6**	**W. Germany**	**17.7**
	Mazut oil	16.9	Synthetic fibre	5.6	France	9.5	U.S.	16.8
	Motor, aviation gas	13.5	Cotton fab.	5.0	U.S.	7.2	U.K.	11.5
	Raw cotton	7.0	Tea	5.0	W. Germany	4.9	U.S.S.R.	6.2
	Kerosene	5.8	Motor cars, pass.	4.9	U. of S. Africa	5.5	France	3.4
		72.0		32.4		43.7		55.6
Afghanistan Kabul	No data		No data		**U.S.**	**30.8**	**U.S.S.R.**	**33.4**
					U.S.S.R.	26.5	U.S.	17.1
					India	16.2	Japan	15.7
					U.K.	9.3	W. Germany	15.3
					Pakistan	8.3	India	8.9
						91.1		90.4
South Asia[b] *Pakistan* Karachi	**Jute, raw**	**46.4**	**Cotton piece gds.**	**5.5**	**U.K.**	**15.9**	**U.K.**	**13.9**
	Cotton, raw	22.5	Iron, steel, ingot, slab	3.5	Japan	12.5	U.S.	6.2
	Gunny bags, cloth	5.6	Drugs, medicines	4.7	India	10.8	W. Germany	5.4
	Wool, raw	4.3	Textile machinery	3.4	U.S.	9.2	Japan	4.9
	Tea	3.3	Iron, steel, ingot, slab	3.2	W. Germany	7.4	Belgium-Luxemburg	2.5
		82.1		20.3		55.8		32.9
India Delhi	**Tea**	**25.1**	**Iron, steel, crude metal**	**9.8**	**U.K.**	**30.9**	**U.K.**	**25.5**
	Jute, gunny cloth	10.4	Cotton, raw	5.9	U.S.	14.7	U.S.	11.6
	Cotton piece gds.	9.9	Iron, steel, sheet, plate	5.1	Japan	5.0	Japan	5.4
	Jute, gunny bags	9.3	Petroleum, crude	3.9	Australia	3.8	Iran	3.4
	Tobacco, unmanuf.	2.5	Textile, manufs.	3.3	Ceylon	3.4	Italy	3.2
		57.2		28.1		57.8		49.1

TABLE XLIV (CONTINUED)

Territory and capital	First 5 export items, millions of dollars	% of total export	First 5 import items, millions of dollars	% of total imports	First 5 countries, dest.	% of total	First 5 countries, source	% of total
Ceylon Colombo	**Tea**	**63.2**	**Rice**	**16.2**	**U.K.**	**29.2**	**U.K.**	**21.3**
	Nat. rubber, gums	17.7	Sugar	5.9	China	10.6	India	13.0
	Coconut oil, raw	5.6	Petroleum	7.4	U.S.	8.2	Burma	8.9
	Edible nuts	4.4	Cotton fab.	5.4	Australia	5.6	China	8.2
	Copra	3.0	Road motor veh.	4.4	Canada	5.4	Japan	7.0
		93.9		39.2		59.0		58.4
Burma[b] Rangoon	**Rice**	**73.0**	**Textile yarn, thrd.**	**10.8**	**Japan**	**14.3**	**U.K.**	**20.8**
	Fodder, other	4.6	Cotton fabrics	11.4	India	15.2	Japan	16.7
	Cotton	4.4	Machinery, other	6.7	Indonesia	11.7	China	11.1
	Rubber, crude	3.8	Petroleum prod.	4.8	Malaya	9.0	India	10.0
	Tin ore, conc.	3.2	Iron, steel	4.4	U.K.	7.4	W. Germany	6.9
		88.9		38.2		57.6		65.5
India 1957 Delhi	**Tea and maté**	**12.0**	**Iron, steel**	**23.0**	**U.K.**	**25.0**	**U.K.**	**23.3**
	Cotton fab.	6.4	Machinery, other	18.2	U.S.	20.5	U.S.	16.6
	Misc. fab.	5.8	Petroleum prod.	12.2	Japan	4.2	Germany	11.9
	Jute bags	5.7	Elect. machinery, appar.	9.6	Australia	3.8	Japan	5.3
	Silver-plat. gp. metals	3.7	Cotton, raw	7.6	U.S.S.R.	2.7	Ethiopia	5.4
		33.6		70.6		56.2		62.5
Southeast Asia:								
Thailand Bangkok	**Rice**	**42.6**	**Petroleum**	**10.2**	**Malaya**	**28.8**	**Japan**	**16.4**
	Rubber, crude	22.7	Cotton fab.	9.5	U.S.	24.9	Hong Kong	16.1
	Tin, tungsten conc.	8.3	Iron, steel	8.3	Japan	8.6	Malaya	11.4
	Wood, shaped	5.1	Road motor veh.	5.4	Hong Kong	8.5	U.K.	11.4
	Oilseeds, kernel	2.9	Elect. machinery, appl.	4.7	Indonesia	6.3	W. Germany	6.0
		81.7		38.1		77.1		61.4
Malaya Federation Kuala Lumpur	**Rubber, crude**	**51.7**	**Petroleum prod.**	**17.8**	**U.K.**	**16.5**	**Indonesia**	**27.7**
	Tin alloys, unwrought	11.9	Rubber, natural	14.3	U.S.	15.1	U.K.	18.2
	Petroleum prod.	10.0	Rice, not in husk	5.0	Japan	8.1	Thialand	7.4
	Coconut oil	1.8	Cotton fab.	2.7	Indonesia	5.4	Japan	6.2
	Pepper, pimento	1.5	Iron, steel	2.7	Australia	3.7	Sarawak	5.1
		76.9		42.5		48.8		64.6
Cambodia Phnom Penh	**Rubber**	**42.7**	**Cotton piece gds.**	**9.9**	**France**	**28.2**	**Hong Kong**	**24.7**
	Rice and prod.	21.0	Machinery, appar.	7.0	U.S.	25.8	Japan	19.4
	Maize	14.8	Other petroleum prod.	4.0	Malaya	11.8	France	16.4
	Kapak	3.9	Pharmac. prod.	3.5	Hong Kong	11.2	U.S.	10.4
	Pepper	3.4	Motor cars, parts	4.3	Vietnam	7.5	Vietnam	7.7
		85.8		28.7		84.5		78.6

TABLE XLIV (CONTINUED)

Territory and capital	First 5 export items, millions of dollars	% of total export	First 5 import items, millions of dollars	% of total imports	First 5 countries, dest.	% of total	First 5 countries, source	% of total
South Vietnam Saigon	**Rubber**	**87.0**	**Cotton piece gds.**	**9.1**	**France**	**67.3**	**U.S.**	**28.1**
	Feathers	1.1	Dairy prod.	6.4	U.S.	18.9	France	23.4
	Rice flour	0.8	Rayon piece gds.	6.1	Cambodia	4.2	Japan	25.7
	Tea	0.5	Pharmac. prod.	5.1	Malaya	2.9	Indonesia	6.5
	Leather	0.2	Machinery, non-elect.	4.9	Hong Kong	2.0	W. Germany	4.2
		89.6		31.6		95.3		86.9
Indonesia Jakarta	**Rubber**	**40.2**	**Livestock for food**	**20.0**	**Malaya**	**24.1**	**U.S.**	**16.5**
	Petroleum prod.	18.3	Rice, not in husk	13.1	Netherlands	19.5	Japan	15.7
	Petroleum, crude	7.2	Cotton fab.	11.8	U.S.	16.1	Netherlands	10.7
	Nonfer. conc.	7.2	Machinery, other	5.7	U.K.	8.9	W. Germany	9.0
	Oil seeds, kernels	5.1	Iron, steel	5.1	Japan	8.4	U.K.	6.1
		78.0		55.7		77.0		58.0
Sarawak Kuching	**Petroleum, crude**	**45.8**	**Petroleum, crude (re-export)**	**67.7**	**Malaya**	**43.2**	**Brunei**	**68.2**
	Gas, diesel, fuel	28.4	Rice	3.0	Australia	14.8	U.K.	8.6
	Rubber	14.7	Tobacco manuf.	1.7	Japan	12.4	Malaya	4.7
	Pepper, pimento	5.3	Petroleum prod.	1.5	Netherlands	11.3	Hong Kong	2.2
	Lumber, nonconif.	3.3	Iron, steel	1.0	U.K.	7.7	U.S.	1.8
		97.5		74.9		89.4		85.5
Brunei Brunei	**Crude oil**	**93.6**	**Iron, steel**	**15.4**	No data		No data	
	Rubber	1.2	Machinery, other	11.8				
	Natural gas	.2	Exposed film	12.5				
	Rubber, jelutang	.1	Road motor veh.	6.4				
	Firewood, mangrove	....	Petroleum prod.	2.4				
		95.1		48.5				
North Borneo Jesselton	**Rubber, natural**	**33.8**	**Rice**	**7.1**	No data		No data	
	Saw, veneer logs	20.0	Copra	12.6				
	Copra	19.5	Petroleum	5.1				
	Tobacco	2.8	Iron, steel	4.0				
	Lumber, nonconif.	2.4	Tobacco, manuf.	3.6				
		78.5		32.4				
Philippines[d] Manila (transitional)	**Copra**	**29.8**	**Mach., other than elec.**	**15.2**	**U.S.**	**53.6**	**U.S.**	**59.3**
	Sugar, centrifugal	22.3	Tex., yrn., fab.	11.8	Japan	17.8	Japan	10.1
	Logs, lumber	10.8	Base metals	8.8	Netherlands	8.7	Indonesia	4.4
	Abaca	7.8	Dairy prod.	6.6	W. Germany	3.1	W. Germany	3.4
	Coconut oil, ined.	5.3	Cereal prod.	5.1	Colombia	2.4	Canada	3.1
		76.0		46.7		85.6		80.3

TABLE XLIV (CONTINUED)

Territory and capital	First 5 export items, millions of dollars	% of total export	First 5 import items, millions of dollars	% of total imports	First 5 countries, dest.	% of total	First 5 countries, source	% of total
East Asia: China, Taiwan Taipei	**Sugar, refined**	**51.2**	**Ammonium sulphate**	**8.6**	**Japan**	**37.2**	**U.S.**	**43.7**
	Rice	14.1	Wheat	8.2	Iran	8.6	Iraq	10.5
	Fruit, fresh, pres.	7.5	Cotton, raw	7.2	Malaya	8.1	Japan	36.3
	Camphor, citronella	4.5	Soybeans, peas	5.8	India	6.8	W. Germany	4.5
	Tea	4.2	Diesel, fuel, crude	5.3	U.S.	5.7	Malaya	1.9
		81.5		35.1		66.4		96.9
South Korea Seoul	**Nonfer. conc. (tungs.)**	**40.7**	**Beet, cane sugar**	**22.2**	**U.S.**	**44.3**	**U.S.**	**84.1**
	Graphite	8.2	Cotton fabrics	22.2	Japan	33.3	Japan	2.4
	Bristles	3.1	Alcoholic bev.	18.4	Hong Kong	7.7	Hong Kong	1.3
	Agar agar	2.7	Fertilizer	11.3	France	5.3	W. Germany	1.2
	Fresh fish	2.5	Elect. machinery	8.1	U.K.	3.6	Formosa	0.7
		57.2		82.2		94.2		89.7
Japan Tokyo	**Fabric, silk, wool**	**10.2**	**Cotton**	**14.9**	**U.S.**	**22.1**	**U.S.**	**33.0**
	Cotton fab. (synth.)	9.4	Wool	8.0	Hong Kong	5.4	Australia	7.7
	Iron, steel	7.8	Petroleum, crude, partly ref.	6.9	India	4.2	Canada	4.5
	Fish, preserved	3.0	Iron, steel scrap	5.7	Malaya	3.1	Malaya	4.2
	Textile yarn, thrd.	2.5	Wheat, unmilled	5.1	Formosa	3.1	Saudi Arabia	4.3
		32.9		40.6		37.8		53.7
China Peiping	No data		No data		**U.S.S.R.**	**49.1**	**U.S.S.R.**	**56.1**
					Hong Kong	11.7	E. Germany	7.3
					E. Germany	5.5	Japan	5.1
					Japan	5.4	Czechoslovakia	4.9
					Czechoslovakia	4.3	Poland	3.8
						76.0		77.2

[a] Sources: First five exports 2nd first five imports, *Yearbook of International Trade Statistics*, Vol. 1, United Nations, New York, 1958, Tables 2 and 3 for each country. Countries of destination and source, *Direction of International Trade*, United Nations, New York, 1958, Tables of individual countries.

[b] Pakistan is transitional between S. W. Moslem Asia and S. Asia.

[c] Burma is transitional between S. Asia and S. E. Asia.

[d] Philippines is transitional between S. E. Asia and E. Asia.

perimeter from Gibraltar to the Bering Strait, is there any difference in this pattern. The Japanese data in Table XLIV shows that none of the first five items in Japan's 1956 exports accounted for more than 10 per cent of total Japanese export trade, which is an indication of a diversified economy. The data shows, further, that each of the first five items were manufactured goods, such as fabrics, iron and steel, ships and boats, clothing, etc. Data on imports show that incoming items are primarily raw materials and food. In this respect Japan is more like Europe than her Asian neighbors.

Economic Nodality of Europe, United States-Canada, Japan, and the U. S. S. R.

The destinations of exports also reveal the continuing economic nodality of the principal exchange-world regions in Europe and North America, even though political independence has come to almost all of Eurasia. Of the thirty-three separate territories listed in the table, only nine (a little more than one-quarter) showed another Asian nation as the primary destination. Three of the nine were Jordan, Syria, and Lebanon, which must be regarded as a special situation since the distances involved are small and the trade is almost local in nature. Jordan and Syria exported more goods by value to Lebanon; and Lebanon returned the favor to Syria. It should be remembered, also, that prior to 1944 Syria-Lebanon was a joint protectorate of France. Another set of three which are more involved in trade with Asian neighbors than outsiders involves Malaya-Singapore (now the separate Federation of Malaya and the port city of Singapore on the crown colony island of the same name), Sarawak, and Indonesia. Leading exports of crude oil from Sarawak and rubber from Indonesia reported as shipment to Malaya were largely re-exported at Singapore, a major transhipment port. Rice is imported to feed the large urban population of Singapore which possesses relatively little agricultural land within the colonial island limits. Only three Asian countries are major exporters to Japan, which is the only Asian exchange-type economy. *Oil* from Saudi Arabia, *rice* from Burma, and *sugar* from Taiwan are the three commodities which make Japan the largest recipient of exports from the three countries mentioned.

The map in Figure 244 shows by lines from the capital of each of the thirty countries or territories involved destination for the first five exports, respectively. Four regions of exchange organization are designated as corelands which prove to be major destination and source regions—core regions of the United States-Canada, Western Europe, the Soviet Union, and Japan. Aside from these clusters of one or more national areas, each country is treated separately on the maps. The largest common focality is that of Western Europe. Out of 150 lines, 62 interconnect territories of the Eurasian perimeter (including territory in North Africa) with the industrial nations of the European coreland. Next in order of frequency are the lines interconnecting twenty major export items with the United States and Canada. Japan is followed by the Soviet Union. Two-thirds of the trade of the Eurasian perimeter regions is with the four Northern Hemisphere core regions of the world's exchange-type area organization.

Europe's share of the trade declines eastward from North Africa. The number of interconnections to Europe out of the total from North Africa is 21 out of 35 (60 per cent). The ratio is 55 per cent from Southwest Asia, 27 per cent in South Asia, 25 per cent in Southeast Asia, and reaches a low of 13 per cent of the interconnections recorded from the offshore countries of East Asia and peninsular South Korea.

The Moslem world is divided between North Africa and Southwest Asia and is the southern half of the western Eurasian "square" examined earlier in Figure 203. Countries of these two regions are primarily oriented toward Europe in foreign trade. By contrast, however, the percentage of focus on Europe from the three monsoon regions of the Asian "square" is more evenly balanced between Europe, North America, and Japan. From the three regions of monsoon Asia taken as a unit, 54 lines radiate outward symbolizing exports from 14 nations to the five top countries. Twelve lines (22 per cent) focus on the United States-Canada, 8 on Japan (15 per cent), and 14 (26 per cent) lead to countries of the European industrial core region. Despite the distances involved European orientation of Asia as a whole, while reduced, is still the most influential by a small margin.

Data concerning *imports* of the countries and territories of the Eurasian perimeter (including North Africa) demonstrates substantially the same type of nodality from exchange-world industrial regions commented on with respect to exports. One difference worthy of note is the greater importance of the United States in providing imports than as

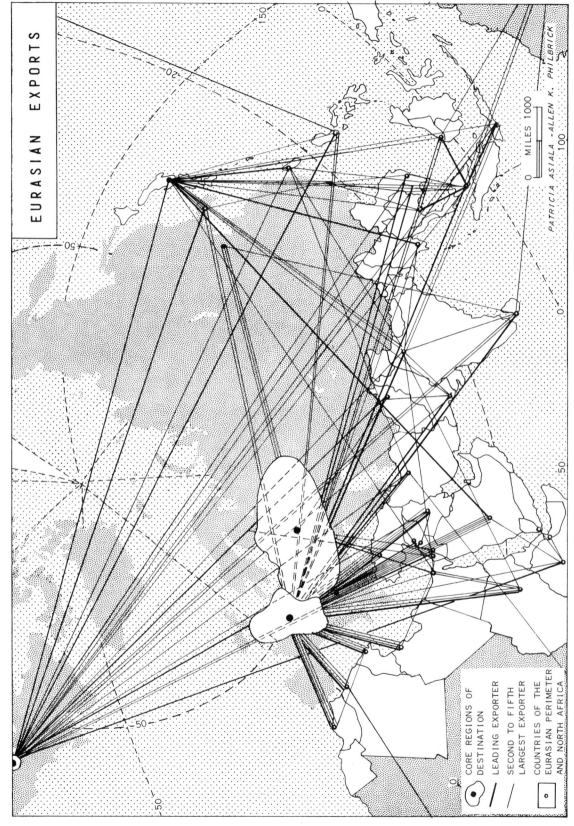

Figure 244

a market for Asian exports. This represents American competition with Japan as a supplier of goods to Asia. In 1956 Japan was the primary source of imports only into Thailand.

This chapter has characterized the six regions of the Eurasian perimeter which surround the Communist Bloc. Discussion has proceeded from west to east. In the next chapter the eastern Eurasian perimeter will be examined in somewhat greater detail with special emphasis on India and Japan.

19 *Regions of the East Eurasian Perimeter*

The purpose of this last regional chapter is to complete the outline of the world portrait by examining two selected countries of the eastern perimeter of Asia which illustrate problems of development in non-Communist Asia—the Republic of India and Japan. They will be examined within the framework of the three regions which represent the "Orient,"[1] as a general cultural concept, in South, Southeast, and East Asia.

The Indian Subcontinent

Once again, the familiar three-fold division of subsurface zones describes a region—the Indian subcontinent. Ancient metamorphic rocks of the Deccan Peninsula are a stable block or "shield" region which extends southward into the Indian Ocean. The highest and most rugged mountains of the world rise out of that part of the zone of weakness occupied by the Himalayan Mountain system which topographically isolates India from the rest of Eurasia. One of the world's important sedimentary lowlands lies between the first two structural zones and is traversed by alluvial river valleys of the Indus and Ganges-Brahmaputra.

Patterns of monsoon precipitation and subtropical growing season have already been described in the discussion of the agricultural resources of Eurasia. Mining activities have been generalized for major mineral-producing regions of the subcontinent. The present concern is with patterns of human life—cultures and organization of area within the Republic of India.

The population of the Union of India alone is more than 400 million persons (408,050,000). An additional balance of more than 100 million persons lives in the subcontinent, principally in Pakistan (87,000,000), divided between East and West Pakistan. South Asia, which exceeds half a billion persons in population, is therefore second in population after East Asia, which is dominated numerically by China's more than 670 million. The total population of East Asia, including Communist China, Taiwan, North and South Korea, and Japan, was more than 800 million (808 million) in 1960.

A complete presentation is far beyond the scope of this book, but the most distinguishing features of India will be described under the following headings: "Hinduism and the Caste System," "Agricultural Subsistence," "The Impact of British Occupation," and "Problems in the Emergence of National Regional Organization."

Hinduism and the Caste System. The population of India after separation from Pakistan was at least 85 per cent Hindu. India is therefore dominated by Hindu culture. The complex Hindu religion itself is a combination of beliefs and rituals which has expanded over thousands of years. It has no unified textual ideology embodied in any one or more commonly accepted written forms, in marked contrast to the Old and New Testaments of Christianity or the Koran of Islam.

The unique socio-religious system known as Hinduism is an amalgam of traditions from Indo-Aryan, Dravidian, and Pre-Dravidian sources. By reasons of its variations in beliefs and customs it is more correctly described as a Brahamanical civilization than as a single religious creed.[2]

"Brahamanical" refers to the caste system which is an integral part of Hinduism. In the beginning there were four social castes into which Hindu society was divided.

. . . the Brahman priesthood, the Kshatriya military group, the Vaisya artisan cultivator, and the Sudra menial group made up of varied low-ranking elements.

[1] The simple geographical meaning of the term "Orient" as "East" has been almost obscured by other connotations. The term *oriental* has acquired inaccurate racist meaning. Prejudicial overtones convey the idea of racial inferiority and low standards of living. The term should be reserved for use in its historical perspective to mean the eastern position of Asian regions in relation to Europe, where the term originated.

[2] John Brush, "South Asia, Peoples and Cultures" in Norton Ginsburg (Ed.), *Patterns of Asia*, New York: Prentice-Hall, 1958, p. 475.

Slowly this simple grouping has become a host of over three thousand social strata today, eighteen hundred of them being Brahman subdivisions as the upper crust surrounded itself with more and more restrictions. . . .

The chief factors in caste distinctions are the rules of marriage, rules covering domestic food consumption, rules covering conduct of the individual, and rules concerning economic work habits. Individuals are born into their caste and cannot raise themselves. Every transgression that is not atoned for through elaborate ritual results in an individual sinking lower in the social order. . . .

And as time has gone on multiple transgression of caste rules was inevitable, resulting in the accumulation at the sheer bottom of the Indian social order of some 60,000,000 "untouchables," outcasts to whom, and to whose descendants there is no prospect other than the lowest of menial labor. . . . Though this one-way road, all down hill, is not a material piece of the physical landscape of India, it is of utmost significance in the cultural geography of the country. India now is moving legally toward abolition of many of the restrictions upon the untouchable, but many decades will pass before caste and its problems are banished.[1]

It is probable that the caste system was an expression of the

. . . genetic classification by the Aryans of the hybrid progeny of Aryans and Dravidians. The Aryans before their invasion had only three castes, which were functional, the Priests, the Fighters, and the Artisans. The Sudras or Dasyus, who formed the fourth class in Aryan nomenclature were generally the Dravidian people.

In India today, caste is neither functional nor genetic. It essentially defines a mating and eating group, chiefly the latter. Having been a fluid institution it became rigid during the British occupation. The tendency during the last century has been toward multiplication of caste divisions, so much so that anyone who disbelieved in caste created a new caste. . . .[2]

Maps of Eurasia in Figures 205 and 239 show that India is easily accessible from the west and northwest. Throughout a very long history waves of population have come into India from these directions, including aboriginal Dravidians and later Indo-Aryans, Moslems, and Western Europeans. The Indo-Aryans, a white-skinned monogamous pastoral people, began infiltrating through the passes in the northwest mountain wall from Persia and southern Russia in approximately 2,000 B.C. The early Dravidian and Indo-Aryans were not united peoples, but many individual tribes, with a common language, in each case.

Two cultures represented by multitribal societies are contrasting—*agricultural (Dravidian)* and a *pastoral (Indo-Aryan)*—peoples. A similar situation existed between the *agricultural Chinese* and the *nomadic Mongols* in North China, and between the sedentary agriculturalists of the *classical Mediterranean world* and the *pastoral Germanic* tribes from the northeast in Europe.

The Bronze Age Aryans brought with them their dairy and cattle culture, which gradually fused with the mainly agricultural culture of Pre-Aryan India.

The ancient Aryans, who were practically patriarchal, met the strong matriarchal Dravidian peoples of India somewhere in the Punjab, and intermingling of the two peoples resulted in the present hybrid Aryo-Dravidian population of the Indo-Gangetic Valley. This process of fusion is still in progress farther south . . .

The highly developed Dravidian culture, together with its Gods, Shiva and Vishnu, and the cult of the mother Goddess, was assimilated into the simple nature and clan cults of the Aryans to result in what is known as Hindu culture. This is a synthesis of all types of thought which have originated or have been introduced since man existed in India.[3]

This geographical hybridization of culture accounts for the extraordinary complexity of Hinduism. The position of cattle is striking. (See Figure 245.)

The inordinate reverence paid to cows in India, especially on the Gangetic Plain, is undoubtedly a relic of . . . mystic relationship of an earlier pastoral people with their herds of cattle. So strong is this primitive tie between man and cow in India, that in the *Code of Manu* killing a cow was considered more heinous than killing a Brahman. Today cow protection is a political issue in India. It is highly probable that the antagonism of the Hindus to beef-eaters is based chiefly on this ancient mystic link with the cow.[4]

Agricultural Subsistence. During the twenty-year period from 1931 to 1951 in India there was little change in the ratio of agricultural to nonagricultural population, and India is still predominantly an agricultural country. Seventy per cent of her population is engaged in agricultural occupa-

[1] J. E. Spencer, *Asia, East by South*, New York: John Wiley and Sons, 1954, p. 129.
[2] E. K. Janaki Ammal, "Introduction to the Subsistence Economy of India," in William L. Thomas (Ed.), *Man's Role in Changing the Face of the Earth*, Chicago: University of Chicago Press, 1956, p. 326.
[3] *Ibid.*, p. 326.
[4] *Ibid.*, p. 328.

Figure 245. Emaciated cattle graze in the shadow of this new thermal electric plant producing nonanimate energy from low-grade coal mined only five miles away. The plant is one of a series of power stations built as part of the multipurpose Damodar Valley development in northeast India. It supplies nearly one billion kilowatt hours of electrical power annually. (*Courtesy of United Nations.*)

tions. Even though the percentage of arable land to total area, as shown by Table XLIII, is unusually high (48.1 per cent), the total population is so numerous that there is less than one acre (0.9 acre) of arable land per capita. This compares with more than three acres per capita in the United States and the U. S. S. R., but it is more than three times as great, in turn, as the per capita ratio estimated for land-hungry China and Japan, which have only 0.29 and 0.20 acres per capita, respectively.

The Indus-Ganges-Brahmaputra alluvial plains associated with the great Himalayan Mountain ranges to the north are the greatest single group of contiguous *alluvial* plains on the globe. Together they occupy some 420,000 square miles, and extend from the Indus Valley in West Pakistan in an uninterrupted belt through northern India for a total distance of nearly 2,500 miles with an average breadth of 200 miles (never less than 90 miles). The alluvial belt ends in the upper Brahmaputra Valley in eastern India.

Despite the relatively large size of these alluvial plains, the characteristic description of the agricultural population of India is that of a life of grinding poverty. Reasons for this are many and complex. They can best be understood when examined in combination. Attention is redirected to the map of agricultural resource regions of Eurasia in Figure 215. On that map India is divided between an eastern region characterized as *plains and low highlands of the humid and wet tropics with little or no frost,* and a northwestern region with *similar topographic conditions and little or no frost under mostly arid circumstances.* This means that over the most densely populated and cultivated areas chemical processes of nitrogen depletion continue at a relatively rapid pace throughout the year with no respite induced by winter cold. The period of nongrowth is induced by drought rather than by cold. This circumstance still further reduces the fertility of the alluvial plains of India. To put it another way, tropical growing-season conditions require more attention on the replacement of soil nutrients through fertilizer and soil management practices than corresponding alluvial soils under more temperate climatic conditions. It is, however, in just this matter that Indian agriculture is particularly weak. Five thousand years of continuous tillage with a perennially deficient return to the soil of plant nutrients has meant that the soils of these alluvial plains have become chronically impoverished, as reflected in crop yields.

Average yield of the annual rice crop of India in 1953–1956–1957 was 13.1, 13.4, and 11.8 hundred kilogram per hectare, respectively. The average for 1948–1952 was 11.1 hundred kilograms. In China the corresponding figures were 26.7, 24.8, and 27.0, respectively, and the average for 1948–1952 was 21.7 hundred kilograms per hectare. Thus the rice crop of China averages twice as much production per unit of area as the same crop in India. Comparison with Japan is even more striking. The rice yield in Japan in 1955 was 48.1 hundred kilogram per hectare, which is well over four times the average for India.

Even though the livestock population which is a source of fertilizer is excessively large—over 200,000,000 cattle, including dairy cows—it is estimated that only one-fourth of the fertilizer need is supplied. Much of the cattle population is underfed and nonproductive. Due to the sacredness of the cow and the refusal to eat beef, the Hindus derive little direct nutritional benefit other than from dairy products which are supplied by a minority of this huge animal population. Cattle represent a burden on the land and its capacity to support people. This burden is not even compensated for by the supply of animal fertilizers because underfed cattle do not produce good fertilizer. To make matters still worse, furthermore, the traditional agricultural village dwellers burn large quantities of animal dung as a fuel substitute for fire wood which is in short supply, and this further depletes the supply of fertilizer. Individual members of a primarily self-sufficient subsistence economy could not afford to purchase commercial fertilizers in adequate amounts even if they were available, because they are outside of the exchange economy. Because of the soil fertility problem, as much as one-sixth of all cultivatable land is left fallow each year and only a relatively small proportion of the land is double cropped. This is true despite the fact that the length of the growing season makes double cropping feasible nearly everywhere.

Another reason for not double cropping is the lack of sufficient water. The map in Figure 246 showing the major crop associations of the subcontinent also shows the regions under irrigation.[1]

[1] Norton Ginsburg (Ed.), *The Pattern of Asia*, New York: Prentice-Hall, Inc., 1954, map, pp. 512–513.

The combined area of land under irrigation in India-Pakistan exceeded 120,000 square miles in 1955—an irrigated territory greater in extent than the total land area of the states of Michigan and Wisconsin combined (111,727 square miles). Even so, somewhat less than one-seventh of the arable land can be double cropped, while approximately one-fifth is irrigated, and one-sixth lies fallow annually as a result of these combined circumstances.

Cultivation of 47,000 square miles of arable land from the combined agricultural economies of Pakistan and India in *nonfood* crops such as jute, hemp, cotton, tobacco, and copra, while an integral part of the total national product, places an additional burden on the ability of the land to support population through the production of food. Within the framework of a continuing subsistence economy and the village organization of peasant agriculture within India, the continuation of the high rate of population increase which has characterized India until now is considered by most demographers and official policy-making agencies of the present Indian government to be highly improvident.

The Impact of British Occupation. The map in Figure 247 after J. E. Spencer shows the expansion of British occupation from 1700 until independence was achieved two and one-half centuries later in 1947. From the map it is apparent that all portions of British India were not directly occupied or ruled. Thus even the British occupation did not by any means represent a unification of all India, but rather a patchwork for the purpose of effective colonial control and development. British occupation may be divided into two principal periods, that of the East India Company until 1857 and partial direct British government control thereafter under a newly created British cabinet post, the Secretary of State for India.

The pattern of Indian areas ruled directly by the British as opposed to the states ruled indirectly is shown on the map in Figure 247. A number of significant facts stand out. First, the areas of direct British control isolated the indirectly ruled portions from one another. Second, the areas of direct British control held all of the coastal portion of India except the southwest, bottling up, so to speak, the areas not directly controlled within the interior. Third, the pattern of railroads and major ports constructed and developed by the British are located in the most productive parts of the whole region: the crescent-shaped plains rimmed by mountains to the northwest, north, and northeast; the principal

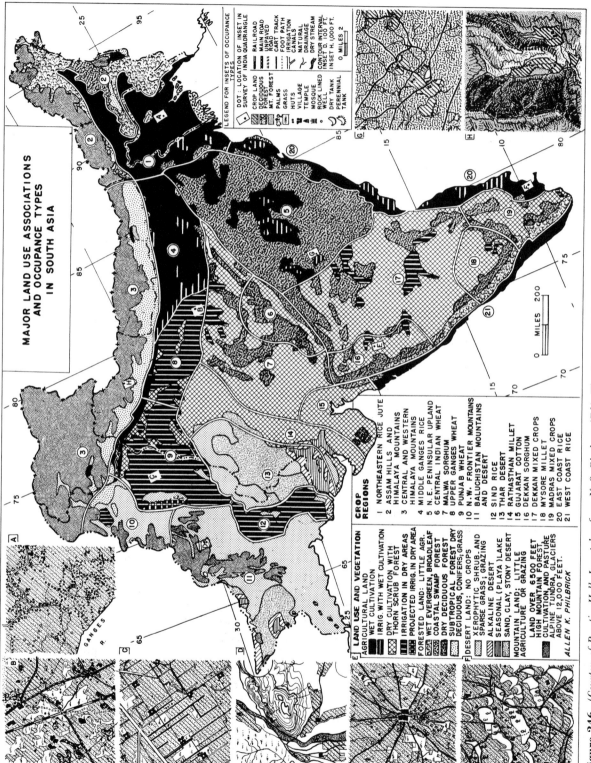

Figure 246. (*Courtesy of Prentice-Hall, Inc., taken from N. S. Ginsburg (Ed.), The Pattern of Asia, 1958.*)

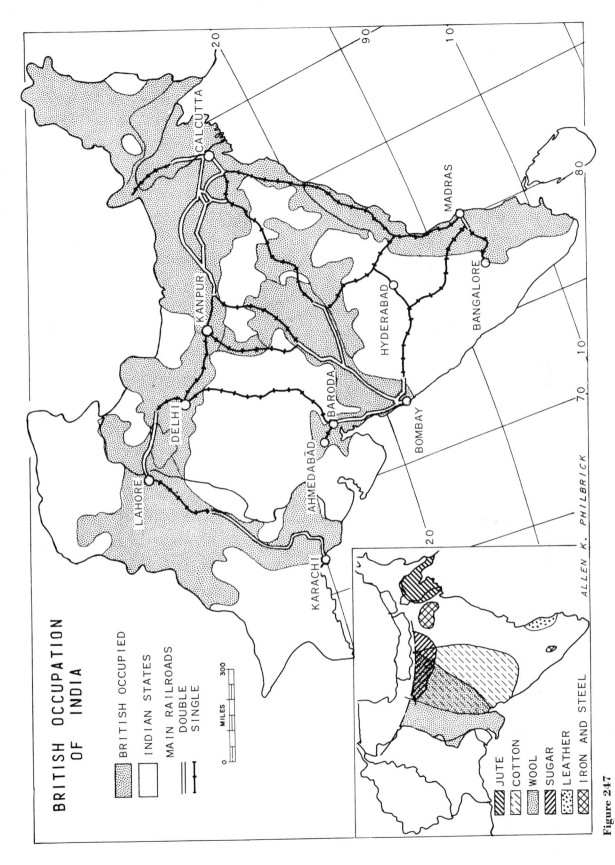

BRITISH OCCUPATION
OF INDIA

BRITISH OCCUPIED

INDIAN STATES

MAIN RAILROADS
DOUBLE
SINGLE

MILES
0   300

CALCUTTA

KANPUR

DELHI

LAHORE

AHMEDABĀD

KARACHI

BARODA

BOMBAY

HYDERABAD

BANGALORE

MADRAS

ALLEN K. PHILBRICK

JUTE

COTTON

WOOL

SUGAR

LEATHER

IRON AND STEEL

Figure 247

cash-crop (cotton) region east of Bombay; and the humid east coast. The largest cities of India are the four ports which are the points of attachment of overseas trade with the best-developed rail networks serving the respective hinterlands. These parts are Calcutta (*5,909,000*), Bombay (4,941,000), Madras (2,208,000), and Karachi (1,916,000). The latter was the first capital of Pakistan, which function has been moved to Rawalpindi, pending construction of a new city to be called Islamabad. The port of Calcutta is shown in Figure 248.

Each of these cities evolved as railhead and port center commanding a large productive hinterland. Each port became the focus of production from the interior district attached to it. British organization of area within South Asia was primarily externally oriented to Britain. In colonial Burma the corresponding port and railhead was Rangoon, which, on the basis of this activity, has grown in 100 years from a town of 50,000 to the capital city of the country and a population of 774,676. As a direct result, however, of the development of the pattern of transportation designed for external trade, the interconnection of the three regions gave ready access to almost all parts of the subcontinent. These larger regional interconnections are also shown on the map in Figure 247. Improvement in transport alleviated the effects of locally occurring famines. Movement of foodstuffs from one part of the country to another or by imports, construction of transportation and irrigation works, and sanitary and disease prevention measures of the British occupation brought about a marked lowering of the Indian death rate.

Coupled with a traditionally high birth rate, these circumstances lie behind the phenomenal population growth in the Indian subcontinent from the middle of the nineteenth century to the middle of the twentieth century. It has been estimated that the combined population of India and Pakistan grew from 200 million persons (206.2) in the 1870s to well over 400 million persons (432.7) in eighty years, by the 1950s.[1] The 1960 estimate for India-Pakistan of just under 500 million (495.0) means a total increase of approximately 290 million in ninety years. Such a huge increase in population during so short a period of time indicates the magnitude of the problem of overpopulation in the Indian subcontinent. Several additional character-

istics of this increase in population should be mentioned. It is significant that the rise in population in India parallels a similar increase in the population of Europe. The important difference, however, is that Europe's increase was accompanied by a great rise in the standards of living which was achieved by industrialization and mechanization. Industrialization and mechanization have as yet scarcely touched India. Instead the increase in Indian population has taken place within the peasant farm villages where it has depressed standards of living.

For comparison purposes, the United States, which is agriculturally a land of dispersed farms, has no more than 20,000 settlements ranging all the way from the world's largest city, New York, to tiny crossroad hamlets. In India, on the other hand, in approximately half the total area and with more than twice the population, there were in 1941 a total of 658,595 towns and villages. No fewer than 450,000 of these had less than 500 inhabitants. There were less than 4,500 villages with more than 5,000 persons each. In India the subsistence peasant village of small size has obviously had a long and deeply rooted existence. Increase in city population, though steady, is still very much in the minority. In 1951 only 17.3 per cent of the population was urban.

Problems in the Emergence of National Regional Organization. India's basic solution to the population problem must be the transformation of its subsistence organization of area to exchange organization. The government has provided leadership in the form of five-year development plans, but the economy remains in private hands, while government develops only the types of enterprises which will not be in competition with private business. Throughout the country, however, the pattern of the subsistence peasant village still has remained intact. The countryside is not yet being systematically reorganized on the basis of a wage economy. Industrial sectors of the national economy as they are developed will have impact on the subsistence portions of the economy only if increased productivity in agriculture makes it possible for the village peasants to sell surplus and buy manufactured products with the proceeds of such sales. Lack of real progress in that respect will have a dampening effect on the results of technological progress elsewhere in the economy.

Internal reorganization of the nation's domestic economy, replacing the former *external orientation*

[1] A. M. Carr-Saunders, *World Population*, Oxford, England: Clarendon Press, 1936, p. 269. The estimate for 1872 population is 206.2 million persons for the then Empire of India.

Figure 248. Improvement of transport, especially of major ports and railways, has been given the highest priority in India's development plans. With the help of a World Bank loan, the port of Calcutta on the Hooghly River, one of the distributary channels in the Ganges delta, is being improved to enable it to handle eleven million tons of traffic annually, an increase of two million tons. (*Courtesy of United Nations.*)

of production which in the British period was destined primarily for export, is a second problem. During the British occupation processing and manufacturing were located in relation to *resources* and ease of *shipment*. In keeping with the latter aim, for example, Calcutta and the towns on the Hooghly River (a distributary on the Ganges delta) became the main *jute* manufacturing centers in the world. Bombay along with Ahmedabad (1,040,000) to the north became associated with cotton spinning and cloth weaving; Madras, on the southeast coast, became the focus for the export of partially or half-tanned leather. Southern Indian wattle bark and a realtively high natural death rate among cattle in the south ensured a supply of both tanning materials and hides. Other items of production were resource and colonial market oriented. Kanpur, a military strong point and rail center in the mid-Ganges Plain, became the center of a wool-processing industry. Sheep from the dry northwest supplied the wool, and the need for military clothing provided a market.

In the central Ganges Plain subtropical sugar-cane production provides the resource base for the Indian sugar-milling industry. India is the largest raw cane-sugar-producing country in the world.

West of Calcutta in southern Bihar Province, large deposits of high-quality iron ore, limestone, and adequate, though not plentiful, supplies of coking coal are the basis of a resource-oriented steel industry. India's largest manufacturing enterprise, the Tata iron and steel works at Jamshedpur (Figure 249), employs nearly 25,000 persons. A second smaller works, the Indian Iron and Steel Company, is located on the coal fields near Asansol (102,000). A third, much smaller, mill which uses charcoal rather than coke (with a possibility of converting to electrical smelting) is based on iron ores of high quality in western Mysore state in south peninsular India. Each of these important Indian manufactures is shown on the map in Figure 247. Note, however, the scattered and peripheral locations of industrial cities of Madras, Bombay, Ahmedabad, Amritsar (371,000), Kanpur (*965,000*), Jamshedpur (*283,000*), and Calcutta. In the British period this dispersed pattern made sense because the economy was geared to exporting the main production outside the country. Today, however, integration of the geographically scattered manufacturing activities into a coherently organized national economy presents a problem.

The national capital at New Delhi occupies the

Figure 249. The crane and molds into which pig iron is cast are shown in the newly built extension of the Tata Iron and Steel Company. The crane is the largest in Asia, with a capacity of 250 tons. The privately owned Tata works (TISCO) is the largest and oldest steel producer in India. The plant, in which production is being doubled, is located at Jamshedpur. Expansion is being accomplished with the help of a joint loan from the World Bank and nine United States and Canadian commercial banks. (*Courtesy of United Nations.*)

site of ancient Delhi which commands the low divide between the Indus and Ganges drainage to the Arabian Sea and the Bay of Bengal, respectively. This site is the ancient crossroads region of northern India, located on the margin between the dry northwest and the humid-to-wet southeast. In this respect, the position of Delhi (2,409,000) resembles that of Peiping, China. Delhi also marks the northwestern end of India's most populous region—the middle and lower Ganges Plain along with the Indian part of the Ganges delta. The 109 million people in 1951 on an area of 141,266 square miles in this region represents a population average of 770 persons per square mile. No other region of like magnitude rivals this within India. The only others might be the continuation of the same type of environment in East Pakistan and the coastal areas

of southern India. The area of East Pakistan is 54,500 square miles with an average density per square mile of 745 for the 40.6 million people occupying the territory in 1951. The Malabar and Madras coastal areas of southern India approach these concentrations of population, but their totals are much smaller. On the Madras coast 30.7 million within 55,421 square miles constitute an average concentration of 554 per square mile; and 16.3 million on the Malabar coast within 21,602 square miles represent an average concentration of 756 persons per square mile.

India, accordingly, lacks a well-developed core region from the viewpoint of national organization of area. The upper and lower Ganges, West Bengal, and the heavy industrial district of Bihar Province are a potential core region for India, from Delhi (2,409,000) on the northwest to Calcutta (5,909,000) on the southeast; but the patterns of manufacturing in India are so dispersed as to make the long-range reorientation of the country's factory production a matter of national necessity. Such reorganization of area requires a basic reversal of the former direction of interconnections between regions from an external to an internal focus. It was all right for the internal focus to be a pattern of scattered production when the sites represented the origins of a movement outward to foreign markets. But this pattern of production and movement is illogical for an internally diversified and coherently organized domestic national economy. Furthermore it cannot simply be reversed but must be shifted for efficiency of operation into one or more core regions.

India is barely self-sufficient in food production (Figure 250). Under its present standard of living it is self-sufficient in wool, cotton textiles, leather goods, paper, and in sugar and vegetable oils. India could now produce iron and steel in nearly sufficient quantities for most of its current needs. However, such statements are virtually meaningless in view of national desires for improvement in the context of present low standards of living. Actual production in India is practically at a preindustrial level of development in machine tools and basic industries.

For example, Indian steel production in 1956 was less than 2 million tons (1,766,000 tons) for a population (estimated for that year) of 387,350,000. On a per capita basis this represents less than 10 pounds of steel per person. Contrast this ratio with 21 million tons of steel divided among 51,430,000 people in the United Kingdom, which is more than

Figure 250. This view of a narrow street in Calcutta leading to a Hindu temple illustrates the population problem of India. The shops under the awnings sell food. In a long line in front of them sits part of the surplus population awaiting the gift of money or food from those who come to patronize the shops. There are many thousands of individuals, displaced persons, and unemployed, as well as professional beggars, whose sole means of survival is charity. (*Courtesy of United Nations.*)

800 pounds of steel for every man, woman, and child. In the United States that ratio is more than 1,200 pounds of steel per capita. China's steel production of 5 million tons in 1956 divided among 600 million persons averaged 18 pounds per capita. Plans to greatly enlarge steel production in India are being implemented. The capacity of the Tata steel works is being doubled and new plants are being constructed. (See Figure 251.)

Another index of the stage of manufacturing development is the number of industrial workers in proportion to the total economically active population. Figures in Table XLV compare the level of development in India with that of the United States and the United Kingdom. The numbers of people and points of application of their activities in three categories are shown as an expression of the degree of geographical division of labor within the national economies—manufacturing, commerce, and transportation-communication; whereas the number of people engaged in agriculture is an index of the opposite—the relative lack of development of a geographical division of labor.

The data in the table show that economically active population is less than one-third of total population (28.5 per cent) in India as compared with two-fifths (40 per cent) of the population of the United States and nearly half (46.2 per cent) in the United Kingdom. Of the economically active population, 70 per cent are engaged in agriculture in India, while the total of the three categories which are centrally or focally located in urban or market-oriented places—manufacturing, commerce, and transportation-communication—is only 16.9 per cent of the labor force. By contrast, in the more developed countries characterized by an exchange-type area organization, the proportions are reversed. In the United Kingdom, which supplies only half of its own food requirements, only 5 per cent of the economically active population is engaged in agriculture. So highly developed is the geographical division of labor in that island country that a total of nearly 60 per cent of the labor force (58.7 per cent) is engaged in manufacturing (37.2 per cent), commerce (13.9 per cent), and transportation-communication (7.6 per cent). Reference should be

Figure 251. Stones and excavated material are being manually dumped into a pond behind a new Indian Iron and Steel Company plant at Burnpur, India. The steel mill is one of several industries now receiving electrical power through the grid of the Damodar Valley Corporation in northeastern India. (*Courtesy of United Nations.*)

made again to the discussion in Chapters 6 and 9 concerning the area organization of the British economy regionally in the United Kingdom, in the Commonwealth, and in the world.

The United States is far more self-sufficient than the United Kingdom since it is a much larger continentwide country. With the resources and technology at their disposal, they require only 12 per cent of the labor force to more than feed the nation, if the stockpiling of foodstuffs under the government price-support programs is any criterion. By contrast, again, more than half the work force

TABLE XLV STRUCTURE OF INDIAN ECONOMY COMPARED WITH UNITED STATES AND UNITED KINGDOM[a]

			ECONOMICALLY ACTIVE POPULATION, THOUSANDS									
			Manufacturing		*Commerce*		*Transportation, communication*		*Agriculture*		*Factory wage earners*	
Country	*Population, thousands*	*Per cent*	*Number*	*Per cent*	*Number*	*Per cent*	*Number*	*Per cent*	*Number*	*Per cent*	*Number*	*Per cent*
India	356,879 (101,775)[b]	28.5	9,176	9.2	5,901	5.8	1,902	1.9	71,809	70.6	1,500	1.4
United Kingdom	50,225 (23,215)[b]	46.2	8,647	37.2	3,235	13.9	1,767	7.6	1,232	5.3	6,000	25.8
United States	150,697 (60,037)[b]	40.0	16,113	26.8	11,082	18.4	4,184	6.9	7,331	12.2	12,000	20.0

[a] Based in part on United Nations, *Statistical Yearbook,* New York, 1957, pp. 55, 58, 65, and 190.

[b] Parenthetical numbers indicate economically active population.

Figure 252. A view of the carding machines in the Keshoram Cotton Mills, Ltd., one of the largest textile mills in West Bengal. (*Courtesy of United Nations.*)

is active in urban-focused activities—manufacturing (26.8 per cent), commerce (18.4 per cent), and transportation-communication (6.9 per cent).

Of existing manufacturing industries in India, the majority produce consumer goods (Figure 252). In the long-range view, India must continue to devote a larger proportion of her productive activity to producer goods and machine tools if she desires to develop a truly integrated national economy.

Summary. The problems of India are two in number. She must support an increasing population at an improved standard of living in such a way that agricultural production increases at a faster rate than population. In order to unite her fourteen-language nation economically and politically she must develop an exchange-type organization of area on the basis of expanded industrial production with particular attention to iron and steel and machine tools.

In the attainment of these objectives India faces a series of practical problems relating to water, soil, and other resources. Some of these are made more complex in the light of cultural practices inherited from the past. The externally oriented pattern of area organization inherited from the British development of a colonial economy is geographically dis-

persed, and an internally focused commercial economy must be developed to replace it. The subsistence base of peasant-village area organization represents an extremely conservative majority of the population which it is extremely difficult to reorient toward an exchange economy. In the locating of new economic activities and the relocation of older ones, it is logical to expect that more and more manufacturing will gravitate toward the larger masses of agricultural population in the Ganges Valley. Existing widely dispersed centers of manufacturing at Calcutta, Bombay, Madras, etc. will grow even larger but additional market-oriented manufacturing centers must also be developed. As agricultural production improves manufacturing will absorb surplus population from the countryside. In this way a better balance between farming and nonfarming sectors of the national economy will be developed.

Southeast Asia

The fragmented nature of the region of Southeast Asia is well illustrated by maps in Figures 205 and 209. Nearly a million square miles of the South China Sea between the mainland Indochina-Malayan peninsula and the islands of Sumatra, Java,

Figure 253. These four pictures emphasize the subsistence organization of life in Southeast Asia.

(A) U Aung Tin and his wife, Daw Nyun Yee, who live in a small farming hamlet 35 miles north of Rangoon, Burma, clean a wooden plow and harrow before storing it away for another season. They have just completed harvesting a bumper crop and now await next year's monsoon.

(B) The threshing of wheat near Vientiane, Laos, by hand methods.

and Borneo are less than 500 feet deep. This very large continental shelf, the peninsular mainland, Borneo, and the inner halves of the islands of Java and Sumatra constitute a partially submerged sedimentary lowland in the form of a huge oval. The long axis of the region extends from the northwest to the southeast, in the same direction as the southeast alignment of folded mountain ranges which separate China from the Indian subcontinent. This huge region composed of peninsulas, islands, and shallow seas is encircled by the great arc of the zone of crustal instability as previously noted. Southeast Asia may be thought of as a partially drowned or submerged subcontinent, ringed by mountain ranges whose peaks form island chains which are bordered in turn by an intermittent ring of deep ocean trenches.

The region may be divided into mainland and insular portions. Major divisions of the mainland have been indicated on the maps in Figures 205 and 213 in Chapters 15 and 16 on the peoples and resources of Eurasia. The highland-enclosed alluvial deltas of the Irrawaddy, the Menam, the Mekong, and the Red and Black rivers provide rice-crop subsistence bases for Burma, Thailand, and South and North Vietnam, respectively. The upper and lower Mekong River valleys provide the principal agricultural basis of two other countries, Laos and Cambodia. Both of these are primarily subsistence-rice economies also. Southern Malaya, the newly federated independent Malayan state, is so nearly insular in character, like its Indonesian island neighbor, that it will be classified with the island portion of the region.

The organization of area in southeast Asia closely resembles that of tropical Africa from the standpoint of the impact of Europeans. The background of rice economies is Asian and self-sufficient (Figure 253A, B, C, and D) but the participation in world trade on the basis of externally oriented mineral and plantation-type agricultural production for export is European. The one exception in this characterization is the export of surplus rice.

Mainland countries of the region possess some characteristics of a frontier. They are not densely populated as are India and China. There is still a considerable quantity of land of agricultural quality to be cleared of forest and put to use. Mainland Southeast Asia has traditionally been a rice-exporting territory from which some of the more crowded of their neighbors could purchase supplementary food.

(D) The hand grinding of rice is preceded by a final tossing to eliminate chaff.

(C) Rice is husked in a hand-powered husking mill in Kedah, Malaya.
Photographs courtesy of United Nations.

Japan

Japan is the only East Asian exchange-type core region of world significance, and it is the only well-developed example of this type of area organization which has been created by non-Europeans. The nation consists of four major islands, Honshu, Hokkaido, Kyushu, and Shikoku, located off the coast of China. They are a continuation of the chains of volcanic mountains discussed earlier in connection with island archipelagoes of Southeast Asia (Figure 205). The tropical archipelagoes of Southeast Asia draw close to the mainland at the island of Formosa (Taiwan) which is now occupied by the Nationalist Chinese. From Taiwan northeastward, the Ryukyu Islands enclose the East China Sea, and loop toward the Korean Peninsula and the southernmost of the Japanese Islands—Kyushu. From a position marked on the mainland by the occurrence of the south tip of South Korea, the Japanese Islands are northeastward again in a festoon of land more than 1,200 miles long enclosing the Sea of Japan. Hokkaido, the north island, has two northern peninsulas, one pointing toward Sakhalin Island and the Soviet mainland, and the other pointing to the Kurile Island chain. The latter chain of islands came under the control of the Soviet Union after World War II. They are yet another arc of submerged mountain tops which enclose the Sea of Okhotsk and end at the tip of the Kamchatka Peninsula in eastern Siberia. From a point midway along the eastern shore of the latter peninsula the Aleutian Islands chain encloses the Bering Sea and joins the North American mainland in Alaska.

Challenge. The challenge of Japan rests in the fact that her people have accomplished so much in the development of an exchange organization of productive activity on the basis of such relatively limited natural resources for such activity within Japan itself. As might be expected from their mountainous character, the islands have only small and scattered plains. These are either coastal alluvial plains and diluvial terraces on the margins of rugged interior mountain ranges, or they are relatively small debris-filled interior basins. In all, something less than 15 per cent of the total area of 142,788 square miles is level land. Only 13.7 per cent (19,490 square miles) is considered arable land. On the basis of arable-land area, offshore fishing banks, and imported food from other lands, a population of more than 96 million persons lives. The average of 4,600 persons per square mile of arable land is perhaps the largest concentration of population in the world for so large a total population. The map in Figure 254 shows the general pattern of small agricultural plains and detailed samples of associations of agricultural land use in various parts of the islands.

As a nation Japan has grown rapidly in population since it was opened to the influence of Western ideas after the visit of the American Admiral Perry in 1853. Population has nearly trebled from 35 million people to a nation approaching 100 million in little more than a century. This growth is similar to that of India; but, unlike India, the economy and culture of the Japanese people have undergone remarkable changes. From an almost entirely subsistence-agricultural economy characterized by an estimated agricultural population of 80 per cent in relation to the total in 1860, Japan accomplished a transformation of herself to an exchange-type organization by the mid-1920s. By 1930 the per cent of population engaged in agriculture and forestry had dropped to 47.7 per cent. Parallel to the shift in agriculture from subsistence to commercial farming, planned and governmentally encouraged development of manufacturing industries and foreign trade also took place.

The Japanese have created an industrial-economic base first developed on silk and cotton-textile manufactures. They continued to reinvest the proceeds of commercial earnings in the expansion of basic iron and steel and producer-goods industries as well as a variety of consumer-goods manufactures. In so doing they have created the most commercially active national economy in Asia, which participates vigorously in world trade. Despite the lack of sufficient coal, iron, and petroleum necessary to the development of a manufacturing industry, Japan has developed a manufacturing economy based on *imported* raw materials. Of the more than 3 billion dollars of imports into Japan in 1956, 53 per cent were inedible raw materials, not including mineral fuels. The latter, including lubricants and related products, accounted for another 13 per cent. Semiprocessed raw materials, such as chemicals and processed metals such as iron and steel, copper, nickel, aluminum, lead, zinc, tin, and others, represented another combined share of import trade amounting to 8.7 per cent of the total. Supplementary food imports were 17 per cent of total imports. Accordingly 92 per cent of the inputs into the national economy from abroad were of an industrial raw material and food variety.

Imported machinery and transport equipment were another 5 per cent of total imports in 1956. It is clear, therefore, that Japan's economy functions primarily on the basis of a geographical division of labor between her own people and those of territories outside her borders. Raw materials and foods are brought in, and Japan manufactures products using these raw materials and prospers or suffers privation on the basis of the sale of those products.

Foreign Trade. The maps in Figures 255 and 256 show that this geographical division of labor on which Japan depends is worldwide. The map in Figure 255 portrays the countries of origin for twenty selected types of items in the functioning of the national economy.[1] These include coking coal from the United States, North Vietnam, and Australia; iron ore from Malaya, India, the Philippines, the United States, and others; and scrap iron from the United States, India, and Australia. Raw materials for the important textile industries of Japan come from many widely separated places. There are imports of wool from South Africa, Brazil, and New Zealand, and cotton from the United States, Mexico, Pakistan, India, Brazil, and Egypt. Through technological improvements of mechanization and the use of commercial fertilizers, Japan is now self-sufficient in rice production, although increasing numbers of Japanese now eat bread. The latter shift means importation of wheat. In 1956 wheat imports from the United States and Australia exceeded Japan's imports of rice from Burma, Thailand, and Taiwan by a wide margin.

The map in Figure 256 shows the companion picture of exports from Japan. *Textiles* are still the most widely exported product, and move to the United States, Hong Kong (for re-export), Thailand, Singapore (for re-export), the Philippines, Burma, Australia, the Republic of South Africa, Venezuela, Ceylon, England, Canada, Communist China, and Indonesia. In the process of developing manufacturing industries, regions such as Japan which were far away from the original culture hearths of the industrial revolution often started their industrial economies by processing raw materials for consumer markets rather than by the construction of basic industries. This was certainly true of Japan in terms of her early concentration on the textile industry.

While textiles are still important in Japan's manufacturing economy, they are no longer the predominant industry. Japan is now a major ex-

[1] *Asahi Yearbook*, Tokyo, Japan: Asahi News Company, 1959, pp. 563–565.

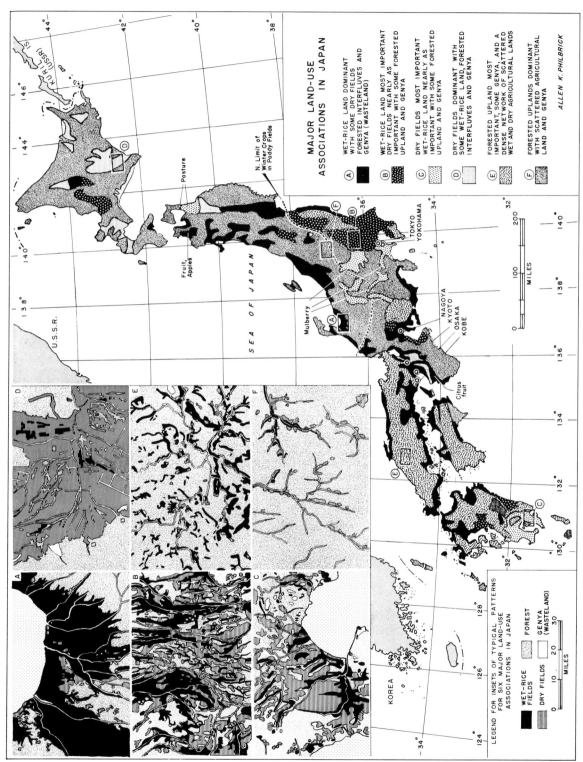

Figure 254. (*Courtesy of Prentice-Hall, Inc., taken from N. S. Ginsburg (Ed.), The Pattern of Asia, 1958.*)

449

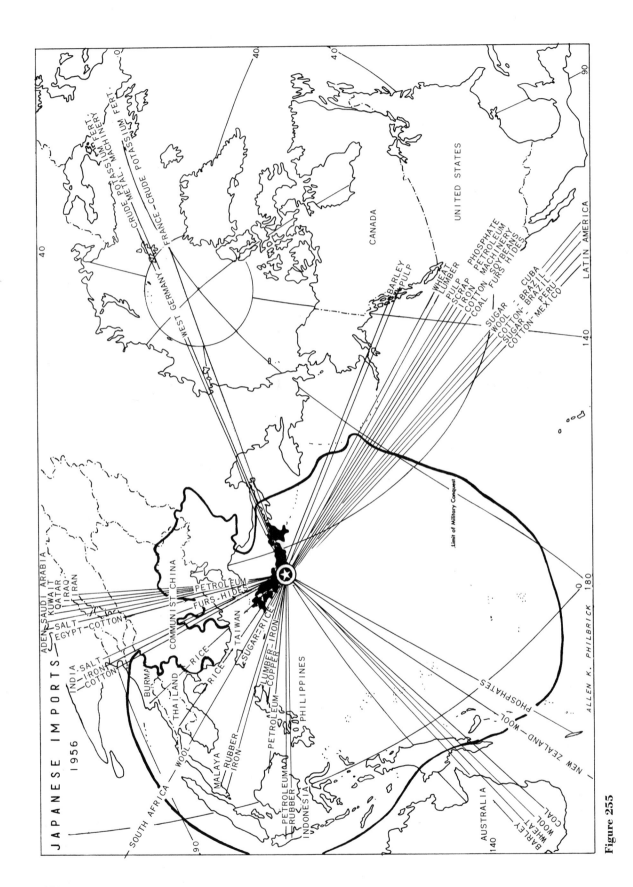

JAPANESE IMPORTS 1956

Figure 255

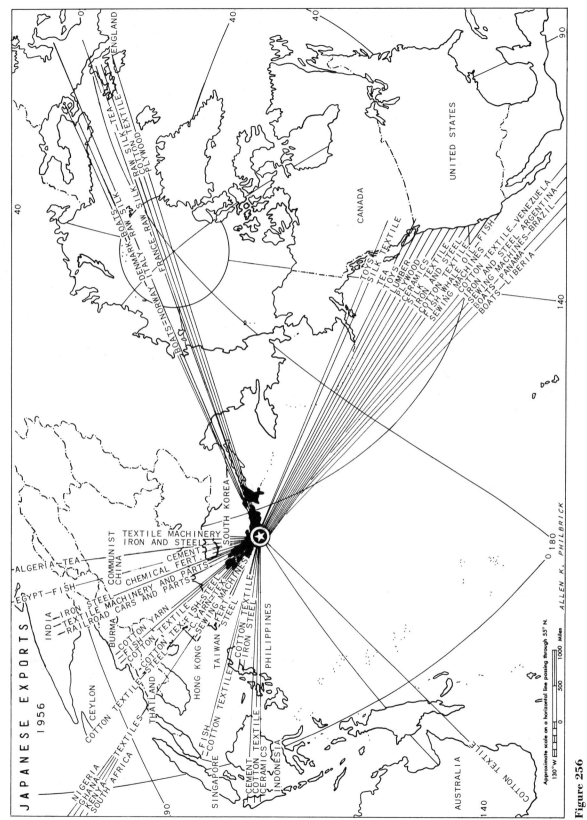

Figure 256

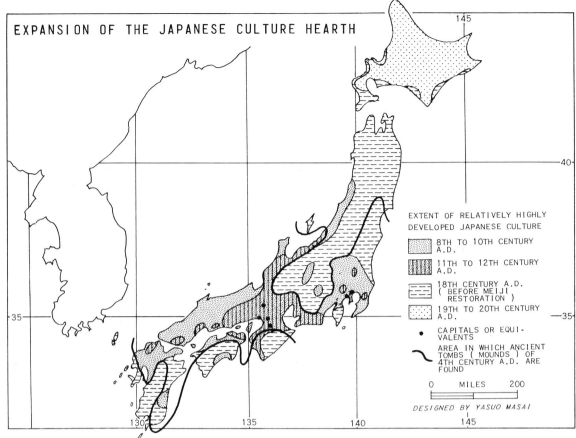

EXPANSION OF THE JAPANESE CULTURE HEARTH

EXTENT OF RELATIVELY HIGHLY DEVELOPED JAPANESE CULTURE

8TH TO 10TH CENTURY A.D.

11TH TO 12TH CENTURY A.D.

18TH CENTURY A.D. (BEFORE MEIJI RESTORATION)

19TH TO 20TH CENTURY A.D.

CAPITALS OR EQUI- VALENTS

AREA IN WHICH ANCIENT TOMBS (MOUNDS) OF 4TH CENTURY A.D. ARE FOUND

0   MILES   200

DESIGNED BY YASUO MASAI

Figure 257

porter of iron and steel to India, Argentina, the United States, Hong Kong, Thailand, Taiwan, and the Philippines. In 1956 Japan exported textile *machinery* and parts in significant quantities to India, Communist China, and Hong Kong. Ships and boats were an important export item from Japan, also, made primarily for registration under the Liberian and Danish flags. Less important in quantity but significant were the railway cars and parts manufactured for India and Thailand.

The map in Figure 256 shows that Japan is now an important supplier of *manufactured goods* of both producer and consumer categories. In this connection Japan dominates the shipping lanes of the Pacific trunk-line routes at right angles to the main line of world trade on the Asian side of the Pacific. Her exports follow the great circle route northwestward to the west coast of North America and southwestward to the nations of East and Southeast Asia. Around the "corner" of Asia at Singapore Japan trades with South Asian, Southwest Asian, and European ports. In 1939 Japan's merchant fleet was the third largest in the world, after those

of the United States and the United Kingdom. Japan has now rebuilt her merchant marine, which was virtually destroyed during World War II, to the point that in 1958 it was fifth in registered tonnage in the world.

Expansion of Japanese Culture. In attempting to understand Japanese progress geographically the spatial evolution of her culture is of key importance. The map in Figure 257 illustrates the expansion of Japanese culture from its original centers in southern Honshu in the eighth century A.D. Subsistence culture of the Japanese developed slowly and in isolation from its original source areas outside the islands. It is believed that these were from mainland China and Southeast Asian island cultures of Malaysia and Polynesia. By the eighteenth century Japanese people had carried their ways of doing throughout the three main islands of Honshu, Shikoku, and Kyushu, and had begun the penetration of Hokkaido. The significance of the map in Figure 257 lies in the fact that the original culture hearth of Japan has remained the core of Japan to the present day.

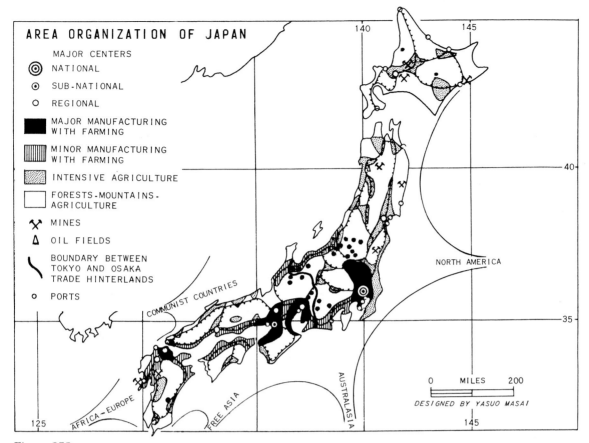

Figure 258

After the opening of Japan to the impact of European and American technologies, the influence and extent of territorial control by the Japanese increased sharply. The map in Figure 255 also shows the conquests of the Japanese Empire before and during World War II. Marked by a series of military and political acquisitions of territory, the list includes Okinawa in 1875, Formosa (Taiwan) in 1895, the southern half of Sakhalin Island in 1905, Korea in 1910, German Pacific islands and the Shantung concession in China from Germany after 1918, and Manchuria in 1931. The high point of expansion occurred during World War II and is shown by the outer line of military conquest on the map in Figure 255. From this high-water mark Japan was reduced to the four main islands as the result of losing the war. The country is now engaged in rebuilding her prestige and economic well-being by peaceful industrial productivity and vigorous competitive merchandising, along with United States aid.

Exchange Area Organization. The map in Figure 258 shows the area organization of Japan and its principal offshore ocean fisheries. The country depends on the latter for a very considerable share of the protein content in its food supply. The core region of Japan extends from Tokyo southwestward to northern Kyushu. The latter island is in a sense no longer separated from southern Honshu, since it has been connected by both a rail and a highway tunnel in 1944 and 1958, respectively. The core region is an alignment of great urban centers interconnected by the country's major axis of double-track railroad, by the Inland Sea in the southwestern half of the core, and by the Pacific coast in the northeastern half.

There are four main urban-industrial clusters in Japan's core alignment. Each cluster is located within one of the larger plains areas. From Japan's meager total area of level arable land, the largest is the Kanto Plain on which the Tokyo-Yokohama (*13,787,766*) industrial complex is located. The region, within a sixty-mile radius of Tokyo, contains the world's largest urban-focused population agglomeration. New York is still the world's largest metropolis from the standpoint of concentrated, purely urban population within the first thirty miles outward from their respective city centers. The addition of several million farmers and part-time farmers whose activities also primarily focus on Tokyo's metropolitan markets makes the Tokyo region on the Kanto Plain a unit of combined agricultural and manufactural-commercial activity without equal in the concentration of its population or in the diversity of its peoples' activities. Tokyo is the nation's industrial, financial, political, social, and cultural capital. With respect to some of these functions it is a relative newcomer, for the traditional capital of Kyoto (1,254,000) and other centers of preindustrial Japan at the head of the Inland Sea were in the past more centrally located in the cultural core region than Tokyo. The general coincidence of the region into which Japanese culture had expanded by the twelfth century A.D. with that of the present core region of the country is striking. Osaka-Kobe is a second set of cities, located at the northeastern end of the Inland Sea. Kobe (1,086,000) is the port for Osaka (2,887,000) as Yokohama (1,302,000) is for Tokyo (9,504,997). Both Osaka and Tokyo were inhibited by shallow waters from early port development in the past, but are now, by the dredging of channels, ports of increasing importance.

Kyoto, ancient capital of Japan, was laid out in 793 A.D. on the model of the Chinese city, Sian, capital of the Chinese Sui dynasty. Today, Kyoto (1,254,000), located twenty-five miles from Osaka, is a city of a million and a quarter inhabitants but retains more of the "atmosphere" of "old Japan" than any other large city in the country. Osaka and Kyoto are on the margins of the seaward and landward limits, respectively, of the Settsu alluvial plain. The Settsu Plain, however, is not so occupied by urban population that it is not a significant producer of food. The Nobi Plain, located between Kyoto and Tokyo, contains Nagoya (1,502,000) as its principal urban focus. The fourth major urban industrial cluster is a group of cities at the western end of the Inland Sea, primarily located on northern Kyushu. Associated with the coal fields of northern Kyushu is a group of industrial cities—Moji (165,000), Kokura (276,000), Tobata (105,000), Yawata (332,000), Wakamatsu (106,000) and, across the straits in Honshu, Shimonoseki (252,000). These cities comprise the most important specialized heavy-industrial district of Japan, although there is heavy industry (steel) in each of the four urban regions mentioned above.

Within sixty miles of Tokyo there are twenty million people. The Nagoya composite urban hinterland has a radius of approximately forty miles around its central city and a total population of six million. Within thirty miles of Osaka are eight million, whereas the industrial prefectures of northern Kyushu total six million persons. The directly urban-focused population agglomerations of the four main urban clusters of the Japanese core region accounted for a total of forty out of ninety-two million persons in 1950 (43 per cent), in the nation as a whole. There are at least another ten million persons within the core region as indicated on the map in Figure 258, which brings the core region's total population to fifty million, 55 per cent of the nation.

A view of the Yawata steel mill in Figure 259 gives an indication of the maturity of the heavy industrial development there. It is the largest integrated iron and steel works in the eastern Eurasian perimeter. The fact that each of the four major industrial complexes has iron and steel works, that each of them focuses on one major port, and the fact that each is the major center for a considerable area attests to the idea that each separate segment of the economic core region functions separately and independently. Each is dependent on imports and exports to and from *overseas* regions as much or more than it is dependent on internal domestic sources of raw materials or markets. Special development of heavy industry in Kyushu is partly a reflection of the prewar orientation toward raw-material imports from the Asian mainland as well as resource orientation to Kyushu coal fields. Decentralization of heavy industry in each of the four main urban clusters of the Japanese core region reflects the relative poverty of domestic mineral resources.

In addition to the major industrial developments in the larger cities, Japan has a vast array of small manufactures and cottage-type industries in all cities. The latter are primarily consumer goods producers.

The map in Figure 258 shows the distribution of activities outside the core region which are of fundamental importance to the operation of Japan's exchange economy. Among these are the food production from the many smaller plains and interior mountain valleys, the fisheries off the coasts which supply protein, and the major hydroelectric plants in the interior mountains west of Tokyo and east of Osaka which provide power for

Figure 259. Part of the Yawata Iron and Steel Works on Dokai Bay, the largest integrated iron and steel operation in the Orient. Originally built by the Japanese government, it stimulated subsequent development and so contributed heavily to making the Kita Kyushu Industrial Zone what it is today. (*Courtesy of The American Geographical Society, taken from John H. Thompson and Michihiro Miyazaki, "A Map of Japan's Manufacturing,"* Geographical Review.)

the nation's major industries. There are also a number of peripheral industrial districts which repeat on a smaller scale what has been noted for the larger centers. Principal among these are the industrial cities on the coast of the Sea of Japan, from Niigata and Toyama to Kanazawa.

In developing an exchange economy, the Japanese have "Japanized" what they have absorbed from European and American culture. The resulting new Japanese culture demonstrates the power of ideas in determining the direction of development in this human world.

Summary

Basically, the development of occupancy in the east Eurasian perimeter is passing through the same phases of development as are Africa and Latin America. Such developments represent the fourth stage of the worldwide dispersion of the industrial revolution begun in eighteenth century England. Exchange organization of area is replacing subsistence. As colonialism is replaced by nationalism, each people strives to develop a more diversified and coherently organized domestic economy with the resources at hand. India exemplifies the extreme difficulty of accomplishing this transformation starting with a very high population and a low standard of living. Japan faced the same situation but began the transformation before her population had increased to the same degree as India's. Japan's energetic development of an exchange society has maintained a higher standard of living.

20 *World Regional Organization*

In bringing the examination of world regional geography to a close it is desirable to review briefly the findings with respect to worldwide *regional organization* in relation to *resources* and to the *cultural forces* which will shape the future of this human world. It is appropriate, after examining the regions of the Eurasian perimeter, which ring the Communist Bloc, to place this huge regional pattern of contrasting cultures and the two major groupings into which they have been classified into the wider context of the world as a whole. This final regional chapter is thus placed within the perspective of the world as a series of realms of regional organization in competition for world leadership.

Within this perspective it can be better appreciated how fundamental are these divisions of the world that threaten the peace. In this way we can understand the physical and cultural bases of the problems which must be solved before the people of the world can hope to achieve a genuine regional interdependence based on mutual understanding, respect, and common sense. Such regional interdependence may yet bring, at some time in the future, a truly unified world regional organization into being.

Four Map Bases for Worldwide Comparison

Four particular maps in earlier parts of the book afford expressions of basic concepts. These maps are:

1. World Regional Organization, Figure 21, Chapter 2.
2. Composite Culture Systems, Figure 54, Chapter 4.
3. Arable Land, Figure 47, Chapter 4.
4. Population, Figure 21, Chapter 2.

Most of the world occupance regions in Figure 21 of Chapter 2 have been discussed in some detail with respect to the three subject threads, *nature*, *culture*, and *area organization*. These threads of thought have shown how the physical materials or conditions which collectively constitute the re-

sources of the world are used by people to build what we understand as human culture in systems of area organization.

"Composite Culture Systems," Figure 54 of Chapter 4, dealt with the cultural aspect of geography. Consideration of selected world regions from the standpoint of culture has shown in each case the tremendous impact of *European culture*, particularly with respect to technology and the development of science and industrial revolution. This concept includes stages of geographical dispersion of know-how from England and Europe in the beginning, and now from the United States-Canadian core region and to some extent from Japan, as well as the Communist Bloc core regions within the Soviet Union and China. Dissemination of know-how embodied in industrial technology as it has evolved and developed from its eighteenth century beginnings in England to the present has occurred in stages expressing the primary leadership of European culture, from the organization of area based on local subsistence to one of regional and worldwide exchange. In the progress of this transformation to date, the world has become divided into a number of significant realms of regional organization.

The third and fourth maps to which attention is drawn are those of "arable land" and "population." Despite the development of regional division of labor between the production of food and the manufacturing of machinery and its products, the bulk of the world's population is still relatively closely tied to the land from which its sustenance is produced. Many countries import food. England, which imports half of its food needs, is perhaps the country most dependent on distant farm lands for basic sustenance. Even in the case of England, however, during wartime emergency, dependence on outside food was greatly reduced by quick changeover within England's basic economy. This demonstrates that food production is probably not the most sensitive category of change or of long-range security in the developing strategy of economic competition.

Five Major Realms and Three Power Blocs of World Regional Organization

The world is divided into five realms of world regional organization. These are the *Commonwealth of Nations, mainland Western Europe*, the *Americas*, the *Communist Bloc*, and the *uncommitted* or *neutral countries*. These realms are interrelated by their position with respect to the two major powers of the world, the United States of America and the Union of Soviet Socialist Republics. A third power bloc is Western Europe, including the United Kingdom.

The maps in Figure 131, 173, and 244 show the focal organization of the majority of the world's territories with respect to one or another of three regional nodes of the exchange world, comprising the world core region previously defined on the map in Figure 21 of Chapter 2. These centers of power come under the headings of (1) United States-Canadian core region on which all of the Americas focus; (2) European core region, combining the Commonwealth and other European commitments; and (3) Soviet core region, including the other Communist Bloc commitments. The remaining uncommitted or neutral nations, which are to be found primarily within the Eurasian perimeter and include North Africa and Africa south of the Sahara, comprise the remainder of the world.

Mineral-Producing Regions as Indices of Strategic World Power

Probably the most significant bellwether of long-range economic potentiality and present strength is to be found in accessible mineral wealth. For it is from the minerals of the earth that the works of man characteristic of the industrial culture of the last 250 years have been made, and it is minerals which must be fed to the machinery of production to determine the strategy and tactics of the economic struggle between Communist and non-Communist realms and between nations and regions within nations. It is to the mineral fuels that humanity turns increasingly to do the work demanded by its creativity. Availability of food to the peoples of the five major world realms is more evenly distributed than the availability of the particular minerals necessary for an advanced industrial economy based on the latest scientific advances in knowledge and technology. Thus the production of significant quantities of the major metallic minerals and min-

eral fuels may be used as the basis for striking a balance in estimating the strategic power of the three major power blocs which dominate "this human world." Against such a perspective, relative significance of the resource characteristics, cultures, and areal organization of the world's major regions may be most usefully summarized.

The map in Figure 260 shows fourteen major world mineral-producing regions.[1] The regions are highly generalized in order to minimize the subjectivity involved in evaluating the *number* of separate producing areas. A selected sample of important minerals is used in Table XLVI to provide a measure of relative importance of the three major power blocs in strategic mineral production. The minerals used in "scoring" are divided into four categories. These are (1) the basic minerals needed in quantity—coal, iron, and petroleum; (2) secondary metallic minerals—copper, tin, lead, and aluminum (bauxite); (3) ferrous alloy metals—manganese, tungsten, and chromium; and (4) radioactive minerals.

In Table XLVI a value of five points is given in the case of each of the three basic minerals produced in significant amounts; a value of three points is assigned to each of the secondary minerals; one point is given to the production of either the representative minerals of the ferrous alloys or radioactive materials.

Regions 1 and 2 on the map in Figure 260 and Table XLVI are (1) the mineral-producing region of the eastern North American continent, including the Canadian Shield; and (2) that of the great western cordilleran region, except Alaska. A pair of regions, 3 and 4, yield the mineral production of (3) northern and (4) southern Europe west of the "Iron Curtain." The great mineral production of the Soviet Union is also paired in two major regions, (5) that designated as eastern European, comprising the Ukraine of the Soviet Union and the satellite countries of East Europe, and (6) the Siberian minerals from and including the Urals districts eastward throughout southern Siberia. Thus, there are two generally comparable mineral-producing regions within the land borders of the national states comprising the respective realms of economic, military, and strategic power.

In addition to those regions *within* the national land space contiguous to the industrial core regions themselves, there are others which are outlying but

[1] Generalized after Charles C. Colby and Alice Foster, *Economic Geography*, New York: Ginn and Company, 1940, p. 43.

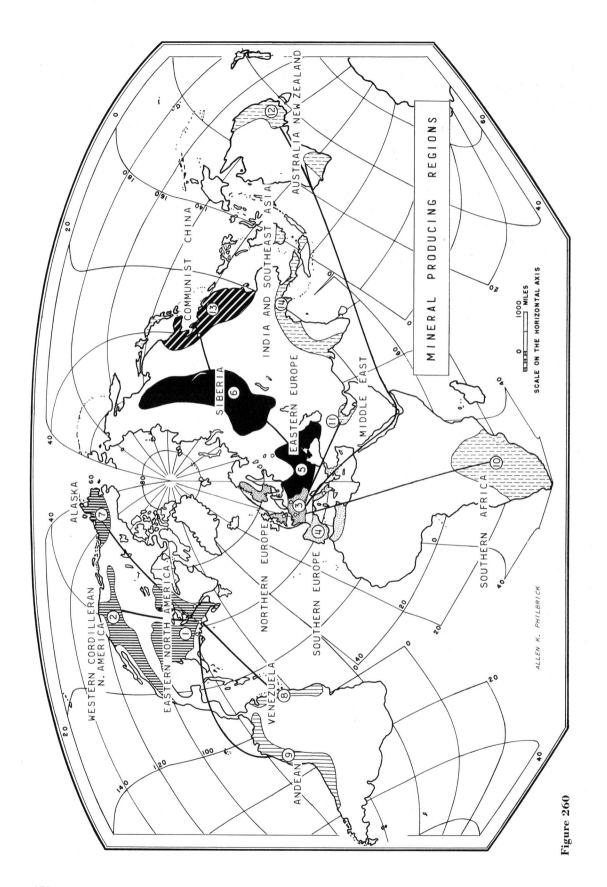

MINERAL PRODUCING REGIONS

SCALE ON THE HORIZONTAL AXIS

0   1000
MILES

ALLEN K. PHILBRICK

WESTERN CORDILLERAN
N. AMERICA

EASTERN NORTH AMERICA

ALASKA

VENEZUELA

ANDEAN

SOUTHERN EUROPE

NORTHERN EUROPE

COMMUNIST CHINA

INDIA AND SOUTHEAST ASIA

AUSTRALIA NEW ZEALAND

SIBERIA

EASTERN EUROPE

MIDDLE EAST

SOUTHERN AFRICA

Figure 260

which either politically or economically focus primarily on one power bloc more than either of the other two. Focusing on the United States-Canadian core region are three additional major mineral-producing regions in the Americas—numbers 7, 8, and 9. European industrial countries draw upon the great storehouse of minerals represented by the African mineral-producing region south of the Sahara (10), and from the fabulously oil-rich region of the Middle East (11). The Commonwealth's ties with the mineral-producing regions of Australia and New Zealand (number 12), taken as one major source of supply, bring to the European core region its third outlying region. The increasing mineral production of the Communist Chinese mainland (region 13 on the map) represents both a partner and outlying mineral-producing region in relation to the Soviet Union; in this case it is not so much the actual shipment of mineral raw materials over land to the Soviet Union which makes this mineral-producing region significant, as it is the potential development of Chinese industrial

economic strength based on those mineral resources. This potential is capable of transforming China's large population from a subsistence to an exchange economy. In this region the share represented by Japanese domestic production is discounted. The last region, number 14 on the map, represents mineral production from widely separated points within the politically uncommitted and neutral states of the Asian perimeter from the Indian Peninsula and Southeast Asian island archipelagoes.

The World Balance of Power

The subtotals and totals of the tentative scoring of Table XLVI for the two major power realms of the world, the Americas and the Communist Bloc, are approximately even. It is true, of course, that the American production of minerals far surpasses in total *quantity* and probably also in quality that of the Soviet sphere; however, the relative commitment of the production to consumer needs are probably much greater in the American regions. In the absence of accurate intelligence on the true sig-

TABLE XLVI TENTATIVE SCORING OF MINERAL PRODUCTION AREAS IN RELATION TO MAJOR POWER AREAS AND OUTLYING AREAS OF THE WORLD

Resource	Score	U.S. Canada 1	2	West Europe 3	4	East Europe 5	6	Principally United States outliers 7	8	9	Principally West Europe outliers 10	11	12	E. Asia, Soviet part 13	Other 14
Petroleum	5	5	5	..	..	5	5	..	5	5	..	5	..	..	5
Coal	5	5	5	..	5	5	5	..	..	..	5	..	5	5	..
Iron	5	5	5	5	5	5	5	..	5	..	..	..	5	5	5
Copper	3	3	3	3	..	3	3	3	..	3	3	..	..	3	..
Tin	3	..	..	..	..	..	..	..	..	3	3	..	3	3	..
Lead	3	3	3	3	3	3	3	..	..	..	..	..	3	3	3
Zinc	3	3	..	3	..	3	3	..	..	..	..	..	..	..	..
Bauxite	3	3	..	..	..	3	3	..	..	..	..	..	..	..	..
Manganese	1	..	..	1	1	1	1	..	1	..	1	..	..	1	1
Tungsten	1	..	..	..	..	..	..	..	..	..	..	..	..	1	1
Chromium	1	..	..	..	..	..	1	..	..	..	1	..	..	1	1
Total by regions	33	27	21	18	17	28	29	3	11	11	13	5	16	22	16
Total by groups		48		35		57		25			34			22	16

Total by major power areas and doubtful: 73 | 69 | 77 | 16

nificance of specific quantities, scoring is based only on the *fact* of significant production of the *variety* of minerals necessary for an industrial economy. The scores lead to an inescapable conclusion that an uneasy balance of power or stalemated strategic situation exists today between the United States and Communist power.

In this circumstance the strength of two other realms—Europe and the Eurasian perimeter—becomes increasingly significant. Europe at the present time holds the balance of power between the Communist Bloc and the Americas; for Europe, even though politically divided, is economically nearly as powerful as the Soviet Bloc and the Americas individually. Only the lack of significant amounts of petroleum reduces the European score in comparison with those of the other two mineral-producing realms.

This fact gives to European economic well-being and successful operation a political and strategic importance which has dominated the international politics of the post-World War II era. Three examples of area organization within Europe stand out as of primary importance in this connection. These are (1) the rapid and successful recovery of West Germany based on the Ruhr coal fields and the iron and steel-producing capacity reconstructed there since World War II; (2) the emergence of the European Common Market or the Iron and Steel Community based on the success of the Schuman Plan for elimination of tariff barriers and other restrictions between Belgium, Luxemburg, the Netherlands, France, West Germany, and Italy; and (3) the economic come-back and continued leadership of the United Kingdom as the focus of the economic organization of the Commonwealth. The continuing commitment of Western Europe along with the Americas in a common political and economic organization based on the principles of competitive free enterprise outweighs the economic strength of the Communist Bloc.

In the face of this latter fact the position of the uncommitted nations and of outlying mineral-producing dependencies and partners of the American and European core regions takes on added importance. Communist economic and political penetration into Latin America and the Eurasian peripheral regions, including North Africa, could change the balance of power just as surely as would the loss of Europe.

Because all three of the major power blocs are represented by nations which have demonstrated the capacity to explode and use atomic weapons— the United States from the Americas, the United Kingdom and recently France from Europe, and the Soviet Union from the Communist Bloc—it is clear that radioactive minerals are sufficiently evenly distributed not to constitute a significant advantage or disadvantage. The nuclear-space age is making effective use of some of the world's larger so-called "empty" spaces for atomic explosion and missiles testing: the American Southwest, former French Sahara, the Australian interior, and Soviet Siberia. The testing range for intermediate intercontinental ballistics developed by the United States in the Atlantic, the atomic testing region in the Pacific used by the United States, and the use of the Pacific as a terminal target area for missiles tests from the Soviet Union demonstrates that the centers of nuclear power meet and overlap one another even in the empty spaces of the world's surface. The nuclear sword of Damocles hangs equally over everyone's head.

In view of the stalemated circumstances between major realms with respect to world economic and ideological leadership, the world's people are apparently to be subjected to a prolonged period of competitive development. It may well be that the struggle for men's minds will be won or lost on the basis of the fourth stage of the dispersion of culture begun in the first period of the industrial revolution more than two centuries ago, and now reaching into the underdeveloped regions of the world under the competitive egis of Soviet and American and European foreign-aid programs in areas as different from one another as China and India, or Egypt and Ceylon.

So long as such competition can be kept within the bounds of peaceful development, no matter how bitterly or how fiercely the struggle is waged, the ultimate result will surely benefit human society. If the issue of the direction and character of the future of world regional organization is determined by interaction between competing systems of thought rather than of arms, neither side in the struggle is apt to impose its will completely on the other. It is to be hoped that the strengths of competing ideas will tend to survive and be adapted, developed, and perfected by the proponents of both sides for the benefit of all.

Such reasoning, however, presupposes that eternal vigilance against either trickery or force will succeed in maintaining the balance of power. This balance is necessary for an indeterminate period, long enough for the yearnings of the world's peoples for permanent and stable peace with justice to find adequate expression. Toward this end, geographical understanding of resources, cultures, and the patterns of area organization has much to contribute. It is hoped that the preceding pages, for their part, may contribute something to the kind of geograph-ical understanding which will help in the development of a genuinely unified worldwide regional organization. Such a framework is a prerequisite for the stability within which regional, national, local, and individual patterns of activity and the organization of area can truly evolve with logic and hope for a better world.

Appendix

AVERAGE TEMPERATURES AND PRECIPITATION OF SELECTED STATIONS (TEMPERATURE IN DEGREES FAHRENHEIT, PRECIPITATION IN INCHES)

Map, graph ref. no.		Altitude, ft.	J	F	M	A	M	J	J	A	S	O	N	D	Year	Range
			S-1 Small H													
1	Rangoon, Burma	18	77	79	83	87	85	81	81	81	81	82	80	77	81	10
			0.2	0.2	0.3	1.6	12.0	18.0	21.4	20.0	15.3	6.9	2.8	0.3	99.0	
2	Leopoldville, Congo	1,066	79	79	80	80	79	75	73	74	77	79	79	78	78	7
			5.3	5.7	7.7	7.7	6.2	0.3	0.1	0.1	1.2	4.7	8.7	5.6	65.4	
3	Manaos, Brazil	144	79	78	78	79	79	79	80	81	82	82	81	80	80	4
			10.3	9.8	10.8	10.9	7.9	4.4	2.7	1.5	2.4	4.7	6.1	8.9	78.7	
4	Singapore	16	78	78	79	80	81	80	80	80	79	80	79	78	79	3
			9.9	6.8	7.6	7.4	6.8	6.8	6.7	7.7	7.0	8.2	10.0	10.1	95.0	
			S-2 Small C-W													
5	Walvis Bay, South Africa	24	66	67	66	65	63	61	58	57	57	59	62	65	62	10
			0	0.1	0.1	0	0	0	0	0	0	0	0	0	0.3	
6	Port Nolloth, Africa	22	60	61	60	59	57	56	55	55	55	56	59	59	57	6
			0.1	0.1	0.2	0.2	0.4	0.4	0.3	0.3	0.2	0.1	0.1	0.1	2.5	
			S-5 Small W-H													
7	Callao, Peru	coast	69	70	71	70	67	65	63	62	62	64	65	69	67	9
			not available													
8	Harar, Ethiopia	6,071	66	68	69	69	69	68	66	65	67	68	67	67	68	4
			0.4	1.3	3.0	4.7	5.0	3.5	5.1	6.3	3.7	1.4	0.6	0.2	48.7	
			M-1 Moderate H													
9	Daly Waters, Australia	692	87	85	84	80	75	70	69	73	80	86	88	88	80	19
			6.1	6.6	4.6	1.1	0.2	0.3	0.1	0.1	0.2	0.8	2.2	4.1	26.4	
10	Beira, Africa	30	81	81	80	77	73	69	68	69	73	77	78	80	75	13
			10.3	9.6	9.5	4.4	2.5	1.3	0.8	1.0	0.6	1.6	4.7	9.9	56.4	
11	Zinder, Africa	1,676	72	77	85	91	93	90	83	81	84	87	81	75	83	21
			0	0	0	0.1	0.7	2.7	6.4	8.4	3.3	0.1	0	0	21.6	

Map, graph ref. no.	Altitude, ft.	J	F	M	A	M	J	J	A	S	O	N	D	Year	Range
12 Vera Cruz, Mexico	52	70 1.0	71 0.6	74 0.5	78 0.6	81 1.8	81 11.4	81 13.0	81 10.7	80 12.0	78 5.7	75 3.1	71 1.0	77 60.2	11
13 Poona, India	1,846	70 0.1	74 0.1	80 0.1	84 0.6	84 1.2	79 4.8	75 7.0	74 3.7	74 4.8	76 3.7	73 1.0	69 0.2	76 27.1	15
								M-5 Moderate W-H								
14 New Orleans, Louisiana	51	55 4.5	57 4.1	63 5.0	69 5.5	75 5.2	81 5.0	82 6.8	82 6.1	79 5.3	71 4.1	62 3.1	56 4.9	69 59.7	27
15 Cairo, Egypt	67	54 0.2	56 0.2	61 0.2	68 0.1	75 0.1	80 0	81 0	81 0	77 0	72 0.1	65 0.1	57 0.2	69 1.1	27
16 Casablanca, Morocco	56	53 1.5	54 1.8	57 2.3	59 1.5	62 0.7	68 0.4	71 0.1	73 0.1	71 0.1	67 1.1	60 4.0	56 2.9	63 16.3	20
17 San Diego, California	93	55 2.0	55 2.2	57 1.6	59 0.7	61 0.3	64 0.1	67 0.1	69 0.1	67 0.1	63 0.5	60 0.7	56 1.8	61 10.1	14
18 San Paulo, Brazil	2,690 2,425	69 8.8	69 7.5	68 5.8	65 2.5	60 2.5	59 2.0	58 1.1	59 2.0	61 3.0	64 4.4	65 5.4	68 7.1	64 52.1	11
19 Perth, Australia	197	74 0.3	74 0.4	71 0.8	67 1.7	61 5.1	57 7.1	55 6.7	56 5.7	58 3.4	61 2.2	67 0.8	71 0.8	64 34.7	19
20 Sydney, Australia	138	72 3.6	71 4.1	69 5.0	65 5.3	59 4.9	55 4.7	59 4.7	55 2.9	59 2.8	64 2.9	67 2.8	70 3.0	63 46.6	19
21 Alice Springs, Australia	1,916	83 1.7	82 1.5	77 1.2	68 0.7	60 0.6	54 0.6	53 0.4	58 0.3	65 0.4	73 0.7	79 1.0	82 1.5	70 10.8	30
22 Salisbury, Rhodesia	4,831	69 7.7	69 6.9	68 4.7	65 1.1	61 0.4	57 0.1	57 0	59 0.1	66 0.2	71 1.1	70 4.0	69 7.1	65 33.4	14
								M-6 Moderate C-W								
23 Kokstad, Africa	4,280	67 4.4	66 4.0	64 3.8	59 1.5	53 1.0	48 0.5	48 0.5	52 0.7	56 1.2	61 1.9	63 3.5	65 4.2	59 27.2	19
24 Valdivia, Chile	16	62 2.7	62 2.8	59 5.5	54 9.5	50 13.9	47 18.1	47 15.6	47 13.0	49 8.4	53 5.0	56 5.0	59 4.0	54 103.5	15

APPENDIX (CONTINUED)

Map, graph ref. no.		Altitude, ft.	J	F	M	A	M	J	J	A	S	O	N	D	Year	Range
25	Dunedin, New Zealand	240	58	58	55	52	47	44	43	45	48	51	53	57	51	15
			3.4	2.8	3.0	2.8	3.2	3.2	3.1	3.0	2.7	3.0	3.2	3.5	36.9	
26	London, England	18	41	41	43	47	55	59	63	62	57	51	44	41	50	22
			1.8	1.5	1.7	1.5	1.7	2.1	2.2	2.2	1.9	2.7	2.2	2.3	23.8	
27	Bordeaux, France	246	41	43	47	53	58	64	68	68	64	55	47	41	54	27
			2.4	2.0	2.2	2.5	2.6	2.8	1.8	1.9	2.6	3.3	3.0	2.5	30.0	
28	Olympia, Washington	coast	38	41	45	49	55	59	63	63	58	51	45	41	51	25
			8.3	6.3	5.2	3.2	2.3	1.6	0.6	0.7	2.3	4.5	8.4	9.0	52.4	
29	Bergen, Norway	72	34	34	36	42	49	55	58	57	52	45	39	36	45	24
			8.8	7.1	6.1	4.4	4.6	4.2	5.6	7.7	9.3	9.2	8.7	8.7	84.4	
M-8 Moderate C-W-H																
30	Buenos Aires, Argentina	89	74	73	69	62	55	50	49	51	55	60	66	71	61	25
			3.1	2.8	4.3	3.5	3.0	2.4	2.2	2.4	3.1	3.4	3.3	3.9	37.4	
31	Canberra, Australia	1,906	69	69	65	61	55	49	43	45	50	56	62	67	56	26
			2.1	1.8	1.9	2.1	1.6	1.7	1.6	2.0	1.5	2.3	1.8	1.7	22.1	
32	Sacramento, California	71	46	51	54	59	63	70	73	73	70	63	54	46	60	27
			3.3	3.1	2.4	1.0	0.5	0.2	0	0	0.3	0.8	1.5	2.7	15.9	
33	Naples, Italy	489	47	48	51	57	64	70	75	75	71	63	55	49	60	28
			3.7	2.9	2.8	2.6	2.0	1.4	0.6	1.1	2.9	4.6	4.5	4.4	33.4	
G-5 Great W-H																
34	In Salah, Africa	919	55	59	68	76	86	94	99	97	92	60	68	58	78	45
			0.1	0.1	0.0	0.0	0.0	0.0	0.0	0.1	0.0	0.0	0.2	0.1	0.6	
35	Biskra, Africa	410	51	55	60	67	75	84	89	88	82	70	59	52	71	38
			0.9	0.4	1.0	0.3	0.7	0.2	0.1	0.4	1.2	0.9	1.0	1.0	8.1	

Map, graph ref. no.		Altitude, ft.	J	F	M	A	M	J	J	A	S	O	N	D	Year	Range
									G-7 Great D-C							
36	Ivigtut, Greenland	0	19	19	24	31	40	47	50	47	41	34	26	21	33.1	31
			3.3	2.6	3.4	2.5	3.5	3.2	3.1	3.7	5.9	5.7	4.6	3.1	44.6	
37	Vardo, Norway	33	22	21	23	29	35	42	48	48	43	35	28	24	33	27
			2.5	2.5	2.3	1.5	1.3	1.3	1.5	1.7	1.9	2.5	2.1	2.4	23.5	
									G-8 Great C-H-W							
38	Rome, Italy	208	45	47	51	57	64	71	76	75	69	62	53	47	60	31
			3.3	2.6	2.9	2.6	2.2	1.5	0.7	1.0	2.5	5.0	4.5	3.9	32.6	
39	Athens, Greece	351	47	48	53	59	67	75	80	80	74	66	57	51	63	33
			2.2	1.5	1.3	0.9	0.9	0.6	0.3	0.4	0.6	1.7	2.8	2.6	15.6	
40	Albuquerque, New Mexico	5,200	35	40	47	55	64	73	76	74	68	56	44	35	56	41
			0.3	0.3	0.4	0.7	0.7	0.7	1.5	1.3	0.9	0.7	0.5	0.5	8.4	
41	Madrid, Spain	2,148	41	44	48	54	62	70	78	77	68	57	47	40	57	38
			1.3	1.3	1.6	1.7	1.7	1.3	0.4	0.6	1.5	1.8	1.9	1.4	16.5	
42	Washington, D.C.	75	34	35	43	53	64	73	77	75	68	57	45	36	55	43
			3.3	3.1	3.7	3.3	3.5	4.1	4.5	4.2	3.5	2.9	2.5	3.1	41.7	
43	Shanghai, China	23	38	39	46	56	66	73	81	81	73	53	53	42	59	43
			1.9	2.3	3.3	3.7	3.7	7.1	5.8	5.6	5.1	2.8	2.0	1.4	44.7	
44	Tokyo, Japan	19	39	39	45	55	62	70	76	79	73	61	51	42	57	40
			2.2	2.6	4.4	5.2	6.0	6.4	5.5	6.4	8.9	7.5	4.1	2.2	61.4	
									G-9 Great D-C-W							
45	Lhasa, Tibet	12,090	32	34	43	49	56	63	61	60	59	48	40	33	48	31
			0	0.1	0.3	0.2	5.1	6.3	25.8	17.8	7.2	0.3	0	0	63.0	
46	Berlin, Germany	187	31	32	38	46	56	61	64	62	56	47	38	33	47	33
			1.9	1.3	1.5	1.7	1.9	2.3	3.1	2.2	1.9	1.7	1.7	1.9	23.1	
47	Stockholm, Sweden	144	27	26	30	38	48	57	62	59	53	43	35	29	42	36
			1.4	1.3	1.3	1.5	1.5	1.7	2.4	2.9	1.9	1.8	1.9	1.9	21.6	
48	Leningrad, U.S.S.R.	30	18	18	25	37	49	58	63	60	51	41	30	22	39	45
			0.9	0.8	0.9	0.9	1.7	1.8	2.7	2.7	2.0	1.7	1.4	1.2	18.8	
49	Calgary, Alberta	3,540	13	17	26	40	50	56	62	60	51	42	28	19	38	49
			0.5	0.5	0.8	1.0	2.3	3.1	2.5	2.3	1.5	0.7	0.7	0.6	16.7	

Map, graph ref. no.		Altitude, ft.	J	F	M	A	M	J	J	A	S	O	N	D	Year	Range
								G-10 Great D-C-W-H								
50	Ankara, Turkey	2,789	31	33	42	51	61	67	73	73	65	56	46	35	53	42
			0.7	0.9	1.0	0.9	1.8	1.0	0.3	0.4	0.4	0.4	0.7	1.6	10.1	
51	Salt Lake City, Utah	4,366	29	34	42	50	58	67	76	75	64	54	41	32	52	47
			1.3	1.5	2.0	1.9	1.9	0.7	0.6	0.9	0.9	1.4	1.3	1.3	15.8	
52	Chicago, Illinois	824	24	26	36	47	57	67	73	71	65	54	40	29	49	49
			1.7	1.6	2.7	2.6	3.4	3.4	3.1	3.3	3.5	2.4	2.1	1.9	31.9	
53	Denver, Colorado	5,272	30	33	39	47	57	67	72	71	63	51	40	32	50	42
			0.3	0.5	1.1	2.1	2.0	1.3	1.6	1.5	1.2	1.0	0.6	0.7	14.0	
54	New York, New York	314	31	31	39	49	60	69	74	72	67	56	44	34	52	43
			3.3	3.4	3.6	3.4	3.1	3.6	4.2	4.2	3.7	3.5	2.5	3.3	41.6	
								E-9 Extreme D-C-W								
55	Yakutsk	330	−46	−35	−10	16	41	59	66	60	42	16	−21	−41	12	112
			0.9	0.2	0.4	0.6	1.1	2.1	1.7	2.6	1.2	1.4	0.6	0.9	13.7	
56	Verkoyansk, U.S.S.R.	330	−58	−48	−22	8	35	54	59	51	36	6	−34	−52	3	117
			0.2	0.1	0	0.1	0.2	0.5	1.2	0.9	0.2	0.2	0.2	0.2	3.9	
								V-4 Severe D								
57	Little America, Antarctica	...	22	9	−7	−24	−27	−29	−34	−34	−29	−14	8.6	23	13.3	58
								not available								
58	Eismitte, Greenland	...	−43	−53	−40	−25	−6	+2	+10	−1	−8	−32	−45	−37	−23	63
			0.6	0.2	0.3	0.2	0.1	0.1	0.1	0.4	0.3	0.5	0.5	1.0	4.3	
								V-7 Severe D-C								
59	Hebron, Labrador	60	−6	−5	6	18	32	40	47	48	41	31	20	4	23	54
			0.9	0.7	0.9	1.1	1.6	2.1	2.7	2.7	3.3	1.6	1.1	0.6	19.3	
60	Pt. Barrow, Alaska	13	−17	−17	−15	0	20	35	40	38	31	17	0	−12	10	57
			0.2	0.2	0.1	0.1	0.1	0.3	0.9	0.7	0.5	0.6	0.3	0.3	4.2	
61	Edmonton, Alberta	2,219	6	11	23	40	51	58	62	59	50	41	25	13	37	56
			0.9	0.6	0.8	0.9	1.9	3.1	3.3	2.3	1.3	0.7	0.7	0.8	17.4	

Map, graph ref. no.	Altitude, ft.	J	F	M	A	M	J	J	A	S	O	N	D	Year	Range
							V-9 Severe D-C-W								
62 Quebec, Ontario	296	10	12	23	37	51	62	67	64	56	44	30	16	39	57
		3.5	2.7	3.0	2.3	3.1	3.7	4.0	4.0	3.6	3.4	3.2	3.2	39.9	
63 Moscow, U.S.S.R.	480	14	17	25	39	55	61	66	62	51	40	28	19	40	52
		1.1	0.9	1.2	1.5	1.9	2.0	2.8	2.9	2.2	1.4	1.6	1.5	21.0	
64 Irkutsk, U.S.S.R.	1,532	−6	0	15	34	47	58	64	59	47	33	13	−1	30	70
		0.5	0.4	0.3	0.6	1.3	2.2	3.1	2.8	1.7	0.7	0.6	0.6	14.9	
65 Churchill, Manitoba	44	−19	−17	−6	14	30	43	54	52	42	27	6	−11	18	73
		0.5	0.6	0.9	0.9	0.9	1.9	2.2	2.7	2.3	1.4	1.0	0.7	16.0	
66 Coppermine, Northwest Territory	13	−19	−19	−16	0	22	38	50	46	36	18	−6	−16	11	69
		0.6	0.4	0.6	0.8	0.5	0.8	1.3	1.9	1.0	1.2	0.8	0.6	10.7	
							V-10 Severe D-C-W-H								
67 Peiping, China	125	25	29	42	56	69	75	80	77	70	56	39	29	54	55
		0.1	0.2	0.2	0.6	1.5	3.4	8.3	6.1	2.5	0.7	0.3	0.1	24.1	
68 Inchon, North Korea	231	25	28	37	49	59	67	74	77	68	57	43	30	51	52
		0.8	0.7	1.2	2.6	3.3	3.9	10.9	8.8	4.3	1.6	1.6	1.1	40.8	
69 Astrakhan, U.S.S.R.	−50	19	23	33	48	64	73	77	74	63	49	36	27	49	58
		0.5	0.3	0.4	0.5	0.6	0.7	0.5	0.5	0.5	0.4	0.4	0.5	5.9	
70 Minneapolis, Minnesota		14	16	30	46	58	67	73	70	62	50	33	20	50	59
		1.0	1.0	1.6	2.3	3.4	4.4	3.4	3.4	3.4	2.1	1.4	1.2	28.6	
71 Harbin, China	526	−1	6	24	43	57	67	73	70	58	40	21	4	39	74
		0.2	0.2	0.4	0.9	1.7	3.7	4.1	4.1	1.8	1.3	0.3	0.2	19.2	

Index

Place names on maps are indicated by italicized page numbers; subjects of maps, photographs, or tables are indicated by (map), (photo), (table) after page number.

bazaar street scene, 443 (photo)
jute manufacturing, port of, 441 (photo)
Calgary, Canada, *50*
California, 225
from Mexico, 1848, 323
California region, oil and gas, 274
Callao, Peru, 42, *48*, *309*, 310
Calvinism, 171
Calvinist faith, 235
Cambodia, *345*, 353, 355, 415, 446
rice exports, 424
Cambrian Mts., Wales, 105
Camel, role of in North Africa, 199
Cameroon Mts., 191
Cameroons, *197*, 198
Cameroons upland, Bantu source region, 183
Campine, Belgium, *176*
Canada, *6*, 247, *250*, 257, 278-279, 286, 311, 314
core region in southern Ontario and St. Lawrence Valley, 341
culture region of North America, 299
emergence of regional organization, 338
linear arc of regional organization, 342
northern and eastern, 261
racial composition, 314
specialized economic regions, 341
Canada-United States, 30, *31*, 32, 59, 340-342
Canadian Arctic, and the Northwest Passage, 252
Canadian Ford Motor Co., Ford in Australia, 243
Canadian National Railway, 301
Canadian regional organization, 290 (map), 291 (map), 299
Canadian Shield, 64, 68, 261, 270, 271 (map), 301
Canadian West, 301
Canberra, Australia, *48*, *227*, 239
Canterbury, *125*
Canterbury Plain, 230
Canton, China, *399*
Canton Delta, 66, 379, *396*, 401
Canton industrial district, *404*
Canton Plain, *352*
Cape Breton I., 299
Cape Horn, *10*, 11, 252, 254
Cape Province, 224, 235
agriculture of, 225, 237
grape harvest and winery, 226 (photos)
Capetown, S. Africa, *25*, 183, *203*, 221, 235, *237*, 284
Capital accumulation, 115
Capitalism, 98
Caracas, Venezuela, *309*
Caravan routes, ancient, Middle East, 414
Carbon dioxide, 71, 74
Carboniferous regions, contrasting extent of in the Americas, 255
Cardiff, Wales, U.K., *110*, 112

Caribbean, 66
Caribbean coast, 252
Caribbean region, 257
Caribbean-South Atlantic route, ocean trade, 284
Carlson, Lucille, 170, 406
Carmarthen, *125*
Carol, Hans, 201, 207
Carolinas-Georgia Coast, *321*
Carpathian Massif, *147*
Carpathian Mts., 146
Carron, Scotland, 130
Carr-Saunders, A. M., 440
Carrying capacity, range in Australia, 229
Cartagena, Colombia, *309*, 310
Casablanca, Morocco, *49*
Cascade Range, 265
Caspian Sea, 149, 358, 367
Caste system, 434
Catholic, 171, 412
Catskill Mts., *319*
Cattle, Alice Springs, 231 (photo)
American West, 338
Europe and the Near East, 155 (map)
India, 436 (photo)
pastoral subsistence, 200 (photo)
role of in pastoral subsistence economies in Africa, 199
sacred position of in India, 435
Soviet Union, 388
Cattle breeding, heat-resistant strains, 261
Cattle ranching, Australia, 225, 231, (photo)
Caucasian race, 182
Caucasian S.S.R.'s, 378
Caucasoid race, *86*, 87
Caucasus mineral region, 374
Caucasus Mts., 64, 146, 351, *352*, 379
Caucasus petroleum, 376
Celebes, *352*, 357
Celtic Europe, Atlantic fringe, 134, 156
Celtic languages, 172 (map)
Centers, local regional cultural, 164
Central African Republic, 198, *345*
Central Alberta, 304
Central America, Mexico, selected crops, 264 (map)
Central American culture hearth, 94, 97
Central American Isthmus, 252
Central Asia, 379
Turkic, *345*
Central Asia industrial district, *404*
Central Asian highlands and basins, *31*, 32
Central Asian manufacturing district, 403
Central Asian S.S.R.'s, 378
Central basin plateaus and mountain ranges, Asia, 371
Central East Europe mineral region, *374*
Central England, urban area, 141
Central Mexican Plateau mineral district, 271 (map), 273

Central Middle West, focus on Chicago, 289
Central mountain regions, the West, 290 (map), 297
Central plateau, Spain, 152
Central Rockies, *271*, 273
Central Saskatchewan, focus on Prince Albert, 304
Central Statistical Board of the U.S.S.R., Council of Ministers, 386
Central Valley, California, 66, 265, 285, 297, 336
soils, 261
Central Valley, Chile, 268
Cerro Bolivar, Venezuela, 68, *271*, 275
Ceylon, *6*, 180, *250*, 361, 415, 422, 460
mineral region, *376*
rice imports, 424
subsistence rice sowing, 370 (photo)
tea, 422
Chad, 198, *345*
"Champagne," Paris Basin, 152
Champagne fairs, 169
Champlain, 300
Champlain Valley, *319*
Chandernagor, India, 415
Changchun, China, 397, *399*
Changing China, 409 (map)
Changsha, China, 401
Charleston, S. Carolina, *25*, 315, *319*, *321*, 329
Chateau Frontenac, symbol, 300
Chekiang, *399*, 400
Chelyabinsk, U.S.S.R., *407*
Chemical exchange, 61
Chemical precipitation, 79
Chemical weathering, 61, 79
Chengtu, China, 401
Cherbourg, France, *25*
Chernozem-like soil group, subhumid margins and southern African highland, 191
Chernozem-prairie-grassland-gray-brown forest soils combination, 261
Chernozem soils, black, 82
Cherrapunji, India, precipitation, 361
Chesapeake Bay, 314, 318
Chester, England, *167*
Chiang Kai-shek, 415
Chiaraviglio ranch, 18 (map)
Chibchas, South American Indians, 310
Chicago, Illinois, *48*, 244, 284
Board of Trade, 288
control center of the Middle West, 289
emergence of as railroad center, 336
focus of both corn belt and American Manufacturing Belt, 288
industry, 285, 286 (map)
rail hub by 1860, 329
stockyards, 27, 288
Chichester, England, *125*
Chile, 32, 57, 78, 82, 276, *286*, 311
central, *271*
copper, 279
soils of Mediterranean, 261